W9-AIP-965

THE INSTANT ASTROLOGER

THE INSTANT ASTROLOGER

BOOKS

Winchester, U.K.
New York, U.S.A.

Copyright © 2003 O Books
46A West Street, Alresford,
Hants SO24 9AU, U.K.
Tel: +44 (0) 1962 736880
Fax: +44 (0) 1962 736881
E-mail: office@johnhunt-publishing.com
www.o-books.net

U.S. office
240 west 35th Street, Suite 500
New York, NY 10001
E-mail: obooks@aol.com

Text: © Lyn Birkbeck 2003
Illustrations: Lyn Birkbeck/Nautilus Design
CD: www.horoscopeservices.co.uk

Design: Nautilus Design, Basingstoke, UK
Cover Design: Krave Limited, UK

ISBN 1 903816 49 1

All rights reserved. Except to brief quotations in
critical articles or reviews, no part of this book may
be reproduced in any manner without the prior written
permission from the publishers.

The rights of Lyn Birkbeck as author have been asserted
in accordance with the copyright, Designs and Patents Act 1988.

A CIP catalogue record for this book is available from the British Library.

Printed by Tien Wah Press, Singapore

ACKNOWLEDGEMENTS

The Instant Astrologer, as an innovation in the field of astrological endeavour, required the synchronous coming together of an astrologer with the vast amount of written material required, a software producer with the expertise and resources, and a publisher with the will and vision to make it into a commercial reality. Merely one or two of these components could not make available both the wealth of astrological information and the easy means of accessing it in technical and financial terms. I like to think therefore that the Planetary Powers had something to do with convening such a team that would provide such an astrological bounty.

And so my thanks go to Michael Mann, John Hunt, Eric Biss and Chris Nelis for all being with me in the right place at the right time, and of course to the Planetary Powers themselves, who are always in the right place at the right time.

*'Everything conspires
to bring us to our rightful place'*

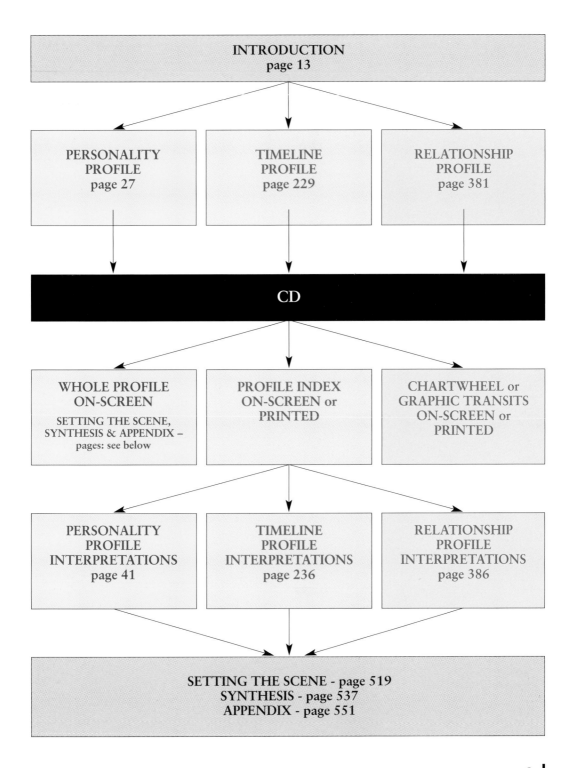

INTRODUCTION
page 13

PERSONALITY
PROFILE
page 27

TIMELINE
PROFILE
page 229

RELATIONSHIP
PROFILE
page 381

CD

WHOLE PROFILE
ON-SCREEN

SETTING THE SCENE,
SYNTHESIS & APPENDIX –
pages: see below

PROFILE INDEX
ON-SCREEN or
PRINTED

CHARTWHEEL or
GRAPHIC TRANSITS
ON-SCREEN or
PRINTED

PERSONALITY
PROFILE
INTERPRETATIONS
page 41

TIMELINE
PROFILE
INTERPRETATIONS
page 236

RELATIONSHIP
PROFILE
INTERPRETATIONS
page 386

SETTING THE SCENE - page 519
SYNTHESIS - page 537
APPENDIX - page 551

CONTENTS

INTRODUCTION

The Profiles
What Astrology is
What Astrology is Today
Why Astrology Works

1. THE PROFILES

*T*he *Instant Astrologer* can create for you straight away any of the Profiles outlined below – or you can simply use it as you would any other astrological resource as an aid to chart interpretation and research. However, if you are not 'astrologically literate' (or even if you are), it is strongly recommended that you read the three short preceding chapters (starting overleaf) that give you a description of this ancient and profound subject, along with some explanations of why and how astrology works.

The Personality Profile, based upon the positions of the Sun, Moon and Planets at the precise time of birth, for anyone of your choosing. It will also produce the ChartWheel, the actual image of your unique Birth Chart. If a birth time is not known, it will still give pages of individual information about your personality. The Personality Profile also includes the highly important Ascendant or Rising Sign, and covers all dimensions of personality from the most obvious to the most secret, your background and purpose, and your very destiny. Go to page 28 if you wish to know more of what a Birth Chart actually is. Go to page 38 if you wish to get straight on with obtaining a Birth Chart and its interpretation.

The Timeline Profile, drawn from the effects upon your Birth Chart of the Planets as they travel through the sky – what are called Transits – during any Timeline period of your own or anyone else's life. Your Timeline Profile regards your life as having a definite direction, which the planetary influences nudge, encourage and challenge you to find, while at the same time helping you to better manage and enjoy it. Your life and personality are seen as an unfolding adventure of your spirit. Go to page 229.

The Relationship Profile, derived from the Inter-Aspects between two individual Birth Charts, that is, how the Planets in one interact with those of another. This is the Chemistry Between You Both, describing the connections that exist between the personalities and lives of two unique human beings. Including Key Connections, Relationship Challenges, Relationship Strengths and Minor Connections. Go to page 381.

● With all three Profiles, most information and descriptions are geared towards practically dealing with difficulties and making the most of assets.

● The scope of astrology is endless and so it is emphasised that although *The Instant Astrologer* meets a great variety of requirements and goes into some depth, it does not profess to take you as far as you might want to go with the subject. To this end you are referred to other fields of astrology (see page 564) and to reading matter that specializes in areas utilized and explored in *The Instant Astrologer* (page 563).

Important – Whilst reading any Profile, please bear in mind that although the interpretations are as accurate and informative as possible, there is no guarantee that every word will apply at this moment in time, or in the past or future. This is because astrology maps out one's *potential* and is not able to say what one has made, or will make, of that potential. Whilst reading, you should rely upon your own judgement and individual choice, will and inclination – which are precisely what astrology is aimed at shedding light upon. Consequently, no responsibility can or will be taken by the author of *The Instant Astrologer* for choices made or impressions gained by the reader as a result of its use.

2. WHAT ASTROLOGY IS

'Sir, I believe in astrology because I have studied the subject. You do not because you have not!'
– Sir Isaac Newton (in retort to one of his peers who was ridiculing his belief in astrology)

Possibly astrology has a greater range of images, concepts and meanings than any other subject known to man. This is not too surprising when you consider that it is one of the oldest subjects, for as soon as he turned his head upwards man was looking at the Heavens and trying to understand what all those points and patterns of light meant.

So before describing why and how it actually works, we need to define what astrology actually is. But first let us point out what, to the displeasure of the true practitioner of this art/science, astrology is *not*.

Astrology is not...

The 'horoscopes' that you read in newspapers or magazines, or on a screen, or hear on the radio.
All these may have some bearing on what astrology is, but they are usually astrology with its teeth drawn. You can take it or leave it, or be merely entertained by it. Such 'false astrology' also suits those who denounce astrology, for they are right, it *is* rubbish, with a few notable exceptions. This does not mean to say that it has no place, for it is often the first step that anyone takes along the path of studying the real thing. It is just that such astrology should carry a 'government health warning' for a 'forecast' that applies to one twelfth of the population is going to be right for a very small percentage – but misleading nonsense for the rest.

Astrology is not...

Solely a means of predicting the future.
It is possible to do this, very occasionally, but then mostly it should be done in the manner of 'If you do so-and-so then such-and-such could happen'. In this way the individual is given some power over their own fate. But to baldly predict an event as if it is unavoidably bad or good - regardless of what you do in the meantime - is irresponsible because it implies that one is a mindless slave to fate, be it negative or positive. All this goes against the idea implicit in genuine astrology, which is that, primarily, it is a tool for consciously living in an increasing awareness of what and who we truly are (see A Tool for Self-Awareness below, and Psychological Astrology on page 21), and that ultimately we are expressions of a Higher Power and are thus co-creators of the world in which we live.

Astrology is not…

Defining personality traits as being fixed and unchangeable.
The whole idea of life is that it evolves, and life obviously includes those who live it. A Birth Chart, properly drawn up and interpreted in a way that *The Instant Astrologer* does, will reveal what it is in the individual that needs to change or improve, along with what is already positive and well developed. This now leads us to say what authentic astrology *is*.

Astrology is…

Something that reveals us to be part of a far greater and all-encompassing, totally interconnecting reality.

The image arises here of the old physics experiment at school where iron-filings on a sheet of paper are seen to be gathering into the patterns of the field of a magnet being held against the other side of the paper. We and our little lives are governed by forces of which we are mostly unaware, and so we go about our business under the illusion of having free will – or rather with *an illusory sense of free will*. And at the same time, we are coerced and regimented by other 'iron-filings' that have more apparent power than us 'little' iron-filings. True free will is paradoxical because it has something to do with choosing to 'follow one's own star', that is, to recognize what truly exerts a pull on one and go with that. This is called one's fate. A genuine and unique Birth Chart, properly interpreted, is precisely that – 'your own star', the character and course that is your destiny, something which we are all simultaneously liberated and limited by. This is truly the power in your life, like the magnet is in relationship to those iron filings, or like a little sailboat trying to get somewhere (your free will) on the open sea in the midst of the elements (fate). In this respect, astrology is a map, compass and weather forecaster.

Astrology is…

A key to true freedom.

Throughout human history people have 'toed the line' and then rebelled against whatever that line might be – boss, state, spouse, religion, etc. But this leads nowhere for it can be seen that we are still a collection of hapless serfs or wicked barons, of power-wielding 'haves' or downtrodden 'have nots'. These are all 'false gods' whereas true astrology puts us in touch with the 'true gods', with that true magnet, the real force that plays upon us little 'iron-filings', that is, the Sun, Moon and Planets of our Solar System. And then our Solar System itself is intimately connected and influenced by the Galaxy through which it moves, the Milky Way, which is in turn an integral part of the whole Universe. This is all part of what is called 'The Macrocosmic-Microcosmic Theory'. This says that the greater is reflected in the lesser, like the structure of the Solar System is reflected in the structure of an atom, that is, a central object orbited by other objects. This in turn gives rise to something that is absolutely essential to understanding what astrology truly is.

Astrology is...

The Law of Correspondence or 'As above so below'.

Through observing the movements of the Sun, Moon and Planets and what is happening down on Earth it is seen that certain positions of these heavenly bodies correspond to certain Earthly qualities, experiences and events – which includes the births of individuals and therefore the nature of the individuals themselves (see Table of Correspondences on page 552). The Birth Chart, accurately calculated for this precise moment in time, is then seen to depict your 'celestial signature', a complex amalgamation of various energies in play that are seen through interpretation to correspond to a set of dynamics of personality with a direction and purpose. So we can see that there is far more to astrology than just one's Sun- or Star-Sign. One's Sun-Sign is rather like the part of one's address that gives the town you live in, whereas a full and proper Birth Chart gives not just your street and house number, but every nook and cranny of your home itself, including your loft and basement!

Astrology is...

A practical guide to everyday living.

And the 'Below' of 'As above so below' reaches right down into the street of everyday life. Days when you feel positive and right with the world; days when you feel short-tempered; days that are good or bad for shopping; days that are great or disastrous for a social occasion; days when the poetry of love and romance is heard. Astrology can shed light on everything form the cosmic to the commonplace. Because of this it can also be seen how the smallest or most trivial occurrence can figure in the far greater scheme of life itself, or your life in particular. 'To see the universe in a grain of sand' as William Blake put it.

Astrology is...

A body of wisdom.

Through seeing how the Macrocosmic-Microcosmic Theory and the Law of Correspondence are borne out through the verses and chapters of your life it is gradually and progressively revealed that there is a right and a wrong way of living. The Greater Will that is symbolized and sky-written by the Sun, Moon and Planets informs the Lesser Will of its true path, for it corresponds to the path of the Greater Will, as seen in the movement of the heavenly bodies in their heavenly courses. This is not a judgemental Will any more than the Law of Gravity is judgemental.

Astrology is...

A tool for gaining self-knowledge.

Through witnessing how one behaves in reaction and in comparison to planetary rhythms and influences – much as a musician keeps time and in tune – one becomes aware of how one is working or playing, of what is truly profitable and enjoyable about oneself and life, and what is not.

Astrology is...

A mystery.

As much as gazing at the stars fills one with a sense of wonder where no conclusion is reachable, astrology is also endless and defies any reduction to some neat formula. Such is life, such is the nature of being human. Astrology is the Science of Life, but practising it is an Art.

3. WHAT ASTROLOGY IS TODAY

Predictive Astrology

This is what most people, and most dictionaries, regard as astrology, that is 'the art or science of predicting events through studying the movements of the sun, moon and planets' – or words to that effect. So the predictive astrologer would be somewhat fatalistic, predict the event, and more or less leave it to the individual concerned to either wait in gleeful anticipation of good fortune, or prepare themselves to deal with a negative occurrence in a way they saw fit, in terms of their aims and disposition. Or with respect to predicting the 'planetary influences' for a planned occasion, such an astrologer would set out the pros and cons for that time and situation. This is rather like the king who is advised about the astrological conditions prevailing during a battle and is therefore better equipped to fight it – or not fight it, as the case may be. A comparatively recent version of such predictive astrology is what now infests the 'horoscopes' and 'stars' of mainstream media, and is an entirely hit-and-miss affair. However, an authentic predictive astrology, be it for the individual or the collective, is trying to make a comeback of late. But apart from its lack of a practical way of meeting and managing some unwelcome situation in an only too modern and complex world, its reputation rests rather too precariously on predicting events accurately.

If astrological predictions of actual events were even as reliable as weather forecasting we would by now, as a civilization, be using it at a governmental and cultural level. So, for example, even though a few astrologers did actually predict the attack on the World Trade Center for September 11th 2001, they weren't about to be listened to because of the track record of such astrology. And even if they had been, putting on alert fighter planes in the skies around New York City to meet an attack predicted by a few stargazers does rather stretch the imagination. Nevertheless, the popular conception of astrology remains as this predictive kind, and books on the spurious predictions of Nostradamus – arguably the most famous predictive astrologer of all – still sell very well. The reason for this strange state of affairs is largely because human beings have been led to believe that they are as sheep, slaves to what fate and the system dish out.

The case for Predictive Astrology is that it equips one with a means to plan one's life, to prepare to meet the bad times, and to be reassured by the prospect of the good times. And although at the lower end of its spectrum it can make one quite neurotic as one lives in dread of something awful that might happen but in fact does not, or holding one's breath until that 'bad influence' is past, at the higher end of its spectrum it can attune one to life's cycles and meanings in a quite extraordinary way. But in any event, because of all this, it then became necessary to investigate the nature of the beast that was actually being subjected to these predictions, influences and cycles – the individual human being – with a view to having some say in the matter.

Psychological Astrology

This is the astrology largely employed in *The Instant Astrologer*, wherein the 'prediction' side of it takes the form of defining potential (what you have the power to be) or suggesting future possibilities, or providing confirmation of your own feelings and intuitions. The modern or 'psychological' astrologer is one who uses a Birth Chart to investigate and reveal one's essential nature, the effect of one's past upon one's present, what and who one attracts, and how one 'works'. He or she can therefore put at one's disposal a more conscious choice as to the kind of life one leads, and would advise his or her client on how to meet or handle an adverse influence from or to, say, the Planet Mars, in another manner entirely to the predictive astrologer. This could be done by viewing it as a reason or opportunity to get more in touch with, or be wary of, their 'Mars energy' (as described in the Mars Profile of the Personality Profile) and of the possible ways it could manifest in their life – rather than by predicting how it would manifest purely as some fated event. Then progressively one could learn to express it better and avoid its pitfalls. 'Mars energy' is the nature of one's own, or someone else's, powers of assertion or measure of anger (which is basically self-assertion that is distorted due to it previously being thwarted). It is also, among many other corresponding qualities, one's sense and experience of masculinity. Alternatively, negative Mars could manifest as some *thing*, like an aggressive animal, a fever, an inflammation, or anything fierce, hot, sharp or dangerous. Or just as an internalized feeling such as sexual desire, impatience or restlessness. Seeing how many ways Mars's effect can be experienced goes to show that predicting an event accurately is largely down to the predictive astrologer's intuition rather than a purely technical or scientific method. And as some wit once said, 'Intuition when it works is brilliant, but when it doesn't it's plain stupid'.

It can be useful just to know that the hot and uncomfortable grip of Mars's negative influence can be alleviated to some degree by simply counting to ten and/or just sticking it out. But again that would be more the 'predictive' approach – that you were caught up on the conveyor belt of some immutable fate and could do little or nothing about it. Alternatively – and this is very important in these days of victimhood and abuse – a negative Mars can all too often be experienced as someone or something else attacking or intimidating one (as alluded to above). But the astrological fact would be that such a negative Martian experience would be seen as a negative Mars in one's own Birth Chart! The Personality Profile (page 27) would reveal this quite clearly, as it would anything important and significant. It will also, where possible, indicate how to remedy attendant problems and transform them into something positive.

The growing importance of Psychological Astrology since its beginning in the first half of the twentieth century stands as a testament to the accent astrology now places upon the gaining of self-knowledge and the assuming of self-responsibility as a means of living one's life and thereby having some control over it, rather than merely predicting a path through it as if one had booked some kind of terrestrial package tour, or as pointed out above, as if one were a slave to fate and the system.

The case for Psychological Astrology is a strong one because it is saying that it is useless and fanciful to predict what lies ahead upon the road of life if you have no knowledge of the vehicle that's travelling down it – that is, you. For example, if you break down, you'll have some idea of how to fix it. And if you are headed in a direction that is not appropriate for you as an individual, then you will know it and not waste time and energy going that way. Most importantly of all, self-knowledge teaches and promotes self-control. As the Chinese saying goes 'A moment's loss of self-control can ruin a whole life'.

Furthermore, the predictive aspect of astrology is incorporated into Psychological Astrology by forecasting not so much actual events but rather the kind of 'psychological weather' that lies ahead. As you will see in The Timeline Profile (page 229) all ongoing planetary influences are there to inform you of something, like a meteorologist would inform you of the strength and direction of the wind. Equipped with this astrological intelligence, you become the informed and seasoned sailor of life's oceans, as opposed to floundering helplessly or struggling against the tide, and possibly winding up 'shipwrecked' or 'drowned'. With respect to Timeline Profiles, the psychological astrologer should constantly remind himself or herself that they are an aid to understanding what is happening and what *could* happen, not predicting what *will* happen.

With regard to relating and relationships, as you will see in The Relationship Profile (page 381), Psychological Astrology very much interprets human interaction in terms of what a relationship is saying about you as an individual, that they are there (or not there) to teach one more about life, relating and yourself, and that in the end any 'other' is really an extension or projection of oneself. All this serves to enrich a relationship and put it into a healthy perspective through gaining a greater understanding of why you are with, or without, someone in your life.

4. WHY ASTROLOGY WORKS

At the time of writing there is no conclusive or generally and scientifically accepted evidence that supports the validity of astrology, or that explains why it works or that it could work. However, here are some of the reasons to believe that it does work.

Practice

The most obvious, but purely anecdotal from a scientific viewpoint, reason for saying that astrology works is because it is seen to do so by an ongoing study of it, as neatly encapsulated in the words of Sir Isaac Newton, the father of material science, that are quoted on page 17. That he believed in astrology and other metaphysical subjects such as alchemy is little known mainly because it suited the world at the time to settle upon his theories that appertained to a more concrete, and therefore seemingly controllable, version of Nature and reality. So, all that can be said is 'See for yourself!' through using *The Instant Astrologer*.

Synchronicity and the Cosmic Clock

Synchronicity, a term coined by the genius psychologist Carl Jung, is the concept that says that time is not merely linear – i.e. one thing occurring after another and causing another thing to occur – but that things happen together because they somehow correspond to one another. Or, as Jung simply put it, 'because they like happening together'. It is all part of the cosmic pattern of it all. Everything is connected. The word 'universe' does after all mean 'the whole turning', one thing happening.

So the movements of the Sun, Moon and Planets – and the Stars behind them – can be seen as the 'hands' of a Cosmic Clock. The astrologer is someone who has learned to tell the 'cosmic time'. Through reading a horoscope, meaning 'view of the hour', he or she can divine the nature of what or who is happening, and when further 'influences' will occur, and what they mean. But, in this context, the word 'indication;' is actually more appropriate than 'influence'. This is because clocks *indicate* the time, they do not in themselves *influence* what is happening or *make* things happen. And the most potent moment in cosmic time is when someone or something comes into being – birth. Hence the importance of your Birth Chart, for that is truly 'your time', and all other 'times' are related to it, as we shall see later.

The Solar Wind

A more scientific reason that accounts for the validity of astrology is demonstrated by a theory put forward by engineer and independent scientist Maurice Cotterell in *The Mayan Prophecies* by Adrian G Gilbert and Maurice M Cotterell (Element). The Solar Wind is a stream of energy particles that is 'sprinkled' from the corona of the Sun, and in which our Planet Earth is 'bathed' via her magnetic field. The point is that the nature of the Solar Wind varies according to what region of space one is positioned in relation to the Sun. Furthermore, it has been proven that DNA, the building block of all life, and therefore of personality as well, is directly affected by the Earth's magnetosphere, which, as just pointed out, is influenced by the Solar Wind. So as the Earth moves through differing regions of space and the Solar Wind, throughout the year as it orbits the Sun, so too is our DNA affected in different ways, creating different personality types in accordance with the Zodiacal Sign through which we are passing. And as the Planets themselves influence the Sun itself – with respect to sunspot cycles that in turn affect the Solar Wind – it can be seen that this theory also covers the part that they play astrologically.

Electromagnetism and Resonance

The above theory is greatly augmented and expanded upon by the work of astrophysicist Dr Percy Seymour. The reader is therefore directed to his book *The Scientific Basis of Astrology* (Quantum) in which he explains in depth and at length how we, as electromagnetic beings, are resonating – via the Earth's magnetic field – with the Solar System and beyond. This makes quite literal the ancient idea of the Music of the Spheres, which sees everything as part of a cosmic symphony where everything is 'playing' with and upon everything else. Furthermore, 'musical themes' played at certain times resonate with earlier themes. One earlier theme that is particular memorable is, of course, the one played at one's birth. Consequently, ongoing astrological influences through life are related to one's own particular 'opening stanza'. Amongst the many other areas he explores, Dr Seymour also explains how such electromagnetic influences also affect the embryo in the womb. This could be likened to the orchestra tuning up or, more intriguingly, to an overture where the themes to be played are run through in preparation for life. In astrological terms this concerns the Twelfth House, which will be explained later.

Dr Seymour's work paves the way for a reconvening of science and mysticism, and thereby the realization that we truly are cosmic beings, intrinsic parts and co-creators of Life within the arena of Nature and the Universe – not masters of it.

Astrological Renaissance

It could be said that we are going through a rebirth of astrology in the light of modern scientific awareness and means, especially with regard to Quantum Physics. As such, many of the old astrological theories and methods are progressively seen not to hold water. It cannot be claimed that *The Instant Astrologer* is free of these 'bugs', but it is hoped that as part of the astrological tradition its users will discover what is and is not true (at least for them), and thereby add to the ever-growing astrological body of wisdom.

THE PERSONALITY PROFILE

The Birth Chart – How it Works
The Birth Chart – What it Means
Creating a Personality Profile
Using a Personality Profile
The Personality Profile Interpretations

1. THE BIRTH CHART –
HOW IT WORKS

Below I explain what a Birth Chart comprises, but if you wish to get on with obtaining a Personality Profile right now, then turn to page 38. However, you will find the following information an important aid to understanding better the Profile interpretations, and to making more use of them.

A Birth Chart is simply an image of both the visible sky and non-visible sky as viewed at the time and place of birth – or of the beginning or occurrence of anything for that matter, because astrology can be used to look at things and events, not just human beings.

Opposite you will see a *pictorial* version of a Birth Chart for someone born in London, England almost exactly at the time of a Full Moon – 8.40 p.m. This is a picture of the Sun, Moon and Planets in the sky as it appeared at this time and place in relationship to the southern Horizon (with the little figure standing in the middle of it). If your incoming soul had a console, this is probably what would be at its centre!

Using, if need be, the Pictorial Birth Chart Key to the left you will recognize the familiar twelve Signs of the Zodiac that form an imaginary band encircling the Earth (shown here as the Signs and 3-letter abbreviations), and this is seen on the Birth Chart as bisected by the Horizon. The Sun, Moon and Planets are positioned in the Signs they were in at that time. The Sign that the Sun is in (in this case, ARIes) is what you know as your Sun-Sign or Star-Sign. The Moon is directly opposite (which is what a Full Moon is, the Moon in Opposition to the Sun) in the Sign of LIBra.

The Sun, Moon and Planets are travelling through the

Planet	Picture	Sign	Picture
Sun		Aries	
Moon		Taurus	
Mercury		Gemini	
Venus		Cancer	
Mars		Leo	
Jupiter		Virgo	
Saturn		Libra	
Uranus		Scorpio	
Neptune		Sagittarius	
Pluto		Capricorn	
Ascendant	'EAST'	Aquarius	
MidHeaven	'SOUTH'	Pisces	

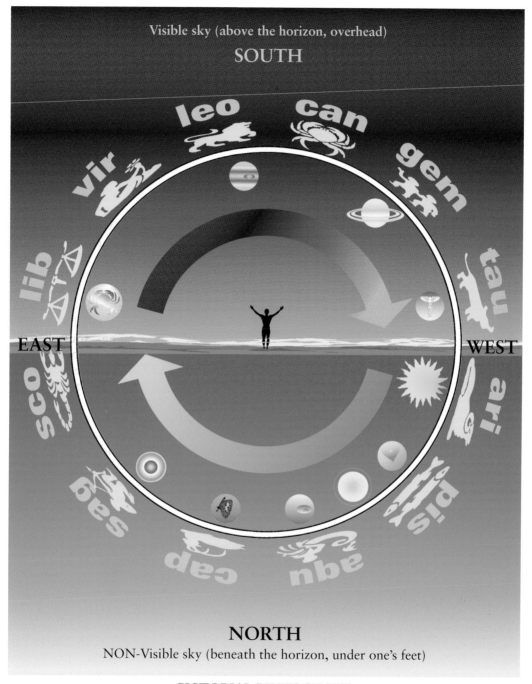

PICTORIAL BIRTH CHART
Example: Full Moon on April 16th 2003 at 8.40p.m in London, England

Zodiac of Signs in a progressively anti-clockwise direction (Aries, Taurus, Gemini, and so on). **But** as the Earth is turning in the same direction at a faster rate, the Sun, Moon, Planets and Signs are therefore seen to move in a **clockwise** direction, rising in the East (as the Moon here is doing), culminating overhead (as Jupiter is doing here) – this is approximately South in the Northern Hemisphere and North in the Southern – and then setting in the West (as the Sun has just done here), disappearing behind the Earth (as a number of Planets have done in this Chart) and reappearing as they again rise in the East (the first one to do this here will be Pluto as it rises in Sagittarius). The Birth Chart is simply a snapshot of where they all are in their movement at that moment in time when one was born.

Now let us look at the Birth Chart proper. Opposite you will see what is simply a more diagrammatic version of the pictorial Birth Chart shown on the previous page. The Horizon is now just a horizontal line going from left to right, broken in the middle by a smaller, numbered, circle containing a collection of lines. There is now also a more or less vertical line with MC at the top of it. And then there is a table of data below it all. So the 'real' Birth Chart contains more information about exactly where the Sun, Moon and Planets are placed in the Zodiac and in relationship to the Horizon and to one another. Namely...

The left-hand or East point of the Horizon is called the Ascendant (AS) and in this case is in Scorpio, which means that this person was born with Scorpio Rising. Note that in the Southern Hemisphere everything is reversed, but the astrological convention is to have the East still on the left. So the actual sky in the Southern Hemisphere does not match the image of the Chart unless you face South, lie down and tilt your head backwards and look North! In any event, the vertical line is called the Meridian and the top end is the MidHeaven (MC), which is where the Sun is at midday. Both the Ascendant and MidHeaven are important points in a Birth Chart as you will find out in the interpretations in the Profiles. The Zodiac, you will see, is now just glyphs only, and calibrated. Each calibration is 1 degree of arc, a Sign being 30 degrees. The table below the Birth Chart gives all the exact positions of the Sun, Moon, Planets, Ascendant and MidHeaven in the Signs by Degree (°) and Minute ('). For example, the Sun is at 26° 24' of Aries, usually just written 26♈24, and so is in the last five degree segment, near the end of the Sign. The Ascendant is 04♏39, in early Scorpio.

Then there are the Houses. These are twelve segments of space in relation to the Horizon, and are indicated in the Chart with a number near the smaller inner circle. The Houses always begin with the First House just below the Eastern Horizon or Ascendant (also called the First House Cusp) and unfold anticlockwise, finishing just above the Eastern Horizon with the Twelfth House. The Sun in this case can be seen to be placed in the Sixth House, both graphically and as given in the table beneath, where can be found the House positions of all the other Planets and Points.

Finally there are the Aspects which depict certain relationships between the Sun, Moon, Planets, Ascendant and MidHeaven, which are determined by being a particular number of degrees apart at the centre of the Chart, and to within a certain 'orb of influence'. The closer this Orb is to 00°00' the more exact and consequently powerful will be the influence of that Aspect, with 8°00' being usually the absolute maximum (and so weakest influence)

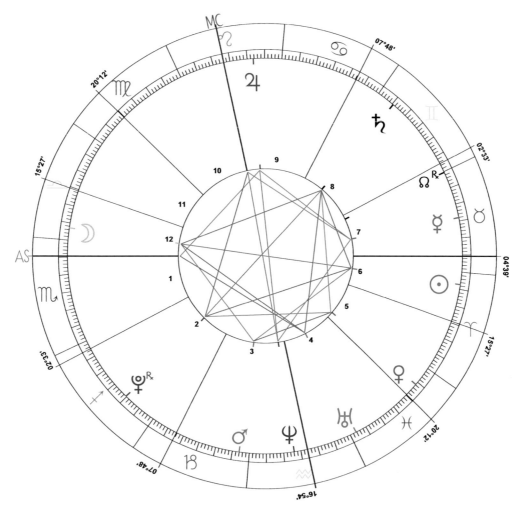

Full Moon Wednesday 16 Apr 2003 20.40 BST – 1.00 London, United Kingdom 51N30 0W10

Planet/Point	Glyph	Sign	Glyph	Position	House
Sun	☉	Aries	♈	26°24′	6th
Moon	☽	Libra	♎	26°26′	12th
Mercury	☿	Taurus	♉	15°58′	7th
Venus	♀	Pisces	♓	24°07′	5th
Mars	♂	Capricorn	♑	26°52′	3rd
Jupiter	♃	Leo	♌	08°18′	9th
Saturn	♄	Gemini	♊	24°39′	8th
Uranus	♅	Pisces	♓	01°46′	4th
Neptune	♆	Aquarius	♒	12°57′	3rd
Pluto	♇	Sagittarius	♐	19°47′℞	2nd
Ascendant	AS	Scorpio	♏	04°39′	ᴄ
MidHeaven	MC	Leo	♌	16°54′	ᴄ
North Lunar Node	☊	Taurus	♉	29°46′℞	7th

℞= Retrograde motion, meaning that this planet *appeared* to be going backwards at this time. This is owing to its position relative the Earth. When a planet goes from Retrograde to Direct, or vice versa, it slows down, goes stationary, then speeds up again.

that is allowed by *The Instant Astrologer*. The Aspects in the Chart itself are depicted by coloured lines in the inner circle, coloured according to the type of Aspect. The Table on page 36 tells what these Aspects and their colours actually are. The Table below gives all the major Aspects in this example Birth Chart along with the closeness of Orb.

Be aware that the Chart shown here is in only one of quite a number of styles used. What the Planets, Signs, House and Aspects mean or symbolize is explained in the next section.

Full Moon 16 April 2003 8.40 p.m. London 51N30 0W10
PLANETARY ASPECTS

Planet Aspect	(mode of relationship)	Planet or Point	Glyphs	Orb
Sun	Opposition (confronting)	Moon	☉ ☍ ☽	00°02′
Sun	Square (challenging)	Mars	☉ □ ♂	00°27′
Sun	Sextile (co-operating with)	Saturn	☉ ⚹ ♄	01°44′
Sun	Trine (harmonizing with)	Pluto	☉ △ ♇	06°36′
Moon	Square (challenging)	Mars	☽ □ ♂	00°25′
Moon	Trine (harmonizing with)	Saturn	☽ △ ♄	01°47′
Moon	Trine (harmonizing with)	Uranus	☽ △ ♅	05°19′
Mercury	Square (challenging)	Jupiter	☿ □ ♃	07°39′
Mercury	Square (challenging)	Neptune	☿ □ ♆	03°01′
Mercury	Square (challenging)	MidHeaven	☿ □ MC	00°56′
Venus	Sextile (co-operating with)	Mars	♀ ⚹ ♂	02°44′
Venus	Square (challenging)	Saturn	♀ □ ♄	00°31′
Venus	Square (challenging)	Pluto	♀ □ ♇	04°20′
Jupiter	Opposition (confronting)	Neptune	♃ ☍ ♆	04°38′
Jupiter	Square (challenging)	Ascendant	♃ □ AS	03°39′
Saturn	Trine (harmonizing with)	Uranus	♄ △ ♅	07°07′
Saturn	Opposition (confronting)	Pluto	♄ ☍ ♇	04°51′
Uranus	Trine (harmonizing with)	Ascendant	♅ △ AS	02°53′
Neptune	Opposition (confronting)	MidHeaven	♆ ☍ MC	03°57′
Pluto	Trine (harmonizing with)	MidHeaven	♇ △ MC	02°52′

2. THE BIRTH CHART –
WHAT IT MEANS

Now that I have explained what are the component parts of a Birth Chart, we can look and see what they actually mean in general terms before revealing what they all indicate about an individual human being. The four main ingredients in a Birth Chart are: The Sun, Moon and Planets; The Signs of the Zodiac; The Houses, which include the Ascendant (also called the First House Cusp or beginning of that House) and MidHeaven (also called the Tenth House Cusp or beginning of *that* House); and The Aspects.

  The Sun, Moon and Planets symbolize energies or forces, which you personally express, feel or embody according to their positions in your Birth Chart by Sign, House and Aspect. Here are some keyword meanings for the Sun, Moon and Planets:

The SUN represents your Will, Heart and Purpose.
The MOON represents your Emotional Needs and Responses.
MERCURY represents your Mentality and powers of Perception.
VENUS represents your sense of Harmony and your powers of Attraction.
MARS represents your Sexual Drive and powers of Self-Assertion.
JUPITER represents your sense of Growth and Faith.
SATURN represents your sense of Necessity and Duty.
URANUS represents Awakening and your sense of Freedom and Originality.
NEPTUNE represents Oneness and your Sensitivity and Imagination.
PLUTO represents Transformation and your sense of Power and Destiny.

The Signs are symbols of quality of expression (see chart overleaf). So the Sign position of each Planet (as well as your Ascendant and MidHeaven) determines how that Planet's energy is seeking to symbolically express itself through your life and personality.

MODES: Cardinal Signs are Initiating; Fixed Signs are Persistent; Mutable Signs are Adaptable. (For more about Modes see page 528.)

ELEMENTS: FIRE Signs show Eagerness   EARTH Signs embody Practicality
                  AIR Signs engender Principles   WATER Signs imbue with Feelings
(For more about Elements see page 521.)

Ruling Planets: These are the Planets that correspond to the qualities of the Signs that they rule or govern. Their significance will become apparent in the interpretations given in the Profile. There is some dispute amongst astrologers about the Signs, if any, that the Outer Planets – Uranus, Neptune and Pluto – govern. These Planets were discovered in 1781, 1846 and 1930 respectively, long after the rulerships had been established. However, they were seen by some to be more suitable or modern rulers over Aquarius, Pisces and

SIGN	QUALITY	ELEMENT	MODE	RULING PLANET
ARIES	Action & Challenge	Fire	Cardinal	Mars
TAURUS	Stability & Productivity	Earth	Fixed	Venus
GEMINI	Communication & Inquiry	Air	Mutable	Mercury
CANCER	Security & Nurture	Water	Cardinal	The Moon
LEO	Creativity & Self-Expression	Fire	Fixed	The Sun
VIRGO	Purity & Improvement	Earth	Mutable	Mercury
LIBRA	Balance & Harmony	Air	Cardinal	Venus
SCORPIO	Power & Intimacy	Water	Fixed	Pluto (formerly Mars)
SAGITTARIUS	Furtherance & Enthusiasm	Fire	Mutable	Jupiter
CAPRICORN	Control & Organization	Earth	Cardinal	**Saturn**
AQUARIUS	Freedom & Reform	Air	Fixed	Uranus (formerly Saturn)
PISCES	Acceptance & Inspiration	Water	Mutable	Neptune (formerly Jupiter)

Scorpio. This is the view taken in *The Instant Astrologer*, but the former rulers are also given and can be used if one sees fit when references are made to Rulers of these Signs.

Using the Keywords: One of the best ways to come to an understanding of what a Birth Chart is 'saying' is to use the Keywords relevant to the various astrological indications, as given here. So, for example, the person born with the Birth Chart we have been using here (16 April 2003 at 8.40 p.m. in London, England) has the Sun in Aries and would or should express their Will and Purpose through taking Action and accepting Challenges. Any Planet in Aries would be prone to taking the Initiative Eagerly (Cardinal Fire). The drive and assertiveness of this Sign is also expressed by its ruler, Mars.

The Houses: These symbolize fields of experience. They represent where, in what areas of your life and personality, the Planets in their respective Signs, most readily find expression. There are a number of different House Systems used in astrology, there being some question as to how to divide up the segments of sky between those physical and undisputed points, called the Angles, which are the Eastern Horizon (Ascendant), the Zenith (MidHeaven), Western Horizon (Descendant or DS) and Nadir (Lower MidHeaven or IC). *The Instant Astrologer* employs the most popular House System, called Placidus. The shaded Houses opposite are called the Angular Houses for they correspond to these Angles. As such they are the same in all the House Systems (with a few

HOUSE	FIELD OF EXPERIENCE
FIRST (incorporating Ascendant)	Birth, Self, Presentation, Persona, Identity, Character
SECOND	Finances, Income, Self-Worth, Material World, Property
THIRD	Communication, Primary/Secondary Education, Siblings, Everyday Encounters
FOURTH (inc. Lower MidHeaven)	Inner or Private World, Security, Home-Life, Roots, Origins, Gene Pool
FIFTH	Creative/Self Expression, Children, Pastimes, Romance, Gambling, Play
SIXTH	Health, Training, Work, Preparation, Techniques, Order, Colleagues, Service
SEVENTH (inc. Descendant)	Relationships, Others, Projected Self, Spouse, Adversaries
EIGHTH	Intimacy, Transformation, Occult/Hidden Matters, Others' Resources
NINTH	Foreign Parts, Law, Higher Education, Travel, Beliefs, Academia, Philosophy
TENTH (incorporating MidHeaven)	Outer or Public World, Profession, Earthly Purpose, Status, Reputation
ELEVENTH	Associations, Friends, Politics, Aspirations, Groups, Ideals, Movements
TWELFTH	Karma, Spiritual Realm, Collective Unconscious, Confinement, Womb-life

exceptions) and are also the most influential Houses in real terms, as can be seen by what they represent: Self-Roots-Relationship-Purpose. This, as can be seen in the Birth Chart or ChartWheel itself, is literally the 'cross we bear'.

Using the Keywords: To continue with our example then, this individual with Sun in Aries in the Sixth House could seek to express their Will through Health Challenges or Active, even Pioneering, Work, Training themselves or others for something (Sixth House) that was close to their heart (Sun).

The Aspects: These indicate the combined effect of certain planetary pairs and the angular relationship in degrees of arc between them (formed at the centre of the Birth Chart). They therefore reveal how one part of your being gets on with another part. These could be called the inner dynamics of your personality, and as such they also affect your interaction with the outside world. There are quite a number of different (and sometimes quite obscure) Aspects, but *The Instant Astrologer* only uses the five Major Aspects, which are as follows (including when there is no Major Aspect formed at all):

ASPECT	GLYPH	DEGREES APART	TYPE OF RELATIONSHIP	BASIC QUALITY
CONJUNCTION	☌	0°	Uniting with or Intensifying (initiating)	Hard & Soft
SQUARE	□	90°	Challenging (urging resolution)	Hard
OPPOSITION	☍	180°	Confronting (awareness increasing)	Hard
TRINE	△	120°	Harmonizing with, or Supporting	Soft
SEXTILE	✳	60°	Co-operating with, or Assisting	Soft
UNASPECTED	⊘	None of the above	Indeterminate/Free to choose	Hard & Soft

HARD Aspects: These are demanding, and create tension that produces awareness, and challenges that could lead to achievement. They motivate one to do something because it is unacceptable staying where one is. Too many Hard Aspects can lead to mental, emotional or physical ill health.

SOFT Aspects: These are harmonious, and create flow that supplies confidence, and ease that allows well-being. Too many Soft Aspects can however give rise to complacency, laziness or a lack of motivation.

MUTUALITY of Aspects: This means that the two Planets involved in an Aspect are influencing one another, not just one to the other. In the Personality Profile Interpretations each Aspect is described from the perspective of each Planet in the Chapter that is relevant to that Planet.

Using the Keywords: Continuing with our example, Sun in Aries in the Sixth House in Opposition to the Moon in Libra in the Twelfth House, would be Confronted by Confinement brought on by a Need for Harmony. In other words, the forcefulness of their Aries Sun would be compromised by their Libra Moon's need for pleasantness which, in itself, is a result of what happened in the womb, which would have a karmic issue behind that.

Information and Intuition: Through using the information given in the Personality Profile, and using your intuition, and with the help of the **Synthesis** on page 537 and more **Keywords** on page 553, you will become versed in the art of astrology.

3. CREATING A PERSONALITY PROFILE

1. If you haven't already, **install** *The Instant Astrologer* software from the CD according to the instructions.

2. Open the program and you will see you have FOUR CHOICES:
1. Personality Profile
2. Timeline Profile
3. Relationship Profile
4. Quit

Select 'Personality Profile'

3. Input Birth Details. If *The Instant Astrologer* cannot find the Birth Place (entered against **City of Birth**) it'll be because it is too small, and you will be prompted to re-enter the nearest town. It could also be queried if spelt wrong, or because the country is wrong (which may be due to historical border changes). For a United States Birth Place select the relevant State.

If you wish you may **Save Birth Details** by selecting that button. If you have already saved the Details you want to use, select **Load Birth Details**.

Unknown or Vague Birth Times: If you do not know the Birth Time at all, then tick the **'Time not known'** box. This will automatically enter 12 p.m. (noon) as this will give the 'mean' positions of the Sun, Moon and Planets. You should then disregard the Ascendant Profile, MidHeaven Profile and the House Positions for the Sun, Moon and all Planets (unless it turns out that the actual birth time was around noon) for all of these indications are determined by Birth Time. In some cases of unknown or just a vague Birth Time, even the Moon Sign cannot be relied upon for it may have changed Signs during that day. If you find that the Moon-Sign does not ring true, then calculate a Chart for earlier or later in the day and you could find a different Moon-Sign. Read that interpretation and that could fit, and also lead you closer to what the Birth Time really is. Another way of getting a clearer idea of Birth Time is to check all the Rising Signs in the book (page 43), see if one sounds right, then work it backwards by looking for the time when that was the Rising Sign. If the Birth Time is merely vague, within a few hours, then this will affect the Rising Sign and House Positions, possibly to within one or two Signs or Houses either way. For example, if you know you were born between, say, between 4 and 6 in the morning, then do Charts for 4, 5 and 6 o'clock, and deduce from the interpretations which one appears to have the most appropriate positions. Doing this will also give you some idea of the rate at which a Chart changes. The Rising Sign, for instance, changes on average every two hours, some Signs quicker or slower, depending on the latitude of birth place.

Namefile Notables: The Instant Astrologer has already stored the birth data of a number well-known people for you to create Profiles for if you so wish.

4. You now have FOUR CHOICES:

a) View Full Profile – To read the whole Personality Profile *on screen only.*

b) Print/View Index – To read the Personality Profile Index* *on screen only*, then if you wish, select the Print option to print the Index.

c) Print/View ChartWheel – To see the Birth Chart itself (plus data) *on screen only*, then if you wish, select the Print option to print it.

d) Return – To return to the Select Profile window.

* **The Personality Profile Index** simply gives all the astrological configurations in the Birth Chart along with the page numbers in this book where they are interpreted. When printed, the Index enables you to study a Profile at your leisure wherever you may be.

5. If you have chosen:

a) View Full Profile - All you have to do is read what is on the screen, scrolling up and down as you require. You can exit at any time or place you wish.

b) Print /View Index - Simply read what the Personality Profile Index says on the screen or on the page, and you will be directed to the pages in the book where the interpretations for the relevant astrological configurations will be found. It is strongly recommended that at first you read these interpretations in the order they are given in the Index for they are composed in such a way as to follow on from one another, helping you to see how the various parts of personality are interrelated. Later, when you want to look at a certain configuration that interests you, or that is referred to in a Timeline Profile or Relationship Profile, or for whatever reason, you can dip in where and when you choose.

d) Print/View Chartwheel - You will have an actual Birth Chart (plus data) to look at and use alongside the interpretations, use for Setting The Scene (page 519) or Synthesis (page 537), keep on file, mount and frame, or do with as you wish.

With all of the above options, you can return to the Personality Profile page at any time.

4. USING A PERSONALITY PROFILE

Whilst reading a Personality Profile – whether you view it as a whole on-screen or in the book via the Profile Index – please bear in mind that although the Birth Chart and its interpretation are as accurate and informative as possible, there is no guarantee that every word will apply at this moment in time, or in the past or future. This is because a Birth Chart maps out one's *potential* and is not able to say what one has made, or will make, of that potential. Whilst reading, you should rely upon your own judgement and individual choice, will and inclination – which are precisely what your own Personality Profile is aimed at shedding light upon.

Sometimes you will notice certain contradictions between certain traits. This is simply because such contradictions exist, which can be seen as what makes for an interesting character, or, as inner conflicts that must be resolved. Conversely, you may observe the repetition of certain characteristics, which simply implies that such are particularly strong ones. Ideally, before reading a Personality Profile you should 'set the scene' by determining some basic energies in the Chart, namely, the Elemental, Modal and Hemispheric emphases, and the Lunar Nodes. Equipped with Planetary Placements given at the beginning of the Profile or Profile Index, this is quite simple and fun to work out – see page 519 **Setting The Scene**. This section and the one following it, entitled **Synthesis** on page 537, will help you read the Profile in a manner that enables you to piece together the various traits and influences, which is what the skill of 'astrologizing' is actually about. However, this is only recommended and not essential, so you can just carry on reading the Profile right away if you wish.

Finally, the overall accuracy of the Personality Profile depends upon the accuracy of the given Birth Time. If the Birth Time is unknown you should have drawn up a Noon Chart (12 p.m.) – see *Unknown or Vague Birth Times* in **Creating a Personality Profile** above, where this procedure and certain important observations are explained.

Introducing Yourself To You - Here follow
the Personality Profile Interpretations...

5. THE PERSONALITY PROFILE INTERPRETATIONS

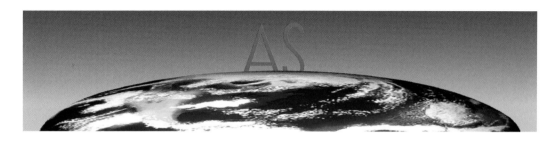

CHAPTER ONE – YOUR ASCENDANT PROFILE
APPEARANCE AND PERSONA

The Rising Sign is simply the Zodiacal Sign that is rising in the East – that is on the Ascendant – at the time of birth, and the Setting Sign is the one that is setting in the West – or on the Descendant – at that time. The Ascendant and Descendant are therefore always in opposite Signs. For example, anyone who has Scorpio Rising (Scorpio on the Ascendant) would always have Taurus Setting (Taurus on the Descendant) because Scorpio and Taurus are opposite Signs (see this graphically in The Birth Chart on pages 29&31). The House just below, or beginning with, the Ascendant is the First House. The House just above, or beginning with, the Descendant is the Seventh House.

What the Rising Sign (and any Planets in the First House, to which your Profile or Profile Index will refer) represents and describes is SELF-EXPRESSION, that is, what it is about an individual that is presented to the world as their IDENTITY, CHARACTER or IMAGE. The event this stems from, and also describes the nature of, is BIRTH, when what you APPEAR to be EMERGES into the world. And it continues to describe the FIRST IMPRESSION, both given and taken.

What the Setting Sign (and any Planets in the Seventh House, to which your Profile or Profile Index will refer) represents and describes is the equal and opposite reaction to this expression of Self. It is OTHER – that is, anyone or anything that we pull in as a compensation and response to our Ascendant or Self-Expression. Consequently, PARTNERS will often have your Setting Sign prominent in their own Birth Chart – like having the Sun, Moon, Ascendant or a group of Planets in that Sign. Or they will embody the qualities of any Seventh House Planets. For this reason, the Descendant and Seventh House are also indicative of your ALTER EGO, BETTER HALF or PROJECTED SELF (that is the parts of yourself that you look for or see in others) and so hate or love them.

The following interpretations describe the Rising Sign and in turn what it attracts in the form of relationship – referred to as 'OTHER' – in terms of the Setting Sign and its Ruler, which will include your Shadow. In each case, it will also be explained why you are alone if you happen to be so. The Ruling Planets (see page 33) are given for both and you are referred to the chapters where they are described (viewed either on screen as your whole Profile or on the pages given in your Profile Index), as this will shed further light on how you express yourself and the type of people or relationships you attract.

RISING SIGNS

Aries Rising

AS ♈

You take on the role of leader, so invariably you act first, decide what's to be done, and get things moving. Other acts as a counterbalance to this, depending upon how agreeable they find it, and whether it fits in with the general consensus or not. Other will usually try to be diplomatic in the face of your unequivocal stance. If Other is particularly unsure of their own standpoint they will go along – happily or not – with whatever your decision or action happens to be. If or when they have a more definite opinion, and they are not entirely happy with your tack, they will deal with your forcefulness in the following way. First they'll try to get you to see their own or another's position. Failing that they'll argue a bit, and failing that they'll use passive resistance. But any soppiness or superficiality on Other's part would be vigorously attacked by you.

You are uncomfortable with having to wait things out, or with letting things develop outside of your initiative. It is as if you see any passivity or consideration of other people's opinions as flabby indecisiveness, and as being a sure sign of asking to be beaten to the punch. But what you see as precarious indecision is really a weighing of the pros and cons of a situation, a look taken at any possible repercussions, and a generally more harmonious manner. Taking this on board would prevent the strife, dissatisfaction, and even disaster which your pushiness, egocentricity or impetuosity can attract.

Your optimum relationship should be balanced and fair, with yourself and Other having equal say in all matters – very much the partnership, in fact. Despite what you might think to the contrary, other people tend or like to see you both as the couple, the social touchstone, even an example of how a relationship ought to work. What you need – despite your wilfulness, or rather because of it – is quite a conventional relationship, the social unit that your milieu comes to rely upon as 'always being there'. All this acts as a stabilizer to your dynamic persona, and as a safe haven to which you may return after one of your sorties.

When or if alone, it is because your selfish and inconsiderate behaviour has caught up with you and there are no takers. But your pushiness, although it can be sometimes downright rude or thoughtless, does not as a rule have malice behind it. It is just that having to get your oar in first can lead to you being the only one on board. Seeing that the kind of Other you attract is usually a deferential, socially aware person, they will probably put up with you for quite some time, then unexpectedly turn the tables on you. It is important for you to soften your hard edge enough to let your softness show, rather than being seen by Other as a challenge or a threat.

Mars is your Ruling Planet, which governs the link between your exterior being and your interior being. So study Chapter Seven – Your Mars Profile, with this in mind. Your Setting Sign is Libra and therefore the Planet Venus governs your relationships, so study Chapter Six with that in mind.

Taurus Rising ♉

AS ♉

You are very much the creature of Nature and the physical senses, exuding an aura of permanence and constancy. You do not like to be hurried or pushed into anything unknown or too new, and are happiest when surrounded by whatever is familiar to you. No matter how you actually look, there is a tactile, even huggable, feel about you – an animal magnetism, in fact. But it is just this slow and physically strong presence that attracts an Other who is not content to leave things as they are. Other is more inclined to dig beneath your placid or stubborn surface in search of the soul and passion that they detect underneath. This ruffles you as much as it excites you – and there's the rub. It is as if you need that 'sting' to stop you from sliding into the mud of your resistance to change – and the sting that works best is sexual in nature. But should Other push you too far, or excite you too much even, you dig your hooves in deeper than ever.

You are uncomfortable with feelings that are too arousing or provocative – a bit like a red rag is to a bull, one could say. Your reaction to such intensity of feeling is to bear your weight down upon it, which means to flatten it with earthy logic, or to simply not acknowledge it or even see it. But the more you deny this, your Shadow, the more you will attract what you'll interpret as disruption. Your pleasure-seeking and sensual persona is bound to evoke deep passions in Other, so it would be wise to understand the secret and psychological workings of human nature, then they won't take your earthy straightforwardness unawares.

A deeply committed relationship is definitely the fodder for you, the type of partnership that can endure quite heavy conflicts or tests of fidelity. At times you may feel trapped and manipulated by such an arrangement, as if you have been bought body and soul. But yours is a rich and fertile pairing, the kind that produces and provides. Rather like a farm that is dependent upon its soil, you have to keep nurturing it, occasionally turning it over, ploughing the goodness back in to regenerate it, letting it lie fallow, etc. Indeed, the seasonal cycle of birth and rebirth, prospering and dying, epitomizes your style of relationship.

When or if alone it is simply because you have not been prepared to accept the deep commitment and mutual possession that this Rising/Setting combination demands. Possibly you fear your depths being plumbed, or that Other would not like what they found beneath your attractive surface. Because of that surface you have no difficulty attracting a mate, but you make the mistake of doubting the profound value of what lies beneath it. After all, a garden is only as good as its soil.

Venus is your Ruling Planet, which governs the link between your exterior being and your interior being. So study Chapter Six – Your Venus Profile, with this in mind. Your Setting Sign is Scorpio and therefore the Planet Pluto governs your relationships, so study Chapter Twelve with that in mind.

Gemini Rising

AS ♊

You approach life in the spirit of enquiry, like the eternal student. You love making connections between one thing and another, without necessarily having to feel any sense of where it is all heading or what it all means. You are also a keen maker of contacts, priding yourself on being acquainted with all types of individual and scene. Not surprisingly, you are equipped with quick wits and word-power. Quite what all this amounts to, that is, who it is that is doing all this talking, thinking and enquiring, can be very elusive. And so you attract an Other intent on teaching you to become some kind of comprehensive whole. Because of this, Other can organize you into an entity of more meaning and emotional integrity – if you let them. However, this can make you feel preached at, and you may wriggle even more in order to remain the free agent you identify with being, even chopping and changing identities to facilitate this.

Your friendliness and conversational ease give the lie to the fact that behind such affability there languishes a quite aloof and even supercilious being. It is as if there is a dimension to your personality that you feel is apart from the world, that no one can ever reach or understand. But because this is your Shadow and as such is denied, you wind up feeling there is a part of you that you must keep out of sight, and so you use your agile tongue and wits to throw Other off the scent. If you accepted your Shadow, you would find that is not so much superiority but more a sense of your higher self – looking out for you, in spite of yourself.

You love a relationship that feels as if it is going somewhere. The trouble is, with your dilettante-like nature, you will interpret this quite literally as going on a trip or travelling abroad with someone. Really, this means that your relationship has to amount to something in a philosophical or even religious sense, like a moral statement. It is as if the relationship is a hair-clasp that holds together all the disparate strands of your Mercurial temperament. Without understanding or accepting this style, you had better resign yourself to a series of inconsequential affairs posing as a love life – the sum being *less* than the total of the parts.

When or if alone, you will, apart from anything else, have your alter ego for company. And this is the clue as to why you are alone: you are disinclined to allow an Other to see the side to your nature which is the 'dark twin', that is, the one who you assume would not be accepted by Other. What characterizes this dark twin you may know in your heart, and it could be described somewhere in these pages under the influence of some Planet. But whatever it is like, let it out so that it might grow to be seen, known, loved, and transformed.

Mercury is your Ruling Planet, which governs the link between your exterior being and your interior being. So study Chapter Five – Your Mercury Profile, with this in mind. Your Setting Sign is Sagittarius and therefore the Planet Jupiter governs your relationships, so study Chapter Eight with that in mind.

Cancer Rising BM
AS ♋

You are all 'feelers', picking up the emotional climate around you with instinctive ease. It can seem at times that you are purely response and react to whomever you are with or wherever you are. This can result in your not being at all sure whether it is your feeling or someone else's. In any event, you have to respond in some way, usually giving care or sympathy, or needing it – or you simply withdraw into your famous shell until it's 'safe' to come out again. Cancer Rising has been described as the 'Emotional Waste Paper Basket', for you can be 'dumped upon' as a result of appearing too available emotionally. With such moodiness being the hallmark of your identity you are inclined to attract an Other who is more emotionally controlled, restrained or repressed even. They may also be somewhat older than you, biologically or psychologically, and therefore more adult or worldly. Other provides you with the equipment and technique that make it possible to function in the harsh material world that your childlike persona can blanch at. If Other's more mature stance appears cold or calculating to you, though, you will give a commensurate display of fearfulness and/or withdrawal.

Your dreamy, sensitive and sentimental response to life makes you react negatively to anything that appears to be coldly realistic and unfeeling. But that is often all it is – a *reaction* that interprets a businesslike and objective approach to things as being alien and unfamiliar, and therefore uncaring. Such a subjective response has at its root a feeling of insecurity that has your mother, father, and childhood as the reason behind it. Take a step back and see that this impersonal attitude is the very objectivity, seriousness, and sober sense of purpose that you need to learn and acquire so as to feel more safe and secure in the world.

You require a traditional type of relationship, where each of you has a clear sense of their role and position in it. This may feel restrictive and limiting at first, but eventually, and paradoxically, this feeling of having and knowing your boundaries and responsibilities is what makes you feel secure and protected enough to go out and explore your potentials and make the most of yourself. An open, easy-come-easy-go kind of relationship would not give you this. As the Chinese proverb says 'Limitation is the key to freedom.'

When or if alone, it is very likely because you have not accepted the limitations or lessons of a relationship in the way outlined above. Without doing this, a relationship, or Other, can wither on the vine. Seeking some kind of unrealistic 'freedom' can be the culprit behind this, and the reason behind that can be a very basic and unconscious distrust of finding any Other whom you can rely upon at all. Alternatively, not taking a tough enough 'impersonal' stance with Other can leave you feeling emotionally exhausted, if not on your own.

The Moon is your Ruling Planet, which governs the link between your exterior being and your interior being. So study Chapter Three – Your Moon Profile, with this in mind. Your Setting Sign is Capricorn and therefore the Planet Saturn governs your relationships, so study Chapter Nine with that in mind.

Leo Rising
AS ♌

Like a king or queen you express yourself with apparent confidence and style, with a regal air that names the game and sets the rules. This attracts Other who, like the court jester, positively responds only when you are aware of what is popular and have at heart the interests of Other. Failing this, you are met with cool indifference, mockery or outright rebellion. Conversely, Other's views and theories about life and society, if only slightly tinged with political correctness, are shot down by you with a blast of passionate self-justification. When, on the other hand, Other's populist point is expressed in such a way as to make it clear that noting it would lead to elevating your individual position, then you graciously and happily accept it.

You have a dread of being merely one amongst the grey mass of human society, so you rankle when Other shows signs of being a member of this large and unexclusive club with values that subscribe to fitting in but at the same time want to be slightly different too. Such naffness is what you yourself live in fear of being seen as. But being a bit so-called ordinary can be paradoxically quite quirky, and more to the point, helps you to be less self-conscious and more at ease with the world. This is like the monarch who is far more popular with his subjects because he is seen to be like them than if he held himself apart from and above them.

Unusual and unprecedented types of interaction, with the accent of freedom, are what suit you, despite the hassle and unpredictability they engender. It is as if you are inventing a set of values that will suit you and Other exclusively. This quality of your relationships reflects what the poet Kahlil Gibran advised any couple: 'Let the winds of the Heavens dance between you.' In other words, don't ever fall into complacency by thinking you really know, let alone own, one another, or shock and upset will descend upon you. In any event, you are inclined to run hot and cold, go on/off, as needs for freedom and companionship alternate.

When or if alone – or without success in, or recognition from, the world at large – it is no doubt because you have been sticking stubbornly to an egocentric viewpoint or value system that failed to appeal to Other. So Other had to follow the only course open to them in the face of such overt self-righteousness. If in future you began to show that behind your magnificent facade you are an ordinary, feeling human being, then Other – either in their current form or a new one – will be only too pleased to bask in your light or appreciate your creative expressions. Just so long as your bright persona is not just a defence system against a world you feel does not understand you. The truth is that it will not do so as long as you fail to show the mere human inside.

The Sun is your Ruling Planet, which governs the link between your exterior being and your interior being. So study Chapter Two – Your Sun Profile, with this in mind. Your Setting Sign is Aquarius and therefore the Planet Uranus governs your relationships, so study Chapter Ten with that in mind.

Virgo Rising
AS ♍

You approach life with a view to improving the quality of it in some way, and so you have an eye for detail, and more to the point, an eye for what is flawed, unclean, untidy or unhealthy. Consequently, you are almost constantly on the go – there is always something or someone that needs seeing to from where you stand. This means that Other will very often fall into this category of what 'needs seeing to'. So Other may be vague, unkempt, absentminded, weak or in some way in need of practical attention – or at least, that is how they'll seem to you. And this is the point, because you can make a rod for your back with all manner of lame-ducks, hopeless cases, addicts or invalids becoming your Other – or workload rather – simply because you see Other as something in need of your attention. Other's response to this will be to be even more vague, unkempt, etc, for you are only too willing to take the strain. But if you dropped your critical gaze for long enough you might see that Other is showing a way to be more accepting and laid back about life.

Your need for things to be 'just so' masks a fear of collapse and confusion. Put more accurately, your Shadow is actually a profound doubt that life and Other will be alright without your constant attention, especially to those details. You find it hard to trust the fact that, in life, some things (just have to) work themselves out in their own way and time. As if to show you that you can no more control Other than a sailor can control the sea, the 'confusion' can leak in with your being particularly messy in one area of your life, and quite indiscriminate in some of your relationships. Pick what you ought to let go of – then do so.

A mixture or purity and 'anything goes' would be a shorthand if somewhat contradictory description of your ideal relationship. Unconditional with distinct no-go areas would be another. What all this amounts to is that you are attempting to find that perfect relationship, and the nearer you get to it the more you appreciate that such a thing is a paradox. And the further you get from it the more impossible it seems. The answer is to keep working at it until you have distilled that blend of discernment and acceptance.

When or if alone, it is simply because you have priced yourself out of the market. Virgo is the Sign of the Hermit so you are more likely than most to get left on the shelf – out of choice, you'd protest. You may well like it that way, but if you did you'd hardly be reading this – unless you were sorting someone else out. More to the point though, you are inclined to find no one quite right because there is some deep-seated flaw of your own which you have classified as untouchable or hopeless. Not so – just simply in need of practice.

Mercury is your Ruling Planet, which governs the link between your exterior being and your interior being. So study Chapter Five – Your Mercury Profile, with this in mind. Your Setting Sign is Pisces and therefore the Planet Neptune governs your relationships, so study Chapter Eleven with that in mind.

Libra Rising

AS ♎

You want to make yourself out to be an agreeable and sociable person. Having a partner in life is more important for you than any other Rising Sign for it is a testament to this aspiration. Furthermore, you are willing to bend over backwards, make all sorts of compromises, and endlessly groom yourself in order to achieve this end of being the Other to an Other. This is all very well and very pleasant too, but the irony is that you attract someone who forces you ultimately to stand up for yourself, to be your own person and not just someone who harmonizes with someone else. Other to you can be quite disagreeable or lacking in the social graces, and could learn from your innate good manners and powers of diplomacy. But Other may be particularly acid should your style be merely a fashionable but superficial display of socially correct verbiage and mannerisms. However, there is also the possibility that Other will play along with you (such is our culture's programming to please and gain approval) and that eventually and shockingly the raw and crude reality of each of you bursts out, presenting your very real sense of harmony with a very real challenge.

If you often find yourself being unjustifiably attacked or mistreated by Other, you can be sure that you are being caught in your own Shadow. The image of charm and pleasantness that you project can fool you into thinking that there isn't an offensive bone in your body – or at least, apart from the ones that you choose to be aware of. But the fact is, being so nice is asking to be pushed around – which is a way of getting Other to act out the aggression that you have but only otherwise experience as anger, frustration or illness. Getting off the fence, stating your case, and being prepared to engage in conflict would resolve matters. A mean alternative to this is your Shadow taking the form of looking for an 'easier', supposedly conflict-free, relationship in an affair.

It is desirable that both you and Other regard yourselves and each other as individuals in your own rights. So a healthy sense of competitiveness is to be encouraged for it helps to keep each of you mindful of your individual worth and effectiveness. Being physically active, together and individually, is also recommended. Without creating or maintaining this theme, outright and destructive conflict could surface

When or if alone, it because the time has come for you to develop and come to terms with yourself as an individual being – that is, someone who has only themselves to contend with life. Although, or rather because, you need a partner more than most, it is inevitable that you will encounter such aloneness quite acutely at some point in your self-development. Naturally, such a state will not come upon you, or be embarked upon, easily – but it should be seen as a positive turning point, with a better relationship following upon it in due course.

Venus is your Ruling Planet, which governs the link between your exterior being and your interior being. So study Chapter Six – Your Venus Profile, with this in mind. Your Setting Sign is Aries and therefore the Planet Mars governs your relationships, so study Chapter Seven with that in mind.

Scorpio Rising
AS ♏

Your persona is like a probe, seeking out whatever lies beneath surface appearances to satisfy your hunger for passions, secrets, intrigues, and powerful emotions. At the same time you cloak your own feelings and intentions, becoming as impenetrable as you are penetrating. Other finds this intensely suggestive approach and personal style quite irresistible, succumbing like a hypnotist's subject or even a lamb (or bull – Taurus Setting!) to the slaughter. This is until it dawns on Other that they are not so sure about being under your spell – or who you are behind that cloak – and whether there's a dagger there too. At this point, when Other comes to suspect your secretiveness and the intentions behind it, they will dig their heels in and become impassive, immovable, intransigent – but still remain. In turn, this is the juncture when you must realize that you want Other to resist you because it is a sign that they are solid and loyal enough not to be perturbed by your sexual power plays and extremes of emotion. Great fulfilment can follow upon this 'deal' being made.

Considering that shady areas are what you are drawn to, it is not surprising to find that your own Shadow is quite ironic. All your secretiveness, devious ploys, and the tabs you keep on Other leave you curiously unaware of the obvious about yourself – that if you behave secretively then you must have an area of your personality that is particularly vulnerable. And you can be so busy protecting it that you can be caught unawares; what you feared most comes upon you. So when you identify and admit to this vulnerable area, what was gullibility then becomes an intense candour, which Other finds extremely binding and endearing.

A steady, traditional, almost 'down on the farm' kind of set-up suits you. What you may find wanting in the area of psychological acuteness or emotional intensity is made up for in a peaceful and natural relationship that is more concerned with creature comforts and natural appetites and values.

When or if alone, it is often the case that you are actually in a relationship but are alone within your heavily protective shell. You are caught between the need for an intimate relationship where Other knows your darkest secrets, and a fear of that vulnerability being disclosed. If you err in favour of the latter, you effectively shut Other out from your emotional interior. Inevitably Other will make the best of their own space, which effectively and progressively has less and less to do with you. If you are entirely on your own the same equation applies: to be as close to an Other as you need to be necessitates being aware enough of your own emotional hang-ups to trust an Other with them, rather than manipulating them through a knowledge of *their* hang-ups.

Pluto is your Ruling Planet, which governs the link between your exterior being and your interior being. So study Chapter Twelve – Your Pluto Profile, with this in mind. Your Setting Sign is Taurus and therefore the Planet Venus governs your relationships, so study Chapter Six with that in mind.

Sagittarius Rising

AS ♐

Like the superior being that you are inclined to present yourself as, you express yourself with a larger-than-life sense of confidence and apparent self-assurance. This attracts Other who, as the eternal gatherer of pieces of information, is impressed by your seemingly broad and effortless grasp of all manner of things. Other sees your persona as a role model for how to give off a cosmopolitan air that makes them look as knowledgeable as they potentially or actually are. However, should Other become aware that behind any particular facet of your self-advertisement there is no product to live up to it, then a kind of intellectual scorn towards what is seen as smugness or pretentiousness on your part can color their idea of you. Conversely, Other's array of endless but unrelated bytes of information, which is simply diversity, is helpful to you just as long as it doesn't annoy you.

What can really bug you about Other is a certain downmarket, irrelevant or inept quality, with a worrisome nature to match. But this is actually a reflection of your fear of being provincial or in *doubt*. Remind yourself that such 'inferiority' is an example to you of the common touch and concerns that would greatly complement, even complete, your talent for seeing the bigger picture. Being honest about your doubts will put Other at their ease and, consequently, they will feel more confident in themselves.

Variety and not getting too tied down are important to you. But so too is having the commitment to a lasting relationship. This contradiction is symbolized by having dualistic

Gemini on your Descendant. The resolution to this dilemma is to accept the fact that you lead a two-tone lifestyle and hope that Other will love you for the adventurous and exciting being that you are. Having more than one partner would be stretching this a bit, but, if such is the case, it would mean that you found it hard to be honest and share all of your light and shade with just one Other. Then again, it could fall to your partner to act out any suppressed duplicity or lack of commitment on your part!

When or if alone, it is most likely because you have simply found it so hard to commit yourself to a relationship that you have either been given up as a hopeless case, or you have never dared take any sort of plunge even into the shallows of a relationship. When it comes down to it, you hate being alone, for then you have to confront what are at the root of relationship problems: your own inconsistencies as opposed to those you see as belonging to Other. Sooner or later, this is the one plunge you will have to take – into your depths.

Jupiter is your Ruling Planet, which governs the link between your exterior being and your interior being. So study Chapter Eight – Your Jupiter Profile, with this in mind. Your Setting Sign is Gemini and therefore the Planet Mercury governs your relationships, so study Chapter Five with that in mind.

Capricorn Rising
AS ♑

You approach virtually everything and everyone in a tactical, businesslike manner; you certainly do not lead with your feelings. You generate an aura of material, political awareness and if anything needs organizing you'll be the first to offer – or rather start doing so without even being asked. Life to you is something to be managed and controlled, so when it comes to emotionally relating or social interplay you're not exactly one to let rip and let your hair down. Dependability and respectability are what you have on offer, not passion and drama. This is not to say that you have no sense of fun, but even that would have a certain limit placed upon it. Other cannot help but respond to all this serious, grown-up stuff in a commensurately emotional, childlike, and needy fashion. Either that, or you are not about to get much response at all, other than an equally restrained display. Hopefully then, Other will get you to melt and loosen up a bit, and appreciate that life can be a soulful adventure and not a matter-of-fact affair where you squash Other at one sign too many of playful romanticism or unscripted unworldliness. This would be a mistake because you need their caring, sympathetic, and comparatively immature input to get past your tough hide of an exterior

You live in dread of losing the control of keeping what's really on the inside becoming visible on the outside. You feel that to appear unworldly or naïve would amount to some kind of self-demolition. And because you are petrified of letting this child in you show, what you see as that guileless part of you becomes increasingly like a time bomb of a baby that one day is going to bawl the house down. This means that if you do not confess to having that naïve and innocent part to you, the part which Other truly loves, a time will come when it causes you to make the very gaffe that destroys what you so painstakingly built up.

Your ideal relationship is a home-from-home, traditional type of one where you and

Other each know your respective roles, duties, and boundaries. Family values and sentimentality should be the lifeblood of your relationship. If such appears claustrophobic to you, or just doesn't seem to happen in this day and age, then you must be still on some wide arc of self-discovery that will lead back to this basic set-up – one day, soon or far off.

When or if alone, it is because you have yet to realize that relationships are born and maintained in the unconscious mind, that very pool of emotions and longings that you work so hard to keep under control. You are like a dam that holds all the water in to generate power for material use but there is no natural flow, which would bring about fertility and growth. Open the sluices, release your emotions, relinquish control, surrender your fears!

Saturn is your Ruling Planet, which governs the link between your exterior being and your interior being. So study Chapter Nine – Your Saturn Profile, with this in mind. Your Setting Sign is Cancer and therefore the Moon governs your relationships, so study Chapter Three with that in mind.

Aquarius Rising
AS ♒

Your approach is cool but friendly. A person's intellect and social or political viewpoint is what appears to interest you most, for you engage on that level first and foremost. Emotional and sexual vibrations are kept beneath your surface, from depths of merely scratching to find rich, intense feelings, to them being somewhat unavailable or virtually non-existent. This measure of how emotionally accessible you are is critical with regard to how Other responds or reacts to you. They may coast along with your apparently airy coolness for quite some time until either they explode with boredom or frustration – or you do. In either case, it is this distance that you create and keep between Other and your true inner feelings that is responsible for this kind of reaction. Consciously or unconsciously, Other is trying to show you that it's all right to have human emotions, to have highs and lows and not just hover in some safe and socially acceptable place in between. On the other hand, your impartial and intuitive assessment of Other's nature and worth, and life in general, is something which Other should take note of – so express it with some confidence and style!

Unless there are Leo Planets in your chart, you are inclined to feel uncomfortable with sticking out in a crowd or having a high profile. You cringe if Other should be showy, exclusive or blow their own trumpet. This is a sign of a classic kind of Shadow because it misses or obscures your own sense of specialness. Possibly, you choose to display your uniqueness by appearing unusual or unconventional, but in a fashion that is acceptable in itself – that is, you are 'conventionally unconventional' or put on an act in a professional capacity. In truth, what you might regard as elitism in Other is just your own specialness which is unexpressed or suppressed because you doubt it for some reason. Let it show and it will grow!

As if to confirm much of the above, you like your relationship with Other to be special or in a class all of its own. An 'ordinary' or lacklustre relationship is not for you, and even if you think it is, it's not what you'll get. In fact a fiery, dramatic relationship is quite likely because it serves to keep you in touch with your ego and emotions, things that you are inclined to disassociate from in order to appear 'civilized'.

When or if alone, it is a logical outcome of your being too detached – that is, you become completely detached. You may well like this state of being, but more than most Rising Signs, you are pulled back into relationship again quite quickly and easily – in the same way that cool air draws in heat. If it then gets too hot for you again, you detach and retract, and so and so on, in an on/off fashion. But overall, and paradoxically, you are quite constant in this.

Uranus is your Ruling Planet, which governs the link between your exterior being and your interior being. So study Chapter Ten – Your Uranus Profile, with this in mind. Your Setting Sign is Leo and therefore the Sun governs your relationships, so study Chapter Two with that in mind.

Pisces Rising
AS ♓

You are very sensitive, as if the whole surface of your skin were picking up on Other and the environment in general. You channel or deal with this in a creative/mystical or evasive/dreamy fashion. You're not quite sure where you begin and Other ends, and will dart off into the shadows if things get too barbed emotionally. Yet at the same time there are some things about Other that you find very hard to resist – are addicted to, in fact. Other will probably view all this popping in and out as chaotic and in need of sorting out. This, of course, can make you even more evasive, but if you value Other's perspective, you will receive their practical assistance. In return, you are quite dedicated to Other, helping or healing them in a subtle, psychic way. Negatively, Other can become a slave to your elusive charm as they try to order your chaos. More than most Rising/Setting combinations, this one depends upon meeting one another halfway.

Other's critical attitude toward you is really the form your Shadow takes. This means that for all your vague and dreamy manner there lurks behind it a scientific and sceptical attitude that finds it hard to accept certain things – but not anything – that does not have a rational explanation. You still like to maintain an area where you can be totally illogical, so it can be pretty difficult to determine where you're coming from. Suffice to say that making clear what you accept and what you question would in itself clarify relationships.

More than anything, you require a relationship that is crystal clear about its own nature and status. The trouble is that you can confuse having such a thing as an impingement on your freedom to meander where you will. This can be a big mistake for vague relationships for you are rather like what uncharted waters are to a rudderless boat. A clean, wholesome, and definite arrangement is, despite your suspicions or apparent aversions, your best bet. A sailor without a homeport can eventually get lost or washed up.

When or if alone, or adrift more like, it is down to one or more of the illusions described above. Whether it is your need to roam the Seven Seas of the yet to be experienced, your over-sensitivity that makes you allergic to being close to an Other, or one of your many brands of evasiveness – they all have behind them one thing. This is your fear of facing your own music – that is, your own hurts, egotism, lack of faith or anything else that strands you between the devil and the deep blue sea. The flip in your own slippery tail is that in being alone you are ultimately forced to face this music of yours. And when you do, you'll know the score and thereby attract the Other who can and will help you in just the way that you need to be helped.

Neptune is your Ruling Planet, which governs the link between your exterior being and your interior being. So study Chapter Eleven – Your Neptune Profile, with this in mind. Your Setting Sign is Virgo and therefore the Planet Mercury governs your relationships, so study Chapter Five with that in mind.

CHAPTER TWO – YOUR SUN PROFILE
WILL AND PURPOSE

The Sun is The Life Force. It is the Creator of everything in this Solar System. In your Birth Chart therefore, it represents what is most IMPORTANT to you. The Sun is what is actually giving you VITALITY. The Sun, according to its Sign, House and Aspects, portrays the nature of your WILL and PURPOSE in life. Negatively it is CONCEIT and EGOTISM. The Sun is the CENTRE of your being, and all other planetary influences are arranged around it.

Birth Chart therefore, it represents your SPIRIT, your HEART, and you. The Sun is what is actually giving you VITALITY. The Sun, according to its Sign, House and Aspects, portrays the nature of your WILL and PURPOSE in life. Negatively it is CONCEIT and EGOTISM. The Sun is the CENTRE of your being, and all other planetary influences are arranged around it.

SUN SIGNS

Sun in Aries

Your essential purpose in life is simply to do something that makes you feel an independent and effective individual. At heart you are a pioneer, a champion of the underdog, the warrior – so therefore you must find a cause to fight for in life. As an Arian, you need to point yourself in a definite direction. In doing so you will encounter adversaries, but it is through them that you can discover your cause. In other words you have to push. If you don't you will find others pushing you instead.

You are egocentric and see life as an extension of yourself. This can appear to others as headstrong or selfish; but it is also what makes you able to act, rather than just think about acting. Aries is the Sign of the leader. It is the First Sign and it likes to be first. If you do not have a competitive spirit then you probably have a fairly strong fear of failure and a lack of self-worth, possibly born of bad experiences of someone else's assertiveness, such as violence, anger or abuse, that have occurred in your life. If such is the case, championing those similarly abused could be the cause for you.

Seeing that independence is what Aries is largely about, convoluted emotions such as self-pity and resentment should be ruthlessly weeded out for such deny you your essential nature and right, which is to be straightforward. This right is like the outpouring of life itself, and nothing should be allowed to get in the way of its innocence and freshness, for this is what enables your Sign, like no other, to set the ball rolling.

Sun in Taurus

Your essential purpose in life is to maintain the stability of Earthly things, and so you have a highly developed sense of earthy harmony and wholesomeness – and you know and feel what appeals to the senses. Your Sign is common amongst the artistically talented. Another one of your solid virtues is the ability to endure change, while at the same time conserving those habits and traditions that are so important to a healthy and wholesome physical life. You have to be careful not to let this talent become blunted into a mere ability to resist change when it is for the good, otherwise one day you would find change foisted upon you in a rather non-negotiable way. Your broad Taurean back can carry more than you sometimes believe.

Your sensuality – possibly your defining feature – has little trouble attracting sex or affection. Where it can go wrong is in failing to appreciate the more psychological dimension of life, giving rise to not seeing and catering to your own or someone else's more intangible needs. It could also find you being assailed by something that you couldn't just stubbornly resist, or find you having to provide for more than you could afford, either materially or emotionally.

Ultimately, as a Taurean you have to discover your truest, deepest and highest values. This is symbolized by ascending terraces of sweeter and sweeter clover. When you know what is truly valuable, you are no longer chained to people and things that are concerned with lesser values. And the greatest indication of value is beauty – either touched, heard or seen. And this cannot really be owned, only appreciated and created – a talent essentially Taurean.

Sun in Gemini

Your essential purpose in life is to make contact with, and connections between, whatever or whoever you regard as important – which is more or less everything! This you do because at heart you find everything interesting in some way or another. You are very alive to the variety of animate and inanimate objects on this planet, and you want to get to know as many of them as possible. As a rule though, 'get to know' is all you want to do.

As long as you have a 'taste' you are satisfied; getting deeply involved is not really to your taste, and you will flip like a coin from one interest or person to another as it suits you. There may be other parts of your Personality/Birth Chart that need or are attracted to more intimate situations, in which case a more profound sense of human interaction will be asked of you.

Like the many facets of life that you are acquainted with, you are able to turn your hand to many tasks and skills; indeed, it is your hands, as well as your quick mind and wits, that are your most excellent tools. You are, or should be, the communicator. There is nothing like a Gemini for keeping itself, the world and society in touch with each other and with what is happening.

Sun in Cancer

Your essential purpose in life is to nurture and care for whatever or whomever you believe needs it. So you have an instinct for survival, marked by a sense of what best constitutes protection and nourishment. But what essentially gives you this instinct is your sense of need, sympathy and emotional receptivity. As Cancer is such a female and maternal Sign, if you are a woman, you are usually a natural wife and mother, and you meet your own needs through meeting the needs of others. The limitation here is that such a life can become dull and automatic, with the Cancerian priority, home, turning into a prison.

However, a Cancerian man may seek to have his unfulfilled need for security met by making his partner into his 'mother'. This can wind up being very restrictive to her for obvious reasons, and to him too because he is so dependent upon her staying that way. However, there is a pronounced tenderness inside him that makes for being a good carer or parent, and that women find very attractive. Whether male or female, having someone or something to selflessly care for is the key to being a secure and happy Crab. What were clinging claws, or would 'clam-up' at the slightest sign of emotional intrusion, then become a pair of open arms that holds firmly, cradles gently. The acute awareness of another's feelings, which negatively can feel threatened and be used to emotionally blackmail, becomes a ray of healing. Cancer's motto could be 'Who cares is cared for.'

Sun in Leo

Your essential purpose in life is to bring warmth, light and vitality to whatever you regard as important. Thus you generate more brightness and creativity. In order to achieve this, you have a radiance, an inner glow, that quite magically draws the attention of others. This same quality then lends an air of certainty to whatever it is that you have involved yourself with. What could be called your royal seal of approval bestows a confidence upon whoever or whatever meets with your favour.

The trouble is that your curse is as disastrous as your blessing is great. And the curse of Leo is, of course, pride. Your pride makes you vulnerable to being taken in vain, and when you feel taken in vain, your bright sun goes behind a dark cloud. Some Leos are even born with their sun behind that cloud. And when it comes out again, you are very wary of having your pride wounded again, and anything that alludes to this – like advice or criticism – you disdainfully ignore or patronizingly put in its place.

However, when you are the Leo who does put your pride aside, and realizes that the sun cannot see its own shadows and so gracefully accepts constructive advice or criticism, you become like the Sun itself – utterly inextinguishable, ever-giving and ever-warm, funny and romantic, the noble ruler, the creative teacher – the healing heart. You, of all Signs, have the Light. All you need do is shine.

Sun in Virgo

Your essential purpose in life is to improve the expression or state of whatever it is that you regard as important. To enable you to accomplish this you are analytical, and are well able to spot the best and the worst in any given person, thing or situation. The danger here is that you can be over-critical and become anxious about things not being right or going wrong.

This can apply especially to the functioning of your own body and mind, although such an attitude could also mean that you are particularly good at caring for health generally. However, you need to cultivate tolerance and acceptance of things as they are. As a consequence of all this, on the one hand, you will attract or be attracted to circumstances and relationships which require your accuracy and eye for detail, and that employ your sensitive and helpful disposition. Yet on the other hand, they could try your fastidiousness to the point of isolating you.

Sun in Libra

Your essential purpose in life is to bring balance, justice or harmony to whatever it is in your world that you regard as important. You are naturally equipped for this in that you are only too aware of the fact that there is a right and a wrong, a rough and a smooth, a pleasant and an unpleasant, etc, etc. side to every situation and person.

It is this innate awareness of the ambiguities of life that gives rise to Libra's renowned indecisiveness. But really there is only one basic decision that you have to make. This is that you arrive consciously at a firm set of social values. This means that you have to ascertain what you think is important to society in your eyes, and what you can do that will contribute to society in that respect.

Indeed, that contribution may be simply the establishing of a balanced relationship, or a balance within yourself. Anyhow, until you have begun to achieve this end, this social contribution, you will most likely vacillate between what you feel others expect of you and what you really want to do – something of which you are only partly conscious.

This in turn can lead to your being rather superficial as you use your innate sense of harmony to blend in with everything and everyone. Or, perversely, you may even be quite deliberately uncooperative as a kind of overreaction to your basic but vapid agreeability. No other Sign can draw attention to beauty and justice, in such a beautiful and just way, as Libra can – when you know what your pitch is.

Sun in Scorpio

Your essential purpose in life is to deepen and make more genuine whatever it is that you regard as important. To enable you to accomplish this you have an ability to see into the heart and soul of a person or situation, and to heal or transform what you find there.

The response that you get to this insight of yours varies. You can elicit from others extremes of mistrust or devotion, and consequently be either mistrustful or utterly devoted yourself. Your probing intensity can certainly reach the parts that other Signs cannot reach. But if you wish to not emotionally exhaust those people who matter to you, give the probing a break occasionally, for the world will get by for a while without it. This ability of yours to penetrate into another's emotional reality is sexually based. This means to say that Scorpio's renowned sexuality is more to do with your mind and feelings than your body.

This is what sets you apart from other Signs, for you are able to 'enter' someone else's space without even touching them. This psychological insight, and the powerful influence that it can wield, is compromised by one thing only: you suspect that others are doing the same to you with dubious intentions. This in turn gives rise to a downward spiral of discord that appears to prove your suspicions correct. Behind all this is your fear of having the chink in your armour – your vulnerability – spotted and taken advantage of. Spot it yourself first, and you are invulnerable.

Sun in Sagittarius

Your essential purpose in life is to further and discover more about whatever it is that you regard as important. To enable you to accomplish this you are very able to grasp the whole meaning of any subject that appeals to your sizeable enthusiasm.

There is always a danger of running away with yourself and overlooking details, as you get carried along by your zest and full-blown opinions. However, because you are a good manager of things and know how to get the best out of people and circumstances, you have probably equipped yourself with something or someone that keeps you grounded by practical considerations. Some kind of goal, vision or belief is of paramount importance in making sense of your life and use of your prolific nature.

By the same token, you need to bear in mind that your ability to make a lot of anything should not be employed solely for material ends – otherwise you could get stumped by a need for something that money or influence just can't buy. You also, in an impersonal way, like to create friction for it gives you the feeling that things are on the move. Yours is probably the most positive Sign for the simple reason that you see life as an opportunity. So it does not matter too much how difficult the road ahead may look, for it is still a road – and roads go places!

Sun in Capricorn

Your essential purpose in life is to establish a material position in the world that you regard as useful. In order to accomplish this you have an innate sense of ambition and organization. You make a point of knowing how the world of politics and business works – along with anything else which your canny mind determines as being practical and relevant to your overall intentions.

Such earthy common sense is something that others depend on you for – and at times can feel rather inadequate in comparison to. However, your weakness is that you tend to overlook or simply not see matters of emotional significance, which are patently obvious to types less pragmatic than yourself.

So although you are more likely than most to achieve some sort of success in the world as a result of your industriousness, you are at some point more than likely to encounter a collapse or a profound sense of pointlessness because you have only taken into consideration the practical side of life, and underestimated the importance of unseen factors like human longings and weaknesses, and the mystery of life itself.

When your sense of what matters begins to include these more invisible and mystical aspects of existence, you then become the true organizer that you were born to be. When you apply your worldly, responsible and hard-working nature, to making a sound base for the furtherance of collective or spiritual interests, then you truly feel that you are the success, which you originally thought you would be.

Sun in Aquarius βM

Your essential purpose in life is to view and approach all things in an impartial and humanitarian way. In so doing, you hope and intend to liberate yourself and others from guilt, fear and conditioning. To enable you to accomplish this, you are emotionally detached to one degree or another.

If you like, you choose not even to recognize the emotional shortcomings of yourself and others – or if you do, you shrug them off or distance yourself from them in some way. Being such a cool observer of life makes for your being a natural psychologist, counsellor, scientist – or simply a good friend.

However, this distancing of yourself from awkward emotional areas that reflect your own discomfort can have the effect of divorcing you not only from them but from some of your best qualities. Consequently, you stand in danger of being someone who has been processed and packaged by what you think should be you, rather than what is actually you.

And others find it very hard to relate to this, then get very emotional, and cause you to do more of the same! When you eventually immerse yourself in the pool, well or cess-pit of your own rejected feelings, you lend a power and conviction to your outward expression that convinces, influences – and liberates – both yourself and others. The reason for this being that others, and your emotional self, can then identify with you.

Sun in Pisces

Your essential purpose in life is to make acceptable to yourself and others whatever you regard as being important in this respect. Your ways of doing this are manifold. In fact you have more facets and possibilities than any other Sign – and you also have as many ways of disguising them. But you are usually trying to do one or both of two things: to inspire or escape.

Inspiration can take the form of being an artist of some kind, or of being some kind of reliever of suffering. Equally, you could be on the receiving end of inspiration, as, say, a lover of beauty and mystery. Your escapist tendencies on the other hand are seen in your inclination to look away from what is really bothering you – probably quite unconsciously. And your means of doing so can range from being ever so intellectual and logical (thereby dodging emotional dilemmas), to being extremely vague – possibly assisted by drugs or alcohol.

Underlying these two extremes of inspiration or escape is one thing: your acute and unrelenting sensitivity to life. Probably the easiest way to handle this in a positive way is with a limited means of escapism. That is, you have say, a drink or two, but not three, so to speak, in order to ease the pain, to deaden the sensitivity to manageable proportions.

However, the nature of the beast in you is inclined to slip and slide, so inevitably a more reliable and healthier means of handling your sensitivity is required – such as meditation, yoga or some other spiritual practice. It is very desirable that you keep on the right side of your sensitivity, for it then enables you to catch and express both the comedy and the tragedy, the heaven and the hell, of the human condition.

SOLAR ASPECTS

NOTE that Sextile (co-operating with) and Opposition (confronting) Aspects are usually described similarly to Trine (harmonizing with) and Square (challenging) Aspects respectively, or they are occasionally described similarly to the Conjunction (uniting with). However, when this is the case, it should be borne in mind that a Sextile Aspect may require conscious awareness and effort to realize the assets and potential so described – and that the Opposition Aspect may indeed be experienced exactly as described, but in reality such can initially be felt or seen to come from someone or something else because you have projected or externalized such traits in order to make yourself aware of them.

Sun Conjunct (uniting with) Moon
☉ ☌ ☽

You were born on or around the New Moon. This means that you are setting about something new or in a new way – most probably with respect to your Sun Profile as a whole. You express this sense of something budding in one of two ways. You could be either childlike and lead with your feelings without much thought of what resistance you are going to encounter, or, you hang back as a result of feeling inhibited by old habits and attitudes – the very things that you're supposed to be emerging from, in fact. In either case, you'd do well to imagine yourself, like a bud, unfolding through time in a natural, spontaneous and unforced manner.

Sun Square (challenging) Moon
☉ □ ☽

What is mainly responsible for your difficulties here are the negative traits of your Moon Profile (see next chapter). You could be said to be at war with yourself in that your habits and fears born of childhood keep eclipsing your brighter and better intentions. Possibly you have a 'piggy-in-the-middle' background where you had the impossible demand of meeting your parents' very different requirements. Relationships with members of the opposite sex are particularly prone to strife because they re-evoke these conflicts, and those with your parent of the opposite sex, which initiated this clash between your conscious intentions and your unconscious reactions. You have to discover what pleases you, and satisfy that!

Sun Opposition (confronting) Moon
☉ ☍ ☽

You were born around the time of a Full Moon, which means to say that the dynamics and indications of your Sun Profile appear to run into trouble with those of your Moon Profile. Your heart and mind want one thing, while your habits and needs pull you in the opposite direction. This results in your being split, between, say, creative opportunities and family duties, or of always having someone or something opposing your wishes or affronting your sensibilities.

Every so often, it might seem that one side of you is cancelling out the other. Basically, you have the task of learning to take a back seat when things are against you, and of going all out when the way is clear. Also bear in mind that others will find you hard to relate to at times when either you appear to be living in two camps, or you blame the side of yourself that you cannot cope with upon the other people. Like it or not, you are working towards gaining a profound grasp of life's extremes, with a well-rounded personality as your reward.

Sun Trine (harmonizing with) Moon
⊙ △ ☽

A very basic and natural quality of yours is that everything that you do in this respect is backed up by your feelings. And just because it is so natural you can tend to overlook or underestimate it. Most people do not have this good relationship between what they are and what they feel. There is something fundamentally wholesome about you that provides a sound basis to whatever else you are endeavouring to do. Again, do not underestimate this.

Sun Sextile (co-operating with) Moon
⊙ ✳ ☽

Your will is happily aligned with your feelings, so others feel confident in your presence – initially at least. The more you cultivate your innate air of knowing and expecting to get what you want, the more you will do so. You are basically wholesome, and notwithstanding your more complex traits, you fare well in life.

Sun Conjunct (uniting with) Mercury
⊙ ☌ ☿

To assist you in these matters you do have a particularly active mind, and you take pride in making good use of it. Your powers of reason are therefore higher than average. However, this can incline you to worrying as you try to work everything out in your head. So every so often remind yourself that there is far more to life than just what you are thinking. Be that as it may, your bright intellect is a more or less constant source of information and stimulation to others, and so you attract interest fairly easily.

Sun Conjunct (uniting with) Venus
⊙ ☌ ♀

What is bound to help and positively enhance all of this is your decidedly pleasant disposition. You have a will to please and love to create a friendly and harmonious social atmosphere. And your in-built grace and charm can accomplish this, as well as attracting people and material benefits. As long as you do not let this lull you into expecting a deceptively easy life, you always lend a certain appeal and panache to any situation.

Sun Conjunct (uniting with) Mars
☉ ☌ ♂

You have quite a strong and resilient nature. You are built for action, and as a rule you have no trouble getting on with the job in hand. You are decisive, forthright and competitive, and other people pick up on this and respond to it – although not necessarily that favourably. You need to know what you want, otherwise what could be a mixture of desire and aimlessness or sheer wilfulness will create far more enemies than allies. Bear in mind that your undeniable drive and energy is ultimately only as good as what you are directing it towards. Your primary requirement is finding a worthwhile cause to promote.

Sun Square (challenging) Mars
☉ □ ♂ *OR*

Sun Opposition (confronting) Mars
☉ ☍ ♂

You have quite a strong and resilient nature, or you feel fearful and feeble in the face of what seems a hostile world. So on the one hand, you are built for action, and as a rule you have no trouble getting on with the job in hand. You are decisive, forthright and competitive, and other people pick up on this and respond to it – although not necessarily that favourably.

On the other hand, you must realize your timidity is being felt by the child in you, which poses the need to develop the tougher adult side of yourself. In either case, you need to know what you want, otherwise what could be a mixture of desire and aimlessness or sheer wilfulness will create far more enemies than allies. Bear in mind that your undeniable drive and energy is initially discovered through encountering similar competitiveness in others. Your primary requirement is finding a worthwhile cause.

Sun Trine (harmonizing with) Mars
☉ △ ♂ *OR*

Sun Sextile (co-operating with) Mars
☉ ⚹ ♂

Fortunately, you have quite a strong and resilient nature. You are built for action, and as a rule you have no trouble getting on with the job in hand. You are decisive and forthright, and other people pick up on this and respond favourably to it. You know what you want and therefore pursue your aims in an unfettered way. Bear in mind that not everyone has this drive, and that they look to you for leadership.

Sun Conjunct (uniting with) Jupiter
☉ ☌ ♃

Furthermore, you have an enthusiastic and philosophical bent, and you travel far, inwardly and/or outwardly. In this way you cultivate as broad an awareness and viewpoint as possible. As a rule, you are optimistic and have faith that life is positive and is going somewhere. There is a danger though, of your being too abstract and conceptual, and of overestimating or over-dramatizing things. But, overall, others are greatly attracted to your expansive and essentially joyful nature. You can also be one of life's travellers or wanderers.

Sun Square (challenging) Jupiter
☉ □ ♃ *OR*
Sun Opposition (confronting) Jupiter
☉ ☍ ♃

You tend to look for the confidence that you lack in yourself in other people – a need for confidence however, which your bright and optimistic air gives the lie to. When you do find it in another, though, after initially being excessively admiring, you can then come to resent or envy them for having what you have not, and are pompously defensive.

It is almost as if you are afraid to live up to your own very real generosity and sense of goodwill. To put it another way, you have a strong faith in life and yourself, but unless you learn to accept your own inconsistencies or what is foreign or morally objectionable to you, then that 'faith' will prove unreliable in the face of real challenges. Bearing goodwill to others is the key to your having goodwill towards yourself, rather than merely expecting too much of others, or of yourself for that matter.

Sun Trine (harmonizing with) Jupiter
☉ △ ♃

There is a supremely positive dimension to your personality that bestows both wisdom and good luck upon you. You have an essentially benign and philosophical nature that attracts funds and opportunities, help just when you need it, and people in foreign parts who are well-disposed towards you. The paradox is that because you can so easily conceive of an easier life, you tend to let negative matters build up to a point where you then have to use your luck in earnest.

Sun Sextile (co-operating with) Jupiter
☉ ⚹ ♃

There is a positive dimension to your personality that bestows both wisdom and good luck upon you as long as you cultivate your essentially benign and philosophical nature. This then attracts funds and opportunities, help just when you need it, and people in foreign parts who are well-disposed towards you.

Sun Conjunct (uniting with) Saturn
☉ ☌ ♄ *OR*
Sun Square (challenging) Saturn
☉ □ ♄ *OR*
Sun Opposition (confronting) Saturn
☉ ☍ ♄

You either have an unshakeable discipline about you, or an impenetrable wall around you – or both. Yours is a life where your will is having to be built and tested, tested and built some more, in order to achieve the goals described by your Sun Profile as a whole. You therefore have, or need to construct, a highly objective attitude to life situations, and adopt conventionally laid down, tried and true, methods in order to achieve those ends. In the process though, take yourself less seriously, or else your innate sense of duty can amount to nothing more than a lonely twenty-four-hour-a-day guard around your fragile ego.

Sun Trine (harmonizing with) Saturn
☉ △ ♄

What serves you well in so many respects is your sense of discipline and practicality. You also have an inherent awareness of how the status quo works. You are well able to deal with the challenges and difficulties of your life and of the material world in general for you have a sort of self-stabilizing mechanism within you.

You usually adhere to a formal and conventional lifestyle, and subscribe to traditional standards – or you would make life easier if you used the system as opposed to bucking it. Paradoxically, it is this very sense of order that can cause you to miss some vital but radical point. So it is when taking a chance on something that your marked sense of reality comes into its own.

Sun Sextile (co-operating with) Saturn
☉ ⚹ ♄

As time goes by, you become more and more practical and realistic, disciplined and organized with regard to these matters. This ensures, therefore, that eventually you attain some degree of success, or at the very least, those in positions of influence and authority will deem you worthy of their attention.

Sun Conjunct (uniting with) Uranus
☉ ☌ ♅ *OR*

Sun Square (challenging) Uranus
☉ □ ♅ *OR*

Sun Opposition (confronting) Uranus
☉ ☍ ♅

However, in respect of much of all this you take up a decidedly radical position, and aim to introduce to the world a strong sense of the original and innovative. This could well involve science and technology or metaphysics. You are heavily challenged in all the areas described here with regard to this revolutionary stance that you adopt, especially by the more conservative elements of society, or even of your own personality.

You can be quirky and cranky, and at times downright rebellious, but you are certainly your own person. Alternatively, you would attract someone who embodies these individualistic traits, thereby forcing you to develop your own uniqueness, and possibly go your own way.

Sun Trine (harmonizing with) Uranus
☉ △ ♅ *OR*

Sun Sextile (co-operating with) Uranus
☉ ⚹ ♅

Because of, or despite all this, you have a well-evolved sense of how life actually works.

This means to say that you possess a sound awareness of human nature and the human condition, which should be rounded off with a healthy air of detachment. You are also well attuned to the uniqueness of yourself, and you are able to draw it out of others. In response to this, you would attract sound friends, and what is right for you would happen at the right time.

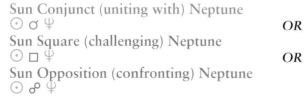

Sun Conjunct (uniting with) Neptune
⊙ ☌ ♆

OR

Sun Square (challenging) Neptune
⊙ □ ♆

OR

Sun Opposition (confronting) Neptune
⊙ ☍ ♆

Most significantly though, pervading your sense of individual will and being is something that causes you to feel at one with the world around you, especially the natural world, and sometimes acutely sensitive and vulnerable to outside influences. There seems to be only a vague boundary that separates you from everything and everyone else. On the positive side this does equip you with great imagination and compassion as you cannot help but identify with the greater whole.

Negatively, though, it may be difficult for you to find a solid place in the material world, or you undermine the position you have, or simply your physical state, with addictions or the indulgence of your weaknesses. Ultimately you have to see your purpose in life as being patently spiritual in the sense of doing something that employs and is aware of divine or invisible forces, or that meets the needs of others. Resisting or merely playing at this will find you deceiving yourself and feeling increasingly helpless and looking for artificial means of escape. Behind all of this is the probability that your father's values confused your own, as if his 'poison' was more important than you.

Sun Trine (harmonizing with) Neptune
⊙ △ ♆

OR

Sun Sextile (co-operating with) Neptune
⊙ ✶ ♆

Pervading all of your being is a very natural sense of love and acceptance. Because this makes for a rather passive disposition, you are inclined to turn the other cheek rather than take issue. Any more aggressive instincts that you might have are more likely to be used defensively. All in all though, you have the wisdom to know that letting life take its own course is bound in time to deliver you to your rightful place. However, do not underestimate, and therefore fail to make something of, your innate ability to inspire and be inspired – be it through music, visual art, drama, literature or in the sphere of healing.

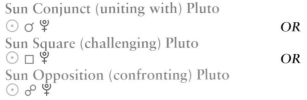

Sun Conjunct (uniting with) Pluto

☉ ☌ ♇   *OR*

Sun Square (challenging) Pluto

☉ □ ♇   *OR*

Sun Opposition (confronting) Pluto

☉ ☍ ♇

Deep in the core of your being lies something profound and powerful. You may not have a particularly conscious idea of what it is, but you are not going to let anyone take it, or you, lightly. It gives, or rather burdens, you with the feeling that there is a dark force in life that could be out to get you. If you identify too closely with this notion then you are on your way to being either a megalomaniac or a self-destructive manic-depressive, or being in the clutches of one.

If, on the other hand, you purify your own intentions, and recognize yourself as being a steward of or a channel for this power, then whatever you do in life will be deeply effective. But through self-study or intimate relating, you have to reach your own depths first, for that is where the power lies. You may find that your father plays or has played some part in what could be called this power complex, with him being highly influential in your life in some way, for good or ill.

Sun Trine (harmonizing with) Pluto

☉ △ ♇   *OR*

Sun Sextile (co-operating with) Pluto

☉ ✶ ♇

You have enviable stamina and powers of regeneration. You also have a healthy sense of power, which enables you to deal with big issues and important people. However, just because you do have this extremely reliable energy supply, you can tend to steam through things and not notice subtle details – like the fact that you have this powerful character trait!

Sun Unaspected by any other planet

☉ ∅

As the Sun is symbolic of your ego, that which around all other parts of your personality are gathered and organized, when Unaspected it can pose difficulty in marshalling your talents and forces. It can therefore be some time before you do what you want to do for yourself, rather than responding purely to what you feel is expected of you. Until then, this could mean your living through someone else in your life, or through your Moon Profile, (Chapter Three) which would mean that your lifestyle was limited by your needs, rather than defined by your own conscious choice.

A strong alternative to this, however, can be that you feel entirely free to follow your own star, without paying any heed at all to what others want of you. If you're this type, you could become noted for your originality, but somehow still remain an enigma. John F. Kennedy was a good example of this.

In either case, a significant feature of your psychological profile consists of your having a father who is or was hardly there at all for you, or who's very much there to the point that one day you either have to detach yourself from his influence, or that he departs from your life relatively early. The ideal father would be one who is kind of there but not there, which means to say that he'd be a figure of strength but not in the least intrusive or dominating.

Perhaps in the final analysis, having an Unaspected Sun poses having to be a father to yourself.

If you have difficulty in establishing your own will and living with a sense of conscious purpose, try deliberately involving yourself with the affairs of the House in which your Sun is placed (see above, this chapter).

Also, thoroughly familiarize yourself with your Sun's Sign (see above). If you use meditation, meditate upon the actual symbol of your Sign – e.g. Scorpio: A Scorpion.

Finally, pay special attention to the Sign, House and Aspects of the Planet that rules your Sun's Sign (see 'The Birth Chart – What It Means' on page 33).

Sun Conjunct (uniting with) Ascendant and in the First House
⊙ ♂ AS

You were born at or just before dawn. This is highly significant, for potentially you are able to be what you are and also come across to others in that way at the same time. Read my comments under Sun in the First House below, for they further describe this very important aspect of your personality.

Sun Conjunct (uniting with) Ascendant and in the Twelfth House
⊙ ♂ AS

You were born at or just after dawn. This is highly significant for you are able to be what you are, and also come across to others in that way at the same time. However, read my comments under Sun in the Twelfth House below, for they describe qualities and circumstances that would inhibit and/or promote this potentially pure and bright light of personality that you could be shedding around and about.

Sun Square (challenging) Ascendant
⊙ □ AS

You need to recognize that your individual talents or potentials are not going to be immediately appreciated by others. This may be because they feel threatened by them, or jealous of them. More likely still, your own self-doubt gets in the way of your expressing yourself only too easily – and so they pick up on that rather than what you are really trying to put across. If this pattern is not checked you can attempt to bully others into applauding or agreeing with you. The answer lies in your accepting the fact that only faith in yourself will win through, and then you could be genuinely in a commanding position.

Sun Opposition (confronting) Ascendant
⊙ ☍ AS

You were born at or near sunset. Your life force, your ego, is about to disappear from view for the night. This symbolizes a situation in which it will take quite some time before you are recognized for what you are – by yourself, as well as by others. As you also possess a strong sense of how others tick, and can identify with them quite easily, when you do eventually re-emerge, it might well be in this field that uses this talent – such as counselling or public relations. In the meantime, and off and on thereafter, you tend to imagine that everyone thinks and feels as you do.

Sun Trine (harmonizing with) Ascendant
☉ △ AS   *OR*
Sun Sextile (co-operating with) Ascendant
☉ ✳ AS

Outwardly you express your intentions in a manner that inclines others to co-operate or agree with them. One could say that you are simply a good advertisement for yourself and what you regard as significant, interesting or important.

Sun Conjunct (uniting with) MidHeaven and in the Ninth House
☉ ♂ MC

You were born when the Sun was at or near its zenith. This is highly significant for potentially you are able to excel in your profession for you have a natural sense of worldly position. All your Sun Profile qualities should be geared for success.

Sun Conjunct (uniting with) MidHeaven and in the Tenth House
☉ ♂ MC

You were born when the Sun was at or near its zenith. This is highly significant for potentially you are able to excel in your profession for you have a natural sense of worldly position. Read the comments under Sun in the Tenth House below, for they further describe this very important aspect of your personality.

Sun Square (challenging) MidHeaven
☉ □ MC

Something either gets in the way of your amounting to something in life, or you have an ambition that brooks no resistance. In either case that something is your ego, and as such it is afraid of failing – which could be regarded as a failing in itself. You'll need to be clearer about what you are really trying to prove to prevent you, and those you work or live with, feeling too pressured.

Sun Opposition (confronting) MidHeaven
☉ ☍ MC

You were born when the Sun was at or near its nadir. This is highly significant for you will have to overcome many obstacles to achieve true success, but when you do get there it will be built on a rock. You are a layer of foundations.

Sun Trine (harmonizing with) MidHeaven
⊙ △ MC   *OR*
Sun Sextile (co-operating with) MidHeaven
⊙ ✶ MC

Whatever else may happen in your life, you are unlikely to lose or fail to catch sight of your goal. This is because life and purpose are synonymous to you. You are alive to the fact that you have what it takes to get somewhere in life – or you can acquire what it takes to do so

SUN HOUSES

Sun in the First House
⊙ 1st

All these qualities should be quite obvious in the way that you come across. You should allow and trust your identity to shine forth – warts and all. But just because you do wear your heart on your sleeve, you can feel rather self-conscious. This could then lead to a feeling that all your worst aspects are showing, and so you retreat behind what turns into a cloud.

This hiding of your own light must be resisted, otherwise you'd be missing the point of having a naturally sunny personality that can shed light on whatever you regard as important. At the other extreme you can turn your self-consciousness into arrogance, which prevents you from taking on board any useful feedback for fear of it being negative. So whether you're prone to cutting off your nose to spite your face, or perpetually blowing your own trumpet, I think you'll find that working up an enthusiasm for yourself, tempered with a bit of modesty, will put a smile on the faces of both yourself and others.

Sun in the Second House
⊙ 2nd

All of this is most likely to centre upon what you regard as being of true worth. So anything that you put your vital energies into has to have a very real and material value. You could simply translate this into accumulating plenty of money and property, and for as long as you truly regard this as important, then that is what you are able to do.

But at some point it is no longer as simple as that, for the issue becomes one of establishing what YOU are worth, and what it is that you have, know or believe in that you must prove to be of worth in the material world. How much money you have or don't have is really only an indicator of what you believe it, and therefore yourself, to be worth.

Sun in the Third House
⊙ 3rd

All of this is most likely to centre upon various forms of communication, such as the written or spoken word, and interactions with your regional environment. A maxim for you could be 'Think globally – act locally'. Your siblings, or lack of them, as well as neighbours and everyday encounters, and your education, will also figure strongly here for these are what have particularly affected the forming of your mind.

In turn, your mental attitude strongly influences your day-to-day situation, and so with you it is very much a case of a positive outlook creating a positive reaction, and of pessimistic expectations breeding precisely what you feared. You find that making short trips here and there, and generally keeping in touch, are what keep you vitalized and interested in life.

Sun in the Fourth House

☉ 4th

All of this is most likely to be centred upon and affected by your home and background. So your roots are very significant in determining what you make of life. You can either get buried in them or use them as a base from which to launch yourself. If there are negative qualities in your early home life, this will dog your progress more than is usual, so it is not until the latter part of life that you begin to prosper.

Even then, this would entail your coming to terms with blocks created in childhood. Your father has a lot to do with all this, for his character has affected you in more ways than you possibly care to admit. Your career or reputation may well involve being the proprietor/owner of some form of establishment or foundation; or simply that you work at or from home. Whatever the case, making a deliberate effort to get away from the home and family scene occasionally is very therapeutic because you can become so bound up in it as to lose your sense of vitality and individuality.

Sun in the Fifth House

☉ 5th

All of this is most likely to centre upon the means and products of your creative expression. This would involve things like pastimes, romance, children, art, speculation, drama, partying, etc. What this entails or even demands of you is that you celebrate your uniqueness in an unreserved, even abandoned way.

You find brightness simply through shining; and in company you do seem to glow. Being proud of your own life and personality, as long as it does not devolve into conceit, encourages others to be proud of themselves as well. The making of something or someone is your essential quality. To you the world really is a stage, so the power and ability to play is vital, as too is your understanding that life is for living.

Sun in the Sixth House

☉ 6th

All of this is most likely to centre upon developing some kind of method or technique with which you can practise gainful employment or perform some sort of service. Without doing this it is probable that you'd suffer from unemployment or a string of aimless jobs. Your life is very much concerned with improving or preparing for something.

Initially, it is quite likely that you find yourself in a subordinate position where you are answerable to someone else – possibly even under their thumb. This would be because you are having to learn the importance of modesty and being in earnest. A career in health or hygiene or veterinary care could suit you well. Your own health can be quite an issue in that it is very much a barometer of your efficiency in life.

Sun in the Seventh House
☉ 7th

All of this is most likely to centre upon and be caused by how you deal with and experience other people and their responses to your ego expression, as described in this your Sun Profile. So what tends to happen is that you live out your will and life through others, and one other in particular. Such an automatic putting yourself in someone else's shoes does give you a profound ability to function well in counselling, public relations or any other people oriented activity.

What you have to constantly be wary of is losing yourself in the identity of another or others, or looking for some heroic figure or father figure in them. Remember that as you live and find yourself through others, they revolve around you. Others are the rim of the wheel – but you are the hub.

Sun in the Eighth House ßⲘ
☉ 8th

All of this is most likely to centre upon intimate involvements and deeply shared experiences – or else you can feel desperately lonely and cut off. Although this commonly means the ties of jointly owned resources with their advantages and problems, there is also the closeness experienced through sex and crisis. This is an intimacy with life itself – which also includes death. And so you can be mediumistic, in touch with the 'other side', or at least have an interest in the occult and the hidden causes behind outer phenomena.

You are the researcher or delver, and can have a profound sense of the soul. And so you are looking for a profound union – which poses the surrender of your separateness. This is a purging of the 'little self', your petty values, and consequently yours can be a hard but transformative road through life. This means that you go through many changes, relationships, and ways of expressing yourself until you begin to see the light at the end of the tunnel – the light of your own life.

Sun in the Ninth House
☉ 9th

All of this centres mostly upon activities which serve to further and explore – or it certainly should do. Such activities could therefore include publishing, travel, philosophy, law, religion, teaching, sports and further education. It is important for you to find a meaning to your life, and to gain a sense that everything is ultimately going somewhere. For then you'd have a broad view of life issues, possess an evolving sense of right and wrong, and also make a good travelling companion. Sometimes your ability to see things as a whole means that you overlook important details. On the other hand, your prophetic sense of the shape of things to come – and your personal growth itself – would be severely hampered by having to consider too closely the pedestrian issues of life.

Sun in the Tenth House
☉ 10th

Your Sun Profile potentials are most likely to be central to the nature and pursuance of your actual career. In other words, having a professional position is vitally important to you. This can mean that you proceed quite quickly up the career ladder because you know what you want early on.

It could also mean that you get involved with busy professional types whom you are either happy to support emotionally, or that at some point you feel you too should have a place of your own in the world. Rising to a position of prominence is probable, but falling from grace is also a possibility if you ignore your home, family or inner life. Behind all this ambition is your mother who wanted so much to have a successful child. Whether her intentions ultimately coincide with yours is another matter.

Sun in the Eleventh House
☉ 11th

All of this is most likely to centre upon some kind of goal or social ideal. You innately believe John Donne's line that 'no man is an island', and so you gravitate or strive towards groups or teams that share the same aspirations. For the same reason, friendships are very important to you. In addition, you often display an interest, or passion even, for freedom and reform in some field of activity.

You tend to get buried in the group you belong to; or sensing this possible loss of your individuality, you rebel against the group you initially rebelled with! But then splinter groups and sudden endings to friendships and associations are all part of your life's course of development. Today's radical is tomorrow's conservative. In the end, it is all part of your striving to uphold some humanitarian cause, through campaigns, inventions or programmes that aim to help mankind. You greatly appreciate people-power.

Sun in the Twelfth House
☉ 12th

All of this is most likely to centre upon and be caused by experiences of the dim and distant past – of this life, womb-life, or even before that. Whether these experiences are felt like heavy shadows or like paradise lost, your will must bend itself to clearing out that closet of repressed longings, regrets and vague reservations. You are open to unseen forces – for good or ill – and this could also incline towards addictions or strange phobias and notions, but at the positive end you can be inspired artistically or as a channel for spiritual messages. The Twelfth House can be the 'hell of the horoscope' or the 'heaven of the horoscope' – everything depends upon your essential integrity of being.

Depending upon your Sun Profile as a whole, managing all this can be quite some task, and may restrict your life to a degree that is proportionate to how much that closet has not been cleared. In the process, or eventually, you can become a light in the darkness to others who are similarly confined by their fears and weaknesses. Inner peace for one and all is the only ultimate goal for you, so meditation, selfless service and psychological awareness (or sometimes practice) are your essential ways of living. Because of your basically reclusive nature, you prefer to work behind the scenes, go into retreat occasionally, and not be too much in the public eye (unless there are indications in your chart that contradict this – like strong Leo placements, for example). Looked at another way, your public persona may be very different to the inner you.

CHAPTER THREE – YOUR MOON PROFILE
NEEDS AND EMOTIONAL RESPONSES

The Moon reflects the light of the Sun, your will, and as such it symbolizes your FEELING RESPONSES and your REACTIONS to others' wills. In CHILDHOOD, before your will had started to become conscious, the fulfilling of your SECURITY NEEDS made you totally DEPENDENT upon others, especially your MOTHER. The Moon is therefore your PERSONAL UNCONSCIOUS, your PAST, and the CHILD and your INNER CHILD. Consequently, much of your personality became conditioned by the HABITS and BIASES not only of your mother, but also of your FAMILY, RACE, CLASS, etc. These influences relate to your SURVIVAL INSTINCTS, SYMPATHIES, RECEPTIVITY, and sense of BELONGING and inner SUPPORT. But the negative expressions of the Moon – like CLANNISHNESS, FEAR OF THE UNKNOWN, INSECURITY, DEFENSIVENESS and being too SUBJECTIVE – need (more than any other Planet except perhaps Mars) to be brought into conscious awareness and sorted out. What is SAFE, COMFORTABLE and FAMILIAR is fine just so long as it is not just a case of CLINGING to the past and eclipsing your individuality. The Moon is your SOUL and can also be looked at metaphorically, or literally if you wish, as being the Sun in the chart from your previous lifetime. So, if I have my Moon in Aries now, that means I had Sun in Aries then. Whether you believe in reincarnation or not, this gives a good feel of what the Moon is – a memory or how and who you once were filtering through as a PREDISPOSITION in the present.

MOON SIGNS

Moon in Aries
☽ ♈

Your reigning need is to be independent or out in front in some way. So you are predisposed to staying as childlike and as unattached as possible, and you have a competitive soul. What you want is all-important to you – even though you may not be quite conscious of what that is! Others will find your single-mindedness either stimulating or exasperating. You run on a kind of 'battle-stations' programme, operating on the assumption that a moving target is harder to hit.

This is all very exciting, but at some point you have to settle for the fact that if you wish to have security you will have to make some kind of commitment. But then again, you might just go for being the eternal youth in the eternal now, and let security take care of itself. Your mixed feelings about security mainly have two things behind them: an insecure or pushy mother, or the sense that feeling too secure would dull your spontaneity and need for action.

Moon in Taurus
☽ ♉

Your reigning need is to feel emotionally stable and materially secure. The former is taken care of by the fact that you are reluctant to pursue any idea or activity that is going to rock the boat, coupled with the fact that you do have a fairly unflappable nature. Ironically, however, when a change is required you could be slow to act, or become bored, to the point of destabilizing your position.

Where material stability is concerned, you have a natural sense of the importance of property and income. From the word go, you use your developed market instincts and sense of value to satisfy this need. The danger here is that you can let material considerations blind you to your emotional and psychological requirements. In any event, though, you are unlikely to get caught without the material wherewithal and, providing there isn't a mean streak in your personality, you can be of great material support and assistance to others who are less financially together.

Moon in Gemini
☽ ♊

Your reigning need is to feel constantly in touch with what is going on around you. Equally, you have a natural sense of what is happening at street level, so to speak. Such a common touch as you have, and the ready wits and gift of the gab that accompany it, are only too able to keep things light and manageable. That is, until your emotional responses to life around you become inappropriately superficial.

You then find that what you are doing on either a personal or professional level ceases to have enough permanence or depth of satisfaction – and is therefore worrying you to death and keeping you awake at nights. The formula that you only get as good as you give, is a very apt one for you. Perhaps you originally devised your blend of affability and flippancy to deal with a mother who was not easy to relate to in an honest or consistent way. An important point in your development is when you consciously commit yourself to a deeper involvement with whatever life is demanding of you, and then trust your mental alacrity and your ability to dodge and weave when necessary in order to negotiate the trickier reefs of human interplay.

Moon in Cancer
☽ ♋

Your reigning need is to feel familiar with your surroundings. So the establishing of a home and garden is something that is important to you and something that you are good at. You are also a sympathetic and caring soul, and you make others feel at home as well. However, if you let your need for security and the familiar get the better of your will-power and faith in life itself, then you can wind up feeling uncomfortably needy of others, and limiting your sphere of involvement to the point of stagnation.

Behind this is your mother's influence that probably consisted of the best and the worst of maternal love. She cared greatly for you, but used emotional blackmail to ensure that you cared for her. The chances are that you also tend to do this with those to whom you are emotionally attached. It would be wise to put a bit of space between yourself and your mother and anyone else in your emotional life. Your emotional responses are wonderfully fluid and elicit strong feelings from others. You yourself can go up and down like a yo-yo! Owing to the fact that your caring ability is so natural, you can tend to overlook its value – and so then will others. So – without being a mother hen – realize this as a very positive asset of yours.

Moon in Leo
☽ ♌

Your reigning need is to receive attention and acclaim. This is most likely owing to the fact that you either did not get enough attention as a child (for probably quite unavoidable reasons), or you got a lot of it and grew to expect it. In the first case, when you do get attention, you may feel uncomfortable and not quite know what to do with it. In the second, you can get disproportionately upset when you aren't noticed or appreciated.

In both cases, what you do require is a means of getting attention, holding it, and justifying it. Because you do have a generous sense of drama, fun, and creativity, this should not be too difficult. At the same time, be prepared to take some constructive criticism of your 'act'. The child in you, which is precious about being unconditionally admired as a sign of love, must not be allowed to run the show, otherwise others could express their discomfort at this in a far more dramatically distressing fashion than merely criticising you. Not surprisingly, with the child so strong and alive in you, you can be a wow with children themselves.

Moon in Virgo
☽ ♍

Your reigning need is to feel pure and that everything is in the right place. This predisposition of yours leads to your having a well-ordered emotional lifestyle as, or when, you consistently weed out influences that are detrimental to your well-being. This can also you give you an instinct for healthcare. The catch here is that your own 'impurities' – such as lusts, dirty habits, peculiarities – can get overlooked, and so you brand others too easily as being not good enough.

Or, conversely, you can become obsessed with your own impurities and not feel good or clean enough to be closely or emotionally involved with anyone for very long. Your mother's fastidiousness, or her lack of it, has something to do with all of this. You like animals, possibly more than humans, because of their innate purity. But then observe how natural animals are with their earthy habits.

This is an example of one of those grey areas, which you can fail to see, or avoid seeing, as you are predisposed to seeing life in black and white, as profane or pristine with nothing in between. Your sense of purity, and of service too, are best employed in dealing with what is inaccurate or polluted. Quite simply, you are aware of what needs cleaning up in this world, but should not take it quite so personally and thereby fight shy of your own 'dirt' or 'mess'.

Moon in Libra

Your reigning need is to have a partner, to have people around you, to have a definite social position. In order to satisfy this need you have an instinct for what pleases, and possess or acquire talents for things like cooking, decor, fashion, entertaining or anything that introduces a sense of harmony or togetherness to a situation. Perversely, not trusting this social sense can make you rather antisocial.

Your weakness is that you become so dependent upon life being nice and pleasant that you find it hard to confront the darker or less attractive parts of your personality. And because you do have grace and charm it is only too easy to maintain a superficial sense of things being all right. It is quite likely that this need to please has its roots in your having felt that you had to please your mother, father or whoever brought you up.

The irony is that your over-riding need for a partner ensures that sooner or later you do have to face what it is about yourself that is not at all easy to relate to – either because you have lost a partner or cannot find or keep one. An important advance is made when you have a partner with whom you can rationally discuss your mutual shortcomings without feeling rejected or unattractive – which is basically what you're so sensitive about.

Having confronted this issue, you then discover that your talent for making others, and therefore yourself, feel good is increased a hundredfold because feeling at ease with your own dark spots enables others to feel at ease with theirs. Ease indeed.

Moon in Scorpio

Your reigning need is to feel close to someone or something. In order to satisfy this need, you have a profoundly intuitive sense of the emotional nature of people and situations. The trouble for you is that your need for closeness is compulsive, and so you can feel lonely or abandoned only too easily.

And then your intuitive sense becomes a radar that picks up anything which bears the slightest suggestion of abandonment or threat towards your vulnerable emotions. The mistake you are making is that you are interpreting others' negative emotional states as being aimed specifically at you. It is then only a matter of time before such paranoid behaviour does actually attract a negative attitude or act towards you. So you need to identify how and where in your past you initially felt betrayed or abandoned, and exorcise that demon.

Until then you will either be haunted by a fear of being alone, or you will find yourself in solitary confinement. Having overcome what must be the oldest human fear, that of abandonment – or at least, when you're not feeling threatened by it – you have an emotional perception of others that is accurate to the point of being deeply reassuring. At your best, you can make personal sacrifices for the good of the whole.

Moon in Sagittarius

Your reigning need is to believe in something, and to have the freedom to discover what that is. This need for freedom can be so pronounced in you that you instinctively reject anything that smacks of limiting or restraining you, be it physically, emotionally or spiritually.

Paradoxically though, you can be rather gullible, because unconsciously you are still looking for some kind of philosophy or adventure. Alternatively, you may just as well be atheistic or amoral for that can appear to be a system of belief with absolutely no laws to keep to.

Behind all this, you probably had an upbringing that indoctrinated you in either a dogmatic or free-and-easy way, and so now you fancy the open road, so to speak. Deep within you there lies that gypsy soul, that wanderer, who trusts life purely for the adventure that it is.

However, if your own life's not to disappear into the boundless, some definite philosophy or set of laws to guide you is what you need. This, combined with your natural sense of humour and of life's 'story', can make you into a warm and optimistic teacher, the raconteur, or just someone who is wise as a result of being cheerful and understanding.

Moon in Capricorn

Your reigning need is to feel needed. This can prove quite precarious for you, as others, especially your parents, can come to see you for what you can do rather than for what you are. Or, one of your parents was not there for you physically or emotionally.

From the word go, your need for external approval put you in a situation where your own emotional nature was not taken into consideration. As a child, you were not recognized as a child, and neither perhaps is the child in you now. And because your emotional interior was not nurtured, and was possibly even abused, you grew up with only a poor idea of how to cherish and value it.

Such emotional denial can cause you to be quite a survivor in the harsh outside world as a kind of substitute for a feeling of inner support. But this can turn into a rather grim and lonely alternative, although your cool efficiency would possibly conceal this fact. Or again, in a partner you may look for the nurturing parent that you never had.

Conversely you could be a parent to your partner, and others too, as you deftly manage material affairs. But this eventually only serves to isolate you further. What you have to set about doing with your innately industrious nature is to look for and find that sad child inside of you, and possibly with professional therapeutic help, look after it yourself. In becoming the parent of your own inner child in this way, you then develop into an extraordinarily balanced and capable human being.

Moon in Aquarius

Your reigning need is to become free of feelings that compromise your freedom. As if to precipitate this, emotional experiences early on in life were shocking, unusual or alienating in some way. Your mother probably related to you mentally rather than emotionally, or she may not have wanted you. And so you learned to distance yourself from raw feelings like anger, fear and desire – or even from soft and sentimental ones. All this made you a bit too tolerant of others' emotional natures, or indifferent to them.

You became an observer of life and so consequently you can be a good listener and provide impartial advice. This might be fine for others, but it all leaves you rather out of touch with the power of your feelings – because you maintain a space between you and them, as you had to do in the past. What you have to do is actually get back in touch with what caused you to feel so intensely in the first place and then prompted you to take that step back.

If you do not do this consciously then you will find yourself in emotional situations that force your real feelings to the surface in quite an unpleasant or disruptive way. But either way, you can then see, with your cool and objective eye, what is preventing you from emotionally responding freely, which is not the same thing as emotionally not responding at all.

Moon in Pisces
☽ ♓

Your reigning need is to feel accepted for what you are, and to gain acceptance for others, whom you feel need it. What is responsible for this is your enormous compassion and sensitivity. I have to say that an equally important need of yours is to find a means of managing this sensitivity.

Without properly handling this openness to the feelings of all and sundry, you can be overwhelmed by something or someone in particular to the point of being emotionally incapacitated. Probably owing to your mother's unstable feelings, or perhaps even her selflessness, you are unconsciously on the look-out for someone to save or someone to be saved by. Such a predisposition is asking for trouble, in the form of being hopelessly in love, or craving something or someone unattainable.

And even if you do have your dream come true, it is then only too likely that the dream fades and ordinary reality – which you loathe – then returns. Any of these eventualities can lead to quite dubious means of easing the pain of disappointment – drugs and alcohol being the favourites.

Ultimately, you have to appreciate that you are a soulful being in a rather soulless world, and take the necessary steps to protect yourself – like meditation or some other spiritual discipline. Your dream for a better world – through art or healing – can then be more safely pursued and surely maintained.

LUNAR ASPECTS

NOTE that Sextile (co-operating with) and Opposition (confronting) Aspects are usually described similarly to Trine (harmonizing with) and Square (challenging) Aspects respectively, or they are occasionally described similarly to the Conjunction (uniting with). However, when this is the case, it should be borne in mind that a Sextile Aspect may require conscious awareness and effort to realize the assets and potential so described – and that the Opposition Aspect may indeed be experienced exactly as described, but in reality such can initially be felt or seen to come from someone or something else because you have projected or externalized such traits in order to make yourself aware of them.

Moon Conjunct (uniting with) Sun
☽ ☌ ☉

No matter what, your feeling nature is quite energized. Negatively, this means that you overdo things and concentrate your energies too much on one or two activities. You then swing to being quite quiet and impassive – increasingly, to the point of exhaustion. Positively, if you can deliberately and regularly involve yourself in others' interests, your pet subjects then become healthy areas of expertise.

Moon Square (challenging) Sun
☽ □ ☉

When expressed negatively, these feelings of yours play havoc with achieving your more creative goals. It is as if you unconsciously undermine your best interests. You are your own worst enemy, in fact. All of this stresses the importance of your becoming less self-protective and of accentuating your more positive and vital qualities. Live life – and let survival take care of itself!

Moon Opposition (confronting) Sun
☽ ☍ ☉

These qualities of your Moon-Sign and Moon-House act as a deep need that has to be met by the conscious and wilful intentions of your Sun Profile. The trouble is that your lunar inclinations will try to eclipse your solar intentions. In other words, your innate habits and dispositions may obscure your more creative view of life. You must fix your attention consciously upon some end that endures, an end to which your emotional requirements must adjust themselves. Eventually, you find that you are then far more able to meet those lunar needs, such as I have here described them.

Moon Trine (harmonizing with) Sun
☽ △ ☉

All these emotional or instinctual qualities of yours are not just passive ones waiting around for someone to make use of them. Well at least, they need not be. You are well able to employ them in a creative and profitable way, as distinct from living them out solely in a private or personal world. Your emotional make-up is vibrant and alive, so make it shine forth!

Moon Sextile (co-operating with) Sun
☽ ⚹ ☉

You enjoy a healthy interplay between these feelings and your conscious means of expressing yourself. Consequently, you work at getting the best out of your emotional nature, and weeding out the worst. In turn, others feel at ease in your presence. For the same reason, you are able to maintain harmony with your partner, children and friends.

Moon Conjunct (uniting with) Mercury
☽ ☌ ☿ *OR*
Moon Square (challenging) Mercury
☽ □ ☿ *OR*
Moon Opposition (confronting) Mercury
☽ ☍ ☿

You have a pressing need to communicate or rationalize these feelings. This is a good thing inasmuch as it enables you to understand how you and others tick, and consequently to interact readily with them. But when you overdo this you can lose touch with your feelings on their own level. Yet if you don't think about how you feel – or again, think about it too much – then your feelings prevent you from thinking straight. Either case can also incline you to chatter on as a kind of verbal overflow for your unfelt feelings.

Obviously you need to find a balance between thinking and feeling, and between talking and listening. Merely going out and doing something can shift you into a clearer perspective.

Moon Trine (harmonizing with) Mercury
☽ △ ☿ *OR*
Moon Sextile (co-operating with) Mercury
☽ ⚹ ☿

You have little trouble in conveying your feelings with the written or spoken word. Consequently, you are able to keep social situations flowing and relaxed with your ready wit and natural poise. There is a slight danger of using your natural eloquence to evade pondering in much depth on anything. But when your mind and soul have something worth chewing on, you have the prized knack of putting it across to all and sundry. You also possess basic common sense.

Moon Conjunct (uniting with) Venus
☽ ☌ ♀

What comes to the rescue in all your emotional interactions is a certain softness that you have about you – whether you are male or female. Others find it easy to bathe in your pleasingly familiar aura. This talent of yours for soothing and making people feel good has many uses and can take many forms. What you do have to guard against though is being too soft and easygoing, because you can get taken advantage of, or seriously compromise your powers of assertion.

Moon Square (challenging) Venus
☽ □ ♀ *OR*
Moon Opposition (confronting) Venus
☽ ☍ ♀

There is a certain softness that you have about you – whether you are male or female. Others find it easy to bathe in your pleasingly familiar aura. This talent of yours for soothing and making people feel good has many uses and can take many forms. What you do have to guard against though is being too soft and easygoing, because you can get taken advantage of, which seriously compromises your powers of assertion.

Moon Trine (harmonizing with) Venus
☽ △ ♀   *OR*
Moon Sextile (co-operating with) Venus
☽ ⚹ ♀

What comes to the rescue in all your emotional interactions is a certain softness that you have about you – whether you are male or female. Others find it easy to bathe in your pleasingly familiar aura. This talent of yours for soothing and making people feel good has many uses and can take many forms.

Moon Conjunct (uniting with) Mars
☽ ☌ ♂   *OR*
Moon Square (challenging) Mars
☽ □ ♂   *OR*
Moon Opposition (confronting) Mars
☽ ☍ ♂

What is more, your emotions are highly charged. You react energetically to the situation in hand, which in turn energizes the feelings of others. But there is a danger here that some of this energy is an unconscious anger about something or at someone from your past – probably your mother. Any jagged emotion such as this can cause havoc in close or domestic relationships as it gives rise to inappropriate responses to others.

For as long as this remains unattended to you can be very spiky and overly defensive when anyone gets close to your raw spot.

Moon Trine (harmonizing with) Mars
☽ △ ♂   *OR*
Moon Sextile (co-operating with) Mars
☽ ⚹ ♂

You do have a very available supply of energy to meet your needs. You possibly take this for granted simply because it is always there as you work and relax with enviable ease. The more aware you are of this healthy balance that you have between your feelings and body energy, the more vibrant and confident you will feel, enabling you to achieve success in your chosen field of endeavour.

Moon Conjunct (uniting with) Jupiter
☽ ☌ ♃   *OR*
Moon Square (challenging) Jupiter
☽ □ ♃   *OR*
Moon Opposition (confronting) Jupiter
☽ ☍ ♃

Everything about your Moon Profile is greatly emphasized. The best and the worst qualities are taken to extremes. You have a definite emotional gusto, which also bestows upon you a healthy body that maintains itself brilliantly and automatically. Because this can allow you to overindulge with apparent impunity you could wind up with weight or liver problems. By and large, though, your physical and emotional zest can be a tonic to all and sundry.

Just beware of doting upon others too much, or of expecting others to dote too much upon you – for in either case you'd just drive them away.

Moon Trine (harmonizing with) Jupiter
☽ △ ♃   *OR*
Moon Sextile (co-operating with) Jupiter
☽ ⚹ ♃

Come what may, you have an innate faith in life and that things will work out for the best. Because of this sense you have that caring and believing are an excellent combination, there is very little that you cannot make come out all right in the end. You also have green fingers – and maybe even the 'Midas Touch'. There is an emotional ease about you that can make a success of any of the positive issues mentioned, or to rectify the negative ones for yourself and others.

Moon Conjunct (uniting with) Saturn
☽ ☌ ♄   *OR*
Moon Square (challenging) Saturn
☽ □ ♄   *OR*
Moon Opposition (confronting) Saturn
☽ ☍ ♄

Your better nature is certainly tried and tested by unloving or less charitable influences in your life. One of these could well have been a coldness or separation between your father and mother. Such has left you with an ingrained feeling that the world is cold and unfeeling.

If you are to avoid being dogged by this negative conditioning, or being cold and unfeeling yourself, you must learn to be more objective and take life's blows a lot less personally.

Moon Trine (harmonizing with) Saturn
☽ △ ♄   *OR*
Moon Sextile (co-operating with) Saturn
☽ ⚹ ♄

As a kind of back-up to all this, you have a natural sense of caution and economy. You lean to conventionality when in doubt. This serves you well as ballast – but not when you want to hoist the sails and get somewhere else. You should make the most of the more fiery, imaginative and animated traits of your personality, and then use this conservative trait as a stabilizing influence.

You are reliable and responsible emotionally, but can lack an outgoing expression of warmer feelings, even though they're there. Instinctively you know that in time everything will work out – that is unless you turn to stone!

Moon Conjunct (uniting with) Uranus
☽ ☌ ♅   *OR*
Moon Square (challenging) Uranus
☽ □ ♅   *OR*
Moon Opposition (confronting) Uranus
☽ ☍ ♅

Now a major theme of your emotional life is one of your becoming progressively more cool and detached about your needs and feelings. However, until you have made some headway in this respect, you are prone to definite, even violent, mood swings. This is caused by your being wrapped up in your emotions one moment, and then being icily aloof the next. Possibly you feel that your mother didn't really want or connect with you in some way, and so you zip back and forth between needing and not needing.

If you are a mother, you make an unusual one. In the meantime, no one could accuse you of being dull or of lacking intuition!

Moon Trine (harmonizing with) Uranus
☽ △ ♅   *OR*
Moon Sextile (co-operating with) Uranus
☽ ✶ ♅

You are very able to suss out people and situations. You are the natural psychologist. Such a great sense of the truth may even frighten you, but it need not because this intuition of yours enables you to deal with most matters that life presents. You possess a lively and humorous mind that is also able to conceive of or manage quite large projects – that is, providing you have not used such a wonderful intuition merely to avoid life's challenges.

Moon Conjunct (uniting with) Neptune
☽ ☌ ♆   *OR*
Moon Square (challenging) Neptune
☽ □ ♆   *OR*
Moon Opposition (confronting) Neptune
☽ ☍ ♆

It is your emotional sensitivity that is both one of your greatest liabilities and one of your greatest assets. There is undeniable pain from your childhood that haunts you in the present as it prevents you from looking at the truth of your feelings. But this just attracts situations that make you feel vulnerable or overwhelmed.

Behind all this is the probability that your mother's values confused your own. But when you have broken through the ultimate human illusion – that vulnerability is life-threatening – then you really can become a healing presence, a voice in the wilderness. You have strong psychic tendencies, but you'd need to get clear of that emotional over-sensitivity (with mental objectivity – possibly through therapy) for it to be relied upon.

Moon Trine (harmonizing with) Neptune
☽ △ ♆   *OR*
Moon Sextile (co-operating with) Neptune   *BM*
☽ ✶ ♆

One of the finer dimensions to all this is your well developed empathetic and psychical nature. Because of this you have the makings of the natural therapist or psychologist, possessing a healing ability of the soothing, relaxing kind. You have an excellent bedside manner and a feel for the mood of the moment.

Moon Conjunct (uniting with) Pluto
☽ ☌ ♇   *OR*
Moon Square (challenging) Pluto
☽ □ ♇   *OR*
Moon Opposition (confronting) Pluto
☽ ☍ ♇

Beneath all the surface expressions of how you feel there lurks a deep distrust of human nature. This emotional seam was probably laid down long ago, in childhood, the cradle, or even before then. Other people with similarly deep-seated fears can spot this and find YOU untrustworthy.

To stop this kind of rot you need to purge such negative emotions – otherwise the power of these negative emotions will attract relationships and situations that force you to purge them anyway.

Moon Trine (harmonizing with) Pluto
☽ △ ♇   *OR*
Moon Sextile (co-operating with) Pluto
☽ ✶ ♇

Like a solid core running through your emotional make-up you have a profound instinct for survival. You may just use this to get by, but this would be rather a waste for when you get right down to the root of the matter, you are capable of regenerating and improving any situation you choose.

Moon Unaspected by any other planet
☽ ∅

As the Moon moves relatively quickly, it is quite unusual for it to form no Aspect at all to any other planet. It could be said that the nature of this unusual situation is that you have 'chosen' to establish your security in life through conscious means, rather than letting your instincts decide, for they often prove unreliable. In other words, you really have to work out where you belong and what you genuinely feel as an individual, because you are unlikely to have inherited such a feeling of inner support.

Your mother could well be, or have been, at a loss in some way, causing her provision of emotional security to be wanting. The Sign and House placement of your Moon shows the nature of such instability, which probably got passed on to you.

So you are inclined to be quite erratic with regard to emotional states and feelings of security. With an Unaspected Moon, you have great ups and downs, interspersed with periods of total emotional absence. It is therefore quite difficult for others to know where you are coming from emotionally, for you are often out of touch with your own and others' feelings.

Matters concerning the House placement of your Moon will be especially subject to erratic swings and unpredictability. Generally, with an Unaspected Moon, you have got to gain a firm mental grip on your Moon's Sign and House indications, and learn to go with the flow, and not take things too personally.

The pearl of positivity that you are diving for is an emotional freedom, where you are not overly swayed this way or that by passing moods or fears. Depending upon how much you are in touch with your centre or individuality, such emotional freedom will allow you to return naturally to your own sense of equilibrium.

Moon Conjunct (uniting with) Ascendant
☽ ☌ AS

You respond to the world around you in an immediate way. It is as if you are having life, the world, society and everything constantly poured over you. How you manage this inundation depends greatly on your Moon Profile as a whole, but I myself would take care to enquire how you really feel, rather than take you at face value, which could merely be your response to me!

Moon Square (challenging) Ascendant
☽ □ AS

All of these feelings of yours tend not to be so readily apparent to others because your way of expressing yourself gives them the lie in some way. Or, conversely, you are rather unconscious of your feelings coming across even though they are doing so, for they run counter to what you think you are putting out. Seeing yourself on video or film would do much to enlighten you here. It could even shock you. With a bit of work, you can become highly aware of the marked effect you have on other people – and improve it or expand upon it.

Moon Opposition (confronting) Ascendant
☽ ☍ AS

You have such a great need for company that you could lose yourself in partners or the concerns of the general public. Sooner or later, though, you have to come to terms with the fact that you do have a feel for others that, when balanced out by a stronger sense of yourself, bestows upon you a fine way with people. You then find they need you more than you need them.

Moon Trine (harmonizing with) Ascendant
☽ △ AS

You are able to make your feelings known to others quite easily – individually or collectively – in a direct and simple way that attracts a relaxed and natural emotional interplay. In short, you know how to fit in.

Moon Sextile (co-operating with) Ascendant
☽ ⚹ AS

With a little conscious application, you are able to make your feelings known to others – individually or collectively – in a direct and simple way that attracts a relaxed and natural emotional interplay. You know how to fit in.

Moon Conjunct (uniting with) MidHeaven
☽ ☌ MC

Your mother's influence in respect of all these emotional qualities of yours is paramount – for good or ill. I therefore think it important that you make absolutely sure that what you are doing in life is happily your choice – and not just hers. Be that as it may, the overall character of your Moon Profile should be embodied in your career. You have a natural feel for the world's needs – just don't become too much of a mother hen to them all!

Moon Square (challenging) MidHeaven
☽ □ MC

A difficulty you have that underlies all your emotional dealings is one of not really feeling at ease with the way of the world in general. Although this could be regarded as understandable, considering the state of things globally, you should bear in mind that such dis-ease is more to do with your emotional conflict with your parents and background rather with than society as a whole.

Moon Opposition (confronting) MidHeaven
☽ ☍ MC

Basically, you need a secure home base where all these feelings of yours can feel protected and have room to adjust to changes, or simply to the end of the working day. You also have a strong sense of your roots, which can mean anything from feeling well established family-wise, to having to dig down deep to discover where you truly belong; it depends upon what your Moon Profile indicates overall. Your father is the real key to your emotional state, whether it is a feeling of security or insecurity.

Moon Trine (harmonizing with) MidHeaven
☽ △ MC   *OR*
Moon Sextile (co-operating with) MidHeaven
☽ ⚹ MC

A blessing you should frequently remind yourself of is that your background and instincts consciously guide you in your dealings with the world – securing both domestic and career interests in the process.

Moon Houses

Moon in the First House
☽ 1ˢᵗ

This need and emotional disposition of yours is what you constantly live by for it is how you immediately respond to all life situations. There is a childlike quality to how you put yourself across, and therefore like a child you can be anything from ingenuously enchanting to acutely annoying.

You wear your emotions on your sleeve for all to see – at least, such as I have described them under your Moon-Sign. This is important to bear in mind, for others are inclined to take you at face value – for better or worse. Your have a naturally caring approach and a sympathetic touch – particularly if you are female.

Moon in the Second House
☽ 2ⁿᵈ

Many of these needs and feelings apply especially to how you estimate your own worth, or earn an income, and to finances generally. Income and self-esteem are also subject to fluctuations, as your moods and the market itself are. By the same token, you may have an instinct for money and property. For better or worse you have inherited the same attitudes to money and self-worth as your family and especially your mother. Money can be earned catering to the public's needs.

Moon in the Third House
☽ 3ʳᵈ

All these feelings are greatly reflected in your relationships with siblings, your school years, and in how you go about your everyday affairs. Your feelings can lend themselves to the climate of the moment with some ease. This favours occupations running from counsellor to shopkeeper, from writer to local gossip. Such an ongoing curiosity as yours both dislikes routine and can dispel it.

Indeed, you have the common touch, and are invariably aware of what's happening locally. You can be intellectually stimulating, but may prattle on somewhat – it all depends what you fill your mind with, but fill it you will. Your ear-to-the-ground awareness is very useful in serving your Moon-Sign's needs, and it also enables you to keep your neighbours, and even the general public, in touch with whatever you regard as nourishing, reassuring or emotionally significant.

Moon in the Fourth House
☽ 4ᵗʰ

Whatever your feelings or needs, you instinctively know how to protect and feed them. In fact, you are a natural homemaker. You exude a home-from-home, hearthside familiar atmosphere. This fosters all domestic and catering talents, be it on a professional or amateur basis. You also have a closeness to Nature. A feel for flora and fauna is in your blood, and you could have green fingers. You can, however, be overly attached to your roots – never leaving the region, or even home, you were born in.

This could amount to a security-blanket syndrome where certain habits and things are clung to – especially in times of stress and unpredictability. Your feelings may be more or less totally bound up or invested in your actual home or family, so that you do not readily express them in external social intercourse. If you are this extremely homely type, then as long as you're happy keeping the home-fires burning, that's fine. But if you are just cooped up on your own, learn to share or express your inner nature.

Moon in the Fifth House
)) 5th

All these needs and feelings are especially drawn to situations where fun and creativity are in the offing. How you respond to this has a great deal to do with your Moon-Sign traits, which I have just described. One way or the other, though, you are instinctively drawn to one type or another of creative self-expression – be it art or drama, children, romance, hobbies or gambling. Because you naturally have a feel for such areas, there is an infectious and familiar quality about you, and others gather round this like a campfire.

You have a great need to enjoy yourself – and the capacity to do so. If your personality is generally rather unrestrained, you can become quite wanton – or just never grow up – and wind up being as unreliable as you were formerly desirable. If, however, you cultivate a serious centre to your being that does not need amusement as a security blanket, then you become someone who not only knows how to make a party go or an affair sparkle, but also knows when it's over.

Moon in the Sixth House
)) 6th

All these needs and feelings largely revolve around health and work. If you are happily or gainfully employed you feel right with the world – when you are not, you don't. So although you put your heart and soul into your job, there can be the danger of your investing emotions into work that don't really belong there. As a consequence of this, you can get too wound up about your work, or use work as a substitute for emotional involvements, which have nothing to do with work. You may also get to thinking that emotional life can be run in the same logical way that work is.

Health itself can then become an issue as your system plays up as a result of overwork or emotional frustration. What your emotional preoccupation with work is really in aid of is making sure that you work out a balance between your job interests and your social ones – that is, a healthy situation. A patently evolved expression of all this is your having an active interest in health itself – based upon balanced habits and lifestyle.

Moon in the Seventh House ♄♏
)) 7th

All of these needs and feelings particularly affect your partnerships, for you are inclined to look for security primarily in a relationship with another person. This can mean that you marry merely for security, and then find out that the price you pay for this is that your partner embodies much that you don't like or don't want to know about yourself.

In other words, you go for your own dark reflection – unconsciously. The important thing to bear in mind is that a mutual nurturing is required in your relationships, which means that occasionally you have to put aside your romantic illusions or intentions, and look for what it is that both of you need from one another – and this may not be in the least romantic.

And, initially, it will probably make you feel insecure, but later you will feel a far deeper sense of familiarity and security with your mate. Generally speaking, you have a good sense of how others are feeling, and this can serve you well in any person- or public-orientated activities.

Moon in the Eighth House
☽ 8th

All these needs and feelings about yourself are kept very much to yourself. It is only in a very intimate situation, such as a sexual relationship, that you show your true emotions. Even then, you can be quite hard to reach. But this is owing to the fact that you are instinctively attuned to private feelings and subtle atmospheres.

You are only too acutely aware of how closeness can be abused, probably owing to your sensing and taking personally something that happened between your parents. Positively, this mediumistic awareness of yours of unseen forces enables you to comfort others in a deeply subtle way. On the negative side though, you can manipulate them to keep them where you want them – but this can give rise to a painful game of cat and mouse.

Ultimately you have to trust and use your magical sense of what lies hidden from common view to heal yourself and others too, rather than feeling increasingly cut off.

Moon in the Ninth House
☽ 9th

Whatever your feeling nature is, there is an energy and enthusiasm to it because you are instinctively aware that the World is more than we can ever know. And so you perennially sense the possibility that around the corner waits another enthralling clue to the mystery of life. For the same reason, you can be adept at readings signs and omens.

Anything that gives you the feeling of life in motion is very reassuring to you. This would include any form of physical or astral travel, religious and philosophical pursuits, outdoor sports and activities. Indeed, your home itself could be distant from your place of birth – even in a foreign land.

Any caring or nurturing ability that you have takes on a religious or crusader-like tone. You regard well-being as an essentially spiritual matter, and you cannot conceive of a God without there being a Goddess too.

Moon in the Tenth House
☽ 10th

All these feelings and qualities are most likely reflected in your professional life and how the world sees you. And, accordingly, your standing and achievements are subject to the same ups and downs as your moods. Your emotional security is dependent upon professional success, and your career itself has to involve you personally.

Merely doing a job will not suffice. Furthermore your success rests upon your ability to sense and cater to the moods and needs of the public – and this ability has a great deal to do with your Moon Profile as a whole. And your mother will have had a lot to do with how you see yourself in the world, in the sense that her ideas, fears and outward mannerisms have strongly influenced you with regard to the ways of the outside world.

Initially you feel about as secure professionally as you did as a child. Ultimately, it is how much you have come to terms with the self-image you acquired in childhood that determines your professional well-being.

Moon in the Eleventh House
☽ 11th

All these needs and feelings are most likely to be met through friends, clubs, social movements, or the nurturing of some ideal. All these matters will go through phases, causing your goals and allegiances to fluctuate. Overall, you manage to keep your emotional life fairly light and breezy.

You prefer not to get morbid and heavy in one-to-one relationships, and if things get that way, you will go out with friends or to somewhere impersonal. This can be a good safety valve, but a bad habit if you make your friends or associations into an emotional crutch. It is wise to take a break from them every so often in order to re-establish your own identity, not to mention facing any more intimate emotional commitments.

All the same, you are capable of appealing to the crowd on an emotional level, which means that you have a finger on the pulse of the public's attitude to political, sociological or cultural issues.

Moon in the Twelfth House
☽ 12th

These needs and feelings of yours may be, or may have been, repressed. The emotional problems that you have are deeply rooted and hard to pin down. They probably go back to babyhood or as far as the womb – or even to previous lives. Needless to say, your mother will somehow be tied up with all of this – in an obvious or more mysterious way.

Often, psychic links with your mother are in evidence and these should be positively used by your mother meditating upon or visualizing you in a positive light, or through yourself doing likewise to the child within you. You are emotionally wounded or very sensitive, or both. Because of this you are inclined to cut off from your feelings and anything to do with them – often with cynicism or a work schedule that allows no emotional access. Consequently, a sizeable dimension of your being may get clouded or closed off from your conscious mind.

This in turn can seriously inhibit emotionally relating, and maybe some mental functions too. Yet at the same time you want emotionally feeding. If you wish some of the weight to be taken from this rather private and idiosyncratic cross you bear, at some stage you will have to own up to your feelings – acutely painful though this will probably be.

You will then find that you are in fact remarkably in touch with the collective mood and its hopes and fears (probably what made you feel invaded in the first place), thus giving rise to creative inspiration. Initially, you can experience and express all of this as being somewhat otherworldly (or in a world of your own), or be very much of this world and into material things, by way of compensation.

CHAPTER FOUR – YOUR MIDHEAVEN PROFILE
CAREER AND STATUS

The MidHeaven or MC (Medium Coeli) is the point in the sky where the Sun would be at noon. The quality of the Sign placed there, and any Planet that might be placed in the area to the left of it (an area called The Tenth House) at the time and place of your birth, symbolizes the nature of your POSITION IN THE WORLD – STATUS, PROFESSION, REPUTATION, RECOGNITION and where you experience AUTHORITY. Bear in mind that this is not the only indicator of profession, for there can be other dimensions of the Personality or Chart that contain, express or contribute to your potential for material success. For example, any Planets in the Tenth House are highly influential with regard to this area of life, as shown elsewhere in this Profile. More fundamentally, the MidHeaven Sign shows you the basic quality needed for AMOUNTING TO SOMETHING IN LIFE, for actually getting there. The other important clue to this area is the Planet that rules the MidHeaven Sign, and this is referred to in all cases.

Finally, the opposite point to the MidHeaven, the Lower MidHeaven or IC (Imum Coeli), indicates the opposite to the public and professional life, that is, the PRIVATE and DOMESTIC life, your BACKGROUND and ROOTS. This too is described along with the significance of the Planet that rules that point and the Fourth House that extends to the right of it. Any Planets in the Fourth House, shown elsewhere in your Profile, will also strongly contribute to the nature of your home and FAMILY background.

MidHeaven Signs

Aries at the MidHeaven
MC ♈

You need a certain boldness to make your way professionally in the world. So the nature of Chapter Seven – Your Mars Profile – will bear greatly upon this, indicating in what style, and with how much ease or difficulty success may be accomplished. You would do well in any profession that entails some kind of pushing, selling or pioneering – which could include the military.

Holding a leading position in your career is also quite desirable, as is having the freedom to do things your own way. At times you may have to fight pretty hard to maintain or achieve a certain position. This proves to be worth it in the long run, when you are at last way out in front.

To compensate for this often-hectic outer world activity it is important for you to have a harmonious home life. Making a priority out of this is desirable, and a beautiful home atmosphere is very possible. All this is symbolized by having the Sign of Libra on your Lower MidHeaven (IC), making the Planet Venus (see Chapter Six) the ruler of your background, home and inner life.

You achieve success more easily when matters are kept straightforward, clean-cut and simple – and, most of all, if you are patient.

Taurus at the MidHeaven
MC ♉

Your profession involves things of substance, such as the physical body's care and maintenance, any kind of production or management, real estate, finances, building, horticulture or agriculture, etc. You prefer a steady position with assured assets and income to pie-in-the-sky projects. Material status is important to you.

Conversely, your private life can be very private, not so plain to see, secret even. You have deep roots, possibly even dark ones! All this is symbolized by having the Sign of Scorpio on your Lower MidHeaven (IC), making the Planet Pluto (see Chapter Twelve) the ruler of your background, home and inner life.

The condition of your Venus by Sign, House and Aspect will reveal more about the nature of your career, as well as the ease or difficulty encountered in pursuing it (see Chapter Six).

Gemini at the MidHeaven
MC ♊

Your profession should involve communication in some way. An ability to make contact with others (e.g. writer, agent, trader), or to enjoy repetition (e.g. typist, printer, production line) proves very useful for your professional advancement.

Two or more careers – one after the other or simultaneously – is likely and practical. This feature of Gemini MidHeaven should be followed up if you are bored or restless with your role in life – or not getting enough money.

An occupation that does not hold your interest can lead to your going from job to job interminably. Unless a chequered career is actually desirable, you had better sit down with pencil and paper to work out what kind of work you believe to be mentally stimulating, and then go for it. Also, a superficial interest in your work means a superficial interest from those you work for. The possible reason behind this lack of commitment is divided attention from your mother. On the positive side, though, her possibly light and easy-going attitude will be reflected in your professional attitude and style.

To balance all this out, your private or inner life needs to have something about that is less secular and divided. A large or foreign abode or roots could be indicated. All this is symbolized by having the Sign of Sagittarius on your Lower MidHeaven (IC), making the Planet Jupiter (see Chapter Eight) the ruler of your background, home and inner life.

The condition of Mercury by Sign, House and Aspects will reveal more about the nature of your career, as well as the ease or difficulty involved in attaining some position (see Chapter Five).

Cancer at the MidHeaven
MC ♋

This suggests that your professional arena is very much a home-from-home. In other words, catering to the physical and emotional needs of the public is a very likely role for you. The fluctuating whims of society need to be sensed in order for you to find success. Your own home could be directly or indirectly involved in your profession, possibly a family business.

You have an inclination to mother the world – and this could range from being very much in demand in business, to being a housewife, which is kind of the same thing! In either case though, beware of going around wiping everyone's noses to the point where you have no strength left and they haven't found theirs either.

Not surprisingly your private life can be rather caught up with your business life. Limits should possibly be placed upon such an occurrence, for you need a personal world to retreat to. This could be owing to your background being somehow deprived in the first place. A disciplined and orderly home and family life is most desirable, and you should strive to achieve this through not being compromised by your sympathies. All this is symbolized by having the Sign of Capricorn on your Lower MidHeaven (IC), making the Planet Saturn (see Chapter Nine) the ruler of your background, home and inner life.

The condition of your Moon by Sign, House and Aspect will tell more of how your nurturing and instinctual abilities may be employed professionally, as well as revealing how easily a professional position may be secured (see Chapter Three).

Leo at the MidHeaven
MC ♌

Your life and identity are best found and expressed through some position of prominence and authority. You do not want to be an 'also ran'. Studying the qualities of your Sun by Sign, House and Aspect (see Chapter Two) will reveal much concerning the nature and success of your professional life.

It is important that you stand proud in the face of the public and the world at large. Your ego wants and needs to be put on the line. Your target is one of being seen to shine – and your mother was probably very instrumental in showing you how to do this, or how not to – or she may have tried to eclipse you in some way.

An unusual home life could be in evidence, possibly unpredictable or used for alternative or scientific activities – gadgets could abound. All this is symbolized by having the Sign of Aquarius on your Lower MidHeaven (IC), making the Planet Uranus (see Chapter Ten) the ruler of your background, home and inner life.

Virgo at the MidHeaven
MC ♍

Professions that require a sense of service or precision are very likely – examples of this being things like healthcare, graphic design, editing, critique, quality control, etc.

However you should guard against feeling slave-driven or being too exacting in your career and what you feel the world expects of you. All the same, you can gain a reputation for high-quality work.

Much as you are a perfectionist and very conscientious in your outer dealings, your home or private life gives this the lie by being mysterious, disorderly or vague in some way. Music and art should be an important part of domestic activities and atmosphere. All this is symbolized by having the Sign of Pisces on your Lower MidHeaven (IC), making the Planet Neptune (see Chapter Eleven) the ruler of your background, home and inner life.

The Sign, House and Aspects of Mercury (see Chapter Five) will reveal more about the nature and conditions of your professional development.

Libra at the MidHeaven
MC ♎

Your profession needs to be concerned in some way with beauty and harmony. So this would suggest the arts, fashion, diplomacy, law, sociology, etc.

There could be a tie-up with your partner professionally. In fact, your career greatly depends upon your mate – directly or indirectly.

Home life, by contrast, could be a bit frenetic as people wrestle for independence. Or it means that living alone becomes the only option. All this is symbolized by having the Sign of Aries on your Lower MidHeaven (IC), making the Planet Mars (see Chapter Seven) the ruler of your background, home and inner life.

The condition of your Venus by Sign, House and Aspect (see Chapter Six) will reveal more details concerning the nature and prospects of your career.

Scorpio at the MidHeaven
MC ♏

You need to be deeply and intensely involved in any professional endeavour. In the end you would find superficial or compromising careers intolerable.

You are ambitious – and you have, or should develop, the steely and ruthless nature, which ensures that ambitions are realized. Indications of idealism or sensitivity elsewhere in your Chart will naturally make this achieving somewhat less straightforward.

Your mother's influence is likely to be quite significant regarding choice of profession and ideas of respectability. You should check as to whether this is really what you want for yourself – for this sort of maternal influence can be so insidiously coercive that major career changes or doubts will occur later in your life if you don't deal with this.

To compensate for the gut-wrenching and possibly obsessive outer activity in the world you require a more solid and unchanging home and private life. Close to nature; farming roots are possible. All this is symbolized by having the Sign of Taurus on your Lower MidHeaven (IC), making the Planet Venus (see Chapter Six) the ruler of your background, home and inner life.

Generally speaking, your career should involve anything Scorpionic, which essentially has to do with delving for and using any type of power or influence – such as politics, medicine, big business, undercover work, the occult. The condition of your Pluto by House and Aspect will reveal more detail concerning the nature and development of your career and reputation (see Chapter Twelve).

Sagittarius at the MidHeaven

MC ♐

For your professional life to be satisfying and successful it needs to be ever expanding, growing beyond itself. So this poses some work or subject that is never finished – teaching, religion, philosophy, archaeology, anthropology, history, law, publishing; anything that is seeking to include and understand more and more, and physically this of course implies any kind of sport or travelling.

You are happiest trying to reach as many people as possible; Sagittarius likes to bring and bind people together with a sense of enthusiasm. You also like plenty of room to operate. A restricting sort of work life is very inadvisable. Furthermore, religious influences in your life greatly affect your choice of profession or the moral way that you conduct it.

Your inner or domestic life is or can be somewhat unsettled. You do not as a rule like to put roots down to deeply – in case you suddenly want to up sticks. A mentally rather emotionally oriented family background could be what is behind this. All this is symbolized by having the Sign of Gemini on your Lower MidHeaven (IC), making the Planet Mercury (see Chapter Five) the ruler of your background, home and inner life.

The Sign, House and Aspects of your Jupiter (see Chapter Eight) will reveal more about the style and conditions of your professional position and development.

Capricorn at the MidHeaven

MC ♑

Your place in the world has very much to do with the conditions and tradition in which you were brought up. There is an unconscious tendency to accept or go for your prescribed lot – be it prince or pauper, tycoon or secretary. Careers that involve the building or maintenance of any kind structure can be suitable for you, whether it is an actual building, a corporation, or government – or medically, concerning teeth or bones.

Conservative values prevail in that you naturally subscribe to hard work and discipline as being necessary to amounting to something in life.

The traditional flavour is also in evidence in your home and background. Family and roots are very important to you. All this is symbolized by having the Sign of Cancer on your Lower MidHeaven (IC), making the Moon (see Chapter Three) the ruler of your background, home and inner life.

The condition of Saturn by Sign, House and Aspect will reveal further details with regard to your professional fortunes and inclinations (see Chapter Nine). Overall, you subscribe to the traditional attitude that it is desirable to reach a position of authority through discipline and hard work.

Aquarius at the MidHeaven

MC ♒

Professional and public status is best geared towards interlinking various peoples and subjects. This could include mass media, linguistics, cross-fertilization of cultures, world services/organizations, etc. In fact anything that aids and furthers the ideal of one united world civilization.

The House and Aspects of Uranus in your Chart (see Chapter Ten) will indicate in more detail the nature of your profession, as well as the obstacles or advantages encountered in pursuing your ambitions. For example, if you had Uranus in the First House, your actual physical presence and personal idiosyncrasies would be very much a part of your professional 'equipment'.

To some extent, you will have to 'invent' your own position in life. Looking for precedents can be missing the point, considering that Aquarius is about innovation and creating precedents. Scientific or so-called alternative disciplines are a very likely career path, also electronics, computers, media, etc.

Teamwork is usually part of your professional scheme. A reluctance to be involved in this way will prove very frustrating unless you are prepared to go out on quite a long limb – even to the extent of being or feeling an outcast.

You have deep convictions arising out of your background, gifting you with a sense of personal significance – or else it forced you to assume it. You like to rule your own roost – which could mean living alone. House proud. All this is symbolized by having the Sign of Leo on your Lower MidHeaven (IC), making the Sun (see Chapter Two) the ruler of your background, home and inner life.

Pisces at the MidHeaven

MC ♓ ♍

Pisces is open to many interpretations and can come in many disguises. Because of this your professional life is hard to identify unless you have already focussed upon one of the more typical careers of this Sign – music, dance, healing, chemistry, cosmetics, visual art or anything that is mystical or glamorous, or has to do with the sea.

You can lose your career path through being undone and side tracked by drugs or alcohol or 'wool gathering' generally. On the other hand your public position may be involved in dealing with or in these issues.

Background was exacting in some way – as if something or someone was always watching what you were doing and how you were doing it, or you had to watch them. This supplies you with a fundamental sense of conscientiousness, but an underlying feeling of never being good enough could undermine your attempts to be more expansive or creative. All this is symbolized by having the Sign of Virgo on your Lower MidHeaven (IC), making the Planet Mercury (see Chapter Five) the ruler of your background, home and inner life.

Generally speaking, Pisces here poses careers that have to do with enlightening (art and entertainment) or relieving (medicine and healing). Also, something which involves compassion and reaches out to the suffering masses: the caring professions.

The House and Aspects of Neptune in your Chart (see Chapter Eleven) will give further and possibly more precise clues as to the nature of your career and public position. For example, Neptune in the Fourth House could mean working from home, or in a home, i.e. institution. Hard Aspects to Neptune would indicate difficulties and confusion in finding or keeping a position; too many Soft Aspects could mean laziness and a lack of objectives. A balance of Hard and Soft Aspects is most favourable with slippery Neptune.

CHAPTER FIVE – YOUR MERCURY PROFILE
PERCEPTION AND MENTALITY

Mercury symbolizes REASON and the THINKING function and the ability to make CONTACT, whether this is externally via COMMUNICATION and PERCEPTION, or internally in the form of your NERVOUS SYSTEM. WIT and SPEED, DEXTERITY and the capacity for LEARNING – and therefore EMPLOYMENT and COMMERCE – are the essence of Mercury. Negatively, Mercury can make for OVER-RATIONALIZATION, leading to DRYNESS and a LACK OF FEELING, as well as SLEIGHT OF HAND and SHARPNESS OF TONGUE, including SARCASM and CYNICISM as Mercury can block or be blind to empathy, belief or intuition.

MERCURY SIGNS

Mercury in Aries
☿ ♈

Your mind is readily energized, and you want thoughts and words to be acted upon rather than just left in the head. So this terrier-like mentality of yours enables you to learn, communicate or teach quickly and effectively. It is also confers a flair for selling and promotion. The shortcoming of such cerebral impetuosity is that you can have an incomplete point of view and are prone to making decisions before all the facts are taken into account. It is then not surprising that there is a lack of follow through on certain projects. You also worry at the heels of anyone you are working with, or talking to or selling to. Yet all these could be described as occupational hazards of a mind and tongue that just have to strike while the iron is hot. But a dash of diplomacy would make for smoother and steadier progress.

Mercury in Taurus
☿ ♉

Yours is a mind that likes to cogitate, to taste and absorb the pros and cons, rather as you would a good meal; and you also prefer the traditional rather than the newfangled – at least, until such has undeniably proved itself to you. Once you have learned or accepted anything, you will probably never forget it or let go of it easily.

All this confers upon you a practical bent. Arts and crafts or construction skills come naturally to you. Or else your practical sense is expressed in handling money or property, or product managing. You are a steady worker and give value for money. Dependable and reassuring as your conservative way of thinking is, if it is carried to the extremes of resisting a move or a change in attitude, then life or others might have to resort to more dramatic or emotional methods to make you see the need for that change.

Mercury in Gemini

Your mind is efficient in that it is quick and precise, but its quality is only as good as what you feed it with. You can be eloquent or just a gossip, clever or facile, fluent or flippant. It all depends on what you read and the people that you mix with. To avoid incipient nervousness and restlessness, and possible mischief making, it is equally important that you actually have something worthwhile to do. This should not be too difficult for you are a fast learner and can lend your native wits and dexterity to any number of jobs, especially those that involve the use of your tongue or hands.

Mercury in Cancer

Your mind is like a pair of feelers or antennae. You pick up all sorts of vibrations and implications sensitively. The problem is that you will probably take them personally and get upset. You may then experience the dilemma of wanting to know at the same time as not wanting to know. You have a good memory, which can do things like recall conversations word for word. Additionally, you have a sympathetic mentality, and the way that you speak can have a 'stroking' quality, which is very agreeable. With such a sensitive perception as yours, it would be well to cultivate a liking for the truth – even though it might hurt – for that is what you are so capable of sensing. Otherwise, a failure to look at the truth is followed by a failure to recognize it just when you need to.

Mercury in Leo

Yours is a creative mind, a mind that likes to play and thereby come up with creative ideas. Consequently you can be known for your distinctive and humorous verbal style. You identify strongly with the way you think and take pride in doing so. The price that you pay for such a vital mentality is that of either overplaying or underplaying your hand; the reason being that you are frightened of not making a big enough impression or of looking ridiculous. In the end, you have to have the courage to put your money where your mouth is – and rely upon your undeniably bright mind to pick up the mental thread should you lose it.

Mercury in Virgo

Your mind is rather like a precision instrument, which can perform more or less any mental task that is set before you. This does, of course, depend on whether you, the owner of that mind, wants to do that task. On the other hand though, just because your intellect is so very capable, you can be inclined to try and work out everything in your head to the point where your mind is running you rather than the other way around. With such a mind as yours, it should not be too difficult to programme your formidable mental machine to turn off occasionally and enjoy the purely physical or emotional aspects of life, and not specialize too much. Then not only will it perform its mental tasks better, but it will not be bothering you with such things as insomnia, irritability or being overly critical of others.

Mercury in Libra

The way that you think is based largely on how you feel in relating to others. Consequently, you are inclined to agree at the expense of failing to contact how you yourself actually feel about a given issue – until later when you're then having to 'agree' with someone else. All this results in the person to whom you relate most intimately becoming frustrated through not knowing which side of the fence you're on. What they don't see is that you are striving to keep the peace amongst a wide variety of people and opinions. However, the point that any close associate is trying to make is that you have to have a yardstick of your own, otherwise no one will get your measure, and consequently they will find you hard to take seriously. And this would be a shame, considering that your decision – when finally made – is the one most likely to be the fairest.

Mercury in Scorpio

Yours is the mind of the interrogator or spy. So any occupation that needs or uses this kind of delving mentality is bound for some measure of success. This particularly favours psychological, research or police work. You do not miss many tricks. Your failing, however, is that you can suspect malice of intent where there is none; and this can lead to mental convolutions which are almost impossible to work out or work through. It is likely that you create intrigue in order to keep your mind on its stealthy toes. This is probably okay, just as long as you don't get foiled by your own mental swordplay. Essentially, you have a good, sharp mind, because there is always something or someone that needs looking into, and so your mental muscle is constantly exercised.

Mercury in Sagittarius

Your mind is searching for a meaning to life, and it wants to be employed in a meaningful way. You perceive things with an eye for opportunity, and you have an enthusiastic way of expressing yourself verbally, although you can say a bit too much on occasions. You have a broad grasp of general life issues and cultural trends. Sometimes this can cause you to overlook details and mistake opinions for facts. Your vibrant mentality should avoid occupations that make you feel confined and restless, and should pursue situations which involve travel and/or variety, and that have some social significance.

Mercury in Capricorn

Yours is basically a constructive mind, or one that is rather too matter of fact – depending on what you are using it for or directing it towards. This is because it is a methodical mind that likes procedural ways of performing tasks, and being in possession of solid facts – so you can make a good organizer or successful businessperson. But you can also be inclined to get stuck at one level of thinking, which leads to intellectual constipation and professional stagnation. To avoid this, incorporate an element of risk, idealism or the unusual into your normally pragmatic way of going about things. Your inventive or even wild ideas, or somebody else's, are what gets something off the ground. Your innate practical way of thinking comes into its own sorting out snags and paperwork, and keeping things on the rails. You have a wry humour, and a sense of irony bordering on the wise.

Mercury in Aquarius

Yours is a scientific and detached mentality. Naturally, any occupation that has to do with technology or deals in clinical facts and figures is something to which you are well suited. On a more personal level you are able to stand back and subtract the emotional charge out of a given situation and thereby keep free of awkward feelings. The danger here is that you can become so good at sidestepping the emotional significance of things as to attract problems with relationships, and situations in general, whose resolution defies a purely logical approach. By the same token though, you can also be very efficient at keeping a cool head where it is needed to guide and maintain objectivity in occupations such as counselling, psychotherapy or group leadership. You also have a quirky sense of humour!

Mercury in Pisces

Yours is a sensitive mind, which absorbs information rather than consciously learning it. Ideas and solutions seem to surface rather than being actually worked out. Because of this process of mental osmosis you are sometimes not quite sure whether it is your own mind that is doing the thinking. If you are happy to let your mind be a kind of nozzle, which directs the stream of pictures and words that issues from your fertile imagination, then you'll be happy with what you do and say. If, however, you have the notion that you must be in logical control of your thought processes, you become adept at poking at the blind-spots and irrational ideas of others because they seem to threaten your own concept of mental order. But sooner or later your imagination will demand its due; that you express your dreams and confront your own doubts in a creative or honest way. Otherwise you will be further driven to suppressing them unhealthily with drugs or alcohol, or with an even fiercer rationality.

Mercury Aspects

NOTE that Sextile (co-operating with) and Opposition (confronting) Aspects are usually described similarly to Trine (harmonizing with) and Square (challenging) Aspects respectively, or they are occasionally described similarly to the Conjunction (uniting with). However, when this is the case, it should be borne in mind that a Sextile Aspect may require conscious awareness and effort to realize the assets and potential so described – and that the Opposition Aspect may indeed be experienced exactly as described, but in reality such can initially be felt or seen to come from someone or something else because you have projected or externalized such traits in order to make yourself aware of them.

Mercury Conjunct (uniting with) Sun
☿ ☌ ☉

These mental attributes of yours are further empowered by having the strength of your will behind them. You are an intellectual force to be reckoned with and your Mercury Profile as a whole will reveal just who and what you have to pit your mental muscle against. It will also reveal in what way you have a clear field of mental endeavour. In either case you sometimes could be accused of being a know-it-all. But then a shining mind like yours just cannot but help cast a few shadows.

Mercury Conjunct (uniting with) Moon
☿ ☌ ☽   **OR**

Mercury Square (challenging) Moon
☿ □ ☽   **OR**

Mercury Opposition (confronting) Moon
☿ ☍ ☽

It is not easy for you to divorce your thoughts from your feelings. Trying to do so merely attracts emotional types whose irrationality drives you mad. The more you cling to reason, the less reasonable things become. Or else it could be that your own unresolved emotional issues are getting in the way of clear thinking. Once you have given your feelings their due and dealt with them accordingly (as described in your Moon Profile) your mental powers are released and increased.

Mercury Trine (harmonizing with) Moon
☿ △ ☽   **OR**

Mercury Sextile (co-operating with) Moon
☿ ✶ ☽

You have an instinctive awareness of the day-to-day workings of people and life in general. This could be called the common touch, and favours any occupation where you have to deal with the public on their own level. You are, in a word, streetwise.

Mercury Conjunct (uniting with) Venus
☿ ♂ ♀   **OR**
Mercury Sextile (co-operating with) Venus
☿ ✳ ♀

Added to all this you have an artistic flair or a way with words. You don't just do or say something – you do it with style, humour or grace. Any activity where a fine touch is required is well starred. This could be playing a musical instrument, massage or perhaps public relations. Writing well comes naturally to you also. Just be careful that you don't mistake fine words for equally fine feelings.

Mercury Conjunct (uniting with) Mars
☿ ♂ ♂

Once you get a mental grip on something you are unlikely to let go of it until you have got the answer, truth, story or whatever it is that you are after. This terrier-like, foot-in-the-door, attitude of yours is invaluable in any kind of investigative activity. Your sharp and witty mind lights the way. You can also get easily agitated, but this does fire you to act and speak out, and thereby get things done and out in the open. All the same, count to ten when wound up.

Mercury Square (challenging) Mars
☿ □ ♂   **OR**
Mercury Opposition (confronting) Mars
☿ ♂ ♂

You have an inner conflict between what you think and what you want. You tend to express this by being awkward or contrary verbally or physically – argumentative, in fact. But your agitated mind does fire you to act and speak out, and thereby get things done and in the open. Just try not to let your contentious nature become a way of life in itself. To do this, you may need to identify the origin of that inner conflict, that mental anger.

Mercury Trine (harmonizing with) Mars
☿ △ ♂   **OR**
Mercury Sextile (co-operating with) Mars
☿ ✳ ♂

Once you get a mental grip on something you are unlikely to let go of it until you have got the answer, truth, story or whatever it is that you are after. This terrier-like, foot-in-the-door, attitude of yours is invaluable in any kind of investigative activity. Your sharp and witty mind lights the way.

Mercury Conjunct (uniting with) Jupiter
☿ ♂ ♃   **OR**
Mercury Square (challenging) Jupiter
☿ □ ♃   **OR**
Mercury Opposition (confronting) Jupiter
☿ ♂ ♃

When it comes to mental equipment, you have more than your fair share, which can be a mixed blessing. Your mind can scan whole panoramas of thought. When it can follow this up with an equally impressive verbal, visual or aural expression of such large ideas, then the teacher in you shines forth. However, the hazard here is one of being full of great notions but not being able to communicate them without exaggerating to the point of gross inaccuracy or without saying too much. Your aim is actually to expand your sphere of thinking through study and experience, yet also to be practical and relevant and not merely academic.

Mercury Trine (harmonizing with) Jupiter
☿ △ ♃   *OR*
Mercury Sextile (co-operating with) Jupiter
☿ ✶ ♃

In any event, you have a well-equipped intellect. With a little conscious effort you readily attract information and contacts. Your mind is a kind of all-purpose tool with a built-in sense of integrity that can apply itself to any task if you should need to. Law, languages, teaching, journalism, publishing or any subject that requires a grasp of both the general and the particular is something in which you can excel. In short, you have intelligence.

Mercury Conjunct (uniting with) Saturn
☿ ☌ ♄   *OR*
Mercury Square (challenging) Saturn
☿ □ ♄   *OR*
Mercury Opposition (confronting) Saturn
☿ ☍ ♄

There is no getting away from it, the correct development and use of your mental equipment is utterly important. This means that as time goes by, you have a more and more disciplined mind with a satisfying working life to match, or else you will become stuck as a result of inconsistent attempts to get to grips with the situation, possibly due to learning difficulties that gave rise to feelings of intellectual inferiority or speech problems. Alternatively your perception and interests become dulled by cynicism, or mentally depressed through dry intellectualism. A formula here could be: work when your mind feels like working; play with it when it feels like playing.

Mercury Trine (harmonizing with) Saturn
☿ △ ♄   *OR*
Mercury Sextile (co-operating with) Saturn
☿ ✶ ♄

Regardless of whatever else your mental qualities might be, you have a serious, efficient and practical mind. You are well able to organize both your thoughts and those of others. You also have planning ability. You are very unlikely to lose your mental grip, and others rely very much on such mental fortitude.

Mercury Conjunct (uniting with) Uranus

☿ ☌ ♅   *OR*

Mercury Square (challenging) Uranus

☿ □ ♅   *OR*

Mercury Opposition (confronting) Uranus

☿ ☍ ♅

Furthermore, your interests extend to the scientific or metaphysical. There is an unusual cast to your mind that is attracted to the more off-beat and radical avenues of thought. Alternatively, you might find yourself opposed to these realms of thinking and the people involved with them, as you stand by your more logical viewpoint. In truth, though, you are striving to see both sides – the intuitive but unprovable, and the rational – and present a balanced viewpoint as well.

Mercury Trine (harmonizing with) Uranus

☿ △ ♅   *OR*

Mercury Sextile (co-operating with) Uranus

☿ ✷ ♅

A significant quality of your mind is that it is naturally in tune with the times. You are able to grasp information quickly – or even obtain it out of thin air. Being so intuitive, you do well in areas of scientific or metaphysical disciplines, or anything that requires clear, objective and detached thinking.

Mercury Conjunct (uniting with) Neptune

☿ ☌ ♆   *OR*

Mercury Square (challenging) Neptune

☿ □ ♆   *OR*

Mercury Opposition (confronting) Neptune

☿ ☍ ♆

Your thoughts are fantasy-prone, and you cannot but help see what lies beyond the logical. But how you manage and express this highly sensitive perception of yours greatly depends upon not just your Mercury Profile, but your personality as a whole. If you deem it proper to stick with scientific facts, then you most probably scorn the mystically minded dreamers of this world. At the other extreme, you are a mystically minded dreamer who dismisses reason as a way of explaining everything. As a child you probably had a bold line in tall stories – and you are still inclined to bend the truth somewhat if you feel in a tight spot or if you are just bored with reality. If your tall stories were received in the right spirit by adults, then you now feel happy with a mind that can fruitfully follow the flight of your imagination. But when such mental sensitivity as you have is denied, you can be vague or convoluted to the point of not making yourself clear when speaking – even though you might think you are.

Mercury Trine (harmonizing with) Neptune
☿ △ ♆   OR
Mercury Sextile (co-operating with) Neptune
☿ ✶ ♆

Through all of this you should always be aware that you have a cultured and imaginative mind, which should not be wasted on purely mundane pursuits. You have a subtle or poetic perception of the world, and could be an exponent of the literary or visual arts – or at least have a keen appreciation of them. There is also the strong possibility of your being able to attune your mind to the thoughts of others. You have a very valuable mind.

Mercury Conjunct (uniting with) Pluto
☿ ☌ ♇   OR
Mercury Square (challenging) Pluto
☿ □ ♇   OR
Mercury Opposition (confronting) Pluto
☿ ☍ ♇

When it comes right down to it, yours is an extremely profound mentality. At the very least you have a knack for getting to the root of a matter. Taken further, you are able to reach a deep understanding of the actual workings of the Nature of Life itself. But it is just because of this profundity of your thinking that all mind games and mental conceit have to go. If not, you are doomed to a life of intellectual conflict and mental paranoia. Furthermore, it is vitally important that you fill your profound mind with equally profound material, or else you would become like a big gun that only shoots peas.

Mercury Trine (harmonizing with) Pluto
☿ △ ♇   OR
Mercury Sextile (co-operating with) Pluto
☿ ✶ ♇

When it comes right down to it, yours is an extremely profound mentality. At the very least you have a knack for getting to the root of a matter. Taken further, you are able to reach a deep understanding of the actual workings of the Nature of Life itself. You have a powerful mind that is not distorted by power games and mental conceit.

Mercury Unaspected by any other planet
☿ ⦰

But you have difficulty focusing your mind on your true interests. Also, communication can be impeded in some way. If not actually lacking in intellectual ability, you may have a speech problem, such as talking too loudly or too quietly, mumbling or stuttering. Perhaps you are not sure enough of your knowledge and mental capabilities – or you are in need of emotional conviction, or have an emotional block to learning. Essentially, your head is not connecting with your heart – and the accomplishing of this should be regarded as a priority, for your heart contains much that is worth communicating. Studying the Sign and House position of your Mercury will help you to organize your mind and use it better.

At the other extreme of interpreting all of this, you could be said to have a very free mind, in that you are not restrained by the logical procedures, which can so easily slow others down (and the world at large – witness bureaucracy!). You are therefore able to perceive the whole meaning of a given situation, rather than be deceived and preoccupied with just one or two facets of it. However, the issue still arises of whether or not you are able to communicate your overall perception of things. Also, as a reaction to the intellectual self-doubt that this can create, you can be anti-intellectual and attempt to justify your fear of learning by scorning it. For the same reason, such freedom of thinking and perception can be a big problem where employment is concerned. If you lack specialization – which, for good or ill, is a job market convention nowadays – you could get stuck at the bottom of the labour ladder. Yours is a mind that needs something concrete to challenge it and prove its worth.

Mercury Conjunct (uniting with) Ascendant and in the First House
☿ ♂ AS

The indications described below under Mercury in the First House are strongly emphasized and I suggest that you note them as such, and how they relate to the whole of your Mercury Profile.

Mercury Conjunct (uniting with) Ascendant and in the Twelfth House
☿ ♂ AS

Your mental strengths and weaknesses are very much there for all to see. If you can muster the courage to say exactly what you feel inside, others will, in time, come to regard you as a source of psychological wisdom.

Mercury Square (challenging) Ascendant
☿ □ AS

All in all, negative qualities about the way you think, or with regard to your mental attitude, get in the way of your communicating clearly or gracefully. Consequently, personal and professional relationships suffer. Find out what it is that you disagree with in yourself, then other significant people will begin to understand you and co-operate with you.

Mercury Opposition (confronting) Ascendant and in the Sixth House
☿ ☍ AS

When all is said and done, you are having to make a supreme effort to communicate your thoughts and feelings to others. You may expect them to make the running, but then you object to things being entirely on their terms.

Mercury Opposition (confronting) Ascendant and in the Seventh House
☿ ☍ AS

The indications described below under Mercury in the Seventh House are strongly emphasized and I suggest that you note them as such, and how they relate to the whole of your Mercury Profile.

Mercury Trine (harmonizing with) Ascendant
☿ △ AS

You have little trouble in perceiving clearly what is happening around you, and in conveying your interpretation of it to anyone that you come into contact with. In fact, you are an excellent and stimulating communicator.

Mercury Sextile (co-operating with) Ascendant
☿ ✶ AS

You have little trouble in perceiving clearly what is happening around you, and in conveying your interpretation of it to anyone that you come into contact with. In fact, you are an excellent and stimulating communicator.

Mercury Conjunct (uniting with) MidHeaven and in the Ninth House
☿ ☌ MC

Your mental strengths and weaknesses are very much in the public eye. On the one hand, this can make for success in a career that involves communication, word-power and perceptual abilities. Or else you can feel rather inadequate mentally and have to make up for this by bluffing or being attractively dizzy.

Mercury Conjunct (uniting with) MidHeaven and in the Tenth House
☿ ☌ MC

The indications described below under Mercury in the Tenth House are strongly emphasized and I suggest that you note them as such, and how they relate to the whole of your Mercury Profile.

Mercury Square (challenging) MidHeaven
☿ ☐ MC

You have to use your mental powers to the full in order to establish or maintain your career position. Equally, your negative Mercury traits can get in the way of your progress in life. Your mind tends to work in a way that is different to, or in conflict with, your parents and cultural background.

Mercury Opposition (confronting) MidHeaven and in the Third House
☿ ☍ MC

Your mental strengths and weaknesses depend very much upon your early home life and upon the intellectual attention your father paid you. More likely than not, you probably grew up in an educated atmosphere, and you particularly like to dig around for buried information.

Mercury Opposition (confronting) MidHeaven and in the Fourth House
☿ ☍ MC

The indications described below under Mercury in the Fourth House are strongly emphasized and I suggest that you note them as such, and how they relate to the whole of your Mercury Profile.

Mercury Trine (harmonizing with) MidHeaven
☿ △ MC

These, your perceptive and mental capabilities, are successfully employed in your career. By the same token they will describe the actual nature of your profession. Intentionally or otherwise, your mother has or had much to do with your forming a healthy and objective mind.

Mercury Sextile (co-operating with) MidHeaven
☿ ✶ MC

These, your perceptive and mental capabilities, are successfully employed in your career. By the same token they will describe the actual nature of your profession. Intentionally or otherwise, your mother has or had much to do with your forming a healthy and objective mind.

MERCURY HOUSES

Mercury in the First House
☿ 1st

This way of thinking and perceiving is quite obvious upon meeting you. You are known for what you say and how you say it. Your mental attitude is highly important because when you put out a negative idea or remark it will quickly make others avoid you. Conversely, when your mind is in a curious and active mode, you attract interest and stimulation, and people desire to make and maintain contact with you. Your physical appearance itself is usually slim or wiry, mobile or fidgety, and your hands and face are very expressive. Versatility can be your identifying feature – along with your wit and sharp perception. But it is crucial that you do not identify too much with these mental characteristics. Funny and clever as they are, there is far more to you than just your wits and perception. But as they are so upfront, that is all others might choose to see.

Mercury in the Second House
☿ 2nd

These mental qualities of yours are a major material asset, or a major liability. So it is important to get the best out of them and eliminate their weaknesses. The soundness of your mind greatly determines your income, and the nature of your mind has much to do with what you do to earn that income. You may even work at something to do with finances. You prefer to concern yourself with practical issues – or you are forced to by circumstances. You are often fascinated by the small details of the physical world. It is as if by making such a contact you feel in touch with everything.

Mercury in the Third House
☿ 3rd

Whatever kind of intellect you have, you are naturally able to gather and disseminate information, improving your word-power as you do so. You relish making contact with others, and establishing common areas of interest. By the same token you can also get bored easily if the only live wire around seems to be you. Intellectual parity – or the lack of it – with brothers and sisters or fellow students can profoundly affect your mental self-esteem. However, your mental contribution to the world around you should never be underestimated, because whatever else might be said, you certainly influence the minds of others.

Mercury in the Fourth House
☿ 4th

These mental qualities of yours were strongly influenced by your early home life and racial, cultural or national background. So your mind can be somewhat buried in your roots as it treads well established, but possibly habit-ridden paths. As a reaction to this, you might rebel against them, moving about from place to place in a need to find your own mind, or attracting a domestic or family set-up where you are continually having to assert your individual attitude. You like to surround yourself with books and bits and pieces of interest for they give you a sense of security. Another interest in roots, and the security which they provide, may well involve subjects like geology, archaeology, ecology, genealogy, etc. But at the bottom of all this is your father, who was probably an intellectual type, and not easy to get to know emotionally. This would have fed your mind but have frustrated your feelings. In other words, what you are really digging for is your father's soul, for it is the route to your own.

Mercury in the Fifth House
☿ 5th

This mind of yours loves playing. You enjoy mental games, and fun and romance usually need some mental pursuit or content to make them go with a swing. You also have a need to prove yourself and impress others with your wit and intellectual capabilities. This is okay as long as it does not get in the way of or become a substitute for emotional expression. You should avoid mental conceit or approaching emotional involvements too analytically for it could become boring. Nevertheless, you do have a talent for teaching and humour. Your original way of communicating has a memorable effect upon the listener, especially children. Generally, your writing or manual skills make for fulfilling hobbies or successful occupations. Your mind is a major creative tool.

Mercury in the Sixth House
☿ 6th

You utilize these mental capabilities very well and with focus and economy. You have a knack for perceiving what is wrong with a person or situation, and are able to devise or suggest methods to improve matters. Health is one area in particular where your mental powers can be successfully brought to bear. But it is also possible that you are prone to overwork and nervous tension yourself. A definite health regimen and work routine would help to remedy these inclinations. Essentially you are a good worker, and appreciate the true value of work.

Mercury in the Seventh House
☿ 7th

You like to have a partner who thinks and perceives things in this way too and is generally stimulating intellectually. You also prefer to conduct your relationships in a very reasonable way. This is fine up to the point where the emotional side of things can't get a look in. You will then find yourself with an extremely emotional mate on your hands, as they demand that you respond with more than just your head. Alternatively, if you are an emotional type yourself, or lack mental confidence for some reason, then you will get someone else to do your thinking for you. This is fine as long as you are both happy with this arrangement, but there will probably come a time when you will have to sort out your own mental or learning problems. Potentially, your mind is very capable of tuning into the facts and figures about others, so public relations or some kind of demographic or agency work would be well starred.

Mercury in the Eighth House
☿ 8th

You utilize these mental capabilities in rooting out hidden information and the deep causes that are responsible for what appears on the surface. You are therefore able to contact more easily than others the significance of such mysteries as sex and death; what lies beyond the grave can fascinate you. There may well be some reason for this in your personal history, such as the disturbing death of a friend or relative, or early sexual curiosity causing you to bite off more than you could chew. Secret information still seems to come your way, and hopefully you treat such confidential material with the respect that it demands – otherwise you could get your fingers burnt. On a material level, you could show an interest in contracts, financial deals, and others' resources.

Mercury in the Ninth House
☿ 9th

Primarily, you use these mental capabilities to evolve a philosophy of life (through travel, study, conversation, etc.) that keeps you free of stale ideas and biased attitudes that slow so many others down almost to a standstill. You aim to maintain a free and open mind. On the negative side, though, you can be inclined to roll around the world and accumulate not much more than passport stamps and a well-travelled, laid-back demeanour. This, or some other form of being a rolling stone, could be a way you have of not letting life get to you. But it can reach a point where very little gets to you at all – and boredom ensues. Your naturally philosophical bent really does have to continue looking for a meaning to life – an endless journey.

Mercury in the Tenth House
☿ 10th

These mental capabilities of yours will actually find a professional outlet in the form of being a writer, journalist, broadcaster, spokesperson, or anything that has to do with communication or manual or mental dexterity: transport, trading, accounting, secretarial, printing, to name a few. You strongly seek recognition for your mental powers. Using and regarding the intellect as a superior factor in life has its positive and negative sides. For example, you can be very happy in your work because you have 'learned the ropes'; but the more emotional areas of life can give trouble as your intellectually dominated mind fails to grasp the significance of the feeling nature. Then again, your profession may even cater for this dilemma. How you think was particularly influenced by your mother's mental attitude.

Mercury in the Eleventh House
☿ 11th

You employ and improve this mentality of yours by gaining or giving out knowledge and mental stimulation through group involvements. You prefer a class/workshop situation to just book learning. And your opinions gain breadth and depth through sharing them. Because your mind flourishes in this way, you are kind of plugged in to the mind of the group itself. So you can become a natural spokesperson, and also be able to maintain a group's goals and principles. You may, however, attract fickle friends, or be one, through not knowing your own mind. To counter this, you should welcome the fact that you also attract friends with opposing views, which challenge your own, making them stronger.

Mercury in the Twelfth House
☿ 12th

During some period in your past, even before birth, you somehow gained the impression that these mental capabilities of yours were inadequate because you were overwhelmed by an emotional force of some kind. As a result of this – or rather what caused it – you have a mind that can pick up all sorts of intimations, vibrations and undercurrents. These can either haunt you and impair clear thinking, or be useful in determining a subtle way through difficulties, for yourself or those who need it. Establishing regular intervals of retreat – when you may restore your mental composure and safely open your mind to those unconscious powers of the imagination which you are especially privy to – is essential. You have a channelling mind and are therefore prone to 'voices in the head'. If such is the case you have to determine whether such are friendly or not.

CHAPTER SIX – YOUR VENUS PROFILE
ATTRACTION AND HARMONY

Venus symbolizes ATTRACTION – what you need and can give by way of LOVE and AFFECTION, BEAUTY and HAPPINESS. A positive Venus shows as the SOCIAL GRACES and CHARM. Negatively it represents INDULGENCE, SUPERFICIALITY and WANTON PLEASURE-SEEKING – all of which could include simply being ANTI-SOCIAL. Venus also represents your ABILITY TO RELATE, HARMONIZE and to express yourself through ART and a sense of AESTHETICS. Venus also has a great deal to do with FEMALE SEXUALITY and SENSUALITY generally. Venus symbolizes what you LIKE.

VENUS SIGNS

Venus in Aries
♀ ♈

You love in a childlike way, regarding relationships as being natural and uncomplicated – at least initially. You are giving, guileless and forthright – and somewhat naively expect others to be so too. You are upset when you find that they are not, but not usually heart-broken. You get back up again as quickly as you fell in love in the first place. Your freshness and impulsiveness is spontaneously attractive to others, and more or less cuts through any caution they might have.

It also makes you very impatient to give, gain or receive love. So much so that you are inclined to mistake infatuation or lust for love, and it takes a while before you are able to spot the difference. Then again, it could be sheer desperation on your part that sets you up with a poor match. There is something impish and naughty about you that can cause others to do childlike things they wouldn't do normally. This has its good and bad sides in that you are able to introduce a refreshingly primitive glee into your social or romantic sphere. But you can lead others on and then be gone.

Venus in Taurus
♀ ♉

Yours is an earthy sense of love and harmony. You have a strong feel for – or actually embody – what is physically attractive. Such awareness of what satisfies the physical senses can make you successful in a number of areas: art – especially singing, or at least you have a pleasant-sounding speaking voice; cooking, and other means of providing comfort and enjoyment; consumerism – you may have a good market sense; healing – for your sense of touch can be highly evolved.

Not surprisingly, you need shows of physical affection as evidence of your worth and desirability. This can go to extremes in the form of passionate possessiveness – but this could be assuaged, by indulging in some sensuous or artistic pursuit that is more under your personal control. Rather than overdoing it with the creature comforts, you could simply commune with Nature, which will give you a feeling of satisfaction.

Venus in Gemini

You like to keep love at an adolescent level of expression. You like the flirting, chasing and love games, and do not like it when things get too heavy or committed. For you, love is in bud rather than full bloom, so if you want something to last, you have to give it a chance to develop, be more steadfast, and not abandon it to the winds of fate. For you love and beauty are things of the mind, and so you may well have some literary ability.

In real life, though, your predilection for keeping things light and airy can be a serious hazard to maintaining a mature relationship. And your natural flightiness would be better or well employed in some art form like dance or song. In essence, you are having a relationship with yourself. As long as this does not become too narcissistic and wrap you up in yourself, you do keep the love stakes fresh and interesting.

Venus in Cancer

For you, love is bound up inextricably with security; affection cannot exist without care. There has to be something traditional and familiar about your partner, a feeling of belonging, an involvement with and acceptance of their family and your own. The love that was or was not forthcoming from your mother greatly affects how much you show and need affection.

Being unsure of mother-love would incline you to cling blindly to a partner. Your sympathetic and tender style of loving should not be under-rated – go on strike if it is, and they will soon come running! On the other hand, beware of your tendency to behave in a sulky manner when reactions to past hurts are triggered by normal emotional confrontations, for this can hatch a game of cat and mouse which is the last thing that you need. You express love and beauty best in a homely, private way.

Venus in Leo

You are the archetypal romantic. On the face of it you are madly affectionate, filled with fiery passions, and inject masses of fun and imagination into your affairs of the heart. Consequently you can transport your paramour to previously undreamed of emotional heights. Inevitably though, this means that you have to understand that they're playing the role of king to your queen, or vice versa, as far as your love life is concerned.

In other words, the royal qualities of respect and nobility must be very alive in your breast if a relationship is to survive or live up to your fairytale expectations. Respect means that you must be mindful that both of you are entitled to equal amounts of freedom and commitment. Nobility means that both of you must behave in a manner that commands respect. But the salient factor is that first you must set this example in order that your mate be truly impressed by your great love – great because it is both generous of spirit, and respectful of the other's individuality.

Venus in Virgo
♀ ♍

You are a perfectionist and critical where love and art are concerned. At its most extreme, this can find you left on the shelf. More usually though, you demand – consciously or unconsciously – that your partner or other people in general subscribe to some closely defined code of behaviour and social conduct. But this is really hiding some impurity, some feeling of unlovability, that exists within you.

You are afraid of showing your earthy or dirty bits. What is really curious however is that you periodically go right over the top and are decidedly dissolute and even promiscuous by way of release. Essentially you are after accepting yourself, warts and all. Then you'll be able to love and be loved without interminably checking everything. A very positive part of your nature is that you can tune in very finely to another's beauty and love needs. This also shows itself as a fine design sense if you are artistically inclined.

Venus in Libra
♀ ♎

You are a social or artistic touchstone. You therefore have a natural sense of beauty and harmony, which you express in a social or artistic way. The inherent weakness of your aesthetic awareness is that you are very easily attracted to good-looking surface appearances – especially in a sexual, glamorous or romantic context. This is a bittersweet situation for you because your undeniable charm or artistry has no trouble attracting popularity, pleasure and even wealth, but you can become a slave to your vanity and appetites. Nonetheless, you are still a social or creative asset – and you certainly know what pleases.

Venus in Scorpio
♀ ♏

You love deeply and intensely. Perhaps a bit too much so, for you can find yourself consumed by desire – and then mistake this for love. You then wind up trying to satisfy your emotional hunger with sexual indulgence, which doesn't bring you love. Or else you get yourself into a tight relationship where each of you is held hostage by your fearful needs. Or you might attempt to step out of the intimacy stakes altogether, which takes some doing.

What you really have to do is return to first principles: you love deeply because at a deep level you want love to transform you. This presupposes that do not know what love is until it has transformed you and your idea of it. In this way – and in this way only – you can discover the profound commitment that you crave.

Venus in Sagittarius

You have a sense of love's bounty and inexhaustibility, which you aim to express. This means that you can warm and inspire another's heart, or merely squander your affections in a rather wanton fashion. So you need to discover and establish an agreed moral or religious basis to a relationship in order to find and maintain a harmonious one.

Having said this though, it is probably also necessary for you to sow some wild oats before trying to settle down. You are the type that can wander only too easily if you feel that the other side of the hill is greener. For you, love is about exploration, so seeking it can lead you far afield. Your generally positive attitude towards relating would be well expressed by your always thinking in terms of what you have gained rather than lost through love. You see love, and art too, as the great teacher.

Venus in Capricorn

You view love and art, and the values concerning them, very much in a traditional light. Unless something or someone is tried and true through the passage of time you are not likely to trust your sentiments, talents or possessions with them. This inflexible dependence that you have upon fidelity, constancy and work-well-done ostensibly makes for your being quite reliable as you give value for money or for time spent on you, or for money or attention paid to you.

But your insistence upon trustworthiness can become a blind to your own emotional shortcomings, that is, a distrust based on subjective fear rather than objective judgement. What can ensue from this is either you or your partner suddenly being very unreliable; or your being without anyone at all; or severe limitations materially as a result of not giving more of yourself to the world; or marrying or being married for money or status rather than love. Track down the cause of any deep distrust, and then you and others will be as reliable as you think you and they ought to be.

Venus in Aquarius

You are endeavouring to introduce a measure of detachment and freedom into your relationships and into your interaction with society generally. What this means primarily is that you require a lover to be a friend, for when such is the case, you are able to look at each other as human beings with individual ways of living rather than as being extensions of, and totally answerable to, each other. However, such a liberal attitude does require an individual moral code that you live by – as distinct from having no code at all.

Without this code – which is really a sense of commitment to your own principles that overrides emotional game-playing – relationships can float way on the breeze as free and easiness turns out to be case of hedging your bets. In other words, not being committed to anything. If you are artistically inclined, you are drawn to the avant-garde.

Venus in Pisces
♀ ♓

Your sense of love and beauty are never without sensitivity, imagination and compassion. This does make you 'all heart', and therefore you are vulnerable and very prone to being taken advantage of emotionally. So you have to learn to be more discriminating in your choice of partner and in how much of yourself you give away. Anyhow, this total giving of yourself is not all it seems, for as much as you want to see everything in your partner, you want them to see everything in you.

This is what I call the 'Gallon in a Pint-pot' syndrome. Your partner can be drowned by love and affection, feel unable to live up to it, and possibly go off with someone else who they feel is not so demanding, or treat you badly for not recognizing their darker side. Alternatively, such disillusionment may cause you to abandon your mate yourself, or be promiscuous in your desire to love the world. To rectify all this, and allot the right amount of your fulsome love nature to a partner, I advise you to invest most of it in some form of artistic expression or care-work, like nursing. In any event, the use of discrimination is the key to expressing your love of all things.

VENUS ASPECTS

NOTE that Sextile (co-operating with) and Opposition (confronting) Aspects are usually described similarly to Trine (harmonizing with) and Square (challenging) Aspects respectively, or they are occasionally described similarly to the Conjunction (uniting with). However, when this is the case, it should be borne in mind that a Sextile Aspect may require conscious awareness and effort to realize the assets and potential so described – and that the Opposition Aspect may indeed be experienced exactly as described, but in reality such can initially be felt or seen to come from someone or something else because you have projected or externalized such traits in order to make yourself aware of them.

Venus Conjunct (uniting with) Sun
♀ ☌ ☉

Your love nature is very strong. You can heal or change someone's life for the better with it. You could also flood them with your own idea of what love is – with both your positive and negative qualities coming back at you with interest! This means to say that you yourself set up the love stakes, the conditions and expectations in a relationship. So a great deal of responsibility lies with you; your awareness of your emotional needs and urges can make or break a love match. Art, as well as love, is central to your existence.

Venus Conjunct (uniting with) Moon
♀ ☌ ☽

You have an instinctive ability to satisfy these needs and senses. You have an attractive personality – at least, on one level of your being. You are also very accommodating of others, and expect to be equally welcomed yourself. It is vitally important that you place a real and positive value upon this attractively abiding nature of yours, otherwise others can take it for granted.

Venus Square (challenging) Moon
♀ □ ☽   **OR**
Venus Opposition (confronting) Moon
♀ ☌ ☽

These love needs, and the ability to appreciate yourself and someone close to you clearly, are confused by the strong need for security which was or was not satisfied by your mother. In other words, you expect a lover to give what your mother did or did not, or you assume that that is what they want you to give them – but they don't. Your weakness is that you can accommodate others, or be accommodated by them too easily, and so love and need get confused all too soon.

Venus Trine (harmonizing with) Moon
♀ △ ☽   **OR**
Venus Sextile (co-operating with) Moon
♀ ✶ ☽

You have an instinctive ability to satisfy these needs and senses. You have an attractive personality – at least, on one level of your being. You are also accommodating of others, and expect to be equally welcomed yourself.

Venus Conjunct (uniting with) Mercury
♀ ☌ ☿   **OR**
Venus Sextile (co-operating with) Mercury
♀ ✶ ☿

And all of your sense of love and beauty is expressed well verbally. What you say and what you write is naturally lyrical. The quality of your voice is also pleasant. Love and beauty constantly occupy your mind; equally the lack of them perturbs your thinking. Truly, you grace your everyday environment.

Venus Conjunct (uniting with) Mars
♀ ☌ ♂

And you are not about to just sit back and wait for all this to happen. You have a strong desire to make it happen. Furthermore, when you make a move towards someone – be it in a social, business or romantic situation – you expect there to be some definite response. Likewise, you readily respond to others' advances towards you. So you are pretty lively in a sensuous way. You can treat others as sexual objects or as social or business stepping-stones, or be on the receiving end of the same thing. But you certainly keep the pot stirred and sweet.

Venus Square (challenging) Mars
♀ □ ♂   **OR**
Venus Opposition (confronting) Mars
♀ ☌ ♂

The trouble is that wherever you seek love you also find conflict. Your feelings of tenderness never seem to have anger very far away from them. What you have to do is first recognize that love and desire, soft feelings and hard ones, are all mixed up inside of you. Curiously, and owing to our society's current confusion over these matters, this conflict within you makes you both exciting and difficult. By the same token, it falls to you to make a greater than average attempt to show your feelings equally of care and desire, of love and sex. You may treat others as sex-objects, or be treated that way yourself.

Venus Trine (harmonizing with) Mars
♀ △ ♂   *OR*
Venus Sextile (co-operating with) Mars
♀ ✶ ♂

Whatever else you may have, you certainly possess warmth and charm. Others find it easy to like you and relax in your presence, even if you are misbehaving! You demonstrate ease in relating sexually; even in an ordinary social sense there is something undeniably embraceable about you.

Venus Conjunct (uniting with) Jupiter
♀ ☌ ♃   *OR*
Venus Trine (harmonizing with) Jupiter
♀ △ ♃   *OR*
Venus Sextile (co-operating with) Jupiter
♀ ✶ ♃

There should be plenty of opportunity to satisfy these appetites and predilections of yours. This is because you have a naturally generous disposition, which life and the world are only too happy to reward. You have a sense of largesse that can attract success and enjoyment in any number of fields – both socially and professionally. Essentially, what you have is a sense of bounty and joy. This can incline you towards over-indulging in the pleasures of life, but all in all, people find you a pleasure to have in their midst.

Venus Square (challenging) Jupiter
♀ □ ♃   *OR*
Venus Opposition (confronting) Jupiter
♀ ☍ ♃

You can take everything that I have said here about your love nature and multiply it by five! You expect more and give more than most other people. What you need to get wise to, is what is motivating you in this. If you're over-indulging yourself or others because of some neurosis – like feeling unattractive or that someone is your whole life – then you are setting yourself up for a fall. But once you gain a more philosophical understanding of the vagaries of loving and relating, you will learn to keep something back in the knowledge that only you, or the god or law in which you believe, is worth that much attention.

Venus Conjunct (uniting with) Saturn

♀ ☌ ♄   OR

Venus Square (challenging) Saturn

♀ □ ♄   OR

Venus Opposition (confronting) Saturn

♀ ☍ ♄

But your pleasures are not without their price, and your social or artistic involvements are certainly not without their trials. It is as if the love or the value of anyone or anything that you concern yourself with has to be thoroughly tested. You may well grow up to regard yourself as a bit of a loser in this respect and have a poor sense of self-worth and a bank balance to match. But you must always remind yourself of your sincerity and thoughtfulness, and that what you are learning is simply how to love, in the manner described here.

Venus Trine (harmonizing with) Saturn

♀ △ ♄   OR

Venus Sextile (co-operating with) Saturn

♀ ⚹ ♄

It is through a process of gradual development that you learn to get the best, and weed out the worst, from your Venus Profile. This is because, whatever else might be said about you, you do have an in-built awareness of love and fair play, which in time cannot but help come up with the goods. The goods in this case being a rewarding and stable love life or a satisfying means of artistic expression.

Venus Conjunct (uniting with) Uranus

♀ ☌ ♅   OR

Venus Square (challenging) Uranus

♀ □ ♅   OR

Venus Opposition (confronting) Uranus

♀ ☍ ♅

All these social or moral values of yours are going through great changes. Perhaps you are even rebelling against them. It would appear that you have an unstable attitude in this respect as you jump from one relationship to another. You are divorce prone. What lies behind your excitement seeking and unpredictability is your restless quest for a set of values for the future, and a social scene and love life to match. Artistically, you are drawn to the avant garde.

Venus Trine (harmonizing with) Uranus

♀ △ ♅   OR

Venus Sextile (co-operating with) Uranus

♀ ⚹ ♅

Most of these qualities of yours do have a relaxed feel about them, and can, if you let them, attract free social and emotional interaction. Such lively sparkle should always make you desirable company. The essence of this trait of your personality is one of humans loving one another for being the individual humans that they are – so nothing should be allowed to get in the way of this!

Venus Conjunct (uniting with) Neptune
♀ ☌ ♆   *OR*

Venus Square (challenging) Neptune
♀ □ ♆   *OR*

Venus Opposition (confronting) Neptune
♀ ☍ ♆

When all is said and done your social skills, and your sense of love and art, are having to evolve to a higher level. This does mean that you are very idealistic in your love life or where your creations are concerned. Seeking the exquisite and exotic can mean many a disillusionment as loved ones fall from grace, and show themselves to be the mere mortals that they are. Be that as it may, your refined senses serve as an inspiration to others. That you practise, or possibly excel in, some form of artistic or spiritual expression is very likely – or very important, because such is a more suitable means of giving form to your vision of a better world than being merely a hopeless romantic. In any event love the one you are with – with all your heart and soul.

Venus Trine (harmonizing with) Neptune
♀ △ ♆   *OR*

Venus Sextile (co-operating with) Neptune
♀ ✶ ♆

As you see and experience it, love can never be without sensitivity and imagination. And so you are romantic, but without being blinded by illusions for too long. You are also talented in one art form or another, either in a professional capacity or just as a pastime. In either case, such creativity enhances your love life, and generally brings a ray of beauty into your social sphere.

Venus Conjunct (uniting with) Pluto
♀ ☌ ♇   *OR*

Venus Square (challenging) Pluto
♀ □ ♇   *OR*

Venus Opposition (confronting) Pluto
♀ ☍ ♇

At a very deep level your whole idea of what love is and is not, is having to go through a major process of transformation. Your love nature, as described here, has taken on the task of bringing into the light the most fearsome, ugly and taboo-ridden aspects of human nature – in yourself and others. This is challenging indeed, and it is therefore not surprising that your love life is cratered with crises of no mean magnitude. Can you still love in the face of death; be it the death of a cherished ideal, a social norm, or of love or a loved one?

Venus Trine (harmonizing with) Pluto
♀ △ ♇   **OR**

Venus Sextile (co-operating with) Pluto
♀ ✶ ♇

Underlying all of this you have a deep sense of what love is truly all about. You have an enormous capacity to love and be loved. You inject a positive and regenerative energy into your friendships and intimate relationships. Others are the better for having been in touch with your powerful caring – although it might take a while before this sinks in past their superficial concepts of what love means.

Venus Unaspected by any other planet
♀ ⊘

You very much need a partner so that you can feel related and close. The qualities of your Venus Profile can then be experienced, which means that you then feel an integrated member of society. In the process however, you can exhibit a more or less take-it-or-leave-it attitude when it comes to love ties and social commitments. This is because you are predisposed to expect a certain amount of freedom with regard to your social involvements – as if there were no rules or constraints involved.

This kind of floating attitude can either be expressed by you as waywardness or irresponsibility where relationships are concerned or, by way of compensation, you will be attracted to partnerships where limitations and duties are sharply defined. The former expression is more likely if there are indications of restlessness or evasiveness elsewhere in your personality; the latter will be more the case if your personality has a conservative bent or where the safer options are pursued in personal relationships.

With either case, however, at some stage you are liable to feel socially confused, outcast or disinherited as a result of the difficulty described here in finding or knowing your social or romantic place.

Venus Conjunct (uniting with) Ascendant and in the First House
♀ ♂ AS

Your qualities described below under Venus in the First House, and your Venus Profile as a whole, are greatly emphasized in your personality, and figure strongly in your life.

Venus Conjunct (uniting with) Ascendant and in the Twelfth House
♀ ♂ AS

These qualities of love and beauty also express themselves in your actual physical presence, appearance or manner of expression. You are either lovely to look at or pleasant to be with – or both. If you are the former, your looks could take you far in one respect, but hold you back in another, simply because you haven't had to do anything other than just be there. This can be very much the case if you are a female who is past her prime. Essentially you have the great asset of being attractive – which is just that, i.e. others are drawn to you. If you have some inner quality to deliver too, then you have the best of both worlds. Your art is the way you are.

Venus Square (challenging) Ascendant
♀ □ AS

You have to use and evolve your charms and social senses in order to be appreciated. However, in doing this you run the danger of sacrificing your values for the sake of popularity. Conversely, you maintain your values but few people like or understand you. Answer: meet others halfway and cultivate etiquette.

Venus Opposition (confronting) Ascendant and in the Sixth House
♀ ☍ AS

You are inclined to experience these values and senses, or the need for them, as belonging to someone else – like your partner or people in general. But really they are a part of you, which you should own. If you do not, you will be inclined to suffer the negative aspects only. By the same token, you tend to look for your own worth and beauty in someone else, with the result that they at first try to live up to your expectations, and then fail miserably.

The fact of the matter is that you are highly pleasing to other people because you somehow embody their idea of social appeal, no matter what you may physically look like. So rather than constantly seeking to have your own charm, poise, humour or whatever confirmed by the attentions of others, begin to appreciate that your pull is as natural as a magnet's. To prove this, just stop and look at what you attract.

Venus Opposition (confronting) Ascendant and in the Seventh House
♀ ☍ AS

Your qualities described below under Venus in the Seventh House, and your Venus Profile as a whole, are greatly emphasized in your personality, and figure strongly in your life.

Venus Trine (harmonizing with) Ascendant
♀ △ AS   **OR**
Venus Sextile (co-operating with) Ascendant
♀ ✶ AS

For those who have eyes to see, your attractiveness or sense of beauty and harmony is quite evident. This may just be in your physical looks and mannerisms. You have a definite avenue from whatever your Venus Profile consists of, to your external means of expressing it, but you do have to work upon improving it and keeping it clear. You also readily attract pleasant and creative people.

Venus Conjunct (uniting with) MidHeaven and in the Ninth House
♀ ☌ MC

These values and preferences are very important for they greatly determine your reputation and professional standing. Your career itself should involve art, beauty or social skills of some kind. Your personal appeal can have a lot to do with the success or style of your career. Your mother could have a certain amount to do with how attractive you feel towards the world generally.

For example, if she was jealous of your talents or looks she might downgrade your worth and self-esteem; alternatively, her own sense of what appeals could help further your career. A key to finding your professional niche is, that you should simply or even sensuously enjoy what you do for a living. In other words, the degree to which you are in touch with your own pleasure principle has everything to do with your amounting to something in the world.

Venus Conjunct (uniting with) MidHeaven and in the Tenth House
♀ ☌ MC

Your qualities described below under Venus in the Tenth House are strongly emphasized, and if in case you didn't know it, you have a gift to give.

Venus Square (challenging) MidHeaven
♀ □ MC

Your sense of beauty and pleasure has to somehow find a place in your home and working life. Otherwise you will find these areas of life too dull to further to any worthwhile degree. If you don't feel equipped to do this, seek advice.

Venus Opposition (confronting) MidHeaven and in the Third House
♀ ☍ MC

Much of what has been described here concerning your Venus Profile starts off as somewhat buried. In other words your beauty is truly an inner beauty. This means firstly that your attractive qualities are more noticeable in your home atmosphere and private life. Secondly, you have to dig out the jewel of your worth that is submerged beneath your inhibitions and bad memories.

Venus Opposition (confronting) MidHeaven and in the Fourth House
♀ ☍ MC

Your qualities described below under Venus in the Fourth House are strongly emphasized, and I suggest that you take care to absorb their meaning.

Venus Trine (harmonizing with) MidHeaven
♀ △ MC   **OR**
Venus Sextile (co-operating with) MidHeaven
♀ ⚹ MC

You employ the attributes of your Venus Profile as described here in a professional capacity – or if you don't, you certainly should. Your strengths and weaknesses in this respect either advance or hold you back in your career. In any event, art, grace, beauty or a sense of harmony is central to your profession.

Venus Houses

Venus in the First House
♀ 1st

These qualities of love and beauty express themselves primarily in your actual physical presence, appearance or manner of expression. You are either lovely to look at or pleasant to be with – or both. If you are the former, your looks could take you far in one respect, but hold you back in another, simply because you haven't had to do anything other than just be there.

This can be very much the case if you are a female who is past her prime. Essentially you have the great asset of being attractive – which is just that, i.e. others are drawn to you. If you have some inner quality to offer as well, then you have the best of both worlds. Your art is the way you are.

Venus in the Second House
♀ 2nd

You like this sense of love and beauty to take physical shape – which means to say that they probably have a lot to do with how you earn your living. It also means that you are likely to attract and keep things of beauty and worth. And you enjoy this – which is the secret behind keeping this flow going.

Your talents and abilities are most likely to involve art, fashion, social skills, etc. You certainly do have moneymaking potential – you are like a magnet to it. However, the value that you place upon it is crucial for it can make the difference between being loved for what you are and loved for what you have.

Venus in the Third House
♀ 3rd

These values or senses find their expression most easily in all areas of communication, be it in the written or spoken word, or in how you conduct yourself in day-to-day interactions with neighbours, shop-people, siblings, etc. Neither do you like to leave any one day in a negative state of mind (as the result of an argument for example), for you know only too well that it would cast a shadow over the next.

You have a talent for literature, and a naturally lyrical sense. Because of this beauty of mind, other people find it easy to relax or open up in your presence, so this also favours any kind of social or counselling work.

Venus in the Fourth House
♀ 4th

These senses most readily find expression in your private or home life. So it is more than likely that your interior decor is tasteful, and your flair for this might be employed on a professional level. Romance too is more happily pursued in the home or family environment, where there is more likely to be a warm atmosphere and no unwelcome intrusions. Your father and background are the wellspring of your sense of grace and charm, and in times of stress you retreat to regenerate in your nest of pleasingly familiar surroundings.

Venus in the Fifth House
♀ 5th

Your feelings of love and beauty have no trouble finding expression for you have a natural sense that they should be expressed. So you possess the usual graces of a romantically and artistically inclined soul: affectionate, lively, entertaining, attractive to the opposite sex, etc. You also like to seek out such qualities in life and others, so galleries, theatres, parties, etc. exercise a magnetic pull.

You experience all the highs and lows of love and art, for this is essentially what gives you such a vibrant sense of them. You should never let anything get in the way of expressing yourself creatively for your natural style is very real. If you have children, it shows in them too.

Venus in the Sixth House
♀ 6th

These love feelings of yours are going through a process of purification. So whatever is false or unjust or lustful about your social or romantic intentions is having to be eliminated in order that a healthy relationship might happen. In fact, 'healthy relationship' sums up the only kind of relationship that you could really enjoy consistently.

Where there is a lack of purity in your loving you will experience loss, or illness – particularly to the throat, hips, kidneys or reproductive organs. You really have to work at love. Love and work also come together in that your work itself can be to do with harmony and beauty, or simply that you lend an air of grace and charm to your work place.

Venus in the Seventh House
♀ 7th

You are inclined to experience these values and senses, or the need for them, as belonging to someone else – like your partner or people in general. But really they are a part of you, which you should own. If you do not, you will be inclined to suffer the negative aspects only. By the same token, you tend to look for your own worth and beauty in someone else, with the result that they at first try to live up to your expectations, and then fail miserably.

The fact of the matter is that you are highly pleasing to other people because you somehow embody their idea of social appeal, no matter what you may physically look like. So rather than constantly seeking to have your own charm, poise, humour or whatever confirmed by the attentions of others, begin to appreciate that your pull is as natural as a magnet's. To prove this, just stop and look at what you attract.

Venus in the Eighth House
♀ 8th

These love needs and feelings of yours, whatever their nature, are drawn into deep and involved relationships that are compelling and absorbing, but hard to get out of. This urge shows itself as something decidedly alluring about your personality, especially if you are female. As far as you're concerned, love needs to go beyond the shallow and commonplace, so emotional crises should be expected and taken in your stride as unconscious desires pull you closer to that core of intimacy.

If you should attempt to satisfy these deeper sexual or soulful needs in a superficial fashion, like mere physical sex, you'd simply be deeply disappointed. And in order to avoid deep bonds manifesting themselves as difficult divorce suits, binding contracts over property and access rights, etc. you would have to reach and maintain a deep set of moral values.

Venus in the Ninth House
♀ 9th

These love feelings of yours find a clearer focus in your developing a philosophy of love, through your covering mental or physical ground. And so the love you seek is likely to be experienced upon a journey or with a person in or from a foreign land. Places of higher learning are also conducive to your finding love, as well as pleasure and rewards.

As well as love, artistic expression has to have some kind of religious meaning to it. Both love and art must teach you something, and allow you to teach others. For you, the whole issue of morality carries great weight where love and relating is concerned – for good or ill. Love for you is generosity of feeling and greatness of understanding.

Venus in the Tenth House
♀ 10th

These values and preferences are very important for they greatly determine your reputation and professional standing. Your career itself should involve art, beauty or social skills of some kind. Your personal appeal can have a lot to do with the success or style of your career. Your mother could have a certain amount to do with how attractive you feel towards the world generally. For example, if she was jealous of your talents or looks she might downgrade your worth and self-esteem; alternatively, her own sense of what appeals could help further your career.

A key to finding your professional niche is that you should simply or even sensuously enjoy what you do for a living. In other words, the degree to which you are in touch with your own pleasure principle has everything to do with your amounting to something in the world.

Venus in the Eleventh House
♀ 11th

You want to experience these senses and bring this style of loving into an open, friendly, possibly somewhat detached and idealistic sphere of social activity. Your Venus-Sign qualities may or may not lend themselves well to this. You very much want your partner to be on good terms with your friends and associates, and to share your social aspirations.

Conflicting aims or social values can spell disruption or death to a relationship. Knowing a lover initially as a friend is a strong prerequisite to having a harmonious relationship. And the actual meeting of your mate is more likely to occur at a club or some group gathering. Your social sense is quite evolved or future-oriented, but in this respect you are inclined to forget that one person's meat is another one's poison.

Venus in the Twelfth House
♀ 12th

Ultimately, these qualities and senses are discovered, and your needs for love and beauty are satisfied, through some form of confinement or withdrawal. This is because these aspects of your being are highly complex, subtle and quite soulful. As such they need peace and quiet to be developed – rather like exotic blooms in a hothouse. Furthermore, when you have contacted your inner beauty and love of yourself in this way – which very possibly should involve some kind of artistic pursuit – an external relationship becomes more viable and rewarding.

Whether you find yourself in this retreat from the 'normal' world voluntarily or otherwise, you need to recognize that being there is in aid of you contacting that indefinable, and very sensitive, quality that lies deep within. Merely escaping from the world is liable to result in feeling lonely, cut-off, and being regarded as a bit peculiar. Alternatively, this attraction to keeping your sensitive self hidden away may become externalized by falling for someone who is unavailable in some way. Consequently, such a relationship also has to take place in secret or in stolen moments.

CHAPTER SEVEN – YOUR MARS PROFILE
SELF-ASSERTION AND SEXUAL DRIVE

Mars is all about GETTING what you DESIRE. This takes DRIVE, including SEXUAL DRIVE, INITIATIVE and primarily COURAGE. But basically Mars symbolizes RAW ENERGY, and as such needs direction, discipline and conviction, as well as consideration. Without direction or discipline Mars can give rise to VIOLENCE, ANGER, ABUSE and SELFISHNESS. Without conviction or contacting one's anger there is COWARDICE and possibly being a victim of AGGRESSION for Mars is like a WEAPON or TOOL that if not picked up and used can be GRABBED and used against you. Without consideration there is IMPATIENCE and STRIFE. You need Mars to WIN, with its greatest prize being INDEPENDENCE. And in order to win anything or anyone you have to be prepared to RISK losing or getting hurt by being in the FIRING LINE.

MARS SIGNS

Mars in Aries
♂ ♈

You assert yourself quite naturally because you have an innately uninhibited supply of raw energy. The vital issue is that you have something worthwhile to do with such energy, which ultimately means having a direction in life. Notwithstanding any more introverted or introspective traits you might have, you do not seem to allow yourself to be compromised by the complications and considerations that dog the footsteps of most people. And so you plough ahead with gusto and unfettered determination.

Courage and initiative are firmly on your list of virtues, but love and patience and an awareness of more subtle points and undercurrents are not. These need to be learned if you wish stop to battering your head against the brick wall of your blind desire to get what you think you want. As a rule, you have an abundance of sexual stamina too, and if you are female you may well be attracted to macho, energetic, go-getting or even violent type males.

Mars in Taurus
♂ ♉

You assert yourself best in a physical or material way. This means that you are happy pursuing or involving yourself with something that is tangible, and not just a concept.

Mars Conjunct (uniting with) Pluto
♂ ♂ ♇   *OR*

Mars Square (challenging) Pluto
♂ □ ♇   *OR*

Mars Opposition (confronting) Pluto
♂ ♂ ♇

Whether you like it or not, underlying all your sense of self-assertion, there lies something very powerful – like a coiled serpent. It very much depends upon the make-up of your personality as a whole as to how you express this sense of power. At one extreme you could be (more than) a bit on the dubious side and use such forcefulness to get what you want by fair means or foul. At the other extreme, the force within you might even intimidate you, or have attracted abuse of some kind.

For this reason, you keep it under wraps – and you may do this quite unconsciously. But ultimately, such power as is in your possession needs to be tamed and put to some constructive use, or it could back up on you in a destructive way. In the process you may need to forgive yourself or someone else because you have misused it yourself, or another has used it against you. A healthy sexual relationship or intense physical activity, or something like drumming, will do much to absorb this energy, an energy that is basically of the healing variety.

Mars Trine (harmonizing with) Pluto
♂ △ ♇   *OR*

Mars Sextile (co-operating with) Pluto
♂ ✶ ♇

You become increasingly aware that your Mars energies come to you from deep sources. And the deeper you go, the more these energies are forthcoming. You can benefit yourself, and possibly others too, from the practice of physical cultures like martial arts or Hatha yoga or spiritual/sexual disciplines.

Mars Unaspected by any other planet
♂ ⊘

Basically and at first you are not too sure of what you want in life, or of how to go about getting what you want. But all this very much depends on whether you are male or female, and the rest of your Mars Profile.

If you are a male, you are quite likely to over-compensate for a fear that you are somehow lacking in this respect by attempting to be 'extra' masculine. This could take the form of picking fights, body-building, macho or dangerous sports, 'scoring' with females, sexual conquests, etc. The way in which you go about this, and the degree to which you do so, is further described by the Sign and House position of Mars.

If you are female, then you are likely to attract or be attracted to males of the above-described type – that is apparently typical 'men'. In any event, and in the face of this, you would have trouble with consistently asserting yourself.

On the other hand, if you are a male, you might at some stage, sooner or later, realize that it is entirely up to you to define what being 'masculine' means. In this case, you will express the more subtle qualities of Mars Profile. Likewise, if you are female, there can be an attraction to men who have thus begun to redefine, or are in the process of redefining, their maleness. Indeed, you too could want to redefine your assertiveness.

The actual challenge then is to express and integrate your desires and to deal with any anger caused by the frustration of those desires. This means that you are having to distinguish between what you want for yourself and what someone else wants or wanted you to be. This implies your having to find the courage to be true to yourself. Having the freedom to accomplish this is your subtle advantage for, deep down – even though you might not know it – you have your own unique way of asserting yourself.

Mars Conjunct (uniting with) Ascendant and in the First House
♂ ♂ AS

Your qualities of drive and assertion described below under Mars in the First House are strongly emphasized, and I suggest that you note them as such, and how this affects your life and personality as a whole.

Mars Conjunct (uniting with) Ascendant and in the Twelfth House
♂ ♂ AS

Whatever the nature of your drive and self-assertion overall, it is quite readily apparent to others. You could come across as quite forthright and audacious – even though you may not feel that way on the inside.

Mars Square (challenging) Ascendant
♂ □ AS

Your space feels threatened in some way. So you are either actively aggressive or passively aggressive in order to protect it. Whatever the case, this does nothing for your popularity as it creates or draws strife down upon you, either at work or at home, and especially with men in general and in particular. Find out what, and with whom, your real beef is, and work it out.

Mars Opposition (confronting) Ascendant and in the Sixth House
♂ ♂ AS

Now it would seem that you initially experience these qualities of drive and self-assertion as coming from others – and one other in particular. This is especially so if you are female. This being the case, you are also more likely to encounter the negative aspects.

In truth, however, the nature and power of your own self-assertion is innately unconscious and so you encounter it through the reactions from others to it. Indeed, your partner may very well embody these traits, but the fact still remains that he or she is being a role model for you – be it negative or positive. The more you claim this manner of forcefulness as your own, the more you are able to be an effective leader of others, or at least a good example of how to assert oneself.

Mars Opposition (confronting) Ascendant and in the Seventh House
♂ ☍ AS

Your qualities of drive and assertion described below under Mars in the Seventh House are strongly emphasized and I suggest that you note them as such, and how they relate to the whole of your Mars Profile.

Mars Trine (harmonizing with) Ascendant
♂ △ AS   **OR**
Mars Sextile (co-operating with) Ascendant
♂ ⚹ AS

The way in which you assert yourself comes across as natural – whether you are aware of this or not. It is best that you are aware of this, because others readily respond to anyone who appears to be a natural leader. But should you yourself doubt it, they could get quickly disappointed, suspicious even, and you'd lose your advantage.

Mars Conjunct (uniting with) MidHeaven and in the Ninth House
♂ ☌ MC

As long as you maintain your integrity, and have a sound moral sense, you should have no trouble in reaching your targets or promoting your cause. If, however, your intentions are less than spotless, you could dive as fast as you rise.

Mars Conjunct (uniting with) MidHeaven and in the Tenth House
♂ ☌ MC

Your qualities of drive and assertion that I have described below under Mars in the Tenth House are strongly emphasized and I suggest that you note them as such, and how they relate to the whole of your Mars Profile.

Mars Square (challenging) MidHeaven
♂ □ MC

You shouldn't have any trouble piling energy into your career, and thereby getting somewhere. However, this same drive rubs family and friends up the wrong way – and even those in authority. The conflict that this creates may not matter to you now, but at a critical stage when you need emotional support it could be unavailable.

Mars Opposition (confronting) MidHeaven and in the Third House
♂ ☍ MC

Much that I have described here concerning your Mars Profile started off in life as somewhat 'buried'. In other words, your sexual urges and powers of self-assertion were or are submerged beneath your inhibitions and bad memories, and bound up with your father's manner of self-assertion. And so you are having to dig progressively through all this to expose and release your own true personal drive.

Mars Opposition (confronting) MidHeaven and in the Fourth House
♂ ☍ MC

Your qualities of drive and assertion that I have described below under Mars in the Fourth House are strongly emphasized, and I suggest that you note them as such and how they relate to the whole of your Mars Profile.

Mars Trine (harmonizing with) MidHeaven
♂ △ MC   **OR**
Mars Sextile (co-operating with) MidHeaven
♂ ⚹ MC

All these assertive energies of yours find their most satisfactory expression in the pursuance of your career. There is something about your way of physically expressing yourself that attracts support from those in authority and that is suited to your actual or desired position in the world.

You feel at your most forceful when the bit of ambition is between your teeth. This force thus released, along with the material success that it can attain, would also enable you to create a good domestic environment.

MARS HOUSES

Mars in the First House
♂ 1st

All this is quite apparent in your actual physical appearance or presentation. You put yourself forward quite spontaneously, or you feel pushed forward even though you'd rather not be. This natural assertiveness can be negatively or unconsciously expressed in accidents to your head or face, leaving scars. It could be said that your very identity is what you are fighting for, and this could have been apparent at birth with you bursting out, as it were.

In any event, though, you do have undeniable body energy, which needs channelling into some physically competitive activity, sport or martial discipline, such as karate. If you are not quite so aggressive and more pent-up, Tai-Chi, Hatha yoga or the like are more suitable. In short, you just have to assert yourself; it is finding the right method, measure and motive that is the crucial issue.

Mars in the Second House
♂ 2nd

This way of asserting yourself has to, or likes to, express itself most of all in the pursuit of your self-worth and a financial income that matches that self-worth. Looked at in another way, your financial state reflects not so much the value you place upon yourself, but upon the energy that you are prepared to put into improving it.

If you simply desire to have plenty of money and are not too fussed about how you go about it, then money is what you'll get. If, on the other hand, it is an increased and truer sense of self-worth that you are after, then how much money you have should not be regarded as a measure of this. But whether it's money or self-worth that you are in pursuit of, your Mars Profile as a whole reveals the pros and the cons of gaining them. It also indicates something of the nature of your worth, and how your income is best earned.

Mars in the Third House

♂ 3rd

Most or all of this applies especially to your manner of speech or literary expression, your everyday encounters, giving or receiving education, and your relationships with siblings. You could say that these areas are the battleground of your life. Your Mars Aspects above will reveal how easy or difficult that battle is. Ultimately, you should be a strong voice, which is heard above others'.

Mars in the Fourth House

♂ 4th

These powers of self-assertion are somewhat unconscious, buried either by having had the actions of others overwhelm you in some way, or else it has simply never occurred to you that you had a right to get what you wanted. Your father's influence or your early sexual experiences could have contributed to or been the cause of this. Whatever or whoever it was could well be causing you to feel very angry, but probably unconsciously.

Left to itself, this anger can give rise to domestic strife or, at its most extreme, fires or accidents in the home. So sooner or later you have, or have had, to get out from under – possibly as a result of some emotional upheaval – and strike out for what you want and what you believe in. Such angry feelings can be released temporarily through energetic housework.

Mars in the Fifth House

♂ 5th

Whatever your manner of self-assertion, because you have a lust for life you run into plenty of opportunities to exercise it. You are rather like a sparking plug is to gasoline. Be it an affair of the heart, a business enterprise or whatever, things are set in unstoppable motion by your verve and desire.

If you are not aware of this provocative streak in your nature, you will attract rivalry anyway – or else you could have children who are bold or arrogant. But really it is you that is the forceful one, and although there is a danger of being crude and unsubtle, going wholeheartedly for the object of your desires is in order.

Mars in the Sixth House

♂ 6th

You most readily use and develop these powers when in a work situation, or when you have some definite method to use or job to do. You wholeheartedly put your energies into anything to do with employment, which includes finding it for yourself or someone else. Occupations themselves may involve animals, health, or the use of sharp instruments or heavy machinery.

What you have to watch out for is working when irritated or angry, for injury or damage can result, or poor relationships with co-workers could ensue, resulting in bad working atmospheres. Also guard against your emotional desires getting awkwardly mixed up with your work and whom you work with.

Mars in the Seventh House
♂ 7th

Now it would seem that you initially experience these qualities of drive and self-assertion as coming from others – and one other in particular. This is especially so if you are female. This being the case, you are also more likely to encounter the negative aspects. In truth, however, the nature and power of your own self-assertion is innately unconscious and so you encounter it through the reactions from others to it.

Indeed, your partner may very well embody these traits, but the fact still remains that he or she is being a role model for you – be it negative or positive. The more you claim this manner of forcefulness as your own, then the more you are able to be an effective leader of others, or at least a good example of how to assert oneself.

Mars in the Eighth House
♂ 8th

Notwithstanding this, your urges and desires do well up from some quite deep and desperate place. There is an intensity about you that wants to get right down to the nitty-gritty. This can be expressed in certain ways – like sex, wheeling and dealing, dangerous activities, or anything else that makes you feel close to the edge, in touch with the core of life. The occult, the astral plane and any site of power exercise a pull on you.

In other words, you are desirous of getting in touch with forces greater than yourself. This is fine as long as you are conscious of this and exercise some caution – but not too much. Paradoxically, a fear of these forces can prevent you from getting what you want. Put it this way: You are turned on by power – and powerful when turned on.

Mars in the Ninth House
♂ 9th

Your manner of self-assertion most readily finds expression in the field of your beliefs and in areas of furtherance – such as travel, law or higher education. You see – or need to see – your moral convictions as especially valid ones, for they are what determine the strength of your assertiveness. Taken to extreme, you can have a righteous and crusader-like attitude, and this means that you are bound to meet someone or something that challenges it.

If you are aware of the fact that your quixotic temperament can lead to you looking a bit foolish at times, then this trait of your character can be generally regarded as enlivening others' philosophy of life. In a sexual context, this can be regarded as endearingly chivalrous if you are male – or as being deserving of chivalry, if you are female. If you are not aware of this, it could have quite the opposite effect.

Mars in the Tenth House

♂ 10th

How easily you express these qualities of self-assertion can go sharply in one of two ways. You see the outside world as a battleground either in which to prove your mettle and push for what you want professionally and materially or as somewhere intimidating and aggressive. In the first case, as long as you are prepared for the dog-eat-dog conflicts that you encounter in business and the like, then you feel happy amidst such a cut and thrust, rise and fall scenario.

If, however, you feel weak in the face of all this to the point of withdrawal, then some form of assertiveness training is called for. Behind all this was your mother's example of assertiveness. Either you took it on board as suitable to you, or it set the scene, somewhat inaccurately, as the unqualified nature of the world out there. If you are female, you possibly hope that some knight in shining armour will save and protect you – but really you should find your own armour and set forth. Generally speaking, your career should be a physically active one, possibly involving the military, force or sharp instruments.

Mars in the Eleventh House

♂ 11th

Your way of asserting yourself most easily finds expression through initiating activities amongst your friends and associates – which, however, may or may not be welcome. Putting such a lot of energy into group activity and teamwork also means that you can get angry at having to fit in with it.

Alternatively, you could actually discover your assertiveness through involvement or competition with friends and other groups. Your personal drive is often sparked off by your ideals and sense of freedom, or by a lack of freedom. You may well be driven to reform something, or rebel against it. One way or the other, you aim to stand out from the crowd – maybe after first getting lost in it. Ultimately, you can become the leader of the pack.

Mars in the Twelfth House

♂ 12th

Such as they are, your powers of self-assertion are somewhat repressed and hard to get a handle on. Some deeply seated fear or desire seems to force your hand, despite what you think or want. Experiences of forcefulness from your past – even in the womb or before that – have had a profound effect upon your own sense of effectiveness.

Ultimately this enables you to have a more subtle and psychological idea of what drive and assertion are actually about. Generally, you can find maleness or sex confusing or intimidating. Pursuits that serve to benefit others are, you discover, more favourable to your subtle energies.

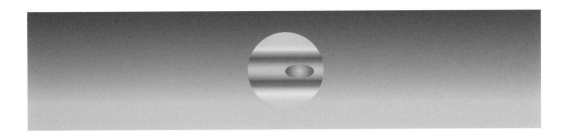

CHAPTER EIGHT – YOUR JUPITER PROFILE
FAITH AND GROWTH

Jupiter is all about GROWTH and the LAWS, BELIEFS and ETHICS that govern it. Jupiter is also a sense of EXPANSION, which leads on to FAITH and JOY, OPPORTUNITY and lead to EXCESS and to being optimistic, over-indulgent, about growth in the sense of RELIGION and BROADENING of UNDERSTANDING. Jupiter is BIGGER PICTURE and GOD. ENTHUSIASM. Naturally, this can 'OVER'- something, like over-overrated, overweight, etc. It is also TRAVEL and PHILOSOPHY, knowledge and anything BIG, as well as the

JUPITER SIGNS

Jupiter in Aries
♃ ♈

You have the faith and zest of a child – whatever age you are. So providing you have some direction, you are likely to attain your goals. However, you need to be careful that your natural eagerness does not become arrogance or blindness to subtler issues, or that your enthusiasm does not merely amount to a waste of time and energy. You have a knack for avoiding getting saddled with too much mental, material or emotional baggage. If you are not travelling light in this way, then this means that you do not believe that life looks after those who live it – which is what you are supposed to believe in.

Jupiter in Taurus
♃ ♉

Faith for you is gained through cultivating solid values and having a philosophical attitude towards material and physical involvements. By nature, then, you believe only in things that have some practical value or material worth, and you can be a good judge of saleability. Your religious persuasions lean towards the conventional and are quite hard to change. You could just be money-minded and not believe in anything 'spiritual' at all. Yet at a more evolved level of understanding, you experience the plenitude of Nature in a religious way.

Jupiter in Gemini
♃ ♊

Faith for you is gained through a gathering of all sorts of information in order to weave it into a comprehensive whole and to attain understanding. In the process of doing this you naturally acquire many contacts, which would serve you well as any kind of agent. Or you could be gathering in order to put together your own particular product or style. What you very much have to watch out for in all this 'gathering' is that you don't get sidetracked by all the distractions that you unavoidably encounter in your travels or interests.

Jupiter in Cancer
♃ ♋

Your faith resides in a feeling that life is basically secure and familiar. So you aspire to or expect the highest standards of sympathy and hospitality yourself. So much so, in fact, that you are liable to retreat out of sight if you feel at any time that these qualities are not forthcoming.

Your feeling nature is broad and deep; you try to accommodate everyone. However, if you find this difficult or taken for granted, you then go to the other extreme of being wrapped up in yourself. To maintain your faith in the milk of human kindness, let others know what your limits are, and bear in mind that being philanthropic can at times require you to allow someone to stand on their own two feet.

Jupiter in Leo
♃ ♌

Faith for you depends upon how much you believe in yourself. So you could say that cultivating an enthusiasm for the sheer fact that you are alive is your key to confidence and growth. There is a danger here of self-importance, but in some ways this is better than being falsely modest or shrewish.

However, as much as your sense of largesse can lead to great displays of generosity and wealth, it can also lead to biting off more than you can chew. Yet, at the same time, this would be a relatively unavoidable aspect of thinking or acting big. Indeed, not taking on a bit more than you can handle would be a sign that you have no great plans or expectations, which is something that should be central to your belief system and the means of developing something impressive.

Jupiter in Virgo
♃ ♍

Your faith rests in work well done, in the sense that you are serving some plan. Without this faith, it can seem that you are getting nowhere at times. Alternatively, you could scale down whatever your project is so that progress was more noticeable. Or you could give it a longer term of development.

Not surprisingly, there is more than a dash of the Puritan in you as you strive in the belief that the harder you work, the better the end product. You are health-conscious as well as conscientious, but at times you can be inordinately excessive by way of release.

Jupiter in Libra

♃ ♎

Your philosophy of life has mainly to do with your sense of justice, as you experience it in a personal way within your one-to-one relationships. It can also come from how you perceive it, or the lack of it, in society in general. In other words, your faith in life rests upon a belief that justice exists. If it does not – or if it appears not to – your faith diminishes.

Conversely, when you are aware that justice prevails, you feel happy to go on. What you have to bear in mind is that justice is not always apparent on a surface level. By its very nature, justice often has to be sought – be it in your mind or a court of law.

Jupiter in Scorpio

♃ ♏

Your faith is discovered in crisis situations. So what or who pushes you to your limits is what you find irresistible. Whatever you are after in life is probably lying deep somewhere, either in earth, water or most likely in the mind or soul. You are enormously confident in your pursuit of such things, but you can also be ruthless too, getting people to do your bidding, often through sexual or financial means.

Because of all this you stand to gain, or lose, a great deal. As ever with Scorpio placements, there is an 'all or nothing' quality about them. And as Jupiter itself has to do with excess, your life will be punctuated with great highs and great lows. The big question is whether the ultimate payback is worth the investment, especially in emotionally terms. In other words, your undeniable ability to get what you want out of people and things could find you wealthy but not necessarily happy. What would prevent this dilemma from occurring is the purging of any greed or dubious ulterior motives.

Jupiter in Sagittarius

♃ ♐

Faith comes naturally to you in that you are basically aware that there is a rhyme and a reason to it all. Consequently, philosophy and mental abstraction is a strong suit of yours. Whatever else your personality might contain, you believe in something, to one degree or another, that goes beyond what is intellectually definable.

Because you have this innate faith that life is going somewhere, life in turn encourages you to travel on, and sometimes even grants you a prophetic glimpse around the bend in the road. Providing that you do not dwell too much in pure and abstract theory, you make a good guide or teacher.

Jupiter in Capricorn

♃ ♑

Your faith in life is built upon some sort of tradition. This could be a certain type of education, a religious, communal or professional tradition, material wealth, or something quite unusual but longstanding all the same. But this background, as much as it provides the backbone of society, is something that can keep you chained to its limitations as well as reassured by its traditions.

So, as much as your traditional set of beliefs and values can serve you well in the day-to-day sense, when change, even in the form of opportunity, comes your way, what normally holds you in good stead holds you back. So if you find yourself stumped for knowing what course to follow – or not believing in anything at all – then take a leap into the unknown, backed by your common sense and an observation of Nature's Laws. You will then find that your faith in life is not only restored but also regenerated.

Jupiter in Aquarius
♃ ♒

You find and seek for faith in your friendships and any club or movement that you subscribe to. In your book, faith hinges on the fact that a sharing of ideas and ideals with others leads to mutual growth and encouragement, and upon your belief that it is your social values that are correctly paving the way ahead.

However, this can lead to your social group being self-righteous, which acts to hide your own doubts. Such 'revolutionary blindness' can then give rise to offhandedness, and associations becoming unreliable. Truly your faith rests upon being able to share with your peers both the bright and the shady sides of your nature. In this way your basically humanitarian philosophy of life gains weight and conviction for both yourself and others.

Jupiter in Pisces
♃ ♓

Your faith in life rests upon an acceptance of things working out as they will. This can cause you to sometimes extend yourself to the point of self-sacrifice. This may even happen unconsciously, with your losing or having to forego something or someone for reasons beyond your control.

And so you may now have come to distrust that accepting attitude in which you innately believe, with your philosophy of life possibly having devolved into something fanciful or insubstantial. However, this all can, or should, be flipped over to reveal that your growth and development in life hinges upon trusting in the power of your sensitivity and goodwill – for such are the true fundaments of acceptance.

JUPITER ASPECTS

NOTE that Sextile (co-operating with) and Opposition (confronting) Aspects are usually described similarly to Trine (harmonizing with) and Square (challenging) Aspects respectively, or they are occasionally described similarly to the Conjunction (uniting with). However, when this is the case, it should be borne in mind that a Sextile Aspect may require conscious awareness and effort to realize the assets and potential so described – and that the Opposition Aspect may indeed be experienced exactly as described, but in reality such can initially be felt or seen to come from someone or something else because you have projected or externalized such traits in order to make yourself aware of them.

Jupiter Conjunct (uniting with) Sun
♃ ☌ ☉

Moreover, such beliefs as you have are central to your life. You place your will behind them and so it is more than likely that you will influence others with them. You have a sense of mission, a mission that involves the whole of your being. You feel that there is something great about life, and you aim to write it large across the sky with whatever means are at your disposal.

Jupiter Square (challenging) Sun
♃ □ ☉   **OR**

Jupiter Opposition (confronting) Sun
♃ ☍ ☉

It's a fact that any negative traits regarding the nature of your beliefs, enthusiasms, cultural attitudes or want of faith, as described here, can get in the way of your progressing much in life at all. So you must pick out the best, and discard the worst, if you wish to get on and enjoy life. Through endeavouring to do this, you create an increasingly alive and original concept of reality with which you can teach and inspire others.

Jupiter Trine (harmonizing with) Sun
♃ △ ☉   **OR**

Jupiter Sextile (co-operating with) Sun
♃ ✶ ☉

By and large, you fall into the positive category with respect to your faith in life and the luck that it attracts. Your beliefs are, or ought to be, the mainstay of your existence and vitality, and others can learn much from them.

Jupiter Conjunct (uniting with) Moon
♃ ☌ ☽   **OR**

Jupiter Square (challenging) Moon
♃ □ ☽   **OR**

Jupiter Opposition (confronting) Moon
♃ ☍ ☽

There is something very natural about the way you express your faith and enthusiasms. One could say that your faith was inborn. This may of course mean that you simply subscribe to the religious persuasions of your family or racial background – whatever they may be – or that you oppose them with equal zeal. Being quite so subjective about your spiritual convictions, you may well under- or overestimate them, and therefore be challenged concerning them.

Jupiter Trine (harmonizing with) Moon
♃ △ ☽   **OR**

Jupiter Sextile (co-operating with) Moon
♃ ✶ ☽

Your emotional background, whatever else it might have lumbered you with, has

Jupiter Conjunct (uniting with) MidHeaven and in the Tenth House
♃ ☌ MC

The indications described below under Jupiter in the Tenth House with regard to how you attract fame or popularity are strongly emphasized – so smile please!

Jupiter Square (challenging) MidHeaven
♃ □ MC

Your beliefs are at odds with your family and background. As if in an attempt to prove yourself in this respect, you aim too high with regard to your profession or home – consequently over-reaching yourself. Model your ambitions on real skills and practical considerations – not on reactions to these others.

Jupiter Opposition (confronting) MidHeaven and in the Third House
♃ ☍ MC

You have inherited this brand of faith and philosophy. This means to say that it is in your blood and so therefore you are not that conscious of it; it is just there. At some stage it may well be necessary for you to become more aware of the nature of this inheritance because either it is a negative faith and it is doing you no good, or it is positive and you are not making the most of it. Your father's beliefs, or lack of them, have a lot to do with all this.

A sign of your innate faith or luck can be seen in your domestic affairs and where you live. Your abode may well be large, mobile or involve human growth activities.

Jupiter Opposition (confronting) MidHeaven and in the Fourth House
♃ ☍ MC

The indications described below under Jupiter in the Fourth House are strongly emphasized and I suggest you note them as such.

Jupiter Trine (harmonizing with) MidHeaven
♃ △ MC   **OR**
Jupiter Sextile (co-operating with) Midheaven
♃ ⚹ MC

Your religious, philosophical and speculative qualities are very much a part of the way you further you career – or actually an integral part of it. As a consequence of this faithful and expansive attitude to the world, the world in turn rewards your efforts in the form of sound opportunities for work, and home too.

JUPITER HOUSES

Jupiter in the First House
♃ 1st

You actually embody your Jupiter qualities. In other words, you put your sense of greatness and growth into your physical presence or appearance. This can mean that you are physically big or rangy. It could also mean that you put your faith primarily in your physical condition and effectiveness.

The traveller, the gambler, the entrepreneur, the teacher, the actor, the fall guy – these are all possible guises you might adopt. You should be outgoing and generous in some way. If not, however, you could well express this in a negative way, such as being overweight, dramatically ungainly or swaggering, or too open. Essentially you are aiming to be a physical example of what faith and enthusiasm are all about.

Jupiter in the Second House
♃ 2nd

You like to have something physical to show for your beliefs. So in proportion to the strength of your faith, you will accumulate money and possessions. The danger here is that this can become a substitute for faith itself. For example, you could amass lots of things around you but feel hollow inside. The wisdom that you are after, or already possess, is that of using your flair for attracting wealth to guide and assist projects and people that are in need of it.

Jupiter in the Third House
♃ 3rd

Most of all, you apply this faith to, or look for it in, your everyday interactions with others. You are the type who brings philosophical concepts into the most ordinary spheres of everyday thought. Sometimes such high-flown ideas as you expound to all and sundry can be impractical and out of place, and you come across as being wordy and abstruse. But, with your broader viewpoint, bend the ear of the common man you certainly will – despite his narrowness or incomprehension.

Jupiter in the Fourth House
♃ 4th

You have inherited this brand of faith and philosophy. This means to say that it is in your blood and so therefore you are not that conscious of it; it is just there. At some stage it may well be necessary for you to become more aware of the nature of this inheritance because either it is a negative faith and it is doing you no good, or it is positive and you are not making the most of it.

Your father's beliefs, or lack of them, have a lot to do with all this. A sign of your innate faith or luck can be seen in your domestic affairs and where you live. Your abode may well be large, mobile or involve human growth activities.

Jupiter in the Fifth House
♃ 5th

Most of all, you apply this faith to, or look for it in, your enjoyment of living life to the full through creative, speculative or romantic pursuits – or children if you have any. Your giving rein to your lust for life can lean towards the excessive, but you have the innate belief that it is only through experiencing something to excess that you will properly absorb the meaning and worth of that experience – and then know for sure where you stand in relationship to it.

You are a great believer that life is a play and the world is a stage – but just make sure you know who the director is!

Jupiter in the Sixth House
♃ 6th

These qualities of faith and understanding become critical issues with regard to health and work. Generally speaking, you are an enthusiastic worker and have a sound constitution to match. You may also be actively involved in healthcare or improving work methods and conditions, in the manner of your Jupiter Sign.

What you have to watch out for mainly is overworking or being overly concerned about getting it right – for this in itself can lead to health trouble. Nevertheless, your recovery rate is good, probably through mind-over-matter methods.

Jupiter in the Seventh House
♃ 7th

You are attracted to relationships that have these kind of expansive and philosophical qualities about them. You and your partner probably travel around together quite a lot – or are happy travelling apart at times. Generally speaking, your relationships have an open and generous nature. However, it is only too likely that you will come to expect rather too much of your mate – and he or she will be forced to break loose from those expectations in a way that challenges your faith in relationships altogether.

The truth is that you hope to find greatness in another, but you won't until you've found it in yourself. Furthermore, you are, or you ought to be, optimistic about relationships. Even when one breaks up, you are aware that someone else is just over the horizon – or that you are now free to make off over that horizon! For you, relationships breed plenty of growth, experience and adventure.

Jupiter in the Eighth House
♃ 8th

And faith for you does not come easily. It is as if an old faith has to die before a new one can be born. There can also be a period of being stuck without any faith at all. However, your faith in life is most likely found or restored when things seem to be at their darkest. Indeed it is from out of the death of someone or something that you draw most benefit.

This could take the form of a legacy, a divorce settlement, a near death experience, a guide from the 'other side', a market insight, or some profound insight born out of a crisis. It is in hidden goodness – especially in your partner – that you find faith and joy.

Jupiter in the Ninth House
♃ 9th

Faith in life for you should always be on the up and up because opportunities for furtherance – through such pursuits as travel, higher education, philosophy or religious seeking – come and go in abundance. However, a lot depends upon whether you make the most of them by putting hard work and effort into making progress an ongoing thing rather than just a chance occurrence that peters out.

You are keen to discover some kind of overall meaning to life, though you can have the attitude that the 'meaning of life' is some kind of joke. What all this amounts to is that you either invest in and capitalize upon your many talents and opportunities, not giving up when the going gets rough or you adopt a cavalier attitude that protects you from having to keep the faith when the odds are against you, but in the meantime your life just trickles away.

Jupiter in the Tenth House
♃ 10th

It is very likely that you will become well known for these qualities of faith and enterprise, as well as for other personal talents – possibly concerning law, drama, teaching, religion or the military. Having a prominent and affluent professional position – or being involved with something or someone prestigious – is more or less inevitable.

It is also quite possible that you could put too much store by your public or professional position and neglect your inner or home life. Generally speaking you have an enthusiasm for publicity, fame and fortune, but you would need sooner or later to develop honesty and integrity in performing your duties – or disgrace could result, and then you'd heartily denigrate success. Your mother's influence was or still is great concerning this inclination to excel and cut a dash in the outside world.

Jupiter in the Eleventh House
♃ 11th

Most of all, you apply this faith to, or look for it in, your friendships and teamwork or group activities. You probably have a wide range of friends. You are attuned to and enthusiastic about new trends of thought, social movements and the like. In turn, you are capable of generating interest in such things, as well as attracting subscriptions towards them.

You can be a fund-raiser for humanitarian organizations. The pitfall here is that you can lose your own good self in all such associations and involvements. Behind this is a reluctance to express your more individual desires because you are afraid of standing out or being censored by whatever group it is that you identify with. The paradox here is that you are probably the strongest link in the chain, not the weakest.

Jupiter in the Twelfth House
♃ 12th

We all have a Guardian Angel, but yours watches over you more than you know. Just when things are looking bleak, out of the blue comes deliverance, a benefactor along the winding road of life. As a sign that you are often unaware that 'someone up there loves you' you can go over the top by either pushing your luck in an attempt to disprove it, or being gushing and dramatic in an effort to prove that you deserve it.

Actually it is more a case of something deep inside that is guiding and looking after you. So you will contact and confirm your faith that life is essentially benevolent through retreat, meditation, researching your past (even as far back as the womb and before), or through working in some form of confinement or institution that ministers to others.

CHAPTER NINE – YOUR SATURN PROFILE LESSONS AND RESPONSIBILITIES

Saturn is all about ORDER. About being in the right place at the right TIME. Above all, Saturn is NECESSITY and FORCE OF CIRCUMSTANCES and the LESSONS they impose, along with the sense of DISCIPLINE and RESPONSIBILITY that is behind the LEARNING of them. Saturn is about TESTING and PRESSURE, and so it can be LIMITING and DEPRESSING as it DELAYS and DENIES. Saturn is also order as it is currently understood, that is, CONCRETE REALITY, the STATUS QUO, or any FORM of AUTHORITY such as PARENTS, ELDERS, TEACHERS and OFFICIALDOM. So Saturn can be a sense of INADEQUACY or INHIBITION for the simple reason that before we have learnt what we have to learn that is how we are most likely to feel. But Saturn is a sense of ACHIEVEMENT and STATUS when we have learned those lessons well.

SATURN SIGNS

Saturn in Aries
♄ ♈

You are learning to be self-assertive, to take the initiative, and to generally manage raw energy and aggressive instincts. Initially, the need to learn such lessons may manifest as being subject to, or fearful of, these very things, such as being on the receiving end of negative versions of them, like strife, violence or anger. Or you could experience this subjectively in the form of a fear of spontaneously being yourself, or a dread of suffering defeat or ridicule. Along the way, you may attempt to react to this through finding yourself being overly forceful, bad-tempered and attacking others in some way.

As time goes by, you should gradually and eventually acquire the grit and inner confidence – or possibly it is a case of reclaiming and reconditioning what you lost along the way – that enables you to function and push ahead in the world, to become an authority in what was at first possibly a weakness.

Saturn in Taurus
♄ ♉

You are learning the basic value of things, mainly including money and your own self-worth, and also to enjoy the physical side of life. Initially, the need to learn such lessons may manifest as losing or being without material security, or anything you regarded as valuable – or as simple a fear of such. Or you could experience this subjectively in the form of a fear of sensual enjoyment, or of becoming involved in getting and spending. Along the way, you may attempt to overcompensate for this through finding yourself being hedonistic, buying and selling, or obsessed with loyalty and dependability.

As time goes by, you should gradually and eventually acquire a healthy sense of worth and values that enables you to function and feel secure in the material world, to become an authority in what was at first possibly felt to be a weakness.

Saturn in Gemini
♄ ♊

You are learning properly to apply rational thought, to communicate well, and to see both sides of an issue. Initially, the need to learn such lessons may manifest as a fear of being stupid, of not finding the right words to express yourself, or as having a one-sided view of things. Such may have been caused by experiences such as a lack of good education, little or no conversation in childhood, or being pushed from pillar to post. Along the way you may attempt to compensate for this through finding yourself being overly intellectual or anti-intellectual, cynical and sarcastic, or torn between extremes. Contrariness.

As time goes by, you should gradually and eventually acquire the knowledge, born of balanced and disciplined thinking, that enables you to rationalize and communicate, to consciously accept opposing values, people and ideas, and to become an authority in what was at first possibly a weakness.

Saturn in Cancer
♄ ♋

You are learning the true meaning of care and sympathy, striving to gain an objective view of emotional involvements, but without becoming uninvolved altogether. Initially, the need to learn such lessons may manifest as a fear of emotional experience or expression, possibly born of coming from an emotionally dysfunctional family, or of sometimes being made to feel emotionally alienated. Along the way you are drawn, consciously or unconsciously, into becoming involved in acutely emotional relationships and situations. So as time goes by, you should gradually and eventually acquire an objective receptivity and the means of emotional expression that enables you to function well in the world of feelings, and to use such genuine but hard-won emotionality and inner strength to help others – possibly even in a professional capacity.

Saturn in Leo
♄ ♌

You are learning to creatively express yourself, build true inner confidence, and maintain a healthy sense of ego without being pompous or inordinately in need of admiration. Initially, the need to learn such lessons may manifest as a fear of being in the spotlight yet of not getting enough attention either, of taking on a superior position, of assuming adult responsibility for your actions, or of having an affluent lifestyle. Along the way, you may attempt to compensate for this through finding yourself being pompous, elitist, overly generous, *demanding* respect rather than *commanding* it, or feeling it incumbent upon you to be 'brilliant' and 'in charge' all of the time. As time goes by, you should gradually and eventually acquire a well-modulated expression of your talents and specialness, along with the ability to accept constructive criticism. This enables you to shine and excel in the world, to become an authority in what you at first possibly felt unsure of, that is, having a rightful and modest sense of self.

Saturn in Virgo
♄ ♍

You are learning to get things right without being too exacting of yourself and others, to be orderly but not rigid, and to know what is healthy and what is not. Initially, the need to learn such lessons may manifest as a fear of entering into emotional areas you are unsure of in case you put a foot wrong, or of being technically inexact or incorrect, or as a reluctance to show your doubts and soft spots. Along the way, you may take this to extremes through finding yourself being overly critical of everyone and everything else, of being fastidious to the point of aversion and reclusiveness or, conversely, by way of compensation, being imprecise, wanton, slovenly or unhygienic. As time goes by, you should gradually and eventually acquire a sense of how to fit in with society while at the same time being genuinely who you are as an individual, of how to balance the needs of your body and soul, of your intellect and emotions, such being the ultimate recipe for health. This could enable you to become an authority in what were at first possibly areas of weakness: health and sociability.

Saturn in Libra
♄ ♎

You are learning the art of grace and harmony, to develop principles concerning relating and justice. Initially, the need to learn such lessons may manifest as a fear of being answerable to something or someone, or of having to subscribe to society's rules. Along the way, by way of compensation, you are therefore drawn to committing yourself up to the eyebrows, either financially, emotionally, or both, or to trying to be all things to all people, or to being caught in the valley of decision.

So as time goes by, you should gradually and eventually acquire a sense of how to compromise without sacrificing your own or someone else's principles, how to be light-hearted yet at the same time sincere, and to make considered decisions. This could enable you to become an authority in what were at first possibly areas of weakness: fair play and keeping the peace without merely glossing over issues.

Saturn in Scorpio
♄ ♏

You are learning to handle and express effectively any kind of power, be it sexual, political, personal, material, occult or whatever. Initially, the need to learn such lessons may manifest as a fear or disdain of being deeply involved, of psychology and the unconscious mind, for such things threaten your feelings of control. For the same reason, fear of death itself could be an issue, it being the ultimate power in life. Along the way, you are therefore inextricably drawn to finding yourself getting caught up in anything powerfully influential or compulsive, or that breaks taboos.

So as time goes by, you should gradually and eventually acquire a sense of how to manage intimate relationships and critical, life-and-death, situations. This could enable you to become an authority in what were at first possibly areas of weakness – sexuality, death and power – with ruthless but just efficiency.

Saturn in Sagittarius
♄ ♐

You are learning to find what has genuine meaning for you, what is a 'practical faith' that applies to the material and physical realities of life, and to gain a pragmatic view of the world and its various cultures and beliefs. Initially, the need to learn such lessons may manifest as being subject to, or fearful of, ardent belief systems, or the constraints of religious dogma, or of something 'foreign' to you. Along the way, you are inexorably drawn to taking the moral high ground, getting caught up in some powerful and probably traditional belief system that is different to that of your own culture, or conversely, to having no belief in anything you cannot touch and see – the stout atheist. However, as time goes by, you should gradually and eventually acquire a sound, tolerant and balanced philosophy of life, quite likely born of the realization that God and religion are not necessarily the same thing. This could enable you to become an authority in what was at first possibly an area of dogma or doubt, that is, what is right and what is wrong.

Saturn in Capricorn
♄ ♑

You are learning to take on responsibilities, to develop a sense of duty, and to amount to something in life. Initially, the need to learn such lessons may manifest as being subject to, or fearful of, situations where there is the possibility of failure, of being tied to circumstances, or of having deadlines to meet. Along the way, you are therefore drawn to being over-ambitious and taking on more than you can achieve, with overly strict regimens or painfully tight schedules. A side effect of this could be that of leaving little or no room for the personal or emotional side of life.

So as time goes by, you should gradually and eventually acquire a disciplined and realistic approach to what the world demands of you. Work projects and other duties get to be well planned and feasible, conferring upon you an authority in what was at first possibly an area of difficulty: organization.

Saturn in Aquarius
♄ ♒

You are learning to identify and develop that which is unusual, quirky and innovative about you – and to cultivate the freedom to do so. Initially, the need to learn such lessons may manifest as being subject to, or fearful of, situations where there is the possibility of being alienated, standing out from the crowd, or being seen as odd. Along the way, you may consciously or unconsciously find yourself in situations where you are restrained and so become demanding of your 'rights', or where you are not recognized for your individuality and so then insist upon special treatment. And so as time goes by, you should gradually and eventually acquire a flair for innovation, become a testament to the uniqueness of the individual human being, yet at the same time make a contribution to, or fit in with, society as a whole. This could enable you to become an authority in what was at first possibly an area of difficulty, that is, individual freedom of expression.

Saturn in Pisces
♄ ♓

You are learning to accept the mysteries and uncertainties of life, to develop selflessness, and be of service to something spiritual or divine. Initially, the need to learn such lessons may manifest as being subject to, or fearful of, chaotic situations where there is the possibility of being emotionally inundated, subject to the wills of others, and generally feeling out of control. Along the way, you are therefore drawn to being in situations where you are in servitude or beholden to someone or something, or wracked by guilt, or in some way at a loss to know what to do. So as time goes by, you should gradually and eventually come to accept that there is much you cannot control in life, that it has you rather than you it, like the sea has the sailor and not the other way around. This could enable you to become an authority in what was at first possibly an area of difficulty, that is, humility and trust in Fate or a Higher Power.

SATURN ASPECTS

NOTE that Sextile (co-operating with) and Opposition (confronting) Aspects are usually described similarly to Trine (harmonizing with) and Square (challenging) Aspects respectively, or they are occasionally described similarly to the Conjunction (uniting with). However, when this is the case, it should be borne in mind that a Sextile Aspect may require conscious awareness and effort to realize the assets and potential so described – and that the Opposition Aspect may indeed be experienced exactly as described, but in reality such can initially be felt or seen to come from someone or something else because you have projected or externalized such traits in order to make yourself aware of them.

Saturn Conjunct (uniting with) Sun
♄ ☌ ☉   *OR*
Saturn Square (challenging) Sun
♄ □ ☉   *OR*
Saturn Opposition (confronting) Sun
♄ ☍ ☉

These issues are central to your life as a whole. Without beginning to understand them and deal with them, you are bound to feel limited or downtrodden in some way. The positive side is that when you do turn to face your own shadow or shortcomings, your bright side becomes even brighter. You stand to become an authority on overcoming fear, or on anything else which is important to you.

Saturn Trine (harmonizing with) Sun
♄ △ ☉   *OR*
Saturn Sextile (co-operating with) Sun
♄ ⚹ ☉

Because you have a natural and increasingly conscious sense of discipline, you work through all this assiduously, and at a steady pace. You get things done simply because you know what has to be done. It is only a matter of time before you hold a position in life of some authority or integrity. In fact, it is your actual ability to structure things that earns you such a reputation.

Saturn Conjunct (uniting with) Moon
♄ ☌ ☽   *OR*
Saturn Square (challenging) Moon
♄ □ ☽   *OR*
Saturn Opposition (confronting) Moon
♄ ☍ ☽

None of the demands indicated in your Saturn Profile is made any easier by the fact that fearful emotions can get in the way of your being objective about these demands. The helpless child in you collapses in the face of them. So you must get in touch with the adult in you, and coolly manage the situation. Yet at the same time do not lose sight of the child in you, your soul, for that was probably not noticed or validated by parents or teachers in the first place.

Saturn Trine (harmonizing with) Moon
♄ △ ☽   *OR*
Saturn Sextile (co-operating with) Moon
♄ ⚹ ☽

Your instincts serve you well here, for you were born with a good working relationship between your inner needs and outer requirements. And so you are able to divide your labour between emotional and family commitments, and those of business and other external ties. This pronounced efficiency of yours can make it seem that you are economical with your feelings – but that's the way you do it.

Saturn Conjunct (uniting with) Mercury
♄ ☌ ☿   *OR*
Saturn Square (challenging) Mercury
♄ □ ☿   *OR*
Saturn Opposition (confronting) Mercury
♄ ☍ ☿

You are learning to become mentally aware of all these matters, and to talk and be rational about them. At times this can cause you to feel quite inadequate intellectually. This needn't be such a problem if you bear in mind that it is being disciplined, objective and successful concerning your Saturn Profile as a whole that enables you to think and communicate clearly, rather than just acquiring a bunch of clever phrases and concepts that weigh you down rather than bear you up.

Saturn Trine (harmonizing with) Mercury

♄ △ ☿   *OR*

Saturn Sextile (co-operating with) Mercury

♄ ⚹ ☿

Where any of the difficulties that I have mentioned are concerned, you readily apply your mind to them and sort them out in a disciplined fashion. Some may regard you as rather cool and clinical in this respect, but that is exactly how you keep a clear head when all about you are losing theirs.

Saturn Conjunct (uniting with) Venus

♄ ☌ ♀   *OR*

Saturn Square (challenging) Venus

♄ □ ♀   *OR*

Saturn Opposition (confronting) Venus

♄ ☍ ♀

You might vainly seek pleasures or distractions in relationships as a way of diminishing or avoiding the difficulties mentioned here. Or you feel that in some way you are not allowed to enjoy yourself. The fact of the matter is that you can only go out to play to your heart's content when you have performed your duties, as I have here described them. Or alternatively, you find that taking pleasure in your work is your ultimate goal.

Saturn Trine (harmonizing with) Venus

♄ △ ♀

Saturn Sextile (co-operating with) Venus

♄ ⚹ ♀

The good news is that you have it in you, as time goes by, to progressively consolidate your own worth and your relationships. This means that you are never alone for too long before someone or something (most likely your good sense of values and duty) rescues you from a difficult dilemma.

Saturn Conjunct (uniting with) Mars

♄ ☌ ♂

For better or for worse, you feel you must act upon what you regard as your duty. You are not the type to take it easy, and you probably have little time for those who do. Such a Spartan-like manner is to some extent self-justifying, for you certainly get things done with an almost mechanical efficiency.

However, if do not wish to seize up one day, you too should take it easy at times, which may involve having to look at your real reason for being so hard on yourself, and others. Alternatively, you could be inhibited to the point of incapacitation, and have to look for the reason behind that.

Saturn Square (challenging) Mars
♄ □ ♂   *OR*
Saturn Opposition (confronting) Mars
♄ ☍ ♂

Many of the difficulties here have to do with the misuse of force, by you or someone in your life. And so you are learning to use force properly, and at the right time. Eventually, you can become an expert handler of raw energy, in yourself and others. Until then, you will continue to collide with things and people.

Saturn Trine (harmonizing with) Mars
♄ △ ♂   *OR*
Saturn Sextile (co-operating with) Mars
♄ ✶ ♂

A solid virtue of yours is a consistent willingness to meet and actually deal with the problems and challenges of life. Indeed, your physical reliability probably prevents the worst from happening. Working hard comes naturally to you.

Saturn Conjunct (uniting with) Jupiter
♄ ☌ ♃   *OR*
Saturn Square (challenging) Jupiter
♄ □ ♃   *OR*
Saturn Opposition (confronting) Jupiter
♄ ☍ ♃

Be aware that the brighter side of life is something that you do have to cultivate. It's not that you're without joy. It is more likely that you were socially conditioned by someone or something that had little joy in them. Be that as it may, you still have to lighten up somewhat, which will mean taking a chance on your intuition, and letting the devil – whatever you fear – take the hindmost.

Saturn Trine (harmonizing with) Jupiter
♄ △ ♃   *OR*
Saturn Sextile (co-operating with) Jupiter
♄ ✶ ♃

Fortunately, you accept your difficulties philosophically, and see the ultimate advantage in learning your lessons and accepting your responsibilities. You may do this a bit grudgingly at first, but as time goes by you come to positively enjoy it. Eventually, you earn the virtues of patience and of performing duties happily.

Saturn Conjunct (uniting with) Uranus
♄ ☌ ♅   *OR*
Saturn Square (challenging) Uranus
♄ □ ♅   *OR*
Saturn Opposition (confronting) Uranus
♄ ☍ ♅

There is a tremendous pressure in you to get free of all the tensions and problems that Saturn imposes upon you. But in truth, the tensions are created by you sticking rigidly with your old ways of looking at the problems. Most of all, you get stuck because you cannot accept anything (like an answer to your problems) which is not logically provable.

When finally you do adopt an alternative approach, you find that you are very efficient in crisis situations. But until then, you merely attract them. You also alternate between conventional methods and unorthodox ones until you find a useful balance between the two.

Saturn Trine (harmonizing with) Uranus
♄ △ ♅   OR
Saturn Sextile (co-operating with) Uranus
♄ ✶ ♅

You stand to alleviate any problems here, both for yourself and for others. You do this through your inventive streak, which employs original means and ideas, or the latest technological, metaphysical or psychological methods. Being flexible and up-to-date are useful assets of yours.

Saturn Conjunct (uniting with) Neptune
♄ ☌ ♆   OR
Saturn Square (challenging) Neptune
♄ □ ♆   OR
Saturn Opposition (confronting) Neptune
♄ ☍ ♆

Like it or not, you have some kind of social or spiritual obligation to fulfil. Until you have accepted this, discovered what it is, and begun to act upon it, you feel dogged by vague feelings of insecurity, or threats of material collapse. Indeed, ambitions or positions that you hold and that are doing nothing for the common welfare are doomed to eventual failure.

Behind all of this lies the fact that you do have the makings of the practical idealist. Your Saturn and Neptune Profiles particularly shed light on these matters.

Saturn Trine (harmonizing with) Neptune
♄ △ ♆   OR
Saturn Sextile (co-operating with) Neptune
♄ ✶ ♆

You have the latent ability to distinguish readily between the real and the imagined, between fact and fiction. Through developing this, you are unlikely to worry about anything unduly. This also means that you would then be adept at allaying anxiety in others. Additionally, your sixth sense could be employed profitably in introducing material awareness to spiritual matters, or vice versa.

Saturn Conjunct (uniting with) Pluto
♄ ☌ ♇   *OR*

Saturn Square (challenging) Pluto
♄ □ ♇   *OR*

Saturn Opposition (confronting) Pluto
♄ ☍ ♇

There is a definite weight and inevitability about all these lessons and tests. It is as if the oppressive figures or situations that you encounter are heavier than average. But when you pass a test or overcome an obstacle you become far more powerful and authoritative. This certainly takes some doing, but then these pressures or adversaries are exactly equal to your own grit and determination.

Saturn Trine (harmonizing with) Pluto
♄ △ ♇   *OR*

Saturn Sextile (co-operating with) Pluto
♄ ✶ ♇

The more that you knuckle down to what has to be done, the more power to your elbow you get. The more you have to handle, the more you are capable of handling.

Saturn Unaspected by any other planet
♄ ⊘

You are inclined to lack the inner sense of order and structure, so you look for it on the outside. This is most likely to take the form of work or a partnership, but this can be ascertained in more detail through studying the rest of your Saturn Profile.

You could have a vague, weak, or non-existent father; possibly he was eclipsed by your mother in some way. In any event you did not, or did not want to, receive much guidance from your father. You still need someone or something to look up to, but this should be seen as a step, not as a permanent dwelling place, because that person or thing could get to feel very oppressive or oppressed. Alternatively, and rather perversely, discovering some figure that lacks order and authority, or someone or something that you cannot respect, can give you by comparison a false sense of stability.

Ultimately you are looking for the inner father, as a consequence of that acceptable sense of order and authority being missing in the first place. This could be regarded as a way of leading you up to following a spiritual path.

Direction, career and status are also likely to be areas of doubt and concern, owing to a lack of discipline, order and guidance earlier on in life. Or your career may be extremely Saturnian as if to drive home the necessary lesson of responsibility. (Saturnian professions involve any creation, observation or maintenance of structures – e.g. architecture, politics, dentistry, etc.)

If you have any planet placed in Capricorn or the Tenth House, this will do much to make up for having an Unaspected Saturn, so you need to make the most of such if this is the case.

Saturn Conjunct (uniting with) Ascendant and in the First House
♄ ☌ AS

Those qualities of yours described below under Saturn in the First House are strongly emphasized and I suggest that you note them as such, and how they relate to the whole of your Saturn Profile.

Saturn Conjunct (uniting with) Ascendant and in the Twelfth House
♄ ☌ AS

Whether you yourself are aware of it or not, you wear your doubts and inner seriousness on your sleeve for all to see. However, they probably do not see what lies behind this. In fact, you can present to the world a very convincing impression of order and earnestness. In practical terms this can be very useful, but be careful that it does not hide your inner sensitivity completely for this could make you feel very isolated.

Saturn Square (challenging) Ascendant
♄ □ AS

Until you have begun in earnest to work through some of the difficulties and setbacks described here, you will experience difficulty in expressing yourself in an emotional sense. This may even manifest itself as skin complaints.

Saturn Opposition (confronting) Ascendant and in the Sixth House
♄ ☍ AS

You not only work hard at your job, you also work hard at your relationships. However, there is a danger of you doing all the work here because your partner or prospective mate somehow embodies authority to you, and therefore there is a threat of punishment if you get it wrong by not pulling your weight. I suggest that a wiser course would be to determine in your own eyes what your duties are and are not, thereby reminding the other party of your own weight and value.

Saturn Opposition (confronting) Ascendant and in the Seventh House
♄ ☍ AS

You work hard at your relationships – or else you make them hard work. This is because there is a danger of you making all the effort because your partner or prospective mate somehow embodies authority to you, and therefore there is a threat of punishment if you get it wrong by not pulling your weight. I suggest that a wiser course would be to determine in your own eyes what your duties are and are not, thereby reminding the other party of your own weight and value.

Saturn Trine (harmonizing with) Ascendant
♄ △ AS   **OR**
Saturn Sextile (co-operating with) Ascendant
♄ ✳ AS

Whatever else might need putting in order in your life, your way of approaching any situation is straight and true, practical and well measured. In turn, you find that others mostly respond to you in the same way, thereby attracting stable relationships. You are good at determining whose duties are whose.

Saturn Conjunct (uniting with) MidHeaven and in the Ninth House
♄ ☌ MC

Through the disciplined development and application of your morals and beliefs you arrive at a worldly position of some standing. Conversely, without this discipline you either get nowhere, or you fall from grace when inevitably your ethics are seen not to match your status.

Saturn Conjunct (uniting with) MidHeaven and in the Tenth House
♄ ☌ MC

Those qualities of yours described below under Saturn in the Tenth House are strongly emphasized and I suggest that you note them as such, and how they relate to the whole of your Saturn Profile.

Saturn Square (challenging) MidHeaven
♄ □ MC

To add to all this, you have your work cut out in making sure that both private and professional commitments are equally maintained. As a negative role model, one or both of your parents is or was probably very bad at this. Apparently it takes you longer than others to get anywhere, but when you do you stay there.

Saturn Opposition (confronting) MidHeaven and in the Third House
♄ ☍ MC

These lessons and necessities also centre upon your home or inner life, and the sense of order that was laid down during your early years – especially by your father. If that sense was absent or restrictive, you now go around with an inner feeling that something is missing or not good enough. You then come to depend upon having very stable domestic security to compensate for this.

But in the long run it doesn't, for it is a want of something emotional rather than something material. In other words, at some stage you will have to reaffirm your sense of belonging, which was not forthcoming in childhood. At the other extreme, your early life might have been highly structured in a supportive way, thus giving you an inner sense of being in the right place at the right time.

Saturn Opposition (confronting) MidHeaven and in the Fourth House
♄ ☍ MC

Those qualities of yours described below under Saturn in the Fourth House are strongly emphasized and I suggest that you note them as such, and how they relate to the whole of your Saturn Profile.

Saturn Trine (harmonizing with) MidHeaven
♄ △ MC   *OR*
Saturn Sextile (co-operating with) MidHeaven
♄ ✶ MC

You have it in you to hold a position of authority. Looked at another way, you sense that there is some worthwhile position earmarked for you, and that you will have to work to get there. And so you do.

Saturn Houses

Saturn in the First House
ħ 1st

Your Saturn Profile is actually etched into your physical appearance and manner of self-expression. So you are probably lean and bony, or swarthy; you certainly are not fleshy unless there is some other contrary planetary influence. You can look rather undernourished, whereas your health is usually reliable, except perhaps for complaints of stiffness.

However, such a look could be said to symbolize that you are a bit mean with yourself. And the stiffness would be a sign that you are being too rigid or formal. Also, you might experience skin trouble as a sign that you are being too self-contained and not showing your true self. Yet another mask could be a very sleek and impenetrable countenance, like highly polished veneer, and this can be very effective in commanding order or respect. But behind this guarded persona is your difficult task in emerging into the world as you actually are, rather than as what you feel is expected of you, which is to be conventional (even if in an acceptably unconventional way).

This can be further expressed as your having to see life in very concrete and logical terms. And behind all this still is your early life, which was difficult in that your own identity was not allowed to emerge, or your birth itself, which was difficult in that perhaps you did not want to enter the harsh reality of Earth-life at all. But finding a face to present to the world, but at the same not confusing it with who you are inside, is precisely what you are having to do.

Saturn in the Second House
ħ 2nd

These lessons and tasks focus particularly upon the issues of self-worth and income or finances. Consequently, it is very likely that you either have trouble as a result of having too little money, or too much of it. In the first case, you are striving to improve your self-worth and thereby attract a better income. In the second case, you find it hard to know what you yourself are actually worth because others seem to judge you by what you own rather than what you are.

Tightfistedness with yourself could arise from the first case; tightfistedness with others from the second. In either case, you are learning what is of real value in life. You could become an authority on quality.

Saturn in the Third House
ħ 3rd

These lessons focus mainly upon your schooling and your daily interactions with others – especially with siblings. Problems and challenges in these areas of book learning and everyday communications are a likelihood, or you make a point of becoming so good at them that you can drive others away with your worship of facts – whatever the subject may be.

What all this really boils down to is your allotting the correct value to reason and factual information. This can take the form of anything from your having learning difficulties to your teaching people with learning difficulties. You may have respiratory problems, for these are symptomatic of difficulty taking things in and giving them out. Whatever the case, you have a specific mental task to perform and possibly even excel in.

Saturn in the Fourth House
♄ 4ᵗʰ

These lessons and necessities focus mainly upon your home or inner life, and the sense of order that was laid down during your early years – especially by your father. If that sense was absent or restrictive, you now go around with an inner feeling that something is missing or not good enough. You then come to depend upon having very stable domestic security to compensate for this.

But in the long run it doesn't, for it is a want of something emotional rather than something material. In other words, at some stage you will have to reaffirm your sense of belonging, which was not forthcoming in childhood. At the other extreme, your early life might have been highly structured in a supportive way, thus giving you an inner sense of being in the right place at the right time.

Saturn in the Fifth House
♄ 5ᵗʰ

These lessons and limitations bear most of all upon your individual means of self-expression. This includes anything that is a creative product or outlet of yours, such as artwork, children, hobbies, games, romance, etc. So delays, difficulties, duty, denial or heavy responsibilities are all possible in one or more of these areas. You are learning to go about such matters in a disciplined way, as if you have to prove something.

Until you do, little or nothing will be forthcoming. When you do, however – which would be through a gradual process – you can become quite an authority in that field. Overall, you tend to feel that your creative efforts are being watched and judged. They are! – by yourself. As you are your own overseer, why not be a positive and generous one?

Saturn in the Sixth House
♄ 6ᵗʰ

These lessons and tests, and the authority that they can earn, are most likely to manifest themselves in your work life, in relating to co-workers, or in matters regarding health. Put the other way around, you do work very hard at learning these lessons, fulfilling your duties, and maintaining health.

All this can make life a bit of a drudge though, or work itself can be hard to come by or get down to – and your health could suffer as a result. One could say that you are either a slavedriver or slave-driven. The real necessity here is that of establishing who or what you are really working for, and of devising a healthy lifestyle.

Saturn in the Seventh House
ħ 7th

These lessons and responsibilities that you are supposed to be working on in yourself can mistakenly be projected on to a partner. You expect them to be putting right what is really your department. When you do get down to it yourself – which essentially means that you are simply learning to relate to others in a responsible way – then you show great honour and discipline with regard to any serious relationship.

In fact, serious relationships are your staple diet, for even casual affairs have a habit of calling you to book. Similarly, having a partner who is cold and remote is a sign that you are only going through the conventional motions of serious commitment rather than owning up to your part in it all. To sum up, failing to commit yourself leads to feeling lonely or being alone. So love for you is very much where you find it and how you make it.

Saturn in the Eighth House
ħ 8th

These lessons and tests mainly relate to involvements of an intimate nature, where sexuality and shared values and shared resources are a critical issue. The challenge to find a position of strength for yourself presents itself in dilemmas centring upon control. For example, seeking to control your partner in order to maintain a closeness, or finding yourself under their control owing to your doubts of how to stand your own ground.

The granting or withholding of sexual favours or secret information are the main instruments of control. Shared property can also become a manipulative device as it has become a symbol of the emotions that have been invested in the relationship, but have not been looked at honestly. Essentially, you are learning what deep commitment means. Ultimately, you have to let go of your fear of closeness, and be honest about your desperate need for it, in order to attain it.

Saturn in the Ninth House
ħ 9th

These lessons and tests, and the authority that they can earn you, focus largely upon issues of belief and morality. As if to set this in motion, you were probably brought up with a very strict morality and rigid religious doctrine, or, in the absence of any kind of faith or divine law. It could also have been a combination of the two – like a political ideology – or you could since have reversed your philosophy of life.

In any event, what you trying to attain is an image of 'God' that is more practical and accommodating of your individual personality. Other areas of trial are higher education, law, foreign affairs, travel. Yet with effort and discipline you stand to excel in one of these fields – including religion. But whenever you feel stuck or held back in life, it will be because you are either resting on your laurels or are following someone else's rules too much, or living by the letter of the law rather than by the spirit of it. 'Beaten paths are for beaten people.'

Saturn in the Tenth House
ħ 10th

These lessons and necessities make themselves known in an obvious way. This is because you either feel that you must definitely amount to something in life and therefore set about pursuing the goals and dealing with the challenges of the material world, or you feel rather weak in the face of the world at large and settle for being nobody in particular. A lot depends upon your Saturn Profile as a whole, and upon your mother's influence in particular, because her ambitions or fears, her confidence or doubts, got readily passed on to you.

Ultimately, and in truth, you must attempt to amount to something in this world for that is the test-bed of your life; worldly success is supposed to be yours and could well be so. But if your ambitions are someone else's, or they have been suppressed by self-doubt, you will first have to fall or sink very low before you realize the true meaning and importance of amounting to something.

Saturn in the Eleventh House
ħ 11th

These lessons and tests focus largely upon friendships and group involvements. In this way you can deal with reserve and self-doubt by objectifying them. A difficulty in forming close associations would indicate that you are trying to keep too much to yourself. It is through perhaps just one close friendship that you may dissolve many blocks and a sense of stiffness.

A trusted friend is a symbol of trust in yourself. Another lesson here is that of learning to work in co-operation with others. In order to do this, it is necessary to accept your own ordinariness, for any elitism could be interpreted as a disguise for your own self-doubt. Out of either of these scenarios you yourself can emerge as the trusted friend or group co-ordinator.

Saturn in the Twelfth House
ħ 12th

None of this comes to you at all easily; nor perhaps does the establishing of a material position in life. It is as if you are first having to make amends for past misdeeds which are reflected as anything negative in your Saturn Profile, which may simply mean failing to act upon it, or that you have never felt enough sense of personal authority to achieve.

So you have to go downwards and inwards in order to discover what lies hidden deep within you that makes you feel as if you've got a monkey on your back. This plumbing of your depths, this contacting and obeying your conscience, is essential. Either you achieve it voluntarily through meditation, psychotherapy, past-life regression or creative work, or you are driven to confronting yourself through some other form of confinement or solitude. The inner stability that you can eventually attain through these means is complete and permanent, for you will have vanquished the most powerful demon of all – the demon within. In other words, your lesson is to learn that true support comes from within, and that could engender the feeling that you are ultimately sustained by some Higher Power.

CHAPTER TEN – YOUR URANUS PROFILE
AWAKENING AND FREEDOM

Uranus is the IMPULSE that AWAKENS, which more often than not amounts to some form of DISRUPTION or SURPRISE taking place. Uranus introduces you to the UNUSUAL or INNOVATIVE, through the TECHNOLOGICAL or METAPHYSICAL, making you aware of what is BUBBLING UNDER, the FUTURE in the making. Uranus represents what is UNIQUE about you as an INDIVIDUAL HUMAN BEING, and ultimately towards the recognition of the goals of the human race itself, something which is essentially the stuff of EVOLUTION. Uranian events and personalities are UNEXPECTED, taking the form of ACCIDENTS or MEANINGFUL COINCIDENCE (SYNCHRONICITY). Uranus is the SPARK of GENIUS, it's ELECTRICITY itself, and MAGIC, that SOMETHING IN THE AIR. In a word, Uranus is CHANGE. Uranus is INTUITION, which is simply a sense of the TRUTH, the only thing that will set you FREE.

URANUS SIGNS

NOTE that the Uranian generations given for each Sign are only the ones dating back to the beginning of the twentieth century. Any further back in time would be a multiple of 84 years before the one given.

Uranus in Aries

♅ ♈

You belong to a generation (born during the late 1920s to mid 1930s or between 2011 and 2019) whose impulse is to assert a most fundamental human right, which is the freedom to act spontaneously upon whatever initially motivates. Such a raw energy can take the form of disorderly and reactionary behaviour at one extreme, to having, at the other extreme, the guts and resolve to conquer or make known some new area or idea.

Uranus in Taurus

♅ ♉

You belong to a generation (born during the mid 1930s to early 1940s) whose impulse is to reform the financial and material side of life. The trouble here can be that such are very resistant to change, which means that you yourself could be too. In other words, your

or more than a bit – of a human thunderbolt.

Uranus Conjunct (uniting with) Ascendant and in the Twelfth House
♅ ♂ AS

Although you possibly suppress or are unaware of what is original about you, others do notice it in you. They could in turn find your ignorance of this rather disconcerting, and then label you as being odd – which would drive your uniqueness further into the shade. Try to identify and actually celebrate what is unique about you; you will be surprised at the changes and effects this creates.

Uranus Square (challenging) Ascendant
♅ □ AS

Your desire for freedom is such that it makes it difficult for anyone to relate to you in a consistent fashion. You do what you want to do when you want to, and this is unlikely to keep a regular guy or girl for long. If this freewheeling style suits you, then well and good, and you are electrically stimulating company. But for a stable relationship, you'd need to be less intransigent.

Uranus Opposition (confronting) Ascendant and in the Sixth House
♅ ♂° AS

Many of the disruptive or original traits that I have been describing in your Uranus Profile actually appear to come from your partner or others generally. This is because you are not recognizing them in yourself.

Uranus Opposition (confronting) Ascendant and in the Seventh House
♅ ♂° AS

Those Uranian qualities of your personality described below under Uranus in the Seventh House are strongly emphasized, and I suggest that you note them as such.

Uranus Trine (harmonizing with) Ascendant
♅ △ AS   *OR*
Uranus Sextile (co-operating with) Ascendant
♅ ✶ AS

Your intuitive perception of life, and your sense of the shape of things to come, is remarkable. So too is your natural flair for presenting yourself in a way that matches this clairvoyant view you have of the future and of how one day we shall all see and relate to each other.

Such uniqueness and singularity of self-expression that you have can alarm or confuse other people, or other parts of your own personality for that matter, which are rigidly conventional or fearful of change. Nevertheless, you are an awakener of others to the truth.

Uranus Conjunct (uniting with) MidHeaven and in the Ninth House
⛢ ☌ MC

The uniqueness of your beliefs and philosophy of life eventually amount to the actual nature of your reputation and status in life. Looked at the other way, the more you develop an original opinion and sense of individual purpose in life, the more successful you will be.

Uranus Conjunct (uniting with) MidHeaven and in the Tenth House
⛢ ☌ MC

Those Uranian qualities of your personality described above under Uranus in the Tenth House are strongly emphasized, and I suggest that you note them as such.

Uranus Square (challenging) MidHeaven
⛢ □ MC

There is something in you that, consciously or unconsciously, rebels against authority, your parental and social background, or anything which smacks of limiting your freedom. This in turn causes you to be unreliable, unpredictable or bored with your work or home life. Unless you wish this disruptive and non-productive influence to continue, you will need to identify and sort out what that 'something' is.

Uranus Opposition (confronting) MidHeaven and in the Third House
⛢ ☍ MC

Your original qualities, which are so important for making your life into something special, tend to be hidden amongst peculiarities of your roots and family – especially your father's. This means to say that you will need to break away somewhat from them all in order to find your own individuality.

Uranus Opposition (confronting) MidHeaven and in the Fourth House
⛢ ☍ MC

Those Uranian qualities of your personality described below under Uranus in the Fourth House are strongly emphasized and you should note them as such.

Uranus Trine (harmonizing with) MidHeaven
⛢ △ MC   *OR*
Uranus Sextile (co-operating with) MidHeaven
⛢ ✶ MC

Through your efforts to make the most of the positive qualities of your Uranus Profile you attain or come to attain a professional position that actually embodies those qualities of scientific, metaphysical or humanitarian progress.

URANUS HOUSES

Uranus in the First House
⛢ 1st

You actually embody the qualities of Uranus, and so you give off an electrically charged aura, which can either be stimulating or shocking – depending on your overall personality. Sparks of genius and eccentricity fly off you. You have a sharp awareness of your very existence; this can amount to being a testament to the uniqueness of the individual or just being downright odd.

You can inspire or move the masses, or just be plain awkward, clumsy and disruptive. Your physical appearance is probably unusual or arresting in some way too. And freedom and rights can become a valid or distorting issue for you, expressed as being stubbornly rebellious just for the sake of it, or as a reformer who actually makes radical changes in the world around you. In any case, you should first reform your own attitudes or be prepared to be drastically transformed yourself in the process.

You are astoundingly intuitive at times – laying bare pseudo or subtle personality traits in others with great precision and *sang-froid*. Indeed, your intuition is your leading edge, and may well find a fruitful expression in psychology, astrology, science and technology, etc. You can also be inventive; in essence, it could be said that you are inventing your very self.

Uranus in the Second House
⛢ 2nd

Your urge for change and awakening reveals itself in those areas of life that are concerned with material substance and self-worth. If you yourself lean to a material view of life, then you probably regard change as something to resist or have well under control. If you can lend stability where there is change or disruption, then this is a good expression of this.

But if you are materially entrenching yourself against any kind of change, at some stage you could encounter something irresistible that forces a change. With regard to your sense of self-worth and the income that reflects it, these are possibly prone to erratic changes. On the other hand, self-worth and income would be made more secure in your having a talent for science, engineering, psychology or something unusual.

Uranus in the Third House
⛢ 3rd

Your urge for change, awakening and uniqueness can show itself as your being the odd-one-out as far as education, relatives, communicating and thinking are concerned. To meet this with feelings of defensiveness and alienation would be missing the point of your having an original and inventive mind that is able to influence and lead. It doesn't run away.

If Uranus has difficult Aspects (see above) shocks and accidents can occur involving travelling or brothers or sisters. Any such events should be investigated for they would profoundly affect your mentality and everyday attitude towards life. You may also move around a lot, or not fit in with neighbours. Again, this is a sign of your restless and unusual mind that when positively expressed can introduce the new and unusual to everyday life, the cosmic into the commonplace.

Uranus in the Fourth House
♅ 4th

Your urge for change and awakening is most likely to manifest itself as upheavals or something out of the ordinary on your domestic scene, in your background or in your relationship with your father. With regard to these situations, you find that you have to adopt an unconventional or even breakaway attitude. You may at times experience feelings of being uprooted or of being rootless. Your father might appear to have disowned you.

The intention behind this, or any other such feeling of being disinherited, is that you re-establish your right to be here – on your own, more consciously conceived, terms. You may find that all of this entails moving home more than average, or of occasional chaos within the home and family. In your home itself, you like to have freedom of movement and not be too tied to it. This is one reason why you may like labour-saving electronic gadgetry. Your home is a testament to the uniqueness of your lifestyle.

Uranus in the Fifth House
♅ 5th

Your urge for change and awakening makes itself felt in your manner of sexual or creative expression. Whatever is original, or shocking, marks the way in which you come across, whether socially or artistically. In any event, taking a conventional route in this respect will either be very boring or unproductive or both. Sexually, too, you are unlikely to be happy with the norm in the sense of settling down with the spouse and children, for this would seriously inhibit your all-important freedom of expression.

Any children you have will themselves be unusual, disruptive or gifted in some way. Creative ideas come and go like lightning, so you have to be ready and quick to catch them. This is important to bear in mind, for potentially you have access to a streak of genius – hence your insistence on the space to make free with your individuality.

Uranus in the Sixth House
♅ 6th

Freedom is an issue for you where your working life is concerned. You are not keen on a rigid routine, so flexi-hours or self-employment are desirable, if not downright essential. Sharp ups and downs, along with interminable changes of fortune in the work sphere would indicate that job security is going to have to take second place to job satisfaction. There is, or should be, something inventive or highly original about your work.

Similarly, unpredictable health – especially intermittent or odd complaints – would point to your being a round peg in a square hole, or that a change of work environment or lifestyle was called for. Further regarding health, you can successfully diagnose the cause of complaints – in yourself or others – by spotting the symbolism involved. For example, trouble with the pancreas, which regulates blood sugar, would suggest that one is bitter or sour about something, that life has lost its sweetness.

Uranus in the Seventh House
⛢ 7th

Forces for change and urges for freedom make themselves felt in an area where most of us would like stability: relationships. But, consciously or unconsciously, you are attracted to unconventional relationships and partners, ones who keep you alive to the fact that you are both individual beings with individual desires for more than just a secure and predictable social and love life. Shared interests, often of a curious or alternative kind, help to keep a relationship alive because it 'marries' your minds together.

This is something you need in addition to a merely emotional or physical bond. You could say that you are awakening to the importance of friendship over romance. Ideal partners are original, inventive types – even with a touch of genius, craziness or both. And whatever is suppressed or denied as odd in yourself is bound to be represented in your mate – at double strength. It can be guaranteed that you will never be able to take each other for granted, for you'll always surprise one another.

Uranus in the Eighth House
⛢ 8th

Your urge for change and awakening, and the freedom that comes with them, makes itself felt in areas of your life relating to intimacy and sexuality, joint or others' resources, and hidden causes. These areas are usually very fraught with intense passions and emotions, which are painfully hard to control. You are trying to gain some detached, scientific objectivity in all this, and more often than not you have to find just that through being flung into the deep end.

So crises like divorce, tax or property problems, sexual difficulties, and death itself, present you with the challenge to be detached but not totally unattached, which would pose an emotional problem in itself. In the process, you can become quite the troubleshooter with respect to such problems, discover important secrets, and ultimately get into the clear as suddenly as you got thrown into the pit.

Uranus in the Ninth House
⛢ 9th

These changes, and advancement through technology or alternative disciplines, are likely to find their way into your life via further education, travelling to foreign parts, or generally seeking to broaden your horizons through religion or philosophical thought and discussion. What you believe in has to have an unconventional, even rebellious, quality about it. You are likely to pursue systems of belief that originate in a culture very different to your own.

You could well decry religion, God or anything divine, and prefer to believe in what you know from your own experience rather than through what you've been taught. Sudden opportunities to travel or mix with the unlikely can come to you out of the blue. Such openings should be jumped at – it is your soul speaking! However, if Uranus has difficult Aspects to other planets, there will be a need for caution while travelling in or to other countries or unknown territories.

Uranus in the Tenth House
⛢ 10th

These changes, and advancement through technology or alternative disciplines, are likely to find their way into your life via your profession or reputation. So your career could involve electricity, science, mass media, aeronautics or anything that is innovative or future-orientated. However, you may at some stage have to 'invent' your position in life as ordinary methods and channels either fail or bore. And in the process of discovering your unique professional niche, many avenues of expression may be experimented with – so a chequered career is likely.

Advancement can be quick, sudden or erratic – and friends or teamwork could play a significant part. Freedom and rights may well be a professional issue – for instance, trade unionist, freedom fighter, social activist, consumer watchdog, etc. The occult may also figure in your career, pointing the way with astrology, magic, or psychology. Your mother figures strongly in how you see yourself in the world, for she either left you very much to your own devices, or caused you to react against her and take a rebellious public stance.

Uranus in the Eleventh House
⛢ 11th

Your urge for change and awakening is most likely to manifest itself quite directly in your pursuance of social ideals and collective goals. Friendships and group involvements also act as clear indicators of how well you are on course with your true path in life, as they stimulate your principles through attack or support.

Groups of friends can change quite radically as you shift gears and get closer to your goal. However, it is important that you do not confuse your goals with your material ambitions, for the former take a lot longer to achieve than the latter. Freedom and friendship are very important to you, and you promote them.

Uranus in the Twelfth House
⛢ 12th

You could be called the 'closet rebel'! Your urge for change, awakening and to be free to do your own thing is somewhat subdued. It is as if the most original and talented part of you is afraid to show itself. This is probably because at some stage in the past – even in the womb or before that – you felt ridiculed, discouraged from taking risks, or your freedom was abused or under-used. This suppressed sense of liberty can give you an acute insight into what lies at the root of inhibitions in both yourself and others. But sooner or later you have to track down what originally held you back, re-live it, and once more find your wings.

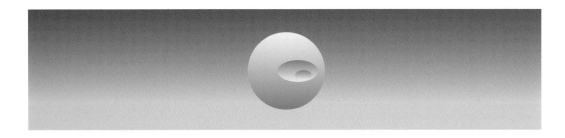

CHAPTER ELEVEN – YOUR NEPTUNE PROFILE
SENSITIVITY AND SPIRITUALITY

Neptune is the SPIRITUAL, the MYSTICAL and the ETHEREAL. It is the sense that there is something 'in there' or 'out there' that has a MYSTERIOUS and SUBTLE effect upon us all. It is the OCEANIC, UNDIFFERENTIATED realm where all is ONENESS – through which we can find AT-ONE- MENT or REDEMPTION. As such it can be anything from ENLIGHTENMENT to DELUSION, DEVOTION to ADDICTION. One could view the saying 'We are all from a grander place' as a key to Mankind's SALVATION or as just a PIPE-DREAM. So wherever Neptune is in your Chart you will find SENSITIVITY and IMAGINATION, whether it is expressed or experienced as a BLIND SPOT or a VISION; as ROMANTIC ILLUSION or UNCONDITIONAL LOVE; as ESCAPE or RELIEF; as SUFFERING or COMPASSION; as VICTIM or SELF-SACRIFICE; as ATTUNEMENT or AVERSION; as MADNESS or INSPIRATION. Neptune is most patently experienced through MUSIC or MEDITATION or SELFLESSNESS.

NEPTUNE SIGNS

NOTE *that the Neptunian generations given for each Sign are only the ones dating back to 1861. Any further back in time would be a multiple or 165 years before the one given.*

Neptune in Aries

You belong to the Neptunian generation born between 1861 and 1875. You therefore came into being during a time that pioneered certain mystical philosophies and art forms.

Neptune in Taurus

You belong to the Neptunian generation born between 1874 and 1889. You therefore came into being during a time that made a religion out of wealth, and attempted to give some kind of material expression to imaginative vision, or to prove mystical phenomena as physical phenomena.

Neptune in Gemini

You belong to the Neptunian generation born between 1887 and 1902. This time witnessed great interest in spiritual ideas, particularly through the written and spoken word – and tried to find rational explanations for them. But a proneness to superficial ideas and acceptance of these was also present.

Neptune in Cancer

You belong to the Neptunian generation born between 1901 and 1916. This time inspired an exquisite sense of Nature, poetry, family and all things concerning one's roots or origins. Strong psychic tendencies were in evidence, but also extreme sentimentalism that obscured the facts – witness the Great War! Consequently, this time embedded a kind of 'divine insecurity' in the collective human psyche.

Neptune in Leo

You belong to the Neptunian generation born between 1914 and 1929, a highly poignant period going from the hell of the Great War to the crazy glamour of 'The Roaring Twenties'. Although this gave rise to great fun and artistic creativity, it also created a very unreal sense of what love and emotion are about.

Neptune in Virgo

You belong to the Neptunian generation born between 1928 and 1943, during which economic chaos prevailed, resulting from the prodigality of the previous Neptune in Leo period. All this inculcated a rather parsimonious attitude towards life, along with a rational dismissal of woolly spiritual ideas and wild notions of better days to come. Scientifically misguided ideas with regard to healthcare, along with the first chemical contamination of food, also arose during this time. Essentially, your generation has the task of employing ideals to more practical ends, entertaining only visions that can be realized.

Neptune in Libra

You belong to the Neptunian generation born between 1942 and 1957. As you came of age, those Libran matters of love and marriage, art and music, and social values, came under Neptune's subtle spell, swinging the Scales so that men became 'softer' and women became more independent. Emotional confusion and soaring divorce rates followed. Whether or not you personally were a part of it, this was the 'Woodstock' generation who marched for peace, gathered in great numbers at music festivals, experimented with psychedelic drugs, and embarked somewhat naively upon a quest for spiritual meaning – or for an escape from ordinary life.

Neptune in Scorpio

You belong to the Neptunian generation born between the mid-1950s and 1970. As it came of age, fashions and musical styles became more sexually explicit and drug abuse became more self-destructive, and also involved the underworld of crime more. Most significant was the appearance of AIDS – a delusional blindness regarding the true and subtle nature of sex. Between the artificial 'highs' that falsely represent Neptune and the dark 'lows' that are the penchant of Scorpio, this time saw grave damage done to the astral body, both individual and collective. The challenge to your generation, and to those living in the wake of it, is no less than one of preventing (further) *de*-generation.

Neptune in Sagittarius

You belong to the Neptunian generation born between 1970 and the mid 1980s. As this generation came of age, there occurred a blurring of the line between right and wrong. The underlying reason for this was a want of distinction between the Law of Man and the Law of God. Where there is seen the unbridled following of the get-rich-quick ethos, later will appear a deep frustration and meaninglessness, and collapse. At the other extreme, fundamentalist religion seeks to overthrow anything that does not agree with it. Between these two extremes a germ of exquisite truth may be found.

Neptune in Capricorn

You belong to the Neptunian generation born between 1984 and 1998. During this time humanity officially began to realize how subtle but very powerful forces affect its Earthly environment – and how it could be doomed if it did not begin to pull together politically and economically as a species. This time, or rather your generation as it comes of age, initiates world government with respect to ecological balance and the distribution of resources.

Neptune in Aquarius
♀ ≈

You belong to the Neptunian generation born between 1998 and 2012. You came into being during a time when humanity seriously contemplates the very real danger of terminating itself. Out of this crisis and the realizations born of it, your generation truly heralds the New Age – the Age of Aquarius.

Neptune in Pisces
♀ ♓

You belong to the Neptunian generation born between 2012 and 2026. You therefore came into being during a time when humanity begun to tune into the truth of its spiritual origins, giving rise to forms of music and healing that previously were only dreamed of. The possibility of great peace – or great chaos.

Neptune Trine (harmonizing with) Mercury
♆ △ ☿   **OR**

Neptune Sextile (co-operating with) Mercury
♆ ✶ ☿

You are blessed with the ability to communicate freely or to give expression to these sensitive areas of your personality in some other way. Innate skills in the healing or performing arts are just a part of your multi-talented nature. Watch out though – for such ease of expression can make you blasé or indolent.

Neptune Conjunct (uniting with) Venus
♆ ☌ ♀   **OR**

Neptune Square (challenging) Venus
♆ □ ♀   **OR**

Neptune Opposition (confronting) Venus
♆ ☍ ♀

You actively look for a means of expressing your finer feelings and more sophisticated ideas, as described by your Neptune Profile as a whole. You seek the sublime or the glamorous in the world of art or society. The sublime leads you forever on; the glamorous seductively leads you round in circles.

Neptune Trine (harmonizing with) Venus
♆ △ ♀   **OR**

Neptune Sextile (co-operating with) Venus
♆ ✶ ♀

Happily, you are able to draw upon both the uplifting and painful experiences that your sensitivity attracts, and put them together in such a way that your personality or your creations touch others' hearts in an inspiring way.

Neptune Conjunct (uniting with) Mars
♆ ☌ ♂   **OR**

Neptune Square (challenging) Mars
♆ □ ♂   **OR**

Neptune Opposition (confronting) Mars
♆ ☍ ♂

What is more, you feel that you must act upon these finer feelings and subtle yearnings. So you can be impatient to reach some artificial high, make a sexual conquest, or save some siren-like figure, or to be saved or conquered by some hero.

Such sexual myth making is both enthralling and confusing, but at times can find you impotent or frigid, chaste or kinky. However, it is through these miasmas that you find your own fascinating blend of desire and imagination.

Neptune Trine (harmonizing with) Mars

♆ △ ♂   *OR*

Neptune Sextile (co-operating with) Mars

♆ ✶ ♂

Furthermore, you are able to act upon these finer feelings and subtle yearnings. Consequently, you are good at educating others concerning higher and better things – possibly in some physical way like yoga or dance. However, subtle as this talent is, it can be overlooked if you yourself have not yet woken up to, or begun to seek, your spiritual or creative path.

Neptune Conjunct (uniting with) Jupiter

♆ ☌ ♃   *OR*

Neptune Square (challenging) Jupiter

♆ □ ♃   *OR*

Neptune Opposition (confronting) Jupiter

♆ ☍ ♃

You probably take all these inclinations to extremes. You yaw back and forth between high hopes and disappointments. And so it will go on until you devise a philosophy of life, which takes human failing into account as a meaningful reality rather than as something to overlook or avoid altogether. You have a big soft heart that can make dreams come true when tempered with some hard thinking.

Neptune Trine (harmonizing with) Jupiter

♆ △ ♃   *OR*

Neptune Sextile (co-operating with) Jupiter

♆ ✶ ♃

You have an innate understanding of how best to make the most of sensitivity, compassion or imagination – in yourself or others. Your generosity of spirit will often reward you by something turning up to save you at the eleventh hour. Or perhaps you are the one that delivers or gives an uplift to others just when they most need it.

Neptune Conjunct (uniting with) Saturn

♆ ☌ ♄

Whenever you try to escape from your difficulties, or indulge in some fantasy or ideal for too long, you are brought crashing down to earth. This is because you are having to come to terms with your blind spots – and then – and only then, help others to confront their blind spots. Conversely, avoid being intolerant of others' dreams or weaknesses, for this would boomerang back on you in some way.

Neptune Square (challenging) Saturn

♆ □ ♄   *OR*

Neptune Opposition (confronting) Saturn

♆ ☍ ♄

Consciously or unconsciously, you are aware that shortcuts to enlightenment do not exist, and so you avoid glamorous religious sects, believing drug-induced ' revelations', marriages made in heaven, etc. However, if you should ignore such innate awareness as you have, there is hell to pay.

Neptune Trine (harmonizing with) Saturn
Ψ △ ♄   *OR*
Neptune Sextile (co-operating with) Saturn
Ψ ✳ ♄

In respect of all of this, you have the great asset of being able to distinguish between fact and fancy, between an impossible dream and a realizable one. This also means that you have, to one degree or another, a talent for giving form to creative ideas – as in photography, drama, music, painting, etc. Your balanced and therefore healthy sense of the importance of both the material and spiritual aspects of life can serve you and others in many ways.

Neptune Conjunct (uniting with) Uranus
Ψ ♂ ♅

Now you were born during a time when the nature of sensitivity and spirituality begun to be better understood. To one degree or another, you will contribute to that increased understanding and appreciation of the wonder of it all.

Neptune Square (challenging) Uranus
Ψ □ ♅   *OR*
Neptune Opposition (confronting) Uranus
Ψ ♂° ♅

Every so often you suddenly swing away from your more sensitive responses to life, and become quite cool and matter-of-fact. This is one way of handling your delicate areas when they go critical, but it makes it very hard for others to relate to you in a consistent fashion. A scientific or psychological viewpoint, which enables you to manage your sensitivity in a balanced way, is what you are really after.

Neptune Trine (harmonizing with) Uranus
Ψ △ ♅   *OR*
Neptune Sextile (co-operating with) Uranus
Ψ ✳ ♅

You find that the more you familiarize yourself with the latest technology, social values, psychological concepts, and your own original way of doing things, then the more you are able to realize your dreams and also relieve, enlighten or entertain others.

Neptune Conjunct (uniting with) Pluto
Ψ ♂ ♇

Now you came into being during a time of great cultural change during the late 1880s – with the Industrial Revolution having by this time affected society in such a profound way as to have begun a process where the world would never be the same again. Quite appropriately, this period saw the coming into being of some impressively creative or heroic figures. You could be one of them!

Neptune Square (challenging) Pluto
♆ □ ♇   *OR*
Neptune Opposition (confronting) Pluto
♆ ☍ ♇

Your spiritual role and development in life is an essential issue. Compromising situations, created by the conflict between your high ideals and dark desires, need to be worked through and transcended. Alternatively, you could just be a part of a generation whose cultural backdrop was coloured by this conflict.

Neptune Sextile (co-operating with) Pluto
♆ ⚹ ♇

You are helped in taking steps towards enlightenment by the fact that doing so has become a more generally accepted pursuit since the horrors of World War II. However, you will need more than this point alone to set you off on this path.

Neptune Unaspected by any other planet
♆ ⊘

This is not a particularly significant influence until it becomes necessary for you to consider the more spiritual or ethereal dimensions of life. The point here is that you are liable to find it difficult to integrate such things into the more material side of your existence (the side which you are likely to regard as your whole existence).

Alternatively, you could go overboard for the mystical and lose sight of land, so to speak. In either case, it will be a help to study closely your Neptune Profile as a whole, or any placement that you might have in the Sign of Pisces or the Twelfth House.

Neptune Conjunct (uniting with) Ascendant and in the First House
♆ ☌ AS

Those complex and subtle qualities of yours described below under Neptune in the First House are strongly emphasized in your personality, and so I hope that you are on your way to becoming a living example of well-managed human sensitivity.

Neptune Conjunct (uniting with) Ascendant and in the Twelfth House
♆ ☌ AS

Your imagination and sensitivity just cannot help but show themselves somehow – even though you might think you are concealing them. On the other hand, you are only too aware of their value and importance. In either case, you do have the bittersweet asset of being an embodiment of what could be called ' in-touchness'.

Neptune Square (challenging) Ascendant
♆ □ AS

Your emotional fears and wounds, and the dreams that compensate for them, get in the way of your having a realistic relationship – or having one at all. You will need to track down what it is that caused them in the first place.

Neptune Opposition (confronting) Ascendant and in the Sixth House
♆ ☍ AS

As much as you tend to lose yourself in your work, you also overlook the subtle emotional state of those you are closely involved with. You may think that you are quite the opposite, and that you are overly concerned with your partner. This could be true, for you are inclined to expect too little or too much from a relationship, and put too little or too much into it.

Understand who your partner really is, or what your prospective partner should really be like, rather than what you fear or yearn for them to be, and things will change for the better.

Neptune Opposition (confronting) Ascendant and in the Seventh House
♆ ☍ AS

Those subtle qualities regarding the way in which you relate to others described below under Neptune in the Seventh House, are strongly emphasized in your personality. I suggest you note them well if you wish to reach the sublime union you crave, and avoid the confusion you can so easily attract.

Neptune Trine (harmonizing with) Ascendant
♆ △ AS   *OR*
Neptune Sextile (co-operating with) Ascendant
♆ ✶ AS

These subtle nuances of your personality are visible to others – but only as you choose to display them. There is a mystique and a healing aura about you.

Neptune Conjunct (uniting with) MidHeaven and in the Ninth House
♆ ☌ MC

Your sensitivity and imagination play a great part in your professional life. Showing the world how you see it in a spiritual or creative sense is extremely important – so you are likely to win some acclaim for your efforts. However, if for some reason you have suppressed or kept your finer feelings too much to yourself, they could be dragged quite embarrassingly into the light.

Neptune Conjunct (uniting with) MidHeaven and in the Tenth House
♆ ☌ MC

Those conditions and qualities of your professional life described below under Neptune in the Tenth House are strongly emphasized in your personality, and I suggest you note them as such.

Neptune Square (challenging) MidHeaven
♆ □ MC

There is confusion about your professional obligations and your domestic ones. You might experience this in a vague way – like feeling a bit directionless or rootless. The cause behind this is possibly some mystery, lie or scandal surrounding your parentage. Looking into this could remove the doubt.

Neptune Opposition (confronting) MidHeaven and in the Third House
Ψ ☍ MC

Spirituality for you is your attunement to Nature. This is also manifest in your sixth sense about certain places and houses. Your home life and where you live is very much in the lap of the gods in that something quite irrational governs this area. Your home itself can be dilapidated, or have a mystical charm about it.

Neptune Opposition (confronting) MidHeaven and in the Fourth House
Ψ ☍ MC

Those subtle qualities about you that not too many others see described below under Neptune in the Fourth House, are strongly emphasized in your personality – so I suggest you note them well.

Neptune Trine (harmonizing with) MidHeaven
Ψ △ MC   **OR**
Neptune Sextile (co-operating with) MidHeaven
Ψ ⚹ MC

Your sensitivity and imagination may be used positively to further your profession, or be an integral part of its nature. So your career should involve the arts, metaphysics, healing, or anything that enlightens, relieves or entertains.

NEPTUNE HOUSES

Neptune in the First House
Ψ 1st

The sensitive issue with you is your very identity. The impression that others get from you is the one that they unconsciously fear or wish for. This is because you are adept at moulding yourself to embody whatever they expect of you. Meanwhile, your own sense of identity proves rather elusive. Another pitfall to watch out for is your susceptibility for seeing things as you want to see them. These difficulties arise because you are seeing everything and everyone as an extension of yourself. Consequently, you get caught up in living out the myths of other people. This can take the form of being glamorous and mystical, or weak and submissive, or anything else that appeals to people's fantasies. Your eyes themselves seem to match this by having a mysterious or far-away quality. Or your sight may be weak, or even non-existent – but in any case you may well have the gift of second sight.

Indeed it is your psychic sensitivity that is behind all this confusion and enigma. When you as an individual learn to use this sensitivity to tune into something that is really fine and beautiful – as opposed to randomly taking on everyone else's idea of such a thing – then your identity becomes a channel for your ideals, visions and dreams. But in order to do this you would need to rid yourself of the illusions created by having used your clairvoyance merely to please others and gain acceptance for yourself.

You can only be truly accepted by others when you have accepted yourself. In order to do this you must train your acute sensitivity through meditation, self-contemplation, or creative activities such as music, drama and dance, or through giving yourself over to some spiritual cause or healing ministry. The point is that you are naturally equipped to identify with, and find your identity through, one or more of these pursuits.

Neptune in the Second House
Ψ 2nd

You are sensitive about your self-worth and earning ability. On the other hand, you could be sensitive to money matters by having a sixth sense about them. But it is more likely that you find it hard to grasp or hold on to what you actually own. This can mean that you are open-handed and do not care too much about money, or that you are forever depending on handouts and maybe have a 'something will turn up' attitude. Or else, when you have money it just slips through your fingers; you are also open to financial deception.

What is going on here is that you are having to settle for the fact that such matters are in the 'lap of the gods' and you should accordingly accept what Providence delivers or takes away. The more you can tune in to the mystery of where it all comes from and goes to (which has something to do with believing that you will be provided for in proportion to your spiritual worth) then the fewer financial problems there will be.

Personal capabilities which are products of your sensitivity or imagination would fall into line with this – such as the arts, photography, dance, healing, psychism or anything spiritual.

Neptune in the Third House
Ψ 3rd

You have in you a poetic or literary talent, or at least the ability to introduce into the commonplace a ray of wonder, a spiritual insight, an element of relief. Alternatively, your intellect may feel confused by apparently irrational notions.

Your early school years would either have found a way for your imagination to flow freely, or would have stamped on it as mere day-dreaming, with the consequence that you now block your imagination and brand it as impractical or irrational. But a failure or reluctance to give expression to the play of your imagination, your finer feelings or your sense of some greater all-inclusive reality can give rise to mental aberrations such as paranoia, unreliable recall, mis-recording of information, obsession with facts, etc. as the greater reality breaks down your mental barriers.

As if to prove the point, any brothers or sisters will embody Neptunian traits that range from the creatively inspired to the glamorous, from the compassionate to that which needs or elicits compassion. Indeed, your relationships with siblings and neighbours either evoke feelings of estrangement through lack of rapport or, more hopefully, a subtle, unspoken understanding.

Neptune in the Fourth House
♆ 4th

For you, such sensitivity and yearning for some ideal focuses upon your home life and family background. It is most likely that you experience this as remembering things in the past as being idyllic. The streets or fields of your childhood have a rosy veil cast across them. Indeed, such childhood dreams are true, even if only because of the way you perceived life in those innocent times.

Actually, this is the whole sentiment underlying Neptune here: that life is as sweet and as secure as you make it. The negative value here is of course one of glossing over the less pleasant or even harsh experiences of early life. This has the effect of making you feel rather rootless, because through denying past pain you are still denying a part of yourself. So you have to go into that pain and then re-emerge, cleansed with a far clearer sense of 'Paradise Lost'; this in turn enables you to go about regaining your 'Paradise', thereby imbuing your own home with a hauntingly familiar quality.

This is very important to you, and creates a haven for others too. It also has something to do with your psychic sensitivity to the Earth and Nature's forces. Without doing this 'regaining', as with the weeds at the bottom of a pond, you can be trapped in the past, or in the self-contained nature of your family and particularly the relationship with your father, who may have been a vague, weak or unavailable figure.

Positively, though, he could be a great example of selflessness and compassion. With regard to finding a home itself, this is often in the lap of the gods in that some power outside yourself grants or takes away quite special abodes. Living by the sea is especially desirable and beneficial to you.

Neptune in the Fifth House
♆ 5th

For you, such sensitivity and yearning for something finer is very suitably and exquisitely bound up with creative expression and romantic involvement. And so you are likely to attract and experience extremes of ecstasy and sorrow as your fertile imagination has a field day placing lovers on pedestals or feverishly striving to express some beautiful vision artistically.

Indeed, the 'Agony and the Ecstasy' are your constant companions, as they are for all romantic and creative souls. With affairs of the heart your inclination to glamorize the object of your affections can certainly set you up for a fall as sooner or later his or her darker, or more ordinary, side stabs through the rosy veil that you have cast over them.

Such great heights are bound to be followed by great lows – and then, if you're truly loving, there can be the sweetness of realizing that your lover is even more loveable than before. Or passion could turn to compassion, the romantic into the platonic. You certainly ought to be artistically talented considering that yours is an artistic and poetic temperament, and your work will be constantly inspired and fed by the peaks and troughs created by your acute sensitivity and imagination.

If for some reason you do not practise some art form, then this has to be because of some unsympathetic figure or factor in your life, which crushed your latent abilities. If this is the case, take up art as a hobby – for your imagination is too good to waste on mere day-dreaming. If you have children, they are highly sensitive or imaginative

Neptune in the Sixth House
Ψ 6ᵗʰ

You have a sensitive constitution; simply because you are rather subtly attuned to the nature of what actually constitutes health. On the one hand this means that you are inclined to contract strange complaints which are hard to diagnose and which are probably best treated with subtle forms of medicine such as homeopathy, acupuncture, Bach flower remedies and visualization techniques.

On the other hand, or as a consequence of this, you yourself are involved in healthcare – and possibly, but not necessarily, using one of these complementary methods. Work too, can be a sensitive issue. If your job does not agree with you, it is because you do not or cannot perform it with a sense of service or devotion.

If this is the case, involve yourself with an occupation that inspires you in some way. On another level you could be inclined to escape into your work because that seems to be a way of avoiding sticky emotional issues – but this can lead to a health problem as such stifled feelings make themselves felt physically.

Neptune in the Seventh House
Ψ 7ᵗʰ

You look for sensitivity and idealism in others – or one other in particular. You project on to your partner all those things that you long for in a mate. This can only too easily give rise to your having great love affairs that are followed by equally great disappointments. Furthermore, your partner becomes like a drug to you, for you are addicted to them and suffer very painful withdrawal symptoms when your 'supply' is threatened or terminated.

It is of vital importance that you find some kind of 'cure' – otherwise you could be doomed to be a 'social junkie'. That cure is in your realization that you yourself are carrying around within your psyche that ideal human being. The people that you long for and are fatally attracted to seem to be supremely gifted and so you worship them, or they are in some way afflicted and seem to need your help.

In either case, you can often wind up feeling the victim in a relationship. The more you find the artist, mystic, healer, musician, visionary or transcendental in yourself, then the more you will be able to relate to your partner as an ordinary human being with ordinary talents and failings.

Neptune in the Eighth House
Ψ 8ᵗʰ

For you, such sensitivity and yearning are a very private affair. Your longing for enlightenment or escape surfaces within intimate relationships, at times of crisis, or in the face of such mysteries as death and other planes of existence. This is a heady mixture and so you can be easily spooked by the unknown and ecstatic, and therefore try to avoid them or rationalize them away.

Or else you could become quite addicted to such things. Sexuality can be particularly elevating, or enslaving, depending on your sexual attitude, stability and inclination generally. A more grounded expression of your marked sensitivity could be a sixth sense about legacies, taxes, investing other people's resources, etc.

Ultimately, you are seeking to surrender and dissolve your illusions of separateness in a wave of transcendental emotion. All or nothing, it would seem – but that in itself is an illusion. More a case of all and nothing.

Neptune in the Ninth House
Ψ 9th

For you, such sensitivity and spirituality manifests itself in a search for some belief or higher meaning to life. Any need that you have to find an 'answer' or a 'way' is strongly coloured by emotional fears and fancies. You are liable, therefore, to convince yourself that anything or anyone who offers an all-inclusive philosophy (or way out) of life is worth giving up a lot for.

This can involve anything from going off on a journey to some exotic foreign part to find what you are seeking, or just dropping out of college for a life of drugs or alcohol. Anything that takes away from the dull, everyday plod of life is what exercises a strong pull.

This can lead you down many a false trail, but this is all part of your search – as you probably know. For you the road really does lead forever on – and with some discipline and creative imagination you can then turn this into a positive feeling and convey this sublime truth to others in some way.

Neptune in the Tenth House
Ψ 10th

For you, such sensitivity and spirituality has to manifest itself in your public or professional life. Initially, this may mean that you are somewhat reluctant to bare your soul to the world – for effectively, this is what you have to do – and so professional status would then be minimal or non-existent.

When, however, you have found a way to express your ideals, visions or finer feelings to the world you may excel in the arts – especially painting, music and dancing – or in some role that furthers or caters for the welfare of the public, which can include anything from nursing to politics. If you continue to keep your shy and subtle side too much to yourself, it is quite possible that it will be dragged into the light in the form of some scandal.

This is because there is something about the emotional truth of your being that has to be openly expressed, whether you are aware of it or not. Still another way in which your sensitivity can show itself in a negative way is through some form of escapism. This could range from being away from home (and its emotional responsibilities) a great deal of the time, to being involved in something a bit shady or criminal, or to being in some glamorous profession which hides your real identity.

All in all, your mother influenced you a lot with regard to how you express your finer feelings to the world at large. Her vagueness or selflessness, her imaginativeness or mental instability, her propensity to inspire or confuse – would have deeply affected how you see the world and a place in it for your own sensitivity.

Neptune in the Eleventh House
♆ 11ᵗʰ

For you, such sensitivity and spiritual striving find a focal point in your friendships, ideals and group situations. Communes and workshops are or have been common on your agenda. Such friends or groups could make or break you, for they could be the typical bad lot that leads you astray, or the band of kindred spirits that lights your way.

Whatever group or social movement you find yourself in the midst of, what you get out of it always depends upon how honest you are being with those associates, and upon how able you are to distinguish your own identity and social values from those of that peer group as a whole. There is a double-edged situation here, which on the one side inspires you through a feeling of being borne on a wave towards the common goals of Humanity and on the other leaves you tossed upon the whims and fancies of the crowd and merely dreaming of a better world and not actually doing anything about it.

Where your imagination is concerned, it is best used socially in the sense that you can inspire others with your fine sense of togetherness. Any artistic talents are well employed to this same end, rather than solely for your own amusement.

Neptune in the Twelfth House
♆ 12ᵗʰ

For you, sensitivity and spirituality are second nature in the sense that you are unavoidably in touch with subtle emotional energies and unseen or mystical realms. But this can have a very distinct down-side to it in the form of feeling that a part of your being is cut off from the rest, or that there is something vague which exercises a certain control over you and keeps you tied to certain people and haunts.

Consequently, you may well suppress any suggestion of what cannot be rationally explained. But sooner or later you have to go into the mystic and make positive use of the fact that there is only a thin veil between your conscious mind and unconscious mind. You then can become aware of being in touch with invisible forces or entities, or memories of past incarnations. These in turn can give rise to rewarding mystical experiences through which you and others may be guided or uplifted.

Before this, however, it is very important that you become firmly grounded through having established a definite grip on the material aspect of life, and an internal sense of control over your life itself, otherwise you are in danger of being like a leaf in the wind as you desperately seek some form of escape or support from something or someone not that reliable. Another means of grounding yourself, which also makes use of your pronounced compassionate or devotional nature, is by working in institutions like hospitals or spiritual retreats. Meditate.

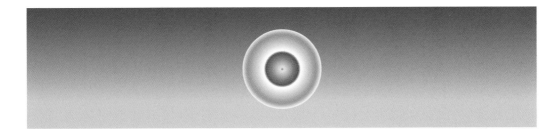

CHAPTER TWELVE – YOUR PLUTO PROFILE POWER AND TRANSFORMATION

Pluto is the SEED of POWER within, like the acorn is to the oak tree. This can amount to a sense of DESTINY or just an OBSESSION. Either way, Pluto is a force to be reckoned with as it, the Lord of the Underworld, urges you to get in touch with DEEP and PROFOUND levels of consciousness. It is the power of DEATH and TRANSFORMATION and of SEXUALITY and the SECRETS of birth and all other things. Pluto governs the HIDDEN (OCCULT) and the DARKER SIDE of life. So Pluto either REGENERATES or DESTROYS - nothing in between. It has the power to harm or heal as no other planetary force, and it shows your DEPTHS (which you might have to sink to) and INSIGHT (that you gained thereby).

PLUTO SIGNS

NOTE that the Plutonian generations given for each Sign are only the ones dating back to 1762. Any further back in time would be a multiple or 248 years before the one given.

Pluto in Aries
 ♇ ♈

You are a member of the Plutonian generation (1823-1852) that witnessed the great pioneers of the New World, giving the world at large a chance for individuals to transform their lives.

Pluto in Taurus
♇ ♉

You are a member of the Plutonian generation (1852-1884) that witnessed the birth of mass production, giant companies and banks, thus giving rise to the reality of corporate power, which materially transformed the world.

Pluto in Gemini
♇ ♊

You are a member of the Plutonian generation (1884-1913) that witnessed the birth of new and powerful communications and transport, like the telephone, automobile and aeroplane.

Pluto in Cancer
♇ ♋

You are a member of the Plutonian generation (1912-1939) that encompassed both World War One and the start of World War Two. In Plutonian terms this was a struggle for power and omnipotence, which threatened the security of the world, thereby permanently transforming our sense of personal and national security.

Pluto in Leo
♇ ♌

You are a member of the Plutonian generation (1937-1958) that witnessed World War Two and the advent of nuclear power and the atomic bomb. These and other events pressed the world into a process of transformation from which it can no more retreat than a nuclear power station can be closed down overnight. Psychologically, the effects of this process have been to dramatize our sense of power, sex and the darker side of life and human nature. How this has affected you personally is revealed below.

Pluto in Virgo
♇ ♍

You are a member of the Plutonian generation (1956-1972) born while irreversible changes began to take place concerning healthcare and working methods and conditions. The processing and pre-packaging of food gave rise to impurities and subsequent health hazards. Working practices became far more automated and consequently depersonalized and less efficient, although the potential and intention was for quite the opposite. Similarly, more efficient means of birth control fostered the illusion of sexual inviolability when quite the reverse (sexual abuse) increased – or at least, it became more noticeable. All these matters were in fact just crises waiting to happen. Ecologically speaking, they manifested as the poisoning of our Planet reaching critical proportions. As an individual, you are a bristle in a gigantic new broom that is supposed to sweep clean. Initially, this can just be experienced as an obsession over work and health as a deeper sense of service and purity arises from your unconscious mind.

Pluto in Libra
♇

You are a member of the Plutonian generation (1971-1984) born during a period when marriage and social values underwent profound change. A typical example of this would be growing up in a single parent family. Fashion took on a darker, more obsessive aspect with styles such as punk and heroin chic, devolving into fixations regarding physical looks, excessive cosmetic surgery, and anorexia and bulimia. So this was, and gave rise to, a time of great uncertainty concerning social justice and the social norm. As a generation you are rewriting the social rulebook, but initially this means having almost no rulebook at all. And because profound Pluto functions poorly in relatively superficial Libra, this will all take quite some time.

Pluto in Scorpio
♇ ♏

You are a member of the Plutonian generation (1983-1995) that witnesses the inevitable surfacing of previously hidden or repressed facts and feelings. The deeper and more profound qualities of human nature appear along with, or in some cases are preceded by, the most degenerate and coarse aspects of it. This is like a gigantic boil that just had to burst and the poison be cleared up, actually forcing us to find more thorough and effective means of healing and dealing with society's ills.

Pluto in Sagittarius
♇ ♐

You are a member of the Plutonian generation (1995-2008) that sees religiosity and international disputes reaching critical mass. So religious fanaticism and conflict will pockmark the way, as will an obsession with centralization. As a response to such simplistic extremism, a more sane and humanistic philosophy will eventually be sought after, based upon a balanced combination of science and mysticism.

Pluto in Capricorn
♇ ♑

You are a member of the Plutonian generation (1762-1777) that witnessed the birth of new forms of government, most notably in the USA with the American Declaration of Independence.

Pluto in Aquarius
♇ ♒

You are a member of the Plutonian generation (1777-1799) that witnessed the transformation of the condition of the common man by granting him the power of freedom to do and act as he chose – or through him having to fight for it. The most notable examples of this being the US Constitution and Bill of Rights, the American Revolutionary War and the French Revolution.

Pluto in Pisces
♇ ♓

You are a member of the Plutonian generation (1799-1823) that witnessed the artistic and cultural expression of the mystical and universal.

PLUTO ASPECTS

NOTE that Sextile (co-operating with) and Opposition (confronting) Aspects are usually described similarly to Trine (harmonizing with) and Square (challenging) Aspects respectively, or they are occasionally described similarly to the Conjunction (uniting with). However, when this is the case, it should be borne in mind that a Sextile Aspect may require conscious awareness and effort to realize the assets and potential so described –

particularly significant in your life and personality, so I suggest that you note them as such.

Pluto Square (challenging) MidHeaven
♇ □ MC

There is something about you that is at odds with authority. You can therefore express this as either having difficulty with knowing who's boss at work, or trying to be one yourself at home – both of which difficulties can lead to loss and upheaval. This all stems back to a feeling of being crushed or subjugated in your early life in some way – so work that one out if you want a happier time of it.

Pluto Opposition (confronting) MidHeaven and in the Third House
♇ ☍ MC

Something about your father's influence or your early home life either gives you a profound ability to make your point verbally, or else it inhibits that very thing. Taking a deep look at this would either further empower your means of communication, or enable you to begin to unblock your mental self-doubt.

Pluto Opposition (confronting) MidHeaven and in the Fourth House
♇ ☍ MC

Those powerful but underlying influences in your life described below under Pluto in the Fourth House are quite profound – so I suggest you take strong note of this.

Pluto Trine (harmonizing with) MidHeaven
♇ △ MC   *OR*
Pluto Sextile (co-operating with) MidHeaven
♇ ⚹ MC

Your power potential, as I have described it here, may be used positively to further your profession, or be an integral part of its nature. So your career could well involve psychology, metaphysics, healing or wielding some form of power.

PLUTO HOUSES

Pluto in the First House
♇ 1st

You actually embody what Pluto is all about. This gives you a powerful presence and a magnetic intensity, as well as an acute and even obsessive self-consciousness. This is because it is your own identity and image itself that is undergoing a process of transformation.

False or outworn ideas of yourself attract drastic upheavals that take you down to more profound levels of consciousness. More and more you see right through to the very core of things – nothing else satisfies. As if to bear witness to this, your eyes have a penetrating gaze, or are like unfathomable pools.

This look and presence of yours has a provocative effect upon others – and this can cause you to feel quite alone at times. It is very much down to you and your psychological attitude as to whether you provoke a healing process in others as you manipulate the way they think and feel, or whether you merely antagonize them, and thereby feel even more outcast. On the other hand, don't make an apology for this unavoidable psychological effect that you have upon others, for that would just make them suspicious of your intentions. Instead, you must learn to use your powerful persona creatively.

Pluto in the Second House
♇ 2nd

Any call to transformation is aimed at your attitude towards money and possessions, and at material values in general. If your attitude is negative in some way – like desiring wealth to avoid closeness with others – then this can lead to financial upheaval, thereby forcing a change in values.

You find it easy to attract wealth in some material form, or very difficult. In both cases, the issue is the same: sooner or later you have to learn what the actual value of material things is. In other words, what is done with wealth is the significant point. If you're out to use material might to bolster a flagging ego, then you either crash or never take off.

When, on the other hand, your material assets are used generously and wisely, a never-ending supply line of material wherewithal is conferred upon you. This can reach a point where your material influence is used to alter substantially the status quo in any given area – like the regeneration of a company, building or some stricken section of the community.

Pluto in the Third House
♇ 3rd

For you, any call to transformation and for depth of experience is aimed at areas of communication such as education, everyday encounters with relatives, neighbours, etc. Indeed, such areas are usually noted for their ordinariness, and so you could well play down heavier and darker emotions such as guilt, desire, phobias and the like. Or, as a child, they may have been kept out of the way for you – or, conversely, thrust under your nose in the form of some crisis at school, the death of a brother or sister, or something that deeply disturbed your ability to learn or communicate.

Hopefully, in time you come to really appreciate the power of thoughts and words and of seemingly commonplace everyday occurrences. This appreciation could show itself as an interest in any subject that requires deep thinking – like psychology, detective work, the transforming of your local environment through tackling pollution or informing your neighbours of something of great importance.

If you actually use the written or spoken word to convey your deeper feelings, your writings will be aimed at altering the very way in which we look at life. In short, in one way or another, you aim to introduce a more profound intellectual tone to your surroundings.

Pluto in the Fourth House
♇ 4th

Your area of power and transformation is your home, family and roots generally. If you are comfortable with your family or racial background, then you truly have deep roots and a firm sense of belonging. If, however, there are shadows cast across the path, which leads back into your past, then they could haunt you with feelings of statelessness and a profound inner loneliness.

Either the positive or negative qualities will be in evidence in your domestic situation. Someone in your life, most likely your father, went about in the time of your childhood in a similarly soul-torn state. But as a child you took it personally and now you feel that the ground could open up and swallow you if you don't keep yourself very much to yourself.

If you are to prevent what amounts to self-isolation from dominating your life – or someone from still dominating your domestic scene with a heavy presence (and that could be yourself!) – then it is imperative that you exorcize such a ghost. To do this you must delve and dig into your past history until you have found what is obsessing you, and what you cannot forgive in yourself or someone else, and then actually forgive them.

Once you have accomplished this, you at last will feel that you have a power base, a home that is your castle – because it will have been built on the only foundation that will satisfy you: a deep feeling of being here on planet Earth.

Pluto in the Fifth House
♇ 5th

Power and transformation enter your life via your creative means of expression or romantic involvements. With the former, artwork, hobbies or drama can be quite heavy, death-defying or macabre. You wouldn't just paint pretty pictures for instance; you'd really be working out some deep psychological matters in your art. The same cloak of intensity affects your affairs of the heart.

Obsessiveness and a strong accent upon sex bear witness to the fact that although you may have been in it for fun at the start, as it wears on, you realize that it is souls and not just bodies that are getting close, with all the highs, lows and deep changes which this entails. And the physical result of sex, children, have an even more than usually profound effect upon you.

As an alternative to all this, you consciously or unconsciously sense what deep and turbulent waters love or art will get you into – and so you back-paddle. But, as Dante said, 'Take away my demons and you take away my angels.' In other words, your choice is between agony coupled with ecstasy, or safety coupled with frustration.

Pluto in the Sixth House
♇ 6th

Your call to transformation, and your sense of power and destiny, is encountered via your work and health. This means to say that any changes that are necessary in the way that you live will show themselves in the state of your body or in your work situation. Putting work and health together, healing and psychology could well be the nature of your actual career.

By the same token, you can be obsessive with regard to health and healthy living. Equally, or additionally, you are very thorough in dealing with any kind of physical disturbance. It is also likely that you subscribe to the theory that all diseases originate in the mind. And indeed, as if to prove it, your own body readily shows up any psychological or emotional problems. At its most extreme, a major illness or physical damage can be the event that alters the course of your life.

You are, or come to be, a great believer in thoughts being powerful and existing in their own right. A negative thought will insidiously breed an unwelcome happening. A positive thought will be the new broom that sweeps clean. Similarly, you are able to solve problems at a profound and deep level for yourself and for others. Because of this, people automatically open up in your presence – like it or not.

Pluto in the Seventh House
♇ 7th

This issue of power and transformation presents itself to you in your dealings with others – especially in a one-to-one relationship like marriage. So you are forced to confront the true nature of your deepest fears and desires, and to establish a balance of power between you and your mate, or whoever.

This is not easy, for it necessitates some in-depth analysis of what or who in your life has been allowed to dominate you. Otherwise your partner could appear to take on the role of being the dominant one, when really it is something in yourself that is unconsciously wanting to be dominated. As if to fit this scenario, your mate may well be powerful, or disempowered too, in some way.

Both of you could possibly even enjoy this dominator/dominated kind of relationship. But sooner or later your relationship has to be psychologically debugged if you are to avoid its going through an agonizingly slow death. It is better to go into the storm, purge your doubts and fears, for upon this will follow either the refreshment of a renewed relationship, or the release of having no relationship at all.

Pluto in the Eighth House
♇ 8th

You experience power and transformation in your most intimate and critical moments and relationships. When you get close to someone or something, a deep and possibly obsessive feeling takes you over. This can lead to any number of scenarios which somehow get you in up to your neck – be it financial in the form of shared property, investments, tax, etc – or emotional in the form of ties that are very difficult to break until you have thoroughly understood what dark or deep part of your being got you into it in the first place.

By the same token, you do have a sense that there is something heavy and omnipotent lurking somewhere in the uncharted depths of your being. But you may be entirely unaware of this until some crisis of the nature I have already described brings it to the surface.

This could be a sexual involvement which elicits previously undreamed of sensations; the divorce that brings out acrimony and greed where previously there was love and tenderness; or even a brush with death itself. These are some of the possible manifestations that may have to occur on order to remind you that there is an undeniably deep and powerful truth in life.

Pluto in the Ninth House

♇ 9th

Power and transformation come to you via your beliefs and moral standards. You have deeply held convictions concerning these matters, or else you will feel hounded until you discover them. Behind all this you could have a 'hell-fire and damnation' sort of image of God, which can either put you off religion altogether or make you into a zealot.

At any rate, you are fiercely opinionated. Sooner or later, you have to forge a reverence for some set of laws and beliefs that will guide you along your way, even though they will constantly go through changes. All this can give a prophetic sense of doom or the 'Judgement Day'. The prospect of death also plays an important part in your philosophy of life. Travel and higher education are activities that can change your life. So if transformation is what you are after, then get thee to a college or an airport!

Pluto in the Tenth House

♇ 10th

Power and transformation occurs for you in the field of your professional life or public position. This means that power can either be bestowed upon you or taken away, or both. The reason for this is that there is a hidden agenda here that says that any such great influence as you might have, is ultimately only maintained when used for the common good. (Ex-President Nixon is a notorious example.) However, this Plutonian condition can strike before you have even grown up and realized any ambitions at all.

This happens as the result of a parent of other figure of authority – but usually your mother – being an overshadowing force imposing their ambitions or agenda upon your own. If this is the case, sooner or later there will occur some kind of catharsis in respect of what worldly position means to you.

Alternatively, such a figure – your mother or someone else – instils in you a pronounced sense of your own destiny. As far as the nature of your career itself, this will most probably have something to do with what is powerful or hidden – like big business, detective, research or undercover work, crime, psychology, astrophysics or anything concerned with delving or dealing.

Pluto in the Eleventh House

♇ 11th

Life's transformations are most likely to occur through friendships, group situations or any pursuit that furthers some cause. In fact, a crisis of some kind could well lead to your taking up a cause. A strong reformist streak can then develop in you, and you'd need to be prepared to stand up and be counted at some stage.

Because you emanate, consciously or otherwise, this aura of social change or upheaval, others are likely to react against it by projecting their own unconscious feelings (good and bad) on to you. They then reject you or are strongly drawn towards you, or both, alternately.

Looked at in another sense, this propensity gives you a talent as a group leader and for paving a way into the future. You probably do not have that many friends, but the few that you do have are friends for life. Such friendships plumb the depths of your being.

Pluto in the Twelfth House
♇ 12th

You have powerful hidden resources, which could also be repressed. This is either because you would abuse them if they were too readily available to you, or because you feel that if they were unleashed, anti-social or even evil forces would spew forth. All of this might be totally unconscious, but the fact remains that eventually, voluntarily or otherwise, this power is drawn out in the form of some crisis or psychological process.

Until then you can feel as if you are carrying the weight of the world around, giving rise to work difficulties, absenteeism, not getting along with co-workers or something more ominous. Essentially, your personal process of transformation is concerned with changing the state of those things, which oppress humanity as a whole. But you have to begin by mucking out your own closet.

A fear of death itself could be the prime occupant, possibly stemming from an early experience – in the womb even. Once you have begun to vanquish some of these demons, then angels in the form of psychological or spiritual insights will take shape to assist you further in your delving and healing.

THE TIMELINE PROFILE

Transits – How they Work

The Graphic Planner

Creating a Timeline Profile

Using a Timeline Profile

The Timeline Profile Interpretations

Transcan

1. TRANSITS – HOW THEY WORK

As the planets move though the heavens in their orbits they form angular relationships (Aspects) with the positions they occupied when one was born. These are called Transits. The Timeline Profile offers interpretations of their influences and possible effects, for any Month or Year of your choice, together with information and inspiration that will help you or someone else to understand their significance and thereby make the most of them. Rather than seeing them as predicting events, a good way of looking at Transits is in much the same way as a farmer would regard the seasons and the weather. Apart from there being 'good' and 'bad' weather forecasts, there are also 'seasons' when certain jobs must be done and when certain 'fruits' can be reaped. But the one depends upon the other; if you do not plant any 'seeds' and tend to their development then there won't be any 'crops' to harvest – no matter how 'good' the 'weather'. Likewise, good deeds from the past will bring good fortune now or in the future, when the time is 'ripe'.

2. THE GRAPHIC PLANNER

Transits *visually* take the form of a Graphic Planner or overview of the Year or Month in question, which you can use to see at a glance what is happening when. It is easier to use if you have this printed separately – see opposite when you come to **Creating A Timeline Profile.** You do not have to use a Planner, you can simply read in plain writing – in the Timeline Profile to come – what influences are happening when, and what they mean.

Referring to the example on the opposite page, in the far left-hand column is written row by row the name of the planet making the influence – the **Transiting** Planet – abbreviated to the first three letters e.g. Nep = Neptune.

This is followed in the second column by the kind of influence it is making, the Aspect, abbreviated thus:

Abbrev.	Full Name	Glyph	Meaning, nature of influence
Cnj	Conjunction	☌	Intensifying; New Cycle beginning
Sqr	Square	□	Challenging/Breaking through effect
Opp	Opposition	☍	Confronting/Awareness-producing effect
Tri	Trine	△	Supporting/Rewarding/Way-opening effect
Sxt	Sextile	✳	Assisting, Rewarding-effort effect

Then in the third column is the planet in the Birth Chart that is being influenced in this way – the **Radix** Planet – abbreviated in the same way as the Transiting Planet.

Finally, to the right of these columns, you'll see the Transit influences themselves depicted as bars as they occur through time, indicated along the top as dates or months. The Transits fade in and fade out and, as a rule, the darker the bar the stronger the influence is. This is because the Aspect being made is then closest to or at its epicentre, but any Transit's effect and timing can be affected by other Transits occurring near it timewise.

So, in our example, we can see that one Transit occurring during 2003 is Neptune Opposition Mercury – Nep Opp Mer. Its first 'wave' of influence is from the beginning of

Year Transits from January 2003 (Example: George W. Bush)

2003	Jan	Feb	Mar	Apr	May	Jun	Jul	Aug	Sep	Oct	Nov	Dec
Jup Tri MC												
Sat Sxt MC												
Jup Cnj ASC												
Jup Sxt Sun												
Jup Sxt Moo												
Jup Cnj Mer												
Jup Cnj Ven												
Jup Cnj Mar												
Jup Sxt Jup												
Jup Sqr Ura												
Jup Sxt Ura												
Jup Cnj Plu												
Sat Cnj Sun												
Sat Sxt Ven												
Sat Sxt Mar												
Sat Sqr Nep												
Nep Opp Mer												
Nep Opp Plu												
Plu Sxt Moo												
Plu Tri Ven												
Plu Sxt Jup												
Plu Opp Ura												

Transits: A Graphic Planner (for a Year Profile)

January to the very beginning of February, then again from ealy September to early December. Note that from the shading of the first period it is apparent that it began before the start date of 1 January (see 'Repeating Waves' on page 234 for more about the recurrence of Transits).

Overleaf it is explained how you create a Graphic Planner – along with the Timeline Profile itself where the influences of all the Transiting Planets in play during the Month or Year of your choice are interpreted.

3. CREATING A TIMELINE PROFILE

1. If you haven't already, **install** *The Instant Astrologer* software from the CD according to the instructions.

2. Open the program and you will see you have FOUR CHOICES:
1. Personality Profile
2. Timeline Profile
3. Relationship Profile
4. Quit

TRANSIT ASPECT TYPE	STRENGTH AND SIGNIFICANCE
Conjunct (intensifying)	This is a very strong influence. It energizes the situation in hand and both forces and enables you to advance and grow. This is a *New Cycle Beginning* and as such may indeed mark the start of some new chapter or outlook – but then so can the Square and Opposition.
Square (challenging)	This is a strong to medium influence that challenges you to develop in proportion to your relevant strengths and weaknesses.
Opposition (confronting)	This is a strong influence, and usually attracts confrontations that in turn increase your awareness of the matter concerned.
Trine (supporting)	This is a medium-strength influence that allows you to make progress with relative ease and support. It rewards past efforts.
Sextile (assisting)	This is a mild influence, and you probably need to apply some conscious effort in order to reap its benefits.

Sun Square (challenging) Sun
☉ □ ☉
Sun Opposition (confronting) Sun   *OR*
☉ ☍ ☉

Key phrases: Ego Conflicts – Me Versus The Rest – Cool It!

This is not a time to see eye-to-eye with others, for you are confrontation prone, whether you like it or not. You can use this effect to get a reading of how you and another, or the world in general, squares up to you, but by and large it is best during these few days either to take the line of least resistance, or to soldier on if needs must.

Sun Trine (supporting) Sun
☉ △ ☉
Sun Sextile (assisting) Sun   *OR*
☉ ✶ ☉

Key phrases: Smooth Running – Opening Doors – No Worries

You are in synch with life today – at least, in the context of whatever else is going on for you astrologically at this time. So now is when you can gain co-operation from others, and be generally in tune and in gear. You could also receive assistance from someone, someone who possibly who has power or authority.

Sun Conjunct (intensifying) Moon – New Cycle Beginning
☉ ☌ ☽

Key phrases: Highlighting Emotions – Starting Out or Over – Vitalizing Feelings

This is a good time to make it clearer to yourself and/or others what the emotional score is. It could also be the beginning of a new and fresh way of relating. Depending on your usual emotional disposition, you feel more energized on a feeling level. If you wish to receive something helpful or advantageous, then put yourself in line for it now because you are likely to get a good result.

Sun Square (challenging) Moon
☉ □ ☽   **OR**
Sun Opposition (confronting) Moon
☉ ☍ ☽

Key phrases: Feeling Split – Emotional Realization – Facing the Facts

You could find yourself in two minds about a certain issue. Such could in turn give rise to discontent and conflict of purpose. You may find yourself in disputes with family members, or feeling generally at odds with the world around you. Succumbing to negative feelings would however be missing the point as this influence offers you the opportunity to see the emotional score, to be less subjective, read the writing on the wall and obey what it says. You can sort out problems as long as you are emotionally honest enough to accept what is your responsibility and what is someone else's – for this is now being made clear.

Sun Trine (supporting) Moon
☉ △ ☽   **OR**
Sun Sextile (assisting) Moon
☉ ✶ ☽

Key phrases: Clear Feelings – Equilibrium – Understanding Needs – Inner Calm

This is an excellent time for getting in touch with both yourself and others. This is because you now experience an optimum balance between what you want and need, between what you think and feel. So you are more than usually able to see things in a healthy light, with a minimum of misunderstanding. Seeing eye-to-eye, creating agreements or settling disputes is also favoured. Moreover, problems arising from childhood traumas may be successfully explored and set on the road to resolution.

Sun Conjunct (intensifying) Mercury – New Cycle Beginning
☉ ☌ ☿   *OR*
Sun Square (challenging) Mercury
☉ □ ☿   *OR*
Sun Opposition (confronting) Mercury
☉ ☍ ☿

Key phrases: State of Mind – Stimulating Interests – Highlighting Anxieties

Life's spotlight is focussed upon the way you think and perceive things now. So this can mean many things, depending upon what you have currently been doing with your mental faculties or to your nervous system. Studying, planning, reading, travelling short distances, making conversation, arguing the point, gossiping, worrying or just plain thinking – these are some examples of Mercurial activities that are presently being intensified. This means that more energy is available to you for putting into one or more of these situations, or that you should learn to slow down, trust, think and talk a little less, and listen and feel more.

Sun Trine (supporting) Mercury
☉ △ ☿   *OR*
Sun Sextile (assisting) Mercury
☉ ✶ ☿

Key phrases: Working Well – Being on the Case – Making Contacts and Connections

You work and communicate well now, and are generally on the ball with respect to any matters that relate to the daily business of living. You also have a better sense of the pros and cons of how you normally go about such things, giving you the opportunity to correct poor attitudes or methods, and to capitalize or improve on the good ones.

Sun Conjunct (intensifying) Venus – New Cycle Beginning
☉ ☌ ♀   *OR*
Sun Square (challenging) Venus
☉ □ ♀   *OR*
Sun Opposition (confronting) Venus
☉ ☍ ♀

Key phrases: Highlighting Love Life, Pleasure, and Material and Social Values

What shows now is the 'state of the art'. In other words, whatever you are doing or not doing with regard to filling your own and others' lives with some love and beauty is brought to your attention. So such areas as relationships, arts and crafts, social activities, buying and spending, or things that add a sweetness to life are presently to the fore. Positively, this can take the form of generosity, a love encounter, a party, a general sense of happiness, or anything that helps to make life attractive and more worth living.

Negatively, finding yourself being mean, lonely, indulgent, excessive, vain or superficial would point to the fact that a genuine sense of worth and the ability to give or receive love is somewhat lacking in your life.

Sun Trine (supporting) Venus
☉ △ ♀   *OR*
Sun Sextile (assisting) Venus
☉ ⚹ ♀

Key phrases: Being In Tune – Social Harmony – Making The Peace

Things are well starred socially right now, and if there is a love interest, then you can be fairly sure that if things are going to go your way at all, they will do so now. Making amends, launching any social event, being artistically creative or entertained – these are all liable to go with a swing at this time.

Sun Conjunct (intensifying) Mars – New Cycle Beginning – HOT!
☉ ☌ ♂   *OR*
Sun Square (challenging) Mars – HOT!
☉ □ ♂   *OR*
Sun Opposition (confronting) Mars – HOT!
☉ ☍ ♂

Key phrases: Highlighting Personal Drive, Sex Life, Courage and Decisiveness

Mars is symbolic of that force within and around you that make it possible to go for and get something or someone; it also represents the urge and the right to do so. How good or bad or indifferent you are when it comes to expressing your Mars qualities is currently an issue. Being active, independent, forthright or bold now is a sign that you know what you are after, and how and when to act. Experiencing – either in yourself or another – anger, abusiveness or excessive use of force would be a sign that you need to look at what you yourself are angry about, at what you want, and at what you must do in order to obtain it or so that you no longer want it.

Sun Trine (supporting) Mars
☉ △ ♂   *OR*
Sun Sextile (assisting) Mars
☉ ⚹ ♂

Key phrases: Getting Things Done – Healthy Self-Assertion – Feeling Fit

Getting down to things, opening doors, launching yourself with energy and enthusiasm, attaining the object of your desires – these are some of the advantages of this influence. In proportion to your usual powers of self-assertion, asserting yourself in any way is in tune with the general way of things at present.

Sun Conjunct (intensifying) Jupiter – New Cycle Beginning
☉ ☌ ♃   *OR*
Sun Square (challenging) Jupiter
☉ □ ♃   *OR*
Sun Opposition (confronting) Jupiter
☉ ☍ ♃

Key phrases: Highlighting Expansiveness and Faith – A Sense of Greatness

Whatever it is that you are like normally, now you are more so! Essentially, you are experiencing an urge to grow beyond yourself, and to understand matters in a more comprehensive and philosophical way. So if you do have something of this nature in mind, then now is the time to make it (begin to) happen. But what you allow yourself, and others, to do or be, has everything to do with your moral viewpoint, which is presently a vital issue. So for a more rewarding life, now and in the future, you would be wise to cultivate an optimistic and big-hearted attitude, and to be mindful that biting off more than you can chew, or making empty promises, is a sure sign that you are pretending to be larger than life, rather than being actually as large as life.

Sun Trine (supporting) Jupiter
☉ △ ♃   *OR*
Sun Sextile (assisting) Jupiter
☉ ✶ ♃

Key phrases: Positive Thinking – Knowing the Plan – Goodwill – Luck

You are in a good frame of mind as you are in touch with the better sides of your life and personality. It is as if you can see how you fit in with the greater whole, you feel that everything is for the best, and you have some sense of how things will pan out alright. So with anything that is particularly oiled by having Lady Luck on your side, now is a good time to go for it, notwithstanding other influences to the contrary. You are also quite likely to encounter positive and encouraging people at this time.

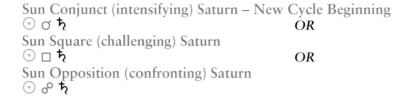

Sun Conjunct (intensifying) Saturn – New Cycle Beginning
☉ ☌ ♄   *OR*
Sun Square (challenging) Saturn
☉ □ ♄   *OR*
Sun Opposition (confronting) Saturn
☉ ☍ ♄

Key phrases: Highlighting Status and Responsibilities, Caution and Doubts

This period doesn't exactly find you in a party mood, but it does put you in a sober frame of mind that should enable you to get down to identifying what is and what is not required of you, and what is blocking your progress or view. The main trouble is that the pressure will be upon you to do just this. It is attempting to duck your responsibilities that would give you a hard time. Equally though, the thanklessness of tasks done out of a blind sense of duty, born of fear also shows up now. Even though this period lasts only a few days, time passes slowly, so use it to reflect coolly and carefully upon your position in life, without feeling panicky or depressed about it. Notwithstanding what else is indicated at present, the time to act comes later, after having made more clear your purpose and obligation.

Sun Trine (supporting) Saturn
☉ △ ♄   *OR*
Sun Sextile (assisting) Saturn
☉ ⚹ ♄

Key phrases: A Sense of Order – Highlighting Discipline and Economy

You should be functioning well over these few days, so it is a good time to get more organised, devise a plan, or even embark upon some important undertaking assuming other indications are not unfavourable. You are presently more than usually inclined to get down to what needs doing without being or feeling sidetracked by issues that do not bear directly on the job in hand. For now you are more disposed towards structure and efficiency than you are towards whims or sentimentality.

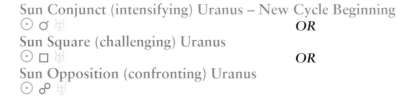

Sun Conjunct (intensifying) Uranus – New Cycle Beginning
☉ ☌ ♅   *OR*
Sun Square (challenging) Uranus
☉ □ ♅   *OR*
Sun Opposition (confronting) Uranus
☉ ☍ ♅

Key phrases: Highlighting Uniqueness and Individuality – Expect the Unexpected

How you experience this influence has everything to do with how in touch you are with what is special about life in general and yourself in particular. If you have allowed your life to become too routine and predictable than something or someone could appear on the scene to give you a shock or a jolt, or at least remind you that the world is a wild and extraordinary place. Alternatively, you could be the one to shock others by revealing what is rebellious or highly original about you. Why not make this a date with the unexpected by doing something you'd never normally do? Then with the element of surprise on your side, there is no telling what new ideas or vistas could open up in front of you.

Sun Trine (supporting) Uranus
☉ △ ♅   *OR*
Sun Sextile (assisting) Uranus
☉ ✶ ♅

Key phrases: Waking up to the Truth – Light upon the Future – The New and Unusual

Whatever else may be going on in your life, this influence helps you to see it as part of a greater pattern or long-term process of development. You also gain insights into what is unique about yourself, and others too – and you begin to appreciate more what freedom actually means. Additionally, this is a good time to involve yourself with subjects that take a greater overview of life, like science and technology, astronomy, astrology, psychology, etc.

Sun Conjunct (intensifying) Neptune – New Cycle Beginning
☉ ☌ ♆   *OR*
Sun Square (challenging) Neptune
☉ □ ♆   *OR*
Sun Opposition (confronting) Neptune
☉ ☍ ♆

Key phrases: Highlighting Sensitivity – Idealism/Escapism – Compassion/Weaknesses

What is brought to light now is something that has been happening outside of your conscious awareness, or has been kept out of sight. Obviously this can mean any number of things: for example, finding out something that's been going on behind your back; discovering a mysterious dimension of reality you only ever dreamt of; realizing that you identify more closely with certain others and their hopes and fears; or weak spots being exposed in yourself or others. In any event, it is important that you keep a firm grip on reality, yet at the same time remain open to the fact or notion that we are all mysteriously united in some way. Generally speaking, your ego is less resilient than usual, so take a back seat and watch life's picture show if you don't feel up to starring in it. Also be extra-careful with drink or drugs for highs and lows are presently very interchangeable.

Sun Trine (supporting) Neptune
☉ △ ♆   *OR*
Sun Sextile (assisting) Neptune
☉ ✶ ♆

Key phrases: Going with the Flow – Attuned to Spirit – Creativity and Entertainment

This is a fine subtle influence, which you could miss unless you are alive to the unseen, mystical or imaginative elements of life and your personality. Any kind of creative or spiritual pursuit – either active or passive – is well starred under this planetary effect. You are more attuned to subtle and emotional vibrations than usual, and possibly sense that struggling with issues only prolongs or complicates them. An enjoyable time listening or playing music, communing with Nature, or any activity involving the sea, are some of the possibilities right now.

Sun Conjunct (intensifying) Pluto – New Cycle Beginning

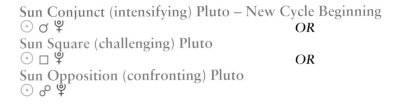

OR

Sun Square (challenging) Pluto

OR

Sun Opposition (confronting) Pluto

Key phrases: Experiencing Power – Degeneration or Regeneration

The underlying fact of life that everything is born, evolves, decays, dies and is born again, now enters your consciousness – in some way, great or small. The opportunity to tune into this cycle of birth and rebirth is well worth taking up, because it gives you a glimpse of the fact that you are a vital part of this cycle. As such, you may sense what is profound and powerful in you and your life, or what is wasteful and degenerate – but you will probably have to peer or delve some way beneath surface appearances in order to do so. You may also encounter manipulators of this power – whether benign or malignant. It could well become necessary for you to let go of decadent elements, and strive towards regenerative ones.

Sun Trine (supporting) Pluto

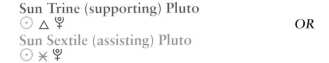

OR

Sun Sextile (assisting) Pluto

Key phrases: Repairs and Regeneration – Getting to the Bottom of It

This is a good time to start any regimen, to turn things around, to eliminate anything that has been bothering you, or simply to put what's wrong right. You feel a power coursing through you, but it is a gentle and sure power – not one that is insisting you express it no matter what. Your powers of concentration, and your stamina – physical, mental or emotional – are stronger than usual, so any demanding activity is better pursued at this time.

Sun Conjunct (intensifying) Ascendant – New Cycle Beginning

☉ ☌ AS

Key phrases: Highlighting Presentation – Putting Yourself Across Well

It's as if you now have some natural spotlight shining upon you – or you yourself are the spotlight for others, illuminating that which needs clarifying or affirming. Any event that needs to look good or go off well can be arranged now – providing you know that your birth time is absolutely accurate, because any influence to your Ascendant (or MidHeaven) depends upon this being the case. In fact, if you feel this spotlight at some time near but not during this time, this would be an opportunity to rectify your birth time; so see an astrologer if this is the case.

Sun Square (challenging) Ascendant
☉ □ AS

Key phrases: Challenging Social/Emotional Equilibrium – Importance of Sharing

Seeing eye-to-eye with others is not easy now, so do not expect to gain any favours, persuade anyone or feel that at peace with the world. This is really a test of your equilibrium, so just balance on that wire and don't try any clever tricks.

Sun Opposition (confronting) Ascendant
☉ ☍ AS

Key phrases: Highlighting Relationship Issues – Acceding to Others

The solar spotlight is now upon your relationships or social life in general. Quite what certain others mean and are doing in your life becomes clearer now – so, pay attention! Significant others will appear even more significant, and what or who does not matter will be obvious, or it should be. Alternatively, or additionally, someone important could now enter your life, especially if there are other more longstanding influences occurring, which indicate such an encounter.

Sun Trine (supporting) Ascendant
☉ △ AS   *OR*
Sun Sextile (assisting) Ascendant
☉ ✳ AS

Key phrases: Highlighting Personal Self-Expression – Being a Social Animal

Your urge and ability to mix with others is marginally increased for the time being; you also come across in a more coherent fashion than usual. So gathering people around you, or getting out and about (depending on what is more suitable), is a good idea, for you make a good impression. If you usually like to 'play to the crowd', you shine even more now. If not, then now you might possibly surprise yourself.

Sun Conjunct (intensifying) MidHeaven – New Cycle Beginning
⊙ ♂ MC

Key phrases: Highlighting or Boosting Career Status – A Lift from Authority

If you want to look your best before those who can help you in the material world, then now is your window – providing of course that there are no deleterious influences abounding. You could also have a better eye for opportunity, and be able to see what is the best course to take with respect to your profession or vocation.

Sun Square (challenging) MidHeaven
⊙ □ MC

Key phrases: Private Life/Public Life Balance – Parental Conflicts

Try and meet both personal and business obligations equally, even though everything will be coming at you from all sides. This only lasts a few days, so don't over-react to difficulties and thereby make things as bad as they momentarily appear to be.

Sun Opposition (confronting) MidHeaven
⊙ ☍ MC

Key phrases: Highlighting Inner, Domestic or Family Life – Importance of Roots

Presently it is better to invest energy in the private side of your life and, as much as possible, to draw in your horns as far as the outside world is concerned. Even though it might seem imperative to deal with pressures from work, officialdom, etc, being around the home and spreading a little sunshine amongst those near and dear to you will be most rewarding, and also avoid conflicts with regard to professional or public affairs, which is a possibility right now. Cutting a low profile and getting more in touch with your roots, closer to what or who is familiar to you, is the ticket right now.

Sun Trine (supporting) MidHeaven
⊙ △ MC   *OR*
Sun Sextile (assisting) MidHeaven
⊙ ✳ MC

Key phrases: Career Advances or Opportunities – Managing Home and Business

At this time you feel more able to see a balance or connection between who you are in public and who you are in private. Examples of this could be bringing a colleague home, or introducing a family member to the way you work. Also, if you have been paying too much attention to one area and not enough to the other, now you can see how to accomplish this, and begin to do so.

2. MOON TRANSITS

As the Moon moves very quickly compared to all the other Planets – one whole cycle in a month – it is not usually worth recording them, so we haven't here. It is possible to track the Moon's Transits, which, although it can be interesting, can wind up making one a bit 'astroneurotic'!

However, it is worth tracking the effect of New and Full Moons on one's Chart. This can be done by ascertaining when they occur (from a diary for instance) and then seeing if they coincide with a Sun Transit. Whatever that Sun Transit is will then be far more noticeable and significant.

3. MERCURY TRANSITS

These are not that dynamic, but can cause you to feel mentally sharper or more on edge – depending on the type of Aspect being made, and your own temperament. Mercury Transits are fleeting (a day or two) unless the Planet has gone stationary (see Birth Chart on page 31) when one will last up to seven days or so. One whole cycle or orbit of Mercury around the Sun is 88 days.

Mercury Transit Interpretations

WHEN READING THESE TRANSIT INTERPRETATIONS, BEAR THE FOLLOWING IN MIND: Because the meanings of Opposition (confronting) Transits are usually similar to Square (challenging) Transits – and both of these are occasionally similar to the Conjunction (intensifying) Transits – the same interpretation is given below the relevant Transit name headings, each separated by 'OR'. Also, Sextile (assisting) Transits are usually the same meaning as Trine (supporting) Transits, and they are set out in the same way, that is, Transit name headings separated by 'OR'. Although any actual differences felt can be fairly subjective, it is worth noting – from the table overleaf – the distinct **Strength and Significance** that each can take on, especially between the Trine and Sextile.

Mercury Conjunct (intensifying) Sun – New Cycle Beginning
☿ ☌ ☉

Key phrases: Connected to your Life – The Thinking Heart – Wired

You feel wired in to what is most important to you now, so it is a good time for seeing to jobs in hand, saying what has to be said, and generally setting to work on affairs. If you start feeling a bit overwrought, then take few deep breaths – or, better still, do some breathing exercises. If you are prone to insomnia this influence could exacerbate it, as you are more than usually inclined to working everything out in your head. As your mind and ego are kind of hooked up together now, try not to blurt out the first thing that comes into your head for you may regret it. For the same reason, for maximum mental harmony, keep your mind focussed only upon serious issues or, paradoxically, upon humorous ones.

TRANSIT ASPECT TYPE	STRENGTH AND SIGNIFICANCE
Conjunct(intensifying)	This is a very strong influence. It energizes the situation in hand and both forces and enables you to advance and grow. This is a *New Cycle Beginning* and as such may indeed mark the start of some new chapter or outlook – but then so can the Square or Opposition.
Square (challenging)	This is a strong to medium influence that challenges you to develop in proportion to your relevant strengths and weaknesses.
Opposition (confronting)	This is a strong influence, and usually attracts confrontations that in turn increase your awareness of the matter concerned.
Trine (supporting)	This is a medium-strength influence that allows you to make progress with relative ease and support. It rewards past efforts.
Sextile (assisting)	This is a mild influence, and you probably need to apply some conscious effort in order to reap its benefits.

Mercury Square (challenging) Sun
☿ □ ☉   **OR**
Mercury Opposition (confronting) Sun
☿ ☍ ☉

Key phrases: Communication Challenges – Pressing Work Issues – Spats

If you start feeling a bit overwrought during this time, then take few deep breaths – or, better still, do some breathing exercises. If you are prone to insomnia this influence could exacerbate it, as you are more than usually inclined to working everything out in your head. As your mind and ego are kind of hooked up together now, try not to blurt out the first thing that comes into your head for you may regret it. For the same reason, for maximum mental harmony, keep your mind focussed only upon serious issues or, paradoxically, upon humorous ones. Arguing for arguing's sake could be a waste of time and energy now, and also could get you into hotter water than you'd bargained for.

Mercury Trine (supporting) Sun
☿ △ ☉   **OR**
Mercury Sextile (assisting) Sun
☿ ✶ ☉

Key phrases: Easy Communication – Getting Work Done

You feel wired in to what is most important to you now, so it is a good time for seeing to jobs in hand, saying what has to be said, and generally setting to work on affairs. You are more able to synchronize your efforts and deliberations with those of other people at this time, so coming to agreements and getting good work done on a co-operative basis are strongly favoured. Travel arrangements and making connections are far likely to go smoothly too.

Mercury Conjunct (intensifying) Moon - New Cycle Beginning
☿ ☌ ☽

Key phrases: Communicating Feelings – Good Memory

The everyday pace and occurrences of life now take on an extra importance. You therefore devote more time to domestic and neighbour relations, and possibly get around your locale more than usual. Time could be wasted with gossiping and small talk – then again, it might be the very thing that makes you feel in tune with your immediate environment. You are more mentally in touch with your feelings at this time, so you may learn a lot on this front, as well as making it clear to others how you feel and, conversely, receiving from them how they feel. Saying too much could be something to watch out for.

Mercury Square (challenging) Moon
☿ □ ☽   **OR**
Mercury Opposition (confronting) Moon
☿ ☍ ☽

Key phrases: Logic Versus Feelings – Gossip and Trivia

Time could be wasted with gossiping and small talk – then again, it might be the very thing that makes you feel in tune with your immediate environment. You are more mentally in touch with your feelings at this time, so you may learn a lot on this front, as well as making it clear to others how you feel and, conversely, receiving from them how they feel. Saying too much could be something to watch out for, as also would be getting into a confrontation with a neighbour, colleague or family member. Then again, it could be precisely such a confrontation that made you more aware of your own and another's feelings, generally speaking or with regard to some specific matter.

Mercury Trine (supporting) Moon
☿ △ ☽   *OR*

Mercury Sextile (assisting) Moon
☿ ⚹ ☽

Key phrases: Contacting Feelings - Easy Conversation - Interest and Sympathy
Things are more likely to fall into place now because you have a greater than usual sense of give and take. You talk but also listen, or vice versa. Enquiry is met with relevant response. Allowed to run on like this, this period can become very stimulating and informative, both emotionally and intellectually. Any intercommunications, personal or business, are favoured at this time.

Mercury Conjunct (intensifying) Mercury – New Cycle Beginning
☿ ☌ ☿

Key phrases: Sharp Mind – Agitated Mind – Busy at Work – Criticism

Your mental processes are to the fore right now, so your usual manner of thinking and of verbally interacting is highly noticeable – for good or ill. You could find yourself being on the ball and very efficient or, alternatively, fretting and fussing as you strive to impose logical order on to all you are involved with. Then again, you may find someone else doing this to you and get very irritated. It should be clear what state your mental powers are in right now. Interactions with neighbours or local environmental issues could now prove significant.

Mercury Square (challenging) Mercury
☿ □ ☿   *OR*

Mercury Opposition (confronting) Mercury
☿ ☍ ☿

Key phrases: Disagreement – Nervous Energy – The Devil Makes Work for Idle Hands

Irritation, a lack of relevance, bad communication, work setbacks, inappropriate thinking – these are some of the things that could dog you at present. To avoid such frustrations or simply feeling at a loose end, find an optimum environment for getting down to what has to be done. This could well mean working on your own somewhere, or keeping intrusions down to a minimum in some other way. All forms of communication could become a nuisance or be unreliable, with the proverbial wires getting crossed. Again, seek to minimize difficulties by avoiding having important decisions dependent upon making a specific contact or travel connection. Look for a more suitable time for such activities.

Mercury Trine (supporting) Mercury
☿ △ ☿   *OR*
Mercury Sextile (assisting) Mercury
☿ ✶ ☿

Key phrases: Flow of Communication – Working and Thinking Well – Connected

All Mercurial activities, such as mental or manual work, studying, communications, travel, contact making, etc., are favoured now. You are generally on good form intellectually, and seem to pick the right moment to make that call, the right way to say something, and put your finger on the easiest solution. Co-operative ventures and interactions with neighbours or siblings are also well starred.

Mercury Conjunct (intensifying) Venus – New Cycle Beginning
☿ ☌ ♀   *OR*
Mercury Trine (supporting) Venus
☿ △ ♀   *OR*
Mercury Sextile (assisting) Venus
☿ ✶ ♀

Key phrases: Loving Words – Artistic Expression – The Art of Diplomacy

You know what pleases now – whether for yourself or someone else. At the same time, you know what does not please! All this gives you a good sense of what appeals or sells, so this is an excellent time for putting together anything that you want to go down well. Art, public relations, discussion, performing, charm and amusement – these are some of the things the positive expression or experience of which are at your fingertips right now. If you wish to make known what is on your mind in an appreciable or agreeable way, do it now.

Mercury Square (challenging) Venus
☿ □ ♀   *OR*
Mercury Opposition (confronting) Venus
☿ ☍ ♀

Key phrases: Not Saying or Seeing it Right – The Need for Diplomacy

This is a time when logical thought is at odds with the emotional or aesthetic side of life. Not seeing eye-to-eye with a member of the opposite sex is highly likely, as one of you wants to make sense of things, while the other wants to feel right about something. One of you might want to talk while the other wants to experience affection or sensual pleasure. None of this need pose a big problem unless you let it, for this is just a passing phase when you are out of phase with whoever is close to you. It is also a time when work issues can get in the way of personal ones, or vice versa, so avoid mixing business with pleasure. If you already have been doing so, then this could prove an awkward time for you. Sorting out love problems is quite likely, and desirable too. But be wary of the above-described inclination of speaking in different 'languages' to one another. Try to meet each other half way – it's the only way at present.

Mercury Conjunct (intensifying) Mars – New Cycle Beginning
☿ ☌ ♂

Key phrases: Forceful Words and Thinking – Count to Ten – Getting a Lot Done

How you experience this influence very much depends upon how sure you are of asserting yourself generally. If such can be a weak point for you, then now you are likely not to speak out when you should have, or to say what was best unsaid, or to say it awkwardly or apparently arrogantly. It is as if everything has bells on, and the slightest wrong word or movement sets them jangling. Conversely, if you are usually good at asserting yourself, then now you do so even more effectively and eloquently. In both cases, however, there is a danger of speaking out of turn or of saying something you come to regret – so try to think before speaking – or acting, for that matter.

Mercury Square (challenging) Mars
☿ □ ♂   **OR**

Mercury Opposition (confronting) Mars
☿ ☍ ♂

Key phrases: Forceful Words and Thinking – Count to Ten – Getting a Lot Done

It is as if everything has bells on now, and the slightest wrong word or movement sets them jangling. There is a danger of speaking out of turn or of saying something you come to regret, so try to think before speaking – or acting, for that matter. You may feel justified in getting heated over a certain issue, but there is a strong possibility that the only satisfaction you get ultimately is from merely feeling justified. If your 'opponent' is so disposed, they could make you eat your words at a later date, or you may not have a 'later date' to say anything at all, justifiable or otherwise. At this time it pays to look at what it is in you that causes you to feel ineffectual or overlooked in any way. This will not only supply you with useful information, which you can then do something constructive about, but it would prevent you having a run-in with someone or something (like a car or sharp object) that has nothing to do with it other than the fact that they trigger your anger and frustration which is born of a complex about self-assertion and getting what you want in life.

Mercury Trine (supporting) Mars

☿ △ ♂   *OR*

Mercury Sextile (assisting) Mars

☿ ⚹ ♂

Key phrases: Healthy Self-Assertion – Getting a Lot Done

Your mind is now in gear with your body, so plan now, if you can, for anything that needs such an advantage. Sports, debate, selling, effective communication, getting your foot in the door – these are just some of the pursuits that you are presently more likely to excel in than you would normally. Any job that has been daunting you, and you have been putting off, set to work on it now.

Mercury Conjunct (intensifying) Jupiter – New Cycle Beginning

☿ ☌ ♃   *OR*

Mercury Square (challenging) Jupiter

☿ □ ♃   *OR*

Mercury Opposition (confronting) Jupiter

☿ ☍ ♃

Key phrases: Saying Too Much – Not Seeing the Forest for the Trees

You are now put in touch with all you need to know. However, this can be a double-edged weapon, for on the one hand it could find you able to organize various items or activities into an effective whole or, on the other hand, find you confused as ideas and conflicting considerations flood your mind, giving rise to a 'brain-jam'. Marshalling your thoughts is therefore both the issue and opportunity at present. Ultimately, you are gaining some kind of understanding now, be it about something specific or something general. Out of this, a philosophical overview can be arrived at, thereby accommodating anything that is presently going on in your life. Another possible expression is thinking, speaking or acting out of a sense of opinion rather than based on a firm fact. Such succumbing to generalizations posing as the truth could set you up for embarrassment or a lot of wasted time, or both, as you bluff and exaggerate your way into or out something. So get the facts straight – that is, unless you are quite happy to pontificate. Dealing with foreign matters or people could also be an issue now – again, worthy of detailed consideration.

Mercury Trine (supporting) Jupiter

☿ △ ♃   *OR*

Mercury Sextile (assisting) Jupiter

☿ ⚹ ♃

Key phrases: Seeing the Whole – Getting a Plan – Philosophical Thinking

Organization and furtherance are the allies available to you at present. Having all the facts at your fingertips, seeing how the general fits in with the particular, linking the local to the global, the everyday to the profound – perceptions like these now come more easily to you, allowing you to put forward, create or resolve whatever issues are in front of you. Whether it is finding the meaning of things, or translating one thing into another, your deductive mind and intuitive mind are now working in concert. Now is the time when you can accurately get the picture, or be put in it.

Mercury Conjunct (intensifying) Saturn – New Cycle Beginning
☿ ☌ ♄   **OR**
Mercury Square (challenging) Saturn
☿ □ ♄   **OR**
Mercury Opposition (confronting) Saturn
☿ ☍ ♄

Key phrases: Need to Organize Thinking – Heavy Thoughts – Officialdom

This is when you can or have to get down to some serious thinking or work. Failure to do what needs doing can give rise to depression or pressure from someone or something that has authority over you. Basically your mind now turns to whatever is your responsibility. Whether or not you are alive to what that is and knuckle down to it, makes the difference between this being a heavy or efficient time. It is definitely not a time for woolly thinking and escapism, because you could put yourself in line for some kind of bad reaction or payback, now or later on. This is not supposed to be a 'fun' time, so do not frustrate or exhaust yourself trying to make out that it is. It is a time for work and effort, and you will feel far better and lighter as a result of simply doing what has to be done – or what you have been putting off.

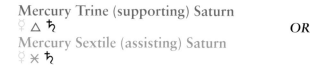

Mercury Trine (supporting) Saturn
☿ △ ♄   **OR**
Mercury Sextile (assisting) Saturn
☿ ✶ ♄

Key phrases: Getting Down to it – Efficient Thinking and Speaking – Officialdom

Now you can do with relative ease those boring tasks that you may usually put off. Mental discipline comes more naturally to you now, and people in authority, like bosses or officials, can be dealt with more effectively – they themselves will also seem more amenable or efficient. Any kind of work, study or communication is favoured now, but more so the practical rather than the creative type. You find it easier, and more immediately satisfying, to get organized. Things fall into place, especially if you do, or have done, the groundwork.

Mercury Conjunct (intensifying) Uranus – New Cycle Beginning
☿ ☌ ♅   *OR*
Mercury Square (challenging) Uranus
☿ □ ♅   *OR*
Mercury Opposition (confronting) Uranus
☿ ☍ ♅

Key phrases: Scattered Thoughts – Intuitive Thoughts – Indiscretion – Crossed Lines

Whatever is new or unusual now catches your interest. Then again it might be a disruptive element that intrudes upon your working and thinking. In any event, some new method or style is available or necessary. If you are in tune and in time with any necessary changes, then, as if by magic, the right person, thing or opportunity appears on your scene. If you are of a nervous disposition, you could feel more jumpy than usual. If this is the case, do some deep breathing or chill out in some way that you know works for you. Your mind is speeded up now, and can be very alive to ideas and inventions. A great deal depends upon how procedure-driven or free-spirited you are. The former will attracts disruption, the latter attracts innovation. Another interesting aspect of this influence is that you either find yourself stuck for words, losing your thread while speaking, or you can be very intuitive and outspoken. Then again, you may find yourself speaking out of turn, or saying something inappropriate. Everything depends on how informed you are regarding a given subject. Machines, especially computers, could play up now.

Mercury Trine (supporting) Uranus
☿ △ ♅   *OR*
Mercury Sextile (assisting) Uranus
☿ ✶ ♅

Key phrases: Synchronicity – Being in the Know – Unusual Connections

Being mentally in tune with new ideas, methods and technology is the advantage that this influence offers you. It is as if you can intuitively put your finger on whatever or whomever you need to make contact with. This is quite simply a time when you are on good mental and verbal form, so earmark it for those tasks and appointments that require such mental acuity.

Mercury Conjunct (intensifying) Neptune – New Cycle Beginning
☿ ☌ ♆   *OR*
Mercury Trine (supporting) Neptune
☿ △ ♆   *OR*
Mercury Sextile (assisting) Neptune
☿ ✶ ♆

Key phrases: The Inspired or Confused Mind – Mystical or Psychic Attunement

If you have been after an answer or inspiration from out of the ether, this is the time you are very likely to receive it. This does not mean to say that it will come whatever you are doing. It may, but it would be better to be focussed upon the issue of your concern, then – magic! Furthermore, not doing anything of a creative, therapeutic or entertaining nature at this time is possibly asking to attract absent-mindedness or strange, even paranoid, ideas. Any experience involving the natural or spirit world is good 'medicine' right now – it may even come to you unbidden.

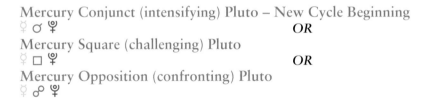

Mercury Square (challenging) Neptune
☿ □ ♆   **OR**
Mercury Opposition (confronting) Neptune
☿ ☍ ♆

Key phrases: The Inspired or Confused Mind – Deceptions or Misunderstandings

Unless you are doing something of a creative, therapeutic or entertaining nature at this time you are possibly asking to attract absent-mindedness or strange, even paranoid, ideas. Crossed lines could also dog any form of communication. So this is not a time to make any crucial decisions or broach delicate matters – it would just not come out right, or what another says or does could be taken in the wrong way. Also, being out and about you may get lost in some way or other. Sitting back and watching the world go by, or taking in a film you know you're going to like, are a few ways of safely, even enjoyably, getting through this one.

Mercury Conjunct (intensifying) Pluto – New Cycle Beginning
☿ ☌ ♇   **OR**
Mercury Square (challenging) Pluto
☿ □ ♇   **OR**
Mercury Opposition (confronting) Pluto
☿ ☍ ♇

Key phrases: Sleuthing it – Mental Preoccupation – Disturbing Undercurrents

Whatever galvanizes you or demands your complete attention is going to appear on the scene now. This could be in the form of a letter, a conversation, a book, or even an old question or feeling that pops to the surface to be looked into. Things that involve a mystery, like a whodunit, can really grab you at this time. Crime or the underworld, or the seamy side of life, can also suck you in – but probably only on a mental level – but watch it, all the same. Having to perform work that requires deep concentration is very possible.

Mercury Trine (supporting) Pluto

☿ △ ♇   ***OR***

Mercury Sextile (assisting) Pluto

☿ ✶ ♇

Key phrases: Sleuthing it – Powerful Words and Thoughts – Deep Study

If you have a job to do that requires your undivided attention, do it now. Not only is your mind on relatively good form, and can work into the night, you are also in the frame of mind where you can repel any interference powerfully, even ruthlessly if need be. You know that you have to see whatever it is through, no matter what.

Mercury Conjunct (intensifying) Ascendant – New Cycle Beginning

☿ ☌ AS

Key phrases: On the Ball – Getting Around Locally and/or Mentally

Life is interesting and busy at this time. Useful contacts and stimulating people and subjects cross your path. If you have to look anyone or anything up, you are more likely than usual to make the right connections, possess good timing. You could also receive a significant communication, or even the one you have been waiting for, especially if there are other activities occurring that indicate positive events.

Mercury Square (challenging) Ascendant

☿ □ AS

Key phrases: Missing the Point – Jumping to Conclusions – Misplaced Interest

You may find yourself in a difficult mediating position right now – or it may be you who is in need of a go-between of some sort. The trouble is, any kind of communication is likely to go awry at present, unless you have someone or something really efficient on the case. Unless you are sure you have such things well in hand, it is best to take a back seat and say very little until this usually brief period is over.

Mercury Opposition (confronting) Ascendant

☿ ☍ AS

Key phrases: Intellectual Encounters – Counselling – Criticism from Others

You now receive mental or verbal feedback concerning the way you come across, getting to know what others make of you – good or bad. You could come across someone or something that is very stimulating intellectually. If you want a reliable soundboard, now is the time to find one – but make sure you listen.

Mercury Trine (supporting) Ascendant

☿ △ AS   ***OR***

Mercury Sextile (assisting) Ascendant

☿ ⚹ AS

Key phrases: On the Ball – Getting Around Locally and/or Mentally

Life is interesting and busy at this time. Useful contacts and stimulating people and subjects cross your path. If you have to look anyone or anything up, you are more likely than usual to make the right connections, possess good timing. You could also receive a significant communication, or the even the one you have been waiting for, especially if there are other activities occurring that indicate positive events.

Mercury Conjunct (intensifying) MidHeaven – New Cycle Beginning

☿ ☌ MC

Key phrases: Business Connections – On the Case – Knowing your Pitch

This can just be a busy day at work, or one where you make an important connection with respect to your career. This could take the form of any kind of communication. Being 'out on the street' doing whatever has to be done to further your interests, is very likely – and advisable too. Someone is out there who could be very useful to you – and/or you to them.

Mercury Square (challenging) MidHeaven

☿ □ MC

Key phrases: Bad Connections at Home or at Work

Your private life and your public life tend to get in the way of one another at this time. Try to create a balance here, and avoid feeling frustrated if nothing seems to gel or if things become unstuck, for this influence is brief as a rule.

Mercury Opposition (confronting) MidHeaven

☿ ☍ MC

Key phrases: Home Interests – Family Connections – Knowing your Patch

This is a time to take an interest in the home. Gatherings that exercise the mind in the family sphere are well starred. Bringing work home could be an issue, for good or ill. Getting in touch with your roots could be very stimulating, and maybe answer a question.

Mercury Trine (supporting) MidHeaven
☿ △ MC   *OR*
Mercury Sextile (assisting) MidHeaven
☿ ✶ MC

Key phrases: Home and Business Connections – Knowing your Pitch

You now see clearly how your home and working life are dependent upon each other, and are able to balance your interests and investments in these respects. Getting private and professional figures and concerns to co-operate comes easier now. You see the whole picture and can organize you and yours more efficiently.

4. VENUS TRANSITS

These are mild and usually pleasant, creating harmony and ease. There can be an inclination to indulgence or indolence, caprice or cupidity, though! Venus Transits are fleeting (a few days) unless the Planet has gone stationary (see Birth Chart on page 31) when one will last up to ten days or so. One whole cycle or orbit of Venus around the Sun is 225 days.

Venus Transit Interpretations

WHEN READING THESE TRANSIT INTERPRETATIONS, BEAR THE FOLLOWING IN MIND: Because the meanings of Opposition (confronting) Transits are usually similar to Square (challenging) Transits – and both these are occasionally similar to the Conjunction (intensifying) Transits – the same interpretation is given below the relevant Transit name headings, each separated by 'OR'. Also, Sextile (assisting) Transits are usually the same meaning as Trine (supporting) Transits, and they are set out in the same way, that is, Transit name headings separated by 'OR'. Although any actual differences felt can be fairly subjective, it is worth noting – from the table opposite – the distinct **Strength and Significance** that each can take on, especially between the Trine and Sextile.

Venus Conjunct (intensifying) Sun – New Cycle Beginning
♀ ♂ ☉

Key phrases: Pleasant Living – Creative Awareness – Happy Day – Love Life Issues

You can now have the classic Venusian experience of, or opportunity for, love, romance, beauty, value or anything else that makes life worth living. It is also a good time to go out or get down to finding such things. On the other hand, what happens is that the level and quality of romantic or social involvement in your life is now apparent and intensified.

The effect can therefore be anything from having a really good time to feeling in need of having a good time, from looking good to feeling how uphill it is trying to look good, from experiencing love and life as sweet and fulfilling to feeling that everything is superficial and of little value.

A purchase can be just what you wanted or turn out later to be an indulgent waste of money. In the end, Venus is about finding love, beauty and value in whatever circumstances you are in, and not fretting after something that is missing or wanting. Stop

TRANSIT ASPECT TYPE	STRENGTH AND SIGNIFICANCE
Conjunct(intensifying)	This is a very strong influence. It energizes the situation in hand and both forces and enables you to advance and grow. This is a *New Cycle Beginning* and as such may indeed mark the start of some new chapter or outlook – but then so can the Square or Opposition.
Square (challenging)	This is a strong to medium influence that challenges you to develop in proportion to your relevant strengths and weaknesses.
Opposition (confronting)	This is a strong influence, and usually attracts confrontations that in turn increase your awareness of the matter concerned.
Trine (supporting)	This is a medium-strength influence that allows you to make progress with relative ease and support. It rewards past efforts.
Sextile (assisting)	This is a mild influence, and you probably need to apply some conscious effort in order to reap its benefits.

wanting and start having; stop craving and start giving. And beauty is only skin-deep if that is only as far as you look!

Venus Square (challenging) Sun
♀ □ ☉
OR
Venus Opposition (confronting) Sun
♀ ☍ ☉

Key phrases: Love At Odds With Life - Love Life Laid Bare - Lover's Tiffs

You can now have the classic Venusian experience of, or opportunity for, love, romance, beauty, value or anything else that makes life worth living. It is also a good time to go out or get down to finding such things. On the other hand, what happens is that the level and quality of romantic or social involvement in your life is now apparent and intensified.

The effect can therefore be anything from having a really good time to feeling in need of having a good time, from looking good to feeling how uphill it is trying to look good, from experiencing love and life as sweet and fulfilling to feeling that everything is superficial and of little value. A purchase can be just what you wanted or turn out later to be an indulgent waste of money.

In the end, Venus is about finding love, beauty and value in whatever circumstances you are in, and not fretting after something that is missing or wanting. Stop wanting and start having; stop craving and start giving. And beauty is only skin-deep if that is only as far as you look!

Venus Trine (supporting) Sun
♀ △ ☉
OR
Venus Sextile (assisting) Sun
♀ ✶ ☉

Key phrases: Pleasant Living – Creative Awareness – Happy Day - Love Life

You should be on good terms with the world around now, and particularly with those who are close to you. If there have been any emotional disturbances of late, then this offers an opportunity to patch up and make up. Also, if you want to go and find a certain consumer item, then you are more likely to find just what you want right now. Artistic expression and appreciation is also well starred – so get thee to a studio, instrument, keyboard or gallery, etc.

Venus Conjunct (intensifying) Moon – New Cycle Beginning
♀ ☌ ☽

Key phrases: Emotional Harmony – Accord with/between Females – Attractiveness

This is a classic time for peace and harmony. This is, of course, relative to whatever else is going on in your life astrologically, for this influence is quite gentle and not that dynamic. However, if you meet it halfway with the conscious intent to give and receive pleasure, then it can actually be a very lovely time. It particularly favours any occasion that involves the female sex coming together. In fact, female power is in the ascendant now!

Venus Square (challenging) Moon
♀ □ ☽

OR

Venus Opposition (confronting) Moon
♀ ☍ ☽

Key phrases: Emotional Discomfort – Discord with/between Females – Let it be

This need not necessarily be a difficult time – it can in fact turn out to be quite pleasurable. However, there is an inclination for social and domestic needs to get in the way of one another. This can also include disharmony on the home front, conflict between mother and lover, or being too accommodating and having to pay the price. Inherent in all this, though, is a need for peace, so that upsets are usually righted quite soon afterwards. Feelings and values may clash, but the requirements of security and harmony eventually hold sway.

Venus Trine (supporting) Moon
♀ △ ☽

OR

Venus Sextile (assisting) Moon
♀ ⚹ ☽

Key phrases: Emotional Harmony – Accord with/between Females – Attractiveness

This is a very 'female' influence in that you are inclined to use charm and receptivity rather than drive and ambition. If you are usually disposed to making things happen, now you are wise to let them happen as they will, for in this way the easiest solution or most attractive outcome will ensue. Any pursuits that require grace, diplomacy or artistic imagination, or occasions like domestic or family gatherings and parties are favoured at this time.

Venus Conjunct (intensifying) Mercury – New Cycle Beginning
♀ ☌ ☿

OR

Venus Trine (supporting) Mercury
♀ △ ☿

OR

Venus Sextile (assisting) Mercury
♀ ⚹ ☿

Key phrases: Loving Thoughts – Sweet Words – Artistic Perception – Eye for Value

The poet, writer, artist or diplomat is now strong in you, so with any situation that requires a way with words, you're the one for the job! People or things that please and interest you are now likely to appear on the scene, so gatherings and shopping trips are well starred – notwithstanding, as usual, any contrary planetary influences possibly active at this time.

Venus Square (challenging) Mercury
♀ □ ☿   *OR*
Venus Opposition (confronting) Mercury
♀ ☍ ☿

Key phrases: Bad Buys – Indiscretion – Feelings at Odds with Words

Feelings and values are presently in conflict with how things are seen or communicated. This can give rise to misunderstandings, especially between loved ones. You should be careful not to let a molehill be turned into a mountain, for really this influence should only amount to a 'life and life only' type of irritation that has no real lasting effect. However, if there is something bigger brewing beneath the surface, then this could bring it out in the open. But it is an ill wind that blows nobody any good, for with a bit of self-control and a few well-chosen, preferably loving, words, a gain rather than a loss could be on the cards. Apart from these more serious areas, be on guard against impulse buys or retorts you later come to regret.

Venus Conjunct (intensifying) Venus – New Cycle Beginning
♀ ☌ ♀   *OR*
Venus Trine (supporting) Venus
♀ △ ♀   *OR*
Venus Sextile (assisting) Venus
♀ ✶ ♀

Key phrases: Pleasure Plus – Love Life Focussed – Spending Sprees – Generosity

Pleasure and harmony are the hallmarks of this time, but so too is indulgence, so watch your pocket and appetite! Be that as it may, Venus says that at times you just must enjoy yourself and not count the cost. The value of having a good time is priceless, and this influence has that very potential. Your love life can also receive a boost now, be it the start of something big, a rekindled romance, or simply an enjoyable evening or two with one or ones that matter to you.

Venus Square (challenging) Venus
♀ □ ♀   *OR*
Venus Opposition (confronting) Venus
♀ ☍ ♀

Key phrases: Spending Too Much – Spending Too Little – Indulgence or Pleasure?

This is not really a problem except that you are inclined to overdo it – or conversely not push the boat out enough. It all depends on what place you give to love and pleasure in your life. If you are naturally generous, affectionate or fun-loving, then this time will probably be enjoyable for you – although you might have a hangover or blown budget to contend with afterwards. If you usually have a hard time giving of yourself and being socially satisfied, this influence is trying to show you why, and how you could remedy such a dilemma. The secret is generosity – on any or all levels – to be aware that another's happiness is ultimately your own too. Without tuning into Venus in a positive way, you can simply feel more anti-social, unattractive or worthless.

Venus Conjunct (intensifying) Mars – New Cycle Beginning
♀ ♂ ♂

Key phrases: Love And Sex – Romantic Opportunity – Attracting and/or Attracted

You are very much in the mood for sexual and/or romantic experience, or simply to feel socially alive. Depending upon your temperament and availability, such an experience, or at least the opportunity for it, could arise right now, or it would be a good time to plan for such an occasion, or, failing all of these, it could be a time of frustration if these matters have been put on the backburner. Then again, out of the blue could come an experience that kind of pleasurably highlights the current state of affairs in your love/sex/social life – even precipitating you into an affair or relationship. All in all though, this has the potential for an enjoyable and exciting time. Attractive, artistic or simply likeable people appear on the scene to sweeten your life – or you could be the one being this for someone else.

Venus Square (challenging) Mars
♀ □ ♂   *OR*
Venus Opposition (confronting) Mars
♀ ☍ ♂

Key phrases: Love at Odds with Sex – Attracting and/or Attracted

You are very much in the mood for sexual and/or romantic experience, or simply to feel socially alive. Depending upon your temperament and availability, such an experience, or at least the opportunity for it, could arise right now, or it would be a good time to plan for such an occasion, or, failing all of these, it could be a time of frustration if these matters have been put on the backburner. Then again, out of the blue could come an experience that kind of pleasurably highlights the current state of affairs in your love/sex/social life – even precipitating you into an affair or relationship. All in all, though, this has the potential an enjoyable and exciting time – but be wary of your own shortcomings with respect to these areas being exposed. Attractive, artistic or simply likeable people appear on the scene to sweeten your life – or you could be the one being this for someone else.

Venus Trine (supporting) Mars
♀ △ ♂   *OR*
Venus Sextile (assisting) Mars
♀ ✶ ♂

Key phrases: Love and Sex – Romantic Opportunity – Attracting and/or Attracted

This should go down in your diary as a time to have a good time socially, sexually or romantically – maybe all three! You are at your best with respect to these areas of your life and personality, so opportunity beckons. Attractive, artistic or simply likeable people appear on the scene to sweeten your life – or you could be the one being this for someone else. There should be signs right now – big or small – that it is good to be alive.

Venus Conjunct (intensifying) Jupiter – New Cycle Beginning
♀ ☌ ♃   *OR*
Venus Trine (supporting) Jupiter
♀ △ ♃   *OR*
Venus Sextile (assisting) Jupiter
♀ ✶ ♃

Key phrases: Love and Goodwill – Fun And Generosity – Joi De Vivre – Lady Luck

Depending on your usual propensity for good fortune or giving/having a good time, this influence will provide you with a strong sense and/or experience of what is enjoyable about life. Taking in anything that enlivens or entertains is very well starred now – whether you are in an active or passive role. You have a lust for life at present – but watch your pocket or appetite, unless you are quite prepared to say it was worth the price, no matter what. Any activity that requires you to put out a good or generous vibe is best booked for now. You are luckier than at other times – but bear in mind that gambling can have an agenda all of its own, so paradoxically, do not bet on it! It is better by far to see and experience this influence as a gift from the gods – but on the gods' terms. This means to say that there is something good in the air, but do not presume on it being 'good' in precisely the way you think you want it to mean. It is really an opportunity to find out what 'good' actually means.

Venus Square (challenging) Jupiter
♀ □ ♃   *OR*
Venus Opposition (confronting) Jupiter
♀ ☍ ♃

Key phrases: Overdoing it – Pleasure Versus Morality – Overspending

Depending on your usual propensity for good fortune or giving/having a good time, this influence will provide you with a strong sense and/or experience of what is enjoyable about life. Taking in anything that enlivens or entertains is very well starred now – whether you are in an active or passive role. You have a lust for life at present – but watch your pocket or appetite, unless you are quite prepared to say it was worth the price, no matter what. You feel luckier than at other times – but that feeling will very likely prove thoroughly unreliable! Any kind of promise now, made by you or to you, could also prove hard to keep, so a bit of caution and a pinch of salt is required at present.

Venus Conjunct (intensifying) Saturn – New Cycle Beginning
♀ ☌ ♄   *OR*

Venus Square (challenging) Saturn
♀ □ ♄   *OR*

Venus Opposition (confronting) Saturn
♀ ☍ ♄

Key phrases: Love and Duty – The Importance of Commitment – Having to Budget

You experience the serious or very real side of love and social involvement now. This is not a time for having fun and letting your hair down, so do not plan for this or get frustrated trying to make it so. More than likely your partner, or people in general, will come across as sober and responsible now – or in need of such qualities. If you are not with anyone, you can feel more alone than usual, or if you are prepared to take a serious rather than cynical look, you can get the measure of why you are unattached. If this is truly not an issue under this influence, then you can probably congratulate yourself on being genuinely self-sufficient. By and large, though, this period is inclined to show up the warts and weaknesses in your love and social life, including the pressure to do something about it. In any event, this means being emotionally mature and responsible and doing what has to be done, even though it is difficult. In time, such commitment will prove to be well worth it. On a financial level, you may well have to read the writing on the wall here, instead, or as well as, economizing or getting real being the call of the day.

Venus Trine (supporting) Saturn
♀ △ ♄   *OR*

Venus Sextile (assisting) Saturn
♀ ✶ ♄

Key phrases: Love and Duty – Serious Attachments – The Importance of Commitment

This brings a period of relative stability in your love life, social involvements or financial affairs. What comprises such is now shown to you, so you can take stock of whatever that is and use it to build and secure these areas for the future. You are now more inclined to be economical and dutiful, without it feeling like a wet blanket. Partners are also inclined to being more responsible and mature at present.

Venus Conjunct (intensifying) Uranus – New Cycle Beginning
♀ ☌ ♅   *OR*
Venus Square (challenging) Uranus
♀ □ ♅   *OR*
Venus Opposition (confronting) Uranus
♀ ☍ ♅

Key phrases: The Electricity of Love – Unusual Attractions – Possible Alienation

Whatever is out of the ordinary regarding sexual, social, creative or romantic involvements can appear out of the blue now. By the very nature of this influence it is hard to say what will happen. For the same reason it is best not to put too much store by whatever does, because it will most probably be a flash-in-the-pan kind of occurrence. Experimental, shocking or odd – whatever happens now can be anything from extremely exciting to somehow detached – or both even. This influence can trigger the start of an exciting relationship, but it does not predict what way it will go, for the only assurances as far as Uranus is concerned is that you can expect the unexpected, be ready to be woken up to something new. Significant coincidences can happen now, trying to tell you something about how love and life tick. Sudden attractions and/or breaks in relationship can occur also.

Venus Trine (supporting) Uranus
♀ △ ♅   *OR*
Venus Sextile (assisting) Uranus
♀ ✶ ♅

Key phrases: The Electricity of Love – Unusual Attractions – Unexpected Pleasure

There is a sparkle to sexual, social or creative activities. A certain type of freeness pervades your involvements that can give rise to new forms of pleasure of expression, exciting contacts and new groups of people. A good time to get out and experiment with life and society, to see what it has on offer. Gatherings go with a swing; people show their more original or quirky sides.

Venus Conjunct (intensifying) Neptune – New Cycle Beginning
♀ ☌ ♆   *OR*
Venus Square (challenging) Neptune
♀ □ ♆   *OR*
Venus Opposition (confronting) Neptune
♀ ☍ ♆

Key phrases: Love Dreams and Illusions – Pleasing Fantasies – Artistic Inspiration

The most romantic and ideal, but equally the most fanciful and illusory, experiences can come your way now. You are more inclined to fall in love or lust, or to be made a fool of for that matter. A more reliable expression or use of this influence is to involve yourself with some creative work, have a special time out with someone you have genuine love feelings for, or simply take in a good movie. A new relationship can arise under this influence – but remember that 'under the influence' can be all it amounts to unless you have at least one foot on the ground. Platonic involvements are quite likely – or they turn out to be! Be that as it may, this can promise to be a pleasurable, if rather heady, time. All of the above could equally just take place in your head. On a more mundane note, you could find just the item you were after, or thought you were! Very much a 'what's real?' type of time, so do not take anything at face value – be it exciting or depressing.

Venus Trine (supporting) Neptune
♀ △ ♆   *OR*
Venus Sextile (assisting) Neptune
♀ ✶ ♆

Key phrases: Love Dreams – Pleasing Fantasies – Artistic Inspiration

Any feelings or ideas regarding love, sex, music or art – or social life generally – are now nicely attuned to your ideals and visions of a better life. None of this is particularly dynamic, but this gentle, almost 'hippie' type, influence can be very enjoyable. This is a good time to put aside for any pursuit or pastime that comes into these categories.

Venus Conjunct (intensifying) Pluto – New Cycle Beginning
♀ ☌ ♇
Venus Square (challenging) Pluto
♀ □ ♇   *OR*
Venus Opposition (confronting) Pluto
♀ ☍ ♇

Key phrases: Deep or Obsessive Love – Powerful Attraction – Sexual Guilt

You find you feel deeply for someone or something, or that you want to, or that you cannot get someone or something out of your system. In any event, you are experiencing the depth and power of love or attraction – and what you do with it is down to your deepest values. Such a feeling can actually materialize as someone whom you feel strongly drawn to. It may or may not be mutual, it all depends upon that deeper state of your emotional being – is it attracting or repelling?

There is this 'Beauty and the Beast' quality to this influence, in that you could experience one of both of these extremes, with someone else on the other end, so to speak. The gulf between what is regarded as appealing and presentable as against what usually has to hide its face, feel anti-social, is a possibility now.

The trick is to go deep but not too deep, to appreciate face values, but not regard them as the entire picture. Be on guard against being manipulated – value yourself above all else – or of manipulating someone yourself, for you would only entrench yourself or get more than you bargained for. Possessiveness and jealousy can rear their heads now, which has something to do with being more in touch with what does and does not constitute genuine love. Handled right, you can get the best of both worlds: intense pleasure, deep feelings, and profound love.

Venus Trine (supporting) Pluto
♀ △ ♇   *OR*
Venus Sextile (assisting) Pluto
♀ ✳ ♇

Key phrases: Loving Deeply – Genuine Attraction – Sexual Pleasure

You are drawn to what is deep and dark – but probably without feeling controlled or compromised by such a feeling, such as can often be the case. If in a relationship, you now have the experience or opportunity of feeling in touch with the nucleus of what binds you together, yet in a way that is very right, fated even. This influence could possibly trigger the start of an important relationship, but there would probably have to be other, longer-standing planetary effects to make it so.

Venus Conjunct (intensifying) Ascendant – New Cycle Beginning
♀ ☌ AS   *OR*
Venus Opposition (confronting) Ascendant
♀ ☍ AS

Key phrases: Love in the Air – Attractive Presentation – Social Pleasures

You have a friendly, attractive aura now. So whatever it is you wish to attract, win over or simply make feel good, now is the time! You may well externalize this effect by having someone attractive come your way. Venus being Venus, however, there is no guarantee as to whether such an encounter is the real thing or just a tease. It all depends what you yourself are prone to right now. Make sure you are aware of your own worth and talent now, and do not lose yourself in someone else's apparent charms.

Venus Square (challenging) Ascendant
♀ □ AS

Key phrases: Appearance Versus Circumstances – Love the One you're with – Bad Hair Day

Venus's trickier ways can dog you now if you are not aware of them. For instance, this means that someone can catch your eye and come to compromise you later. Or your partner can appear to have not as much going for them as you think you'd like. The situation could be reversed, in both cases. In other words, do not fooled by looks or style now; stick to the main plot.

Venus Trine (supporting) Ascendant
♀ △ AS   *OR*
Venus Sextile (assisting) Ascendant
♀ ⚹ AS

Key phrases: Attractive Presentation – Working to Please – Social Investments

This is an excellent time to be seen in your best light. Making presentations, performing, making a play for someone or something, even going down on bended knee – these are all favoured under this influence. Generally, others are glad to have you around, and the feeling will probably be mutual.

Venus Conjunct (intensifying) MidHeaven – New Cycle Beginning
♀ ☌ MC

Key phrases: All the World Loves a Lover – Attracting Status – Finding Favour

This is a good time – other planetary influences willing – to ask for a raise or bank loan because you emanate or can sense the way to success. Your emotional state, reflected by the kind of relationship you are currently involved in, makes itself felt in the world around you, depending upon what that state is. Favourable news, or at least a favourable view, adorns your professional position now.

Venus Square (challenging) MidHeaven
♀ □ MC

Key phrases: Home/Work Conflicts – Spread A Little Happiness

Love and social life is now inclined to get in the way of your professional or domestic concerns. A case of business and pleasure not mixing, you could say. This could just be a passing thing, or then again it could be something more weighty and important, making itself felt. Being diplomatic and as pleasant as possible to whomever you have dealings with is the best course now.

Venus Opposition (confronting) MidHeaven
♀ ☍ MC

Key phrases: Charity Begins at Home – Domestic Harmony – Loving Family

This is a good time to be with your family or whomever you live with. It is also well starred for any home improvement or any creative activity in your home. If there has been any conflict or disharmony in the family, now is the time to make peace. Sentiment and nostalgia could be to the fore, and very pleasurable – but don't overdo this or it could have an ultimately undesirable effect.

Venus Trine (supporting) MidHeaven

♀ △ MC   *OR*

Venus Sextile (assisting) MidHeaven

♀ ✶ MC

Key phrases: Charity Begins at Home – Domestic Harmony – Loving Family

This is a mild influence that should help you to use your skills to blend your working and private life, to get one to serve the other. Any artistic or creative flair or project can now gain support from both official and personal spheres.

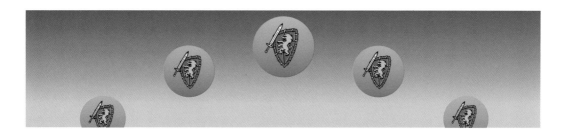

5. MARS TRANSITS

These are highly significant, especially when Conjoining, Squaring or Opposing a Radix Planet (Planet in one's Chart), because they can trigger the bigger, longer Transits of Jupiter, Saturn, Uranus, Neptune and Pluto that are described later, or because they fire you up for good or ill. It has to be said that 'for ill' usually means losing one's temper, or someone losing theirs with you or near you. And so knowing your Mars Transits is vital if you wish to avoid, minimize or be prepared for conflagrations. This can also be crucial with regard to driving or sports, for you may be vulnerable to accident and injury during one of them. Such Mars Transits are flagged: – **HOT! HOT & COLD! HOT & HEAVY! or DECEPTIVE!** and such can also refer to sexual or emotional incidents.

Mars Transits normally only last 3-5 days, but sometimes when the Planet goes 'stationary' (see Birth Chart on page 31), or it transits a number of Radix Planets in quick succession, you can have that hair-trigger energy around for up to a month. It cannot be emphasized enough how much knowing your Mars Transits can help you to prevent upsets and regrets, while enabling you to use that energy wisely and productively. One whole cycle or orbit of Mars around the Sun is 687 days.

Mars Transit Interpretations

WHEN READING THESE TRANSIT INTERPRETATIONS, BEAR THE FOLLOWING IN MIND: Because the meanings of Opposition (confronting) Transits are usually similar to Square (challenging) Transits – and both these are occasionally similar to the Conjunction (intensifying) Transits – the same interpretation is given below the relevant Transit name headings, each separated by 'OR'. Also, Sextile (assisting) Transits are usually the same meaning as Trine (supporting) Transits, and they are set out in the same way, that is, Transit name headings separated by 'OR'. Although any actual differences felt can be fairly subjective, it is worth noting – from the table overleaf – the distinct **Strength and Significance** that each can take on, especially between the Trine and Sextile.

TRANSIT ASPECT TYPE	STRENGTH AND SIGNIFICANCE
Conjunct (intensifying)	This is a very strong influence. It energizes the situation in hand and both forces and enables you to advance and grow. This is a *New Cycle Beginning* and as such may indeed mark the start of some new chapter or outlook – but then so can the Square or Opposition.
Square (challenging)	This is a strong to medium influence that challenges you to develop in proportion to your relevant strengths and weaknesses.
Opposition (confronting)	This is a strong influence, and usually attracts confrontations that in turn increase your awareness of the matter concerned.
Trine (supporting)	This is a medium-strength influence that allows you to make progress with relative ease and support. It rewards past efforts.
Sextile (assisting)	This is a mild influence, and you probably need to apply some conscious effort in order to reap its benefits.

Mars Conjunct (intensifying) Sun – New Cycle Beginning – HOT!
♂ ☌ ☉   *OR*
Mars Square (challenging) Sun – HOT!
♂ □ ☉   *OR*
Mars Opposition (confronting) Sun – HOT!
♂ ☍ ☉

Key phrases: Stimulating or Challenging your Ego – High Energy – Anger or Drive

Finding a suitable and effective outlet for your energies is the main issue at present. This probably means expressing yourself physically as well as mentally. So if there is something you have to do that needs a definite degree of forcefulness, then now is the time to go for it. But this is also a time when you can arouse or be aroused to anger or arrogance. This could be just right for clearing the air or making a breakthrough, but watch out for over-reactions, for they could lead to damage. This is a 'hot' period, and can set things off easily. It is up to you whether it is for good or ill.

Mars Trine (supporting) Sun
♂ △ ☉   *OR*
Mars Sextile (assisting) Sun
♂ ✳ ☉

Key phrases: Forcefulness with Ease – The Door-Opener – A Winning Way

You are able to approach and execute matters as well as is possible now, either in relation to your usual ability to act decisively – or considering the situation that you are currently dealing with. In other words, you are now most likely to know what you want, and how to go about getting it. More to the point, however, you are most likely to assert yourself owing to an instinctive sense of sureness that attracts success and confidence, rather than to being impatient and pushy, which would attract the opposite.

Mars Conjunct (intensifying) Moon – New Cycle Beginning – HOT!
♂ ☌ ☽   *OR*
Mars Square (challenging) Moon – HOT!
♂ □ ☽   *OR*
Mars Opposition (confronting) Moon – HOT!
♂ ☍ ☽

Key phrases: Stimulating or Attacking Feelings – Protecting your Space

The feelings that you have been sitting on need to come to the surface now. So feeling irritable or fit to burst is quite likely. This is a natural safety valve urging you to unload negative feelings such as anger or resentment, and especially those that concern your family and figures or events from your past. Being 'reasonable' at this time would be missing the point, for being supposedly abiding and well-behaved is what made you swallow your true feelings in the first place. So 'cough up the bile' and all concerned will feel the healthier and more secure for it eventually. It is very important now to make it clear how you feel, but to avoid unnecessary conflict, you must make the distinction between a feeling and who or what triggers off that feeling.

Mars Trine (supporting) Moon
♂ △ ☽   *OR*
Mars Sextile (assisting) Moon
♂ ✳ ☽

Key phrases: Strong Feelings – Spontaneous Actions – Feeling Vibrant

At present you experience a natural flow of energy into whatever pursuits further your needs. So any activity that requires lively responses or consistent emotions, such as a challenging task or satisfying a desire, is well starred right now. Also, you are able to stand your ground without appearing defensive and unsure of yourself. Your current emotional

6. JUPITER TRANSITS

These are life-expanding or life-overdoing in some way. Jupiter's influences are therefore growth inducing or excessive, faith-inspiring or promising/expecting more than can be delivered, magnifying or exaggerating, and are generally in aid of showing you the bigger picture and how you fit into it, and how you can make more of yourself and life.

It is a good idea to meet Jupiter with a sense of enterprise, optimism and goodwill that is tempered with a sense of modesty and reality, and to keep an intuitive eye out for signs of where you are supposed to go next – for they will be there; and to cultivate enthusiasm for the overall feel of how things are developing, rather than attempting to prove logically or account for everything item by item.

A Jupiterian period in your life can be likened to having a sense, literally or symbolically, of being on life's highway, with the journeys, adventures, opportunities and destinations that this can lead to, and with the possible realization that all is in aid of some sort of divine plan for this Planet; this can bring religious experiences and philosophical insights. A Jupiter Transit to one Radix Planet (Planet in one's Chart) can be relatively fleeting or last on and off for up to one year. One whole cycle or orbit of Jupiter around the Sun is almost 12 years.

Jupiter Transit Interpretations

WHEN READING THESE TRANSIT INTERPRETATIONS, BEAR THE FOLLOWING IN MIND: Because the meanings of Opposition (confronting) Transits are usually similar to Square (challenging) Transits – and both these are occasionally similar to the Conjunction (intensifying) Transits – the same interpretation is given below the relevant Transit name headings, each separated by 'OR'. Also, Sextile (assisting) Transits are usually the same meaning as Trine (supporting) Transits, and they are set out in the same way, that is, Transit name headings separated by 'OR'. Although any actual differences felt can be fairly subjective, it is worth noting – from the table opposite – the distinct **Strength and Significance** that each can take on, especially between the Trine and Sextile.

Jupiter Conjunct (intensifying) Sun – New Cycle Beginning
♃ ☌ ☉   Start of a new 11-12 year 'Belief-in-Life Cycle'.

Key phrases: Increased Vitality – Exaggerating Everything – Growing Creativity

TRANSIT ASPECT TYPE	STRENGTH AND SIGNIFICANCE
Conjunct (intensifying)	This is a very strong influence. It energizes the situation in hand and both forces and enables you to advance and grow. This is a *New Cycle Beginning* and as such may indeed mark the start of some new chapter or outlook – but then so can the Square or Opposition.
Square (challenging)	This is a strong to medium influence that challenges you to develop in proportion to your relevant strengths and weaknesses.
Opposition (confronting)	This is a strong influence, and usually attracts confrontations that in turn increase your awareness of the matter concerned.
Trine (supporting)	This is a medium-strength influence that allows you to make progress with relative ease and support. It rewards past efforts.
Sextile (assisting)	This is a mild influence, and you probably need to apply some conscious effort in order to reap its benefits.

Theme: A powerful emphasis upon your Sun Profile, thereby inflating your sense of self and of being alive – for good or ill.

This time is all about furthering yourself, through studying, travelling or moving, and launching yourself into a new chapter of your life's story. So anything that is aimed at achieving this has a cosmic stamp of approval. Yet simply because this is a natural time of expansion for you, there is also the danger of you overestimating your resources and possibilities – falling short of them – and then exaggerating your disappointment.

So some sober restraint is a vital ingredient in most of your considerations at present, for this has the effect of stabilizing rather than abusing what is actually a period of promise. Providence smiles on those who don't expect too much (or too little, for that matter) – but it also leaves stranded, at a later date, those who are just plain greedy.

This is essentially a time of experiencing joy, and spreading it around – as wisely as possible. Your most sensible and important investment under this influence would be that of tuning in to the positive feelings that are a very real right now.

Possible Encounters: Big Hearts and Minds – Good Health – The Extraordinary

Jupiter Square (challenging) Sun
♃ □ ☉   *OR*
Jupiter Opposition (confronting) Sun
♃ ☍ ☉

Key phrases: Increased Sense of Self – Full Life – Self-importance – Overextended

Theme: Forced emphasis on your Sun Profile, giving you a stronger sense of being alive – for better or worse.

If you are normally on the shy or self-effacing side, now is a good time to get more in touch with your self-esteem and sense of enterprise, or you will encounter an excess of the same qualities in others. If you are usually fairly (or apparently) confident, you could find yourself being overbearing, too busy and unlucky, through expecting too much. In either case though, there should be an urge to expand – but how you gauge this is the critical issue.

Possible Encounters: Opportunities for Growth – Big Egos – Fat Chances – Joy

Jupiter Trine (supporting) Sun
♃ △ ☉   *OR*
Jupiter Sextile (assisting) Sun
♃ ✶ ☉

Key phrases: Return to Health – Lust for Life – Increased Will and Vitality

Theme: Opportunities to make more of your Sun Profile, through having a greater sense of being alive.

This is a very positive time for you – so make the most of it. Equally, do not waste it, for there can be an inclination to just cruise and then have nothing to show for it later. There is the probability of putting your life on a better footing – or at least, there will be a sense of things being all for the best ultimately. Anything that furthers you physically or mentally can be fruitfully embarked upon now.

Possible Encounters: Successful Launches – Happy Travels – Financial Gain

Jupiter Conjunct (intensifying) Moon – New Cycle Beginning
♃ ☌ ☽   Start of a new 11-12 year 'Belief-in-Belonging Cycle'.   *OR*
Jupiter Square (challenging) Moon
♃ □ ☽   *OR*
Jupiter Opposition (confronting) Moon
♃ ☍ ☽
Key phrases: Buoyant Emotions – Exaggerated Feelings – Security Conscious

Theme: Powerful emphasis upon your Moon Profile, giving you a stronger sense of where you belong and how you behave.

You are liable to get carried away by the mood of the moment at present; so a lot depends upon what is currently preoccupying you. If you are stressed, then count to ten, for you could make a mountain out of a molehill – but then you shouldn't miss this opportunity to get in touch with your emotions. On the other hand, harmonious circumstances (indicated by other planetary influences) will allow you to feel very much a part of your surroundings, feeling closer than ever to others – especially family members and loved ones.

However, make sure that such people do not absorb too much of your psychic energy. All in all, this is a time to start putting your truest emotions on the map, understanding past influences, and setting a positive trend for future security.

Possible Encounters: Sentimentality – Reconciliation – Over-reactions – Mothering

Jupiter Trine (supporting) Moon
♃ △ ☽   *OR*
Jupiter Sextile (assisting) Moon
♃ ✶ ☽

Key phrases: Feeling Good – Increased Security – Happy Families

Theme: Opportunities to make more of your Moon Profile, through understanding better your own and others' needs.

This is not a particularly powerful influence, but you can make the most out of it by investing time and energy in whatever makes you and others feel safe and comfortable. And the more you cultivate what is familiar and nest-like, the more you'll attract goodwill from others. When linked with more dynamic influences, this time could be one of prosperity or securing something important.

Possible Encounters: Nature's Gifts – Religious Influences – Good Women

Jupiter Conjunct (intensifying) Mercury – New Cycle Beginning
♃ ☌ ☿   Start of a new 11-12 year 'Active-Intelligence Cycle'.   *OR*
Jupiter Square (challenging) Mercury
♃ □ ☿   *OR*
Jupiter Opposition (confronting) Mercury
♃ ☍ ☿

Key phrases: Thinking Big – Too Busy – Overlooking Details – Mind-Broadening
Theme: A powerful emphasis upon your Mercury Profile, when the best and the worst of your mental ability and attitude are in play.

Everything seems to happen at once now, which is fulfilling if you are organized and exasperating if you are not. Similarly, you have a more than usually broad perspective and overview of things at present, especially involving work or study programmes – so you are able to plan ahead and achieve a great deal during this period. But if you wish to have the co-operation of others – or not feel let down by yourself – avoid getting carried away by enthusiasm, inflated expectations, or just plain arrogance. Also check the 'fine print'.

Possible Encounters: Mental Activity – Meetings and Journeys – Getting Deflated

Jupiter Trine (supporting) Mercury
♃ △ ☿   *OR*
Jupiter Sextile (assisting) Mercury
♃ ✳ ☿

Key phrases: Increased Knowledge – Seeing Ahead – Happy Talk – Work Improvement

Theme: Chances to make more of your Mercury Profile through better understanding and increased use of your intellectual potentials.

Any kind of negotiation or strategy can be successfully accomplished or devised under this influence. So if there is a point you wish to grasp or convey, a subject you'd like to know more about, a journey to make, or a position you want – then now is the time to go for it. This is mainly because during this period you have the maximum number of facts at your fingertips, plenty of ideas, and a winning way about you.

Possible Encounters: Job Opportunities – Further Education – Adventure Trips

Jupiter Conjunct (intensifying) Venus – New Cycle Beginning
♃ ☌ ♀   Start of a new 11-12 year 'Belief-in-Love Cycle'.   *OR*
Jupiter Square (challenging) Venus
♃ □ ♀   *OR*
Jupiter Opposition (confronting) Venus
♃ ☍ ♀

Key phrases: Increased Attraction – The Joy of Love – Over-indulgence

Theme: A powerful emphasis upon your Venus Profile, making you more aware of your relationships, values, art and love.

Everything about your social and love life – the good, the bad and the indifferent – is now magnified. You might go from the one extreme to another in the space of a few hours – from having fun to being distraught, and back again. Or one day you could be wildly enthusiastic about someone in your life, and next day feel they are limiting your freedom. Needless to say, it is probably sensible to wait until this period is over before making any decisions. But then again, such extremes could well see someone else making a decision for you.

Possible Encounters: Significant Ones – Windfalls/Spending Sprees – Fun and Games

Jupiter Trine (supporting) Venus
♃ △ ♀   *OR*
Jupiter Sextile (assisting) Venus
♃ ⚹ ♀

Key phrases: Pleasant Gatherings – Attracting Joy and Prosperity – Happy Trails

Theme: Chances to make more of your Venus Profile through appreciating your capacity for giving and receiving love better.

This is all about the more you give the more you get. Whatever you have been investing in life, emotionally or financially, can bring about dividends now. And whatever you give out now is sure to breed happiness in the future – if or because you feel the generosity of Life itself flowing through you. You'll get the best out of this influence by fully appreciating its qualities rather than merely indulging in them, which can be the temptation. Spent well or squandered.

Possible Encounters: Romance – Bringers of Goodwill – Value for Money/Windfalls

Jupiter Conjunct (intensifying) Mars – New Cycle Beginning
♃ ☌ ♂   Start of a new 11-12 year 'Faith-in-Self-Assertion Cycle'.

Key phrases: Increased Energy – Fortunate Moves – Devil-may-care – The Joy of Sex

Theme: A powerful emphasis upon your Mars Profile, enabling you to express your personal drive better.

Your spirit of independence is strong now, so whatever you currently desire can be got – or got a lot closer to – by simply going for it. You feel more confident and exuberant than usual – even swashbuckling – during this period, so whatever you want to make happen, happens!

Afterwards, you may just find that you weren't so keen – but taking everything in gigantic strides as you are now, you are equally quick and sure to take your next leap forward. As long as you avoid overdoing it, a great deal can be accomplished during this period, and for as long as you can ride the crest of your own wave. Conversely, failing to express your desires or be sure of your own space at this time could give rise to inner tension.

Possible Encounters: Successful Launches – Sexual Adventures – Physical Exertion

Jupiter Square (challenging) Mars
♃ □ ♂   **OR**
Jupiter Opposition (confronting) Mars
♃ ♂ ♂

Key phrases: Excess Energy – Confidently Assertive – Over-reaching/Over-reacting

Theme: The forced emphasis of your Mars Profile, through an exaggerated urge to put yourself forward or to come first.

You could be rather arrogant at this time – or you'll cross swords with someone who is. It would be a pity to waste this surge of personal drive merely on feeling indignant, so endeavour to channel such energy into a constructive pursuit. But even if you do get on your 'high horse' or fly off the handle, you are likely to discover 'muscles' you didn't know you had. But a mixture of moderation and taking the initiative would be the best way of harnessing this force. However, failing to express your desires or be sure of your own space at this time could give rise to inner tension.

Possible Encounters: Collisions with Authority – Lustfulness – Selling – Sport

Jupiter Trine (supporting) Mars
♃ △ ♂   **OR**
Jupiter Sextile (assisting) Mars
♃ ✶ ♂

Key phrases: Increased Drive – Confident Self-Assertion – Motivation and Initiative

Theme: Opportunities to make more of your Mars Profile, as a result of feeling encouraged to make something happen.

Because at this time you have an air of conviction and generosity, others can tune into it and are therefore willing to support or follow you. But the essential point to grasp is that initial sense of optimism, for this is the seed from which a chain reaction of encouragement and mutual advantage will grow. As soon as you act from this positive starting point, the world at large begins dancing to your tune – simply because it likes it!

Possible Encounters: Successful Launches – Sexual Adventures – Enthusiasm

Jupiter Conjunct (intensifying) Jupiter – New Cycle Beginning
♃ ♂ ♃   Start of a new 11-12 year 'Growth-and-Development Cycle'.

Key phrases: Increased Scope – Great or Inflated Expectations – Expanded Beliefs
Theme: A powerful emphasis upon your Jupiter Profile, thereby granting you a greater sense of what you have and what you can give.

This can be a time of largesse or excess, of a new and positive outlook and understanding of life, or of totally overestimating your prospects. You now begin to envisage and work upon something that will last way into the future, as a result of wise planning and generosity, or else you get carried away on a hot-air balloon of wild speculation that begins to lose height with the first pin-prick of reality.

Opportunity and goodwill certainly come your way, but in the long run, everything depends upon your sense of modesty and practicality. You may well find yourself borne along by all manner of visions and possibilities, and by the people that accompany the smell of success. Yet such are best regarded as merely signs and promises. The true thrust of genuine success at the core of this influence has 'You get back as good as you give' written all the way through it.

Possible Encounters: Offers – Travel – Much Ado – Religiosity – OTT Experiences

Jupiter Square (challenging) Jupiter
♃ □ ♃   **OR**
Jupiter Opposition (confronting) Jupiter
♃ ☍ ♃

Key phrases: Increased Scope – Great or Inflated Expectations – Expanded Beliefs

Theme: Forced emphasis upon your Jupiter Profile, through expecting too much or too little from life and yourself.

This is really a chance to grow and expand, but how you read this has everything to do with how you manage and express it. Most likely, you experience a sense of abundance for some reason, be it real or notional. And so you go about spending this and promising that, and, naturally, most people will be happy to go along with you.

But the danger of over-committing yourself and overestimating your luck is very real under this influence. Later on, you will have to pay for it. So the all too obvious advice here is to guard against excess, but stay in touch with that sense of joy and abundance, and the very real confidence that it can afford you.

Possible Encounters: Misappropriation – More Than Enough – Legal Difficulties

Jupiter Trine (supporting) Jupiter
♃ △ ♃   **OR**
Jupiter Sextile (assisting) Jupiter
♃ ✶ ♃

Key phrases: Positive Thinking – Philanthropic Plans – Increased Scope
Theme: Chances to make more of your Jupiter Profile through simply trusting in your beliefs.

If things are going well right now, this will make them go better – or you could just sit back and coast for a while. If matters are difficult, this period can attract some much needed luck or help. It also favours travelling and studying. You are able to see more and see further, so this is a good time to make plans, or put them forward. Whatever your circumstances, you should feel that someone up there loves you!

Possible Encounters: Financial or Legal Ease – Optimism – Goodwill – Prestige

Jupiter Conjunct (intensifying) Saturn – New Cycle Beginning
♃ ☌ ♄   Start of a new 11-12 year 'Faith-in-Life-Structure Cycle'.

Key phrases: Growing beyond Restrictions – Increased Responsibility

Theme: A powerful emphasis upon your Saturn Profile, enabling you to understand your fears and responsibilities better.

This can be quite liberating and difficult at the same time. Whatever it is in your life that has held you back or down or in chains, you now begin to comprehend more and more. By way of reaction, your doubts and fears could become exaggerated – but you should get wise to this as part of the process of ridding yourself of such rigidity and restriction. What is also part and parcel of this important time for you, is the taking on of a fresh and more conscious set of responsibilities. Finally, there could also arise the decision to break free from or expand within an established situation or relationship.

Possible Encounters: Growing Pains – Father Figures – Lasting New Circumstances

Jupiter Square (challenging) Saturn
♃ □ ♄   **OR**
Jupiter Opposition (confronting) Saturn
♃ ☍ ♄

Key phrases: Growing beyond Restrictions – Increased Responsibility

Theme: Forced emphasis upon your Saturn Profile, through having to understand your fears and responsibilities better.

Now you are looking for – and have the opportunity to discover – a balance between what is realistically possible and desirable to maintain, and what adjustments have to be made to your situations and expectations. You find then that over-optimism is promptly flattened, and that playing it too carefully creates boredom or frustration.

So this is very much a time of trial and error; do not expect to have a ready answer born of some theory. Such reliable guidelines are in fact what you are establishing during this period. However, wherever you are genuinely sure of yourself, this period will eventually confirm it.

Possible Encounters:: Growing Pains – Serious Agreements – Decision-Making

Jupiter Trine (supporting) Saturn
♃ △ ♄   *OR*
Jupiter Sextile (assisting) Saturn
♃ ⚹ ♄

Key phrases: Increasing Order – Alleviating Difficulties – Improving Status

Theme: Opportunities to appreciate your Saturn Profile, through creating a balance between vision and caution.

Whether or not more hectic or exciting planetary influences are around now, this one provides you with a sense of equilibrium and of the value of sobriety. You recognize and accept where your duties lie, and consequently go about performing them in a measured and matter-of-fact fashion. Anything that requires you to be serious or solitary, can be confidently undertaken now. At the very least, this period will help you to accept reality more.

Possible Encounters: Happy Responsibilities – Clear Objectives – Practical Solutions

Jupiter Conjunct (intensifying) Uranus – New Cycle Beginning
♃ ☌ ♅   Start of a new 11-12 year 'Individual Philosophy Cycle'.   *OR*
Jupiter Square (challenging) Uranus
♃ □ ♅   *OR*
Jupiter Opposition (confronting) Uranus
♃ ☍ ♅

Key phrases: Belief Versus Freedom – Increasingly Radical – Exaggerated Uniqueness

Theme: The powerful emphasis of your Uranus Profile, through magnifying your desire to be true to yourself.

You feel that 'something's got to give', and if it doesn't then you'll make it do so! Whatever happens now is in aid of giving you a stronger sense of you as a one-off individual. This can mean being constantly pulled this way and that as your morals conflict with your urge to be free or, for example, it might suddenly land you with the opportunity to do something entirely different.

Restlessness can be a particularly disruptive force in you right now, but you could more than satisfy such feelings through simply doing something that you'd never normally do. The pull or desirability of investing your time and energy in new ways of living and looking at life is strong now. Such involvements can act as a springboard into a fresh chapter in your life, where the world is more your oyster than ever it was before.

Possible Encounters: Unexpected Chances – Significant Coincidences – Release of Tension

Jupiter Trine (supporting) Uranus
♃ △ ♅   **OR**
Jupiter Sextile (assisting) Uranus
♃ ✶ ♅

Key phrases: Increased Freedom – Faith in Originality – Spontaneous Growth

Theme: Chances to make more of your Uranus Profile, through exploring and exploiting the radical and unusual.

This is a lucky influence, so during this time some kind of forward leap can occur. This may happen quite unexpectedly, so be quick on the draw, for much depends on how open you are to change and experiment. Fortunately, your mind is now more than usually geared to taking advantage of such new developments, which could involve science and technology, alternative subjects, or any type of far-reaching pursuit. Advancement is what this period is all about.

Possible Encounters: Happy Surprises – New Ventures – Sudden Opportunities

Jupiter Conjunct (intensifying) Neptune – New Cycle Beginning
♃ ☌ ♆   Start of a new 11-12 year 'Faith-in-Unity Cycle'.

Key phrases: Increased Sensitivity – Exaggerating Blind Spots – Believing the Best

Theme: A powerful emphasis upon your Neptune Profile, granting you a greater appreciation of your visions and ideals.

This is a highly significant influence in your life, but a tricky one, for it can present itself as somewhat more than a glimpse of what a better life truly consists of or as just a 'pipe dream' and a fool's errand. Both cases depend upon how much you are aware of egotistical or glamorous ideas of what the 'good life' means. If you are genuinely concerned with leading a more selfless life of helping other living creatures that need it, then this period will bear you along, elevating your thoughts and feelings as it does so.

On the other hand, if you are merely pretending to be 'spiritual', or just want to have a high old time, then, like a wave of pink foam, you'll be blissfully carried along – only to find yourself later washed up on some barren shore of disillusionment. So this is a time when either you can begin to really open your third eye and see yourself, the world and everything for the whole that it is, or you will just be jamming on a pair of rose-tinted spectacles. In effect, you are now betting on the ultimate winner – or the ultimate loser.

Possible Encounters: Compassion – False Hopes – Charlatans – Enlightenment

Jupiter Square (challenging) Neptune
♃ □ ♆   **OR**
Jupiter Opposition (confronting) Neptune
♃ ☌ ♆

Key phrases: Increased Sensitivity – Exaggerated Compassion – Questionableness

Theme:: Forced emphasis upon your Neptune Profile, giving rise to a greater sense of what compassion and understanding really mean.

The possibility of contacting your ideals, and the sensitivity that goes with them, is great now. But then so is the challenge to express them, and to come to terms with any misunderstandings that have occurred because of sensitive spots in yourself and others not being properly looked at.

   For this is a time when all such issues are put under the magnifying glass, and great honesty and discrimination has to be exercised in order that you may avoid being taken for a ride, feel excessively disillusioned, or simply waste your time and energy with misplaced sympathy. You have to make sure that your good intentions are not merely disguising your own emotional wounds.

Possible Encounters: False Hopes – Charlatans – Do-gooders – The Nature of the Sublime

Jupiter Trine (supporting) Neptune
♃ △ ♆   **OR**
Jupiter Sextile (assisting) Neptune
♃ ✶ ♆

Key phrases: Spiritual Furtherance – Increased Acceptance – Gentle Speculation

Theme: Chances to make more of your Neptune Profile, through a better understanding of your compassion and sensitivity.

This influence is soft, even dreamy, and not particularly dynamic – so it brings a time of being able to tune into the Universe, and go with its intentions more than your own. Consequently, getting the best – or anything at all – out of this period greatly depends upon what you understand this to mean.

   If you are by nature into doing 'good works' or looking into the meaning of life, then this will help you to do so even more. If you are more self-interested, this might just give you a glimpse of a greater and more meaningful life than you believed existed, which may simply be seen in the plight of one other or many others.

Possible Encounters: Guides or Gurus – Idealism – Uplifting Experiences

Jupiter Conjunct (intensifying) Pluto – New Cycle Beginning
♃ ☌ ♇   Start of a new 11-12 year 'Faith-in-Destiny Cycle'.

Key phrases: Increasingly Influential – Hunger for Power – Profound Growth

Theme: A powerful emphasis upon your Pluto Profile, through the appreciation of your influence and potential.

Whatever you regard as your fate or fortune, now is the time when you are most likely to receive a boost from it, or make a blow for it. It is also a time when whatever you have been piling a great deal of energy into is most likely to meet with success. But you could get caught out by this period if you either have nothing much to offer, or if you are too intent upon gaining a position of power.

The consequence being that if you are the former you would feel hard-done-by and at the mercy of the powers-that-be, or if you are the latter you could wind up falling so far short of your expectations as to feel worse off than you were before.

Any obsessions you might have can also get in your way now, for they will preoccupy you more than usual – yet also give you the opportunity to deal with them once and for all. All in all though, the more you are now doing something that reaches out to the masses, or that is for the common good, then the more rewarding this period will be, with material success being a by-product rather than the main objective.

Possible Encounters: Worldly Success – Your Destiny – Powerful Ups or Downs

Jupiter Square (challenging) Pluto
♃ □ ♇   *OR*
Jupiter Opposition (confronting) Pluto
♃ ☍ ♇

Key phrases: Power-Plays – Increased Ambition – Exaggerated Fears or Obsessions

Theme: Forced emphasis upon your Pluto Profile, in order that you appreciate the nature of power and hidden influences in your life.

One way or the other, now is a time when you get more in touch and involved with what needs changing and improving, and with the necessary force and will that can make this possible. But this can be rather like Aladdin and his Lamp, for the 'genie' of power and ambition that you summon up may well turn against you – however well-intentioned you thought you were.

Therefore be ruthlessly honest and careful about your motivation to gain any particular position or object, because the desire to serve the whole rather than just yourself is the only motivation that will truly justify, and indeed guide, your actions now. If your intentions are not honourable, then things could blow up in your face. On the other hand though, avoid being falsely modest, for this would cause you to miss out on the opportunity that is presently in the air.

Possible Encounters: Provocation/Confrontation – Crises of Opinion – Legal Conflicts

Jupiter Trine (supporting) Pluto
♃ △ ♇   *OR*

Jupiter Sextile (assisting) Pluto
♃ ⚹ ♇

Key phrases: Positive Changes – Increasing Insight – Mounting Influence

Theme: Opportunities to make more of your Pluto Profile, through experiencing a stronger sense of wealth and power.

Generally, this is a time when you can improve anything that needs improving. The secret is to approach and launch any such endeavours in a spirit of everyone benefiting from them; you then find that 'the more you give, the more you get' is in fact a Law of the Universe rather than just a nice idea. You also notice during this period that the world itself is more alive to this Law – and is all the more so for your personally taking advantage of it.

Possible Encounters: Favours – Regeneration – Gains – Support from High Places

Jupiter Conjunct (intensifying) Ascendant – New Cycle Beginning
♃ ☌ AS   Start of a new 11-12 year 'Personal-Furtherance Cycle'.

Key phrases: Expanding your Viewpoint – Looking Further Afield – New Hope

Theme: An over-emphasis upon your Ascendant Profile, thereby enabling you to broaden your horizons.

During this time you are inclined to have a more than usually good eye for opportunity, which may well take the form of finding and meeting people who increase your scope and range of possibilities. Positively, such can give rise to your being confident and far-seeing, whereas negatively, it can lead to being arrogant and dangerously over-optimistic.

The trick is to temper the sense of enthusiasm that you currently feel by actively paying attention to the feelings and opinions of people you respect. In this way, apart from equipping yourself with a wiser choice, you will enlist the support of those others. It will also help limit matters to manageable proportions, for being greedy now could find you with a big nothing at a later date. Let generosity and a sense of adventure born of experience and understanding, be your guide.

Possible Encounters: Opportune Ones – Empty Promises – A Full Life – Signs and Omens

Jupiter Square (challenging) Ascendant
♃ □ AS

Key phrases: Expanding your Viewpoint – Looking Further Afield

Theme: An over-emphasis upon your Ascendant Profile, thereby enabling you to broaden your horizons, or causing you to promise more than you can deliver.

During this time you are inclined to have a more than usually good eye for opportunity. But such can range from your being confident and far-seeing to being arrogant and dangerously over-optimistic. The trick is to temper the sense of enthusiasm that you currently feel by actively paying attention to the feelings and opinions of people you respect.

In this way, apart from equipping yourself with a wiser choice, you will enlist the support of those others. It will also help limit matters to manageable proportions, for being greedy now could find you with a big nothing at a later date. Let generosity, born of experience and understanding, be your best guide.

Possible Encounters: Wise or Fanciful Advice – Empty Promises – A Full Life

Jupiter Opposition (confronting) Ascendant
♃ ☍ AS   Start of a new 11-12 year 'Social-Furtherance Cycle'.

Key phrases: Improving Social or Love Life – Expanding your Viewpoint – New Hope

Theme: An over-emphasis upon your Ascendant Profile, thereby attracting people and situations that enable you to broaden your horizons, and to create mutual understanding.

Now you have a green light to make more of yourself through enjoying a greater sense of social involvement. The obvious advantages of this are such things as getting out and about more, joining in with group, educational or sporting activities, and generally meeting types of people who are refreshingly different in some way.

You could well find yourself attracting someone in particular who plays the role of a teacher or guide in your life. For this reason it is also a good time to seek out professional advice, like lawyers, counsellors, etc, for they are more likely than usual to meet your needs successfully. Last, but by no means least, existing partnerships, or ones that begin now, are scheduled for growth.

On the one hand this means that together you have the opportunity to share and prosper together, and possibly do some travelling and exploring. On the other hand, this growth could create problems if one of you is reluctant to break new ground.

Suffice to say 'nothing ventured, nothing gained', and that ultimately you must follow and be true to what you believe is right – for even the friction created by feeling either pushed or limited by your partner will produce some form of realization or understanding.

Possible Encounters: Opportune Ones – Empty Promises – A Full Life – Love Adventures

Jupiter Trine (supporting) Ascendant
♃ △ AS   *OR*
Jupiter Sextile (assisting) Ascendant
♃ ✶ AS

Key phrases: Expanding your Viewpoint – Improving Relationships

Theme: Opportunities to make more sense of being in the world, thereby attracting rewarding relationships.

You feel a growing sense of largesse with regard to your attitude towards other people and life in general. You begin to see more of the total picture of life, and your place in it. This can have decidedly religious or philosophical overtones, and you have less time for petty thoughts and petty people.

But you are also feeling quite philanthropic, and are more inclined to point out the wider issues of a given subject. Naturally enough, your current urge to take more in would be well satisfied through some course of study, for all knowledge and experience is like food and wine to you now. So eat, drink and be merry!

Possible Encounters: Mutual Profit and Understanding – Enlightened Perspectives

Jupiter Conjunct (intensifying) MidHeaven – New Cycle Beginning
♃ ☌ MC   Start of a new 11-12 year 'Professional-Furtherance Cycle'.

Key phrases: Career Boost – Increasing Status – Inflating Position

Theme: The powerful expansion of your MidHeaven Profile, thereby bringing the opportunity for growth and understanding of your position in the world.

Presently in particular, and off and on for about a year, you find that your profession or direction in life will possibly progress in leaps and bounds, or you might overestimate your chances and standing, and wind up spread too thin, letting others down or feeling let down yourself.

Determining what you are able to manage, and carefully planning ahead, as distinct from jumping feet first into what you merely fancy you should have, will help forestall any embarrassing over-extension of your professional ability, and at the same time enable you to spot the real nature of the opportunities that are now liable to come your way. On the face of it, this is a time of outright improvement in your material situation, with perks and travel also possibly being in the offing.

In fact, the more you think in terms of improving the lot of the greater whole now, the more likely you are to make the right choices, and realize that true success is simply a case of being true to your deepest beliefs and moral standards.

Possible Encounters: Worldly Experiences – Greater Sphere of Activity – Promotion

Jupiter Square (challenging) MidHeaven
♃ □ MC

Key phrases: Inflating Status – Increasing Ambition

Theme: A forced emphasis upon your MidHeaven Profile, giving rise to a greater sense of professional or personal scope, but also an inclination to over-estimate your capabilities.

It is best to look upon this time as a 'shot in the arm', which gives you that extra bit of confidence that you need to get on in life. But that's all it is: a leg up the ladder of life. If you go scrambling for fame or recognition, it might work, but it will definitely prove meteoric, with you coming crashing down not much later. Or you could find yourself spread too thinly, leaving personal as well as professional commitments unfulfilled. A push will get you started now, but you'll need talent and persistence to keep going.

Possible Encounters: Bold Ventures – A Step up – Fanciful Promises

Jupiter Opposition (confronting) MidHeaven – New Cycle Beginning
♃ ☍ MC Start of a new 11-12 year 'Home-Improvement Cycle'.

Key phrases: Improving Home Base – Enriching Inner Life

Theme: An emphasis upon the underpinnings if your MidHeaven Profile, thereby giving you the urge to create a positive and inner sense of security.

The point on your Chart directly opposite your MidHeaven, your Lower MidHeaven, represents your roots, background, home and family; where you come from and go back to. With Jupiter crossing this sensitive point you now have an opportunity to understand all these things much better, to make more of them, to feather your nest and feel comfortable with your innermost self.

On a material level this is therefore a good time for home improvements, either through decoration or alteration, or even moving somewhere more suitable to your needs. But perhaps more importantly, it is time to get to know 'where you live' in the psychological sense, through looking into your family background, sharing your deepest feelings and beliefs, maybe laying a few ghosts, and generally putting your house in order.

So this is not so much a time for outer development – but more about investing some time and energy, and money if possible or necessary, in creating a feeling of ease with yourself. Then in about a year's time you will be strong inside, and ready to express yourself through some individual project.

Possible Encounters: Domestic Gatherings – Personal Discoveries – 'Going Home'

Jupiter Trine (supporting) MidHeaven
♃ △ MC   **OR**
Jupiter Sextile (assisting) MidHeaven
♃ ⚹ MC

Key phrases: Furthering Professional Image – Improving Domestic Scene

Theme: Opportunities to make more of your MidHeaven Profile, through a better understanding of your place in the world, and even actually elevating it.

At present you experience encouragement or advancement with regard to your chosen profession. The work you have put in over the previous years now begins to show dividends. You have an aura of success about you, which is what actually attracts it. So do not be dispirited if, say, an offer turns out to be no more than that.

Jupiter is giving you a sign of things to come. So respond to this with increased optimism and an inner sense of self-esteem, but guard against being over-optimistic and feeling crestfallen later. This is also a time when you may make positive changes in your home, which would further increase that good feeling about yourself. Other planetary periods notwithstanding, you are in a 'gain mode' right now. Perceiving and accepting with grace and modesty what that gain actually is will ensure its continuance.

Possible Encounters: Influential Connections – Recognition – Inner Support

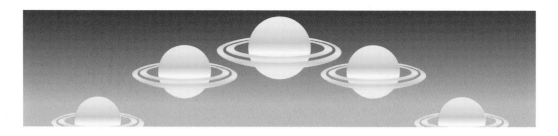

7. SATURN TRANSITS

These are life stabilizing or life-testing in some way. Saturnian influences are therefore materially supportive or restrictive, consolidating or separative, firm or heavy, authoritative or oppressive, and are generally in aid of getting you organized and of making you aware of the status quo.

So it is advisable to meet Saturn with a sense of practicality, preparedness, matter-of-factness, a willingness to confront issues, and through using time as your instrument rather than being ruled by it or wasting it. Saturn is about objectivity – which means to say that seeing things for what they are, and establishing and achieving your objectives, can and must be attended to, or begun to be so, under its influence. A case of ' getting real'.

A Saturnian period in your life is, or is like, an encounter with a figure of authority, and whether this is helpful or hindering, it is still in aid of your getting yourself together. A Saturn Transit to one Radix Planet (Planet in one's Chart) lasts up to a year overall. One whole cycle or orbit of Saturn around the Sun is 29.5 years.

Saturn Transit Interpretations

WHEN READING THESE TRANSIT INTERPRETATIONS, BEAR THE FOLLOWING IN MIND: Because the meanings of Opposition (confronting) Transits are usually similar to Square (challenging) Transits – and both these are occasionally similar to the Conjunction (intensifying) Transits – the same interpretation is given below the relevant Transit name headings, each separated by ' **OR**'. Also, Sextile (assisting) Transits are usually the same meaning as Trine (supporting) Transits, and they are set out in the same way, that is, Transit name headings separated by ' **OR**'. Although any actual differences felt can be fairly subjective, it is worth noting – from the table opposite – the distinct **Strength and Significance** that each can take on, especially between the Trine and Sextile.

Saturn Conjunct (intensifying) Sun – New Cycle Beginning
♄ ♂ ☉   Start of a new 29.5 year ' Life-Structure Cycle'.

Key phrases: Tests of Will – Taking Stock – Consolidation or Liquidation

Theme: A powerful point of reckoning, with your having to be practical and objective about matters relating to your Sun Profile, with the goal of putting your life on a firmer footing. Hard cold reality stares you in the face during this time, checking your every move. If you

TRANSIT ASPECT TYPE	STRENGTH AND SIGNIFICANCE
Conjunct (intensifying)	This is a very strong influence. It energizes the situation in hand and both forces and enables you to advance and grow. This is a *New Cycle Beginning* and as such may indeed mark the start of some new chapter or outlook – but then so can the Square or Opposition.
Square (challenging)	This is a strong to medium influence that challenges you to develop in proportion to your relevant strengths and weaknesses.
Opposition (confronting)	This is a strong influence, and usually attracts confrontations that in turn increase your awareness of the matter concerned.
Trine (supporting)	This is a medium-strength influence that allows you to make progress with relative ease and support. It rewards past efforts.
Sextile (assisting)	This is a mild influence, and you probably need to apply some conscious effort in order to reap its benefits.

find yourself encountering very few setbacks, then you can be sure that you know what you are about. But it is more than likely that there is something you will have to prove now.

This is a good time to start something new providing it has been well thought out, involves some already established situation, or you are prepared to learn as you go, step by step. Don't expect new ventures or involvements to take off overnight. Time should be your instrument now – so take it. The bottom line under this influence is that you keep your spirits up. Even if outwardly things seem discouraging, it is the state of your heart that is the critical issue – so don't lose heart!

You may well have to stand your ground – which means that you'll need to make sure of where you stand and what you stand for. Providing that you apply the maximum amount of disciplined effort now, which also includes your not overworking, you may be sure that anything that does not survive this period was just not supposed to; and whatever does survive will last and prosper.

Possible Encounters: Delays – Authority – Extra Responsibilities – A Heavy Feeling – Feeling your Age – Older, Experienced People

Saturn Square (challenging) Sun

♄ □ ☉   *OR*

Saturn Opposition (confronting) Sun

♄ ☍ ☉

Key phrases: Tests of Will – Taking Stock – Consolidation or Liquidation

Theme Having to be practical and objective about matters relating to your Sun Profile, with the goal of putting your life on a firmer footing.

Hard cold reality stares you in the face during this time, checking your every move. If you find yourself encountering very few setbacks, then you can be sure that you know what you are about. But it is more than likely that there is something you will have to prove now.

Also, this may be a poor time to start anything new – or at least, don't expect it to take off overnight. The bottom line under this influence is that you keep your spirits up. Even if outwardly things seem discouraging, it is the state of your heart that is the critical issue – so don't lose heart! You may well have to stand your ground – which means that you'll need to make sure of where you stand and what you stand for.

Providing that you apply the maximum amount of disciplined effort now, which also includes your not overworking, you may be sure that anything that does not survive this period was just not supposed to; and whatever does survive will last and prosper.

Possible Encounters Delays – Authority – Extra Responsibilities – A Heavy Feeling – Feeling your Age – Being/Feeling Let Down

Saturn Trine (supporting) Sun

♄ △ ☉   *OR*

Saturn Sextile (assisting) Sun

♄ ✳ ☉

Key phrases: Running Smoothly – Healthy Will – Steady Living – Groundwork

Theme Opportunities to be practical and objective with regard to your Sun Profile, thereby consolidating your position.

Whatever needs stability and working upon in your life, now is the time to apply yourself to it, for at present you are more patient and disciplined than usual, and likely to synchronize your activities with those in positions of influence and authority. You can now be the 'well-oiled machine' that gets things done efficiently and on time. Any difficulties are simply taken in your stride.

Possible Encounters: Responsible Individuals – Helpful Elders – Recognition

Saturn Conjunct (intensifying) Moon – New Cycle Beginning

♄ ☌ ☽   *Start of a new 29.5 year 'Emotional-Development Cycle'.*   *OR*

Saturn Square (challenging) Moon

♄ □ ☽   *OR*

Saturn Opposition (confronting) Moon

♄ ☍ ☽

Key phrases: Testing Feelings – Emotional Maturation – Child/Adult Consciousness

Theme: A powerful point of reckoning with regard to your Moon Profile, establishing or calling for a balance between inner/emotional and outer/material realities.

This can be a painful and depressing time, for you are made to feel any clash between your emotional nature and needs, and the demands of the outside world of work, status, and other people generally. On the one hand you are liable to attract difficulties with relationships, women in general, your mother or family, and on the home front.

On the other hand, professional responsibilities and material pressures prevail upon you to measure up, seemingly at the expense of those private needs. But basically, this influence is in aid of making you 'feel' in order that you might learn about your inner child and its current state, and how appropriately or not it (you) reacts to life situations; and consequently how you might make adjustments to your life priorities so that your Saturnian or adult self may remain mindful of, and look after, the lunar child within you.

The child in turn can then lend a genuine lightness and emotional spontaneity to your day-to-day affairs. The care with which you treat yourself during this period is vital, for it will greatly determine your future emotional security and happiness. So definitely 'Try a little Tenderness' – and seek out professional therapy if the going gets too rough.

Possible Encounters: Self-Pity - Alienation - Emotionally Worthwhile Lessons

Saturn Trine (supporting) Moon

♄ △ ☽   *OR*

Saturn Sextile (assisting) Moon

♄ ✶ ☽

Key phrases: Emotional Stability – Domestic Security – Establishing Safety

Theme: Opportunities to be practical and objective with matters relating to your Moon Profile, thereby meeting your own needs, and of those close to you.

This is literally and metaphorically a case of being able to put your house in order. Your life experience is serving you well at this time, and you feel able simultaneously to satisfy both your inner needs and outer responsibilities; home and work life are in harmony and serve one another well. The best of what is conservative in your nature manifests itself, allowing you to plan and set down conditions that will ensure future comfort and security.

You become aware that Heaven and Earth are in their respective and proper places.

Possible Encounters Sobriety and Self-Control – Settled Family – Reliable Care

> **Saturn Conjunct (intensifying) Mercury – New Cycle Beginning**
> ♄ ☌ ☿   Start of a new 29.5 year ' Mind-in-Order Cycle'.   *OR*
> **Saturn Square (challenging) Mercury**
> ♄ □ ☿   *OR*
> **Saturn Opposition (confronting) Mercury**
> ♄ ☍ ☿

Key phrases: Hard Work – Dull/Seriously Minded – Perception Tested – Groundwork

Theme: A powerful point of reckoning with regard to your Mercury Profile, where you have to organize your mental faculties.

Most things on the work and intellectual front are slowed down at this time. You are being tried as to whether any given project is worth the mental effort. If it is, then it will survive this period. You could be given more responsibility at work – or have your position tested. Any woolly thinking or slackness on your part will attract pressure from authority figures, which would include your own conscience.

  Bear in mind that the intention of this influence is to stabilize your attitude, bringing it in line with the reality at hand. Disciplining your mind now will serve you well for a long time to come. If in doubt, take your time and only speak if you are absolutely sure of what you wish to say. Allow for delays, especially while travelling.

Possible Encounters Mental Focus/Pressure – Lack of Work – Dry Intellectualism

> **Saturn Trine (supporting) Mercury**
> ♄ △ ☿   *OR*
> **Saturn Sextile (assisting) Mercury**
> ♄ ✳ ☿

Key phrases: Stable Thinking – Efficient Working – Steady Studying

Theme: Opportunities to be practical and objective with regard to your Mercury Profile, creating mental discipline and a realistic attitude.

This an extremely useful influence, because it enables you to keep your mind on the job in hand, and not let it be deflected by side issues or unrealistic ideas. Such efficiency should not be allowed to blind you to the value of imaginative and intuitive thoughts (of your own or of other people) – for that would give no style, just functionality. Currently, you have possession of a reliable precision tool – your intellect – for organizing and planning your life. So make sure that you are using it, and not it using you; otherwise a stable attitude could become a boringly rigid one.

Possible Encounters: Successful Establishment – Dependable Work(ers) – Promotion

Saturn Conjunct (intensifying) Venus – New Cycle Beginning
♄ ☌ ♀   Start of a new 29.5 year 'Real-Love Cycle'.   *OR*
Saturn Square (challenging) Venus
♄ □ ♀   *OR*
Saturn Opposition (confronting) Venus
♄ ☍ ♀

Key phrases: The Love Tester – Establishing True Values – Art/Cash Flow Problems

Theme: A powerful point of reckoning with regard to your Venus Profile, whereby you have to create a balance between pleasure and duty, and make the distinction between true, practical love aims and needs, and fanciful, unreal ones.

This is one of the hardest periods to handle, because it demands that you be utterly realistic about your emotional or financial involvements, and it is in just these areas of life that most of us are prone to the most confusion or delusion. In effect, Saturn is challenging you to establish a firmer sense of loving and being loved.

You will therefore have to look more closely at what you are giving and getting in any relationship, and at what might be causing you to experience too much or too little of either. A steep imbalance here would suggest a lack of emotional companionship altogether, with the loneliness that goes with this now becoming plainly unacceptable. Existing relationships, or ones that start around this time, have responsibility stamped all over them. The word means the ability to respond – to 'whatever' a particular person means in your life.

The pressure to learn this lesson may be so great as to tempt you to depart or withdraw even more, or go off with someone else; but this would be foolhardy, for as long as Saturn is around – and for a while after – it will present you with the same issue, whoever you're with, and whether you're with anyone or not. At the same time, though, relationships that really cannot stand the test will end, which is perfectly all right as long as the necessary lesson in love has been learned.

Material resources are subject to the same issues – i.e. What do money and possessions really mean to you? Should you be more or less businesslike? And creative flow too has to stand the test, as the worth of your product or idea is evaluated.

Possible Encounters: Fated Relationships – Separation – Worthwhile Trials

Saturn Trine (supporting) Venus

♄ △ ♀   *OR*

Saturn Sextile (assisting) Venus

♄ ✳ ♀

Key phrases: Stabilizing Relationships – Firmer Finances – Practically Creative

Theme: Opportunities to be practical and objective with regard to your Venus Profile, making for a happier life.

This a good time to make ties – whether financial or emotional – for you are at your most level-headed now. You are inclined to take – or accept – a mature point of view, a conservative evaluation. Also, getting down to any creative project is facilitated by a basically balanced attitude. Moreover, whatever ructions or changes might be occurring during this time, this sense of equilibrium acts as an anchor; an anchor that very likely takes the form of a dependable partner or friend.

Possible Encounters: Ordinary Love – Loyalty – A Mature Mate – Mutual Profit

Saturn Conjunct (intensifying) Mars – New Cycle Beginning

♄ ☌ ♂   Start of a new 29.5 year 'Disciplined-Activity Cycle'.   *OR*

Saturn Square (challenging) Mars

♄ ☐ ♂   *OR*

Saturn Opposition (confronting) Mars

♄ ☍ ♂

Key phrases: Blocked or Controlled Energy – Testing Self-Assertion – Sex on Hold

Theme: A powerful point of reckoning with regard to your Mars Profile, where you have to assess and organize how you go about getting what you want.

With this difficult period, hard work is not only the best policy, but quite unavoidable. You have to persist with whatever needs your individual energy and input, while at the same time acknowledging and accepting that circumstances are such that hold-ups are inevitable and that the current way of the world ultimately has the upper hand.

Also, you will have to confront others, yet always be prepared to meet them half way. You are now laying down, or else having laid down for you, a long-term plan, which could even be quite military-like. So hold back, and hold firm, and hold it all together.

Be patient. If necessary, work out your pent-up energies, such as anger, in harmless physical activity, but beware of knocks and strains. It may also be necessary to re-appraise the nature of your sexual activity, with a view to maturing in this area. In general, you will find that relating to men is difficult at this time.

Possible Encounters: Frustration – Opposition – Collisions – Tough Conditions

Saturn Trine (supporting) Mars
♄ △ ♂   *OR*
Saturn Sextile (assisting) Mars
♄ ✶ ♂

Key phrases: Disciplined Activity – Stabilizing Sexuality – Executive Ability

Theme: Opportunities to be practical and objective with regard to your Mars Profile, enabling you to steadily achieve your objectives.

You are now methodical and patient in all that you do – the degree depending on how much you are so normally. But in any event, your measure of self-reliance is increased during this period, and so you execute tasks thoroughly and economically, and furthermore you do not bother yourself with matters that are just not ready to be dealt with, or that only time itself can deal with.

Others find your perseverance and diligence both admirable and formidable; they may also find it boring – but that, you realize, is their problem. This is not supposed to be a scintillating time in your life (notwithstanding other indications): you are happily working towards a time when you can deservedly reap your rewards.

Possible Encounters: Work Well Done – Wholesome Sex Life – Reliable Men or Reliable Masculinity

Saturn Conjunct (intensifying) Jupiter – New Cycle Beginning
♄ ☌ ♃   Start of a new 29.5 year 'Controlled-Expansion Cycle'.   *OR*
Saturn Square (challenging) Jupiter
♄ □ ♃   *OR*
Saturn Opposition (confronting) Jupiter
♄ ☍ ♃

Key phrases: Testing Faith – Controlled or Restricted Growth and Expenditure

Theme: A powerful point of reckoning with regard to your Jupiter Profile, where you are having to assess the practical nature of your plans, with the intention of making steadier progress.

Whatever you are investing time, money or energy in will, at this time, demand that you align it with the reality at hand, and do any necessary pruning. But watch out that you don't over-react through disappointment, and scrap what could be a worthwhile project or opinion. You are being tried now – not condemned! If, however, circumstances do get the better of you, then put it all down to experience, for it just wasn't meant to happen.

But don't throw the towel in too readily, especially if there are more positive planetary influences coming your way, for this period marks a critical point in a cycle of organized growth in your life. So, be sure to check that it isn't just your own outworn principles or beliefs – or not having any at all – that are denying you a brighter future. Do your 'homework', and don't let restlessness get the better of you either. Patience is the virtue.

Possible Encounters: Legal/Financial Difficulties – The Valley of Decision – Resolutions Made or Forced

Saturn Trine (supporting) Jupiter
♄ △ ♃   **OR**
Saturn Sextile (assisting) Jupiter
♄ ✶ ♃

Key phrases: Steady Progress – Stabilizing Beliefs – Consolidating Plans

Theme: Opportunities to be practical and objective with regard to your Jupiter Profile, thereby allowing you to organize and secure future developments.

For as long as this period lasts, you are more than usually aware of how to maintain a balance between your hopes and the status quo. You are therefore prepared to be conservative, yet at the same time speculative. This blend enables you to make the most of your assets and experience, and to invest them wisely. Those in positions of authority are willing to assist you, for what is positive and dependable about you is plain to see. Make your prospects firm now.

Possible Encounters: Sound Judgement – Reliable Agreements – Financial Gain

Saturn Conjunct (intensifying) Saturn – New Cycle Beginning
♄ ☌ ♄   Start of a new 29.5 year Order-Structure Cycle.

Key phrases: Test of Status – Time Tells – Establishing Duty – Order and Necessity

Theme: Progress Report. The powerful necessity of being true to your Saturn Profile, with its lessons, limitations and responsibilities – thereby aligning you with your life's proper direction.

This highly important period is called your 'Saturn Return', and it marks a time in your life when many changes can occur as a result of your having to ascertain for what actual reason you are down here on Earth. Other events that are occurring during and around this year-long period will further define what this life status report is all about. It is very possible that certain elements in your life have been winding down over the last year or two, making way for a more mature expression of your real purpose.

    For this reason, you will at this time experience the shape and nature of your being more strongly than ever before. On the one hand, this could feel like pressure, but only in proportion to how much your life is off course with itself. On the other hand, such a pronounced sensation of who you really are could be highly reassuring and informative. In any event, circumstances and relationships that no longer serve your real purpose will fall or be taken away. However, any partings or meetings that occur now are in themselves essential to your life's lessons and plot.

If this is your first Saturn Return, then you could regard this as when you have become a true adult, in the sense that you must now take full responsibility for your thoughts and deeds. If it is your second (or even your third), what is at stake is your sense of what constitutes a correct attitude to life for someone approaching probably the last chapter of your life, possible retirement, and the ultimate question/experience.

Possible Encounters: Peak Experiences – Parenthood – Developmental Crises

Saturn Square (challenging) Saturn
♄ □ ♄   OR
Saturn Opposition (confronting) Saturn
♄ ☍ ♄

Key phrases: The Test of Time – Progress Report – Ambitions versus Duties

Theme: Having to be practical and objective about matters relating to your Saturn Profile, which is in aid of making your material situation or attitude more sound.

You are going through a period when what you want to happen is measured against what is actually happening; what you are demanding of life against what life is demanding of you. This reckoning of your efforts will be seen more clearly in the light of other planetary influences that are occurring in and around this time. All being well, you will manage to meet both your own requirements and those of your circumstances, dependants or superiors – and soon find yourself in a better position. If, however, more difficult influences are also prevailing during this time, then you will have to bite your lip, read the writing on the wall, and obey what it says.

Possible Encounters: Law and Order – Limitations/Real Strengths – Maturity/Elders

Saturn Trine (supporting) Saturn
♄ △ ♄   OR
Saturn Sextile (assisting) Saturn
♄ ⚹ ♄

Key phrases: Stabilizing Position – Drawing from Experience – Smooth Running

Theme: Opportunities to be practical and objective with matters relating to your Saturn Profile, thus enabling you to manage current situations efficiently.

This marks a stage in your life when it is a sense of authority, be it your own or another's, that assists and guides you. This is not in itself a particularly creative or dynamic influence, but it is steadying. And you will feel the benefit of this when you observe how well regulated certain parts of your life are, and how much respect for work well done serves you. Mature and measured expressions of your personality attract support, and pave your path into the future. For it is your balanced objectivity, which is the hallmark of this period, that can now be profitably used to improve or firm up anything that requires it.

Possible Encounters: Official Approval – Helpful Elders – Good Timing

Saturn Conjunct (intensifying) Uranus – New Cycle Beginning
♄ ☌ ♅   Start of a new 29.5 year 'Freedom-Building Cycle'.   **OR**
Saturn Square (challenging) Uranus
♄ □ ♅   **OR**
Saturn Opposition (confronting) Uranus
♄ ☍ ♅

Key phrases: Inhibiting Freedom – Necessity for Change – Purposeful Liberation

Theme: Having to be practical and objective with matters relating to your Uranus Profile, through establishing what freedom and the uniqueness of self means for you.

Essentially this is a time when you have to ascertain what structures and habits in your life are keeping you chained to people or situations that do not, or no longer, serve your most individual interests and goals. If you are fearful or unconscious of making any necessary changes in aid of this, then you'll be in for a tense time, which could even create (subsequent) health problems. Alternatively, the difficulty will be the disruption any changes will cause not to you but to those closely involved with you.

   The trick is firstly to find a good reason (the actual reason) for making a change; and secondly, to appreciate that resisting this need for change will eventually make a disaster out of a mere dilemma, for both yourself and others. Ruts are only so far from being graves. But most importantly, it is the most individualistic aspects of your life – be it your beliefs, lifestyle or whatever – that are put to the test. This means that at some point you have to create a balance between your principles and material necessities, or sacrifice one for the other.

Possible Encounters: A Parting of Ways – Worthwhile Causes – Feeling Held Back

Saturn Trine (supporting) Uranus
♄ △ ♅   *OR*

Saturn Sextile (assisting) Uranus
♄ ⚹ ♅

Key phrases: Stabilizing Changes – Establishing Freedom – Old Blends with New

Theme: Opportunities to be practical and objective with regard to your Uranus Profile, enabling you to incorporate the unusual or innovative into your life.

During this period you are able to see how changes that began a while ago are now making sense in your life. Also, anything new that you wish to involve yourself with – from studying a novel subject to altering your appearance – you can now do without jarring others or feeling awkward yourself. You feel comfortable being your own person, and are able to express your idiosyncrasies confidently. Being true to yourself is no longer just an ideal, but patently practical.

Possible Encounters: Worthwhile Causes – Sound Ideas – Well-mixed Age-groups – New Solutions to Old Problems

Saturn Conjunct (intensifying) Neptune – New Cycle Beginning
♄ ☌ ♆   Start of a new 29.5 year 'Enlightenment-Building Cycle'.   *OR*

Saturn Square (challenging) Neptune
♄ □ ♆   *OR*

Saturn Opposition (confronting) Neptune
♄ ☍ ♆

Key phrases: Testing Idealism – Imagination versus Reality – Managing Weaknesses

Theme: Having to be practical and objective with regard to your Neptune Profile, in order that you make the distinction between guilt and obligation.

This is a time when the real concrete world 'out there' appears to have tracked down your secret and sensitive world 'in here'. Whatever webs of deceit, escapism, glamour or morality that you have woven to protect you or make you feel special in some way, are now cruelly dragged into the cold light of day. The main illusion here, though, is the one that made you feel you had to pretend in the first place to be anything other than what you actually are: a Spirit in a Body.

If you find that your spirit has not being living up to its spiritual responsibilities – or has been pretending to do so – then you must now put your pride aside, have an objective look at your superficial defence systems, and then get down to being responsible to, and on a level with, your fellow human beings. Just feeling guilty or indignant amounts to masochism because in effect you're merely putting off the inevitable confrontation with past misconceptions. Be thankful for this time when you can begin to rid yourself of illusions (that is, disillusionment), and express your ideals in a modest but real fashion.

Possible Encounters: Unreal Expectations – Coming Down to Earth

Saturn Trine (supporting) Neptune
♄ △ ♆   **OR**
Saturn Sextile (assisting) Neptune
♄ ⚹ ♆

Key phrases: Stable Inspiration – Gentle but Firm – Understanding Weaknesses

Theme: Opportunities to be practical and objective with regard to your Neptune Profile, thereby enabling you, and others, to benefit from your sensitivity.

This influence lets you keep a steady fix on what has been previously elusive or illusory. Fancies become facts as you hold in focus finer feelings long enough for them to become installed as established traits of personality, and real parts of your life, rather than just passing whims. So this is an auspicious time for any pursuits that require you to be both grounded and inspired – such as metaphysics, any form of artistic activity, charity work, yoga, etc, as well as accepting and dealing with soft or blind spots in yourself and others.

Possible Encounters: Practical Idealism – Altruism – Creative Productivity

Saturn Conjunct (intensifying) Pluto – New Cycle Beginning
♄ ☌ ♇   Start of a new 29.5 year 'Hand-of-Fate Cycle'.   **OR**
Saturn Square (challenging) Pluto
♄ □ ♇   **OR**
Saturn Opposition (confronting) Pluto
♄ ☍ ♇

Key phrases: Motivation Check – Necessity versus Desire – Reviewing Matters

Theme: Having to be practical and objective about matters relating to your Pluto Profile, which involves your reconciling deep feelings with reality.

You now have to have a long hard look at whatever it is that you have set in motion, at what caused you to do so, and how and whether you can continue with it – at all or in the same fashion. If your plans and ambitions harmonize with your relationships and circumstances, then you will be free to proceed. In fact, the way could open up powerfully now, meeting your priorities as if by magic, and setting your circumstances for some years to come. If, however, you encounter resistance to your intentions, then either you will have to work extremely hard to satisfy them or you will need to meet others halfway through, making it clear that you both have an equal and valid part to play.

Possible Encounters: Cutting Losses – Powerful Resistance – Hidden Strengths

Saturn Trine (supporting) Pluto
♄ △ ♇
                                                    OR
Saturn Sextile (assisting) Pluto
♄ ✳ ♇

Key phrases: Stabilizing Insights – Steady Concentration – Running Smoothly

Theme: Opportunities to make practical use of your Pluto Profile, through establishing a deeper sense of yourself and your goals.

Whatever else is going on at present, you become more aware of something deep inside of you that is superior to fate. Because of this sense of your own power and destiny, you are willing to bear with difficulties and work long and hard to gain a more profound standpoint. The commencement or continuation of any pursuit that further assists this psychological strengthening process – such as yoga, psychotherapy, meditation, etc – is highly recommended now. This is a time when you can, and maybe have to, get in touch with your own true and essential being.

Possible Encounters: Strong People – Material Advancement

Saturn Conjunct (intensifying) Ascendant – New Cycle Beginning
♄ ☌ AS   Start of a new 29.5 year 'Identity Cycle'.

Key phrases: Testing Presentation – Getting It Together

Theme: The powerful necessity of being true to your Ascendant Profile, through having to brave the world as you put yourself and your interests forward as having definite worth.

This is a highly significant period in your life, for you are emerging, or rather re-emerging, into the world after several years of some degree of withdrawal. It may not have been a particularly conscious retreat because the re-assessing of how you wish to present yourself to the world, and what as, has been taking place in much the same way as your body would assimilate a large meal while you carried on the business of living.

But that 'large meal' was the last 29.5 years of your life – or the whole of your life if you are under that age. And so two main questions arise now: Are there any old issues from the past that still need to be closed or dealt with before you can make a fresh start, and, What has the emergent you got to offer or involve yourself with that is going to give a definite purpose for the future?

Theoretically, and traditionally, you would be advised to clear away the former before getting on with the latter. But, in reality, you are probably finding yourself living out a mixture of both as you strive to straighten out old ties and commitments, while at the same time endeavouring to make that new beginning or launch that new product or project.

Consequently you have your work cut out for you now, while you represent yourself to the material world with all its, and your, strengths and weaknesses being heavily emphasized. If you are trying to do too much, or do it too quickly, Saturn will find a way of slowing you down. Conversely, where you are on target, some influential or authoritative figure will appear on the scene to assist you substantially.

To keep matters as manageable as possible then, you'll need to cut out any dead wood, in the form of outworn habits, haunts and relationships. Later in your life you will look back at this time as the beginning of an important new chapter in your life, and you will see quite clearly what just had to shape up or ship out. For now, though, you are having to thrash this out as best you can – in the knowledge that this new version of you will get through.

Possible Encounters: Firm Impressions – Concrete Reality – Material Resistance

Saturn Square (challenging) Ascendant
♄ □ AS

Key phrases: Limiting Self-Expression – Testing Relationships

Theme: Having to be practical and objective with regard your Ascendant Profile, forcing you to present your case as coolly and carefully as possible.

How difficult you find this particular influence greatly depends on what other events you are currently experiencing. If you have hard ones, then the trouble is likely to focus upon your not feeling able to express yourself in a way that others can appreciate or understand, thereby exacerbating the problem. But really this is just magnifying inhibitions that have always existed between yourself and certain others.

If you cannot see eye-to-eye now, it is very possible that a given relationship could be strained to the point of separation. On its own, however, this period will just find you feeling a bit cut off from people generally. In either case, it would be advisable to make a serious attempt to bridge any such gaps as much as possible, and to avoid being rigidly defensive, for this would further isolate you.

Possible Encounters: Awkward Situations – Outworn Ties – Necessary Withdrawal

Saturn Opposition (confronting) Ascendant – New Cycle Beginning
♄ ☌ AS   Start of a new 29.5 year 'Relating Cycle'.

Key phrases: Testing and/or Consolidating Relationships – A Question of Balance

Theme: Having to be practical and objective with regard your Ascendant Profile, which forces you to present yourself as coolly and carefully as possible.

This is a time when your patience and resolve is tested in the face of matters not moving along swiftly enough or as you'd like them to, for the reason that they now greatly depend upon the will and co-operation of others. Such circumstances can affect any kind of relationship – be it business or personal. If you are married or seriously involved with someone, then the oldest and most entrenched problems now present themselves.

So the most serious block to maintaining a harmonious relationship will now plant itself firmly in your way and demand that it be dealt with – one way or the other. Trying to avoid any such issue would only find you even more compromised – immediately, or at a later date when it might not be so obvious what the problem is. On the other hand, upon passing the test now set before you (and your partner or friend), you will put the relationship upon a firm footing for way into the future.

Essentially, you are at a critical turning point in your life when much of the effort and preparation that you have been making over the previous years is, as it were, presented to the world for its judgement or approval. What the 'world' is to you at this time is what lies in the other side of the scales. You will have to exercise patience and diplomacy, and maturity and skill in relating, if you wish to attract future success or harmony.

Whether it is a personal or a professional relationship that is the issue, it all depends upon your learning to be fair and well-measured, to meet others halfway, and to recognize that their interests may run counter to your own. Balance and respect on your part could win them over, as long as you do have something worthwhile to offer in return.

Possible Encounters: Trials – Marriage – Separation – Blockage or Stability

Saturn Trine (supporting) Ascendant
♄ △ AS   *OR*
Saturn Sextile (assisting) Ascendant
♄ ✶ AS

Key phrases: Playing it Straight – Stabilizing your Image

Theme: Opportunities to consolidate your Ascendant Profile, through being able to present yourself to the world in a conventionally appreciable way.

Whatever else is now going on in your life, to one degree or another you manage to give the impression that you are worthwhile and trustworthy. Consequently, others are happy to go along with you, either on a professional or a personal level. But bear in mind that this is a relatively superficial state of affairs, and that your true intentions will later show through for what they are, or they could suffer as a result of your being too bland and conservative. But, these points apart, this is a good time for expressing yourself in a disciplined and orderly fashion. As a reflection of this, those with whom you are involved are also reliable.

Possible Encounters: Sober Relationships – Helpful Elders – Sound Perspectives

Saturn Conjunct (intensifying) MidHeaven – New Cycle Beginning

♄ ☌ MC   Start of a 29.5 year 'Achievement Cycle'.

Key phrases: Culmination of Effort – Testing Position – Taking Responsibility

Theme: A powerful point of reckoning with regard to your MidHeaven Profile, when your status is put on the line – in the best or the worst sense.

As far as Saturn is concerned, there is no such thing as a short-cut or a game without rules. It rewards or discredits, with absolute accuracy. At this time in your life, Saturn is judging you on its own ground – that is, the material world. Saturn could be personified as the just, strict and successful elder who metes out advantage and responsibility, or demotion and disgrace. He has had his cool eye on you, and now he moves you like a chess-piece – on, up or off the board of worldly endeavour.

If you show promise, or it is required that you show what you're made of, or you have been working assiduously for some time, then you now find yourself deftly placed in a significant or higher position on the ladder of success. If this happens quite swiftly, which it might, try not to back out on the one hand, or be cocky about it on the other, for in some years to come you may regret having wasted the opportunity.

Conversely, if you have been cheating or skiving – that is, not playing by Saturn's rules, then now you will find yourself sliding down a snake, rather than going up a ladder. Ex-President Nixon is the classic negative example here, for the Watergate break-in occurred in the same week as Saturn Conjoining his MidHeaven.

So, in any event, this time is a landmark in your life, when your innate calibre is officially registered, be you pawn or king/queen, rising or falling, or just passing through.

Possible Encounters: A Peak of Achievement – A Fall from Grace – A Glimpse of Success

Saturn Square (challenging) MidHeaven

♄ □ MC

Key phrases: Testing Progress – Professional/Domestic Balance

Theme: Having to be practical and objective about your MidHeaven Profile, through reconciling where you are going with where you are coming from, or where you are with where you ought to be.

This can be the hardest part of the climb, in the sense that the balance between your professional life and your personal life becomes a critical issue. If you have been too involved with feathering your nest and not paid enough attention to amounting to something in the world, then you now feel trapped, and prevented from being 'somebody'.

But this would be because you have taken the line of least resistance and slotted into a niche that has now turned into a prison. To break out of this dilemma, which would probably involve loosening or even severing family ties, will take some doing. But the choice is yours: brave the dog-eat-dog world, or settle for staying in the kennel!

On the other hand, if you have neglected your personal or domestic life for the sake of getting on in the world, you could now feel rather empty. You may even be deserted by those you have taken for granted. So whatever the warning signs here, you must get down to finding out who you are as a person, as opposed to what you are in your job.

The above are extremes of imbalance, but all the same, to some degree it is now necessary for you to check out that you and yours are happy with the current domestic/professional set-up, and to reconsider the validity or feasibility of the course you have taken.

Possible Encounters: Aborted Projects – Necessary Setbacks – Family Crises

Saturn Opposition (confronting) MidHeaven – New Cycle Beginning
♄ ☍ MC   Start of a new 29.5 year 'Foundation Cycle'.

Key phrases: *Establishing a Base – Making Firm your Roots – Beginning Again*

Theme: A powerful point of reckoning with regard to the underpinnings of your MidHeaven Profile, while you begin to discover that a sound home or inner life is the only true basis to worldly success.

When you get to the bottom, there's only one way to go – up! For some years now you have been trapped in neutral, so to speak, although it may not have appeared that way from the outside. But that period is now coming to a close and you begin to build anew with what you have learned from your previous experiences.

The danger to watch out for is an inclination to press on too quickly, born of your sensing that the lights have changed from amber to green. But a structure is ultimately only as good as its foundations, and so you are advised to make firm and clear your domestic and personal situation rather than just racing towards some professional goal. Otherwise, your efforts will only amount to an empire built on sand, which would crumble in about seven or fourteen years' time. Such a mistake would be understandable considering the frustrations that you have been subjected to over the last several years.

But Saturn is Saturn, the Master Builder, and it dictates that the correct procedure must always be adhered to when you are going through one of its more important periods, such as this one. So do not be afraid to 'spring-clean', by weeding out weaknesses or misunderstanding at your home base, work base, or through revisiting, either mentally or physically, your childhood roots, in order that a sound material and emotional foundation may be created to support your process of development that will now unfold over the years to come.

Possible Encounters: False Starts –Domestic Difficulties – Figures from the Past

Saturn Trine (supporting) MidHeaven
♄ △ MC   *OR*
Saturn Sextile (assisting) MidHeaven
♄ ⚹ MC

Key phrases: Consolidating Ambitions – Recognition of Status

Theme: Opportunities to stabilize your MidHeaven Profile, through feeling aware of your rightful place in the world, and able to work steadily towards it.

You now have a definite intention to make your position firm in the material world, not only professionally, but also where you stand on the domestic front. And so you are likely to create a procedure whereby you are able to achieve your ends in a disciplined and regular fashion. If you work on your own, then you keep to a schedule more than you usually do. If you work for someone else, you find it easier to keep time and meet deadlines.

   In either case, people in positions of influence or superiority are liable to recognize your worth and efforts, and are therefore willing to assist you. The only drawback could be one of keeping too strictly to your work-plan, with the result that it limits your goals rather than serves them, and causes you to overlook whether or not you actually like what you're striving towards. So deliberately incorporate some flexibility and freedom of choice into your schedule and then progress will be happily achieved.

Possible Encounters: Advancement – Sense of Reality – Genuine Authority

8. URANUS TRANSITS

These are, or should be, life changing – often in an unexpected way. Uranian influences are therefore those of revolution, rebellion, liberation, innovation, suddenness, explosiveness, originality, accident, coincidence, and are awakening or disrupting and out of the ordinary.

The ideal way of responding to Uranus is with open-mindedness, a sense of experimentation, a willingness to look at things with alternative means that may well surprise or shock others, and by appreciating that you are receiving a message or an instruction from your unconscious, even though you might be unaware that such a thing could happen!

In effect then, Uranus is loosening up your idea of reality in order that you may adopt a more scientific, technological, alternative or esoteric overview of life processes. So a Uranian period in your life can be likened to flying or seeing the world from a higher vantage point. A Uranus Transit to one Radix Planet (Planet in one's Chart) lasts around a year to eighteen months in all. One whole cycle or orbit of Uranus around the Sun is 84 years.

Uranus Transit Interpretations

WHEN READING THESE TRANSIT INTERPRETATIONS, BEAR THE FOLLOWING IN MIND: Because the meanings of Opposition (confronting) Transits are usually similar to Square (challenging) Transits – and both these are occasionally similar to the Conjunction (intensifying) Transits – the same interpretation is given below the relevant Transit name headings, each separated by 'OR'. Also, Sextile (assisting) Transits are usually the same meaning as Trine (supporting) Transits, and they are set out in the same way, that is, Transit name headings separated by 'OR'. Although any actual differences felt can be fairly subjective, it is worth noting – from the table overleaf – the distinct **Strength and Significance** that each can take on, especially between the Trine and Sextile.

Uranus Conjunct (intensifying) Sun – New Cycle Beginning
♅ ♂ ☉   Once-in-a-lifetime start of a 'New-You Cycle'.   *OR*
Uranus Square (challenging) Sun
♅ □ ☉   *OR*
Uranus Opposition (confronting) Sun
♅ ☍ ☉

TRANSIT ASPECT TYPE	STRENGTH AND SIGNIFICANCE
Conjunct (intensifying)	This is a very strong influence. It energizes the situation in hand and both forces and enables you to advance and grow. This is a *New Cycle Beginning* and as such may indeed mark the start of some new chapter or outlook – but then so can the Square or Opposition.
Square (challenging)	This is a strong to medium influence that challenges you to develop in proportion to your relevant strengths and weaknesses.
Opposition (confronting)	This is a strong influence, and usually attracts confrontations that in turn increase your awareness of the matter concerned.
Trine (supporting)	This is a medium-strength influence that allows you to make progress with relative ease and support. It rewards past efforts.
Sextile (assisting)	This is a mild influence, and you probably need to apply some conscious effort in order to reap its benefits.

Key phrases: The Awakening Will – Disrupting Life in General – Life Changes

Theme: Being made forcibly aware of your Sun Profile, through the shattering of your routine, and through sudden developments and altered circumstances.

This should be a time of liberation for you! If you have got yourself entrenched in a situation or relationship that is not allowing you to be true to yourself, then expect the unexpected, for that'll be the only way to get you to move into the next chapter of your life, and breathe some fresh air into your lungs that will remind you of what you've been missing.

The more stiffly you resist any such necessity for change now, the more disruptive the occurrence or individual will be that comes along to enforce it. To be smartly in step with this wind of change, you would be well advised to plan in advance to make some sort of definite move during this period that will increase your self-awareness, and set you apart from the world you know too well, and that knows you too well.

Meeting fate halfway in this fashion will effectively 'absorb' the potentially shocking influence of Uranus. Alternatively, the issue in your life may now well be that you have to persist with something in the face of circumstances that are anything but encouraging. To change or not to change, that is the question! The factor from which to make your decision here, is how much tension or pressure is bearable – for you and yours.

If you see that a breaking point is fast approaching, then be as quick off the mark as possible, and be assured of the fact that change relieves stress, just as a thunderstorm releases atmospheric tension. Making a blow for freedom now would also put you in touch with new people and experiences that make the clouds of past skies seem very far away. This could be the beginning of the rest of your life!

Possible Encounters: Freedom – Rebellion – Restlessness – Innovation – The Unusual

Uranus Trine (supporting) Sun
♅ △ ☉   *OR*
Uranus Sextile (assisting) Sun
♅ ✶ ☉

Key phrases: Freeing Your Will – Awakening Creativity – Renewing Vitality

Theme: Opportunities to become more keenly aware of your Sun Profile, thereby enabling you to make positive changes in your life.

Under this influence you can, if you wish to, revolutionize your lifestyle. This is because prevailing circumstances offer you the chances and facilities to develop or redevelop yourself. The kinds of people and situation with which you are now involved allow you to make the most of your original and creative attributes.

Also the studying or utilizing of anything that is concerned with advancing knowledge and broadcasting information – technology, astrology, metaphysics, media – is now well starred. Essentially, this is a time for making all things NEW! And it is an especially good time for beginning any programme that will make you feel a new person – particularly with regard to your health. The more eager you are to make creative changes now, the more opportunities will arise to help you do just that.

Possible Encounters: Stimulating Friendships – Alternatives – Expert Assistance

Uranus Conjunct (intensifying) Moon – New Cycle Beginning
♅ ☌ ☽   Once-in-a-lifetime start of a new 'True-Security Cycle'.   *OR*
Uranus Square (challenging) Moon
♅ □ ☽   *OR*
Uranus Opposition (confronting) Moon
♅ ☍ ☽

Key phrases: Emotional Freedom? – Domestic Disruption – Awakening True Feelings

Theme: Being forced to refresh your Moon Profile, as inappropriate reactions and patterns of behaviour are no longer tolerable or tolerated.

This influence from your unconscious mind has the effect of jolting you out of ruts. What you think (or do not think) actually is a rut is one thing – what your unconscious thinks is probably something else. In other words, and in spite of what you reckon, the fact is that you have by now, through a series of instinctive and security-seeking reactions, got yourself into a living situation that is in some ways holding you back. Jarring, hectic and unpredictable as this time is, it does intend you to feel considerably lighter and more liberated by the end of it.

The trick is to remain as open as possible to what actually needs changing – in you, more than in others – and to make conscious attempts at dealing with each 'shock-wave' in a way that is distinctly different to your usual reactions. This will have a surprisingly freeing effect upon you, and others – although at first they might think you're being unpredictable, unstable or even unhinged.

On the other hand, battening down your emotional hatches through either blaming someone else for current upsets and frustrations, or simply suppressing them, is liable to attract occurrences that are even more designed to shock – such as you or your partner suddenly having an affair (which probably has a very unlikely quality about it, with short-term prospects to match), or perhaps a domestic accident, or something else that reflects inner tensions trying to break out.

If a relationship or any other important part of your life is seriously at odds with your real needs, then a parting of the ways is inevitable. Life and the ones who live it are hardly ever what we think they are, and this period is trying to trick you into getting a glimpse of what your own emotional truth is. Looked at in this way, and once you have accepted and got over the pain of waking up, this planetary experience can be exhilarating – a word which means 'enlivening'!

Possible Encounters: Odd Situations and Females – Unusual Behaviour – Home Moves/Home Changes – Unusual Accommodation

Uranus Trine (supporting) Moon
♅ △ ☽   **OR**
Uranus Sextile (assisting) Moon
♅ ✶ ☽

Key phrases: Freedom from Conditioning – New Feelings – Leaving the Past Behind

Theme: Opportunities to make original use of your Moon Profile through a change of needs, habit, home, or in the way you experience family or femininity.

If you are thinking of taking a chance, now is the time to do so. It is also a time when any changes that you have set in motion begin to take effect, possibly quite suddenly. This is an excellent period for gaining a new and refreshing sense of yourself, and proclaiming a big HELLO to your future.

Your relationships with women, mother, and the female side of your life and personality generally, will now become lighter, more open and aware. Many shadows that have previously darkened your path through life may now be lifted by simply moving into the light of truth.

Possible Encounters: Close Friendships – Liberating People – New Horizons

Uranus Conjunct (intensifying) Mercury – New Cycle Beginning
♅ ☌ ☿   Once-in-a-lifetime start of a new 'Perception-of-the-Truth Cycle'.   *OR*
Uranus Square (challenging) Mercury
♅ □ ☿   *OR*
Uranus Opposition (confronting) Mercury
♅ ☍ ☿

Key phrases: Awakening Perception – Revolution in Thinking – Disrupting Ideas

Theme: The powerful awakening of your Mercury Profile, through your mental attitude being radically altered.

This is a time when the mental lens through which you view life is changed. During this process you will adopt new theories and methods that challenge both yourself and others to change with the times and get fitted up for the future. With such a powerful but erratic current going through your mind you can also expect to be changing it quite often.

Likewise, be ready for 'jumps' in your perception that suddenly cause you to take off in a new direction with irresistible force. Or you might crash into an immovable object, for resisting this influence with rigid thinking would find you feeling tense and out of step, even to the point of snapping.

Conversely, mental flexibility enables you to snap into different modes or unconventional techniques – which could include the study of some alternative or technological subject – that in turn allow you to cut corners and break new ground. But beware of being too impulsive and not stopping to think, or of forgetting that something else again will come along to alter your course. You are being 're-routed' now, so enjoy the 'diversion'.

Possible Encounters: New Ideas – Job Changes/Home Moves – Nervous Complaints

Uranus Trine (supporting) Mercury
♅ △ ☿
Uranus Sextile (assisting) Mercury
♅ ✶ ☿

Key phrases: Awakening Perception – Original Methods and Ideas

Theme: Opportunities to make original use of your Mercury Profile, through discovering different ways of thinking.

Your mind now is more lively than usual, so you make connections and associations between one thing and another that enable you to see the pattern of life more clearly. You are also drawn towards alternative or metaphysical subjects such as astrology, magic, yoga, etc. It is an auspicious time to pursue any new mental discipline for your intellectual cogs are well oiled right now.

Unusual ways of coping with problems present themselves; indeed, an unlikely solution may be the only one that works. Being free to think your own thoughts – and to enjoy the free thinking of others – is a virtue of this influence that is its own reward. A fresh outlook, mentally or physically, paves the way to your future.

Possible Encounters: Surprise News – Stimulating Company and Journeys

Uranus Conjunct (intensifying) Venus – New Cycle Beginning
♅ ☌ ♀   Once-in-a-lifetime start of a new 'Freeing-Love Cycle'.   *OR*
Uranus Square (challenging) Venus
♅ □ ♀   *OR*
Uranus Opposition (confronting) Venus
♅ ☍ ♀

Key phrases: Awakening Love/Beauty – Disrupting Relationships – Changing Values

Theme: Forced or renewed awareness of your Venus Profile, through the manner of your social or artistic expression being radically altered.

You now attract or are attracted to anything or anyone that gives you a stronger sense of emotional satisfaction. If current involvements or pursuits are alive to change and experimentation, then you will get the best out of this influence. Existing relationships can have new life breathed into them; new relationships, which are very likely to happen now, are the breath of life itself, and are in aid of getting you in touch with relating freely and honestly.

As such, you find yourself drawn not to your usual type, for this gives you a sharper and fresher sense of yourself as a lover or social being. You would do well to appreciate Kahlil Gibran's injunction concerning love between two people: 'Let the winds of the heavens dance between you.'

If you are stuck in any kind of rut socially or romantically, morally or artistically, then be ready for something to shake you out of your complacency – such as you or your partner being drawn to someone or something else. But the more you go to meet this transitional period with an awareness that life, significant others, and you yourself are worth more than you presently think, then you will ultimately be pleasantly surprised.

Yet passing through this phase wondering what you're doing and who you're doing it with, would be an unavoidable part of your redefining and coming to terms with both your true sense of what brings you and others happiness, and an individual moral code that allows you to do so. This should be a time of stimulating, although not particularly stable, relationships, and of original expression and experience.

Possible Encounters: Liberating Relationships – Short-lasting Affairs – Divorce

Uranus Trine (supporting) Venus
♅ △ ♀
Uranus Sextile (assisting) Venus
♅ ⚹ ♀

Key phrases: Liberating Relationships – Creative Innovation – New/Renewed Love

Theme: Opportunities to gain original experience of your Venus Profile through changing your manner of relating, and your social or artistic expression.

This period can be quite uplifting as you find yourself with more freedom to be and show who you really are as a social and creative being. You appreciate now that there is no one exactly like you in the whole universe, and as such you feel more able to express your unique values and style.

During this time, you attract people and experiences that recognize and appeal to your special-ness. Existing relationships can have new life breathed into them; new relationships are the breath of life itself. You appreciate Kahlil Gibran's injunction concerning love between two people, 'Let the winds of the heavens dance between you.'

Possible Encounters: Unusual and Stimulating People and Experiences – New Pleasures

Uranus Conjunct (intensifying) Mars – New Cycle Beginning
♅ ☌ ♂   Once-in-a-lifetime start of a new 'Freedom-to-Act Cycle'.   *OR*
Uranus Square (challenging) Mars
♅ □ ♂   *OR*
Uranus Opposition (confronting) Mars
♅ ☍ ♂

Key phrases: Awakening Self-Assertion – Disruptive Raw Energy – Freeing Sexuality

Theme: The powerful awakening of your Mars Profile, leading to a forceful expression of desires, consciously or unconsciously.

This is rather like being plugged into the mains! How you apply such energy depends greatly upon the manner in which you usually assert yourself, go about getting what you want, or simply maintain your right to be here. If you are inclined to repress such desires to some degree, then you are now likely to find yourself restless and easily irritated, and given to unusual outbursts of anger. This would be a sign that you first need to look into what it is that has been compromising your freedom to say and do what you feel.

Secondly, contact precisely what it is that you do want – and set about attaining it in a fashion that is, ideally, direct but not harsh. If, on the other hand, you are normally quite able to express your wishes, you could experience this period as others rebelling against your assumption that you can always get what you want.

Whether you believe you belong to the second or the first category, or somewhere between the two, you are now called upon – often in a quite sudden and unexpected way – to assert yourself afresh. Failure to do so could result in such raw energy manifesting itself in the form or accidents, physical traumas, etc. And unless it is absolutely unavoidable, beware of making snap decisions during this period – you could regret it.

Oddly enough, though, it may be some impulsive and apparently foolish action that precipitates you into a new and challenging situation. One particularly significant area during this time is your sex life: fast, furious, experimental, tense, exciting, unpredictable – these are a few words that could now apply!

One way or the other, now is the time to stand up for your rights, and thereby create a more self-determined lifestyle for the future. This influence provides a strong dynamic for men who are trying to discover their true masculinity, and for women looking for the true place in their lives of their own 'maleness'.

Possible Encounters: Fast-changing Energy Levels – Explosive Realizations – Risk-Taking – Surgery

Uranus Trine (supporting) Mars
♅ △ ♂   *OR*
Uranus Sextile (assisting) Mars
♅ ✶ ♂

Key phrases: Awakening Self-Assertion – Original Moves – Surprising Courage

Theme: Opportunities to express your Mars Profile, through finding it easier to know and get what you want.

If you normally have no trouble asserting yourself, this influence will add an extra sparkle to the way that you do this. If, on the other hand, you are somewhat reticent or feel ineffectual, this period will offer you chances to take not just one step forward, but two or three. Circumstances and coincidence seem to favour any attempt to make yourself felt. You may even find yourself helping others who have a hard time finding freedom of movement.

Possible Encounters: Advancement – Liberating Sexuality – Successful Surgery

Uranus Conjunct (intensifying) Jupiter – New Cycle Beginning

⛢ ☌ ♃   Once-in-a-lifetime start of a new 'Intuition-of-the-Divine Cycle'. **OR**

Uranus Square (challenging) Jupiter

⛢ □ ♃   **OR**

Uranus Opposition (confronting) Jupiter

⛢ ☍ ♃

Key phrases: Unusual Opportunities – Awakening Faith – Disrupting Beliefs

Theme: The powerful awakening of your Jupiter Profile, through your philosophy and world-view being radically altered.

Your life is now slipping, or rather jumping, into a different and higher gear. This is an 'anything can happen' period, so the more free and open to new experience you are, the more you will profit from it. Whatever does happen, though, will be in aid of broadening your horizons – whether through travel, study, a job, a move, a stroke of luck or a relationship.

As time goes by, you see more and more what 'it' is all about, and this sets a long-term pattern of how you go about determining and reaching your goal in life. For this reason, it is important that you do seize any significant opportunity that comes along now – because it has 'Made in Heaven' written on it – rather than your just continuing to amble along with a safe but stale lifestyle, which would be a possible but rather indifferent way of responding to Chance or Lady Luck.

In other words, a definite turn is now occurring in your life's road – so be ready to drop what you're doing which is of lesser importance than your higher hopes. At the same time, though, be prepared for a 'double-bend' – one change after another. Having a contingency plan would also be a good idea, but avoid using it at the expense of taking that opportunity to lead a greater and more fulfilling life.

Possible Encounters: Sudden Growth – Magic in the Air – Release of Tension

Uranus Trine (supporting) Jupiter

⛢ △ ♃   **OR**

Uranus Sextile (assisting) Jupiter

⛢ ✶ ♃

Key phrases: Awakening Faith – Quickening Understanding – Reaching Further

Theme: Opportunities to better express your Jupiter Profile, through strokes of good luck, and being able to see the bright side more easily.

During this period you can begin to realize that you are more free than you think you are. This may be quite obvious, or you may have to take a step back from whatever or whoever you are involved with in order to appreciate this.

In any event, you are unlikely to become unstuck by any harder influences that are presently around, for positive thinking or timely events will deliver you. This is a time when you could experience some outright good fortune – but if you are not used to this, you might have to open your eyes wider in order to spot it. Count your blessings now – for you have more than you think.

Possible Encounters: New Vistas – Joyful Individuals – Unusual Opportunities

Uranus Conjunct (intensifying) Saturn – New Cycle Beginning
♅ ☌ ♄   Once-in-a-lifetime start of a new 'Individual-Life-Policy Cycle'.   ***OR***
Uranus Square (challenging) Saturn
♅ □ ♄   ***OR***
Uranus Opposition (confronting) Saturn
♅ ☍ ♄

Key phrases: Disrupting Rigidity – Awakening to Fears – Re-Ordering and Reform

Theme: The powerful awakening of your Saturn profile, through being suddenly confronted with what is holding you back, thus enabling you to free yourself of such restrictions.

During this time, whatever you have suppressed or have simply come to regard as normal, re-presents itself in the form of tension that needs to be released in some way. Such tension can appear in your material world, your relationships or your physical body. You may need to seek help in backtracking to the cause of this stress, because by its very nature it is hard to approach and deal with on your own.

Merely keeping a stiff upper lip is not advisable here, for not only would this make for far greater stress or disease at a later date, but you would be missing the chance to free yourself from the icy grip of ancient fears. Now you really have to let go – and have the opportunity to do so. And in the process, you will re-establish yourself as the physical reality that you truly and actually are.

Possible Encounters: Nervous Complaints – Sudden Release or Breakdown – Friends Indeed

Uranus Trine (supporting) Saturn
♅ △ ♄   ***OR***
Uranus Sextile (assisting) Saturn
♅ ✶ ♄

Key phrases: Removal of Restriction – Time to Move on – Awakening to Duty

Theme: Opportunities to understand anew your Saturn profile, through making original use of your limitations and experience.

This is a time for making necessary changes in your material circumstances, but without creating instability or impossible expectations. You are presently at your most 'scientific', for you are equally aware of both theory and practice.

As such, you proceed in an orderly fashion, clearing away in the process anything that has outlived its usefulness. Those in authority recognize this and reward it; they may even clear away those obstacles for you, but do not bank on this. Consequently, you see your path ahead of you – and your new responsibilities – far more clearly.

Possible Encounters: Professional Advancement – Technical Studies – New Systems

Uranus Conjunct (intensifying) Uranus – New Cycle Beginning
♅ ☌ ♅

Key phrases: Awakening Uniqueness – The Moment of Truth – Disrupting Complacency

Theme: Becoming suddenly aware of your Uranus Profile, through your normality being upset, and your real self revealed.

If you've got this far, then WELL DONE! – for 84 years of age is the symbolic lifetime in astrology. This means to say that you have run the gamut of human existence and are eligible for some great insights concerning the nature of being human, which you can use as freely as you like – for freedom is precisely what you have now earned.

If you are not alive to this fact, then some more negative Uranian event – such as your being the victim of someone abusing your freedom – could occur. A classic example of this superbly significant point in life was the 84-year-old man who chose to stay where he lived on Mt. St. Helens when it blew its top in May 1980!

Possible Encounters: Unusual Happenings – Explosive Events – Young People

Uranus Square (challenging) Uranus
♅ □ ♅

Key phrases: Awakening Uniqueness – The Moment of Truth – Disrupting Complacency

Theme: Becoming suddenly aware of your Uranus Profile, through your normality being upset, and your true self revealed.

What is happening now is that you are being 'reminded' of what and who you really are. So any elements of your life that are in any way not conducive to your expressing your true identity now begin to play up, get in your way, and generally seem to limit your freedom. This experience occurs twice in your life: first around age twenty-one, and secondly around age 60-63.

If it is your first, then it is now a natural step for you to move on and do your own thing, which may incidentally mean going against someone else's grain – probably some authority figure. If it is your second, you are entering a stage of life that probably involves imminent retirement, and the prospect of working out what your life means on an inner, spiritual level rather than an outer, material one.

If you've already begun to ponder upon this question, this influence won't feel like an approaching vacuum, but actually be quite stimulating. If, on the other hand, you have not begun to 'inquire within', then you'd better get down to some pondering! Whatever your age, though, bringing things out in the open, speaking your mind, and asking some radical questions, is a very constructive way of dealing with this period.

Possible Encounters: New Circumstances – Youthful Viewpoints – Your Origins

Uranus Opposition (confronting) Uranus – Mid-Life Crisis
⛢ ☍ ⛢

Key phrases: Awakening Uniqueness – The Moment of Truth – Disrupting Complacency

Theme: Becoming suddenly aware of your Uranus Profile, through your normality being upset, and your real self revealed.

This is the astrological indication of the so-called mid-life crisis, occurring between 38-44 years of age. What is happening is that you are being 'reminded' of what and who you really are. How this works is by blowing a few 'fuses' – the fuses being whatever resistances, habits or conformities of behaviour were installed earlier on life in order to get by or fit in. All those things that 'one does' for the sake of convention, stability and social acceptability – most likely without knowing about it at the time. So any elements of your life – job, partnership, attitudes, beliefs, etc – that are in some way not conducive to your expressing your true identity, now begin to play up, get in your way, and generally seem to limit your freedom. And you want to be free of them.

The knee-jerk reaction would be to leave your job or your spouse or your home, and possibly become madly involved with something or someone highly unlikely. But this would be owing to an urgent feeling that you had fallen into a rut of predictability, and hadn't really done what you once dreamt you'd do. Be on your guard against this desperate manner of relieving a feeling that life has passed you by, or that you want to relive your adolescence in a fortyish-year-old body. But then a fuse that's about to blow does not usually give one much warning! If we were aware of it, it is quite likely we would resist it in some way – but that would be missing the very point that Uranus is trying to make.

What this highly significant period of your life is actually asking you is: 'What is unique about you, and how are you going to express that uniqueness?', which doesn't mean throwing the baby out with the bathwater by rejecting or ejecting anything or anyone that appears to represent what is stale and unstimulating. For one thing, maybe existing elements in your life could do with a shot in the arm themselves.

If they don't, and are quite happy with the way things are, then you need to start making some radical changes, which they can accept or reject. But as freedom is presently the name of the game, make sure that everyone has a chance to express themselves freely too. Bringing things out in the open is a very constructive way of dealing with this period.

Study very carefully any other events that are also occurring now, for they indicate in what ways and areas of your life changes may or must be made – and where you could be fooling yourself too. Overall, this is a great time to introduce something fresh and far-reaching into your life – particularly anything that furthers an ideal or that looks at things from a different perspective. So, having a goal or aspiration is your truest guiding star right now.

Possible Encounters: New Faces – Younger People – Unusual Happenings – Your Origins

Uranus Trine (supporting) Uranus
♅ △ ♅   *OR*
Uranus Sextile (assisting) Uranus
♅ ✶ ♅

Key phrases: Ringing the Changes – Awakening Originality – Befriending the Truth

Theme: Opportunities to attune yourself to your Uranus Profile, thereby enabling you to think more freely, and then act and feel more freely.

Now you see, or should be seeing, the future in a positive light, with your true reason for being alive as a primary consideration. By the same token, you could well be reflecting upon where you have not been true to your real sense of self and purpose, and upon using this chance to break away from stale patterns and introduce something new into your life that blows away the cobwebs and helps you to see life in a more hopeful and inventive way, where the unexpected is (again) seen to be a vital ingredient to life's recipe.

Possible Encounters: Youthful Ideas and People – Alternative Approaches

Uranus Conjunct (intensifying) Neptune – New Cycle Beginning
♅ ☌ ♆   Once-in-a-lifetime start of a new 'Spiritual-Awareness Cycle'.   *OR*
Uranus Square (challenging) Neptune
♅ □ ♆   *OR*
Uranus Opposition (confronting) Neptune
♅ ☍ ♆

Key phrases: Disrupting Illusions – Shocking Realizations – General Awakening

Theme: Forced awareness of your Neptune Profile through experiencing extremes of emotion, such as grief, ecstasy, allergy, anti-climax, enchantment, etc.

How you experience this time has a lot to do with how alive you are to the wonder of it all. There could be the extreme of feeling so high or low that you find it hard to function normally at all, or the extreme of feeling very bored or frustrated as a result of habitually resisting the mysterious, intellectually unfathomable or your spiritual obligation.

In any event, yours is now a case of waking up to the more subtle, sensitive and universal issues and areas of life; finding out how they work, how you can positively involve yourself in them, and not getting caught out trying to avoid them – either through rationalizing them way as being merely 'strange', or through abuse of drugs or alcohol.

Either of these escape routes could lead to mental or physical health problems later on – or simply waste years of your life. It is better that you now plunge into an alternative philosophy of life that offers some form of creative or practical explanation of what is happening to you. But try to exercise some discrimination in how you go about this.

Possible Encounters: Startling (In)Sights – Generational Revolutions and/or Disillusionment

Uranus Trine (supporting) Neptune
♅ △ ♆   *OR*
Uranus Sextile (assisting) Neptune
♅ ✶ ♆

Key phrases: Awakening Compassion – Stimulating Idealism or Inspiration

Theme: Opportunities to make original use of your Neptune Profile, through tuning yourself into others' emotions and needs.

The possibility of seeing the truth is relatively strong during this time – depending upon how much you are naturally inclined to try doing so, and upon what else is going on in your life at this time. So, you may now begin to see far more clearly how life works, which could also include your helping others to see as well, or you may just be marginally more easy-going. You could really hit some high notes – or just hum along.

Possible Encounters: Spiritual Ones – Profound Emotions – Enlightenment

Uranus Conjunct (intensifying) Pluto – New Cycle Beginning
♅ ☌ ♇   Once-in-a-lifetime start of a new 'Rebellious-Instinct Cycle'. *OR*
Uranus Square (challenging) Pluto
♅ □ ♇   *OR*
Uranus Opposition (confronting) Pluto
♅ ☍ ♇

Key phrases: Disruptive Obsessions – Awakening Power – Sweeping Changes

Theme: Forced awareness of your Pluto Profile, through unconscious fixations and motivations being brought to the surface.

When the 'mains' need replacing or mending, first the road has to be dug up! Whatever it is in your life that is holding you down, now expect it to be shattered or become more than usually troublesome. Once you have let go of those things or people that you have clung to, or those phobias that have clung to you – then you will begin to experience a great release of energy that will allow you to breathe freely and get on with the rest of your life with renewed vigour and conviction.

Possible Encounters: Necessary Collapse – Revelations – Upsetting People

Uranus Trine (supporting) Pluto
♅ △ ♇   *OR*
Uranus Sextile (assisting) Pluto
♅ ⚹ ♇

Key phrases: Awakening to Power – Freedom through Depth of Understanding

Theme: Opportunities to make original use of your Pluto Profile, through being able to see the greater picture, and your place in it.

You presently have the chance to tune into and more easily perceive the forces that are actually shaping our lives. Where you personally are concerned, certain fixed ideas and attitudes that have been getting in the way of a more fulfilling life can now be focussed upon and dealt with. And as you reveal or release one thing, so another is revealed or released.

  This is therefore a good time to take up any sort of metaphysical subject, such as yoga or astrology – or to undergo some therapy and receive favourable results. The more you probe into the workings of life and yourself now, the more effective and insightful you become, which in turn can virtually improve any area of your life. All it requires is that you look inside yourself.

Possible Encounters: Spiritual Perspectives – Psychological Awareness

Uranus Conjunct (intensifying) Ascendant – New Cycle Beginning
♅ ☌ AS   Once-in-a-lifetime start of a new 'Personal-Image Cycle'.

Key phrases: Change of Outlook – Freedom of Expression – The Awakening Self

Theme: The powerful awakening of your Ascendant Profile, whereby your view of the world and how it works is radically altered.

This period really rips the veil away from your eyes, allowing – possibly even forcing – you to see things in such a different way as to make what has hitherto been your role in life seem dull and restricting. It is very likely that someone now enters your life in response to such feelings of restlessness and hungering after something new. And indeed, it is a revolution in life that you are currently experiencing. But to be more precise it is a revolution in consciousness, which means to say that for as long as this period is effective you will be going through a number of changes in your view of things – so don't jump on the first train out of town, thinking that you have discovered the truth.

The chances are you have merely perceived a hint of the truth. The next clue could take you off in another direction again. Unpredictability is the name of the game at present, so be careful not to chuck the baby out with the bathwater by suddenly leaving your job, marriage, home or whatever. If any of these things is now seriously unsuitable to your newly perceived sense of reality, then you will have to move. But burning your boats and bridges, although a common effect of Uranus crossing one's Ascendant, would be a rather immature way of handling this major turning point in your life.

If you actually are quite young when this is occurring, then you probably will up sticks and move extremely impulsively, or you may simply have no say in the matter because someone whom you are dependent upon does the moving. Whatever the case, though, what happens now is mainly in aid of changing your perspective.

Ideally your change in circumstances should occur as a result of this alteration in how you view things, rather than the other way around. This could very likely take the form of your becoming involved with New Age Thought, alternative medicine, astrology, the latest technology, etc – and then your taking it from there. Consequently, other people who are accustomed to the 'old you' may well find you odd and unpredictable at this time.

If you are jumpy and reactionary in the face of this influence, then their vote of no confidence will be hardly surprising. Then again, whatever you do might appear to them as off the wall. But one way or the other, finding an avenue of free expression, and a system of thought to guide it, is what you must, can and ultimately will pursue now – above and beyond all other considerations.

Possible Encounters: Radically New and Different Relationships and People

Uranus Square (challenging) Ascendant
♅ □ AS

Key phrases: Disrupting Relationships – Altering Outlook – Freely Relating

Theme: Waking up to your Ascendant Profile, through a need for change in your manner of self-expression and interpersonal relating.

How others relate to you – and if you have a partner, how he or she relates to you – has a lot to do with how you come across yourself, and how much freedom you do or do not allow them. At this time, the issue of having an evolving relationship with one other person or society in general becomes critical; and it may do so quite suddenly.

If you have just been drifting along in a habitual kind of fashion, and not cultivating an ongoing exchange of thoughts and feelings that is mutually stimulating to each other, then expect at least one person in your life to rebel against your stiff and stale style of being. How that person will do this is unpredictable; suffice to say that the level of shock value will be in direct proportion to how much you have been 'asleep' to what and who that other person is.

Essentially, this is a time when you have to relate as one human being to another human being, with all the honesty and friendliness that this requires. It would also help greatly if you did not assume that you totally knew one another. Leaving room for surprise and individualism magically refreshes any relationship.

Possible Encounters: Unexpected Ones – Short-lasting but Stimulating Affairs

Uranus Opposition (confronting) Ascendant – New Cycle Beginning
♅ ☌ AS   Once-in-a-lifetime start of a new 'True-Relating Cycle'.

Key phrases: Disrupting Relationships – Changing Partners – Free Love

Theme: Waking up to your Ascendant Profile, through a need for change in your outlook, presentation and social interaction.

How others relate to you – and if you have a partner, how he or she relates to you – has a lot to do with how you come across yourself, and how much freedom you do or do not allow them. At this time, the issue of having an evolving relationship with one other person or society in general becomes critical; and it may do so quite suddenly.

If you have just been drifting along in a habitual kind of fashion, and not cultivating an ongoing exchange of thoughts and feelings that is mutually stimulating to each other, then expect at least one person in your life to rebel against your stiff and stale style of being. How that person will do this is unpredictable; suffice to say that the level of shock value will be in direct proportion to how much you have been 'asleep' to what and who that other person is.

If, consciously or unconsciously, you have actually been restricting them in some way, then you are in for a bit of an explosion! In fact, any kind of coercion or suppression on your part will attract rebellion or a bolt from the blue, like being left or sued. Or the whole thing could be the reverse way round, with you being the restricted partner suddenly making a blow for freedom, maybe through being attracted to someone radically different.

If, on the other hand, you have been open and fair with your partner or others in general, then this is a time of increased freedom within your relationship, with you both enjoying an ease of movement and expression, within and outside that relationship. This just might include a stab at a so-called open relationship, but that is likely to blow up in your face if you are prone or oblivious to feelings of insecurity, possessiveness or jealousy.

Essentially, this is a time when you have to relate as one human being to another human being, with all the honesty and friendliness that this requires. It would also help greatly if you did not assume that you totally knew one another. Leaving room for surprise and individualism magically refreshes any relationship.

Possible Encounters: Unusual, Odd or Young People – Alternative Society

Uranus Trine (supporting) Ascendant
♅ △ AS
Uranus Sextile (assisting) Ascendant
♅ ✶ AS

Key phrases: Freely Relating – Unique Presentation – Unusual Circumstances

Theme: Opportunities to refresh your Ascendant Profile, through adopting a new and different way of relating and expressing yourself.

This is not an especially powerful influence, but the more you spot the fact that you are now seeing the world in quite an original fashion, then the more you will enjoy the interesting and highly individualistic connections that you are attracting.

And one thing can lead to another, with you possibly getting to know certain people who can introduce you to a world that is more to the fore of social evolution. So don't sit on what might appear to be quirkiness in your manner of behaving, for such is the hallmark of your individuality – which is currently your most valuable asset.

Possible Encounters: Stimulating Company – Alternative Occupations

Uranus Conjunct (intensifying) MidHeaven – New Cycle Beginning
♅ ♂ MC   Once-in-a-lifetime start of a new 'Individual-Achievement Cycle'.

Key phrases: Awakening to Purpose – Revolutionizing Professional Identity

Theme: A powerful quickening of your MidHeaven Profile, giving you sharp indications of how your professional life can be devised, or should be altered, to fit the shape of things to come.

Events can occur now that raise the issue of whether or not your professional position or social standing is a true expression of who you are as a unique individual. The less it is so, then the more unexpected and disruptive will be the invasion of your normality. And the more you resist such as being out of order or as being a dereliction of duty, then the more disruption you will invite.

In truth, a radical change is what is required now – particularly in the way you work, or even the type of work that you do; but the impulse to do this may just as well occur in an apparently unrelated quarter – such as your home and family. Ask yourself, 'Am I staying in this out of a fear of insecurity, or merely because it is expected of me?' Such reasons will be insufficient, for there is something in you that wants you to be true to your real self, and it's calling very loudly now.

Alternatively, if your individuality is aligned with your position in life, you now experience opportunities to leap forward. This could take the form of anything from the introduction of new technology, new ideas, new people, special people, friends or some sudden change or coincidence that precipitates you into future development. This can and ought to be a very stimulating time for you out in the world of people and things. The changes are now being rung.

Possible Encounters: A New Direction – Shocks to Reputation – Your True Purpose

Uranus Square (challenging) MidHeaven
⛢ □ MC

Key phrases: General Shake-up – Loosening Parental Ties – Fighting for Freedom

Theme: Disruption of your MidHeaven Profile, giving rise to changes and upsets on the domestic and/or professional scene.

During this time you experience tremors that are designed to dislodge outmoded attitudes that have probably been around since you were a child. The object of such is to force you to liberate yourself from stale and limiting ways of being that are possibly holding you back professionally, personally or both. Seeing that it was your parents who apparently instilled these negative attitudes, you are very likely to struggle against their influence quite strongly now, whether or not one or both of them is alive, or is living with you.

The more you put some emotional or physical space between you and them, or rather what it is in them that appears to compromise your freedom, then the more you will be adapting yourself for the future. Unless there are no signs of such friction – which if you are being honest is very unlikely – then attempting to maintain the status quo could find your life severely limited at a later date.

Possible Encounters: Clashes between Family and Friends – Liberating Realizations

Uranus Opposition (confronting) MidHeaven – New Cycle Beginning
⛢ ☍ MC   Once-in-a-lifetime start of a new 'Inner-Freedom Cycle'.

Key phrases: Constructive Uprooting – Family/Domestic Changes – Rumblings Within

Theme: Waking up to your MidHeaven Profile through the need for change on the home and professional front.

Events from your past and background that are getting in the way of future development are now surfacing and possibly creating disturbances in your home and family. If you have taken this cue from Fate and are actually making radical changes, then you can regard yourself as being in tune with your life's true direction. If you are blind to the need for alterations, then expect some form of unexpected disruption at home or at work.

Possible Encounters: Home Moves – New Direction/Profession – Domestic Upsets

Uranus Trine (supporting) MidHeaven
⛢ △ MC   *OR*

Uranus Sextile (assisting) MidHeaven
⛢ ✶ MC

Key phrases: New Directions – Aspirations Guide Ambitions

Theme: Opportunities to revolutionize your MidHeaven Profile, thus enabling you to align your profession with your ideals.

If you wish to, you may now update your career, in that you have opportunities that offer you the chance to do something in life that has more to do with what you like to do, rather than with what you usually do or think you ought to do. There is no actual pressure to break away from the norm with regard to your professional and personal position – notwithstanding other events – but doing so could well help you to clarify your life situation generally, as well as satisfy your heart and not just your pocket. This is also a time when you could successfully begin to utilize or work in science and technology, or some unusual subject, like astrology.

Possible Encounters: Innovation – Positive Changes Professionally and/or Domestically

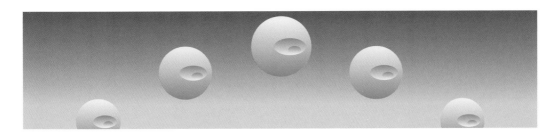

9. NEPTUNE TRANSITS

These are, or should be, life changing in a subtle way. Neptune's influences are those of sensitization, softening, mystification, fascination, temptation, inspiration, compassion, delusion, addiction, aversion, irritation, and are enlightening or undermining. While very much under its influence – for Neptune is like a drug or gas, literally or metaphorically – you are advised to let things take their course without struggling or resisting too much, go with the flow, but at the same time avoid giving in to your weaknesses. One can get quite exhausted under Neptune if you are trying to push against the tide or go for what you erroneously think you want. Any pursuit that relieves, enlightens or entertains is a positive way of channelling Neptune's influence – like healing, music, painting, writing, dancing, acting, any activities involving water, or that transcend the ego or attune one to a Higher Power, like meditation, yoga, mysticism, etc. Most of all, an attitude of acceptance is appropriate.

A Neptunian period in your life can be likened to a voyage across or beneath, or an encounter with, the sea, attuning you to personal undercurrents or collective moods. A Neptune Transit to one Radix Planet (Planet in one's Chart) lasts around two years overall. One whole cycle or orbit of Neptune around the Sun is 165 years.

Neptune Transit Interpretations

WHEN READING THESE TRANSIT INTERPRETATIONS, BEAR THE FOLLOWING IN MIND: Because the meanings of Opposition (confronting) Transits are usually similar to Square (challenging) Transits – and both these are occasionally similar to the Conjunction (intensifying) Transits – the same interpretation is given below the relevant Transit name headings, each separated by 'OR'. Also, Sextile (assisting) Transits are usually the same meaning as Trine (supporting) Transits, and they are set out in the same way, that is, Transit name headings separated by 'OR'. Although any actual differences felt can be fairly subjective, it is worth noting – from the table overleaf – the distinct **Strength and Significance** that each can take on, especially between the Trine and Sextile.

TRANSIT ASPECT TYPE	STRENGTH AND SIGNIFICANCE
Conjunct (intensifying)	This is a very strong influence. It energizes the situation in hand and both forces and enables you to advance and grow. This is a *New Cycle Beginning* and as such may indeed mark the start of some new chapter or outlook – but then so can the Square or Opposition.
Square (challenging)	This is a strong to medium influence that challenges you to develop in proportion to your relevant strengths and weaknesses.
Opposition (confronting)	This is a strong influence, and usually attracts confrontations that in turn increase your awareness of the matter concerned.
Trine (supporting)	This is a medium-strength influence that allows you to make progress with relative ease and support. It rewards past efforts.
Sextile (assisting)	This is a mild influence, and you probably need to apply some conscious effort in order to reap its benefits.

Neptune Conjunct (intensifying) Sun – New Cycle Beginning
♆ ☌ ☉   Once-in-a-lifetime start of a new 'Inspired-Life Cycle'.   *OR*
Neptune Square (challenging) Sun
♆ □ ☉   *OR*
Neptune Opposition (confronting) Sun
♆ ☍ ☉

Key phrases: Sensitizing Sense of Self – Undermining Your Will – The Spiritual Life – Let it be

Theme: Having to experience the subtleties and illusions of your Sun Profile, through being painfully but inexorably drawn away from your ego's control, and hopefully drawn towards a more developed sense of spirituality.

In truth, this is a time when your higher self is attempting to get you more in line with its intentions, which are very likely to contradict, confuse or compromise what you think you want. How much it does this depends entirely upon your current awareness of the direction in which your spiritual path lies. But remember that 'All roads lead to Rome'. In other words, the more attuned you are to where your life really wants to go, the less confusing and more inspiring this period will be.

For most people, however, this time is largely a case of first having to realize how lost you are before you can begin to find yourself. What or who now tempts or leads you astray, or calls you away from what you are presently doing, is very likely to be what others point a finger at, admonishing you for being impractical or misguided. Indeed, you could well be deceiving yourself as some aspect of your being craves some high – or some escape – that will take you away from the banalities of life and into the sublime or mystical, the glamorous or the fascinating. So you are very vulnerable now to anything that appeals to the romantic or the gambler in you, or to the idealist or the seeker after a greater and more meaningful life. The unanswerable question is whether you are being inspired or deluded; only time – possibly many years – will tell.

The chances are that you will lose something physical, which is of passing value, and gain something spiritual, which is of eternal value. At times you may feel totally lacking in vitality, as your unconscious mind tries to inform you that you're wasting your energy on whatever or whoever; or is it testing your resolve to see things through? But the subtle thing about being very much under this influence, is that it is almost impossible to be entirely wise and prudent by avoiding or pursuing what to others may seem obviously dubious.

There is no drug like experience! However, be warned against those blatantly dangerous people and things that promise instant ecstasy or profit – like drug or alcohol abuse, or get-rich or get-wise quick schemes – for you'd really find yourself undone. Unless you are in the unlikely position of being totally free of illusions, the only 'safe' way of handling this period is through some disciplined form of enlightenment such as retreating into meditation, compassionate service or creative activity. Even then there is the possibility of having no one to point out your blind spots, but you would be tuning into your own music – which is the real key to Neptune. But whatever your response is to Neptune here, you will still be taking a step into the beyond, and asking yourself – and hopefully finding out a bit more of what Life is really all about!

Possible Encounters: Mystery/Confusion – Disappointment/Frustration – Glimpses of Bliss

Neptune Trine (supporting) Sun
♆ △ ☉   *OR*
Neptune Sextile (assisting) Sun
♆ ✱ ☉

Key phrases: Spiritual Will – Concern for Life in General – Self-Transcendence

Theme: Opportunities to become more subtly aware of your Sun Profile, through aligning your intentions with others'.

This can be a very enlightening time as you become more sensitive to what is going on around you – and within you – and furthermore, are able to manage that sensitivity in a way that makes matters more easy-going for all concerned. The key opportunity here is to find and follow the line of least resistance. At best, this can mean that you feel happy and able to sacrifice your more selfish interests for the universal welfare, and thereby you attract opportunities to help or serve – which in turn help you. Or, at least, you can smooth your own path through being less insistent upon getting your own way.

One of the many subtle realizations that occur now is that what you thought you wanted for yourself becomes rather irrelevant as you allow life to take its own wise and all-inclusive course – a course to which you become increasingly attuned. It should be stressed, however, that this 'going with the flow' style of living does not and should not preclude your being self-actualizing or assertive; in fact under this influence you finely tune in to exactly what you truly wish to assert. And so this is also a good time for any metaphysical discipline, such as meditation.

Possible Encounters: Compassion – Acceptance – Inspiring People/Experiences

Neptune Conjunct (intensifying) Moon – New Cycle Beginning
♆ ☌ ☽   Once-in-a-lifetime start of a new 'Emotional-Sensitivity Cycle'.   *OR*
Neptune Square (challenging) Moon
♆ □ ☽   *OR*
Neptune Opposition (confronting) Moon
♆ ☍ ☽

Key phrases: Sensitizing Feelings – Undermining False Security – Susceptibility

Theme: Enforced sensitization of your Moon Profile, making it important that you make the distinction between fact and fancy, and that you adopt a more psychologically aware, or spiritually enlightened, view of life.

This is a time when many of your emotional weaknesses and blind spots become more acute. Positively, this gives you the opportunity to get a clearer picture of them through understanding that evasive responses born of childhood fears and insecurities are and have been giving you certain false impressions of what is actually happening. The major difficulty here is that it is this vulnerability that still makes it hard for you to look at how things actually are.

Consequently, this is a time when your reluctance to confront the truth can subject you to the very experiences that make you feel helpless or used. For example, any emotional involvement occurring or commencing during this period is prone to your trying to make it 'fit' your ideal; and the more you try, the more the comparatively harsh reality forces itself upon you. This is because your 'ideal' is actually a version of security that is acting as an anaesthetic for something that was missing or hurtful in your childhood.

The antidote for all of this quite painful stuff is firstly to recognize and then admit it. This is a time when self-honesty not only relieves but also enlightens. But initially it will hurt. The next way that you can positively go with this period is through your pursuing some very real ideal – rather than an illusory one. This influence makes you extremely open to the plights of everyone around you, and helping to relieve such conditions will channel your increased sensitivity correctly. But be very careful here as well, for you can attract all manner of hard luck story and lame duck, and they could suck you dry. Again, this is your own unlooked-at wounds or misconceptions visiting themselves upon you through the demands and suggestions of others.

Your 'openness' at this time can also affect you physically, so guard vigorously against infection and any kind of toxin, including alcohol, drugs and bad foods. On the same account, and in order to create much-needed security now, maintain maximum order and hygiene in your home. Additionally, such openness will boost any existing or latent psychic sensitivity that you may have. Again, seek to balance this out with more concrete knowledge of how to use and manage this correctly: metaphysical texts and practitioners (healers) will help you here – but yet again, check out their credentials too! How you handle this part of your life sets a trend that will affect the emotional reality of the rest of your life.

Possible Encounters: Strange and Fast-changing Moods – Confidence Tricks(ters)

Neptune Trine (supporting) Moon
♆ △ ☽   *OR*
Neptune Sextile (assisting) Moon
♆ ⚹ ☽

Key phrases: Sensitizing Feelings – Security through Spirituality

Theme: Opportunities to be subtly aware of your Moon Profile, through being able to tune into the emotional states of others, and into your own finer feelings.

This is a positively mild influence, in that it finds you ready to go along with the state of things as they are without becoming too agitated by any disruptive elements. It also inclines you to being soft and compassionate with others – or else you invite the same from those around you. This sense of common humanity that you experience now may vary from just feeling comfortable with your roots, family and domestic surroundings, to a more all-encompassing openness to your fellow beings. In fact, the more you can cultivate this spiritual aspect, the more receptive you'll be to helpful advice and making wise choices. Your hunches are reliable now, so follow them.

Possible Encounters: Helpful People – Spiritual Women – Psychic Phenomena

Neptune Conjunct (intensifying) Mercury – New Cycle Beginning
♆ ☌ ☿   Once-in-a-lifetime start of a new 'Heightened-Perception Cycle'.   *OR*
Neptune Square (challenging) Mercury
♆ □ ☿   *OR*
Neptune Opposition (confronting) Mercury
♆ ☍ ☿

Key phrases: Mental Inspiration or Confusion – The Deluded or Guided Mind

Theme: Enforced sensitization of your Mercury Profile, through having the doors of your perception opened.

If you usually like to run your life with logical thinking, then this influence will knock you sideways as circumstances arise for which you cannot find any rational explanation or solution. The more your intellect struggles, the more confused you'll become. If, on the other hand, you are less structured in your thinking and go more on your feelings, then this will be a time when you may gather a lot of wool and are too easily swayed by the ideas and opinions of others. In either case, you now perceive life more intuitively, in that you are extra-aware of forces and factors that the mere intellect normally misses.

By tuning into this higher frequency through some form of creative use of your imagination (writing, music, meditation, dream-work, painting, journal-keeping, etc), you will profit from this potentially inspiring stage of your life as you become increasingly able to express your finer thoughts and feelings, and to let problems apparently solve themselves. It is NOT a time for making important decisions concerning material issues, as your mind is going through a 'poetical' rather than 'technical' phase. It is however, a time for great honesty with yourself, which is ultimately rewarded with a more complete and sophisticated view of reality.

Possible Encounters: Channelling – Paranoia/Gullibility – Sensory Changes – Sensory Defects

Neptune Trine (supporting) Mercury
♆ △ ☿   *OR*
Neptune Sextile (assisting) Mercury
♆ ✶ ☿

Key phrases: Sensitizing Thinking – Heightening Perception – Inspiring Thoughts

Theme: Opportunities to subtly enhance your Mercury Profile, through finding yourself more able to read between the lines, and to be mentally creative.

Imagination is now the name of the game. If you already use your imagination as part of your lifestyle, then you now enjoy a richer and easier creative flow. Your mind resonates beautifully with whatever you regard as your source of inspiration. You readily tap into the stream of words, images and sounds that fills the pool of artistic divination. And even if you do not usually practise some form of creative expression, but have just dabbled or always meant to, now is the time to begin doing so, for you will invite encouraging results. Generally speaking, you are now more able to find creative solutions to everyday problems.

On a social or psychological level, this period enables you to perceive more intuitively – and therefore more clearly – the thoughts and feelings of others. At the same time, your own thoughts and feelings are in harmony rather than at odds with one another. So during this period, a healing for yourself and others can occur as a result of this attunement of Heart and Mind.

Possible Encounters: Art/Literature – Psychic Understanding – Subtle Realizations

Neptune Conjunct (intensifying) Venus – New Cycle Beginning
♆ ♂ ♀   Once-in-a-lifetime start of a new 'Higher Love Cycle'.   **OR**
Neptune Square (challenging) Venus
♆ □ ♀   **OR**
Neptune Opposition (confronting) Venus
♆ ♂ ♀

Key phrases: Selfless Love – Love's Illusions Undermined – Artistic Inspiration

Theme: The powerful sensitization of your Venus Profile, through your attracting or being attracted to fascinating and enlightening people and pursuits. These can be dangerously deceptive though, and can require you to adopt more psychologically aware values and live by them.

This is a very important influence for it appears to bring to you what we are all after: love and happiness. Or it can make you feel that your life lacks a certain special quality. In either case, it begins with your envisaging, consciously or unconsciously, some romantic ideal. This image is so powerful that you eventually find someone on whom you can project it. Whether this person is available is not really relevant to you – for you use a mixture of imagination and desire to make him or her into what you wish for.

The trouble with all this is that what you are really looking for is something that can only be found in the deepest recesses of your own being. But as looking in that direction involves your confronting emotional shortcomings, it seems easier to seek it in someone else, or to feel frustrated because you cannot see it in the one you are already with. The agony and the ecstasy of love, which is what this influence is putting you in touch with, could also be experienced as the loss of someone (or even something) that you regard, or once regarded, as your ideal.

The central question here is are you seeking or escaping? Owing to society's current confusion regarding love, sex and relationships, which stems from our lack of inner or spiritual awareness, you are probably trying to escape into something more sublime, heady or transporting, as a release from the drabness that is the spiritual void of your usual day-to-day life; and to escape from having to do what is emotionally necessary to inject that ordinary life with a piece of your soul.

In the meantime, you may enjoy that heady experience of rarefied or stolen moments – but when this period is over, or even during it, you'll come down to Earth and see that other person as another lost and vulnerable soul like you. But therein lies the truth and the beauty, which is what Neptune through Venus is trying to bring you. For the best way of giving expression to this influence is through some form of creative, spiritual or self-discovering pursuit.

If you already have an artistic outlet, or wish to, you currently find that inspirational flow is far stronger. Alternatively, you may express the spiritual, unconditional love of this influence through selflessly helping another – but just be very careful that you are not playing that well-known escape trick of 'saviour and victim', which is still another way of disguising who you and the other person actually are, as well as the conditions that you are secretly setting. Whatever is happening now, you do feel under some sort of spell. It is up to you whether it's bewitching or enchanting, a curse or a charm!

Possible Encounters: Mysterious Liaisons – Clandestine Affairs – Confusion or Elation – Dissolving Relationships – Falling in Love

Neptune Trine (supporting) Venus
♆ △ ♀   **OR**
Neptune Sextile (assisting) Venus
♆ ✷ ♀

Key phrases: Higher Love – Artistic Inspiration – Fine Romance

Theme: Opportunities to tune into and enjoy the finer features of your Venus Profile, through attracting tender and inspiring people or situations.

This particularly soft and sweet influence stimulates your imagination – romantically, artistically or both. You are able to perceive and experience the beauty and poignancy of life to a very fine degree. The classic manifestation of this period is a relationship that is extremely soulful – even to the point of not being physically sexual. This influence does not preclude physical intimacy, but its inherent idealism inclines either you or your partner, or both of you, to steer around anything that might diminish the refined and subtle nature of the feelings you have for one another. In effect, during this period, you are being made aware of the higher aspects of love, such as compassion and acceptance; and if you are active in some form of artistic expression, your creative flow is now more than usually strong and your imagination vivid.

Possible Encounters: Beautiful People or Places – Communion with Nature

Neptune Conjunct (intensifying) Mars – New Cycle Beginning
♆ ☌ ♂   Once-in-a-lifetime start of a new 'Psychic-Energy Cycle'.   **OR**
Neptune Square (challenging) Mars
♆ □ ♂   **OR**
Neptune Opposition (confronting) Mars
♆ ☍ ♂

Key phrases: Confused or Subtle Self-Assertion – Undermining/Refining Raw Energy

Theme: The powerful sensitization of your Mars Profile, where you either adjust your desires to someone or something other or higher than yourself, or get more and more confused and frustrated.

This is a difficult time for you as you are caught between two dimensions of your life, which are diametrically opposed: the desire to do and get what you want; and the inclination to submit to the needs of others. The most important thing to bear in mind is that during this period the latter will ultimately get the better of the former. But at the same time, you are being made to feel aware of any weaknesses regarding the way you usually go about getting what you desire. And so whenever you make a stab at something in the same old way, which could mean waiting for someone else to make the first move, you find that you become unstuck and fall from grace with egg on your face.

Before long, you may well feel apathetic and too tired to bother. In other words, Neptune is winning. So what does Neptune want of you? Essentially it wants you to appreciate that much of what you think you desire is actually an illusion. This can be acutely obvious where your sexual expression is concerned, where the stress upon physical 'performance' is particularly hard to keep up. Very much a case, sexually or otherwise, of the flesh only being willing if the spirit is! Neptune is calling you to let yourself just be with things as they are and not try to force issues Alternatively, you may at this time experience a quite fine and delectable type of physical relationship; but beware of hidden traps, like infections, deceptions, or relying too much upon fantasies or artificial stimulants to give you the illusion of mutual desire.

All of this does necessitate your initially getting in touch with the nature of your desires and forcefulness (or the lack of either), in order to let go of what it is about them that is delusory or unnecessary. A constructive way of getting the feel of the subtle but powerful emotional undercurrents that are prevailing right now, is to practise some physical activity that engenders putting your own little individual will in touch with or at the mercy of something far greater – like Hatha yoga, dancing, surfing, paragliding, etc. Such pursuits also tone up your physical body, which could otherwise become a problem now. This is a time when through learning to improve grace and poise you later emerge as far better equipped, and with a greater measure of personal charisma.

Possible Encounters: Energy Drops – Sexual Delusions – Weak or Gentle Masculinity

Neptune Trine (supporting) Mars
♆ △ ♂   *OR*
Neptune Sextile (assisting) Mars
♆ ✳ ♂

Key phrases: Sensitive Self-Assertion – Psychic Energy – Softening Hard Edges

Theme: Opportunities to become more subtly aware of your Mars Profile, through aligning your desires with others' needs.

Because you do not feel so pressured to prove yourself now, you are able to settle into a more comfortable gear. Wherever the road of life is uphill, you manage to see a way around it, or are simply prepared to wait until it levels itself out. In fact, helping others along is what seems to give you the greatest satisfaction during this time, for discovering the effectiveness of a gentle and selfless touch is the hallmark of this period.

Possible Encounters: Charitable Works – Healing – Fine Sexuality – Charisma

> Neptune Conjunct (intensifying) Jupiter – New Cycle Beginning
> ♆ ☌ ♃   Once-in-a-lifetime start of a new 'Vision-of-God Cycle'.   *OR*
> Neptune Square (challenging) Jupiter
> ♆ □ ♃   *OR*
> Neptune Opposition (confronting) Jupiter
> ♆ ☍ ♃

Key phrases: Elevating Noble Feelings – Undermining False Hopes – Blissfulness

Theme: The subtle empowerment of your Jupiter Profile, through the sensitizing of your beliefs and philosophy.

This is a very spiritual influence in your life. Quite what this means to you greatly depends upon what the current state of your faith in any particular god or goddess or cosmic law happens to be. If yours is a negative vision, be it cynical or dogmatic, then expect to feel either pointless or gullible, as you are liable to being left out or taken in. On the other hand, a sound faith in the essential goodness of the Universe will reward you with opportunities to become more involved in ministering to others, as you yourself see the Light more and more clearly.

Tell yourself that 'Heaven can wait' under this potentially giddy-making influence, for far-flung visions and easy options present themselves seductively now. Schemes for making a material killing should be avoided, or at least heavily scrutinized. Opportunists will see you coming a mile away, but when the dream fades and the going gets rough, they won't be seen for dust. It could be said that this period is out to make a fool of you.

Positively though, it is out to discover how firmly you can keep your feet on the ground in the face of the opportunity to improve greatly the lot of your fellow creatures. If you are merely seeking to gain something for yourself, or to avoid looking at yourself through 'helping' others, then expect to be greatly embarrassed. But if you experience compassion for what it truly is, without any urge to 'do good', then you may enjoy the greatly uplifting sense of being one soul amongst many. And from this sentiment, a true expression of faith and generosity will spring.

Possible Encounters: Idealism – Religious Fervour – Cults and Sects – Teachers

Neptune Trine (supporting) Jupiter
♆ △ ♃   **OR**
Neptune Sextile (assisting) Jupiter
♆ ⚹ ♃

Key phrases: Refining Understanding – Philosophical Acceptance

Theme: Opportunities to become more subtly aware of your Jupiter Profile, through appreciating more the Way of the Spirit.

Under this influence, you are more able to perceive life in a way that does not depend so much on material considerations. Because of this, many things of a physical or financial nature that you would normally worry about begin to be seen as something that is more in the lap of the gods than the hands of your bank manager.

In other words, you benefit from discerning an invisible reason for the way things are, and consequently are more able to create or maintain an optimistic outlook. You increasingly understand that the quality of life has everything to do with how you're looking at it. Hand in hand with this positive sense of the world, you may well experience the wish – and the opportunity – to relieve the plight of your fellow creatures.

Possible Encounters: Mystical Philosophies – Compassion – Gentle or Wise People

Neptune Conjunct (intensifying) Saturn – New Cycle Beginning
♆ ☌ ♄   Once-in-a-lifetime start of a new 'Enlightened Reality Cycle'.   **OR**
Neptune Square (challenging) Saturn
♆ □ ♄   **OR**
Neptune Opposition (confronting) Saturn
♆ ☍ ♄

Key phrases: Sensitizing Fears – Undermining Rigidity – Dissolving Inhibitions

Theme: A subtle confrontation with your Saturn Profile, through disappointing your limited viewpoint, and through realizing, and beginning to remove, what has been holding you back.

This period of your life is more or less unavoidably confusing. This is because the foundations and principles upon which you have built your life, now begin to show a few cracks. Reality is now no longer what it always seemed to be. We all adopt a certain set of rules quite early on in life, in order to have something concrete and reliable to live by. But this set of rules eventually becomes more limiting than it was reassuring; and this planetary period is particularly indicative of such a situation.

The first thing to do is to accept it. Then, to appreciate that Neptune will take about a year to introduce you to a more subtle and sophisticated concept of reality. And thirdly, because of this, take with a pinch of salt the depression and disorientation that this will

353

bring, for it would be unwise to make a fixed evaluation of your condition when it is your actual view of it that is constantly shifting. Also, and for the same reason, avoid as much as possible making weighty decisions.

Your main concern during this time is one of contacting and coming to terms with anything in your life – work, relationships, health, etc – that is giving you pain. Then seek to relieve that pain by discovering the blockage that is causing it. In the process of making this discovery – for which you must seek professional help if needed – you also find that there are dimensions to life and your own being that are far more subtle, mysterious and inspiring than you hitherto dared imagine. Having found your 'factory setting', you can then alter it – that is, your sense of reality – to include the miraculous and the mystical.

Possible Encounters: Odd Complaints – Otherworldliness – (Need for) Compassion – Loss of Unnecessary Possessions

Neptune Trine (supporting) Saturn
Ψ △ ♄
Neptune Sextile (assisting) Saturn
Ψ ✶ ♄

Key phrases: Dissolving Inhibitions – Practical Idealism – Imagination Takes Form

Theme: Opportunities to express your Saturn Profile, more subtly, through bringing your dreams and sensitivity into line with concrete reality.

During this time you are more than usually able to maintain a balance between your inner/emotional life and your outer/material life. So therefore you feel able to look at your doubts and fears for what they are, without feeling intimidated or inadequate; you are able to accept weaknesses and do something about them. As a result of this, you feel prepared and strong enough to incorporate your finer, idealistic opinions into your everyday reality, in a sound and substantial fashion.

Possible Encounters: Creative Projects – Rewarding Introspection – Wise Counsel

Neptune Conjunct (intensifying) Uranus – New Cycle Beginning
Ψ ☌ ♅   Once-in-a-lifetime start of a new 'Inspired-Originality Cycle'.   *OR*
Neptune Square (challenging) Uranus
Ψ ◻ ♅   *OR*
Neptune Opposition (confronting) Uranus
Ψ ☍ ♅

Key phrases: Confusing Changes – Sensitizing Ideals – Tuning Into Individuality

Theme: Being made subtly but forcibly aware of your Uranus Profile, through having your quirks and original traits exposed.

This could appear to be a strange time for you, because you are now experiencing the 'dark side of your moon', which means to say that those peculiarities about yourself and about life, of which you were previously unconscious, kind of sneak up on you. In actual fact, you are becoming increasingly attuned to what it is about you that is unique – and this could come as a shock or a surprise, or a bit of both. So it is advisable to inwardly digest, as calmly as possible, what is currently being revealed to you, and to avoid reacting to it or denying it, for this would only further confuse issues. Humbly observe what is unique about you, even though it (and the way it is shown you) may appear rather weird. You are not going mad – you are expanding your awareness.

Possible Encounters: Mysterious Associations – Disappointing or Special Friends

Neptune Trine (supporting) Uranus
♆ △ ♅

OR

Neptune Sextile (assisting) Uranus
♆ ⚹ ♅

Key phrases: Higher Mind – The Sense of Freedom – Discovering the Truth

Theme: Opportunities to become more subtly aware of your Uranus Profile, through reaching out for a greater understanding.

The more you are now involved with the spiritual, artistic or metaphysical dimensions of life, the more you will get out of this influence. As a result of this boost to your intuition and inspiration, you progressively further your finer interests and at the same time are able to perceive your own and others' place in the scheme of things. If you are looking for a cause, you will find one.

Possible Encounters: Idealistic Movements – Other Realities – Special Qualities

Neptune Square (challenging) Neptune
♆ □ ♆

OR

Neptune Opposition (confronting) Neptune
♆ ☍ ♆

Key phrases: Super-sensitivity – Blind Spots go Critical – Inspiring Visions

Theme: Mandatory immersion in your own delusions and fantasies in order that you become more acutely aware of your Neptune Profile, and thereby perceive the more subtle dimensions of life, yourself and others.

This is a time when you can really be a led a dance. Actually, it is you yourself that is leading the dance, but it is a side of yourself that you may not be that aware of – the blind side in fact. The more in touch you are with your illusions and fantasies, and the more you observe and express your dreams and ideals, the less trouble this period will sink you in. Where you continue to be blind to your blind spots, you must expect to experience spectacular flops and confusion within confusion. Bear in mind that disillusionment does rid you of illusions, which you no longer need – painful though this may be.

Possible Encounters: The Mystical or Illusory – The Spiritual or Glamorous

Neptune Trine (supporting) Neptune
Ψ △ Ψ   *OR*
Neptune Sextile (assisting) Neptune
Ψ ✳ Ψ

Key phrases: Divine Inspiration – Easy Sensitivity – The Line of Least Resistance

Theme: Opportunities to become more subtly aware of your Neptune Profile, through attuning yourself to the Way of the Spirit.

This is not a particularly powerful planetary influence, simply because by its very nature it inclines you to passivity. This is in order to help you become more in sympathy with those currents and occurrences in life that can usually escape one's notice, but are fascinating and important for that very reason. And so, while your sixth sense is being thus enhanced, you may perceive more clearly your individual part in the cosmic scheme of things.

Possible Encounters: Mysticism – Compassion – Selflessness – Spiritual Rapport

Neptune Square (challenging) Pluto
Ψ □ ♇   *OR*
Neptune Opposition (confronting) Pluto
Ψ ☍ ♇

Key phrases: Sensitive to Hidden Matters – Undermining Obsessions

Theme: Being made subtly aware of your Pluto Profile, through tuning into or being confronted with certain home truths.

Those undercurrents of emotion that have been secretly but powerfully affecting you all your life now become apparent, but as a result of something or someone no longer being there. That is, unless you are deliberately seeking to discover your most hidden motivations and power complexes. Either way, though, expect to make contact with those aspects of life and yourself which cannot be easily explained away. In fact, the more you try to avoid gut issues now, the more trouble they'll give you. So, the more you adopt a spiritual perspective and an attitude of acceptance, the more likely you are to experience enlightenment rather than deception; self-realization through isolation, rather than depression through desolation.

Possible Encounters: Mysterious Insights – Secrets Revealed – Disappearances

Neptune Trine (supporting) Pluto
♆ △ ♇   ***OR***
Neptune Sextile (assisting) Pluto
♆ ⚹ ♇

Key phrases: Sensitizing Insight – Generational Enlightenment

Theme: Opportunities to become subtly aware of your Pluto Profile, thereby tuning into your deeper motivations and the power within life processes generally.

This influence enables you to understand the way of the Universe, human evolution, the occult, etc. without getting out of your depth. And so, if you are just beginning to know yourself, you will get off to a good start; or if you have already been seeking cosmic or psychological awareness for a while, you could now take a leap forward and find yourself very much a part of the movement towards a greater appreciation of what constitutes the meaning of life on this planet – and maybe even others!

Possible Encounters: Mystical Groups – Consciousness Raising

Neptune Conjunct (intensifying) Ascendant – New Cycle Beginning
♆ ☌ AS   Once-in-a-lifetime start of a new 'Alignment-with-Spirit Cycle'.

Key phrases: Rose-coloured Spectacles – Spiritual Renaissance – Refining Image

Theme: The powerful sensitization of your Ascendant Profile, thereby altering and redefining your view of the world.

You are now seeing the world in a manner that essentially makes you want to see life and others in a better light. You also want to see yourself as something more than ordinary. Consequently, you are inclined to glamorize who or what comes into your space, and are reluctant to see the material truth of the matter. When this period is over – or even before then if some more down-to-earth influence comes to bear – you once again are aware of the reality of these people and things, with all their weaknesses and failings. And so a profound feeling of anti-climax and disillusionment can descend upon you.

But this need not necessarily be how it turns out, if you can understand that behind all this is a deep-seated desire to see life from a more enlightened perspective; to see everything and everyone as an expression of the spiritual notion that we are all one, and therefore beyond being separated or alienated, judged or found wanting in any respect.

Without such an understanding, though, it is this same desire that seduces you into seeing another, or yourself, as what you have always longed for or longed to be. This fantasy can take the form of a saviour, prophet, martyr or whatever it might be that transports you to some apparently rarefied place, to which mere mortals do not go.

Friends and family who know you as an ordinary fallible being are hard-put to point out that you are kidding yourself in this way, that it will all end in tears, some form of loss, or just fizzle out.

But the fact remains that you are now seeing life in this idealistic way. If you can exercise some discrimination in the midst of such a mist, and catch the point that it is the WAY in which you are seeing things, rather than the things themselves, then you are far less likely to be caught out when your ordinary perception of reality returns.

Positively, this is a time when you can immerse yourself in a situation where you are living an ideal through some form of service to others, or are endeavouring to transcend the illusions or apparent reality of things, and to get away from a purely materialistic way of life and looking at life. But above all, take pains to exercise that discrimination, for otherwise, despite your idealistic convictions, you could wind up as merely a slave or a loser.

Possible Encounters: Guides, Genuine of False – 'The Ideal' – Spiritual Ones

Neptune Square (challenging) Ascendant
♆ □ AS

Key phrases: Confusing Relationships – Relating Subtly

Theme: An air of deception hangs around your Ascendant Profile, thereby either undermining or making more sophisticated your perception of and dealings with others.

Things are just not what they appear to be during this time. So do not take anything at face value, but rather just allow whatever tempts or foxes you to pass on by. Presently, you are rather like a fish that is inclined to go for anything that catches its eye, whether of an emotional, mental or material nature. But beware; there could be a hook – or a catch.

Notwithstanding other more reliable or stabilizing influences, the chances are that if something is going to go awry, it will now. So avoid committing yourself to anything that incurs any serious responsibilities, yet have an eye open for snags surfacing from existing involvements. Being scrupulously honest, maintaining a sense of the ridiculous, avoiding trying to be clever, and gently contemplating life going by, will save you from falling foul of the reefs that could beset your current passage.

Possible Encounters: Misleading People – Strange Experiences – Sod's Law

Neptune Opposition (confronting) Ascendant – New Cycle Beginning
♆ ☍ AS   Once-in-a-lifetime start of a new 'Fine-Relating Cycle'.

Key phrases: Confusing Relationships – Relating Subtly – The Tender Trap

Theme: Introducing a hidden agenda to your Ascendant Profile, thereby either undermining or refining your dealings with others.

Whatever longings or fears you have been harbouring with regard to one person in particular, or others in general, now emerge and take some sort of form. It is more than likely that this will be experienced initially as a difference between how you are seeing things and how others are seeing them. And so a longstanding discrepancy between your idea of fears and longings and theirs now begins to reveal itself.

But unless you have a mutual understanding that is above average, you are probably going to try to avoid looking at this difference of ideas for fear of disillusioning or being disillusioned. However, it would be advisable for both parties to put their cards on the table as soon as the first signs of discontent or deception begin to show themselves. This will take courage, but it would forestall the despondency or lies that would otherwise descend upon the relationship and poison it. Then again, at its extreme, this influence could put you and another in a situation where sacrifice, surrender or both are quite unavoidable.

Another expression of this period could be that of someone or something entering your life that puts you under a spell, in the sense that they appeal to your weaker or better nature. If it is your weaknesses that they appeal to, then that someone will have the character or state of being to match. In other words, beware of lame ducks or offers of easy profit or enlightenment, for they will suck you dry.

Initially this would give you, by comparison, a sense of superiority but it would devolve into a horrible trap later on. On the other hand, a more spiritual or gentle way of life may now begin to open up in the form of some opportunity or personality. But again, without becoming paranoid, test the water before taking any plunges.

Possible Encounters: Misleading People – Strange Experiences – Infatuation

Neptune Trine (supporting) Ascendant
♆ △ AS   *OR*
Neptune Sextile (assisting) Ascendant
♆ ✳ AS

Key phrases: Sensitizing Relationships – Refining Personal Presentation

Theme: Opportunities to tune into the subtleties of your Ascendant Profile, thereby lending a spiritual tone to your environment and social interaction.

You are now more inclined to recognize the wisdom in serving the needs of other people, and in the process seeing the world and your place in it from a greater and more enlightened perspective. This could be ever so slight, but this is not in itself a dramatically noticeable influence. In fact, it is characterized by the sense of softness that you may now feel towards life and all who live it. And so, it is a compassionate outlook and charitable people that will guide and bless you now and the meek and the lowly that most appeal to you.

Possible Encounters: Inspirational Ones – Fine Understandings – Mysticism

Neptune Conjunct (intensifying) MidHeaven – New Cycle Beginning
♆ ♂ MC   Once-in-a-lifetime start of a new 'Spiritual-Direction Cycle'.

Key phrases: Refining Sense of Purpose – Undermining Public Position

Theme: The powerful sensitization of your MidHeaven Profile, giving rise to a sense that there is, or ought to be, a higher purpose to your life.

How you experience this period very much depends on how you currently see your role and standing in life. The less this has to do with meeting some kind of social or worldly need, and the more it has to do with just making a living or maintaining material status, then the more likely it is that you now feel some kind of unsettling undercurrent. On the one hand, you may feel that what you are doing in life is rather meaningless or self-serving.

From this can arise a wish to immerse yourself in some completely different pursuit that relieves, enlightens or entertains in some way. But as they say, don't give up your day-job – yet. It is more advisable to slide yourself gently into any occupation that puts a different interpretation upon what is a valid work role. Firstly, this is because you have a tendency now to 'make good' or 'go professional', and that could find you in a seriously ill-paid position, to which you would find it hard to adjust materially, and you would have only your ideals for comfort. Secondly, it is very possible that you are now prey to charlatans or pie-in-the-sky schemes.

If, however, you feel very sure of your position in life, be prepared to encounter something that could embarrass or expose you. If there are genuinely no chinks in your professional armour, then adjust your halo and carry on. But chances are that there is some element in your public life that is vulnerable and needs your sensitive and imaginative attention.

Over and above all of this, though, this influence can be very inspiring. Once you have managed to see through the probable miasmas previously described, you stand to be in line for some kind of calling or insight regarding your direction in life. The warning here is to avoid playing God, because there would be the Devil to pay! Essentially, you now have the opportunity to recognize why you are here, and what you can begin to do about it. Just avoid the extremes of thinking too big or too small.

Possible Encounters: World-weariness – Compassion for the World – Glamour

Neptune Square (challenging) MidHeaven
♆ □ MC

Key phrases: Refining Sense of Purpose – Undermining your Position

Theme: An air of deception hangs around your MidHeaven Profile, giving rise to a temptation to use questionable means, or to come clean.

How you experience this period very much depends on how you currently see your role and standing in life. The less this has to do with meeting some kind of social or worldly need, and the more it has to do with just making a living or maintaining material status, the more likely it is that you now feel some kind of unsettling undercurrent.

On the one hand, you may feel that what you are doing in life is rather meaningless or self-serving, and from this can arise a wish to immerse yourself in some completely different pursuit that relieves or enlightens in some way. But if you allow your ego to get in the way, or it has not yet occurred to you that there some things in life that are more important than how others see your position in the world, then you are likely to try bluffing your way through current difficulties. This will actually do nothing to diminish your feelings of uneasiness; on the contrary it would complicate things further.

Ultimately, it would be better to be as honest and upfront about any matters that threaten to make you look a fool, for this is far more preferable to actually being one! So face the music and don't try faking it by coming on weaker or stronger than you really are. Such honesty will eventually attract a quite revelatory display of help and compassion from others.

Possible Encounters: Embarrassment (Great or Slight) – Defeat (Dignified or Otherwise)

Neptune Opposition (confronting) MidHeaven – New Cycle Beginning
♆ ☍ MC   Once-in-a-lifetime start of a new 'Psychic Origins Cycle'.

Key phrases: Refining Inner Life – Undermining External Position

Theme: The powerful sensitization of the underpinnings of your MidHeaven Profile, thereby making it necessary for you to look within.

If you are one to concentrate more deliberately upon what is happening out there in the world of people and things than you do upon what is really going on in the most deeply private recesses of your being, then this influence makes itself felt through your becoming gradually aware of an insidious feeling that something has given way or fallen in somewhere. You may not be able to put your finger on it too easily, you may discard it as just a vague sense of insecurity, or then again it could manifest itself as problems closer to home, illness of a family member, or the like. Possibly some long taken for granted aspect of your background now turns out to be an illusion or just disappears.

Whatever the case, Neptune is calling your attention to the importance of your roots, for your outer life is ultimately only as healthy as they are. Now is therefore a good, or highly necessary, time to withdraw into the personal world of your past, your dreams, your family, etc, and get a better idea of where you are coming from. Otherwise you will have an increasingly weaker idea of where you are going.

If, on the other hand, you are usually inclined to being introspective or housebound, this is a time when some objectivity must be gained as to why you tend to bury yourself so. Being amidst the safe and predictable can now feel as if you are caught at the bottom of a well and slowly drowning. So you would need to make an effort to wrench yourself away from the ties that bind you to the past or to apparent safety.

Whichever case is yours, you may need to seek professional help in sorting out and freeing yourself from your particular form of entrenchment – and this could involve losing or saying goodbye to certain habits or people that are holding you back. But however you go about such digging, there is gold to be discovered in the form of an inner depth and beauty that will enrich the rest of your life and provide a true foundation for future developments.

Possible Encounters: Inner Mysteries – Deep Deceptions – Rising Damp

Neptune Trine (supporting) MidHeaven
♆ △ MC   *OR*
Neptune Sextile (assisting) MidHeaven
♆ ✳ MC

Key phrases: Spiritual Directions – Enlightening Ambitions

Theme: Opportunities to finely tune into your MidHeaven Profile, through acting upon your sense of social obligation – and thereby finding guidance.

Without allowing yourself to become a dogsbody, you can now do your work in a spirit of service and selflessness. Depending upon how sensitive you usually are to such things, the spiritual or social value of what you do out in the world, or at home, now becomes more of an issue.

Such a sense of being able to serve the welfare of others through your occupation or in your personal circumstances, may only be faint – but a subtle shift in emphasis upon what you see as being a worthwhile role in life could eventually lead to it being central to your life as a whole. So the more you tune in to subtle inner promptings now, the more on course you will feel. Any pursuit that involves entertaining, comforting or campaigning for those in need, or working behind the scenes, is also presently favoured.

Possible Encounters: Philanthropy – Inspirational Changes Professionally or Domestically

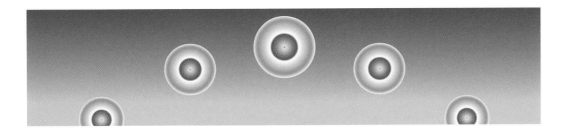

10. PLUTO TRANSITS

These are, or should be, life changing in a profound way. Pluto's influences are those of intensification, upheaval, elimination (of what is outworn), probing and deepening, purging, obsessing or concentrating, and are empowering or disempowering, regenerative or degenerative.

The best way to respond to Pluto is therefore through letting go of what or who you no longer need or is no longer there; getting more in touch with your deeper urges, feelings and fears; recognizing what or who is powerful in your life; and making the distinction between a positive expression of power and a negative one.

A Plutonian period in your life can be likened to a journey down and through, or an encounter with, the Underworld – that is, your deep subconscious mind and therefore your destiny itself. A Pluto Transit to one Radix Planet (Planet in one's Birth Chart) lasts around two to three years overall. One whole cycle or orbit of Pluto around the Sun is 248 years, so when Pluto makes a visit he means it!

Pluto Transit Interpretations

WHEN READING THESE TRANSIT INTERPRETATIONS, BEAR THE FOLLOWING IN MIND: Because the meanings of Opposition (confronting) Transits are usually similar to Square (challenging) Transits – and both these are occasionally similar to the Conjunction (intensifying) Transits – the same interpretation is given below the relevant Transit name headings, each separated by 'OR'. Also, Sextile (assisting) Transits are usually the same meaning as Trine (supporting) Transits, and they are set out in the same way, that is, Transit name headings separated by 'OR'. Although any actual differences felt can be fairly subjective, it is worth noting – from the table overleaf – the distinct **Strength and Significance** that each can take on, especially between the Trine and Sextile.

> Pluto Conjunct (intensifying) Sun – New Cycle Beginning
> ♇ ♂ ☉   Once-in-a-lifetime start of a new 'Life-Destiny Cycle'.   **OR**
> Pluto Square (challenging) Sun
> ♇ □ ☉   **OR**
> Pluto Opposition (confronting) Sun
> ♇ ☍ ☉

Key phrases: Profound Change – Intensified Will – Days of Destiny – Life Crises

TRANSIT ASPECT TYPE	STRENGTH AND SIGNIFICANCE
Conjunct (intensifying)	This is a very strong influence. It energizes the situation in hand and both forces and enables you to advance and grow. This is a *New Cycle Beginning* and as such may indeed mark the start of some new chapter or outlook – but then so can the Square or Opposition.
Square (challenging)	This is a strong to medium influence that challenges you to develop in proportion to your relevant strengths and weaknesses.
Opposition (confronting)	This is a strong influence, and usually attracts confrontations that in turn increase your awareness of the matter concerned.
Trine (supporting)	This is a medium-strength influence that allows you to make progress with relative ease and support. It rewards past efforts.
Sextile (assisting)	This is a mild influence, and you probably need to apply some conscious effort in order to reap its benefits.

Theme: The empowerment of your Sun Profile, through being forced to get in touch with what is truly motivating you – possibly through what is frightening or possessing you.

This important period is spread over one or two years, and is in aid of provoking in you a deeper sense of what you have been doing, and what you are doing, with your life. All of us have a destiny, a 'deep programme', which contains the plan of what we must grow into – as an acorn is to an oak tree. During this period, whatever you have allowed to get in the way of your destiny – a relationship, a lifestyle, or your sense of ego – will be broken down, or at least be severely dented.

If you find yourself fighting a losing battle to maintain – or avoid – some such factor in your life, then you will have to let go – of it or into it. But some form of deep change MUST be implemented. Attempting to resist could eventually poison your soul or do damage on a physical level. The issue to grasp here is what is of real importance in life in general, and in your life in particular.

Concentrate ruthlessly on that; which will mean making the distinction between an obsession and a conviction, or between a need and a fear – and then as a result of doing what you have simply got to do, any cause for regret will be ultimately outweighed by a thoroughly renewed sense of what and who you are.

Possible Encounters: Powerful People/Experiences – Breakdowns/Breakthroughs

> **Pluto Trine (supporting) Sun**
> ♇ △ ☉
> **Pluto Sextile (assisting) Sun**
> ♇ ✶ ☉

OR

Key phrases: Regenerating Life – Restoring Vitality – Power-Assisted Changes

Theme: Opportunities to lend power to your Sun Profile, thereby deepening and strengthening your will and sense of purpose.

This is a real boost to your confidence. Or, if you are having to contend with difficulties, you have the staying power and an insight into the reason behind such problems. Whatever you regard as the central issue of your life is now attracting advancement, along with a deeper conviction of what that basic aim is.

The powers that be smile upon you now. This is therefore a great time for practising any activity that transforms or renews – be it your body, your mind or preferably both. During this period, the 'life force' that is 'you' is rather like a mine to be explored and exploited – by you.

Possible Encounters: Promotion – Positively Influential Figures – Profound Ideas

> **Pluto Conjunct (intensifying) Moon – New Cycle Beginning**
> ♇ ☌ ☽   Once-in-a-lifetime start of a new 'Emotional-Regeneration Cycle'.   **OR**
> **Pluto Square (challenging) Moon**
> ♇ □ ☽
> **Pluto Opposition (confronting) Moon**
> ♇ ☍ ☽

OR

Key phrases: Emotional Purification – Elimination of Outworn Dependencies and Behaviour Patterns

Theme: The empowerment of your Moon Profile, through being put more intimately in touch with your feelings, security needs and ingrained reactions.

The idea of yourself, which you have grown up with, and which dates from childhood experiences, is now due for an overhaul. This is necessary because the habitual responses and defence mechanisms that you devised in your early years in order to protect yourself from real or imagined threats to your well-being, are now getting in the way of a healthy and continuous emotional interplay. In effect, you need to contact what your key emotional fears are, but it is more than likely that they are focussed on a deep and central fear of abandonment.

Doing this is extremely painful, and the temptation to use your old unconscious defence systems is almost as intense as the need to get rid of them. But the more you succumb to this temptation, the more you will attract situations that actually make you feel abandoned – by a loved one, material resources, health, professional support – or whatever you rely upon for a feeling that you belong somewhere or to someone or something. Or alternatively, you could feel horribly invaded or taken over by someone or something. But they won't let go of you until you have let go of your old defences.

You are like the snake that is shedding its old skin, and as it sloughs it off it reveals the new and tender skin underneath. You may need help, in the form of psychotherapy or an intimate and trusted friend, to get that 'old skin' off, and to reassure you that when the new skin has weathered a bit, you will feel like a new person, free of fearful schemes and imaginary enemies.

This enormously important time in your life has the potential to set you up for rich and rewarding emotional experiences in the future, as a result of not being limited by negative habits and reactions. Miss this opportunity, and you could be consigning yourself to an emotional scrap heap.

Women will figure strongly in your life now, as they symbolize the death and rebirth of your emotional nature. Your mother could be particularly significant now. Anything or anyone that is an inextricable part of the old you must fall or be taken away. The new you eventually shows itself to have qualities and depths that were once fearfully hidden.

Possible Encounters: Powerful Females – Domestic Difficulties/Moves/Repairs

Pluto Trine (supporting) Moon
♇ △ ☽   **OR**
Pluto Sextile (assisting) Moon
♇ ⚹ ☽

Key phrases: Regenerating Security – Renewing Self-Image – Domestic Improvements

Theme: Opportunities to deepen and empower your Moon Profile, thereby enabling you to feel more emotionally self-confident.

This positive influence amounts to a general overhaul of your life and personality. It is as if something deep and powerful were presenting you with people and things that give you a far stronger sense of being here as a person in your own right. It could be said that, to some extent, you are now being reconnected with your soul. And so, during this time, faces and places have a caring, reassuring and familiar feel about them.

Every so often, you feel that you have really 'come home'. And in physical terms, this could be literally the case, because housing and domestic affairs are favoured by both invisible and material forces Accompanying all of this, or more likely what is causing it, is your deepened understanding of what makes you tick, and your reconciliation with your past and those who figured in it – especially your mother and family. And the more that you are aware of this, the more rewarding and stabilizing the people and experiences that inhabit your life become – for now and in the future.

Possible Encounters: Profound Ones – Effective Healing – Powerful Female Bonds

Pluto Conjunct (intensifying) Mercury – New Cycle Beginning
♇ ☌ ☿   Once-in-a-lifetime start of a new 'Mind-Power Cycle'.   *OR*
Pluto Square (challenging) Mercury
♇ □ ☿   *OR*
Pluto Opposition (confronting) Mercury
♇ ☍ ☿

Key phrases: Intellectual Regeneration – Elimination of Outworn Thinking Patterns

Theme: The empowerment of your Mercury Profile, through the intensification of your thinking processes, and thereby the birth of a new mental attitude.

This is a time to question your own and others' opinions and ideas very deeply. It is as if nothing but the most radical reasons for acting or thinking will satisfy you. Such probing consequently creates changes in your mental environment, which mainly includes work and all forms of communication. If your burgeoning mentality is positive and alive to the need for thoroughness and change then the influence of your thoughts and ideas may well attract promotion or furtherance career-wise, and a more rewarding interaction with friends and loved ones.

However, if you find yourself resisting certain ideas and concepts, and insisting that your view is the only correct one, then you are in for a battle, where the winner will be absolute, and the loser sorely vanquished. So it is advisable to think things through to the roots of the matter, and not flinch at entertaining ideas that initially seem to threaten your model of reality; for now is a time when it is precisely that which is being targeted for any necessary alterations.

You should bear in mind that this urge to think and communicate more deeply is just as likely to be thrust upon you through finding yourself in situations where relatively superficial thinking simply does not wash. In other words, you are forced to dig down deep in order to resolve or discover something of vital importance.

Similarly, this period very much favours any kind of research or delving for the truth. Whatever happens during this period, your way of thinking will have changed by the end of it, and effectively introduced you to how powerfully your mental attitude influences what happens to you and around you.

Possible Encounters: Profound Insights – Job Changes – Obsessive Thinking

Pluto Trine (supporting) Mercury
♇ △ ☿   *OR*
Pluto Sextile (assisting) Mercury
♇ ⚹ ☿

Key phrases: Refreshing Thoughts – New Ideas – Work Improvements – Deep Thinking

Theme: Opportunities to make profound use of your Mercury Profile, through being able to apply concentration and insight, and thereby communicate better with others and see your way more clearly.

This is a time when you can tap into your mental resources and thereby further yourself at work – or at least, begin the groundwork that will breed successful results later on. This is a good influence to have around when sustained mental effort or concentration is needed. Physical activity that requires concentration is also well starred, and could lead to the discovery and regeneration of other dimensions of your being. The vital information that is needed for enriching or rationalizing certain areas of your life now becomes available. Restoring or repairing damage to any kind of communication links can also be successfully dealt with now.

Possible Encounters: Psychology/Metaphysics – New Jobs – Profound Realizations

Pluto Conjunct (intensifying) Venus – New Cycle Beginning
♇ ☌ ♀   Once-in-a-lifetime start of a new 'Love-Destiny Cycle'.   *OR*
Pluto Square (challenging) Venus
♇ □ ♀   *OR*
Pluto Opposition (confronting) Venus

Key phrases: Regenerating Love/Social Life – Eliminating Outworn Relationships

Theme: The empowerment of your Venus Profile, giving rise to the need for a deeper sense of relatedness, beauty and values.

What you want now is a feeling of having a more intimate and passionate quality in your life. Consequently, anything that would involve such a rich dark feeling – a relationship (or the lack of one), a creative pursuit, or your social life as a whole – has a hunger and an intensity about it that in turn attracts situations that compel you to live out these more profound and gut-wrenching emotions. With an existing relationship, it will be necessary to delve consciously into what is not satisfying you or your partner.

This is bound to entail a degree of confrontation with negative unconscious attitudes concerning intimate relating – in both of you. If this unearthing of such fears and desires that have previously been unexpressed is successful, then the bond between you will become far stronger and more deeply satisfying. Conversely, failure to achieve this for any reason – most likely a fear of looking at one's hidden motivations, or simply that your respective life-paths are unavoidably diverging – would lead to the death of the relationship, or an ongoing game of manipulation and emotional blackmail – a slow death, in other words.

If you have no intimate relationship, (or if you are failing to deal with an existing one in the way described above) then this influence is very likely to attract a new one. Such an attraction has a fated quality about it – as if you just HAD to meet. Indeed, a relationship beginning at this time will often last and last. But it should be borne in mind that the very force that brought you together also has a hidden agenda to it, which means to say that what keeps you attached is liable eventually to reveal itself as being more compulsive than romantic, and ridden with taboo rather than convention.

The underlying reason for this is that in order to have a deep involvement with another human being, you also need to be more in touch with your own deeper feelings, which are bound to include ones that have hitherto been repressed and now need to be drawn to the surface. Resisting this unconscious urge to get closer to yourself would result in the relationship being fraught with negative emotions such as guilt, jealousy or possessiveness, or the relationship collapsing in a painful and ugly way.

If you have a particularly deep fear of intimacy, and no such attraction arises during this time, then that is the very reason for it. If this is the case, and if it distresses you, it is advisable to contact that fear through professional help, or through expressing your feelings creatively in some art form. In fact, whatever the case, where artistic or emotional expression is concerned, this influence will supply you with profoundly deep inspiration.

If this need for a deep change in the quality of your life and in how you evaluate it is not experienced in your emotional relationships, then such a desire for re-evaluation is very likely to occur on the material level, with problems arising with regard to money, property or anything you deem as belonging to you. In other words, the question is 'What genuinely IS the quality of life?'

Possible Encounters: Moving or Fated Relationships – Marriage or Divorce – Profound Sensations

Pluto Trine (supporting) Venus
♇ △ ♀   *OR*
Pluto Sextile (assisting) Venus
♇ ⚹ ♀

Key phrases: Regenerating Love/Social Life – Deepening Sense of Worth and Pleasure

Theme: Opportunities to become more profoundly aware of your Venus Profile, through experiencing a combined sense of grace and intensity.

This is a very fruitful time for you, when existing relationships enjoy a new lease of life, and/or a new one can begin which has a transformative effect upon your whole concept of love. Dimensions of your being that you did not even know existed take form as you experience new depths of beauty and affection.

For this reason, any form of creative expression also takes on a greater vibrancy and influence. As you are carried along by this rich dark wave of genuine emotion, your social involvements become more dramatically meaningful. And in proportion to the increase in your appreciation of life generally, so your financial state and earning capacity will also receive a boost.

Possible Encounters: Passionate Romance – Paradise Regained – Restored Value

Pluto Conjunct (intensifying) Mars – New Cycle Beginning
♇ ☌ ♂   Once-in-a-lifetime start of a new 'Deep-Self-Assertion Cycle'. **OR**
Pluto Square (challenging) Mars
♇ □ ♂   **OR**
Pluto Opposition (confronting) Mars
♇ ☍ ♂

Key phrases: Enforced Independence – Surfacing of Power Drives – Transformation

Theme: The empowerment of your Mars Profile, through your manner of self-assertion or sexual expression being changed in some way – deliberately or otherwise.

Mars supplies you with the uncompromising desire to get what you truly want from life, which includes the mettle for preventing others from abusing you – something that could happen if you continue to ignore your own desires now. However, this does not mean being merely selfish – if you were you would find yourself very much out on your own or drawing someone or something else's superior fire-power.

Such isolation or defeat could occur in any event though, because the main dynamic here is one of getting you in touch with a deeper and truer sense of survival or sexuality or sheer self-determination. So this is quite a tough one, for it involves you having to confront, or be confronted by, forces within you and/or outside of you that are extremely raw, powerful and uncompromising.

This means that you should endeavour to put yourself forward as boldly as possible, and tell yourself that it is unlikely that you will be able to weather the storms that either threaten or descend upon you now through just being nice or reasonable. At the same time, however, avoid unnecessarily dangerous situations, and aim to come through it all with a far stronger sense of identity.

Possible Encounters: Power Trips – Intense Sexuality – Ego Conflicts – Violence – Hot Flashes

Pluto Trine (supporting) Mars
♇ △ ♂   **OR**
Pluto Sextile (assisting) Mars
♇ ⚹ ♂

Key phrases: Reinforcing Self-Confidence – High Energy – Physical Regeneration

Theme: Opportunities to tap deeply into your Mars Profile, thereby enabling you to assert yourself anew and take definite strides forward.

This is a time when your psychic energy aligns itself with your physical energy, which effectively means that you are performing efficiently and economically. You are thus very able to meet any targets successfully, or at least to put yourself in better shape for doing so later on.

General repairs can also be effected now. This is a period when strength leads to strength, things whip along, and the more you do – the more you feel capable of doing. As long as you avoid overdoing it, and bear in mind that most others do not possess the same drive as you do at present, you will easily climb several of life's ladders.

Possible Encounters: Powerful Masculinity – Little or No Resistance – Sex Boost

Pluto Conjunct (intensifying) Jupiter – New Cycle Beginning
♇ ☌ ♃   Once-in-a-lifetime start of a new 'Deep-Belief Cycle'.   *OR*
Pluto Square (challenging) Jupiter
♇ □ ♃   *OR*
Pluto Opposition (confronting) Jupiter
♇ ☍ ♃

Key phrases: Regenerating Faith – Eliminating Outworn Beliefs – Great Plans

Theme: The empowerment of your Jupiter Profile, forcing you to become more profoundly aware of your world-view, through the intensification of what you do or do not believe in.

The questions that you have to be asking yourself now are: What is my philosophy of life? How important is it? What am I prepared to give up for my beliefs? In what way, if any, should I temper my opinions? Can I live up to my own promises, convictions or expectations? Other people challenge you over these issues, and difficulties arise from your being unsure whether to compromise or not, or from being absolutely unwilling to bend at all.

This obviously involves your deepest principles – or insecurities resulting from not really having any. This period will determine whether or not you are over- or under-estimating your potential for success or for influencing others. You may well find yourself making an important journey, a date with fate. Whether this journey takes place outwardly or inwardly, it will or should shake you to the core, make the Earth move, even cause you to tremble with a sense of some Superior Being – for that is what you are instinctively after.

Possible Encounters: A Great Leap Forward – A Big Step Backwards – Righteousness

Pluto Trine (supporting) Jupiter
♇ △ ♃   *OR*
Pluto Sextile (assisting) Jupiter
♇ ⚹ ♃

Key phrases: Restoring Faith – Deepening Understanding – Powerful Growth

Theme: Opportunities to become more profoundly aware of your Jupiter Profile, thereby enabling you to make positive improvements in your life.

This is a time when you have the chance and are given the encouragement to shift your life into a higher gear. This is naturally relative to what gear you are presently in, but whatever you pursue now would prosper most if it had something to do with the general welfare, rather than solely serving yourself.

What, in this sense, could be called 'strength in numbers', is where the power lies now, and so that is what you can capitalize upon. Merely indulging yourself in the sense of wealth and opportunity that this influence can bring, is liable to give you a buoyant feeling – but you won't float very far! It is your immersion in the deeper waters of belief and philosophy, and the goodwill that goes with them, that really makes you feel vital, and that we are all on our way to a grander place. A feeling of generosity works wonders now.

Possible Encounters: Favourable Judgement – Good Companions – Philanthropy

Pluto Conjunct (intensifying) Saturn – New Cycle Beginning
♇ ☌ ♄   Once-in-a-lifetime start of a new 'Deep-Stability Cycle'.   *OR*
Pluto Square (challenging) Saturn
♇ □ ♄   *OR*
Pluto Opposition (confronting) Saturn
♇ ☍ ♄

Key phrases: Eliminating Outworn Structures – Forced Material Change or Loss

Theme: The empowerment of your Saturn Profile, through your physical circumstances being changed in some way – deliberately or otherwise, for good or ill.

This is a time when the manner in which you have structured your life materially is due for renewal – if it needs it. If such changes are required and you resist them, then expect things to happen which will make this point to you. At the very least, part or all of how you see yourself fitting into the status quo is up for review. In effect, you are challenged to remove stale patterns, habits and standards from your life that are holding you back.

Then, when this period is over, you should feel reality resting more lightly upon your shoulders. For now, you are driving deep into the bedrock of your being in order to build the rest of your life on firm foundations – so expect to meet with some resistance (from within or without) as you're doing so.

Possible Encounters: New Environments – Dubious Situations/People – Struggles – Physical Degeneration – Need for Repairing/Replacing

Pluto Trine (supporting) Saturn
♇ △ ♄   **OR**
Pluto Sextile (assisting) Saturn
♇ ⚹ ♄

Key phrases: Eliminating Fears – Power With Authority – Long-lasting Changes

Theme: Opportunities to regenerate your Saturn Profile, through renovating or replacing material structures in your life.

This is a time when steadiness of purpose – either born of your experience or of someone else's – is what will carry you through. This can either be in aid of your making actual physical improvements in your life, or of keeping you going through difficulties. In any event, a sense of maturity will be deepened and appreciated. Any tasks or programmes that need discipline and reliability can be effectively undertaken now.

Possible Encounters: Patience/Endurance – Influential Elders – Material Uplift

Pluto Conjunct (intensifying) Uranus – New Cycle Beginning
♇ ☌ ♅   Once-in-a-lifetime start of a new 'Genuine-Freedom Cycle'.   **OR**
Pluto Square (challenging) Uranus
♇ □ ♅   **OR**
Pluto Opposition (confronting) Uranus
♇ ☍ ♅

Key phrases: Enforced Change – Tunnelling to Freedom – The Tremor of The Truth

Theme: Having to become more deeply aware of your Uranus Profile, through intensifying your sense of uniqueness and the need to change with the times.

This can be quite an earth-shaking time – for you as an individual, and for the area of society in which you presently find yourself. Essentially, this influence is in aid of shaking you out of any complacency, and putting you in touch with who you really are – and the right to be so. How conscious you are of this impulse to explode out of the class–race–creed myth in which you are possibly buried, determines whether you feel a victim of change, or are stimulated by it.

And this can be a very exciting time if you let it. On the other hand, though, avoid being too keen to alter or overthrow everything, for later on you could find yourself more lonely than free, with a sense that something or someone is sadly missing. A measure of tradition or sentimentality serves to balance the see-saw effect of current circumstances.

Possible Encounters: Agents for Radical Change – Extreme Wilfulness – Shocks

Pluto Trine (supporting) Uranus
♇ △ ♅   **OR**
Pluto Sextile (assisting) Uranus
♇ ✶ ♅

Key phrases: Radical Transformation – Thorough Overhauls – The Power of Freedom

Theme: Opportunities to become more involved with your Uranus Profile, through identifying your individual effect on the greater whole, and your place in it.

This is a good time for feeling more a part of the positive changes that are occurring generally in the world around you. Chances offer themselves now to use your own uniqueness in order to further such changes, or to simply contact what is utterly original about you. So you can begin to feel a 'Citizen of the World' – or at least take a rewarding and alternative look at your own potentials, with the view to expressing them better.

Possible Encounters: New or Regenerated Friendships – New Insights and Liberties

Pluto Conjunct (intensifying) Neptune – New Cycle Beginning
♇ ☌ ♆   Once-in-a-lifetime start of a new 'Vision-of-Destiny Cycle'.

Key phrases: Old Order Passing - Eliminating Blind-spots - Inspiration Boost

Theme: The empowerment of your Neptune Profile, through the intensification of your ideals and yearnings, and a keener suffering of your illusions.

During this time you experience a power surge from your unconscious mind, which means to say that you receive a kind of 'course correction', which more likely than not involves quite dramatic changes in a number of areas of your life. It is all in aid of getting you more attuned to who you are, where you've come from and where you're supposed to be going. In the process of this happening therefore, you have to dig a lot more deeply into understanding yourself, through such pursuits as psychology, astrology, creative expression, or anything that gets you more in touch with the real you.

Of necessity, this involves the gradual, yet sometimes quite drastic, elimination of the old you, with its relatively superficial values and pastimes. However, you probably won't notice just how much you have changed over this period until some years hence. Indeed you will look back then, and regard this as a major turning point in your life; so it is advisable to live through this time with a sense of destiny being at work, and not to treat it lightly.

The actual experiences that you have now can vary enormously, but they are probably deeply moving, with moments of great significance and intimacy. There are also times of acute pain as you strive towards whatever you are trying to express or make contact with - or as you wrestle with what you're attempting to evade! Be mindful that it is these very moments of poignant pain and pleasure that are a testament to the fact that you are a lot closer than usual to the heart and soul of the matter. And to differing degrees, this roller-coaster ride will be shared by other people of your own age, for this is a generational influence.

But you experience it very much in your own special way, or at least you should, for this influence is in aid of putting you in touch with what is essentially 'you', and certainly not about going along with the crowd, although at times paradoxically you find yourself being wonderfully carried along by a tide of collective emotion. So mixing with people of a different age-group to your own is a good idea now, for the contrast will give you a sharper idea of where you're at. You are now setting a trend for the rest of your life that will profoundly influence your future work and relationships: so enjoy, and endure, and envision.

Possible Encounters: Shattered Dreams / Renewed Visions - Powerful Influences

Pluto Square (challenging) Neptune
♇ □ ♆

Key phrases: Old Order Passing – Eliminating Blind Spots – Spiritual Delving

Theme: The empowerment of your Neptune Profile, through the intensification of your ideals and yearnings, and a keener suffering of your illusions.

What place your dreams and ideals have in the modern world concerns you now. If you are prepared to sift through them in order to discover and honestly admit to any that are unrealistic, fanciful or escapist then you will find yourself more attuned to the eternal and ageless truth of being a spirit in the material world. On the other hand, insisting upon clinging to overly sentimental or outmoded notions will alienate you, and make life more difficult for those close to you.

Possible Encounters: Shattered Dreams/Renewed Visions – Powerful Influences

Pluto Trine (supporting) Neptune
♇ △ ♆   **OR**
Pluto Sextile (assisting) Neptune
♇ ⚹ ♆

Key phrases: Deepening Spirituality – The Power of Acceptance

Theme: Opportunities to become more involved with your Neptune Profile, thanks to

1. INTER-ASPECTS – HOW THEY WORK
The Chemistry Between You Both

Inter-Aspects are the interactions, in the form of angular relationships, between the Planets in one person's Birth Chart and the Planets in another person's. They and their interpretations are what a Relationship Profile consists of. The Interpretations mainly focus upon emotional/sexual/romantic relationships, but friends, family and business partnerships are also covered. Generally speaking, Inter-Aspects reveals how each person makes the other feel, and what each brings to the other by way of worth, experience and opportunity.

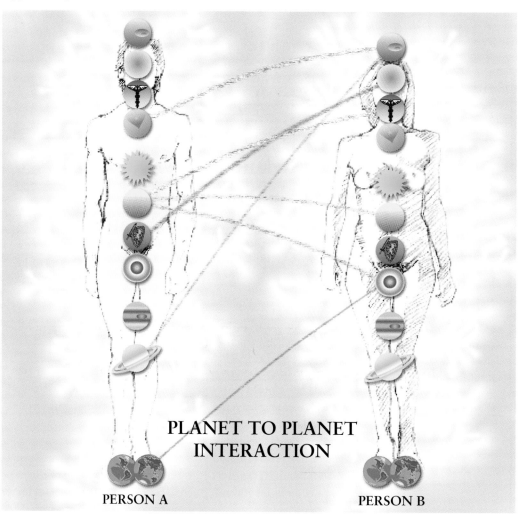

PLANET TO PLANET INTERACTION

PERSON A   PERSON B

2. CREATING A RELATIONSHIP PROFILE

1. If you haven't already, **install** *The Instant Astrologer* software from the CD according to the instructions.

2. Open the program and you will see you have FOUR CHOICES:
1. Personality Profile
2. Timeline Profile
3. Relationship Profile
4. Quit

Select 'Relationship Profile'

3. Input Birth Details for 'Person A'. If *The Instant Astrologer* cannot find the Birth Place (entered against **City of Birth**)it'll be because it is too small, and you will be prompted to re-enter the nearest town. It could also be queried if spelt wrong, or because the country is wrong (which may be due to historical border changes). For a United States Birth Place select the relevant State.

If you wish, you may **Save 'Person A' Birth Details** by selecting that button. If you have already saved the Details you want to use, select **Load 'Person A' Birth Details**.

Unknown Birth Times: If you do not know the Birth Time then enter 12 p.m. (noon) as this will give the 'mean' positions of the Sun, Moon and Planets. You should then disregard altogether any Inter-Aspects with *Person A* that involve their Ascendant, Midheaven and Moon, for these would only be reliable if they just happened to have been born around noon. (See also *Unknown or Vague Birth Times* on page 38 for more concerning this issue).

Namefile Notables: The Instant Astrologer has already stored the birth data of a number well-known people for you to create Profiles for if you so wish.

4. Input Birth Details of 'Person B'. Enter the birth details of the second person – 'Person B'. Again, if *The Instant Astrologer* cannot find the Birth Place it'll be because it is too small, and you will be prompted to re-enter the nearest town. Again it could also be queried if spelt wrong, or because the country is wrong (which may be due to historical border changes). For a United States Birth Place select the relevant State.

If you wish, you may **Save 'Person B' Birth Details** by selecting that button. If you have already saved the Details you want to use, select **Load 'Person B' Birth Details**.

Unknown or Vague Birth Times: See previous page, but apply to person B.

5. You now have THREE CHOICES:
    a) View Full Profile – To read the whole Relationship Profile *on screen only*.
    b) Print/View Index – To read the Relationship Profile Index* *on screen only*, then if you wish, select the Print option to print the Index.
    c) Print/View Data Only – To see the Planetary Placements and Inter-Aspects only.
    d) Return – To return to the Select Profile page if you wish to start over.

* The Relationship Profile Index simply gives all the various planetary Inter-Aspects for the two individuals in question, along with the page numbers in this book where they are interpreted. When printed, the Index enables you to study a Profile at your leisure wherever you may be.

7. If you have chosen:
    a) View Full Profile - All you have to do is read what is on the screen, scrolling up and down as you require. You can exit at any time or place you wish.
    b) Print /View Index - Simply read what the Relationship Profile Index says on the screen or on the page, and you will be directed to the pages in the book where the interpretations for the relevant Inter-Aspects will be found.
    c) Print/View Data Only – Read the raw data only.

With all of the above options, you can exit to the Relationship Profile page at any time.

3. USING A RELATIONSHIP PROFILE

As a rule, a Planet referred to in an Inter-Aspect's interpretation corresponds to the person whose Planet it is. For example, with the Inter-Aspect **A's Moon Conjunct (uniting with) B's Saturn**, where it says the Lunar person or the Moon, it means Person A; when it says the 'saturnine person' or just 'Saturn', it means Person B. However, there are often exceptions to this rule because of Interchangeability (see below). For the same reason, each person is sometimes referred to in terms of the role they are playing in the relationship that corresponds to one of the Planets involved, but not necessarily the one that is technically theirs.

These Inter-Aspects are divided into four general types:
    1. Key Connections
    2. Relationship Challenges
    3. Relationship Strengths
    4. Socio-Cultural Interactions

Also, as you read them in the whole Profile on-screen, or in the Profile Index on page or screen, the following should be noted:

'Close Ones'

Given to the far right of each Inter-Aspect name is a figure (in degrees and minutes of arc) denoting how close that Inter-Aspect is. Usually, the closer it is to 00° 00′ the more strongly that Inter-Aspect will influence the relationship as a whole, whereas the nearer the absolute maximum of 8° 00′ the weaker will be its effect. Sometimes, even when the Inter-Aspect is 'challenging' or technically 'negative', a Close One that is very close, like less than a degree, can be felt to be positive simply because the two people 'fit' so closely. Whenever an Inter-Aspect is actually classed 'Close One' this is because it forms a tight connection (3 degrees or less). Such interactions compose the core of your relationship, be it good or bad. As a general but not absolute rule, no less than around a third of all the Inter-Aspects should be 'Close Ones' for a relationship to be called 'close'.

Remember that the classification 'Close One' will not appear in the Interpretations that follow because it refers strictly to the Inter-Aspects between the two people in question, and as such it will only appear in the Profile Index, the Datasheet, or the whole Profile on-screen, for that couple.

'Birth Time Sensitive'

This means the interaction will be technically correct only when the birth times are accurate to within fifteen minutes. Also, if a birth time is only to within several hours, then any interactions involving the Moon of that person should be regarded as possibly being unreliable.

Double Whammies (identify these yourself)

When any Inter-Aspect, along with its interpretation, is repeated – because that Inter-Aspect goes both ways, for example, 'A's Moon Conjunct (uniting with) B's Pluto' followed by 'A's Pluto Conjunct (uniting with) B's Moon' – then it affects the relationship very strongly.

Interchangeability (identify this yourself)

With any Inter-Aspect, individuals can swap roles in relationships, due to psychological projection, cultural and gender roles, individual status and inclination, etc. That is, Person A can be playing the part of what appears to be Person B, and vice versa.

The One Golden Rule

No one interaction or Inter-Aspect can make or break a relationship. In a healthy relationship, there is always a strength to deal with a stress or a strain. Through time and love, challenges, if met, can always be overcome. Needless to say, many relationships do not turn out to be long lasting or permanent, but they are there for a reason – and the Inter-Aspects will tell you what that reason was.

The Chemistry Between You Both – here follow
the Relationship Profile Interpretations…

4. THE RELATIONSHIP PROFILE INTERPRETATIONS

1. KEY CONNECTIONS

These are usually the most powerful and dynamic points of interaction between you, but do not be put off if you find little or none, as other interactions will provide strong connections. They can be either harmonious, difficult or a bit of both – depending on the Planets involved.

Ascendant and MidHeaven Inter-Aspects: Note that when a Planet of one person is Opposition (confronting) the Ascendant or MidHeaven of another person, then it is at the same time Conjunct (uniting with) their Descendant or Lower MidHeaven, respectively. This is simply because the Descendant is always the opposite point to the Ascendant, (see page 42) and the Lower MidHeaven is always the opposite point to the MidHeaven (see page 95). Conversely, when a Planet of one person is Conjunct (uniting with) the Ascendant or MidHeaven of another person, then it is at the same time Opposition (confronting) their Descendant or Lower MidHeaven, respectively. The interpretations will cover these cases.

IMPORTANT

Remember that the name of the Inter-Aspect may be written the other way around to how it is given in the Relationship Profile INDEX or on-screen. For example, an Inter-Aspect given as **Saturn Conjunct (uniting with) Sun** ♄ ☌ ☉ in the INDEX will be given here as **Sun Conjunct (uniting with) Saturn** ☉ ☌ ♄ . Also, the As and Bs are not included here because they are individual to the particular relationship as given in the INDEX or on-screen.

KEY CONNECTIONS: INTERPRETATIONS

Sun Conjunct (uniting with) Sun
☉ ☌ ☉

Two Hearts Wanting To Beat As One
This means that your birthdays are within a week or so of one another, and that your Sun Signs could very well be the same. If they are the same, the strong similarity in basic make-ups is of course noticeable. The best and the worst of shared Sun Sign is expressed, experienced and intensified by being together. The Air Signs, Gemini, Libra and Aquarius,

profit from this intensification because they are naturally co-operative. The first two Fire Signs, Aries and Leo, would tend to bring out the competitive streak in each person – for good or ill. The third Fire Sign, Sagittarius, has an expansive, philosophical and impersonal quality, so they lope along rather well. The Earth Signs, Taurus, Virgo and Capricorn, are more territory conscious, which could give rise to problems – but apart from that, very stable, and a lot would get done. Virgo to Virgo could be a bit exacting though. Finally, the Water Signs, Cancer, Scorpio and Pisces. Once two Crabs have locked claws there is probably no parting them, and Scorpios nest down, but if they do fall out, Hiroshima's got nothing on it! Pisceans tend to lose sight of one another. If the two of you are not the same Sign, then you will be one Sign apart, which means that some kind of compromise will have to be made at some point. This is because your similarities can blind you to your dissimilarities and find you in an awkward place where the best way out is to meet each other half way. All in all, same Sign or not, this is a pretty positive interaction, but a common goal or direction, with some rules of how to go about getting there, should be seen as the important thing.

Sun Conjunct (uniting with) Moon
☉ ☌ ☽

Soul Mates?

Whatever your sexes, ages or positions in life, this interaction gives a definite feeling of being connected in some way, if not many ways. There is a feeling of familiarity, despite anything else that might or might not be happening between you both. It is as if one of you, the 'Sun', has the other, the 'Moon', fixed in their beam, as if they are illuminating their inner or emotional being. Depending on other factors, particularly sexual or status ones, this can make the 'Moon' feel overwhelmed or greatly impressed, or somehow inferior or even at the 'Sun's' command. As the 'Moon' person reflects this back, the 'Sun' feels this happening, and depending on what kind of ego they have, can feel empowered and then become anything from dominating to feeling strangely or uncomfortably superior. At another level – when there are plenty of other strong interactions – you may feel like soul-mates. After a short while though, it can make a great difference as to what sex the 'Sun' and the 'Moon' are. When the 'Sun' is male and the 'Moon' female, the above descriptions lean towards the positive, for the male solar 'radiating' and the female lunar 'receiving' are in their natural and comfortable roles. In fact, if this is the case, it almost acts as a demonstration of this phenomenon, flying in the face of contemporary ideas of men and women being the same (as distinct from equal). When it is reversed, the female can uncomfortably feel that the man should be making the moves but he doesn't for he is waiting, possibly quite awkwardly, for her to do so. If the man should make the move, the woman then feels equally uncomfortable. Then again, it could be a case of you both actually getting something out of such a role reversal. But here too, yet this time not so obviously, the basic differences between male and female are experienced. If both of you are the same sex, then one might say the 'Sun' determines who is the 'male' and the 'Moon' the 'female'. There is also a sense of the 'Sun' as being the 'parent' and the 'Moon' as being the 'child'. This may literally be the case, and this interaction would then be highly suitable. However, an older 'child' and a younger 'parent' could be curiously enlightening or plain awkward. To sum up, basic connectedness is what this interaction is all about, but other more personal and idiosyncratic interactions would indicate whether such a basis has anything worth building upon it.

Sun Conjunct (uniting with) Mercury
☉ ☌ ☿

An Emphasis On Communication

Communication between the two of you is highly important, but does not indicate in itself whether or not it is good or bad communication. If as a pair you have a sound mental rapport indicated elsewhere, then this interaction will give it more strength and energy. If you have a poor intellectual link, or ongoing emotional conflict, then this will make it all the more exasperating – simply because efficient communication is more sorely needed. One way or the other, you will highlight the mental condition of each other. This can take the form of aiding and encouraging mental muscle, and/or belittling any weakness that is perceived. Work issues can also be spotlighted in these ways. If you both have strong intellects, you will give as good as you get, whether positive or negative. Ideas can fly like sparks, just as readily as disputes. To create the former, some mutual respect and understanding is called for, especially where it comes to appreciating where either of you has an educational or mental work background that is better or worse than average.

Sun Conjunct (uniting with) Venus
☉ ☌ ♀

Love And Happiness

This is a classic indication of a love relationship. One of you bathes in the other's expression of their personality, responding with an appreciation and affection that is immediately pleasing and attractive to that person. Simultaneously, the first person feels warmed and filled with loving energy from the second person. As long as this mutual admiration and pleasure in each other's company does not devolve into a fanciful and superficially romantic relationship where heavier emotions build up unattended to, then you can develop a loving, caring and creative relationship. Such an interaction also greatly favours any artistic endeavours that you might be involved in for it is evident that you make pleasing 'music' together, literally or figuratively. Socializing and having fun together are also strong points, again as long as they do not become so indulgent or hedonistic that you lose sight of each other as individual emotional beings.

Sun Conjunct (uniting with) Mars
☉ ☌ ♂

All Fired Up

You have here an interaction that makes for a sexual or active relationship, but not necessarily a loving or affectionate one. In itself then, this aspect gives you a greater energy together as a couple than you'd have individually, and so you can get a lot done, go many places together, and, if it is a sexual relationship, find each other very stimulating. Whatever the case, you arouse one another. You can also be quite competitive. But there comes a point where a lack of care and tenderness can cause you to actually wear one another out. This can also be the case if you do not allow one another the time and space to do your own thing as individuals. So fighting can easily replace passion and the enjoyment of the physical aspects of life and yourselves. If you find that the sexual or sporting/competitive area is 'hot' for you, make sure that there are also some harmonious and intellectual connections between you. Otherwise it will just become rather basic and dissatisfying, if not downright combative. Your combined energies can achieve a great deal in whatever field you choose, but there is always a danger of pushing yourselves or others, or both, too hard.

Sun Conjunct (uniting with) Jupiter
☉ ☌ ♃

Warmth And Goodwill
You have an affinity with each other that is very healthy and honest. Not only are you mutually supportive and encouraging, but as a couple you both go out of your way to be helpful and generous towards others. Owing to this, and a generally good feel about the pair of you, you are popular. Naturally enough, this interaction favours being parents or anyone in authority, not least because there is always a benign quality about you and between you. This is one of the few interactions that is entirely positive, and it goes a long way to overcoming friction and disagreement indicated elsewhere. This could be further aided, even transcended, owing to the fact that, together or individually, you might follow some definite moral code or spiritual discipline. It must be pointed out that this is not an emotional interaction – it can even be quite impersonal – and so it does not in itself indicate romance, just that good feeling. This all promises that – mentally or spiritually, materially or emotionally – to some degree you will grow, as partners or as individuals, as a result of your time together.

Sun Conjunct (uniting with) Saturn
☉ ☌ ♄

A Serious And Important Connection
One of you brightens the dark or doubtful areas of the other's personality or life, while the other gives in return a sense of purpose and position in life. Negatively, however, the second person can resent or suppress what is bright in the first person, while the first person can make the second person feel (even more) dull or inadequate by comparison. There is also something rather timely about your coming together; a serious reason for your being involved. This is not a romantic connection in itself – it could very much be a business relationship – but it is highly significant. Both of you should become more worldly and responsible as a result of interacting; this may even mark a first step towards adulthood, parenthood or maturity. As long you both appreciate that one of you provides the light and confidence, and that the other provides the sense of order and limitation – and you don't allow one to dazzle or blot out the other – then this can contribute to a very stable and long-lasting, or simply learning, relationship.

Sun Conjunct (uniting with) Uranus

The Odd Coupling

This is a bit like Sunshine and lightning coming into exciting and flashy contact. You can both feel very plugged into one another, but it is rather like trying to hold a 10,000 volt charge steady. This is an odd interaction because it seems to promise or threaten so much but, like lightning or Sunshine, it can be gone in an instant. However, for as long as you can stay steady enough or even manage to be in each other's presence, you can both experience some strange and extraordinary sensations – some thrilling, some uncomfortable. There is also an underlying sense of 'where is this supposed to be going?' and 'what happens next?'. This of course adds to the crackle and sizzle between the two of you, but it also points to the innate instability of this contact – at least, for any kind of ongoing emotional relationship. It has to be said that this is very unlikely, a word that could also be used to describe you as a couple should you become one. But still this sort of electromagnetic connection persists. It may be that this unusual interaction is only really for doing unusual things, like some kind of magical or esoteric activity, or just having fun. Or perhaps it would put one or both of you in touch with the alternative side to life. One of you may be an outsider while the other is quite conventional, and you both have something to show one another in this respect. In the end, this interaction is rather like a firework display, lots of ooh-ing and aah-ing, but rather anticlimactic. Keeping or living up to what it so erratically promises would necessitate having a decidedly odd lifestyle, one that precludes the normal routines that make things manageable but at times comparatively dull. Whether or not it occurs to either of you, there is the notion that your encounter should have happened, or will happen, at another time, another place. More to the point though, it is some kind of 'wake-up call' to both of you, right here and now.

Sun Conjunct (uniting with) Neptune

A Karmic Link

The range of feelings and experiences that this interaction can create in and for you both is vast. Perhaps the spectrum could be described as stretching between the spiritual and creative at one end, to the addictive and confusing at the other. This spectrum of feeling and experience could itself be called one of mutual fascination or inspiration. But then again it could be or become quite one-sided where one of you is, or is seen to be, in a weak position and the other in a strong one. So one scenario could be that one of you is fascinated by the other for some reason – bewitching eyes, a psychic sense of having met in a previous life, artistic talent, or some such thing – but the other is not that interested. Or you could both be under each other's spell and lose all sight of the real world and its responsibilities. Or you embark on some kind of inner journey together. Or one of you is by a peculiar twist of circumstances having to help the other with some affliction or addiction. The list is endless, but it will always be somewhere on that spectrum. And underlying whatever the scenario might be, consciously or unconsciously, there is some mysterious or karmic tie, or a debt to be repaid, or something to be lived out for reasons that are hard to fathom. Because of all this, deception and/or illusion are quite likely to be somewhere on the menu. A more precise reason for this could be that one of you is trying to keep to something, while the other is trying to avoid it. This interaction can take you to Heaven and then to Hell and then back to Earth. A spiritual or creative reason for your being together is the healthiest and sanest way of handling this interaction. This means to say that the seeking of enlightenment or relief, for yourselves or others, gives your relationship a path that it is designed for. Imagination and sensitivity are the stuff of the chemistry between you, and it is highly important that you use them both wisely and constructively – guided by something inner or divine – rather than let either of them get the better of you.

Sun Conjunct (uniting with) Pluto
☉ ♂ ♇

Darkness And Light

This is a journey into the Underworld – with or without a torch! The first person, 'Pluto', takes the other, the 'hero', down to levels of experience they would not have agreed to visit had they first seen a brochure. 'Pluto' sees the 'Hero' as the light they want in their lives, but that too often means that they try to convert and remake them in the image of what they feel their hero/heroine ought to be. Psychologically speaking, that hero/heroine may be what 'Pluto' feels their father is or ought to have been like. Depending on what their father was/is actually like, they can also resent and even despise the 'Hero' – especially if the 'Hero' is forced to brandish their torch in order to maintain their individuality. If, however, such psychological complexes do not loom or are suitably dealt with, then this interaction can take on the form of a mutually empowering and regenerative relationship. But it has to be said that some sort of purging has to take place first as your respective ego defence systems are given the once over – the reason being that they get in the way of the vibrant intimacy that is the true and deep intention of this interaction. Whether this happens or not, you are each bound to become somewhat closer to your real selves, if not each other. In the fullness of time, you will realize how deeply affected you have been by the experience of being involved – or even nearly involved – with one another.

Sun Conjunct (uniting with) Ascendant *Birth Time Sensitive*
☉ ♂ AS

The Lighted Way

Your meeting should mark a new beginning for one or both of you. The first person is rather like a beam of light who shows the second person the path towards what they are supposed to become. If the second person is looking for some way forward (or out), either consciously or unconsciously, encountering the first person is a bit like a light being switched on for them. Not only are they made to see their way ahead more clearly, they also get a clearer idea of what their current circumstances are about. In fact, this may come before seeing their way ahead, but only a little. Naturally enough, such a ready and positive response to their ego causes the first person to behave in a confident and magnanimous fashion. Consequently, the two of you get off to a good, even dynamic start, which can, as I say, lead to a new path for one or both of you, either together or individually. A possible downside to all this bright interaction is owing to the fact that your respective egos and images are so intensified as to make you act rashly, and take on more than you originally thought you were taking on. So, eventually, competitiveness and being too much in each other's faces may be a problem. However, if there are other fast and furious interactions between you, then the immediacy of this one will be irresistible. Sometimes life is running along rails, and all you can do is apply the brakes a bit, but if Fate wants you to switch tracks – you will. Seeing that this interaction leads to a far stronger sense of yourselves and your abilities, you may as well toot your whistle and move on down the line – but watch out for amber or red signals!

Sun Opposition (confronting) Ascendant *Birth Time Sensitive*
☉ ☍ AS

Two Halves Make A Whole
This is one of the two most significant interactions of all. This is because the will or ego of one of you finds its mirror or shadow in the manner and presentation of the other person – and vice versa. Essentially, each of you is the other's 'other half' – or at least, seems to be. Depending on your respective levels of self-awareness, each of you may or may not like some of this because it reflects back a part of yourselves that you have yet to come to terms with: your shadows. But just because you are embodying or reflecting each other's other half, there is a strong attraction between you – at least initially. As time goes by, seeing each of your alter egos externalized in the other in this way can provide a feeling of being made complete by each other. But, as I have just pointed out, it can at times be objectionable to one or both of you. The great secret for success here, is to 'take back your projection', that is, to recognize and accept that it is your 'other half', warts and all, that makes you a more complete, and a stronger and better, person. In turn, this would possibly give you a relationship to match. As ever, a great deal depends upon the other interactions between the two of you. But even if this does not turn out to be a marriage or meeting of soul-mates, this interaction can so sharpen your sense of who you are or appear to be that, as a result of it, you are more able to recognize and attract someone who really is your other half – because of having learned what this really is in you.

Sun Conjunct (uniting with) MidHeaven *Birth Time Sensitive*
☉ ☌ MC

Mutual Illumination
There is a mutual recognition of status and individuality here, so you boost each other's egos and confirm each other's place upon your respective paths. This can also be a 'way-showing' interaction where one or both of you is shown by the other the best direction to take in life. Alternatively, or subsequently, there can be some competition between you, but this would depend upon, or take on the quality of, the Sign in which the Sun and MidHeaven are placed.

Sun Opposition (confronting) MidHeaven *Birth Time Sensitive*
☉ ☍ MC

Home Fires Burning
One of you, usually the Sun person, brings light, warmth and energy into the home or

inner life of the other, usually MidHeaven, person. Conversely, the other provides them with somewhere or something that acts as a practical base or opportunity to be creative or enterprising in some way – possibly concerning the qualities of the Sign in which the Sun is placed (and which is the opposite to the MidHeaven, i.e. Lower MidHeaven). Family or family-like ties are in evidence.

Moon Conjunct (uniting with) Moon
☽ ☌ ☽

Emotional Surfers
Your emotional rhythms and dispositions are very alike, which means that you not only mirror each other's highs but also your lows. You crest together and you trough together! Yet because you are so emotionally in sync, you kind of surf side-by-side through these troughs and peaks. It also has to be said that a great deal depends upon the actual Moon Sign(s) in question. Check out the positive qualities and help one another to make them more so. Check out the negative qualities and make a pledge to each other to keep a wary eye out for getting simultaneously caught in any downward spiral. The trick here is to not go over the top when you're both on a high, otherwise the inevitable low could wipe you both out for a while or more. By and large though, you are excellently and instinctively well matched – peas-in-a-pod type of thing. Whatever or whoever is under your care should count themselves lucky – troughs notwithstanding!

Moon Conjunct (uniting with) Mercury
☽ ☌ ☿

Instant Rapport
There is great immediacy and spontaneity in how you connect with one another. It is as if a part of one of you is plugged into a part of the other. If this sounds sexual it is not supposed to be, for this interaction in itself has no specific indication of your being that way involved or attracted. However, such is your mutual ability to tune into each other and communicate what you find there, either verbally or kinaesthetically, that a sexual relationship – if you have one – would certainly not find you lost for words. Then again, just talking for the sake of it can be a bit of a waste of this excellent rapport that you possess – rather like watching television with the colour and contrast turned right down. In other words, the link between you is a sophisticated one, and is supposed to be used for conveying something of value and meaning. Because of this smart 'wire' that you have between you, you would also make a good team in any work situation. Again, though, a constant 'brother/sister/schoolkid' kind of banter could drive colleagues nuts. If you have avoided or got out of this possible 'loop' of gossip, giggles or meaninglessness, then you can do wonders for helping each other – as well as friends, family and associates – by putting straight any emotional or intellectual problems you or they might have. In the process, however, the more rational of the two of you should avoid being too dry and lacking in empathy as they rationalize the other, more emotional person's feelings in an attempt to clarify, and they in turn best make some effort to keep their feelings in check and not be too subjective or stuck in a rut. All the same, this interaction is a testament to the saying 'A trouble shared is a trouble halved,' or for that matter, 'Two heads are better than one.'

Moon Conjunct (uniting with) Venus
☽ ☌ ♀

Sweet And Lovely

You have a feeling for each other that is both sympathetic and affectionate, caring and loving. If this sounds good, you're right, it is! This interaction favours love, marriage, friendship and family relationships like no other. The natural occurrence of what could loosely be termed 'native' pursuits is something that you draw great pleasure from, as well as providing it for others. Such things are singing, dancing, crafts, artistic expression, etc – but all done on a personal or domestic level, and not necessarily a professional one. This is a very gentle and 'female' interaction because you both tune in to what are loveable and likeable, rather than desirable and admirable. The former qualities are accommodating and flexible, whereas the latter can be brittle and distance inducing. For this reason, this interaction very much favours female-to-female relationships. If there is a 'but' to this lovely interaction, it is the possible excess of this 'femaleness', for it can incline you to be too passive as a couple. So unless there are some more dynamic interactions between you, this means that you can get led down whatever path presents itself rather than be consciously self-directing or discriminating, with the result that pleasure- and comfort-seeking becomes your sole directive, and aimlessness your only product. Apart from that possible hitch, together and with each other, you are 'Sweet and lovely.'

Moon Conjunct (uniting with) Mars
☽ ☌ ♂

Intense Attraction, or Reaction

There is a strong and basic reaction to one another – very possibly sexual. In fact, this interaction is so basic as to be almost primitive for it embodies the meeting of the two most fundamental drives – desire and need. If the more assertive person is male and the more receptive person female, then this mutual attraction is usually more intense. It would also be more straightforward than the other way around, in which case a 'receptive' male would be having to passively respond to an unusually 'assertive' female. In any event, such a strong tug towards one another seems to defy any more social or sensitive considerations about your becoming intimately involved. It is plain that there is no problem with mutual attraction here, but when the initial burst of animal enthusiasm is over, and the relationship tries or has to settle down to something more humdrum and domestic, then trouble can begin. One expression of this could be that the two of you keep trying to maintain that original intensity which then leads to a sense of urgency and/or disappointment. Another could be that the mundanities of life take over and these hot feelings have no choice but to burst out as anger or aggression in one of you, which elicits a hurt or threatened feeling from the other. A great deal depends here upon the balance of other interactions you have between you. Positive aspects will harmonize and maintain this rather fruity bond, whereas negative ones will lead to ongoing conflict, frustration and hurt – and eventually, and maybe even gratefully, separation.

Moon Conjunct (uniting with) Jupiter
☽ ☌ ♃

Emotional Abundance

There is a great and natural feeling of understanding for one another. Whatever might be occurring in your lives, together or individually, it is always within both of you to explore it if it is positive, or to accommodate it if it is not. There exists an innate faith and trust in one another, to whatever degree it needs to be there. For these reasons, this interaction has more the nature of furthering and maintaining a relationship rather than initiating or creating one. And so, if your relationship is ongoing, you can be sure that together you will progressively overcome any difficulties, and prosper in the process. It also favours child-rearing and caring for the spiritual or physical health of anyone or anything – as long as you avoid doting on each other and pious do-gooding or proselytising. But do not expect this aspect alone to fire you up. Indeed, the ultimate expression or energy of this interaction may go beyond emotional and physical gratification, as it leans more and more towards altruism and philanthropy. Kindness towards one another, and to those around you, is the great key to emotional well-being bestowed upon you by the benign effect of this interaction.

Moon Conjunct (uniting with) Saturn
☽ ☌ ♄

A Fated Contact

This is an important interaction, but unfortunately not for the most cheerful of reasons. Whereas the one of you, the 'lunar' person, expresses their feelings only too naturally, the other 'saturnine' person has a commensurately difficult time positively expressing their feelings. The writing on the wall with this contact is saying that both of you have an important lesson to learn from each other. The 'lunar' person needs to discipline their emotions and be more mature, less childish, in this area. The 'saturnine' person, on the other hand, could take some lessons from the 'lunar' person in how to live up to their emotional potential. The trouble here is that the 'lunar' person feels suppressed or chilled by what is really only the 'saturnine' person's inadequacy in this respect, for in the face of the 'lunar' person's emotional ease, they feel awkward and in need of controlling their behaviour. And so a downward spiral is only too likely if the two of you are not emotionally very objective. For this to happen, there will certainly have to be a good supply of mutually loving and caring interactions present also, because this interaction certainly doesn't fit that bill. This has been called a 'fated contact' because it is quite timely in the sense of both people having to become more conscious of free-flowing feelings on the part of the 'lunar' person, and inhibitions on the part of the 'saturnine' person. Family responsibilities and domestic arrangements can be a very likely area for these lessons and difficulties to surface, as too can the 'saturnine' individual's professional duties getting in the way of the 'lunar' individual's needs, and vice versa. Having said all of this, if the writing on the wall is read and obeyed, a very stable and mutually responsible, though possibly somewhat sober, relationship can be established.

Moon Conjunct (uniting with) Uranus

☽ ☌ ♅

Emotional Reorientation

This interaction between you provides excitement but little, if any, security. The more needy of you in particular should guard against expectations of comfort and predictability because they are not about to get it from the other, more cool, person. In fact, the very reason 'needy' has been attracted to 'cool' is because their unconscious is trying to tell them, via 'cool', that it is time for them to review past attachments and outworn ideas of being settled. This interaction also spells out for the 'needy' person the necessity of not being so attached to another human being (or anything else) for this smacks of their inner child running the show – or rather ruining it – with past agendas that now need seeing to. The 'cool' person is a catalyst for this process, and as such can feel anything from uncomfortably distant to quite taken with being an agent of change in someone's life. There is a more subliminal effect that 'cool' should be aware of, and this is that they should perhaps become more emotionally aware and expressive, while the 'needy' person is being forced to be more cool and detached. In English this means that the 'cool' person has possibly become too remote and emotionally distant, and the 'needy' person can show them how to be more in touch with their feelings. By way of exchange, the 'needy' person learns to cultivate a measure of emotional distance. This is not a stable interaction for its dynamic is one of emotional change and reorientation. But because the experiencing of this is so important for both of you, you are strongly attracted to one another. For this reason, this interaction can at times appear 'unfair' or 'impossible' as it seems not to offer anything that is expected of a conventional relationship. But the only thing you can expect from this interaction is the unexpected, as it will bring about surprise events that are in aid of waking you up to the need to change your respective emotional dispositions or situations.

Moon Conjunct (uniting with) Neptune

☽ ☌ ♆

Two As One

This is a highly sensitive connection, which can create a wonderful emotional and spiritual rapport. However, there is also the danger of each partner losing themselves in the other. So it is important to establish and maintain individual identities and not live in each other's pockets. As Kahlil Gibran said: 'Let the winds of the Heavens dance between you.' Having achieved this, the psychic sensitivity of the one can nurture the inspirational nature of the other, while at the same time you delicately show one another your own individual emotional needs and state. This interaction strongly favours any creative or spiritual pursuits of a joint nature. You are somewhat like twin radio receivers rather than one on its own, so you pick up more ideas and guidance than you would otherwise. So exquisite is the melding of your two personalities under the influence of this interaction that it can, indeed has to, overcome any separative tendencies indicated elsewhere. Having said this, though, you are also exceptionally able to accept whatever the river of life might bring you, even if it wishes you to go your separate ways. But then again, if there comes a point when your mystical link is made complete, probably through some acute emotional suffering, then no man can put asunder what God has joined together. Domestically or as a family, you emanate a subtle and gentle feel that is very special. In some respects this will need maintaining by being quite discriminating about what type of energies, physical or otherwise, you allow into your space – but without letting this become too precious. Basically, yours is a psychic bond and as such can pull in all manner of psychic phenomena, good, bad and indifferent. For the same reason, you as a couple are adept at creating a quite enchanting atmosphere which can be both healing and entertaining for those in its midst.

Moon Conjunct (uniting with) Pluto
☽ ☌ ♇
Emotional Intensity
This very intense interaction will take you both down to some very deep emotions and churn them to the surface. In fact, you could go so far as to say that this is some form of emotional initiation, for it will transform the way you feel about yourselves, as individuals and as a couple. The sexual dimension, real or imagined, is a key area for it is the compulsions of desire and need that drive this interaction, cementing you together or driving you apart, depending on how such intense feelings are managed. Sometimes you can feel overwhelmed with such intensity, causing one of you, the 'susceptible' person to withdraw from the onslaughts of the other 'obsessive' person – but it can also happen the other way around. But the emotional 'elastic' persists in bringing you back together again and again, no matter what. Such swinging back and forth between feelings of extreme closeness and painful distance (or painful closeness!) can be very trying, even despair inducing. It is well to remember the old French adage, 'A woman is like a man's shadow, go towards it and it will walk away from you, walk away from it and it will follow you.' No matter what the gender is, though, this means that if the one of you can resist hungering after the other when the chips are down, they will come back – or it will be seen not to matter. Conversely, abandoning the other will only make them more persistent. Recognize that you do have a very deep bond – or that you are forging or letting go of one – and that you will have to confront inappropriate feelings and eliminate them. As a result you will both be purged and therefore reunite with renewed and purer feelings of connectedness – or not. This process will go on inexorably until your respective emotional states are such that you either have an indestructible bond between the two of you, or you both agree that enough is enough. But until then neither of you will really have any choice in the matter other than how you handle such an intense interaction.

Moon Conjunct (uniting with) Ascendant *Birth Time Sensitive*
☽ ☌ AS
Familiarity
There is an instantaneous emotional link between the two of you. This means that you feel like 'family' to one another – and in fact, you could actually be related. Whatever the case, you 'go way back' either literally or figuratively. And so the water-under-the-bridge issue can be an important one for you both, as memories of past experiences, shared or individual, form a great part of your lives and relationship together. On the positive side, you have an easy rapport as you share, instinctively or experientially, common emotional

attitudes and habit patterns. Negatively, though, it can be difficult for either one of you to break out of, or be seen to break out of, the mould in which each has cast the other. The making of a little distance, in time, space or both, can be very helpful in your both getting a clearer idea of who each of you are as distinct individuals rather than merely jigsaw pieces, with no identity of their own, that fit into each other's puzzles.

Moon Opposition (confronting) Ascendant   *Birth Time Sensitive*
☽ ☍ AS

Emotional Contentedness
Here you really do have what is called an 'emotional relationship'. You have a mutual as well as natural need of one another, and endure and enjoy the ongoing highs and lows that are part and parcel of your being together. Even if this is not a marital, sexual or family relationship, you still interact in a quite intimate and familiar fashion. And where family is concerned, respective family members can be either a great mainstay or quite a burden to your own emotional harmony. This is a 'love me, love my family' sort of thing. Each of you responds very well to the needs and expressions of the other; so well, in fact, that sometimes one of you knows where the other is emotionally coming from way before they do. The down side to this, though, is that the both of you instinctively 'catch the shadow' of the other. This means that whatever one of you is unsure of in themselves, they can project it on to the other and blame them for what is actually their 'stuff'. Yet at the same time, this is the price you may have to pay for being so dependent on each other for displaying those positive qualities that you each wish you had. Again, this can be seen in the family sense of one member taking care of a certain area of life, and another member something else. Traditionally, for instance, father brings home the bread, and mother makes the home and looks after the kids. So, in effect, yours is a symbiotic relationship, to one degree or another. As such it can work very well, and this interaction, when accompanied by other favourable aspects, really can make one out of the two.

Moon Conjunct (uniting with) MidHeaven   *Birth Time Sensitive*
☽ ☌ MC

Kindred Spirits
There is a very profound connection between the two of you, especially with regard to home and work, family and business. You look out for one another emotionally and professionally, almost as if you are related – but then you well may be. It is as if you belong to the same 'tribe' and share the same interests at a fundamental level. The personality of the one of you acts as beacon to the status of the other, and vice versa. Literally or figuratively, there is a parent and child dimension to this Inter-Aspect. Following in one's father's or mother's footsteps is also a likelihood. The main pitfall with this otherwise close and mutually supportive interaction is confusion arising between the domestic commitments of one of you with the career commitments of the other.

Moon Opposition (confronting) MidHeaven *Birth Time Sensitive*
☽ ☍ MC

Feeling At Home

You both share similar roots – you may actually belong to the same family or district. Consequently, you feel a basic sense of familiarity that allows you to settle comfortably with one another. This is, of course, providing that the Moon is not badly aspected to other Planets in one person's chart or to the other person's. So you feel like family even if you are not literally so, and each of your families tend to intermix fairly spontaneously.

Mercury Conjunct (uniting with) Mercury
☿ ☌ ☿

Of Like Mind

Your minds work very much the same way if you both have Mercury in the same Sign, which will usually be the case. In any event, you still connect well mentally – or sometimes too well. This latter point is owing to your sharing both the best and worst of the same kind of mentality. And so one of you can get irritated with the other if they are still stuck at a certain level of thinking or worrying, because it uncomfortably reminds them that they suffer, or used to, from the same complaint. You approach problems and work matters in a similar fashion too, and so can be efficient co-workers. However, the same issue can arise when one of you regards the other's methods as wanting or outmoded when really it is just reflecting back their own doubts or shortcomings. If both of you are pretty aware of the plusses and minuses of your intellectual states and attitudes, then you can go from strength to strength as you develop your communication or work skills further and further. This is somewhat like how brothers and sisters learn to communicate through interacting with one another, and indeed, this interaction can make for a brotherly/sisterly feel. Whether you are discussing some abstruse and complex issue or merely indulging in gossip, you do it brilliantly together.

Mercury Conjunct (uniting with) Venus
☿ ☌ ♀

Creative Rapport

If the two of you do not enjoy talking together, then there must be something really wrong. Even then, you are drawn to discussing 'love problems' anyway, so on one level or another, this interaction is always getting what it wants. This is apart from the fact that you do like your conversations to be pleasant and harmonious, and so may gloss over the nastier or more difficult issues that arise. On the other hand, it is your combined awareness of what looks and sounds right that is one of your stronger assets. So notwithstanding the tendency to gloss over, you can be an adept pair at finding a pleasing solution, one which is agreeable to most people concerned. As such, on a professional or merely social level, you excel at being diplomatic and discreet, and so should be welcome or in demand. You could also be creative together in some way – with one of you providing the appeal and aesthetics, and the other the interest and technical know-how – you may alternate these roles quite easily too.

Mercury Conjunct (uniting with) Mars

☿ ♂ ♂

The Hot Wire

Ideas, attitudes and discussions are nearly always upfront with the two of you, and rarely left on the back-burner. This is because your thoughts and desires are like fuel to one another. Naturally enough, this can go in the direction of energetic and effective communication, outright disagreement or hot debate. A great deal depends here on what other interactions that you have between the two of you. This can make the difference between feeling pushed or stimulated by one another, one or both of you feeling impatient with the other for being all talk and no action, or enjoying each other as a source of information and a guide to your actions. On a sexual level, this can be a case of talking about or around it but never doing it, to being quite turned on by sexy ideas or sheer mental force.

Mercury Conjunct (uniting with) Jupiter

☿ ♂ ♃

Good Companions

You feed one another's minds and understanding to a great degree. Such an interaction therefore favours any mental, educational or cultural pursuits that you might be involved in. One of you is more of an ideas and visions person, whereas the other helps put them into words or some other appreciable and practical form. These roles can also be interchangeable. Also, if one of you has a problem, the other can help alleviate or even solve it by helping them see it in a larger context, or by providing contacts or techniques to deal with it. Humour can also play a part in this, and may also be a central part of your relationship overall. Moreover, you make good travelling companions, and show one another where to go and how to get there – in more ways than one. There is a small danger of getting stuck in your heads with this interaction, with perhaps one of you being too conceptual and the other being too pedantic, or of both of you blowing things out of proportion. But sooner or later you could make each other aware of that too, and actually use it to further benefit your communication and understanding.

Mercury Conjunct (uniting with) Saturn

☿ ♂ ♄

Seriously Cerebral

You feed one another's minds and understanding to a great degree. Such an interaction therefore favours any mental, educational or cultural pursuits that you might be involved in. One of you is more of an ideas and visions person, whereas the other helps put them into words or some other appreciable and practical form. These roles can also be interchangeable. Also, if one of you has a problem, the other can help alleviate or even solve it by helping them see it in a larger context, or by providing contacts or techniques to deal with it. Humour can also play a part in this, and may also be a central part of your relationship overall. Moreover, you make good travelling companions, and show one another where to go and how to get there – in more ways than one. There is a small danger of getting stuck in your heads with this interaction, with perhaps one of you being too conceptual and the other being too pedantic, or of both of you blowing things out of proportion. But sooner or later you could make each other aware of that too, and actually use it to further benefit your communication and understanding.

Mercury Conjunct (uniting with) Uranus
☿ ♂ ♅

Mental Stimulation
You should have quite a strong and stimulating mental connection. Between the two of you, you can work through original ideas, give them verbal expression, and generally spark one another off. Metaphysical or technological subjects could be an area of interest – or one of you may introduce the other to such a pursuit. One of you is usually more grounded in the everyday world, down on the street, kind of thing. As such, they are able to help the other to get a practical handle on their inventiveness or apparently eccentric notions – but at times they just will not be able to understand their more 'spacey' mate who seems to be too 'far out'. The 'spacey' one, on the other hand, can awaken their partner to new attitudes of thought and perception – or simply blow them away. If there are several indications of rapport given elsewhere, then this can be a very innovative and mind-expanding interaction.

Mercury Conjunct (uniting with) Neptune
☿ ♂ ♆

The Thinker And The Dreamer
If both of you are fairly mature and have sorted your ideals from your illusions, and your fantasies from your visions, then this interaction will enable you, individually and as a couple, to a see lot further and more clearly than many other people. If there are other intense or harmonious mental and emotional links between you, together you can tune into higher levels of intelligence. This amounts to 'channelling' or creative inspiration which may be used artistically, esoterically or therapeutically. One of you, the 'dreamer', is the psychic half who channels, inspires or visualizes, while the other, the 'thinker' gives it practical form and 'edits' what the 'dreamer' has received. It must be pointed out that these roles can at times be interchangeable. The difficult side to this potentially inspired and inspiring combination, is one of seeing only what you want to see, and reinforcing each other's illusions and wishful thinking. It should really be a case of you both checking out whether either of you are being this way or, for that matter, being too rationalistic or cynical. And this could also go too far, with the 'thinker' doubting and questioning the visions and impressions of the 'dreamer' – or just finding them vague and hard to understand, while the 'dreamer' regards the 'thinker' as being too critical, linear or lacking in imagination. In some respects this sifting process is an essential part of sorting the inspiring from the fanciful, for it is this that ensures that the gold of this mine of mystical information is real and not of the fool's variety. It would also guard against your day-to-day communications becoming garbled or misleading. In effect, you jointly possess a blend of imagination and the means of giving it some form of expression, and if you don't use it, it might well confuse you

Mercury Conjunct (uniting with) Pluto
☿ ☌ ♇

'Mind Sex'

What one of you has to say to the other, or even think about, makes a lasting impression. So, be it positive or negative, expect it to eventually come back to you in some way. Also, the powerful effect of this combination has a great deal to do with the direction in which such power is expressed. For example, if both of you are involved in some sort of research or psychological work together, which is quite likely, then the mental power of it is seen to go outwards into the world and have some kind of effect which you can both monitor and work upon. If, on the other hand, that probing mentality is aimed at one another, a kind of psychological game of cat and mouse can ensue. Each or one of you can be intrigued by the insights the other has into your mind and make-up. But at a certain point this can feel like psychic invasion. So the issue that then arises is one of trust with each other's darkest secrets. Am I being helped or selfishly manipulated? Do I want to know more and get in deeper – or not? These could be the kind of questions that one or both of you might find that you're asking. This contact is rather like 'mind sex' because it is both mentally compelling and threatening; or a therapist/patient relationship where confidentiality and trust are vital. One of you is most likely to feel 'invaded', and by way of defence will try to dodge or trivialize what they see as the other's mind-probes. The other can find this reaction despicably superficial, but they should look to their motives for trying to rip away their opposite number's apparent veil of pretence or cleverness. To a certain extent, or rather by its very nature, this mutual mind-probing will be unavoidable. When such an exercise is part and parcel of how you express yourselves to the world, individually or as a partnership, then you can wield a profound influence with great conviction and sound effect. In any event, this interaction should make you both mentally or psychologically stronger. Black humour could also be on your mutual mental menu.

Mercury Conjunct (uniting with) Ascendant   *Birth Time Sensitive*
☿ ☌ AS

Food For Thought

One individual will act as a sounding board to the other, who will in turn give them back food for thought. In fact, 'food for thought' describes well what you both are to one another, in direct proportion, however, to your current states of mind as individuals. You put one another in touch with not only ideas and ways of translating the meaning of things, but also introduce one another to interesting people. You also stimulate each other's wits, and humour can be a strong component to your interaction. Together you can bring alive the phrase 'body language' as you connect so well through word and physical expression. But this does not mean to say that what is communicated is always pleasant, you may even get on each other's nerves – a case of the media being good, but not necessarily the message.

Mercury Opposition (confronting) Ascendant *Birth Time Sensitive*
☿ ☍ AS

Mental Rapport

Straightaway, something clicks on a mental level when you first meet. It is as if one of you is a mental mirror to the other. In fact, this contact is entirely cerebral and does not in itself pose anything emotional or physical between the two of you. However, because of the excellent communication and intellectual rapport that it potentially bestows, any physical or emotional (or intellectual) issues that do arise can be thought through and talked out very efficiently between you. Notwithstanding any other interactions you might have that are detrimental to communication, if there is a mental solution at all, you'll find it. You are also of great help to one another in accurately observing and helping to improve your respective manners of self-expression and outlook, as well as aiding each other in verbally expressing yourselves with more effect and style, perhaps through putting each other in contact with interesting and useful people. This interaction can therefore give rise to intense verbal and intellectual interplay. If and when you have communication hitches, it is because one or both of you is failing to accept the other's ability to complement their thinking or point of view. The reason for this being that one of you thinks they have all the answers – when of course, they do not.

Mercury Conjunct (uniting with) MidHeaven *Birth Time Sensitive*
☿ ☌ MC

A Useful Connection

What one of you says and what the other one does in the world have a lot in common and therefore provide contacts and avenues of thought that help further the interests of both of you. Business-wise, you talk the same language, walk the same street, and benefit greatly from sharing ideas and knowledge. Practical and constructive communication is what this interaction is about.

Mercury Opposition (confronting) MidHeaven *Birth Time Sensitive*
☿ ☍ MC

A Root Connection

One of you is able to connect with where the other lives. This can mean that they, probably the Mercury person, makes mental or verbal contact with what is most personal and private to the other, probably MidHeaven, person. In return they provide a base of operations for Mercury's work. You both provide one another with information that is precisely what is required at the time. This could simply take the form of one knowing something that leads the other to coming a step nearer what they are after. The pooling of information could be a significant issue.

Venus Conjunct (uniting with) Venus
♀ ☌ ♀

St. Valentine's Own

This interaction is called 'St. Valentine's own' for it confers all the romantic and social graces upon your coming and being together. Your likes and dislikes are very similar, and you take great pleasure in each other's company. Others also like to be around you. Your style of relationship will fit very well with the respective requirements of your Venus Signs which will usually be the same. Aesthetically and artistically you also have a lot in common – and you resonate creatively with one another. The only pitfall to be wary of here, is an inclination that you both have to base the relationship upon superficialities such as appearance and manners. Just tell yourselves that the insides of each of you are as good, if not better, than the externals. Then, hopefully, this will not only avert disappointment, but enable you both to attract more and more, both materially and spiritually, into your lives together.

Venus Opposition (confronting) Venus
♀ ☍ ♀

Opposite Poles Attract
This is rather like two magnets coming together in that both pull together at once rather than just one attracting the other. So this is a classic mutual attraction, but after the initial clinching has occurred, both of you will find that you are a strange mixture of similar and dissimilar tastes and social standards. This can give rise to either being very happy doing the same thing together, or being annoyingly out of sync. What lies behind this is the need to become increasingly aware of what turns each other on – or off. In the process of doing this, both of you can become more aware of what appeals and doesn't appeal on a general level rather than just a personal one. This means that your combined sense of what is popular can give rise to a more commercial awareness – something about which your partnership may become quite astute. As hard aspects go this isn't particularly 'hard' because it is about the pursuit of happiness and harmony and this is what you consistently drive one another towards. A very real danger is simply that you will overindulge in whatever it is that you both like. Conversely, one of you can be happy indulging in something when along comes the other and looks on disapprovingly, thereby spoiling their enjoyment. But probably the greatest hidden asset of this interaction is that whatever happens between the two of you, those two magnets keep you together – at least until you have had your fill of one another. Studying your respective Venus Sign positions would tell you a great deal about differences and similarities.

Venus Conjunct (uniting with) Mars
♀ ☌ ♂

Cupid Scores A Bull's Eye!
There is a natural and immediate sexual attraction between you. If this is not a sexual relationship – but it probably is – then this would certainly be a warm and tactile one. Not that this interaction is troublesome – except that you may not be able to keep your hands off one another. Usually, it is the male who will be the one who makes the moves, while the female gladly responds. When it's the other way around, the female's inclination to call the shots and do the chasing may find the male feeling slightly awkward, occasionally frustrated or even repulsed. If there are more difficult contacts between the two of you then such can be made more acute. Even so, the role reversal can be a turn-on in itself! Generally, you are both made to feel more sensual and responsive, and to go

spontaneously and directly for what you desire. Incidentally, sometimes this contact can occur between two people where one or both of you is already spoken for. The reaction of one or both of your parts can be to deny this attraction, but this is possibly just as well, for seeing it is pure 'Cupid' you could both wind up looking more than stupid! Then again, it could lead to greater things – but first be absolutely sure what lies behind that immediate attraction.

Venus Opposition (confronting) Mars
♀ ☍ ♂

Adam And Eve
This interaction is a classic indication of mutual, and very possibly sexual, attraction. However, it is also a classic re-enactment of the basic differences between the sexes. The male's maleness is what turns the female on, but at a later date this very thing becomes the forcefulness that she objects to. Conversely, what is initially experienced by the male as her female allure and mystique can later be seen to be inaccessibility or over-sensitivity. Alternatively, there can be confusion because the female is having to be the one who calls the shots while the male feels passive and submissive. If this is the case, then it can be managed as long as both of you can accept this role reversal with grace, otherwise it will prove too uncomfortable to maintain. In either case, the awareness to aim for is a sharply increased sense of what it is to be male or female – quite possibly in contrast to what you previously felt or believed such to be. The first kind of coupling is by far the simpler, especially if each of you can accept the traditional, even biological, roles of masculinity and femininity as being valid, comfortable and enjoyable. Failing this, your interaction on this level could give rise to falling out over such typical issues as respective rights and property – not least of all the perceived ownership of each other. But mutual frustration would become the most damaging element, which is a shame when considering the fact that this contact should act as a reminder that men and women were made for one another.

Venus Conjunct (uniting with) Jupiter
♀ ☌ ♃

The Joy Of Love
This is a particularly favourable interaction because it ensures a benevolent and good-hearted feeling between the two of you. You tend to see the best in each other and this furthers positive development for both of you as individuals and as a couple. This can mean a number of things, from attracting wealth to helping you through hard or tense times together. There is an enthusiasm for life and each other, which ultimately leads to a quite religious or spiritual understanding and expression of what your relationship means. Along the way, however, there can be quite a strong indulgent streak that had better be curbed if your life together is to be more than just a feast of eating and drinking and social rounds. One of you can help give the other a social direction and context to their visions of a better life, while they in turn encourage that partner to make more of their talents. This giving could also go both ways. Through, or apart from, any storms that your relationship may have to endure, this interaction will maintain a constant flow of joy and optimism.

Venus Conjunct (uniting with) Saturn
♀ ♂ ♄

Marriage Lines

Whatever else goes on between you, there is certainly a serious and committed side to your relationship. Potentially, this has the makings of a classic marriage – given time. Ideally, you should be able to maintain a good balance between being playful and loving on the one hand, and order and duty on the other. In order to do this, you should each be progressively taking a page out of one another's books. If, however, a balance and exchange of this type is not created, then one can seem to become a wet blanket or not be forthcoming at all, while the other appears wanton and capricious – and the rot could set in. Alternatively, your relationship could be quite formal, or for reasons of convenience or money. If this is the case, it may only be a matter of time before one of you would crave a more romantic relationship, and the other would have their possible expectation of 'love being for fools' effectively borne out. Whatever happens, unless there is some very negative event in your lives, such as an acrimonious parting, you will always give and receive from each other a sober kind of affection. Most importantly, this contact really demands that you draw up some form of conscious agreement or arrangement – and that you keep to it.

Venus Conjunct (uniting with) Uranus
♀ ♂ ♅

Love Brings Change

This is one of the most powerful mutually and instantly attracting interactions in the book – literally. One, or probably both, of you is swept off their feet by the extraordinary, possibly otherworldly, quality they perceive in the other person. You are also both drawn to the style and/or beauty of each other. In fact the actual circumstances of your meeting could be otherworldly in some way, presaging the unusual nature and course of your relationship itself. If we take a brief look at the Greek myth of the god Uranus it will give us some idea of why this is such an irresistible attraction. Uranus was the 'god of gods', Heaven, who lay across Gaia, the Earth, and Creation then came about. One of his sons, Saturn, strongly disapproved of his random way of ruling and deposed him by scything off his sexual organs and casting them into the sea. From the blood and foam of his severed genitals Aphrodite ('born of foam') or Venus was born. So you can see what a strong pull there would be between the man and his member! But the symbolism of this is that Uranus wants his power back and Venus wants the freedom to wield it. What all this adds up to is that each of you sees in the other an opening to make more of yourselves and life – although at the time of meeting the feelings are mainly sexual, not surprisingly. But then surprise is the element here, because the wind or tide of this interaction sets you off on a course you wouldn't have accounted for – and quickly too. It is important to recognize and understand the process that is going on here – namely that one or both of you is being given a sharp awakening with regard to the nature of your social/aesthetic values and style. Furthermore, one or both of you is being made to see the reality of your own, possibly unconscious, desire for change, and of the unusual effect you can have upon others. Effectively then, this interaction launches both of you into a very different orbit to the one you've been used to. But once the excitement and pyrotechnics of the launch is over there is that journey into the unknown to be reckoned with. What this is saying is that your relationship is only going to be as stable as your awareness of what it's really about and of where it's going. Failing this, an 'abort mission' light may well start to flash as the intensity of the interaction becomes too hard to handle. But this could simply be owing to your trying to repeat the thrill of the launch when you are already in flight. Once airborne, the force of this relationship could progressively take you somewhere new, refreshing itself as it goes. But whether or not you continue to experience this together depends greatly upon the presence of more long-lasting and stabilizing interactions – otherwise it could just be a case of 'Wow! What happened there?'

Venus Conjunct (uniting with) Neptune
♀ ☌ ♆

Unconditional Love
You have a very fine feeling flowing between you, and potentially the kind of love that survives many ups and downs. But 'transcends' might be a more accurate term than 'survives' because this interaction does not necessarily make for durability in the sense of an everyday, steady but unsensational sort of bond. It is a highly romantic love, but it can also adjust itself to whatever else is going on around you – and that includes more or less everything. You are both inclined to go along with whatever happens to you as a couple; even if someone else should come along and woo one of you away, the other would be inclined to accept this. If there are any more possessive links between you, then such 'unconditional love' may have to rise to the occasion, identify any illusions, and walk its talk by bowing out gracefully. A very pure and eternal, even platonic, relationship can be the fate of this interaction. Whatever the case, this certainly has a quite uplifting influence upon both of you. Creative pursuits, such as music and dance, or simply artistic appreciation, could very much be a part of your time together.

Venus Conjunct (uniting with) Pluto
♀ ☌ ♇

Self-regenerating Love
This interaction exercises a powerful pull towards each other, but to quite a degree it is unconscious. This means to say that the two of you would probably not realize how deeply involved you are with one another until later. Feelings of possessiveness or jealousy surfacing could be signs of this depth, especially on the part of one of you, who will also try to make the other person 'fit' their emotional requirements. From their intensely emotional and possibly isolated viewpoint, the other seems to give off a take-it-or-leave-it attitude, which is not really the case, even though the other would sometimes like to think so. Be that as it may, there is a quality to your relationship that keeps on bringing you through one crisis after another, and renewing yourselves and the relationship itself – sometimes in spite of yourselves. The sexual dimension to this interaction is also deep, and intense. Sexual feelings and activities go through significant changes as you are both inevitably, and sometimes painfully, made aware of what works for you – often through a process of occasionally getting stuck with what doesn't! Money can also be a very

significant or even bargaining factor in your relationship. The fact that this bond is so powerful and deep is what makes you endure these deep changes and feelings. Unconsciously you are both aware that something won't let you go until it is satisfied, and then it won't matter. Till death us do part?

Venus Conjunct (uniting with) Ascendant *Birth Time Sensitive*
♀ ♂ AS

Mutual Affinity
There is an immediate attraction towards one another, whether either of you admits it or not. This is an interaction of 'style' for both of you focus your overall interaction upon matters of love, art, pleasure, play, money, social pros and cons, etc. Whatever your sexes, there is an affection between you that is shown or not shown, depending on the personal inclinations of each of you. With a few natural exceptions, you tend to share the same likes and dislikes regarding people and things. If one of you is more socially or artistically aware they can help the other to improve greatly. Your great enemy is most probably boredom owing to a failure to amuse or be amused by each other or whatever social or aesthetic situation you find yourselves in. Having said this, though, together you can possess a huge talent to entertain.

Venus Opposition (confronting) Ascendant *Birth Time Sensitive*
♀ ♂° AS

Real Or Fanciful Love
On the face of it, this interaction is highly favourable for marriage or any kind of romantic or affectionate relationship. One of you senses that the other is the one who will make them happy and socially complete, while they respond accordingly. And so all these matters can be excellently starred – but there is always the danger of superficiality and/or social convention. This means to say, that the 'idea' of marriage and living-happily-ever-after, or simply being too 'social', can superimpose itself on the emotional reality of both of you. How long it takes before any cracks show is very dependent on what other interactions you have between you. If there is plenty of harmony or depth elsewhere, then this interaction would live up to its promise and, indeed, contentment with one another will persist. If there are difficulties with the gilt fading, then one or maybe both of you should bear in mind that the beauty, worth and lovability that they initially perceived in their partner was really their own unrecognized beauty, worth and lovability projected on to them. On the other hand, one or both of you may need to learn not to please at the cost of losing sight of who they are in their own right.

Venus Conjunct (uniting with) MidHeaven *Birth Time Sensitive*
♀ ♂ MC

A Sound Investment
This is mutually beneficial to both of you. The professional and social standing of the one of you, usually the MidHeaven person, provides a sense of position, worth and belonging to the other, probably Venus, person. In turn, Venus acts as muse or aesthetic touchstone to the other individual, helping them to attune themselves to what pleases and is profitable

in the world of commerce and art.

Venus Opposition (confronting) MidHeaven *Birth Time Sensitive*
♀ ☍ MC
Home Beautiful
Whether it is in the home in the literal sense, or in the sense of one's inner or private world, this interaction confers upon one or both of you an aura of beauty and social grace. You feel happy and comfortable with one another, as if you were harmonious family members – and indeed you may actually be so.

Mars Conjunct (uniting with) Mars
♂ ☌ ♂
Hot! Hot! Hot!
This interaction had better be sexual, sporting or very active in some way. This is because it could otherwise degenerate into interminable battles as the raw or competitive energy created by the two of you being together finds nowhere positive to go. This is not to say that it ought to be sexual or physical in some way, but that it has a hard time expressing itself through other channels. One way or the other, though, you do test each other's mettle quite frequently; a bit like a game of arm wrestling. If one or the other of you is not very assertive or sure of your act, this interaction should teach you to be so – or you'll get knocked down or pushed around. You over-stimulate one another, which can give rise to the kitchen being too hot to stay in for long. This is more of a bout or match than it is a relationship – because you react rather that relate to one another. If you do both manage to harness this drive, this internal combustion engine of an interaction, then you could achieve a great deal together.

Mars Conjunct (uniting with) Jupiter
♂ ☌ ♃
Energy And Enterprise
This is a fiery interaction, which can launch you both to new heights of satisfaction and success in many areas of life, or simply result in burn-out if you merely indulge and behave as if you have more energy than sense. Positive activities together are the key here, and so being up and about the business of living through travel, sports, outdoor activities, are what get your wheels going round. This is an interaction that needs to have constructively employed the prodigious energy that it makes available to you as a couple. One of you stimulates the other to put their ideals and plans into action, thereby helping them to further themselves. In return, the other encourages their partner to be more confident in themselves and their activities. And so this interaction can positively escalate as one boosts the other, who in turn is then able to boost the one, and so on. So much depends upon the direction of such self-propelling. You could merely romp around and exhaust or irritate each other, or launch yourselves anew. Other, more passive or inertia-producing interactions may stifle this one, or be overcome by it. This is a 'get it on' interaction!

Mars Conjunct (uniting with) Saturn

♂ ☌ ♄

Hard Work

This is a key contact because the energies of each of you are so different, but can be strangely attracted to one another because of this. One of you we'll call the 'Martian' is hot, impulsive and boyish/childish; the other, the 'Saturnian', is cool, cautious and adult/mature. Because of these natural extremes, you are liable to bring them out in one another even further. The 'Martian' will become more pushy and impatient, while the 'Saturnian' can become cold and withdrawn. But really there is quite a positive dimension to this interaction if we look at it in terms of 'blade' ('Martian') and 'stone' ('Saturnian'). The 'Martian', rather than feeling confounded and frustrated by the 'Saturnian's' doubts and inhibitions, could see this an opportunity to sharpen their ability to show the 'Saturnian' the exact nature of those doubts and how they might assert themselves more spontaneously. And the 'Saturnian', rather than feeling stiff and awkward, could teach the 'Martian' the value of planning and using time and non-action as instruments for getting what they want. Failing this, things can go from bad to worse. The key phrase for this key contact is Hard Work. If the 'Martian' works hard at controlling their energies and the 'Saturnian' works hard at releasing them, with each other's help, then both of you will obviously gain. Otherwise it really will be 'hard work', a dead-end case of irresistible force meeting immovable object. Ultimately, all this could add up to a lesson in survival.

Mars Conjunct (uniting with) Uranus

♂ ☌ ♅

The Transformer

Here we have a mutual, and probably sexual, attraction that comes about in a very immediate manner, which seems to overlook or bypass what could be regarded as more practical, or even moral, considerations. This is because the energy of this interaction is in aid of freeing up both of your respective senses of who you each are as unique individuals, and as such, forces you uncompromisingly to exercise your right to assert your unique desires and feelings. This may, for example, involve unusual bursts of anger or sexual activity – or simply ongoing or periodic irritation. Of necessity, all this probably includes disrupting the status quo of one or both of you – and even those connected with you. So this is an interaction that has a sort of electrifying urgency about it, for its dynamic is that of pushing each of you on towards the next step in your personal evolution. After the initial catalytic interaction has taken place, there is no guarantee that the relationship will be long lasting, but its effects certainly will be. However, if there are other interactions which do indicate durability, as a couple you could, in an ongoing way, be involved in reforming or overthrowing certain existing norms, whether in your personal lives or in society as a whole.

Mars Conjunct (uniting with) Neptune

♂ ☌ ♆

Subtle Sexual Interplay

This interaction can lead you as merry dance – and sometimes not at all merry. In fact, 'dancing' makes a very apt metaphor for the interaction between these two Planets. First, who is leading who? Owing to current gender confusions and the contemporary styles of dance that reflect them, very few people have a clear idea of this. And in families too, the hierarchy of leadership is often in disarray. But with this interaction between you, some kind of rule had better be established or a lot of bruised shins and trodden-on toes will be the result. If yours is a sexual relationship, the range of shades and preferences is endless. Suffice to say that it can go from the extremely exotic to the peculiarly dissatisfying, from the intense to the infrequent or non-existent. Back to the dance – what music are you trying to dance to? This means, what is the theme or philosophy, if any, of your intimate relations? Generally, it is about sexual refinement, which along the way finds the sensitivity and peculiarities of one of you reacting with disgust, evasion or confusion to the other's hungry and hard pushing. Resort to artificial stimulants such as drugs or pornography can also enter the picture. Ideally, the pursuit of some spiritual–sexual discipline such as Tantra or Taoism is recommended. As far as non-sexual relationships are concerned (or the parts that are not to do with sex) this interaction makes for a subtle interplay between the two of you which can have many expressions, but probably the performing arts, healing and yoga are the major ones. In any event, finding a creative and positive way of channelling physical and psychic energies together is the goal to aim for. Without aiming 'high' in this way, this interaction can sink you quite low with deception, listlessness and frustration.

Mars Conjunct (uniting with) Pluto
♂ ☌ ♇

Healing Or Destructive Passion

This is one of the most powerful interactions there is, and as such, can corrupt or heal, transform or destroy. It is most likely that you are intensely and passionately involved in a sexual way, but such energy could also be used for any pursuit where a superior type of force is utilized, such as martial arts or some dynamic form of healing. In an emotional relationship, this interaction reaches the parts other interactions can't reach! This means to say that the intensity of your involvement brings all manner of feelings and desires to the surface, some wonderful, others hard to handle. A great deal depends upon what is motivating you both, and whether or not there is a higher goal you are aiming for. If you are simply getting off on the power and intensity merely for the sake of it, you are probably unwittingly sowing the wind only to find that you have a tornado on your hands. There is also a big brother/little brother, big sister/little sister, element in your relationship. If such is the case, the 'big' half may try to manipulate or dominate the 'little' half who, in turn, may be tempted to use fair means or foul to get even. It is when such selfish interests creep into this relationship that the destructive element is set in motion, and can escalate horribly. Again, this stresses the importance of having an objective that is regenerative for one or both of you, or someone or something outside of your relationship. Something quite dark, and even dangerous, can, as I say, be surfaced by your coming together. If you are not aware of this and of some means of eliminating or transforming such crude emotions, then you could find yourselves in a sticky situation. Metaphorically, it is as if your relationship is an oil well that draws the black stuff to the surface, but it has to be processed and refined to render it manageable and useful.

impersonal, yet at the same time quite enjoyable. As long as the relationship doesn't become 'academic' through losing sight of any emotional substance, this interaction can bring ethical steadiness and openly expressed goodwill to the relationship. Travelling near or far is also a strong aspect of your coming, or staying, together.

Jupiter Conjunct (uniting with) MidHeaven *Birth Time Sensitive*
♃ ☌ MC

Success!

This is a particularly positive combining of energies that furthers the career of the one and guides the career of the other, especially in an ethical sense. In fact, it is quite reciprocal in that an advantage for one of you is going to give rise to an advance for the other, and then the favour is returned, and so on. You both recognize and confirm each other's place and talent in the world.

Jupiter Opposition (confronting) MidHeaven *Birth Time Sensitive*
♃ ☍ MC

The Treasure Of The House

The home becomes a hive of activity under this Inter-Aspect, with mental and domestic parameters being expanded in the process. Although this is mainly beneficial to home and family life it may create friction with respect to differing values and beliefs within that home or family. But this does serve to make everyone aware of those very things. Overall, the Jupiter person is the 'treasure of the house' as they bring growth and understanding to this scene, while the MidHeaven person provides them with the space to find what their own 'treasure' actually is.

Saturn Conjunct (uniting with) Ascendant *Birth Time Sensitive*
♄ ☌ AS

A Karmic Tie

This key contact is very much a parent/child kind of relationship, literally or figuratively. It falls to the one person, the 'parent', to be the teacher, guide and setter of limits with regard to the other person, the 'child'. This can be experienced by the 'child' as the heavy 'father/mother' who restricts their self-expression, moulds their character and way of doing things, and suppresses their very identity. On the other hand, it could be more a case of the 'parent' showing the 'child' how to be more mature and methodical, objective and businesslike. How patient the 'parent' or teacher is and how receptive the 'child' or pupil is can therefore be the critical issue. What the 'parent' has to be careful of is to avoid projecting their own weaknesses and inadequacies onto the 'child' and becoming the above-described brow-beater, chastising themselves through their 'child'. So this interaction forces the 'parent' to be more mature, patient and responsible too, but with the difference that they are mostly having to teach it all to themselves. If the 'child' resists or rebels against the 'parent', even when they are being a just and level-headed teacher, then they can expect the 'parent' one day to leave them – temporarily or permanently – to their own devices. But the 'parent' has to learn to 'bear kindly with the fool' rather than dismiss the 'child' as being hopelessly naïve, selfish and generally brat-like. The circumstances that you both find yourselves in may well be limiting in some way. This is because it is teaching you both to ascertain what is holding you back in life, get real, and do something about it. By looking at the sign position(s) of the Saturn and the Ascendant in your respective charts, it may be seen what issues this 'parent/child' type relationship revolves around, because such will tell you what you are both supposed to be learning about. It is unlikely that either of you will get out of this 'classroom' relationship until those lessons have been learned. This could take quite some time, and for this reason, if no other, your relationship is probably a long-lasting one.

Saturn Opposition (confronting) Ascendant *Birth Time Sensitive*
ħ ☍ AS

The 'Conventional' Relationship
Your relationship imposes great responsibilities upon one another. These can be regarded as the essence of the relationship, with the enjoyment of the sense of purpose and stability that this confers, or your time together can seem like a long and meaningless haul up a steep and rocky road. A third alternative is that one or both of you is not ready for such responsibility and so the relationship never really gets off the ground in the first place, or that it limps along just for a bit. This interaction is the ultimate acid test of a relationship, for it says 'Can you relate properly?' The ultimate prize here is one of harmony and order combined, and it is your progressive working through all the trials and tribulations that earns you this. If you get to a point along this course and then wonder what it is all for, then you would need to take a less conventional look at the nature of relationship generally and of your own in particular. On this score of 'conventional' relationship, there is a possibility that originally you got together entirely for reasons of status, convenience, tradition or money. If such is the case, you would be fortunate indeed if this need to review your relationship from a more emotionally valid standpoint never arises. Yet another possibility that extends from this is one of marrying someone who is beneath or above you. This can appear to preclude emotional difficulties as the 'lower' person is taken care of and can't complain, whereas the 'higher' person feels in charge and emotionally invulnerable. But this can backfire as one or both people feel less and less emotional satisfaction, and may look for it elsewhere. This interaction demands that each of you own up to your respective shadow – the part or parts of yourself you do not like, openly express or admit to – rather than being married to it in the form of someone who appears un-likeable to you!

Saturn Conjunct (uniting with) MidHeaven *Birth Time Sensitive*
ħ ☌ MC

Win-Win Or Lose-Lose
You are both in positions of power and influence, relatively speaking. This means, for example, that one of you could be in a position of material power, while the other is in a position of emotional or psychological power. Whether or not this is recognized and taken advantage of is the question. Although this is often found between two people running a business or a home together, there is ever the possibility of jealousy and resentment. And this in turn can lead to a fall from grace for one or both parties. Obviously what is

required is that you ascertain and respect your individual strengths and benefit from them, get them to complement each other rather than conflict with one another. This Inter-Aspect is therefore mutually destructive or mutually constructive.

Saturn Opposition (confronting) MidHeaven *Birth Time Sensitive*
ħ ☍ MC

Firm Foundations Or Want Of Them

The fears or sense of order of the one of you, probably the Saturn person, come into direct contact with the inner, private or domestic realm of the other. A great deal depends upon the strength of the Saturn person with regard to their own house being in order if it is a case of the MidHeaven not having their house in order. This will also apply the other way around. So the expression of this Inter-Aspect can, on the one hand, be a dire, cold and chaotic private relationship that undermines the professional life of one or both of you, or, on the other hand, a stable and well-ordered private or domestic life that acts as a sound base for career activities. In effect then, this Inter-Aspect serves to show how well or badly each of you are doing at this particular time of your respective lives. It may therefore be a lesson in the learning, or something sober and firm – but maybe a bit lacking in emotional warmth – that lasts and lasts.

Uranus Conjunct (uniting with) Ascendant *Birth Time Sensitive*
♅ ☌ AS

A Highly Unusual Relationship

You have a unique relationship, and as such it is really up to you what you make it into. When you first met a light flashed on somewhere or a shock-wave went rippling through both of you. The great thing about this interaction is that you should continuously surprise one another. Sometimes this can take the form of sudden breaks in your relationship, which serve to keep you mindful that you must not and cannot put either one of you, or the relationship itself, into some conventional category. You are there in each other's lives to be reminded that there is no one like either of you in the whole Universe! What goes with this territory is that you force one another to evolve as individuals and this will eventually amount to some form of spiritual development. Personal freedom is of paramount importance, and as such it is in some ways better if you are friends rather than lovers or members of the same family. Lovers and family tend to fix one another in some mould for the sake of security, in which case one of you would be forced to break away, rattling the other's cage in the process. Whatever the case, it would probably help to be alive to the fact that you are of the same family – the human one. As such you are born to be ever true to yourselves and not someone or something else. This interaction, through a process of storms, unpredictable occurrences and amazing coincidences, keeps you both keenly aware of this cosmic fact. There is often the feeling that you should both amount to something extraordinary together. And it is through being true to your individual selves that you may well make this a reality.

Uranus Opposition (confronting) Ascendant   *Birth Time Sensitive*

♅ ☍ AS

Freedom And Balance

It could be said that this interaction holds the key to relating. The esoteric reason for this is that Balance, which is what relating is essentially about, is really only found when both people have and allow each other the Freedom to do so. This interaction is all about Balance and Freedom. But before you start opening the champagne and booking the reception, it has to be said that most people either do not know what Freedom actually is, or, if they think they do, when they are offered it they feel quite threatened by it. For example, with this interaction, Freedom can first show its face by not allowing you to plan or fix things as you'd like. It is as if it tests your ability to be free by not letting you have what you expect, by not letting you feel too safe. But from a conventional standpoint, these are the very things that we want from a relationship. And so when either one of you feels shaky about the other being unreliable, think again, it is just this interaction rattling the cage of your conventional expectations. Another clue here is that Freedom has a great deal to do with friends and friendship. And so if this is a love or family relationship, attempt to see each other as friends do – that is, not making unnecessary or, least of all, possessive demands on one another. True friends don't. You may indeed find that you are quite easygoing with one another, and do not live in each other's pockets. This is a good sign that you are being true to one another – because you are feeling free to be yourselves, and allowing each other to be so too. However, if one or both of you is secretly hankering after something more cosy, or is just pretending to be 'modern' and laid-back, then expect the other person, or circumstances, to start upping the dosage of unpredictability! Another very common manifestation of this interaction is one that happens after two people have married and settled down: divorce. But this only happens because you got married for reasons of security and social convention – anathema to this interaction – even though you may have thought along the way that you were free and easygoing, and even open to experimentation. All the same, experimentation is what it is about in a very pragmatic sense. In other words, with this interaction you are both discovering something new, by trial and error, and possibly developing some new social values in the process. In any event, yours is not what others would class as a 'normal' relationship – whatever that is.

Uranus Conjunct (uniting with) MidHeaven   *Birth Time Sensitive*

♅ ☌ MC

Ringing The Changes

The Uranus individual brings the prospect of change, new ideas, even revolution, to the status of the MidHeaven person, and also to their idea of how they see the world work and how they fit into it. A great deal then depends upon how much the MidHeaven person actually wants to change. They might see Uranus as just being off the wall, as an interesting oddity, an outsider. Then again they could provide Uranus with something practical to further their unusual or alternative interests. In any event, Uranus does mark or point to some sort of change in the position of the MidHeaven individual.

Uranus Opposition (confronting) MidHeaven   *Birth Time Sensitive*
♅ ☍ MC

The Bomb In The Basement

The Uranus individual brings disruption to the home and inner life of the MidHeaven person, but this is only because they unconsciously needed to clear out the cobwebs in that area. The trouble is that the home and private interior is usually the very place where one wants peace and stability – and so Uranus may eventually get 'expelled' or not admitted in the first place. However, it is also the place where habits can cause one to stagnate. If the MidHeaven can accept this seeming 'disruption' in this spirit then they can be renewed and liberated. In return they can provide Uranus with the place to realize their uniqueness and accept what is unusual about their nature, and make something of it. Generally, the home and what goes on inside of it are out of the ordinary, shocking even.

Neptune Conjunct (uniting with) Ascendant   *Birth Time Sensitive*
♆ ☌ AS

Psychic Rapport

Because, on first meeting, this interaction allows you both to see through each other's masks, defences or smoke screens, the subsequent reaction of each of you can vary enormously. A great deal depends upon what it is that each of you senses within the other person. The chances are that whatever each of you does see will reflect or enhance some highly sensitive issue of your own. Your individual emotional reactions that follow upon this are what then characterize this interaction, rather than what actually happened in the first place. There are usually two extremes here: one is where a glamorized image or some other smoke screen is quickly put up in order to protect yourself from the other person's psychic perception of your inner truth. The other extreme is that a great openness remains, allowing a wonderful psychic rapport to manifest between the two of you. This psychic rapport causes you to feel as one, to identify very closely with one another, and to detect at any distance the state of one another. However, it must be pointed out that it only takes one of you to adopt the first extreme in order, sadly, to preclude or at least greatly diminish the second one. And even when the second extreme has been maintained by one of you, the psychic defence screen erected by the other person could eventually become actually offensive, which would cause the 'open' person to close down defensively too. The outcome here is then a 'psychic war' of projected and imagined fears, which can be quite sapping, physically and emotionally, to both of you. Generally speaking, because most people are not yet prepared to see clearly their inner truth as distinct from their outer display, the remedy to the negative expression of this interaction is not very acceptable. All the same, here it is. If you are experiencing the negative expression, cast your minds back to when you first met, and visualize slowly and closely what actually transpired at that time. If you can do this, without defensively reacting again, you will gain a great insight into the truth of who you both are, as individuals and to one another. This interaction reminds me of the Mayan greeting 'In lak'ech' which means 'I am another (like) yourself.' One way or the other this interaction will bring you both an insight into spiritual reality or the mystery of being. How you respond to this determines whether you experience it as fascination or confusion, identification or alienation, love or hate – or a strange combination of some or all of these.

Neptune Opposition (confronting) Ascendant *Birth Time Sensitive*
♆ ☍ AS

An Illusory Or Spiritual Connection

One person is fascinated by some quality in the other which they most likely will ascribe to something that may or may not prove to be the case at a later date. It is as if the second person unconsciously picks up what the first finds irresistible and plays that card over and over again in an equally unconscious bid to be accepted or have some special quality in them recognized. But the first person is all the while fitting the other's 'show' or mystique into whatever they fantasize as being their ideal partner. The upshot of all this can be anything from continuing to fit each other's ideal of the perfect partner, or what you make of one another reveals itself to be a mirage. From this point one or both of you can feel disillusioned, with embarrassment and possible parting to follow, or, if you are inclined to see past these misconceptions, and sacrifice your individual illusions for what they are – that is, not seeing things right – you may move on up to a higher vibration of love and relationship altogether.

Neptune Conjunct (uniting with) MidHeaven *Birth Time Sensitive*
♆ ☌ MC

Heaven Or Hell?

This is quite a complex interaction because it involves what can be very disparate energies. The MidHeaven individual will be concerned with the material and professional world, whereas the Neptune person will be drawn to the spiritual, inspirational or dreamy aspects of life. When harmonious, there can be a mutual advantage as worldly position and divine inspiration converge to create some form of successful expression involving music, healing, art or mysticism. On the other hand, the MidHeaven can become undermined or seduced by Neptune, possibly leading to collapse or scandal. Neptune for their part may feel crushed or overlooked by the MidHeaven's more pragmatic, materialistic approach to life.

Neptune Opposition (confronting) MidHeaven *Birth Time Sensitive*
♆ ☍ MC

Inner Psychic Link

At some deep and subtle level the two of you feel joined at the hip. But the nature of this link can very much go two ways, with such a sensitive connection manifesting as a great feeling of being at home with one another, to finding such 'familiarity' disconcerting. Spirituality, music, alcohol or drugs are just a few of the potent influences that can make themselves felt here. Ultimately, everything depends upon your respective levels of psychological awareness and development. At the one extreme this could be the case of the one, relatively needy or weak, person imposing upon the stronger, better positioned, person, or, at the other extreme, of the highly sensitive and psychically attuned individual influencing the private or professional life of the materialistic individual. Owing to the nature of this Inter-Aspect, the roles of Neptune and MidHeaven are quite interchangeable.

Pluto Conjunct (uniting with) Ascendant   *Birth Time Sensitive*
♇ ☌ AS

Empowerment Or Disempowerment

One of you is strongly inclined to feel under the influence of the other person, but it can sometimes work both ways. At first, the feeling of being 'under the influence' could amount simply to being impressed. Later on, however, this can come to be a feeling of empowerment or disempowerment as the person with the influence either feels disposed towards attacking or supporting the one who is under their influence. In either case, this influence is taken in quite compulsively because the 'influenced' feels very dependent upon the 'influencer' in some way. If the influencing is entirely positive, then you can either instil or confirm a sense of effectiveness and worth in each other. One individual benefits particularly from having their image bolstered or their appearance transformed in some way. The other individual, who is doing the bolstering, gets to feel more influential as a person. If, or when, the negative holds sway, then one or both of you will have to look at why your need to gain approval for yourself has degenerated to the point of receiving abuse instead – maybe in the hope of getting a few crumbs of praise. But merely to resist the 'influencer' would not turn things around. Whichever of you is needing such affirmation of their existence – and it could well be both of you – would be far better off seeking something that would do this more consciously and without an emotional agenda. Verbal affirmations (like 'I am that I am' or something more personal), psychotherapy or some course of self-improvement are a few suggestions. If you are both confident enough in yourselves, none of the above should be that much of an issue, one way or the other. Instead, you could both be deeply involved together in a programme of self-transformation or some other kind of psycho-spiritual project. Or you may simply enjoy a very deep emotional and physical intimacy.

Pluto Opposition (confronting) Ascendant   *Birth Time Sensitive*
♇ ☍ AS

Light And Shadow

If one of you is rather unconscious of their shadow side or alter ego, the other person will play this out for them in a manner that makes both people deeply dependent upon one another, or even obsessed with one another. In effect, consciously or unconsciously, the second 'shadow' person can exert an enormous influence over the other, 'light', individual. But as they do so through playing out the 'light's' darker and more dynamic side – or at least the part they cannot seem to easily express – they too become dependent upon the 'light', because of the power this seems to invest in them. All of this sounds rather vampiristic – and it can be, with intense passion and possessiveness also being on the menu. However, if the 'light' can take back or repossess some of the personal power that is theirs, then the 'shadow' will have to come out of the shadows and show their darker side too, with a view to being positively transformed in the process. What can make this difficult is that the 'light' person has grown habituated to depending on the other for a show of power (because they needn't take the flak that expressing their own power would attract), and this interaction marks some sort of reckoning. But the 'shadow' person can also be the 'patsy' here for allowing themselves to be set up as the 'power-player', when really they are playing along with the 'light' person's (unconscious) ruse to manipulate a partner into being what they want them to be – that is, their shadow. It can be the case that both of you are happy with this arrangement, which could, for example, take the form of the 'shadow' person being well-off materially and the 'light' person being dependent upon them for their power to earn, while the 'shadow' is dependent upon the 'light' person's physical charms and emotional support. Whatever, the 'deal' that this interaction translates into, your relationship will attract and go through many changes, some quite cathartic. This is because this interaction's influence is geared to creating deeper and deeper levels of involvement, with usually money and/or sex as the lever. It may appear to one or other of you that at times you have to use your own particular 'lever' to get what you want, but this only invites a game of psychological poker as the other person is forced to then use their 'lever'. A more honest and psychologically aware approach to relating on the part of one, but ultimately both, of you could make this interaction into a deep, lasting and emotionally satisfying bond.

Pluto Conjunct (uniting with) MidHeaven *Birth Time Sensitive*
♇ ☌ MC

Professional Transformation
Pluto somehow remakes the MidHeaven's idea of who or what they are in the world. How the MidHeaven responds to this all depends upon how much they agree to such a professional or status makeover. To Pluto they can appear rather too mundane and conventional for his or her profound sense of what life should be about – but, then again, the MidHeaven could provide them with the practical wherewithal to further such deep interests. Alternatively, you could both be professionally involved in something that aims to transform the status quo itself, or that involves the occult or psychology.

Pluto Opposition (confronting) MidHeaven *Birth Time Sensitive*
♇ ☍ MC

Digging Deep
The Pluto person really gets the other MidHeaven person 'where they live'. This can range from simply getting them to transform their actual home or to purging their most entrenched habits. The MidHeaven person can find such penetration into their most private areas invasive or welcome; it all depends upon what they feel needs changing in this respect. In return, or alternatively, the MidHeaven person can provide Pluto with a base of operations for their transformative practices or simply accommodate their darker side. A case of either intimacy or repulsion ruling.

Ascendant Conjunct (uniting with) Ascendant *Birth Time Sensitive*
AS ☌ AS

Identifying With One Another
There is an immediate and mutual physical attraction between you, as well as strongly identifying with one another. However, the quality of it and how such an attraction develops greatly depends on the Signs which you both have rising (your Ascendants or Rising Signs), which will usually be the same. Certain Signs are destined to get on together

better and longer, like Sagittarius or Taurus, whereas others can fall foul of a doubling up of inherent weakness. For example, Libra can fall in love with love only to find a mirage is all that they're left with; Gemini can amuse and interest each other but never get that involved; Cancer can cling together tightly and securely, but suffer claustrophobia later. Aries or Leo would be exciting but competitive; Virgo just right or just not quite right. Scorpio is a pairing that can definitely merge and stay that way, come hell or high water; but Capricorn would get too dull if it ever got off the ground at all. Aquarius could be a very easy, friendly pairing as long as neither wanted anything more emotionally profound. Finally, Pisces could be blissful if they managed to stay entwined long enough to find out. Furthermore, this interaction is one to get you going in the first place, but the course of your relationship will fall to the other interactions between you.

Ascendant Opposition (confronting) Ascendant *Birth Time Sensitive*
AS ☍ AS

Head-to-Toe
The image here is that of the snake eating its own tail. What this means in plain English is that each of you strongly identifies with the part of yourself that you cannot understand or accept through being attracted to it in the other. If there are a good deal of harmonious or positive connections supplied by planetary interaction between you, then this aspect can eventually make you as one. More often, though, this interaction seems to occur when both of you need to have a good look at what it is about each of you that is dragging its feet. Your relationship with each other is therefore an opportunity to become a more complete person through having demonstrated by your opposite number what it is you usually find hard to accept or express. Either they will simply always act that part out for you, or you learn from them how to do it for yourself.

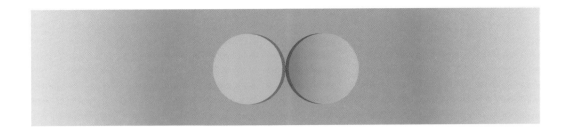

2. RELATIONSHIP CHALLENGES

These are the interactions that are most likely to produce friction and disagreement – some more than others as the interpretations point out. In fact, they often explain why you were attracted in the first place because they define the deeper reasons for your coming together in that they force both of you to become more self-aware and improve your relating skills or ability to love and be loved. Too many of these Challenges, however, (in comparison to the Relationship Strengths below) can make it unacceptably uphill and lead to separation. But it would still have the potential for self-growth.

Ascendant and MidHeaven Inter-Aspects: Note that when a Planet of one person is Square (challenging) the Ascendant or MidHeaven of another person, then it is at the same time Square (challenging) their Descendant or Lower MidHeaven, respectively. This is simply because the Descendant is always the opposite point to the Ascendant (see page 42), and Lower MidHeaven is always the opposite point to the MidHeaven (see page 95). The interpretations will cover these cases.

IMPORTANT: Remember that the name of Inter-Aspect may be written the other way around to how it is given in the Relationship Profile INDEX. For example, an Inter-Aspect given as **Saturn Square (challenging) Sun** ♄ □ ☉ in the INDEX will be given here as **Sun Square (challenging) Saturn** ☉ □ ♄. Also, the As and Bs are not included here because they are individual to the particular relationship as given in the INDEX or on-screen.

RELATIONSHIP CHALLENGES: INTERPRETATIONS

Sun Square (challenging) Sun
☉ □ ☉

A Clash Of Egos
Your individual wills are at odds with one other and so your life tracks tend in different directions. This can lead to interminable battles as you both try to get your own way, sapping one another's strength in the process. From a positive standpoint, it means that you can each become stronger in your own right as you each continually wrestle for supremacy, or better still, accept what one Sun Sign can learn or gain from another. However, unless you are the kind of people to whom harmony is not that important, or who actually need someone to keep you on their mettle, then you should not expect to work together or live in each other's pockets. This interaction can exist in longstanding relationships, but it would seem that, apart from the reasons just given, it would be

between people who both have ego problems of some kind. For example, one would need to learn humility, whereas the other is learning to become more sure of themselves – the hard way.

Sun Opposition (confronting) Sun
☉ ☊ ☉

Two Halves Of An Orange
Here we have a classic case of opposites attracting one another. So although both of you are strongly drawn to one another at the outset, as time goes by you find that you each have quite distinct 'ego zones' and will object quite vehemently to the one being invaded and managed by the other – or even seeming to be. This amounts to an exercise in respecting each other's space and way of living. Having avoided this pitfall, which could otherwise result in quite serious rifts being caused, a very complementary relationship can be created that presents a complete front and lifestyle to anyone, be it children, employees or others in general. A blending of the best of each person's Sun Sign qualities is the goal to aim for. A great deal also depends upon emotional harmony and reasonable communication being provided by other interactions.

Sun Square (challenging) Moon
☉ □ ☽

A Superior/Inferior Problem
This makes for a basic incompatibility. You would need to have a great deal going for your relationship in terms of external and superficial worth, or conversely, inner and spiritual worth, in order to override this one. One of you, the 'Sun' person, cannot seem to appreciate where the other, 'Moon' person, is coming from emotionally. Consequently, they often offend, confuse or dominate the 'Moon' person without even knowing it. The 'Moon' person's background and personal habits do not fit in with the 'Sun's' lifestyle. Another, and decidedly better way of overcoming, or at least diminishing, the negative effects of this interaction, is for the 'Moon' to become very aware of how and why they react to the 'Sun's' way of being. In the meantime, the 'Sun' would have to learn to observe how the 'Moon' is feeling and avoid stepping on their toes. Even so, this is not a desirable interaction, especially between parents, for you can put out mixed messages and double standards to your children – unless these problems are dealt with in the manner suggested.

Sun Opposition (confronting) Moon
☉ ☊ ☽

A 'Full Moon' Relationship
This interaction is like the Full Moon – with one of you, the 'Sun' person, diametrically opposite the other, 'Moon' person, and illuminating the whole of its face. The 'Moon' person is therefore very much in the thrall of the 'Sun' person, dependent upon their words and actions for feeling whatever they feel. The 'Sun' person is bestowing upon the 'Moon' the attention, warmth and sheer vitality that they need to feel alive and comfortable – or they could simply overwhelm them and have them dangling on a string. The 'Moon' person can either take this, gladly or sadly, or retreat into some area of safety where the

'Sun's' ego can't get at them. A great deal can be learned by the 'Sun' as to how they affect others with their will and ego, for the 'Moon' picks up every little nuance and reflects it back to the 'Sun'. The 'Moon', on the other hand, is made to feel acutely aware of every little emotional feature – particularly childhood or childish patterns of behaviour. So much depends upon the spirit in which this illuminating and reflecting is performed. This interaction is far more manageable when the male is the 'Sun' person because traditionally it is his role to 'do', and when the 'Moon' is the female, for traditionally it is her role to 'be' in response. When it is the reverse way around, you could both feel out of your traditional roles to the extent that the female 'Sun' is having to be both mother and partner to the other, while the male 'Moon' feels rather weak and powerless and in danger of crumbling. But if the female 'Sun' can get the hang of having such power and use it benevolently, and the male 'Moon' get the feel of how effective being passive can be, then all will be well. Even so, and common though this aspect is in marriages, it is rather demanding. But then it does promise a great reward: increased awareness of what and who you both are, and of life itself.

Sun Square (challenging) Mercury
☉ □ ☿

Cross Purposes
The two of you often talk or think at cross-purposes, so arranging day-to-day activities can prove to be irritatingly difficult. Another reason for this may be that the one person's daily schedule does not fit the other's plans. All of these little annoyances can build up to being a sizeable problem. It is well known that good communication is one of the most important elements of a successful relationship – and, to varying degrees, this aspect denies you this. To complicate matters, one of you may view the other as intellectually inferior and disorganized, whereas that person thinks the other pompous and overbearing. Sometimes these roles could become reversed. The truth is that you are both shedding light on the affairs of the other, but sometimes in a too-too clever or caustic fashion for it to be appreciated. It would best be viewed as both of you revealing not only shortcomings but positive avenues that could be taken to improve your minds and lives generally and your working lives in particular. But a superior stance taken by one of you can make the other defensive, and so they do not benefit from their 'light', such as it is, by not taking the other seriously. This can even reach a point where one of you sees the other merely as a figure of fun, which causes that person to look down on them even more. If the one or both of you could learn to be more noble and less conceited it would pre-empt such a defensive reaction.

Sun Opposition (confronting) Mercury
☉ ☍ ☿

Monarch And Advisor
Essentially, one of you feels in a superior intellectual position to the other. The 'inferior' person then feels they only have their point of view to offer the other person or confront them with, whereas the 'superior' person has their whole will and lifestyle to either overwhelm, ignore or approve of the other with. Of course, if the 'inferior' person is very

sure of themselves mentally and the 'superior' person's will is not that developed, it would be a different story – but it would not amount to a balanced or satisfying relationship. This interaction is therefore about each of you learning to take on board what the other has to say, and not just resisting or criticising out of wounded or threatened pride. One or each of you should be seen as some sort of advisor to a dignitary, and not presume upon their mental connection or prowess. Bearing all this in mind, you can learn a great deal from one another.

Sun Square (challenging) Venus
☉ □ ♀

Disappointed Love

This interaction can amount to being one of Cupid's most capricious darts. You are drawn together for relatively superficial and indulgent reasons, but at the time it will have seemed quite, even intensely, romantic. But as time goes by the differences between you make it uncomfortably clear that your values and intentions are at odds with one another. One of you seems less and less able to please the other, who then feels that that person is beneath them. It would seem that one individual's point of view is obscured by their chagrin at not having things as they like them, while the other expresses the very traits that rub this in. Love and vanity make poor companions, with the result that there is no real understanding or sympathy between you – or at least, it is not provided by this aspect on its own. If one of you could be less egotistical and the other more sure of their worth then all would be well, but the very nature of this interaction spells out that this is probably just not the case – yet ultimately these are the respective lessons you have to learn, with or without one another.

Sun Opposition (confronting) Venus
☉ ☍ ♀

Love Or Fancy?

This is an odd interaction for it means that your attraction and affection for one another is blighted by a certain sense of distance and dissatisfaction. It is as if one or both of you is drawn to something in the other which you later find is not really to your liking, but you seem stuck with each other all the same. If it is just one of you that experiences this, then the relationship can also wind up being decidedly one-sided. The most likely reason for either case is that vanity and superficial appeal have got ensnared by one another. In other words, you are being confronted with the perils of superficial or romantic notions of love and the only way of putting matters to rights is either by deepening your love through recognizing what it really is that you feel genuinely for in each other, or by accepting the fact that you have been the victims of your own fancies and call it a day. If there are other commitments already in hand, like children, then the former course would appear to be compulsory – or at least something you must try very hard at.

Sun Square (challenging) Mars
⊙ □ ♂

Battle Stations!

This interaction represents a battle zone in your relationship, which unfortunately is likely to spread to other areas as well. And talking of battles, there is a 'soldierly' or masculine quality to the way you interact generally. So there can be an impulsive, 'let's go and do it' approach to things, but little receptivity, tenderness or passivity. This is especially noticeable if yours is a sexual relationship, meaning that it can be very exciting and immediate up until the point where it becomes too coarse or one-dimensional for one or both of you. But more basically, your egos are at war with one another, and only a good amount of harmonious interaction could prevent this interaction from making your lives a misery of conflict, which may even include physical combat. Going back to the 'soldier' analogy, one of you may come on as 'officer' and treat the other as the 'squaddie' who has to be constantly told what to do. This riles them to the point that they eventually mutiny in some way. Or they may simply snap at the heels of the 'officer' in a terrier-like fashion, thereby attracting more scorn and bossiness from them. Through this interaction you could each learn a lot about how effective you are, or need to be, in asserting or defending yourself. Ideally you should learn this after a battle or two, rather than living an ongoing war together.

Sun Opposition (confronting) Mars
⊙ ☍ ♂

The Importance Of Being Independent

Each of you makes the other more aware of their sexuality and independence (or lack of it). This may not be done that consciously. It may in fact be done inadvertently by one of you treating the other as a lesser being, somewhat like an officer would regard one of his men. And so the 'man' may have to strike out on their own – but this is precisely how they find themselves, and the meaning of this interaction. However, it probably will not go as simply as this. The 'officer' will have their ego pricked by the 'man' fighting back, and try to stop them going or get them back. But the 'man' is not what they want back, it is their self-esteem. And so the basic competition or incompatibility that is the core of this interaction plays itself out in this way, with many a fight and a lonely space in between. This aspect is not one of love in the romantically or generally accepted sense of being close and together, for it is stressing the need for each of you being an independent individual in your own right, sometimes in quite a crude and hard way. If yours is a sexual relationship, this hardness and lack of love can be quite noticeable – and add to the separativeness of this interaction. This aspect can exist in long, ongoing relationships, but other things will be holding you together while the battle persists as some form of keeping you both on your toes, or more seriously, as a means of bringing home the importance of independence within a relationship, something which one of you may be resisting and the other contesting.

Sun Square (challenging) Jupiter
☉ □ ♃

A Question Of Morals

The beliefs and philosophy of one or both of you either get in the way of each of you freely expressing yourselves or make you want continually to get the better of each other. At the same time, you both encourage each other's excesses, wasting quite a lot of energy and time as you do so. Your relationship can eventually take on a 'believers versus infidels' quality as you progressively mount one 'holy crusade' after another against each other. It has to be said that you can have quite a lot of fun and horseplay together, but will also regularly fall out with each other. Each of you just has to be right all the time, and so a true intimacy is not made possible, at least not by this interaction. Distance and travel can also be a part of this interaction that brings adventure, but it exacerbates, or simply externalizes, differences in philosophy or cultural outlook. Your conflicting egos and beliefs drive formidable wedges between you. This aspect of your relationship is quite 'male', which tends, on its own account, to exclude the presence of sympathy and tolerance.

Sun Opposition (confronting) Jupiter
☉ ☍ ♃

A Valuable Learning Experience

As you incline each other to be bright and playful, there is a general atmosphere of goodnaturedness between the two of you. But this is called upon again and again to overcome or diffuse the strong clashes that occur between the ego and lifestyle of the one of you, and the philosophy and beliefs of the other. Consequently, one of you is all too likely to regard the other as a hypocritical know-it-all, preaching and moralizing. At the other end of the mat, that person is seen as being too proud for their own good, and unable to view things from what they regard as their superior mental overview. The fact remains that you are poles apart in these important respects, and that it would be wise to take the differences on board and, by contrast, benefit from getting a clearer idea of your individual standpoints. Then you will each become more sure of that standpoint and not waste time and energy trying to defend or prove it to the opposing camp. You both need to remind yourselves that there are three ways of teaching: by example, by example, and by example. Then you will be subtly reminded of how enlightening another's view can be when it is no longer so readily offered – or available at all.

Sun Square (challenging) Saturn
☉ □ ♄

Two Rulers

You are inclined to trigger each other's doubts and defences – so this can prove a difficult aspect to your relationship. It is rather as if one of you is the 'monarch' and the other is 'president/prime minister'. You both have or want a sense of power and position, and feel that the other threatens it in some way. The 'monarch' is brighter and more outgoing in the use and expression of themselves and their way of life. The 'president' is more conservative, traditional, and toes some sort of party line. Possibly the common ground that you do have is one or each of you wishing to maintain your individual integrity. And so it would be fruitful to earn each other's respect through showing that you both stick to your principles – even though they are very different – and defer to the other if they have honourably proved their point. All this will take time, which poses the necessity of there being a commitment to a duty that goes beyond your ego conflict – like being parents, for example. Basically, a balance needs to be struck between the 'monarch's' expansive and generous nature, and the 'president's' restraining and cautious one. You both have an important contribution to make to whatever is the substance of your relationship, but the 'monarch' is being forced to learn that restrictions can have great value, and the 'president' to trust that matters will unfold creatively and should not be controlled too much. Failing to understand these apparently opposing laws of good 'government' can cause one or both of you, or the relationship itself, to fall from grace.

Sun Opposition (confronting) Saturn
☉ ☍ ♄

Strength And Weakness Collide
With what they think they are sure of, the one of you confronts what the other is not sure of in themselves. Alternatively, or as a response to this confrontation, the other person will suppress and dampen the first person's self-expression – they may even sense what is coming from them unconsciously, and withdraw or suppress them from the outset. This very inharmonious and unromantic interaction probably occurs at a time in their life when one of them needs to learn to be sure enough of themselves so as to not overcompensate by over-asserting their strong points at the expense of another person's weak ones. Conversely, the other needs to take a good hard look at the weaker side of their personality, rather then leaving it to rot in the shadows. This is a 'Light versus Shade' interaction; the second person can resent the brightness and apparently strident confidence of the first person, while they find the second person fearful, too cautious or boringly conservative. Both Planets want authority, but of different types. As such, it makes for a poor boss/employer, teacher/student or parent/child relationship – simply because it will not be clear who is actually in charge. As previously stated, so much depends on how sure of their pitch each person is. If one is truly confident then they will feel no need to get into a conflict of wills with the other. But the very nature of this interaction seems to attract individuals and couples who have yet to attain this kind of true self-assuredness.

Sun Square (challenging) Uranus
☉ □ ♅

The Autocrat And The Outcast
One of you is inclined to see the other as being interestingly eccentric but, at the same time, as being a bit of a loose cannon. They, for their part, have mixed feelings of admiration and rebelliousness towards that person. This interaction could be called 'Royalists versus Republicans'. One of you is especially outraged by any signs of autocracy from the other, and will do all they can to rattle their cage. In return, the so-called 'autocrat' will patronizingly humour them or, depending upon their personal influence or social position, cause them to feel an outcast and an outsider whose ideas are totally off

the wall. But the 'outcast' will respond to this with renewed revolutionary zeal. This can amount to anything from actually sabotaging the 'autocrat's' position, to more subtle psychological tactics, such as detaching themselves in a way that piques their pride. In the end, the 'autocrat' needs to be more honourable, and the 'outcast' absolutely truthful. The 'autocrat' is, or appears to be, in the 'ruling position', and as such, should grant the 'outcast' credit where it is due for their laser-like perception of how things actually are. And if the 'outcast' is reacting and uptight, then they themselves should wake up to the fact that this is because they are unable to detach themselves, and so are therefore part of the problem that they are so ready to accuse the 'autocrat' of creating.

Sun Opposition (confronting) Uranus
☉ ☍ ♅

Stimulating But Unstable
You have an exciting but unstable interaction, which demands a great deal of space and freedom for both of you. At least as far as this aspect is concerned, your relationship could never be described as cosy! One of you takes exception to what they see as the other's overbearing nature and intuitively discovers ways of putting a spoke in their wheel. But the more they rattle their cage, the more dictatorial that person becomes by way of reaction, and so on and so on. If both of you have a bit of humility and willingness to learn from one another, you can become aware of the ways in which you might queer your own pitches, rather than the other's. Such a positive way of dealing with this interaction would also need to find the one person somehow eliciting respect from the other, while they in return would have to really put that person on the spot to make them realize that they hadn't got all their bases covered. From out of all this a mutually enlightening friendship could emerge, but a lasting intimate relationship would be a rarity.

Sun Square (challenging) Neptune
☉ □ ♆

Fascination And Illusion
Your relationship can start off as a fatal fascination but eventually encounter disillusionment – or if not dealt with, even end in it. This is because one or both of you, on first meeting the other, will present their most attractive and glamorous idea of themselves, blended with whatever the other expects this to be. This is a bit like Sunshine sparkling on and off the surface of water. But come nightfall there can be just a dull grey limpid mass – that is, sooner or later the mirage evaporates and the real and vulnerable person remains. Unless the one of you is some kind of spiritual master (in which case they wouldn't have been taken in first of all) they then find that what they thought was a knight in shining armour, or a damsel in distress, is by comparison rather pathetic. But, continuing with the Sun-reflected-on-the-water metaphor, they are really seeing what is pathetic about themselves. But again, both of you will most likely try to bluff your way out of this uncomfortable realization, which is when the real trouble begins. One of you takes on the role of the one in charge and can make the other's life a misery by treating them like a slave, fool or fall guy. If not doing so already, then one or both of you may seek solace in some form of escape from the oppression – like alcohol, drugs or work – or eventually

from out of the relationship all together. However, this could prove difficult, because both of you are addicted to your own illusions of strength and weakness, which this interaction so uncomfortably represents. Consequently, all manner of deception (self-, unconscious or otherwise) can creep into the cracks that this interaction opens up. So, unless some rigorous creative, spiritual or therapeutic discipline is, or already has been, embarked upon by both of you, your relationship will become a leaky vessel that has only one fate.

Sun Opposition (confronting) Neptune
☉ ☍ ♆

Karma And Drama
Although this is an interaction that has misunderstanding and delusion built into it, there is also a strange link that is possibly created by the fact that the personality of the first person is a polar opposite to the second – and opposites attract. The first person is bright and outgoing and set upon creating an impression, proving a point, and being seen to be important. The second person, on the other hand, is mysterious and diffuse, passive and evasive. And so the two of you play out this union of opposites. Positively, you can both tune into the ethereal and theatrical, the musical and romantic, feeding each other's dreams and fantasies. Negatively, the second person is inclined to dodge and deceive in the face of what they feel to be the first person's glaring and invasive ego as it attempts to pin their opposite number to the wall, spotlighting their weaknesses. They then respond with more evasiveness and fabrication as they reel against their delicate feelings being thus assaulted. And both the roles are very interchangeable. If there are other interactions which bestow some respect and decent communication, the two of you may eventually tune into the fact that you are both not only as sensitive as one another, but that you also have similar difficulties expressing or protecting that sensitivity. This is, after all, a psychic interaction, and if paranoia can be avoided on one or both of your parts, then a subtle and curiously strong bond can develop. Having said this, though, there is always the chance of some hidden hurt slipping in or of a mutual blind spot being encouraged, thereby sabotaging that bond. This interaction very much depends on respecting each other's emotional wounds and the sensitivity that attracted them or the distressed circumstances that inflicted them.

Sun Square (challenging) Pluto
☉ □ ♇

Regeneration Or Destruction
There is probably a great intimacy between the two of you, but this in itself becomes a problem, especially if this is a sexual relationship. In fact the sexual dimension is the main area of conflict and power struggle, and consequently where your relationship could come to grief. At first the feeling of being invaded and taken over is sexually attractive. But eventually one or both of you feels laid bare and robbed of their own will. One or both of you is also rather like a moth drawn to a flame, but the intensity of such a pull can be interpreted as being deliberately forceful – and it may be. In any event, this interaction demands that both of you attain a more conscious awareness of the powerful effect that you can have on others generally, and on each other in particular. It may come as a

surprise that every human being has this power potential in them but it takes this kind of interaction to spell out what kind of influence this can exert. So this intense and powerful contact is all too often destructive in some way, either partially or of the whole relationship. Basically, it is manifesting the dangers of any negative course either of you have set out upon – probably quite unconsciously, and possibly before your relationship even started. Underhand or morally questionable motives on the part of either of you are inevitably brought to a point of crisis. Whether or not you survive such a crisis as a couple, there is still a deep and lasting effect and lesson built into this relationship.

Sun Opposition (confronting) Pluto
☉ ☍ ♇

Svengali And Trilby

One of you, the 'Svengali' individual, inevitably tries to mould or transform the other – 'Trilby'. What motives and values they have behind doing this are the crucial issue, for they make the difference between it being a negative Svengali type of approach which can rob 'Trilby' of their own will and individuality, or, through connecting very deeply with the core of the 'Trilby's' being, it can empower them and give them a far stronger sense of their own will. More often than not, though, the nature of this interaction will lie somewhere in between. This can mean that 'Trilby', through resisting 'Svengali's' negative or selfish attempts to change them, actually becomes stronger and gets them more in touch with their own individuality. Before this occurs, however, 'Trilby' might be taken quite low, especially with regard to moral or sexual behaviour. Alternatively, 'Trilby' should endeavour to recognise and validate 'Svengali's' positive moves to change and empower them, for the reason behind any of their negative efforts is a lurking doubt in their own personal influence. Whatever the case, 'Svengali' can or should become more aware of their own power-plays and motivations to transform 'Trilby'. Ironically, the more that 'Trilby's' will is empowered by 'Svengali', then the more they can resist and even boss 'Svengali' around. This can be the case from the outset if it is 'Svengali' that is actually the less confident of the two of you. As long as this balance of power is understood and maintained, this interaction can make for a mutually empowering relationship – but a battle of wills is an integral, and potentially healthy, part of this process.

Sun Square (challenging) Ascendant   *Birth Time Sensitive*
☉ □ AS

Ego Versus Image

Neither of you may show it, but one or both of you feels a little in the shadow of the other. To one the other may seem to have more going for them, rather like a child would feel when comparing themselves to an adult. And so you have a mild contest of wills here, which if owned up to, can lead to a rather clear idea of who you each are in your own right. Failing this, this interaction will give rise to a petty competitiveness with each of you egocentrically trying to score points off one another.

Sun Square (challenging) MidHeaven *Birth Time Sensitive*
☉ □ MC

Territory Versus Respect
Although at first the MidHeaven person can find the Sun impressive and fun to have around, eventually they experience them as a threat to their professional position or domestic set-up, something which the Sun person may have seen merely as opportune or convenient. So unless they recognize and respect that it is lot more than that for the MidHeaven, they could wind up being unwelcome – quite suddenly. Then again, they may not have been admitted in the first place. On the other hand, the MidHeaven could forestall such upset by laying down some ground rules at the outset – but then it would probably be the Sun that has to make them aware of them. So that territorial issue persists, whatever the case.

Moon Square (challenging) Moon
☽ □ ☽

A Need To Accommodate
Your backgrounds and habits are different, possibly at odds with each other – or alternatively, there may actually be some sort of friction from the past. It is therefore difficult for you to get in step regarding such things as home and family life, day-to-day co-existence, etc. It is hard for you to find a 'flow' that allows you to relax into a life together. There may well be sympathy for one another, but it can be awkwardly expressed – possibly because of the general inconvenience that this interaction brings. Consequently, this interaction can cause a stale feeling to creep into the relationship – because there is not the fundamental 'soil' for it to grow in. It is very likely that your relationship has another agenda apart from the lunar, settling down, home-from-home type of thing. Sexual interest, or being, say, conflicting family members, could be the agenda. Indeed, the emotional difference between you can actually be sexually stimulating, but obviously the shelf-life of the relationship itself can be limited – unless of course you are both, rightly or wrongly, prepared to live with such basic emotional discord. Most of all, you could learn from it, getting to know a lot more about your respective emotional dispositions, by way of contrast.

Moon Opposition (confronting) Moon
☽ ☍ ☽

Chalk And Cheese
You are involved in an interaction of emotional extremes. You each bring out the other's feelings, good and bad, simply because they are so different. This serves to make you more aware of what kind of emotional animals you each are, but it can a bit like a game of emotional poker as each of you keeps raising the bet. Eventually, it can become only too obvious that emotionally you are on different sides of the tracks. If you have harmony and good communication elsewhere, or a strong sense of them as individuals, then your contrasting personalities can actually complement one another. You can then be a pair who 'cover the board' in whatever area in might be – socially, creatively, family. Two halves making a whole, in fact. And yet, the trouble with 'two halves' is that they meet but

do not necessarily merge or interpenetrate; you complement one another but do not naturally integrate with one another. A great deal depends upon the Signs each of your Moons is in, and what you actually need from a relationship. If you both want to be a 'social unit' then this combination can, as I say, meet and cater for extremes externally. If, however, you need to feel more closely intertwined as an intimate couple in your own right, then this aspect of your relationship will feel like the chalk and cheese that it is.

Moon Square (challenging) Mercury
☽ □ ☿

Thinking Versus Feeling

This interaction seriously affects the day-to-day affairs of both of you because the more feeling-orientated person lives life in an instinctive, emotionally led fashion, while the more thinking-orientated person bases their activities on logic and work routines. There can therefore be disagreements over mundane issues like what food to eat, how to run domestic matters, personal cleanliness, use of time, etc. Habits such as the proverbial 'leaving the cap off the toothpaste' can aggravate the 'thinking' individual, while this kind of order seems irrelevant to the 'feeling' person. The 'feeling' individual may be seen as lazy and dominated by emotional issues such as past involvements and family problems, while the 'thinker' is regarded as clinical and insensitive. If some kind of domestic or mundane, and therefore emotional, harmony is to exist, then the 'thinker' has to either get accustomed to doing all those little tasks which the 'feeler' leaves undone, or become a little bit more laid back with respect to these issues. On the other hand, the 'feeler' could learn to partly organize their lives along more rational lines rather than solely instinctive ones, and recognize the advantages of the everyday maintenance of things. This interaction is very much a case of meeting each other halfway, which is the basic remedy for all conflicts. With such a sense of grace, each of you can benefit from learning from the other: the 'thinker' to become more emotionally aware in the sense of being perceptive of feelings rather than merely being technically 'right'; and the 'feeler' to appreciate that having some kind of method or intellectual overview would actually assuage the emotional aggravation that the 'thinker' gets blamed for inflicting with their demand for mental order.

Moon Opposition (confronting) Mercury
☽ ☍ ☿

Fingertips In The Dark

Because you approach one another from very different perspectives there is the strong likelihood of mutual misunderstanding. It is a bit like trying to connect with each other's fingertips in the dark. In effect, one of you uses a rational, intellectual approach whereas the other is needing or expecting an emotional or sympathetic one, and vice versa, with first person, the 'thinker' not being able to identify what the other's pitch is. Consequently, the 'thinker' perceives the other, the 'feeler', to be vague or moody, while the 'feeler' can experience the 'thinker' as unfeeling or critical. As is usual, this interaction will not be operating all the time, especially if there are more positive interactions between you, but it can tend to kick in at those times when your opposing expectations give rise to getting the wrong end of the stick at the crucial moment. Eventually, such perennial 'misconnections' can render untenable an ongoing, everyday relationship. In small or occasional doses though, this interaction can be quite stimulating or amusing.

Moon Square (challenging) Venus
☽ □ ♀

Conflicting Needs

Needs for pleasure and needs for security, and the clash between them, strongly colour this aspect of your relationship. Such motivations, valid as far as they go, do not make for a deeper bond, or most importantly, a respect and recognition for each other as individuals in your own right. At one level, and also beneath the surface, you are each in the relationship for different reasons. At a superficial level you may appear to both be getting what you want or need, but sooner or later such will not be enough – for one or both of you. Of course, other interactions may supply this, but because this one represents such a pull towards comfort and pleasure you may not even notice what else you have, or have not, got going for you – until one of you suddenly stops supplying the cushions or candy, or some crisis strikes. This means that one of you goes cold or even looks elsewhere – while the other withdraws or sulks. Another possible hitch can be your relationship being complicated by the mother or family of one or both of you, or the domestic set-up, compromising your social/love life. Behind any or all such difficulties is the fact that, in one important area at least, you are not emotionally or socially in tune. Paradoxically though, because this interaction is very 'female', it makes for a basic and instinctual empathy, whatever your sex, which can tolerate and accommodate a great deal of strife, within or outside of your relationship. This also means that you are hospitable to others. But it is this very 'accommodation' that can gloss over the gritty issues that one day will have to surface.

Moon Opposition (confronting) Venus
☽ ☍ ♀

Just Good Friends?

Here you have a soft and tender attraction for each other, but it has an inclination to find you not quite knowing who's supposed to make a move towards anything more dynamic than simply liking and feeling affectionate towards one another. If, because of a more intense feeling between you, things become more intimate, this interaction can cause one of you to want to back out. If you are both fairly emotionally aware, then you will probably both realize you were mistaken in your intentions. If not, however, in the same way that making that move initially towards one another was awkward, it can be equally awkward trying to pull apart, which in turn can wind up with one of you feeling upset and unwanted. Underlying all of this is the probability that one of you is motivated by security needs, but the other by pleasure or social ones. Another expression of this combination of such conflicting needs is that you both become rather indulgent and hedonistic, maybe by way of compensation. When all is said and done, this interaction has really only the makings of 'just good friends', and very sociable and lively ones at that!

Moon Square (challenging) Mars
☽ □ ♂

Fire And Water

If in close proximity for any length of time, you will bring out the worst in each other: in the one of you, over-sensitivity born of childhood and past experiences; in the other, residual anger and desire to get and act in spite of circumstances. It could well cut both ways. If you are contemplating getting together for a protracted period, be warned and give yourselves a trial period with 'get-out clauses' – or just back off altogether. Barbed remarks and acutely hurt feelings having already arisen would be a danger sign here. If you are already in such a situation it is because your respective unconscious minds deemed it necessary. This means that you both had to become more aware of your emotional fears and impulses, and these very things drew you together. So it is a case of the fat being in the fire. Ideally, and put simply, one of you probably needs to toughen up a bit and not be so phased by the slings and arrows of emotional life or, alternatively, not be so comfy or complacent. Equally, the other person had better get in touch with their anger and the reasons for it in some way other than using their partner as a punch-bag. Again, these roles could alternate. Both of you, if you value your relationship or yourselves at all, may well need to seek professional help in dealing with your respective emotional difficulties. Two hurt children are only too able to hurt one another – and other children, perhaps your own.

Moon Opposition (confronting) Mars
☽ ☍ ♂

Of 'Heat' And 'Kitchen'

In a non-domestic relationship, or one where you are not with one another day-in-day-out, this interaction adds a frisson of emotional tension, which gives the relationship a charge of emotional reality – a bit like a live chat show. However, if yours is a live-in, family or working relationship then you're in for a rough ride. One of you is always hitting, deliberately or inadvertently, the other's tender spots. They see them as too soft and emotionally motivated. They want action, the other needs comfort. But psychological projection is particularly rife here, for the 'active' one is hitting out at the 'passive' one as they see in them their own dependency and vulnerability. And the 'passive' one would love to be as spontaneous and forceful as their opposite number, but they dare not be, and so justify this by seeing them as insensitive. Unconscious motivations are the main theme here. Because of this, there is liable to be a strong sexual attraction, but this can too often be the interpretation or expression you both give this interaction at the outset. In other words, you are drawn to one another for reasons of unconscious programmes in each of you that set one another off. But owing to the 'passive' person's inclination to avoid such confrontations, and to the 'active' one's putting it on someone else, such a 'hot' interaction has to be given a site that is acceptable to you both – sex. So it should not be so surprising when you find that your passion is a mixed blessing, as it cooks up both delicious and ghastly dishes. As they say, if you can't stand the heat, then stay out of the kitchen. But once in, you probably won't be able to get out – at least until you know what's cooking!

Moon Square (challenging) Jupiter
☽ □ ♃

Emotional Excess

Although there is a measure of kindness and consideration between the two of you, it is inclined to become a case of emotionally indulging or doting on one another, or conversely, a vague discord caused by the phoniness of such misplaced 'care'. In truth, one of you is after security and home life while the other is after freedom and adventure – but these can be interchangeable. And so a false sense of security or togetherness can grow out of this. It is as if this interaction happens to make it known to one or both of you that what you have been brought up to need or believe in is not actually appropriate for you as individuals. This is not a particularly difficult challenging aspect – but it can cause emotional confusion. Exploring what you both really need or believe could reveal that you are more in tune than you thought – or a lot less, which is possibly why you'd be disinclined to do so.

Moon Opposition (confronting) Jupiter
☽ ☍ ♃

Emotional Indulgence

To a certain degree, this is the opposite of a blessing in disguise. In other words, you both have a genuine desire to help one another, but are misguided as to the form such support takes. For example, one of you senses the apparent confidence or faith of the other, wants to be part of it, so then goes about indulging them in the unconscious attempt to achieve that. The other person interprets this as them being an acolyte worthy of indulging in return – possibly by confidently encouraging some questionable habits and metaphorically patting them on the head. Such a peculiar interaction has a simple truth behind it: one person's beliefs are detrimental to the security of the other, whose responses give off a false idea of those beliefs' value. This interaction ultimately forces one or both of you to be more aware of their own needs and more in command of satisfying them, and to be more sure of their ethics and beliefs before imposing them on someone who too readily accepts them in their need for security or to be caring.

Moon Square (challenging) Saturn
☽ □ ♄

Negative Backgrounds Played Out

This is a highly unsympathetic interaction, even though one of you, the 'lunar' person, may at first feel some of the other, 'saturnine', person's pain. The two of you probably came together for reasons of sex or security – which, when you think about it, could include a family relationship. But as time goes by it becomes apparent that there is a no-go area between the two of you – rather like a patch of black ice. If, for some reason or other, you are initially reluctant to engage it is probably because of an instinct that senses this 'black ice' and so you avoid coming any closer. If this is not the case, however, the 'black ice' can create quite a cold and uncaring feeling between you that can eat away like a cancer at the rest of the relationship. The reasons for this are most likely ingrained fears and inhibitions on the 'saturnine' person's part, and previously unmet or indulged childhood needs on the 'lunar' person's. In other words, negative parental conditioning is dragged to the surface and reiterated under this aspect. The 'lunar' person can play out the fearful side of their mother, while the 'saturnine' one expresses their father's doubts. This mixture, unless you are prepared to go to great effort and depth, is unfortunately separative. Nonetheless, it does teach you this important lesson because that was what was there to be learned. It also goes some way to teaching you both the value of caution.

Moon Opposition (confronting) Saturn
☽ ☍ ♄

Child Versus Adult

The sense of order and social correctness of one of you, the 'saturnine' person, is totally at odds with the natural behaviour and free-flowing responses of the other, 'lunar' person. The result is that the 'lunar' person feels controlled and thwarted by the other, experiencing them as being judgemental and unsympathetic. The 'saturnine' person sees the other as childish and irresponsible. It would seem that a difficult lesson is here in the learning. And just because it is a difficult lesson this interaction can go on for a considerable period of time – until the lesson has been learned or the inherent difficulties make the relationship untenable. The lesson itself is that each of you should learn to accept that what is different to oneself is not wrong. Yet at the same time, the 'saturnine' person probably does have a point in that the 'lunar' person needs to grow up and get the hang of the way of the world. Conversely, the 'saturnine' person needs to let the child in them out more, have more fun, and remember their dreams – as per the 'lunar' person's example. The actual reasons for becoming involved at all are most likely down to insecurity on the 'lunar' person's part, and loneliness on the 'saturnine' person's – a sad, but not very promising, recipe. If there was enough objectivity, a deal could be made here. But alas, objectivity is the very thing the 'lunar' person is learning, and the 'saturnine' person would have to shoulder most of the worldly responsibilities.

Moon Square (challenging) Uranus
☽ □ ♅

Closeness Versus Distance

The needs of one of you for comfort and security are denied by the other individual's erratic nature and urge for freedom and independence. The 'needy' person should view this interaction, when not given its due, as having no place in a stable and enduring relationship. This is more of a home-breaker than a homemaker, and its agenda is that of breaking any outworn or mistaken attachments that the 'needy' person has to mother, home or thoughts of matrimony. The same could also apply to the other 'cool' person, for social conditioning may even have caused them to go against their innate need for space to develop. So strong is this interaction's power to break conventional moulds that it will disrupt the social and domestic lives of those around you as well. The unpredictable and unstable nature of this aspect can be very upsetting to the 'needy' person, and irritating to the 'cool' person. Paradoxically, though, such is the excitement caused by this coupling that it can go on, spasmodically, for quite some time. That is, until the 'needy' person is somewhat freer from their claustrophobic ideas of emotional closeness, and the 'cool' individual recognizes that they are essentially just a catalyst for this process, or that they need to be more emotionally attuned or available.

Moon Opposition (confronting) Uranus
☽ ☍ ♅

Emotional Awakening Through Apathy

This is not an interaction that you should invest in for the future, or at least, expect to have a conventional lifestyle with. One of you needs security and comfort, family values and emotional receptivity. The other wants change and excitement, friendship values and mental freedom. So it is no surprise, or rather it is, when the 'needy' person discovers that after finding the 'cool' individual such a turn-on that they are also unpredictable and hard to keep to anything solid or routine. Furthermore, the 'cool' person is liable to react in this way to an even greater extent when the 'needy' person tries to mother them or be mothered by them. The sooner the 'needy' person realizes that they unconsciously became involved for reasons of freeing themselves from any such blind and immature security needs the less likely they are to have such a hard time of it. The 'cool' individual, for their part, should endeavour to go a bit more gently on the 'needy' person's feelings, and consider the possibility that their reason for allowing themselves to become involved are the opposite to theirs – that is, to recognize that their blows for freedom are more to do with a fear of emotional commitment. It is also possible that one or both of you need to search for and explore something less cosy and more unusual in a relationship. Ultimately, you are in the relationship to show one another that the combining or confrontation of freedom and security takes a great deal of emotional honesty on both your parts. Without waking up to the 'emotional clearing' that this interaction poses, you will find the extreme ups and downs that you experience very hard to endure or understand.

Moon Square (challenging) Neptune
☽ □ ♆

Emotional Confusion

The issue here is one or both of you having personal boundaries that are defined too strongly or not strongly enough. Consequently, there are three possible scenarios. If you both have vague ideas of where you begin and end as individuals, you then accommodate each other only too well, in a rather indiscriminate fashion. This invites emotional confusion, as you tend to drag one another down to the lowest common denominator of living standard. What allows this to happen is the fact that in the first place you kind of melt into each other, fostering the illusion that you are closer than you actually are or were. In this case, one or both of you has to find the strength or help to make a stand, possibly having to be quite ruthless in the process. The second case is when one of you is quite open emotionally, and the other is relatively closed. The open one gets under the closed one's skin, in spite of themselves, forcing them to be more emotionally forthcoming. Unfortunately, this is unlikely to be done consciously, but more in the way of being victim-like and needy, compromising the other 'stronger' person in the process. But the stronger person should read this as having to be more compassionate. The third case, when both of you are quite separate as people, would mean that something occurs or will occur that forces you to be more open about your individual vulnerability. Without dealing with whatever your scenario is in the constructive ways suggested here, your relationship could go from confusion to delusion, from misconception to rank deception.

Moon Opposition (confronting) Neptune
☽ ☍ ♆

Mistaken Identities

There is very likely to be a mutual fascination, but just as with the Sirens in the myth of Odysseus, one or both of you could wind up high and dry, where shortly before it seemed you were in the swim of heady emotions. This interaction really sees love's illusions coming, whereas the two people concerned usually do not. This all has something to do with one of you, the 'needy' person, longing for some kind of womb-like comfort and security that they did or did not get inside their mother, while the other, 'dreamy' person, is wistfully looking for their dream lover. So this interaction has its psychological roots firmly placed in the unconscious – but not really anywhere else. This is why neither of you will see what is actually happening until the child in the 'needy' person freaks out and/or the dream of the 'dreamy' person fades. Incidentally – and strangely – the two can be quite interchangeable because there is a certain sense of oneness felt here. But all this may take a while because the 'needy' person instinctively obliges in reflecting and giving emotional substance to the fantasies of the 'dreamy' person, who in turn pretends to the point of being downright deceptive. However, because this interaction is so unconsciously driven, mutual involvement with the mystical, musical or meditative can take you both to some genuinely blissful and enlightening places. But there is sadness here, which is only too much the tragic legacy of the human soul. As much as you reach for the soul-mate in each other, the image of it fades because it is more likely than not based on wishful thinking.

Moon Square (challenging) Pluto
☽ □ ♇

Susceptibility Versus Manipulation

One of you, the 'susceptible' person, is likely to feel held in a kind of psychological arm-lock by the other person, the 'manipulator. They will probably not let on, or even realize, that this is the case, and this makes it all the more incapacitating. The probable reason behind this is that the 'manipulator's' attitude to the 'susceptible' person can be one of disdain, because they see them as being weak or pathetic in some way. It is also likely that the 'manipulator' is projecting their own emotional vulnerability here, something which they deny. And so the 'susceptible' person will instinctively retaliate in an indirect or passive way. But in both cases, it would not be too obvious what was going on or why. Possessiveness and jealousy are also likely to raise their gnarled little heads sooner or later. Again, suspicious looks and subtle sneers or jibes would, initially at least, be the only signs. This interaction makes for more or less constant erosion of whatever your emotional links are, but with a view to renewing them in the process. This obviously necessitates some pretty good mental and emotional rapport supplied from elsewhere. If this is so, then neither of you will allow the grass to grow under the feet of your relationship, and it will consequently last and last, yet probably with occasional 'blackouts' of communication. The mean alternative is, unfortunately, stagnation – or worse still, destructiveness.

Moon Opposition (confronting) Pluto
☽ ☍ ♇

An Appointment With Fate

Here there is a great contrast between how one of you, the 'susceptible' person, and the other, the 'hungry' person, experience this interaction. The 'hungry' person is somehow emotionally 'feeding' off the 'susceptible' person in order to satisfy – very unconsciously, initially at least – a deep craving to gain, or regain, a position of power. For some reason, most likely a feeling of being disempowered or denied something earlier in life, the 'hungry' individual wants to get their way – and will go through hell and high water to do so. Unfortunately this can be quite oppressive to the 'susceptible' person, whose feelings and security feel threatened by what they experience as the 'hungry' one's emotionally manipulative or merely neurotic onslaughts. How the 'susceptible' person deals with this very much depends upon the position of the Moon in their Birth Chart. As a general rule, though, the 'susceptible' person will feel rather like they did as a child when oppressed by their mother – and this means a sense of powerlessness that only has evasion or passivity, rebelliousness or contrariness, as a way of coping or resisting. Ultimately all of this leads to some sort of crisis which either tears the relationship apart, or which makes you closer and stronger as a couple. In turn, this process of going through the mill could also deeply involve the families, dependants and offspring of both of you. If you reflect for a moment, you will remember that there was always a sense of the inevitable about your coming together, like an appointment with Fate, that has been or will be in aid of putting you far more in touch with your respective emotional depths. However, because this interaction does pose quite cataclysmic upheavals, you both may sense this and choose just to experience the chemistry between you as an almost irresistible tug with distinct sexual undertones – but if circumstances bring you together often enough it may prove fatal.

Moon Square (challenging) Ascendant   *Birth Time Sensitive*
☽ □ AS

Habit Versus Manner

The manner of self-expression of one of you rubs up the wrong way the emotional sensibilities of the other. In return, their reaction to this invites more of same. Also, your respective habits and routines can also prove somewhat annoying to one another. This vicious circle needs to be broken by at least one of you to prevent such disharmony developing into an outright breakdown of any kind of positive interaction. In other words, self-control and some compromises are called for in both of your behaviour patterns. Failure to do this can additionally preclude doing anything together that caters to others or the public. Neither is this interaction that favourable for domestic co-existence.

'spark' is supposed to be the one who is learning some dull but necessary lesson. In this way, it may be seen how you are actually interdependent, like spark and flint usually are. However, at best, communication between the two of you is rather thin and one dimensional and merely functional.

Mercury Square (challenging) Uranus
☿ □ ♅

Logic Versus Intuition
On first meeting the 'intuitive' individual, the 'logical' person is either impressed by their mental originality – or they see them as just a scatterbrained fool. Yet, seeing that unpredictable thoughts, words and circumstances are the hallmark of this interaction, the 'logical' one is very likely to change their mind. In fact, looked at psychologically, the 'intuitive' one is in the 'logical' person's life to challenge and/or wake up the way they think. If the 'logical' one has a strong mind, they will attempt to 'straighten out' their opposite number's more hare-brained ideas, branding them as impractical and off-the-wall. The 'intuitive' one may take this point on board if they are alive to the possibility that they do actually need to ground their thinking in the 'real world'. More usually though, the 'intuitive' one will resort to being even more shocking and outlandish in protest against what they see as the 'logical' one's limited viewpoint. So, all in all, this interaction can give rise to many a misunderstanding or crazy argument, scotching day-to-day plans and arrangements in the process. But occasionally, when 'the Moon is right', between the spark of the one person's intellect and the flash of the other's intuition, a great idea or realization can be conjured into being.

Mercury Opposition (confronting) Uranus
☿ ☍ ♅

Mental Stimulation Or Disruption
Someone once said that intuition when it works is brilliant, and when it doesn't is sheer stupidity. This interaction embodies this statement because one of you is stimulated and impressed by the other's brilliant insights and the new avenues of thought that they bring, but is frustrated and disdainful when any such ideas prove to have no practical substance. What is more, the second person can in this way be disruptive to the first's day-to-day mental functioning – in their workplace, for instance, but possibly giving them a needed jolt in this area. From the so-called 'disruptive' or 'spacey' person's point of view, their opposite number can appear to be slow and pedantic as they seek to find a logical explanation for everything. But all this is really just the mental flak that is a necessary part of clearing out old, impractical or biased ideas in both of you. See past this flak, and your mental interaction can produce quite enlightening and amusing, if sometimes crazy, material. You certainly spark one another off.

Mercury Square (challenging) Neptune
☿ □ ♆

A Need To Re-attune
This can be a bit like trying to plug the telephone into the television. Both are wonderful

transmitter/receivers, but without some radical rewiring (profound change in perception of how you view life and one another) they are not going to communicate very well with each other. The logical approach of one of you, the 'thinker', is annoyed or baffled by the more sensitive and holistic view of the other, the 'dreamer'. The 'thinker' wants to see everything and everyone as separate, categorizable, entities, whereas the 'dreamer' feels everything and everyone to be totally interconnected. What this does for your perception of one another is that the 'thinker' holds the 'dreamer' to be unrealistic and self-deluding – and therefore unreliable, possibly deceptive, even mentally unbalanced. Conversely, the 'dreamer' sees the 'thinker' as not seeing the whole picture, over-simplifying what is complex but beautiful, and generally enchained by intellectual tyranny. The 'thinker's' tunnel-vision of the 'dreamer' as a person is what can be really troublesome for the 'dreamer', because they seem to be seen only as someone who must fit, or will not fit, into the 'thinker's' linear landscape. Eventually, rather than argue the point, the 'dreamer' will, possibly unconsciously, go along with the 'thinker's' idea of them, which ironically means that the 'dreamer' becomes the very shape-shifter that the 'thinker' cannot handle. This is because the 'thinker' is putting out myriad expectations that their rational perception overlooks. But all the while, the 'thinker' thinks they're the one with a firm grip on reality. The point is that they well may be, but they will have to prove it in the face of the 'dreamer's' possibly neurotic and evasive antics. But the reality is not that either of you are right or wrong, but that the telephone and the television are vaguely similar but quite different, and very unlikely ever to make lasting or meaningful contact – unless that 'radical rewiring' is done. For the reason why you experience this interaction at all is so that you can hopefully appreciate the existence of both these modes of perception/communication, and not simply become alienated by getting stuck on the illusory fence between correct and incorrect, real and unreal. Incidentally, the crossed lines that this interaction produces can also manifest as the two of you having some kind of breakdown of communication with others, like neighbours or colleagues. Overall, and basically, this interaction causes a misconception of what one of you is to the other, and the glitches in communication that follow upon this.

Mercury Opposition (confronting) Neptune
☿ ☍ ♆

Mental Confusion
The judgement of one of you, the 'thinker' can get confused by what they see as the vague or obscure behaviour of the other, the 'dreamer'. They may even see it as a subtlety that they cannot grasp. Most probably, the 'dreamer' is not clear what they want or don't want from the 'thinker', and is putting out mixed or indistinct messages. One reason for this could be that the 'dreamer' is not sure of their own pitch, and the 'thinker' puts them on the spot in some way. In any event, crossed lines are very likely, rather like what one would encounter when trying to get by in a country whose language you have little knowledge of. In some instances, the 'dreamer' can seem devious or mysterious or stupid, which may or may not be the case. And seeing as this is about miscommunication, the 'thinker' could appear this way to the 'dreamer'. There may well be some external element like drugs or alcohol that is part and parcel of your interacting generally, and this interaction really

kicks your lack of mental accord into the stratosphere of total non-communication. Even if stone cold sober, there is still the likelihood that your failure to connect will result in confused arrangements and that kind of thing. Any emotional rapport or sympathy between you will do wonders to by-pass this poor channel of communication; maybe this interaction occurs in order to force the development of empathy.

Mercury Square (challenging) Pluto
☿ □ ♇

Mental Interrogation

One of you, the 'logical' person, has a perception of life that is the more practical and 'safe' in comparison to the other, 'delving', person's probing or psychological way of looking at it. In the face of the 'delver's' X-ray gaze the 'logical' one therefore finds that they have to dodge and weave and consequently appear even more superficial and 'reasonable'. On the other hand, the 'logical' one may just refuse to budge from what they see as their more sensible standpoint, branding the 'delver' as being too obsessed with always wanting to get to the very bottom of things. The 'delver's' response to this will be to use every means at their disposal to influence the 'logical' one's thinking with their propaganda of psychological or occult values. Not surprisingly, this is not an interaction to inspire trust – on the contrary, it can lead to 'paranoia' on one or both of your parts. To resolve or prevent the breakdown in communication that this can create, the 'delver' should honestly look at the possibility that the reason they want the 'logical' one to see things their way is that they are not entirely convinced of it themselves. The 'logical' one, apart from getting the 'delver' to lighten up a bit, should meet them halfway and take a deeper look at themselves and the meaning of life. Who knows, they may then be able to give the 'delver' a spot of their own mental medicine.

Mercury Opposition (confronting) Pluto
☿ ☍ ♇

The Delver And The Browser

One of you, the 'delver', penetrates to the core of the mind of the other, the 'browser', and attempts to bend their way of thinking towards what they think is more valid and profound. Although the 'browser' can at first find this impressive and somehow compelling, they sooner or later experience such mental invasion as being nerve-wracking. So they then crave that erstwhile and relatively superficial attitude to life where probing and plumbing the depths is not regarded as essential mental activity. However, the 'delver's' hold on the 'browser's' mentality is as persistent as it is genuine in its profundity and psychological insight; if they have some point rooted in truth then the 'browser' will find it irresistible, despite their objections. If, though, the 'delver' is simply out to suppress the 'browser's' own point of view, then the 'browser' will grow increasingly distrustful of the 'delver's' words and intentions – and ironically be intellectually more robust as a result. But it is important to remember that each of you is supposed to become more aware of your respective strengths and weakness, rather than simply resist or insist. This means that the 'browser' may gain some far more reliable insights into how life works, and get to the bottom of things rather than flitting around rather ineffectually. The 'delver', on the other hand, can learn to take things more at face value and not be quite so interrogatory, letting the 'browser' (and themselves) take time out with a bit of brain candy every once in a while.

Mercury Square (challenging) Ascendant *Birth Time Sensitive*
☿ □ AS

Differing Attitudes
There is a mildly critical atmosphere that pervades your relationship. The perception of the one of you fails to appreciate the body language of the other, and this can lead to an irritation that infects other parts of your being together. Making decisions together could also present a problem in itself. If you can see your two different attitudes as a means of thrashing things out – in a good-humoured fashion – then this not-too-significant interaction will have its 'irritant' value diminished, or even converted into something useful.

Mercury Square (challenging) MidHeaven *Birth Time Sensitive*
☿ □ MC

Out Of Sync
To Mercury's way of thinking and working the other person abuses their position, whereas the MidHeaven person sees the Mercury person as speaking out of turn. It could go the other way, but overall you have conflicting ways of working and organizing. If one of you is obviously subordinate to the other, like employee to employer or pupil to teacher, then this may not be too much of a problem, but in any event it means that your working together, or simply being together, can only go so far. This may simply manifest with it being hard to find time together in the first place.

Venus Square (challenging) Venus
♀ □ ♀

A Need To Accommodate Different Values
Your tastes and values clash in some areas. This may not be too great a problem unless you let it become so. Small things like disagreeing on what to buy, what film to see, what food to eat, etc, if allowed to become a priority, could undermine whatever sharing and harmony you have between you. More seriously, though, an imbalance in terms of how much or what type of affection is shown could amount to a dissatisfaction that is hard to ignore. If such a thing can be regarded as not that important, then well and good. If not, however, dissatisfaction could lead to separation.

Venus Square (challenging) Mars
♀ □ ♂

Sex Objects
A quite immediate and very exciting feeling is evident from early on, even on first meeting. A thoroughly enlightened person would recognize such a sensation as one of Cupid's tricks, and steer clear. However, seeing as there are very few thoroughly enlightened beings around, and that there are probably other more valid agendas or interactions between the

two of you, you succumb. Yet the fact still remains that this aspect does create sexual attraction but, in itself, there is little else. One might say this has a 'one-night-stand' quality about it, for the sex may be gratifying on a physical level, but the lack or intrusion of finer feelings finds it very empty or crude. So what starts out as attracting can end up repelling. Usually one of you will lose interest first and look elsewhere, but the other person may have felt uncomfortable beforehand but carried on succumbing in spite of such feelings. If there are indications elsewhere of the mutual understanding that this interaction definitely doesn't provide, then you will both probably put such impulsive folly down to experience, or the lack of it. One of you could then learn to refine the expression of their desires, while the other learns to recover from any bruised sensitivity, hopefully teaching them how to be more emotionally resilient.

Venus Square (challenging) Jupiter
♀ □ ♃
The Road Of Excess
On the face of it you have, or could have, a high old time, for this makes for a pretty indulgent and hedonistic coupling. You encourage one another to seek pleasure and excitement, which although this may come under the heading of sowing some wild oats, does find you frittering away time, energy and/or money. Apart from someone having eventually to pay the piper, or watch their waistline, it can also be an imposition on others who have more serious things to do. There is also an easy-come-easy-go feel, which can be quite upsetting to one of you if they have more earnest expectations of the relationship. Usually, it is the urge for freedom and experience of one of you that can hurt and offend the sensibilities and desire for companionship of the other. Moral issues come to be a major consideration, sooner or later.

Venus Opposition (confronting) Jupiter
♀ ☍ ♃
Extravaganza!
You both relate to the pleasures and joys of life – so although this is a challenging aspect, you will probably have plenty of fun together. One person loves the other's largesse and excessiveness, their cultural awareness and breadth of mind. They in turn greatly value their partner's charm and social style, for it fits well into their bigger picture. Because of this mutual enjoyment and estimation, many a flaw or sin of omission can be overlooked. But this is the danger of this interaction: you can both be too busy being, or wanting to be, social successes or live wires to notice that you are not actually recognizing each other as individuals in your own right – only as social or cultural appliances. And of course another danger is indulgence in whatever your appetites include – food, drink, partying, social niceties, etc. So, ironically, even though it is the value that you place or placed upon on another that draws you together, it is the failure to see each other's true value, 'warts and all', that can cause you to drift apart. But all the same, it is, or was, great fun!

Venus Square (challenging) Saturn
♀ □ ♄

Work Versus Play

There is a clash here because one of you, the 'player', will want to enjoy themselves while the other, the 'worker', is beset with duties and schedules. Or the 'worker' will try to instil discipline into how the 'player' goes about their aesthetic, social or other pursuits. So the 'worker' feels like the parent who forever has to guide their child in the ways of the world, stressing that effort, economy and objectivity are necessary if one is to get on in life. Unfortunately, the 'player' will too often regard this as being too serious and emotionally suppressive. Because the 'worker' is thus made to feel the killjoy or wet-blanket, or simply socially or emotionally inadequate, it falls to them to realize that they are being forced to become more disciplined and responsible as well, but in the more refined sense of learning to draw the line yet at the same time not react to the 'player's' complaints, games or indulgences. Like the good teacher, the 'worker' should deliver the lessons with the firm inner assurance that sooner or later the pupil will have to learn – maybe the hard way and in their own time – but without becoming embittered because they feel they are being misunderstood, like so many parents, real or metaphorical, so often do. The 'player' should tell themselves that the 'worker' will ease off their pressure in proportion to how much they learn to become responsible and constructive with regard to their talents and moral behaviour. It is important, however, that the 'worker' does not overlook the sublime and childlike charm with which the 'player' can brighten up a dull day or even prevent the 'worker' from becoming a dull or unloving person. All in all, this makes for a serious relationship where each of you is learning to strike a balance between love and duty, pleasure and responsibility. Separation can occasionally threaten, or even become a reality, if the above 'writing on the wall' is not read and obeyed. But given time, and it can go from strength to strength.

Venus Opposition (confronting) Saturn
♀ ☍ ♄

Love Versus Duty

This can be very difficult to handle because you have inclinations that are at odds with one another – one being towards love and play, the other toward duty and work. And so this antipathetic theme can play itself out – or have to work itself out – through your relationship. The 'love' person could appear frivolous or superficial to the 'duty' person, whereas to the 'love' person they seem inhibited or limited by their own feelings or responsibilities. Basically, 'duty' is liable to feel unloved or be unloving, and 'love' more socially flowing or even fancy-free. In the end it is a case of both of you being committed in your own individual ways. 'Love' will have to melt 'duty's' wall, while 'duty' should learn to not be so stiff and be more trusting. Put more simply, 'duty' is learning to love, and 'love' should be a good example of love. But the danger is that 'love' can resort to game-playing or capriciousness in the face of 'duty's' apparent coldness. Needless to say, such behaviour would only increase 'duty's' reserve. Possibly you may both have to look long and hard at what your real motivations are for being in this relationship. Without such serious reappraisal, a sizeable wedge could grow between you, leading to eventual separation. It should always be borne in mind that time is a very important factor in the development and learning that this interaction demands.

Venus Square (challenging) Uranus
♀ □ ♅

Rude But Irresistible Awakening

One of you, the 'awakener', gives the other person, the 'lover', a sharp shock as to what is their real worth and attractiveness. Quite unceremoniously, they will expose what is beautiful or ugly, talented or dull, about their partner. And all of this their partner finds quite irresistible, even though it gives them such mixed feelings about themselves and their other half. It is almost as if the 'awakener' is taking any feelings they have of alienation out on the 'lover'. It can be seen why this peculiar reaction exists between the two of you in the myth of the god Uranus and the goddess Venus. Uranus was the 'god of gods', Heaven, who lay across Gaia, the Earth, and Creation then came about. One of his sons, Saturn, strongly disapproved of his random way of ruling and deposed him by scything off his sexual organs and casting them into the sea. From the blood and foam of his severed genitals Aphrodite ('born of foam') or Venus was born. So you can see where those feelings of alienation came from – especially of the sexual variety! But the symbolism of this is that Uranus wants his power back and Venus wants the freedom to wield it. So Uranus, the 'awakener' thinks, 'If Venus, the 'lover', is still around after so much fast and loose treatment, then they must love me.' Unfortunately, this does not work because all the 'awakener' is getting from the 'lover' is the measure of their lack of self-love, which perfectly reflects the 'awakener's' own lack of self-love. All of this is important to understand, for it explains why you are so attracted to one another but fail to mesh in so many other areas of your respective lives. In a quirky way, you are both learning one of love's most important lessons: You can only truly love someone as much as you love yourself. If this relationship is handled right – which means not expecting it to be predictable – then you can both go some way towards loving more the unusual or outcast in yourselves and each other.

Venus Opposition (confronting) Uranus
♀ ☍ ♅

Excitement Before Love

You were probably attracted to one another in a lightning-like, irresistible fashion. However, there could have been a certain sense of difference and distance at first meeting, something which may have taken place in an unusual place or circumstances. However, such is the electro-magnetism between the two of you that synchronicity conspires to bring you together again, seemingly by accident. The sexual dimension is strong between the two of you, but you may even try to resist this too. But again that electro-magnetic attraction wins, and the whole subject of sex and what it implies becomes a major issue, with coincidence, accident, unusualness, etc. streaking through it. But this is possibly all perennially resisted by one or both of you to a degree where the decidedly disruptive and unstable qualities of this interaction seem to be strangely self-imposed. But then this is life making the point that everything is self-imposed, consciously or unconsciously. And so indeed you are both on a sexual roller-coaster that'll lead you know not where. Socially too, one of you will introduce the other to new ideas and sensations; this could be mutual. But this interaction's intention is to surprise and shock you out of your ruts and awaken you to whatever you need to know next about life and yourselves. And so one of you becomes more aware of what their values and pleasures really are by having them turned upside down by the other, who will just re-throw the dice and hope for better luck next time. As you have probably guessed, this is not a relationship to grow old and grey together with, not unless there other interactions that bestow this, or unless you are both quite kinky or into openly sharing. On this last point, so-called 'open relationships' are more often than not just a reluctance to commit posing as 'liberation' – especially on the part of one you.

Venus Square (challenging) Neptune
♀ □ ♆

Higher Love Or Illusion Of Love

It could be that one of you is in love with their idea of the other rather than the person themselves – it could also be mutual. Depending on many factors, such as image-sustaining material situations and how much both of you wish to please one another by fitting their romantic ideal, this classic indication of 'love's illusions' can persist for quite some time. However, when something happens to bring you both down to earth – such as one of you being attracted to someone else, money problems, a loss, or one of you simply feeling that you are not being loved for yourself – then the real, human, fragile versions of yourselves begin to emerge. It is then that this interaction challenges you to love unconditionally and spiritually. If you rise to this, then you will have put your relationship on a higher and nobler footing altogether. Failure, however, would amount to an uncomfortable and embarrassing separation, perhaps after trying to fake it for a bit longer. Be that as it may, it is also quite likely that you are involved creatively in some way – and this would greatly contribute to stabilizing this interaction by giving imagination and fantasy a positive outlet.

Venus Opposition (confronting) Neptune
♀ ☍ ♆

Romance, Illusions And Spiritual Ties

This is a real falling in love – with all the unreality that this engenders! The longings of one or both of you for the perfect match or soul-mate seems to be initially satisfied with this interaction. But your respective illusions around such concepts are not far behind that original falling. Unless there is some very sound awareness concerning the pitfalls of romantic love, then a deal of hurt and deception (conscious or unconscious) is bound to descend upon the pair of you. But this is not to say that this is an entirely negative aspect – far from it. Its true intention is to lure both of you away from your respective illusions of a loving or satisfying relationship – but at first it does so by playing upon those very illusions. Either one of you may well feel that you have been taken for a ride at some point as the dream fades, but it is precisely at this juncture that you need to perceive what is really happening. For example, one of you has been playing at 'saviour' and then finds that it was far harder work than was first thought. It is just here that you have to tell yourself that such a 'saving' has very real spiritual reasons, but it means that you will have to face up to the fact that you need some saving too! As far as the other person is concerned, when the dream fades for their 'saviour' they may well feel like used or damaged goods, and an unequal or unstable partnership can then seem your lot. But this is precisely the time when you must muster your self-worth and not just be some cipher for the 'saviour' to project first their ideal and then their disillusionment upon. If this mutual realization takes place, then the two of you can enjoy a higher love and an ennobling kind of bond – but it will take time, effort, awareness and, most of all, sacrifice and acceptance. Apart from all of this, this interaction can also make for a very creative coupling – especially with regard to music or the visual arts.

Venus Square (challenging) Pluto
♀ □ ♇

Possessive Love

There is a compulsive or oppressive quality to your relationship that is based upon a heavy need to be loved on the part of one of you, and a need to deepen their sense of what love is on the part of the other. And so possessiveness, jealousy or resentment are the unfortunate hues which colour this interaction. Money too can come into the picture as an issue that makes matters worse, is used as leverage or actually creates the problems. One of you can feel coerced into being loving and affectionate by the other's desperate pleas, bribes and/or threats. Initially there may well be strong passionate feelings for one another, or at least one or both of you could be so swept off their feet so as to mistake lust for love. Although this interaction can bring a certain satisfaction, or at least a greater emotional understanding, the price can be very high in terms of soul-searching and deep hurt – or money.

Venus Opposition (confronting) Pluto
♀ ☍ ♇

Romeo And Juliet?

As this is Romeo and Juliet material, don't go reaching for daggers or poisons, either literal or metaphorical ones. It is just that you are powerfully attracted to one another, yet at the same time you encounter certain taboos on the way to getting or remaining as close as you want to. In the process, however, these 'taboos' won't be so obvious as coming from opposing families or backgrounds – although they might be. In fact, these taboos are more likely to be, or stem from, some internal taboo that may conveniently have an external manifestation, like for example, mixed race, same sex, big age gaps, incest, adultery, etc.. Before going any further, it may be that one or both of you may sense all this difficulty and not enter into intimacy in the first place. The best way of expressing this is mythologically ... it is called *The Rape of Persephone*. Persephone was the daughter of Mother Earth and was closely protected by her for she was very ethereal, unworldly and innocent. Her polar opposite, Pluto, Lord of the Underworld, wanted her for his own, and forcibly took and dragged her down to his realm. After much pain and destruction (mostly on the part of Mother Earth who went on strike causing the world to go barren), a deal was struck after consulting Zeus/Jupiter, and Pluto was allowed to keep Persephone for four months of the year (which is how and when we get the barren winter), and her mother for the remainder. Pluto and Persephone went on to be one of the soundest relationships amongst the gods and goddesses. What all this means for you is that Venus has to go through a purging and steeping process as her superficial values and shallower feelings are eliminated and transformed. She then becomes a strong, emotional figure, capable of loving deeply, despite appearances and conventions – but she takes time out every so often. Pluto, for his part, simply has his loneliness put to an end – or at least, for some of the time, because Pluto's realm is about aloneness, after all. All of this is made possible by ultimately appealing to something higher for help. It has to be said, though, that this process can be so intense and gruelling as to finish off emotionally one or both of you. Apparent or real capriciousness on the part of one of you can do the other in with jealousy and despair, whereas the other's attempts to force their partner into the shape they think they desire can psychologically damage them, forcing them to escape (home to mother?). Handled right, and the course seen through, can find you in a deeply fulfilling relationship – like Beauty and the Beast.

Venus Square (challenging) Ascendant *Birth Time Sensitive*
♀ □ AS

Looks Versus Love
The physical appearance and manner of one of you can seem unattractive or socially inept to the other, or they feel that way in comparison. In return, the other finds their partner's standards here superficial. If there are more emotional and psychological attractions going on between the two of you, then this interaction can seem peculiarly out of place – and indeed, superficial. In the end, or perhaps after it if this interaction becomes really troublesome, it is up to the one hung up on appearances (and it could be both of you) to scrutinize their possibly hollow and insincere feelings. Then again, and as ever, the other individual (or both of you) could make an effort to come halfway by endeavouring to look as good as they can without becoming a slave to such an issue – or just play down the whole appearance thing. The looks thing could be an issue for one or both of you, something which this interaction intensifies.

Venus Square (challenging) MidHeaven *Birth Time Sensitive*
♀ □ MC

Business And Pleasure Don't Mix
Although there is a fun aspect to work interests, the two of you could fall out where these wires get crossed. For example, this could take the form of one of you feeling taken advantage of – which could be the result of not being assiduous enough when called for – with the other feeling that they are feckless and not pulling their weight. Also, the social and romantic interests of one of you interfere with the career and status of the other. If the two of you can learn to determine and maintain the distinction between work and play, this Inter-Aspect need not be too much of a problem.

Mars Square (challenging) Mars
♂ □ ♂

Sparring Partners

What each of you wants and the way that you both go about getting it is very different. Consequently, a lot of friction can develop between the two of you. In extreme cases, or if there is little or no indication of love and tenderness in other interactions, such conflict can even get physically abusive. But this won't happen if both of you are of a reasonable and peaceful disposition. More subtly though, one of you has a different idea of manliness or courage to the other. For example, one of you might see courage as instinctively responding to someone attacking one's family or sense of security – but the other sees courage as holding back, thinking about it, and finding a more circumspect or diplomatic route. Usually, one of you will have a 'hot' reaction, and the other a 'cool' reaction – but you might both be 'hot'! Either way, you can see how this could cause flare-ups or frustrations. Furthermore, such friction can build up to bursting point if there are more 'peaceful' areas to the relationship that you both try to keep to. A good battle or row once in a while is a healthy thing for it clears the air. However, with this difficult interaction, such may be too frequent or not frequent enough. Ultimately, this interaction could be saying that one or both of you are being challenged to fight, to one degree or another, for their own right to be what they essentially are.

Mars Opposition (confronting) Mars
♂ ☍ ♂

Locking Horns

You can have a physical and sexual tie here, but left to its own devices it could well devolve into out-and-out conflict, even violence. A great deal initially depends upon how you both express, or are allowed to express, the sexual tension between you. If you are, for one reason or another, not able or willing to make the relationship physical, then that tension will just persist as ongoing frustration or stimulation. This is a case of what you never catch you never get tired of pursuing. If you do get together in any way, however, it will only be a matter of time before battle commences. If one of you allows themselves to be easily subjugated then it will take longer. Unless there is a substantial amount of tenderness and mutual respect indicated by other interactions, then the shock of how harsh merely sexual or egotistical urges can be will become only too evident. Civilized veneers are inevitably worn away under this aspect. The reasons for being involved through such an interaction are, on the one hand, a case of being too submissive and having to become more assertive and independent. On the other hand, it would be a case of first exercising the 'right' that has hitherto always been assumed, only to find that your opposite number eventually fights back, or is vanquished. Such tough outcomes are probably only avoidable if neither of you need or choose to become thus involved in the first place.

Mars Square (challenging) Jupiter
♂ □ ♃

A Want Of Governing Principles

This is a swashbuckling kind of interaction that attracts plenty of adventure and activity, but may not really lead anywhere. It could even get you into hot water or a brush with the law. Whatever more expansive or philosophical ideas one of you might have, the other probably regards them as too academic, boring or just plain disagrees with them. Or one of you may encourage the other to act unwisely and then not take responsibility for it. Hopefully there are indications to the contrary elsewhere, but this interaction is rather lacking in the honour and ethics department. Conflicts of belief are a keynote for this combination, which may simply mean that one or both of you has yet to find a higher or more enterprising reason for living, and, by this relationship, is being forced eventually to do so. Essentially, one of you stimulates the other's principles by attacking or offending them, thereby forcing them to be more aware of them and develop them. By reaction, the other subsequently comes down heavy on them for having so few principles themselves! It could mean that one or both of you have to either rethink or the relationship could bust up as enthusiastically as it begun.

Mars Opposition (confronting) Jupiter
♂ ☍ ♃

'Holy War'

Initially, there can be the feeling or 'energy' between you that you are together in order to get or gain something. So there can be quite a lot of activity, coming and going, or just horsing around in your relationship. However, it may be a case of more energy than purpose as it eventually dawns on you that you are possibly espousing different causes, motivated by different objectives, or even fighting under opposing standards. But this 'dawning' will not happen until one day you realize that you both, literally or figuratively, share the same address but lead different lives. How uncomfortable this realization is depends upon the level of understanding you have between you that is indicated by other interactions. For any number of reasons, you may choose to stay together while leading your own lives. If there are certain commitments, like family for instance, then this would be a sensible, if not totally desirable, expression of this interaction. Failing this, a kind of jihad or holy war could be your ongoing lot. The freedom to roam is the keynote of this interaction. Whatever you each make of the place of this in a relationship, one or both of you will inevitably go their own way – with or without the other's blessings. But this could actually be the elusive or primary purpose of this interaction: for one of you graciously to grant the other freedom, or at least help them to discover it.

Mars Square (challenging) Saturn
♂ □ ♄

Brakes And Accelerator

The interaction that you have here is bound to give you trouble and stop you getting anywhere as a couple – unless one of you, who we'll call the 'Martian', is prepared to take stock of how they actually go (or don't go) about getting what they want as an individual,

unsuitable, or even unsafe, for a normal relationship.

Mars Square (challenging) Ascendant *Birth Time Sensitive*
♂ □ AS
A Need For Anger Management
The manner that one of you has of asserting themselves is sometimes offensive to the other person. Then there is the possibility that they will react in such a way as to possibly make that assertiveness turn to anger. It could also be said that something about the offended person's demeanour is what gets the 'assertion' going in the first place. The resolution for this possibly vicious circle is for one of you to temper your forcefulness or control your hot reactions, while the other should endeavour to be more assertive, and less defensive, themselves. And patience needs to be exercised on both your parts.

Mars Square (challenging) MidHeaven *Birth Time Sensitive*
♂ □ MC
Independence Versus Status
The Mars individual can be felt as a thorn in the side of the MidHeaven person, particularly with respect to their professional or domestic position. Mars may be tolerated, or even enjoyed, as a loose cannon, but only so far. For their part, Mars can see the other as part of the 'establishment' in that they appear superior, or have more material or emotional might. But Mars actually is more of a free agent, whereas the MidHeaven is tied to certain procedures and responsibilities that Mars finds heavy and stuffy. They may have a point, but this could simply conceal feelings of powerlessness.

Jupiter Square (challenging) Ascendant *Birth Time Sensitive*
♃ □ AS
Having To Walk Your Talk
One of you is inclined to judge the other's moral or spiritual standing purely by their character and manner of expression. Understandably, that person can be offended by this, seeing such as sanctimonious and hypocritical. More constructively, this person can force the other to walk their talk if they wish to be taken seriously. However, what can follow upon this is that if they do walk their talk, then that person who forced this will have to look to the ethical or spiritual dimension of their own life.

Jupiter Square (challenging) MidHeaven *Birth Time Sensitive*
♃ □ MC
Too Great Expectations
The trouble here can be simply that one or both of you is led to expect too much from the relationship. Whether it is the other person or oneself that does the leading is another question however. There is also the possibility of one of you using the other to get on in the world in a mercenary fashion, and the one that is used is seen to be too laid back, full of plans and nothing else, an armchair philosopher. In any event, you mislead one another in some way, but paradoxically you both benefit from the relationship, although possibly not as a relationship. Differing socio-cultural backgrounds could also be a divisive issue.

Saturn Square (challenging) Ascendant *Birth Time Sensitive*
♄ □ AS

Adult Versus Child

One of you, who we'll call the 'adult' because they feel more worldly and responsible, will find the personal manner of the other, the 'child', offensive in some way – it'll be too immature, egocentric, showy, impulsive or anything which the 'adult' feels is not good 'form'. Because of this, the 'adult' tries to discipline or belittle the 'child' into behaving or expressing themselves in what they see as a more appropriate way. Naturally enough, the 'child' finds this stifling, painful and/or boring, and will most probably step up the very behaviour that got the 'adult' going in the first place – either that or sulk. Needless to say, a good amount of love and understanding, hopefully provided by other interactions, is needed to make each of you realize that the other has a point. The 'child' does need to reform their manner of expression and how they physically hold or present themselves if they wish to make a better impression, whereas the 'adult' should focus upon exactly why it embarrasses them or makes them feel uncomfortable – maybe they should take a leaf out of the 'child's' book of self-expression, or heed the same criticism they themselves are dishing out. Failing all of this, this interaction is decidedly separative.

Saturn Square (challenging) MidHeaven *Birth Time Sensitive*
♄ □ MC

A Conflict Of Interests

Your individual ideas of what constitutes order, in the home or at work, are at odds with one another. So joint domestic or business ventures become unstuck, or just never take off. In any event, doubts and reservations are apparent early one – or at least they should be. It may fall to one of you to point them out in no uncertain fashion. There is probably a mutual learning experience going on that is in aid of teaching one another your respective limitations. Another lesson being learned is the place personal feelings have in the professional arena, and vice versa. This lesson could take the form of one person putting too much emphasis on one or the other, giving rise to destabilization generally.

Uranus Square (challenging) Ascendant *Birth Time Sensitive*
♅ □ AS

Disruption

One individual, the 'disrupter', will attempt to change the outlook of the other, the 'disrupted', in some way or other, but they may resist this. The 'disrupter' may do this unconsciously by being unpredictable or unreliable, or actually causing them to move away from their previous environment, thereby forcing the 'disrupted' to adopt a more flexible attitude or simply become more aware that how they look at things is inappropriate and needs changing anyway. For example, the 'disrupter' would not take kindly to the 'disrupted' impinging on their freedom in any way, and so the 'disrupted' would have to adapt to this if they wanted to maintain the relationship. Alternatively, the 'disrupted's' behaviour could put the 'disrupter' through a few shocks and changes. So eventually each of you can become both 'disrupter' and disrupted'! So it has to be said that this is not an interaction that favours a stable and long-lasting bond. In fact, it is actually in aid of shaking off any idea that such a thing is possible with the current state of one or both of your personalities and abilities to relate. So, in any event, this interaction should find you somewhat the wiser with regard to appreciating the place and space that freedom of expression demands in a relationship.

Uranus Square (challenging) MidHeaven *Birth Time Sensitive*
♅ □ MC

Forced To Change With The Times

There is an unpredictability in one individual that occasionally queers the pitch of the other, especially on a career or domestic front. The first person can just think that the second one is being stuffy and not moving with the times – and they may have a point. But the second person is more likely to see them as a loose cannon. In effect, each of you keeps the other on their toes with the advantage being that of the one not allowing the grass to grow under the other's feet.

Neptune Square (challenging) Ascendant *Birth Time Sensitive*
♆ □ AS

Who's Fooling Who?

Initially at least, one or both of you have their own somewhat mistaken idea of who or what the other person is to them. Consequently, the one person can easily get the wrong idea of where the other is coming from, and even come to regard them as dubious or not entirely reliable. Your actual meeting was probably quite spellbinding in some way, but as time goes by, the spell, although quite real, is seen to have a different agenda to what it felt like at the time. If there are not some close and substantial interactions between the two of you, this one can just produce disappointment. Whatever the case, though, it is saying that first impressions can be deceptive, yet in retrospect can be seen to have had a subtle meaning all of their own. This is the kind of interaction that will 'trick' you into an involvement for spiritual or karmic reasons that you would have otherwise avoided. The illusions of the one of you, and the physical looks, manner and state of the other, are what the 'trick' and the karma are based upon. If all this sounds confusing, that's because it is! But it is worth unravelling if one or both of you wish to become clearer about these particular issues so that you are no longer so vulnerable to them. Suffice to say that the fantasies of the one of you, which the appearance of the other seems to elicit, need to be transmuted into compassion for the Ascendant's circumstances.

Neptune Square (challenging) MidHeaven *Birth Time Sensitive*
♆ □ MC

Worldly And Unworldly Collide

Any emotional or psychological weakness in one of you can play havoc with the professional and/or domestic interests of the other. Deceit or addiction problems may interfere with the maintenance of the home or career advancement or position. One of you may find yourself in the role of having to be a tower of strength to the other. Scrupulous honesty is the best antidote to difficulties here – at least, for one of you. The chances are that the other, weaker, person will have a problem with honesty. However, as with all things Neptunian there is no clear-cut line, for the deceitful person may just as well be the one who is apparently in a stronger position, particularly in a financial sense. The Neptune person could just as well be a spiritual influence that is challenging the hedonistic or materialistic ways of the MidHeaven person.

Pluto Square (challenging) Ascendant   *Birth Time Sensitive*
♇ □ AS

The Manipulator And The Manipulated
Initially, and maybe for quite some time, your relationship (or a part of it) has to go on in secret, with few or no one knowing about it. As such, this imposes the pressure and the excitement of forbidden fruit upon your coming together at any time. When and if you are able to 'come out' and show your face to the world there may still be a deal of trouble stemming from conflicting or awkward circumstances, and possibly from someone else who is involved with one or both of you in such a way that is not easily got out of. So although this compulsive sort of interaction is the type that actually forms a relationship in the first place, it does tend to get you off on the wrong foot with convolutions and machinations being apparently unavoidable. Yet the best way to deal with all of this intrigue is to be as open and honest as possible, which would entail one of you dropping their façade and eventually coming clean, and the other eliminating whatever is getting in the way of what they want before getting in too deep. In any event, what is behind this interaction, and what is probably a perennial difficulty, is that of preventing concealed or hard to pinpoint issues getting in the way of any genuine connection that you have between you. This is in aid of eliminating any possibility that all there is to the relationship is compulsion and intrigue.

Pluto Square (challenging) MidHeaven   *Birth Time Sensitive*
♇ □ MC

Power Games
This indicates a situation where the position of one of you, probably the MidHeaven person, is questioned or sabotaged, or merely resented, by the other, probably Pluto person. At first this may be quite unconscious, particularly if there are more straightforward or positive interactions between you. In effect, it is a case of the person with power having it challenged in some way. An example of this would be the boss being less aware than a subordinate of what is actually going on, and being made aware of it either directly by confrontation, or indirectly by insinuation. All this could lead to an outright struggle for power.

Ascendant Square (challenging) Ascendant   *Birth Time Sensitive*
AS □ AS

Sod's law
There can be a strong physical attraction and identification with each other initially, but at a later date you can find yourselves at cross purposes and with circumstances preventing you from being together as much as you'd like – or as much as you think you ought to be together. It is as if what was so important initially eventually becomes secondary at most.

If there is a pronounced mutual attraction and harmony between you indicated elsewhere with planetary interactions, then this denial of each other's physical presence and attention can be steered round and compensated for. You would also be able to see, or maybe have to see, that physical appearance and image are relatively unimportant. Without such compatibility, though, your relationship could be dogged by physical disappointment, inappropriate circumstances and a simple lack of opportunity.

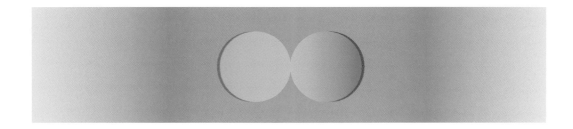

3. RELATIONSHIP STRENGTHS

To varying degrees, these are the harmonious interactions that create pleasure, reward and fruitfulness – as well as providing you with the love, compatibility and understanding to manage and transform the Relationship Challenges.

IMPORTANT: Remember that the name of the Inter-Aspect may be written the other way around to how it is given in the Relationship Profile INDEX. For example, an Inter-Aspect given as **Saturn Trine (harmonizing) Sun** ♄ △ ☉ in the INDEX will be given here as **Sun Trine (harmonizing) Saturn** ☉ △ ♄ . Also, the As and Bs are not included here because they are individual to the particular relationship as given in the INDEX or on-screen.

Trine and Sextile Inter-Aspects: Because the meanings of Sextile (assisting) Inter-Aspects are similar in meaning to Trine (harmonizing with) Inter-Aspects, the same interpretation is given below the relevant Transit name headings, each separated by 'OR'. The difference is essentially between the words 'assisting' and 'harmonizing with' in the sense that the Sextile requires conscious effort to benefit from it, whereas the ease and accord of the Trine come naturally to the couple. Also, in the software settings a far smaller Orb is used for the Sextile than is used for the Trine, which means to say that it has to be fairly strong for it to count as a valid Inter-Aspect. Concerning this though, also note the following …

Ascendant and MidHeaven Inter-Aspects: Note that when a Planet of one person is Trine (harmonizing with) the Ascendant or MidHeaven of another person, then it is at the same time Sextile (assisting) their Descendant or Lower MidHeaven, respectively. The converse will also be the case, with Sextile Ascendant or MidHeaven also being Trine the Descendant or Lower MidHeaven. This is simply because the Descendant is always the opposite point to the Ascendant(see page 42), and Lower MidHeaven is always the opposite point to the MidHeaven (see page 95). Because of this, the difference between the meanings of the Trine and Sextile are even more negligible, and the interpretations will cover these cases.

RELATIONSHIP STRENGTHS: INTERPRETATIONS

Sun Trine (harmonizing with) Sun
☉ △ ☉   *OR*
Sun Sextile (assisting) Sun
☉ ✶ ☉

Egos In Harmony

As a couple you are basically very compatible – but such a statement needs some further definition that focuses on the word 'basically'. This interaction gives a sound foundation upon which to build a relationship and anything that might issue from it, like children or a product/creation. Whatever else might happen along the way, as the relationship is built and progresses, there will always be this basic understanding to refer to and be reassured by. But this does not indicate or determine the more individualistic qualities of the overall interaction. This is done by other planetary pairings, which can amount to anything from a wonderful mansion to an abandoned shell!

Sun Trine (harmonizing with) Moon
☉ △ ☽   *OR*
Sun Sextile (assisting) Moon
☉ ⚹ ☽

Hand In Glove

This is one of the most basically harmonious interactions, and favours any kind of relationship: romantic, family, business or between friends. One of you, the 'Sun' person, is the 'leader' here, and the other, 'Moon' person, is quite happy to follow that lead. Because of traditional gender roles, it is more effective when a male is the 'Sun' and a female the 'Moon'. Nevertheless, if the reverse, it may well be that the male is in need of someone to show the way, and he knows it, and therefore accepts it. In return, the 'Moon's' instinctively positive response to the 'Sun' gives them a sense of being on the right course in life. However, because this interaction has this 'basic' quality of harmony, it does not define or take into consideration the more idiosyncratic qualities of the relationship, be they positive or negative. It simply promises that, come what may, there will be an essential harmony between the two of you.

Sun Trine (harmonizing with) Mercury
☉ △ ☿   *OR*
Sun Sextile (assisting) Mercury
☉ ⚹ ☿

Mental Co-operation

You should have no trouble communicating, especially with regard to the more objective or non-emotional issues of life. This is a good aspect for intellectual companionship, and so also favours any working partnership. Whether or not such good mental rapport touches upon the more nitty-gritty aspects of your relationship would rest with the quality of other more weighty interaction. But you can certainly assist one another in the development of your minds and careers, giving confidence to one another in these areas as you do so.

Sun Trine (harmonizing with) Venus
☉ △ ♀   *OR*
Sun Sextile (assisting) Venus
☉ ⚹ ♀

Social Desirability

Being together brings out a heightened sense of fun and harmony. Not only that but you find each other attractive in an easy sort of way. There is a great deal that you readily agree upon, and so others like to be around you: friends, children or business associates. There can even be a feeling of wealth about you that may very well attract that very thing if other interactions support this. Hopefully there are dynamic and challenging aspects between you that drive you to achieve something, because this interaction can incline you to being a bit lazy, even complacent. But apart from that, you have a delightful and enjoyable chemistry, which graces any situation, but especially social gatherings such as parties.

Sun Trine (harmonizing with) Mars
⊙ △ ♂   *OR*
Sun Sextile (assisting) Mars
⊙ ✶ ♂

Healthy Coupling
This is a very positive interaction for it means that your intentions and actions are in sync with each other. And so activities and projects are executed swiftly, enthusiastically and efficiently. There is also a natural sexual harmony between you, at least on a purely physical level of expression. In fact, this interaction is quite basic for it makes it clear who wants what, who's on top, etc. If this can be accepted as enough then this interaction would act as a strong contribution to your relationship being lasting and satisfying. You are able to keeps things simple with a kind of 'go for it or forget it' attitude. This can ease and overcome many difficulties that might arise, but not those of a more complex psychological variety. The asset of this interaction is that it makes you as a couple quite brisk, as long as it does not cause you to skip more subtle issues. Sporting activities are also something you may enjoy together or even excel in.

Sun Trine (harmonizing with) Jupiter
⊙ △ ♃   *OR*
Sun Sextile (assisting) Jupiter
⊙ ✶ ♃

True And Mutual Generosity
This interaction is bound to give rise to, or at least coincide with, personal advancement in the lives of both of you. The hallmark of this excellent aspect is that you help one another to improve your personal lots in a way that is altruistic. There is no thought of doing what one of you does for the other as requiring or deserving any sort of 'payment' – although one paying the other for something to help them out is a good example of the generosity that this coupling engenders. This is all the more significant when considering that it is not just the individual ambitions of each other that you each assist, but rather something for the both of you. Of course, it could be said that what helps the one in a partnership also helps the other, and indeed this is the essence of such a coupling – but in a more far-reaching way that either of you may yet appreciate. This interaction is all about prospering and growing – but in a wonderfully impersonal way. So this aspect of your relationship is a real gift, a boost to, or restoring of, a belief that life is something great, holy even. You also make good travelling companions for you believe that the road (of life) will take you

where it will – together or apart, as you have a respect for each other's freedom.

Sun Trine (harmonizing with) Saturn
☉ △ ♄   **OR**

Sun Sextile (assisting) Saturn
☉ ✳ ♄

Sober And Industrious

This interaction lends itself well to any kind of organization. As a couple you can function in a businesslike way, with each determining and knowing what roles to play or responsibilities to fulfil. This is by no means a romantic connection for it emphasises the importance of the mundane and material side of life. Because of this, you as a couple can create stability and durability in so far as any more emotional contacts will allow or demand. In terms of what you do for each other, one of you can bring some light and play into the overly serious or even downcast areas of the other's life, while they in return provide a sense of order and tradition. If one of you is somewhat older than the other, then this coupling will accentuate these positive attributes, which means that the sense of order provided by that individual is more likely to be quite real and substantial. In any event, the stability and order, which is the hallmark of this interaction, can be attained if the two of you establish some rules and limitations that you are both happy to keep to. Notwithstanding other interactions, this aspect does confer mutual trust and reliability.

Sun Trine (harmonizing with) Uranus
☉ △ ♅   **OR**

Sun Sextile (assisting) Uranus
☉ ✳ ♅

Friends Until The End

You have a very positive interaction because it has something that all too many relationships lack: a true sense of friendship. This means that you allow each other room to be yourselves, are open with one another, and that there is little or no possessiveness about each other. One of you has a liberating and awakening effect upon the other, giving them new ideas and directions. Alternative or metaphysical subjects are very likely to be the means through which this effect happens, and you may well have met in a situation that was related to such matters. Groups involved in esoteric or unusual pursuits can be a significant part of your time together. In return, the 'liberated' individual validates or furthers the other's more original expressions and qualities, rather like a monarch would patronize an artist. All of this positive interaction makes for a mutual attraction, mentally and/or physically, yet it does not necessarily confer the emotional stability that ensures a lasting tie. Paradoxically though, because you are always surprising one another with hitherto unknown facets of your characters, this relationship has a self-refreshing quality about it. Whatever the case, though, that outstanding friendship should remain.

Sun Trine (harmonizing with) Neptune

☉ △ ♆   **OR**

Sun Sextile (assisting) Neptune

☉ ✶ ♆

A Mutual Blessing

You have a quite spiritual or dreamy connection, and so flow together or apart as the current of life allows. Notwithstanding any other more passionate or possessive interactions, you accept this gentle ebbing and flowing. Imagination, dance, music and the otherworldly can be elements that make up your relationship in a positive and creative way. One person affirms and sheds light upon the other person's sensitive areas, thereby helping them to express and deal with them better. Reciprocally, the second person treats the first with the respect and sensitivity that causes them to feel more sure of themselves. There is a mutual blessing going on here, something which may not be that obvious to others, simply because the process is patently subtle. However, because there is the psychic link between you, others who are psychically attuned will pick up on it. This is not a robust connection by any means, but it knows how to go around obstacles – if you let it take you.

Sun Trine (harmonizing with) Pluto

☉ △ ♇   **OR**

Sun Sextile (assisting) Pluto

☉ ✶ ♇

Mutual Empowerment

One individual benefits greatly from the other's insights or resources, while the other is given much needed confidence by the first person's convincing appreciation or admiration of those very things. Together you can be the new broom that sweeps clean, clearing away obstacles to your progress and well-being, either individually or as a couple – or even for the area of society in which you operate. This is a mutually regenerative relationship, and other interactions considered, can make for a longstanding and self-renewing partnership. With the support of similar interactions, great wealth and/or power can be attained. In any event, you will both be the better for knowing one another.

Sun Trine (harmonizing with) Ascendant *Birth Time Sensitive*

☉ △ AS   **OR**

Sun Sextile (assisting) Ascendant *Birth Time Sensitive*

☉ ✶ AS

Mutual Encouragement

One or both of you makes the other feel more confident about their personal expression and appearance by helping them improve it, or simply appreciating it. Because of this positive effect, the person on the receiving end feels that they have something going for them too. This healthy interchange can lead to a positive escalation of mutual appreciation, contributing a good feel to any romantic or marital relationship. You are both confirming each other's existence and therefore get along consistently well.

Sun Trine (harmonizing with) MidHeaven   *Birth Time Sensitive*
☉ △ MC   **OR**
Sun Sextile (assisting) MidHeaven   *Birth Time Sensitive*
☉ ✳ MC

Mutual Furtherance

Each of you encourage and provide for one another with respect to career and domestic matters. As a result, the one who does the giving is made to feel philanthropic, a reward in itself. If one of you has a position or contact of any power or influence they will directly or indirectly be an agent of good fortune for the other.

Moon Trine (harmonizing with) Moon
☽ △ ☽   **OR**
Moon Sextile (assisting) Moon
☽ ✳ ☽

Soul Children

This is one of the most basically favourable interactions for it bestows upon the relationship personal and emotional harmony. Both of you feel relaxed and at ease in each other's company. So this strongly contributes to the underlying stability that is needed for a domestic, familial, intimate or business relationship – or, for that matter, any kind of relationship. As individuals you see eye-to-eye on such basic issues as what are deemed to be the really important values and qualities of a wholesome and healthy life. This is especially positive for bringing up children because as parents your united front on basic values gives your offspring a balanced and confident feeling about themselves and life. In fact, as a couple, between the two of you there is a mutual emotional nurturing going on that can do much to heal your individual past wounds. Others find it comfortable to be around you, too. The child in the one of you brings out the child in the other – and thereby you find it easy to play with one another.

Moon Trine (harmonizing with) Mercury
☽ △ ☿   **OR**
Moon Sextile (assisting) Mercury
☽ ✳ ☿

The 'Working' Relationship

You have no trouble in communicating how you feel or the point either of you wish to make to the other. The difficult interactions that you have with one another are to a large degree sorted out because you are able to be rational about matters but without becoming divorced from the emotional issues involved. As a rule, the more rational of the two of you is the one who contributes a clear mental viewpoint, while the other, more instinctive person provides a sense of emotional awareness and security, which aids the rational thinking of their partner. Similarly, the rational one helps clarify the instinctive one's feelings, while in return, they help out when the 'thinker' gets stuck in their head. This interaction also favours the workaday environment and makes for a common touch with regard to sensing what appeals to others in general, and what they feel comfortable with. Obviously, this can greatly benefit the job and emotional security of you as a couple, and for the same reasons you could work together well. Running through all this there can be an ongoing banter and sense of childlike fun.

Moon Trine (harmonizing with) Venus
☽ △ ♀   OR
Moon Sextile (assisting) Venus
☽ ⚹ ♀

Pleasant And Pleasing
There is a soft and gracious feeling between the two of you, which others around you appreciate as well. This lends itself particularly well to romantic, family or friendly relationships or any dealings with the public, but because this interaction is quite 'female' in quality, it places the accent upon affection rather than sex. The man, if there is one, in your relationship, is able to get in touch with his female side through this partnership. So both of you are receptive and tender towards one another, showing respect for each other's sensitivity. Again, because this is very 'yin' in feel, such empathy could be entirely passive and not necessarily acted upon. If there are more dynamic or passionate interactions indicated elsewhere, then this one provides a soft base for those harder desires. The home and family of one of you can be beautified or graced by the other, and they in turn provide a vehicle or receptacle for such loving feelings.

Moon Trine (harmonizing with) Mars
☽ △ ♂   OR
Moon Sextile (assisting) Mars
☽ ⚹ ♂

Energetic Accord
You have a vibrant interaction here that enables you, individually or as a couple, to get a lot done for you tend to energize one another. One of you acts as a ramrod to the other, who otherwise may have stayed at home and not achieved or experienced much. On the other hand, the 'passive' person can show the 'fiery' one how fun can be had in a more private and cosy way. Naturally, this aspect is more favourable when the 'fiery' one is male and the 'passive' one is female, for they are then in their traditional roles. But this description can give a limited idea of the great scope that the 'energetic accord' of this interaction affords you both. Sexually, for example, you can be equally physical and emotional, and instinctively lose yourselves in the heat of passion. But just because you are interacting through such instinctual drives (security and sex, need and desire) there is a danger you could consume yourselves, so some moderation would keep the fires burning nicely.

Moon Trine (harmonizing with) Jupiter
☽ △ ♃   OR
Moon Sextile (assisting) Jupiter
☽ ⚹ ♃

Care And Consideration
There exists a 'good feeling' between the two of you. This has its roots in the fact that you

mean each other no harm at a deeply instinctive and moral level. Put more positively, you are generous and considerate towards one another, and genuinely care what becomes of each other. Together you are in touch with some of the best of human nature. You nurture or encourage each other's development, emotionally or materially, mentally or spiritually. Obviously, this interaction goes a long way towards sorting out or preventing any strife or misunderstanding caused by other interactions. In fact, owing to the passivity of this interaction, it may well need some kind of challenge – from within or without your relationship – to call it into being. Such kindness that you create and have between you will also be of inestimable value in looking after or teaching others.

Moon Trine (harmonizing with) Saturn
☽ △ ♄   **OR**
Moon Sextile (assisting) Saturn
☽ ✶ ♄

Stable Stuff
At a very basic level you can rely upon one another: one of you for being there emotionally, domestically and, if necessary, maternally; the other for being materially and professionally committed. Either of you could actually fill both bills. This could be called a 'meat and potatoes' aspect for it provides those essentials of responsibility, duty and durability for home, family or business. Good, solid, lasting stuff. However, unless your coming together was 'arranged' there would have to be more interesting or romantic interactions for you to have come together at all. Then again, this down-home sort of feeling between the two of you may remain just a notion if there are serious conflicts or illusions about and between the two of you. But whenever the boat rocks on choppy seas, this aspect serves as excellent ballast – but it isn't the kind to get you launched in the first place. Perhaps this interaction favours a traditional type of partnership with, for instance, the man being the breadwinner and the woman being the mother and homemaker.

Moon Trine (harmonizing with) Uranus
☽ △ ♅   **OR**
Moon Sextile (assisting) Uranus
☽ ✶ ♅

Emotional Liberation
Notwithstanding the presence of any possessive or more passionate contacts between the two of you, both of you go to some lengths to help one another come to terms with past influences, and if necessary, cut the ties with them. This is also a relationship where a comfortable involvement with occult or esoteric subjects can take place. Practically speaking, unusual or alternative pursuits are accommodated by one or both of you. All of this makes you quite relaxed with each other in the face of making psychological inroads into yourselves or others. You both sort of stroke and poke at the same time, with one of you being the 'stroker' or comforter and the other being the 'poker' or one who lays bare the truth of the matter. A slight danger with this essentially very positive interaction is that you can become strangely detached from each other as your respective feelings become kind of academic, and you fail to see the emotional wood for the theoretical trees. Apart from that, you make a good team.

Moon Trine (harmonizing with) Neptune

☽ △ ♆   **OR**

Moon Sextile (assisting) Neptune

☽ ✶ ♆

The Healing Relationship

As a couple you feel as one at a very fundamental, even unconscious, level. And so there is what could be called a 'psychic familiarity' with each other – that feeling of having known each other before. All of this makes for a fine receptivity and sensitivity that not only enables you to sympathetically tune into each other's feelings, needs and weaknesses in a positively therapeutic fashion, but that also allows other people (and animals too) to feel at home and at ease, even healed, in your presence. In addition, this psychic interaction means that you can operate well together in any creative or spiritual endeavour. Such accord, other interactions notwithstanding, can make for a particularly loving and caring relationship that can eventually spread to alleviating the suffering of certain areas of society as a whole.

Moon Trine (harmonizing with) Pluto

☽ △ ♇   **OR**

Moon Sextile (assisting) Pluto

☽ ✶ ♇

Mutual Regeneration

With this interaction both of you should experience a degree of 'soul reconnection', which is rather like a garden hose that has come adrift from the tap being connected to it again. So each of you in your own way can feel replenished and emotionally renewed by your involvement with one another. Such regeneration can also positively affect the domestic and/or family situation of one or both of you. However, it should be added that this interaction often proceeds out of sight and over a longish period of time – a bit like an underground river. So don't expect to see all the results occurring that soon or that obviously. This interaction, because it is regenerative at a very basic, even unconscious level, can greatly contribute to the durability of a partnership. Having said that, though, positive results may even appear after the relationship itself is over. This is not to say that your relationship has to end for you to realize how good it was, but just to give an idea of the hidden and protracted way in which this connection operates. Whatever the case, the material or personal assets of one of you are given a boost by the other, who in turn feels a sense of power and effectiveness coursing through them. This mutual effect can of course be profited from in areas outside of the relationship itself.

Moon Trine (harmonizing with) Ascendant *Birth Time Sensitive*

☽ △ AS   **OR**

Moon Sextile (assisting) Ascendant *Birth Time Sensitive*

☽ ✶ AS

Emotional Ease

There is a comfortable feel between the two of you provided by this interaction, but it is quite mild in its influence. So it will augment other harmonious links between you, but would do little to withstand or ameliorate deeper conflicts. Be that as it may, you do find that your feelings and attitudes fit well together. This would also mean that your timing was quite good, with you being in the right place at the right time for each other, and in relationship to circumstances around you.

Moon Trine (harmonizing with) MidHeaven *Birth Time Sensitive*
☽ △ MC   **OR**
Moon Sextile (assisting) MidHeaven *Birth Time Sensitive*
☽ ⚹ MC

Mutual Support

This is a mutually supportive influence in that both of you encourage and reassure one another with respect to domestic and career issues. This can take the form of one of you actually providing a home or workplace for the other, and the other giving intellectual guidance and emotional sustenance

Mercury Trine (harmonizing with) Mercury
☿ △ ☿   **OR**
Mercury Sextile (assisting) Mercury
☿ ⚹ ☿

Intellectual Accord

You get along much as siblings who have a healthy relationship would. The flow of ideas and how to verbally express them comes easily to you both. The actual nature of your easy discussions, though, depends upon other interactions that you have between you. At one extreme, if yours is an intensely emotional relationship then your conversations will be rich and rewarding as you readily gain mental understanding of all that flows between you. At another extreme, where, say, you do not quite hit it off emotionally or physically, conversation can be easy but does not seem to get anywhere in particular, for you are able to talk almost for its own sake. Possibly, a working relationship is where most advantage can be drawn from your basically good communication.

Mercury Trine (harmonizing with) Venus
☿ △ ♀   **OR**
Mercury Sextile (assisting) Venus
☿ ⚹ ♀

Friends And Lovers

Both of you have a liking for the same people and pursuits, and have similar tastes. This goes a long way to ensuring a lasting interest and harmony between the two of you, and you are well able to have fun and be creative together. This interaction especially favours any joint artistic endeavours, either as a pair or with one of you being in an advisory role. You are in tune with one another. Most significantly, though, the emotional and intellectual accord of this interaction enables you to see your way through to harmony and agreement even after the most severe conflicts. This is owing to your mutually creating an ongoing sense of what is good and decent about being human, and so co-operation leads to greater harmony, which in turn leads to more co-operation, and so on. You both profit from the simple activity of discussing your likes and dislikes, rather than expecting to either know them already, or assuming that they should be identical.

Mercury Trine (harmonizing with) Mars
☿ △ ♂ *OR*
Mercury Sextile (assisting) Mars
☿ ⚹ ♂

Getting It On

This is very much a 'get up and go' interaction for it enables both of you to transform thoughts into deeds. Rather than leave something to go to seed, you are inclined to thrash out the best way of achieving an objective. You like locking horns in that mental competition comes naturally to you as a healthy means of keeping sharp and effective. If yours is a sexual relationship, you both appreciate the fact that the brain is the most erogenous zone of all, for sexual ideas and verbal interplay turn you both on. You make a clever team, and others are aware of this mental accord and instinctively steer clear of taking you on as a couple – or they better be advised to. So this is a very dynamic interaction, but with a minimum of friction (notwithstanding other more challenging interactions), which is often based upon one of you being the ramrod, forcing ideas into action, while the other plots the best way of going about it. However, these roles can be interchangeable.

Mercury Trine (harmonizing with) Jupiter
☿ △ ♃ *OR*
Mercury Sextile (assisting) Jupiter
☿ ⚹ ♃

A Meeting Of Minds

You have an excellent mental rapport here because one individual can help the other to contact and express their visions and beliefs in a more effective way, while they in turn enable that individual to see how their ideas and attitudes fit into some broader, cultural perspective. These roles are also interchangeable. Put more simply, you both support and further the minds of one another. As a result you can work together on projects where both the general and the particular need to be equally considered. You can also fruitfully discuss ethical matters and reach an understanding that oils the wheels of day-to-day, mundane matters. Literally or metaphorically speaking, this is rather like a positive relationship between writer and publisher.

Mercury Trine (harmonizing with) Saturn
☿ △ ♄ *OR*
Mercury Sextile (assisting) Saturn
☿ ⚹ ♄

Mental Efficiency

If a practical, working relationship is what you have in mind, then having this excellent interaction of 'mental efficiency' will ensure that commercial details and information, and accounts, will be kept in excellent order. Also, relationships that necessitate one person being in authority over the other, like teacher/student or parent/child, are favoured by this aspect. In a romantic relationship, your serious mental approach to things will ensure that problems are dealt with – as long as they are not too emotional or subtle. But day-to-day, mundane bumps are smoothed over and worked through efficiently and easily. One of you will always make sure that other keeps on the case in a practical way, whereas they keep that person informed with the latest 'down on the street'.

Mercury Trine (harmonizing with) Uranus
☿ △ ♅   *OR*
Mercury Sextile (assisting) Uranus
☿ ✕ ♅

The Problem Solver

Whatever else might be going on between you, this interaction provides you with a combined mental awareness of new ways of seeing things, and consequently new ways of being and doing too. What's behind this mental awareness is a brilliant, almost telepathic, communication. It has been said that if we were telepathic as a race, then all our problems would cease to exist. The reason being that we would always know what someone really meant, and also when someone was lying. Such mental accord, of which you have some measure, can overcome or actually prevent disagreements and misunderstandings. One could call this interaction 'The Problem Solver', as you free each other from whatever veils have obscured your perception of how things really are. You may even extend this mental tool to help others as well.

Mercury Trine (harmonizing with) Neptune
☿ △ ♆   *OR*
Mercury Sextile (assisting) Neptune
☿ ✕ ♆

Telepathically Attuned

Each of you represents one of the two sides of the brain – the 'psychic' right and the 'logical' left – when paired harmoniously as in this interaction, the two of you can be expected to evolve progressively toward a greater and greater understanding of one another, and of life and people generally. What facilitates this process is a psychic rapport that you have, which means that you are consciously or unconsciously attuned to where each of you are at mentally and emotionally. The old adage 'Do as you would be done by' is made real with you two as you deftly give each other space and avoid stepping on one another's toes. Not surprisingly, you are capable of working together on literary pursuits, with the 'logical' individual editing and finding the right words or avenues of expression for the 'psychic' person's visions and ideas. In turn, the 'psychic' one shows the 'logical' one that there are subtleties and incongruities to life that the 'logical' may overlook through being too 'scientific'. As is so often the case with all interactions, the roles of each individual can be interchangeable – but it is particularly so with this one. Art and music are an important part of your relationship together, either in terms of actually being creative or being simply appreciative. This interaction is not dynamic in itself, which means it can recede into the background when more hot, forceful and negative interactions come to the fore. It is therefore vital to give yourselves time after any such altercation for this psychic connection will automatically right things in a quite mysterious way.

Mercury Trine (harmonizing with) Pluto
☿ △ ♇   *OR*
Mercury Sextile (assisting) Pluto
☿ ⚹ ♇

Mental Regeneration

One of you can be very instrumental in regenerating or even transforming the other person's career and/or everyday attitude. This may take some time to develop, but its effects are long lasting possibly beyond the span of the relationship itself, for this is no indicator of emotional durability, one way or the other. In return the first person benefits from seeing their 'pupil' burgeon under their influence. This is not an ego-trip on their part, but just that it is gratifying for them to know that their deep and often invisible 'ray' is effective and not just their lonely point of view. On a more mutual level, your discussions are relatively quite profound, and probably include occult subjects, psychology, and anything dealing with the invisible or unknown. Because of this you are usually quite happy to be alone with each other's intellectual company.

Mercury Trine (harmonizing with) Ascendant *Birth Time Sensitive*
☿ △ AS   *OR*
Mercury Sextile (assisting) Ascendant *Birth Time Sensitive*
☿ ⚹ AS

Fun To Be With

You have a fairly easy banter going on between you. You also make good working companions, and possibly even met in your place of work. You get along easily with each other in a day-to-day way, and connect with your respective personal styles. At the same time one of you finds the wit and agility of other fun to be with and work alongside. This may well be mutual, with you bringing out the humorous side of one another.

Mercury Trine (harmonizing with) MidHeaven *Birth Time Sensitive*
☿ △ MC   *OR*
Mercury Sextile (assisting) MidHeaven *Birth Time Sensitive*
☿ ⚹ MC

Finding A Place

The intellect and skills of the Mercury person help the MidHeaven individual find their place in the world, pointing out ways in which they can amount to something in life, advising on career, and putting their house in order. In return, the MidHeaven can give Mercury, or help them find, a place to work or just to think.

Venus Trine (harmonizing with) Venus
♀ △ ♀   **OR**
Venus Sextile (assisting) Venus
♀ ⚹ ♀

So Happy Together

At one level at least, there is great harmony between you, making for mutual pleasure and complementary tastes and values. You are very much the 'couple' in the sense of being seen as a happy pair by others, and your social life could well be a central theme to your own relationship. If, however, you are loners by nature, you are happy in each other's company, playing and loving together on your own. Artistic pursuits and people are also something you can be involved with. However, there is always the danger of there being not enough emotional depth. In fact, the possibility of there being too much ease or of encouraging each other's social/physical indulgences, can render your relationship a little meaningless. Appreciating the true value of the pleasantness that you have and feel as a couple can be a beautiful springboard for plunging into the deeper aspects of your being so much together.

Venus Trine (harmonizing with) Mars
♀ △ ♂   **OR**
Venus Sextile (assisting) Mars
♀ ⚹ ♂

Venus And Mars Are Alright

This is an accurate but low-powered dart from Cupid. You are sexually or socially attracted to one another, but unless there are other more urgent interactions, you are not going to plunge in on the strength of this one alone. A curious thing that comes into focus when studying relationships with astrology is that it is the 'noisy', jagged or sharp-edged feelings that propel us into relationship rather than the gentle, well-modulated kind like this one. The latter are what are (sometimes sorely) needed once a relationship is off the ground. So whatever the case, there is a pleasant spiciness to being in each other's company. This interaction also contributes to any involvement you might have in the creative or performing arts. One to one, the gentler of you can show the other how to be more gracious and stylish in how they conduct themselves socially or go about getting what they want. On the other hand, the more assertive of the two of you can bring the other out of their shell and get them to realize their worth or charm.

Venus Trine (harmonizing with) Jupiter
♀ △ ♃   **OR**
Venus Sextile (assisting) Jupiter
♀ ⚹ ♃

Joy And Abundance

Your being together creates prosperity, or at least a promise of it. It should be said that this prosperity can take many forms – money, property, good living, access to luxuries, and most of all, burgeoning love. You are both good news to one another, in whatever way or context this applies. The crock of gold at the end of the rainbow – or simply a cup of water at the end of a dry and dusty road – is what this interaction symbolizes. But wine will probably flow soon after – 'Good times here, better down the road'. There is one small snag with this combination, which is that it can blind you to or distract you from issues of more serious concern. All the same, this is an interaction of joy and abundance.

Venus Trine (harmonizing with) Saturn
♀ △ ♄   **OR**
Venus Sextile (assisting) Saturn
♀ ⚹ ♄

Love And Duty
There is definite layer of emotional responsibility and physical fidelity between the two of you. Any more flighty or indulgent elements in one or both of you will be prevented or at least brought to heel by this sense of social propriety. Through highs and lows, this interaction acts as a stabilizer, returning you to some kind of balance. The personal interchange behind this is that one of you is validating the worth of the other, but in a sober, understated way that is ultimately more substantial than a more sensational display of appreciation. They, in reciprocation, appreciate this quiet, less sensational, but reliable quality in their partner side, thereby establishing a very personal bond. Although this interaction is no more a guarantee of a sound and durable relationship than any other one aspect, it is or could be the mainstay of a marriage, business partnership or parent/child relationship.

Venus Trine (harmonizing with) Uranus
♀ △ ♅   **OR**
Venus Sextile (assisting) Uranus
♀ ⚹ ♅

Friendly Lovers
Love and freedom co-exist relatively easily, so this interaction is non-possessive – or at least, it diffuses any other indications of jealousy. There is a friendliness between you if you are lovers, and you are loving if you are just friends. One of you really appreciates and is turned on by the other's unusualness, causing them to depart from their usual social or sensual style. This can actually cause fluctuations in this person's affections, however, as they swing back and forth between their old and new values. To the 'unusual' person, their partner is the perfect playmate, as they seem able to pick up on their odd or intuitive ideas – particularly in the sexual department – as well as being excitingly unpredictable. Not surprisingly, such an interaction is a little too open or loose to ensure fidelity and durability, but it is extraordinarily pleasurable. If you are involved artistically in any way, this gives a zing of originality to whatever you create.

Venus Trine (harmonizing with) Neptune
♀ △ ♆   **OR**
Venus Sextile (assisting) Neptune
♀ ⚹ ♆

Creative Love
Here you have a feeling between you that is so loving and harmonious that it is really quite

fine and spiritual. You bring to one another the mysterious and the beautiful. One or each of you can take on the form of the other's imagination and longings, while you both inspire each other socially and/or artistically. This is a wonderful interaction for making music or being creative together in any way. There is a subtle attraction that gently persists and could well exert a healing influence upon those around you too. This is not a 'robust' kind of interaction and so does not in itself confer physical durability, but whatever the outcome of your relationship, there is always likely to be a wistful connection and sweetness between the two of you.

Venus Trine (harmonizing with) Pluto
♀ △ ♇   *OR*
Venus Sextile (assisting) Pluto
♀ ⚹ ♇

Deep Love

There is a profound and deep bond between you that can heal rifts or take you through other difficulties. In fact, such is the strength of this bond that it may insist that you endure and push on through any 'night' of emotional isolation and confusion. One of you can show the other how to come out of their cave of despair or feelings of unlovableness. They in return can lend more weight and authenticity to their partner's affections and emotional values. This interaction is the kind that occurs when one or both people are 'about to believe in love again' after having endured painful experiences in the past. They must tell themselves that this interaction represents the underground river that can take them there!

Venus Trine (harmonizing with) Ascendant *Birth Time Sensitive*
♀ △ AS   *OR*
Venus Sextile (assisting) Ascendant *Birth Time Sensitive*
♀ ⚹ AS

Easy Attraction

One of you is quite simply attracted to the physical appearance and manner of the other – and this could be mutual. This should be immediately obvious to the other who cannot but help feel flattered by such a response to their image. But that is all it is, one person's image and another's liking of it, and as such this interaction in itself could get a relationship started but little else – unless both of you were unbelievably vain or superficial! More profound and lasting interactions should, and probably do, exist between the two of you.

Venus Trine (harmonizing with) MidHeaven *Birth Time Sensitive*
♀ △ MC   *OR*
Venus Sextile (assisting) MidHeaven *Birth Time Sensitive*
♀ ⚹ MC

Bless This House

One way and another you improve each other's lot – especially on the home and work front. The Venus person's social or aesthetic assets cater to, or provide opportunity for, the domestic and career requirements of the MidHeaven person. The MidHeaven brings substance and confirmation to the worth and talents of Venus. As a pair, more than likely others find you good to be around as you exude a sense of harmony and well-being.

Mars Trine (harmonizing with) Mars
♂ △ ♂   *OR*
Mars Sextile (assisting) Mars
♂ ✳ ♂

Pushing Forward Together
A combination of ease and activity makes you move or operate well together, be it on the dance floor or sports field, in the workplace or bedroom. There is also a youthful quality about you as a pair, as you have a physical and spontaneous approach to life. You spur one another on in natural and unselfconscious way, making things easy that once were difficult, for this energy opens doors for both of you. The straightforwardness of this interaction means that you usually press on through any difficulties without getting too bogged down. As time goes by, more fulfilling (or less exhausting) pursuits than these physical ones may be called for, something which this aspect in itself does not provide.

Mars Trine (harmonizing with) Jupiter
♂ △ ♃   *OR*
Mars Sextile (assisting) Jupiter
♂ ✳ ♃

Mutual Encouragement
There is a confident and loping quality to your being together that enables you to get a lot done with ease. It is as if one of you has the drive and the other knows how to direct it – and then you feed each back to one another. You are probably quite keen on outdoor activities and sports, or failing this, get out and about a good deal and know how to enjoy yourselves in a pretty physical manner. As is often the case with 'healthy' interactions like this, they supply energy and decisiveness and therefore a minimum of complications. But a great deal depends upon how much meaning such activities have for you, and whether such ease ever forces you to look within. Hopefully, other more emotionally or psychologically significant interactions will be present to supply this. When you do fix your sights upon some higher goal, the chances are that you'll not only achieve it, but show others how to as well.

Mars Trine (harmonizing with) Saturn
♂ △ ♄   *OR*
Mars Sextile (assisting) Saturn
♂ ✳ ♄

Energy And Control
This is what you could call a very useful interaction because it bestows practicality and industriousness. Apart from favouring a business relationship, it also means that you are well able to assist one another in getting things done or off the ground. This feeling of 'things to be done' that exists between you is of inestimable value for it counteracts any woolly or overly romantic notions that are so common in many relationships. This is a no-

nonsense aspect. One of you is very good at spurring the other to action, even or especially in the area where that person feels inertia and doubt. In return, they show their partner, in a way they can accept, how to be more mature in the choice of their activities, and how to be more responsible where they are possibly selfish or headstrong. Because together you link energy and control, you can become a very effective team.

Mars Trine (harmonizing with) Uranus
♂ △ ♅   *OR*
Mars Sextile (assisting) Uranus
♂ ⚹ ♅

Forever Young
Between the two of you much can be achieved that will make you feel more as individuals in your own right. So, paradoxically, this interaction inclines towards a certain 'looseness' rather than closeness. A great deal depends upon other interactions and your personal attitudes towards relationships, but ultimately this interaction is saying that you can both follow your own stars and not jeopardize what you have between you. In truth, you actually make your feelings towards one another all the more positive – simply because it is evident that you trust those feelings. So there is a youthful and friendly flavour to your partnership that frees you from restrictions and the limiting ideas of life and love that created them in the first place. Very refreshing – and can be quite sexy in a breezy sort of way! Whatever the type of your relationship, you strike a blow of freedom, and maybe not just for yourselves.

Mars Trine (harmonizing with) Neptune
♂ △ ♆   *OR*
Mars Sextile (assisting) Neptune
♂ ⚹ ♆

Sexual Healing
Because you instinctively and psychically pick up on each others feelings and desires, it can mean anything from your becoming exquisitely intertwined emotionally and sexually – or that you avoid having much to do with each other at all. This is not as perplexing as it might seem. You really do sense what is best for each other, even despite your lesser thoughts and feelings. This is not to say that this fine sensibility cannot be overridden, but it will always be there, trying to make itself felt. Such a subtle interaction is actually of the healing variety for it is this unerring ability to tune into areas of trouble and then lance or cleanse them that is the essence of it. If one or both of you are so inclined, this healing ray may be used very effectively upon others as well. In fact, there are many areas of endeavour, from dancing to business to film-making, that can draw from this sensitive interplay you have between body and psyche, muscle and the mystical.

Mars Trine (harmonizing with) Pluto
♂ △ ♇   **OR**
Mars Sextile (assisting) Pluto
♂ ⚹ ♇

Powerful Coupling

There is a powerful and dynamic energy flowing between you, which is basically sexual in nature. But, in itself, it is not an interaction that will force itself upon you, or be forced upon one of you by the other. It is rather like a reservoir of physical and psychic energy that can be called upon by both of you if you both choose to or if you have to in time of need. In any event, it acts as a strong aid to survival, emotionally or physically. If your relationship is a sexual one, then this is the kind of interaction that make the earth move for both of you, especially if you are involved in some sort of sexual discipline like Tantra or Taoism. Apart from such 'specialized' harnessing of this raw power, you are both instrumental in enabling one another to be more effective and independent in whatever fields you are involved in, to a lesser or greater degree. It is quite likely that in some way one or both of you are put back on your feet by the other, either through a prolonged process or simply through pushing one another in the right direction. Being able to eliminate some attachment that is holding one or both of you back could figure in this exercise. Taken some steps further, as a couple you could become effective in performing this service for others.

Mars Trine (harmonizing with) Ascendant *Birth Time Sensitive*
♂ △ AS   **OR**
Mars Sextile (assisting) Ascendant *Birth Time Sensitive*
♂ ⚹ AS

Physical Attunement

This interaction contributes to compatibility with regard to physical and sexual activity. You will find that there is a ready response to each other's desires and bodily movements, with a minimum of inhibition relative to any innate reserve on either of your parts. This is not a strong interaction, but it can certainly oil the wheels of any endeavours you choose to pursue together.

Mars Trine (harmonizing with) MidHeaven *Birth Time Sensitive*
♂ △ MC   **OR**
Mars Sextile (assisting) MidHeaven *Birth Time Sensitive*
♂ ⚹ MC

The Spur To Act

You encourage or motivate one another to do whatever needs doing, at home or out in the world. So yours is an active relationship rather than a purely romantic or recreational type of thing. One of you always seems to have the wherewithal, either material or intellectual, to get the other a step nearer the goal – or even just to point out that there is a goal.

teaching both of you that creating a balance between these two sides of life – namely, growth and limitation – is highly important. As the Chinese philosopher Lao-Tzu said, 'If you wish to contract something, you must first let it fully expand.' This counsels the 'realist' to let the 'idealist' go off on their flights of fancy, possibly fall flat on their face, and come back the wiser. What can stop the 'realist' doing this is their own fear of taking chances or thinking big. So on the other hand, the 'realist' could learn a lesson or two from the 'idealist' by having more faith in life. Underlying all of this can be a fundamental difference in your respective socio-cultural backgrounds and values. The 'idealist' is more loose and fancy-free, while the 'realist' is structured and more formal. You both have something to offer one another, but deeply ingrained standards and opinions will be forced to the surface by the very conflict itself. In the process hopefully both of you will consciously choose the best of each and discard whatever inherited beliefs or conditions are constricting, outmoded or useless.

Jupiter Opposition (confronting) Saturn
♃ ☍ ♄

Left Versus Right

This interaction embodies qualities that are naturally opposed in that one of you is the 'idealist' and the other the 'realist'. And so your basic values are at odds with one another; where the 'idealist' is liberal, adventurous and spiritually orientated, the 'realist' is conservative, cautious and materially orientated. And so you are inclined not to gel in the first place, often purely because circumstances do not seem to allow it, which can be frustrating if there is emotional/sexual attraction indicated elsewhere. If you are involved, then you run into difficulties while travelling, working out any kind of plan or programme, and disagree over matters of religion, education and how to live generally. In such an ongoing relationship it would be a good idea to recognize and accept that the 'idealist' is involved for reasons of learning from the 'realist' to be more practical and exercise more restraint. The 'realist' is involved so that they might be given a glimpse, by the 'idealist', that there is more to life than just what you can touch and see, or that tradition allows. If some kind of equilibrium can be found here, then you could make quite a healthy whole, giving and getting the best of both worlds, but it would be rather like trying to merge two political parties.

Jupiter Trine (harmonizing with) Saturn
♃ △ ♄   **OR**

Jupiter Sextile (assisting) Saturn
♃ ⚹ ♄

Sound Support

If you have other interactions that indicate emotional and personal harmony and stimulation, then you find that you also have an aspect to your relationship that is both enterprising and practical, confident and reliable. With one of you supplying the vision, and the other establishing the structure, you can build a relationship that in some way positively contributes to your society as a whole. On a personal level, the expansiveness and optimism of one of you keeps the other from getting too earthbound and downcast, while they in return make sure that their other half's ideas are grounded in common sense. This can be a relationship that goes from strength to strength if, as I say, there is more than just this mix of one person's sense of growth and the other's sense of order. Otherwise, you'll be culturally, socially and religiously in tune – and on a business level too maybe, but without the interpersonal feelings of love and care it would be a bit like dough without the yeast or heat to make it into bread.

Jupiter Conjunct (uniting with) Uranus
♃ ☌ ♅

A Marriage Of Minds
This is primarily an interaction that suits or indicates friendship and a 'marriage of minds' – at least, in one area of your relationship. As such it tends to by-pass or rise above physical, sexual or even emotional involvement. Yet because you tend to fire one another up with respect to subjects like metaphysics, religion, education, new age thinking, etc, you could be forgiven for feeling that the fire is a bit lower down than it is! Any forays into the sensual are probably isolated incidents or are just titillating prospects that hover around – or more likely down to other, more emotional and physical, interactions. When such misconceptions of your interest in one another are put behind you, or if they never arose in the first place, this interaction can enable you to discover together very unusual and encouraging insights into life, the Universe and everything. So what can start out as a very lively interaction that promises all manner of exciting and unlikely things can evolve into something quite cerebral. However, there will probably always be that frisson of 'what if' whenever you are in each other's company. None of the above is to say that yours cannot be an ongoing relationship. If it is, then this interaction would help to keep it refreshed, not least because your individual opinions cannot resist good-humouredly vying with one another, thereby upgrading your respective viewpoints and ideas of one another – and life itself.

Jupiter Square (challenging) Uranus
♃ □ ♅

The Freedom Stakes
Compared to one person's radical outlook on life, the other person appears old-fashioned, even though they may not be in a general sense. And to the other, the 'radical' person seems exciting and unusual, but impossibly unstable. But the dynamic of this interaction is to shake or even shock one of out of any stale beliefs or outmoded cultural values. Conversely, the other could learn some tolerance and generosity of spirit from their other half. However, the greater difficulty here is when you both 'agree' to charge around and do exactly as you want. This is liable to happen because both of you stimulate the desire for freedom in each other. And so it may not be long before you are more apart than together for reasons of each doing your own thing, chasing your personal rainbow, etc. At some point the question arises as to what takes precedence – your desires for freedom or your needs to maintain a steady relationship. A great deal would depend here upon the amount of emotional compatibility shown elsewhere. If you trust one another then well and good. If you do not, you would wear one another out as you swung between, so to

speak, a cosy home and the open road. This is the kind of interaction that a film star couple might have. Through learning the price of freedom, you gain a clearer idea of what freedom actually is – or is not.

Jupiter Opposition (confronting) Uranus
♃ ☍ ♅

Opposing Viewpoints

Because this interaction embodies qualities of the higher mind – like faith, intuition and collective codes of thought – you can at first seem to have a lot in common. But unless you also do so on a more personal level, it will become plain as time goes by that your ideas on how to live are distinctly at odds. For example, a theme of your relationship could be the seeking or practising of some unusual religious philosophy that progressively becomes a wedge between you as one of you becomes more and more convinced and the other more and more disenchanted. Apart from this kind of thing, there is a restlessness about you, or created by the chemistry between you, that can make things feel as if they are happening and on the move. But at a certain point, probably quite suddenly, you realize that you are on the same roundabout but turning off at different exits. If other more earthy and responsible ties exist between you, then this interaction could provide stimulating differences of opinion that you combine into some meaningful whole. But even then, beware, for this is a pie-in-the-sky aspect.

Jupiter Trine (harmonizing with) Uranus
♃ △ ♅   OR
Jupiter Sextile (assisting) Uranus
♃ ✶ ♅

Lucky Together

A healthy sense of freedom and equality is the keynote here, and it is linked to the fact that your individual philosophies of life, without necessarily being the same, are able to find common ground. Yours is a modern and future-orientated partnership, and you could both be actually involved with new realms of thought and religion. Without any conscious effort, this interaction seems to foster the development of the innovative and unusual. This is not what you would call a dynamic interaction, but it does provide an atmosphere of altruistic and platonic co-operation. This is a harmonious connecting of your higher minds – so to get the best out of this, quite a lot depends upon how consciously or deliberately you invest time and energy as a couple into mind-expanding pursuits. Potentially, you are able to further each other's higher or better interests, and this in turn would attract 'luck' into your life as a couple in the form of good timing and unexpected opportunities or windfalls, and possibly disappearing into the wild blue yonder every so often.

Jupiter Conjunct (uniting with) Neptune
♃ ☌ ♆

Divine Association

This is a subtle interaction that can give you both a sense of connectedness that goes beyond the day-to-day circumstances and requirements of life. A mutual interest in the mystical or unseen realms is present, along with shared experiences in these areas. This can give your relationship a meaning and direction that puts the more mundane ups and downs into perspective, especially if metaphysical practices such as meditation, hypnosis, trance-work, or the investigation of such things as dreams and previous lives is embarked upon. On the other hand, this interaction can make for fanciful and escapist ideas about yourselves as individuals and about your relationship itself. For example, one of you may encourage the weaker side of the other under the mistaken idea that they're being easygoing or compassionate. Or you may indulge in the idea that you as a pair are somehow more special than others. A great deal depends upon how down-to-earth you each are as individuals, for the ability of at least one of you to distinguish a vision from a mirage, or an ideal from an excuse, can make the difference between your having a gentle and spiritual bond or merely living in cloud-cuckoo land until the bubble inevitably bursts. Whatever the case though, and sooner or later, yours is a coupling that should aspire to finding its higher reason for existing, simply because it has one.

Jupiter Square (challenging) Neptune
♃ □ ♆

Unreal Expectations
One person encourages the other to lose their way in fantasies and great expectations, while the other in return confuses their other half's sense of right and wrong. There is a 'hippie' quality here, which is fairly soft and harmless in the usual sense of the word, but it undermines any attempts to achieve anything more substantial. There is also a religious or spiritual feel about your being together, but this is possibly fanciful and notional. So unfortunately the cloud that you tend to float away on finds you resenting one another, being scorned by others, or at least feeling rather aimless. If this combination could be contained in some form of discipline, like meditating, performing, or doing some sort of charity work together, then it would have a positive outlet.

Jupiter Opposition (confronting) Neptune
♃ ☍ ♆

The Importance Of Acceptance
This interaction is likely to occur between two people when one of them has reached a point when their beliefs or understanding of life need to become more inclusive, tolerant or even mystical, while the other individual needs to adapt their ideals and visions to the cultural or social reality they find themselves in. This is, in effect, an interchange of one person's intellectually determined philosophy with the other's emotionally inspired one. However, before either of you accept this – that is if you ever do – you are going to become quite confused or indignant as the 'right versus wrong' attitude of one of you collides with the 'live and let live' outlook of the other. You both have a point, so meeting somewhere in the middle is what you both should aim for. In the process, one of you will have to walk their talk by accepting the other's inability to accept, being tolerant of their intolerance. Curiously, this person may also have to accept from the other that in reality, as opposed to ideally, people fall into different and opposing camps, and that sometimes one is forced to take sides.

Jupiter Trine (harmonizing with) Neptune
♃ △ ♆   **OR**
Jupiter Sextile (assisting) Neptune
♃ ⚹ ♆

Compassion And Goodwill

At a very basic level you have spiritual compatibility. This means that as human beings you are always human towards one another in that you maintain a certain gentle tolerance and respect. Friends and associates will pick up on this harmonious vibration – possibly quite subliminally – and like to be around you, or even seek your help and sympathy in times of trouble. How much you make out of this, or do not, is the question. On the one hand, such passivity is developing towards something of its own peaceful accord. On the other, it can cause you to just coast along in a nice but somewhat ineffectual fashion. Ideally, if you are both evolved to some degree spiritually, then you can 'use' this spiritual energy to achieve greater good. Compassion and goodwill, are, after all, the basic ingredients of this compatibility.

Jupiter Conjunct (uniting with) Pluto
♃ ☌ ♇

Power For The Good

One of you has their beliefs and opinions probed and questioned, influenced and possibly transformed in some way by the other, who would also be inclined to see them as impractical or lightweight in their philosophy of life. But really, that 'lightweight' can shine a ray of hope and goodness into what could be their opposite number's dark and suspicious recesses. Overall this interaction has the potential of deepening and furthering whatever valid convictions either of you have. One of you can spiritually or professionally benefit from any insights or powerful connections possessed by the other, who in return is made to feel less buried and alone by their partner's warmth and magnanimity. If other interactions support or augment this one, you could make a formidable pair in converting the beliefs and ideas of the public at large – and of making considerable amounts of money out of this or some other enterprise.

Jupiter Square (challenging) Pluto
♃ □ ♇

Judge Not Lest Ye Be Judged

Any excesses or incautious behaviour may lead to some kind of crisis. Should this happen you will be confronted with some sort of moral dilemma. One person will attempt to steamroller the other person's thoughts or feelings on the matter, and then that person will resist this with ethical or religious justifications. But the fact is that both of you have been, or are in danger of being, remiss in some matter of judgement or conduct. So this interaction is all about bringing to the surface some quite profound or taboo-ridden issue, possibly one that involves the law, be it made by man or God – or sex. Apart from being wise before the event, whatever that might be, the two of you had better avoid bad feelings as much as possible by accepting that you are only human. But then the trouble with this interaction is that difficulties can arise simply because you forget that human is all you really are. Accepting this, and that neither of you will really have the last word, is probably the only way of resolving the conflict. "Vengeance is Mine," saith the Lord' or 'Judge not lest ye be judged.'

Jupiter Opposition (confronting) Pluto
♃ ☍ ♇

Morals Versus Passions
Moral principles are thrashed out through the sexual or other powerful forms of involvement that make up your relationship. This interaction makes it clear that giving into your passions ultimately leads to some kind of reckoning, or that sooner or later ethical standards will have to prove themselves to be more than just opinions. The possibility of blame and recrimination is strong with this interaction as the emotional urges or convictions of one of you clash with the beliefs of the other. The contrast between the two should serve to make you both more aware of where you stand with respect to these issues. Ultimately, what you are both after is some form of philosophy that goes deep enough to enable you both to understand what it is about human nature that draws us downwards and inwards, despite, or because of, our best intentions or sense of what is right and what is wrong.

Jupiter Trine (harmonizing with) Pluto
♃ △ ♇   **OR**

Jupiter Sextile (assisting) Pluto
♃ ⚹ ♇

When One Door Closes Another One Opens
This interaction is a bit like 'money for old rope' in that you are able to show each other that it is through getting rid of things you do not need that you acquire things that you do. Whatever is obstructing either one of you – an inappropriate belief, a sense of impotence or importance, or a possession of some kind – the other is somehow able to help them let go of it. You make one another live up to the saying 'When one door closes, another one opens.' Great wealth, spiritual or material, can be gained through this simple 'give more to get more' philosophy that is the potential of your being together. One of you knows the way to get there; the other has the power to get there.

Saturn Conjunct (uniting with) Saturn
♄ ☌ ♄

This Relationship Is What You Make It
Having this interaction emphasizes the importance of making commitments and keeping to them, whether they are to one another or someone or something else. On the positive side, you share similar ideas of what these things mean, along with status, politics, material stability and the way of the world generally. However, if any of these issues are ill-founded, then you will reinforce them in each other. This in turn could result in your having difficulties with respect to them. So this interaction is very much a case of what you make it. It is as if you have been given a lump of clay, which you can mould how you both see fit. A sense of constructiveness and order is therefore a prerequisite, while any inclination to just 'see how things turn out' or 'hope for the best' will be met with a

diminishing sense of either one or both of you having any solid ground to stand upon. This interaction is rather like knocking two houses together to make a bigger shared living space. This can work very nicely if it is well planned and there is sufficient harmony indicated by other interactions – but a sheer disaster if not.

Saturn Square (challenging) Saturn
♄ □ ♄

A Need For Caution

You tend to work at cross-purposes, yet at such a basic level that one or both of you may even overlook it until time together, or apart, makes this more obvious. Because of this, it would be wise for both of you to exercise considerable caution in making any kind of substantial commitment. Fortunately, this interaction often implies that one of you won't be that keen on taking the plunge – but they will have their work cut out making this plain to the other, more eager, person. If one of you feels any doubt, it is imperative that you give expression to it, otherwise you could find yourselves in a highly inconvenient situation later on. Beneath it all, there are important differences between you with regard to what you take most seriously, what you define as appropriate behaviour, and your status or positions in life. Having said all of this, if there are positive and harmonious connections elsewhere, this interaction will still tend to slow things down and emphasize the duller side of life over the more uplifting. There is always the possibility that you are learning about the nature and necessity of your respective limitations and duties as a result of such a relationship, which may include having to learn which of those obligations are no longer necessary for you, and which you must break off from.

Saturn Opposition (confronting) Saturn
♄ ☍ ♄

Begging To Differ

What is needed here is a kind of division of labour where each of you deals with your respective duties and objectives without falling into the mistake of insisting the other person has the same duties and objectives or ways of achieving them. Emotionally, we often have a need to feel 'together' with someone in more ways than is possible considering the different life circumstances of each individual, such as this interaction indicates. Saturn as a planetary energy is not interested in such personal inclinations, and this interaction makes that very clear. However, if it is not clear to both of you that you do have different paths and disciplines in certain areas, then this simple material difference can grow into what seems a great block to emotional harmony. Much of the difficulty may simply arise because one of you is 14 to 15 years older than the other, and their responsibilities are simply greater, their perspective more world-wise or world-weary. Ultimately, this interaction could indeed spell out a difference between the two of you that does make untenable an ongoing relationship of any kind. It could be rather as if you pass one another by, test each other's standpoint and objective, and move on – hopefully leaving you both a little wiser as to what is hard but necessary in each of your lives, as opposed to what is easy and pleasurable.

Saturn Trine (harmonizing with) Saturn

♄ △ ♄   *OR*

Saturn Sextile (assisting) Saturn

♄ ⚹ ♄

Running Mates

This is not a powerful interaction in itself. There is a stabilizing and industrious quality created by the two of you being together, but a mature or businesslike streak would have to be present in you as individuals in order to make anything of it. Even so, there is a basic sense of sobriety and mutual respect that will help you through more difficult times, or prevent you from both indulging too much in any feckless pursuits. To put it another way, you have an idea of a good firm road going somewhere, but the vehicle for going down it would have to be supplied by other positive and constructive links and activities. If such is the case, then you are reliability itself, providing a firm base for anything from a family to a business. Another possibility is that you would attract someone or something that provides that firm base. What you do with it is another matter.

Saturn Conjunct (uniting with) Uranus

♄ ☌ ♅

Old Friends, Old Enemies

The parts of you that come, or are forced, together by this interaction are quite dissimilar – but curiously you often 'swap' these roles. One of you, being the 'provocative' one, will help the other, 'reserved' one, to come out of their shell and loosen their inhibitions. The 'provocative' one could do this intuitively or with shock tactics. Sometimes the 'provocative' one can appear icy cold and detached in the way they do this. But the 'reserved' one can understand coldness and impersonality, and so can respond strangely well to the 'provocative' one's provocation – just because they are impersonal. Stranger still, the 'reserved' one's solid response to the 'provocative' one's off-the-wall behaviour gives the 'provocative' one permission to be the unique and maybe shocking or unusual person they feel themselves to be, but may not show others generally. However, with all this ice and cold around, it should come as no surprise that your relationship can go very cool sometimes. Again, this may be, or should be seen as being, all very well because there is a kind of impersonal, on-off process that goes on between you. In this way, you can remain friends until the end – with any romantic, sexual or warmer interludes being just oases along the dusty way. If your two Charts are elsewhere seriously lacking in harmony and understanding, then indeed your relationship could go into an ice age and never come out. But even so, much as you might disapprove of one another, the radical 'provocative' one and the conservative 'reserved' one just cannot resist one another.

Saturn Square (challenging) Uranus

♄ □ ♅

Compromise Or Conflict

This interaction definitely requires that some compromise be made between the both of you with regard to the one of you who is inclined to be relatively conservative, and the other who takes a more radical or liberal stance – at least, in relation to the 'conservative' one. And note that these roles can be interchangeable. So the 'conservative' one needs to loosen up a bit, change with the times and adopt new methods and approaches, and generally take a more alternative view of things. The 'radical' one, on the other hand, should endeavour to toe the line, wait things out, and not get so hot and flustered and reactionary when things do not proceed at the speed and in the direction they desire. Looked at positively, which is the best way of dealing with challenging interactions, the 'conservative' one can benefit from the 'radical' one's intuitive insights and innovative ideas, if they can be made to see a logical and practical reason for them – before it's too late. Conversely, the 'radical' one can draw reassurance from the 'conservative' one's more solid, steady-as-she-goes, attitude – providing there is at least a token display of flexibility from them. Failing this, this interaction can become quite separative or create a stalemate situation as the 'conservative' one regards the 'radical' one as becoming unacceptably unstable and unpredictable, while the 'radical' one sees the 'conservative' one as remaining impossibly stuck or stuffy and closed. This aspect can indicate a marked age difference, literally or psychologically, with the 'conservative' one being the 'older' person.

Saturn Opposition (confronting) Uranus
♄ ☍ ♅

Radical Versus Conservative

This interaction is fraught with tensions as one of you, the 'conservative' one, doggedly sticks with the devil they know, while the other, 'radical' one, consciously or unconsciously endeavours to free the 'conservative' one from that very thing. The 'conservative' one's past involvements, especially those to which they still feel duty-bound, seem to get in the way of both the relationship and their own well-being. The 'radical' one does not offer anything very solid – but has the allure of the wild blue yonder, all the same. And so an impasse can arise here as the 'conservative' one refuses to change but is tempted to, while the 'radical' one maintains a fairly wide orbit, which is in itself provocative and unreliable. The 'conservative' one will also try to restrict or control the 'radical' one's erratic and unpredictable behaviour. Not surprisingly, this relationship can appear impossible – mad even. But the simple truth is that the 'radical' one is merely a catalyst, no more and no less, that is in aid of shocking or tricking the 'conservative' one out of their rut. Once that mission is accomplished, they'll most likely be off, for their own reasons. What they have got out of it will be something entirely different, like being shown how free they are compared to most people in general, and the 'conservative' one in particular. Or they may have learnt (or not) a lesson from the 'conservative' one which states that the 'radical' one's original ideas are only as good as they are practical and appreciable by ordinary folk, and that believing they are an unrecognized genius is misguided, to say the least. So the pay-off is that after the relationship is over the 'conservative' one has been liberated in some way and to some degree, and the 'radical' one has a firmer or clearer idea of what is unique about them and what impact, if any, it can have upon others. Apart from this, in a more ongoing way, the 'radical' one can make the 'conservative' one more aware of their true standing in the world, a place from which the 'conservative' one may be able to help bestow the same upon the 'radical' one. Because of all of this, this interaction is far better expressed and experienced in a friend relationship.

Saturn Trine (harmonizing with) Uranus
♄ △ ♅   **OR**

Saturn Sextile (assisting) Uranus
♄ ✶ ♅

Efficient Teamwork

One of you is able to affirm what is unique about the other, or at least, make them constructively aware of how they should and could fit better into the status quo. In return, the other can show their opposite number new ways of looking at life that clarify difficult issues and impartially point out where they are possibly being their own worst enemy. And so there is a mutual problem-solving element to this interaction which is useful, to one degree or another. This is essentially a contact of sound and sincere friendship, or of working together on some specific project. If yours is an emotionally intimate relationship, you draw upon this resourcefulness and sense of 'unconditional comradeship' to get you through rocky patches. Taken further still, you could, as a pair or part of a team, be instrumental in helping others through difficulties.

Saturn Conjunct (uniting with) Neptune
♄ ☌ ♆

The Dreamer And The Builder

This interaction can amount to either enormous spiritual/creative realization on the one hand, or a boring and frustrating stalemate on the other. So much depends upon the preparedness of each of you to meet the other halfway. This is because one of you is approaching matters from a pragmatic, materialistic and logical viewpoint, while the other is inspired by something idealistic, spiritual and mystical. This is rather as if one of you is the architect with this vision of something wonderful that could be built, while the other is the builder who has the wherewithal to make it a physical reality. But if the builder thinks the architect is just dreaming of castles in the air they will look elsewhere for business, but possibly wind up erecting something dull and meaningless. And if the architect sees the builder as merely suppressive, limited or unimaginative, then they will look for someone who will give form to their dream, but find this an endless search. And yet, you both could have a valid point here, but just not be the 'architect' and 'builder' who are meant for one another – and you'll both have to keep on looking. If, however, your respective ideas and abilities gel, then your relationship will indeed be a monument to harmony, understanding and co-operation. It may even be your combined spiritual duty to make it work, by meeting each other halfway. This could be called a 'Jack Spratt and his wife' interaction.

Saturn Square (challenging) Neptune
♄ □ ♆

Realist Versus Dreamer

The more practical person, the 'realist' tends to experience the weaknesses and peculiarities of the other, the 'dreamer', as being detrimental to their stability and material well-being. The 'dreamer', on the other hand, sees the 'realist's' ingrained fears and inhibitions as being frustrating and suppressive. So a lot of blame and guilt can be generated by this conflict of values and approach. The 'realist' finds themselves in the position of having to hold the fort while the 'dreamer' is being feckless and irresponsible, at least from the 'realist's' point of view. But then the 'dreamer' cannot stand playing by the 'realist's' rules, and regards them as the 'heavy father' who disapproves when they have a little fun. 'The Authoritarian and the Libertine' could be another apt title for this pairing. As far as adopting a more positive attitude, the 'realist' should endeavour to see that the 'dreamer', consciously or unconsciously, is trying to get them to go with the flow more, to stop trying to control everything, and to confess their fears and thereby disperse them. The 'dreamer' should honestly admit to any need for self-control, more practicality and generally cleaning up their act. Ultimately, both of you are forced by this interaction to listen to your consciences, rather than project them on to each other as blame and recrimination. Until this psychological impasse is dissolved, or at least recognized and admitted to, this is not a good aspect for the building of anything together.

Saturn Opposition (confronting) Neptune
♄ ☍ ♆

The Realist And The Dreamer
In one respect at least, you are in natural opposition with one of you, the 'realist', representing material order and responsibility and the other, the 'dreamer', symbolizing spiritual reality and obligation. And so one of you could see the other as being vague and afraid to make certain types of commitment, while the other sees their opposite number as dull, limited or suppressive. It could well work the other way around as well because each of you acts as the shadow of the other and tends to catch their projection. So the 'realist' could conveniently load some of their material shortcomings on the 'dreamer', and the 'dreamer' their emotional weaknesses on to the 'realist'. Consequently, your relationship can often get caught in a muddy pool of not seeing one another at all clearly. On the face of it, you could learn a great deal about how you could be more balanced and stable if you owned up to this projection on to one another of something each of you finds hard to admit to having in themselves. Such self-honesty is best exercised early on, for in time that 'muddy pool' can turn into a veritable swamp.

Saturn Trine (harmonizing with) Neptune
♄ △ ♆   **OR**

Saturn Sextile (assisting) Neptune
♄ ✶ ♆

Creative Teamwork
You have a great thing going for you both here because each of you takes care of and teaches the other just what they need to have or know at the time. This is because one of you has a sound grip on reality just where the other does not, while the other is aware of another dimension of reality that can greatly relieve and enlighten their opposite number. More precisely, they can give them a practical awareness of their psychic abilities and insights, and how they perhaps fulfil their duties in more or better ways than they have allowed themselves to think. In return, thus enlightened, they give substance to their partner's vision and imagination – possibly furthering a creative endeavour – as well as

allaying any unfounded anxieties. As a team, you would be very successful and effective where both a sense of form and imagination is required – like, for instance, film-making, speculation or psychotherapy.

Saturn Conjunct (uniting with) Pluto
♄ ☌ ♇

Power: Healing Or Destructive?

This is essentially a businesslike contact – literally or figuratively. If other interactions comply or contribute, you can further one another, individually or together, in your careers. Usually, one of you will be the organizational side, and the other will provide the thrust and insight – but these delineations should not be taken too literally, for there should be some crossover of roles. Actually, the ability to interchange and trust, give and take power and position, is very important to your getting ahead and not running into a competition of control and manipulation. Together you can present a formidable front that would impress any group or individual. On the other hand, any power politics that go wrong will give off a decidedly nasty smell. So the good and enlightened management of your unmistakably powerful energy combination is vital. In fact, the clean and upright use of power may be the very thing you use, teach or espouse – or are having to learn through this interaction. On a more emotional level, which may or may not be that obvious with this aspect, one of you acts as a limiting and disciplining influence over any degenerate or wasteful qualities in the other, while they in turn are able to penetrate to their opposite number's secret weaknesses and show them the instability they can cause in their life structure. Again, these roles can be interchangeable. How successful you both are with such manipulation of your respective inner workings depends greatly on that trust-building and the debugging of any potentially suspicion-producing elements.

Saturn Square (challenging) Pluto
♄ □ ♇

Power Struggles

This is basically a struggle for power and authority, on whatever level or in whatever field your relationship is operating. Sex and money would be the main stakes here, but so too could be children or property or status. But the underlying matter here is an emotional rather than material one. One or both of you has had a hard time trusting long before this particular relationship began, and now you are experiencing the natural outcome of such distrust – that is, someone whom you feel it is impossible to trust. And so you have to dig down and look at the roots of such distrust and the emotional control that developed in order to defend yourself (or yourselves) against it. It is as if one, but probably both, of you have made some rather rigid rules to life, and they have now become most unpleasantly restricting. The trouble is that you blame the other for it. Without coming to some personal reckoning in this way of self-honesty, your grievances will have to be settled by some external authority, such as a court of the law or the Hand of God.

Saturn Opposition (confronting) Pluto
♄ ☍ ♇

Disarmament Or 'Cold War'

In ordinary terms, this is like the government of the day on the one hand, and the power base of secret services and multinational corporations on the other. So, as a couple, you are vying for control and influence all of the time, or at least some of the time. The wise way to handle this is to make concessions to one another as acts of trust and goodwill. Failing this, mutual 'paranoia' can set in, with the possibility of material and social collapse. But to a degree, this mistrusting of each other's motives can force each of you to study your own quite closely and, if they are suspect, to eliminate them. Again though, using a political analogy, you both have to be seen to 'disarm' at the same time and in equal proportions. Failure to do all this though – whether you are seen to or not – will inevitably sabotage the whole, which means that both of you would lose what you had spent so much time and energy building up. Trust or perish.

Saturn Trine (harmonizing with) Pluto
♄ △ ♇   OR

Saturn Sextile (assisting) Pluto
♄ ✶ ♇

A Businesslike Arrangement

This is an extremely down-to-earth interaction, with one of you helping the other to find their place in the world, and give stability to their insights or feelings of loneliness. In turn, their part of the 'deal' – for this is what this aspect of your relationship amounts to – is to confirm or intensify that person's sense of authority at a deeper level. At the same time, they will also eliminate that individual's dead wood – sometimes quite ruthlessly. But in response to this the other person won't give in easily here, but this is what gives their opposite number's persistence the seal of approval. This no-nonsense element of your relationship is bound to profit both of you, no matter what else happens. You have the businesslike side of relating in hand, and as such this favours a business partnership.

Uranus Conjunct (uniting with) Uranus
♅ ☌ ♅

The Call Of The New?

This interaction is generational and so its significance for you as individuals depends upon what other interactions you have that dispose your relationship towards the unconventional, exciting, unpredictable, open, liberating, forward-looking, detached, alternative, etc. If this is the case, then this interaction is saying that such qualities are central to your being together. On a purely generational level, you were both born and grew up in a time that saw the same technological advances and changes in social or political values.

Uranus Square (challenging) Uranus
⛢ □ ⛢

The 'Generation Gap'

You probably excite or annoy one another, but it is unlikely that you have the makings of a smooth or predictable relationship – more likely a friendship. Your social values and approach to radical ideas is quite different. However, the fact that you differ here is what can be stimulating. It is as if you both give one another tacit permission to do your own thing, be outrageous and unpredictable, and discover or assert your most individualistic ideas or rebellious feelings. All of this could simply be down to the fact that your ages themselves differ by around 21 years, or even 63 years, but from an astrological viewpoint it has more to do with your soul-minds being different 'models', having different 'specifications'.

Uranus Opposition (confronting) Uranus
⛢ ☍ ⛢

A Mutual Wake-Up Call

To have this interaction your ages would have to be around 42 years apart, and so it is unlikely, even for a parent/child relationship. Some other kind of family relationship or a friendship or business relationship is more likely. In any event, though, this is not only an unusual interaction but it would make for an unusual relationship – and not just because of the age gap. It is as if you keep waking one another up to something new you ought to know about, whether you think so or not. This may even be done unconsciously through one of you being disruptive or shocking in some way. The effects of this can range from being constantly stimulating to being like an ongoing crisis.

Uranus Trine (harmonizing with) Uranus
⛢ △ ⛢   *OR*

Uranus Sextile (assisting) Uranus
⛢ ✶ ⛢

An Unusual Understanding

What makes this interaction so distinctive is that although you are one or two whole generations apart in age, but there is an intuitive understanding that seems to go beyond such normal considerations. The unusual quality of rapport that you enjoy is, however, something which few others will be able to tune into. You may even disturb others because of your unique connection. If there are constructive or creative interactions between you, then you could be instrumental in making others aware of facets to life and human nature they never knew existed.

Uranus Conjunct (uniting with) Neptune
⛢ ☌ ♆

Mutual Awakening

If one or both of you are not interested in the metaphysical or mysterious side of life before, then this interaction should herald experience and involvement with it, somehow or other. It may even have had something to do with the way you actually met. One of you is instrumental in making the other far more aware of their psychic or compassionate nature – and of their weaknesses and blind spots too. In turn, this person can suggest to the other a gentler and more collectively appealing way of giving expression to what is unusual, valuable or even brilliant about them. But they will also show them how hurtful and inappropriate it can be when they insensitively, although truthfully, point out the frailties of others. Although this interaction can be quite far-reaching in its effect upon the lives and personalities of each of you because it quickens your awareness of the more subtle side to being and relating it can also be quite easily resisted and reasoned away if one or both of you is of a particularly conventional and scientific bent. If this is the case, then shocking and apparently unwarranted events could dog the relationship.

Uranus Square (challenging) Neptune
♅ □ ♆

Head Versus Heart

You have a clash between intuition and compassion, which means that where one of you, the 'head', takes a scientific, detached and impersonal view of things, the other, the 'heart', is mystical, sentimental and subjective. And so the 'head' can miss the subtle and sensitive messages that the 'heart' puts out, some of which are often complimentary to the 'head'. Conversely, the 'heart' often suffers needlessly for want of seeing things impartially and as part of a greater process by tuning into the 'head's' wavelength. This is an interaction of misunderstanding rather than outright incompatibility.

Uranus Opposition (confronting) Neptune
♅ ☍ ♆

Head And Heart Make A Whole?

This not too common interaction has a range of effects that can vary greatly, depending considerably upon the other interactions that you have between you. One person, the 'head', can either wake up the other person, the 'heart', to their psychic ability, creative imagination or their sensitivity in general. On the other hand, the 'heart' may experience the 'head' as someone who invades their psychic space and offends their sensibilities with radical outbursts and sudden changes. Likewise, the 'head' can find the 'heart' a wistful, healing and soothing influence, or see them as weak, escapist and fanciful. When these energies are worked positively, you can be of great help to one another, and even the world at large, in increasing your spiritual understanding of life.

Uranus Trine (harmonizing with) Neptune
♅ △ ♆   *OR*

Uranus Sextile (assisting) Neptune
♅ ✶ ♆

Head, Heart And Harmony

If the two of you are interested or involved with metaphysical subjects or the frontiers of science and the understanding of human nature, then this interaction will greatly contribute to your progress, individually or together. One person, the 'head', offers scientific explanations and formulas to the psychic impressions of the other person, the 'heart'. In turn, the 'heart' introduces a vision or myth to inspire the 'head's' models or theories. If there are other creative interactions between the two of you, together you can make a very original and innovative duo.

Uranus Conjunct (uniting with) Pluto
♅ ☌ ♇

The Power Of Truth

For better or worse, very powerful and often unconscious dimensions of your respective lives and personalities come to meet – or into collision – with this interaction. An enormous amount depends on how much of a handle one or both of you have upon your radical or rebellious nature – does it just want excitement and to shock, or is it more into creative and constructive change? Similarly, are your respective senses of power and insight expressed as compulsion or deep conviction? Because of these conditions, your effect upon one another can be anything from a positive transformation to an absolute disaster (which would eventually amount to a transformation of some sort anyway). If you are sexually involved, one of you is likely to tune into the other's deepest desires and phobias concerning their sexuality, whereas they in return zero in on the other's sexual quirks. With a good amount of harmony between you given elsewhere, your relationship can be extraordinarily satisfying, and healing too. Even so, this interaction can often indicate areas where and how you can be on the edge of, if not beyond, sexual 'acceptability'. So whatever the individual case for each of you, you should become a lot more aware of how you tick sexually. But as change and transformation is the dynamic of this interaction, it will take one or both of you to a point where you have some kind of sexual reckoning, which may be quite difficult. Ideally, you should both establish and maintain an awareness of this powerful process that you are caught up in, and learn from it rather than get into judging one another. Another area in which this interaction finds expression is through occult or esoteric study and involvement. Handled well, you could become far more aware of the forces of the unconscious that govern your own and others' lives, and then somehow express such awareness.

Uranus Square (challenging) Pluto
♅ □ ♇

Rebel And Ruler

Your relationship has a dimension to it that resembles a nation where there are those in power, the 'state', and those who are the revolutionary group, the 'rebel', who is against those in power. And so the 'state' often sees the 'rebel' as subversive, unruly and a threat to their security or deepest convictions – even if they do not know what they are. The 'rebel', on the other hand, regards the 'state' as underhanded, manipulative and possibly corrupt – or just unaware of their own depth. Far Right versus Far Left, in fact. What is required if your relationship is not to turn into a kind of 'civil war', is that both of you put your cards on the table and make it clear what you each actually want from the relationship. It is then highly likely that you'll find that you are working at cross purposes in a number of areas. If you cannot find an amicable way of satisfying your individual needs and desires by respecting any differences, then an ongoing upheaval will be unavoidable. Eventually, a total breakdown in communication could then occur as you retreat to your own extremes. If yours is a sexual relationship, this power struggle will choose to play itself out in this area, with the 'state' taunting the 'rebel' or withholding what they want, and the 'rebel' resorting to shock tactics such as going off with someone else or becoming, or pretending to become, disinterested.

Uranus Opposition (confronting) Pluto
♅ ☍ ♇

Exposure
You are two people who are some distance apart in age. On the face of it, the two of you are very different, and not just because of your ages. One of you is brash or open, whereas the other is covert and manipulative. But you are both subversive – or rather you bring the subversive out in one another. So your relationship can be quite mischievous or irresponsible, in quite surprising or hidden ways. In no way does this interaction have the makings of a stable, ongoing relationship. If you are together for any length of time, then you'd be the kind of odd couple they could make a film about!

Uranus Trine (harmonizing with) Pluto
♅ △ ♇   **OR**

Uranus Sextile (assisting) Pluto
♅ ⚹ ♇

It's Psychological
This interaction sets a scene that allows each of you to become far more aware of your respective psychological make-up and how it fits in with society as a whole. So this favours your seeking truth and deep understanding, either together or because of the other person's influence. But this interaction is not, as a rule, a powerful one. It simply provides you both with the opportunity to take your investigations into the truths of life further than you could or would have done on your own. If you do happen to have a good handle on this aspect through other Planets in each of your Charts being 'plugged' into it, then you may work together to help others to find what is original and powerful within themselves too.

Neptune Conjunct (uniting with) Neptune
♆ ☌ ♆

Cultural Compatibility
This is a generational contact, meaning that you are more or less the same age and therefore have been subjected to similar cultural, spiritual and musical influences in your lives. Such acts as a general underlay of compatibility in these respects.

Neptune Square (challenging) Neptune
♆ □ ♆

Mist And Fog
This interaction can only occur when there is an age gap of 40 or so years between you. In itself it would be of little influence other than occasionally getting your wires crossed. If,

however, there are other interactions that pose similar communication problems, then this one will scramble it further, laying confusion upon confusion. One of you at least would have to be very clear about themselves and the messages they put out, and how they interpret the other's messages, to overcome the conflicting impressions that you have, not just of one another, but of life in general.

Neptune Opposition (confronting) Neptune
Ψ ☍ Ψ
Possible Poignancy
This interaction would only occur between two people born 80-odd years apart and so there is little chance of there being much interaction other than that of a vague or poignant sense of something of emotional or spiritual significance.

Neptune Trine (harmonizing with) Neptune
Ψ △ Ψ
The Eternal Verities
There can be empathy and psychic rapport and attachment which is, quite simply, indicative of your having a subtle and sensitive feeling for one another. This interaction, one way or the other, keeps or gets you in touch with the eternal verities.

Neptune Conjunct (uniting with) Pluto
Ψ ☌ ♇
Symbiosis Or Co-dependence
Superficially, this interaction can just be regarded as being indicative of a generation gap, with all the classic symptoms which stem from having differing world-views and values. Looked at more personally, though, and dealt with more consciously and creatively, this contact can be quite profound. One of you, the 'intense' one, either through their deep convictions or emotional compulsions, can arouse in the other person, the 'sensitive' one, a sense of the oneness of all creatures and things, and thereby cause them to develop the compassion which is a direct expression of this. The 'intense' one may have to strip away the 'sensitive' one's glamour's or illusions in the process, however. The 'sensitive' one, for their part, can show the 'intense' one that their sense of power and psychological insight are as nothing without the very things which they have aroused, deliberately or accidentally, in the 'sensitive' one: a sense of universality and compassion. So your relationship is deeply symbiotic, something which when viewed less spiritually would be merely seen as co-dependence.

Neptune Square (challenging) Pluto
Ψ □ ♇
Intensity Versus Sensitivity
One of you, the 'intense' one, in their urge to impress or get what they desire, may overlook the subtleties and protective veils that the other person, the 'sensitive' one, has around their being. So what can happen is that in looking for strength in the 'sensitive' one, the 'intense' one finds what they see as weakness or evasiveness, overlooking the fact

that their emotional missile was misguided at the outset. To make things more confusing, the 'sensitive' one just might become quite addicted to these shows of power, yet at the same time try to avoid such invasions. If the 'sensitive' one was given the chance, they could show the 'intense' one how to go more gently into the night – that is, into the unknown of someone's emotional interior. However, unless this interaction is part of a very intimate relationship in itself, it will probably just amount to a general conflict created by the respective differences in your respective world-views as established by your formative years occurring at different times in social history.

Neptune Opposition (confronting) Pluto
Ψ ☍ ♇

Worlds Apart
There is going to be two generations' gap between you both, which could be the problem in itself. Essentially though, one person experiences the other as being too invasive and ruthless emotionally, and lacking in finesse. One of you sees the other either as just strange or overly sentimental and sensitive. Basically, this interaction is academic because two such people are just not about to encounter one another unless they are grandparents and grandchildren. In such a case, the understanding born of experience would be a crucial factor in the grandparent accepting the grandchild for what they are.

Neptune Trine (harmonizing with) Pluto
Ψ △ ♇

Healer And Healee?
There will be at least a generation gap between two people with this interaction, and its effects are not that noticeable anyway. It will give rise to mutual psychological support and guidance, but only if there are other interactions to support this, or if one person is a professional trained in counselling or some kind of therapy.

Pluto Conjunct (uniting with) Pluto
♇ ☌ ♇

Possible Intensity
This is a generational contact, meaning that you are more or less the same age and therefore have been subjected to similar psychological, political and global changes in your lives. If there are a number of passionate or obsessive contacts between the two of you, this would make it all the more so because your social environment would encourage the same.

5. THE MIRROR
Honesty Is The Policy

'If you hate a person, you hate something in him that is part of yourself. What isn't part of ourselves doesn't disturb us' - Hermann Hesse from *Demian* (1919) ch.6

To round off, here is a powerful exercise that you can use to help you with common relationship difficulties and misunderstandings, which can, if left unchecked, prolong emotional tensions and potentially lead to estrangement or separation, or any pain-producing situation.

   The surest way to resolve any relationship difficulty is to identify what it is in the Other that appears to be giving you the trouble, and then recognize that it is reflecting something back at you, about you. This is astrologically seen as the Sun's light (your ego expression) reflected upon the Moon (someone else's response to it), or metaphorically as the projection of an image upon a screen. The point is that you cannot change the image on the screen (other person) other than by changing what is coming out of the projector (you). Upon admitting and taking back this 'projection' you find that you feel less, or no longer, perturbed by the Other – you may even feel greatly relieved and empowered because you have taken back a part of yourself. More precisely, this is what this Reflection and your Projection are:

REFLECTION: What the Other appears to me as, which concerns, confuses, fascinates, obsesses or irritates.

PROJECTION: What I, upon reflection, see that I am 'sending' to the Other and so getting back as the Reflection, or realize is true, fair or a simple solution.

You have to work at it, and you have to be honest. While doing this for yourself, look at an actual Mirror or the facsimile overleaf and jot down your Reflections and Projections as you do so. There is the Mirror Chart at the end of this section which you can use for this purpose. Here follows an example list of Reflections and Projections to help you with your own.

Example Use Of The Mirror

REFLECTION: Being unreasonable.
PROJECTION: Basing things too much on reason. The times I have been unreasonable.

REFLECTION: Not listening to me.
PROJECTION: Me not listening to my own feelings or better judgement, or to the Other. An historical problem with my older brother or sister not listening to little me.

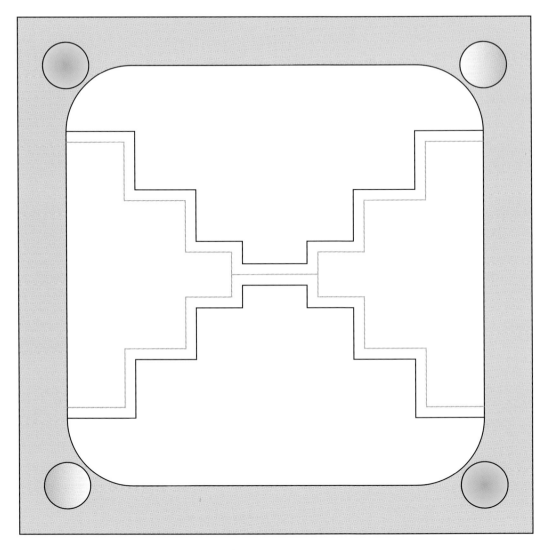

The Mirror

REFLECTION: Being lazy.
PROJECTION: The times when I was lazy owing to a lack of confidence, indecisiveness or a lack of motivation.

REFLECTION: Being obsessed with looks.
PROJECTION: I too am obsessed with looks – and, how do I look?

REFLECTION: Emotionally reacting.
PROJECTION: I do so too at times, or the fact that at other times I uncomfortably suppress my feelings.

REFLECTION: Thinking life should fit some theory.
PROJECTION: I do, or have done, exactly that myself.

REFLECTION: Not liking certain pieces of music which I love.
PROJECTION: Music has emotional associations and so I feel my feelings are not being appreciated – another childhood issue.

REFLECTION: Being a pain/embarrassment in company.
PROJECTION: My internal distress, which I think is under control when really I have merely suppressed or internalized it.

REFLECTION: Being inadequate, a victim.
PROJECTION: The times I too have suffered from this, and how I still do in that I still feel victimized by certain people. That I'm able to protect the Other when they feel weak.

REFLECTION: Not respecting my time and space and feelings.
PROJECTION: That I do not feel entitled to my own time, space and feelings – so I have a right to gently but firmly defend and assert them.

REFLECTION: Being childish.
PROJECTION: Let he/she who is without childishness not throw a tantrum! That I need to be more mature myself.

REFLECTION: Being disinclined sexually to give me what I want when I want it.
PROJECTION: Sex is not enjoyable when I don't want it so why should it be for the Other. What is it about me sexually that I should look at, change or discuss with the Other.

REFLECTION: Not closing doors, turning lights off, or replacing lids and caps.
PROJECTION: Where the Other fails to get the message, in the long run it's easier to do it myself, and teach by example.

REFLECTION: Violent emotions, behaviour and reactions.
PROJECTION: The violent thoughts and feelings that I keep under – a danger to my health – or try to express or sublimate through other means such as sport or sex.

NOTE that you can also project back and forward in time. For example, something the Other is doing now is something you used to do. Or you could be expecting the Other to be, say, aggressive or whatever, and they turn out not to be so. Also, and this is very important, the Other's Reflection may be a COMPENSATION for what you are (sending). For example, you could see the Other as being only ever concerned with themselves, reflecting that you are too much concerned with the Other(s) and not nearly enough with yourself. There can be many versions of and reasons for Compensation.

Discounting Projection: If you genuinely and honestly discover that there is no projection occurring on your part, that the Other's behaviour is entirely their issue and flaw, then you can tell them so or leave them to their own devices in the knowledge that you actually are right in a really objective sense.

THE MIRROR CHART

Instructions for Use

1. Close your eyes and take time to concentrate upon the Image, that is, what is concerning, confusing, fascinating, obsessing or irritating you about the Other, until you have it clearly in focus. Be calm. Be still.
2. Open your eyes and gaze into the Mirror (real or facsimile opposite) until you realize that the Image is actually a Reflection of a facet of your own personality that you have Projected on to the Other. Jot down these Reflections and Projections on the chart below. Again, take your time.
3. Having successfully accomplished this, appreciate how you now no longer feel (so) concerned, confused, obsessed or irritated – because you have now reclaimed possession of a part of your Self, or found a simple answer.

REFLECTION:

PROJECTION:

REFLECTION:

PROJECTION:

REFLECTION

PROJECTION:

REFLECTION:

PROJECTION:

REFLECTION:

PROJECTION:

REFLECTION:

PROJECTION:

REFLECTION:

PROJECTION:

REFLECTION:

PROJECTION:

REFLECTION:

PROJECTION:

REFLECTION:

PROJECTION:

REFLECTION:

PROJECTION:

REFLECTION:

PROJECTION:

REFLECTION:

PROJECTION:

REFLECTION:

PROJECTION:

REFLECTION:

PROJECTION:

SETTING THE SCENE

Elements
Modes
Hemispheres
Lunar Nodes

Here are ways of assessing four basic energies in the Birth Chart/personality that you can use once you have calculated the Birth Chart with the CD (see page 38). These will not only describe fundamental traits but also inform you of general biases and inclinations that 'set the scene' onto which you can place your own 'customized interpretations' of the interpretations given in the Personality Profiles you create. This entails reading between the lines and intuitively integrating the various pieces of information supplied. This is the stuff of being an astrologer and you are assisted in this further with the **Synthesis** which follows this chapter on page 537.

Whilst reading these 'scene-setters' below, refer to:

The Elements, Modes and Hemispheres Chart overleaf in order to see how these three factors intermesh graphically, and, how each Sign opposes another.
Photocopy and use the Chart Calculation charts on pages 565-570.

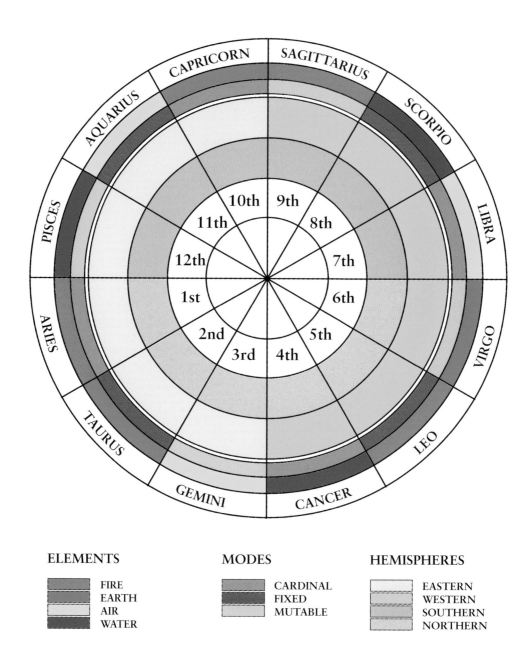

ELEMENTS

FIRE
EARTH
AIR
WATER

MODES

CARDINAL
FIXED
MUTABLE

HEMISPHERES

EASTERN
WESTERN
SOUTHERN
NORTHERN

Elements, Modes and Hemispheres

Elements, Modes and Hemispheres

1. Elements

There are four Elements in astrology: Fire, Earth, Air and Water. Each Sign belongs to one of these:

FIRE	EARTH	AIR	WATER
Aries	Taurus	Gemini	Cancer
Leo	Virgo	Libra	Scorpio
Sagittarius	Capricorn	Aquarius	Pisces

They have these basic qualities:

FIRE	EARTH	AIR	WATER
Intuition	Sensation	Thinking	Feeling
Creativity	Practicality	Concepts	Receptivity
Initiative	Objectivity	Ideals	Empathy
Adventure	Material Stability	Principles	Instinct
Vision	Reliability	Impartiality	Security seeking
'Fired with enthusiasm'	*'Down to Earth'*	*'Air your views'*	*'Going with the flow'*

Assessing Elemental Emphasis

Having created a Personality Profile, you will know from the Planetary Placements what Sign the Sun, Moon and each Planet is in. If birth time is accurate, you will also see what Sign the Ascendant and MidHeaven are in. Equipped with this information we can now calculate for the Chart the Planetary Weight of each Element with the following point system:

SUN and MOON = 4 points each
MERCURY, VENUS and MARS = 3 points each
JUPITER and SATURN = 2 points each
URANUS, NEPTUNE and PLUTO = 1 point each
ASCENDANT (Rising Sign) = 4 points
MIDHEAVEN = 2 points

Let's use as an example *George W Bush born 6 July 1946 at 7.26 a.m. in New Haven, Connecticut, USA*. His Chart is shown opposite, and his Planetary Placements and Aspects are shown on pages 524 and 525. Go through the Planets in the order they appear in the Planetary Placements, that is, Sun, Moon, Mercury, etc. Make notes as you go, as I advise you to do with a whole Profile in the next chapter, **Synthesis**

FIRE placements	pts	EARTH placements	pts	AIR placements	pts	WATER placements	pts
Mercury in Leo	3	*Mars in Virgo*	3	*Moon in Libra*	4	*Sun in Cancer*	4
Venus in Leo	3			*Jupiter in Libra*	2	*Saturn in Cancer*	2
Pluto in Leo	1			*Uranus in Gemini*	1		
Ascendant in Leo	4			*Neptune in Libra*	1		
MidHeaven in Aries	2						
Total Fire	13	Total Earth	3	Total Air	8	Total Water	6

Check to see that you have included all the Placements; there should be **ten** if you have not used the Ascendant and MidHeaven (because of unreliable birth time) or **twelve** if you have included them.

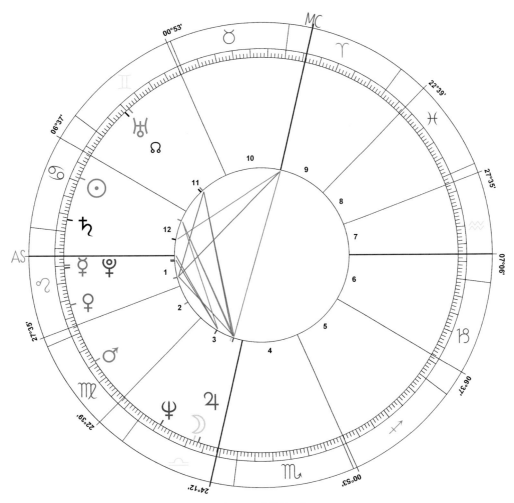

George W Bush
Born Saturday 6 Jul 1946 07.26 EDT +4:00
New Haven, Connecticut 41N18 72W55

George W Bush
Born Saturday 6 July 1946 07.26 EDT +4:00
New Haven, Connecticut 41N18 72W55

Planetary Placements

Planet/Point	Glyph	Sign	Glyph	Position	House
Sun	☉	Cancer	♋	13°46′	12th
Moon	☽	Libra	♎	16°42′	3rd
Mercury	☿	Leo	♌	09°49′	1st
Venus	♀	Leo	♌	21°29′	1st
Mars	♂	Virgo	♍	09°18′	2nd
Jupiter	♃	Libra	♎	18°08′	3rd
Saturn	♄	Cancer	♋	26°30′	12th
Uranus	♅	Gemini	♊	19°09′	11th
Neptune	♆	Libra	♎	05°56′	3rd
Pluto	♇	Leo	♌	10°34′	1st
Ascendant	AS	Leo	♌	07°06′	↷
MidHeaven	MC	Aries	♈	24°12′	↷
North Node	☊	Gemini	♊	20°34′	11th

With the ten placements there is an overall total of **twenty-four points**; with the twelve there would be an overall total of **thirty points**. So we can assess the Elemental Weighting, as the averages being roughly six or seven points per Element, as follows (page 526):

Planetary Aspects

Planet	Aspect (mode of relationship)	Planet or Point	Glyphs	Orb
Sun	Square (challenging)	Moon	☉ □ ☽	02°55'
Sun	Square (challenging)	Jupiter	☉ □ ♃	04°21'
Sun	Square (challenging)	Neptune	☉ □ ♆	07°50'
Moon	Conjunct (uniting with)	Jupiter	☽ ☌ ♃	01°26'
Moon	Trine (harmonizing with)	Uranus	☽ △ ♅	02°26'
Mercury	Sextile (co-operating with)	Neptune	☿ ✶ ♆	03°53'
Mercury	Conjunct (uniting with)	Pluto	☿ ☌ ♇	00°44'
Mercury	Conjunct (uniting with)	Ascendant	☿ ☌ AS	02°42'
Venus	Sextile (co-operating with)	Jupiter	♀ ✶ ♃	03°21'
Venus	Sextile (co-operating with)	Uranus	♀ ✶ ♅	02°20'
Venus	Trine (harmonizing with)	MidHeaven	♀ △ MC	02°42'
Jupiter	Trine (harmonizing with)	Uranus	♃ △ ♅	01°00'
Jupiter	Opposition (confronting)	MidHeaven	♃ ☍ MC	06°03'
Saturn	Square (challenging)	MidHeaven	♄ □ MC	02°17'
Neptune	Sextile (co-operating with)	Ascendant	♆ ✶ AS	01°10'
Pluto	Conjunct (uniting with)	Ascendant	♇ ☌ AS	03°27'

4 points or less makes that Element UNDER-EMPHASIZED
12 points or more makes that Element OVER-EMPHASIZED
5-11 points makes that Element BALANCED, with strength of that Element according to how near 5 or 11 its weight is.

This is what they would mean to the general disposition of the personality you are looking at:

EMPHASIS	FIRE	EARTH	AIR	WATER
UNDER (4 points or less)	Lacking drive and initiative. Little get-up-and-go. A want of burning desire.	Impractical. Poor sense of time and physical/material needs. Unsensual. Ungrounded.	Finds it hard to relate or view things impartially. Non- or even anti-intellectual.	Out of touch with own and others' feelings. Lacking in empathy. Prone to toxicity.
OVER (12 points or more)	More energy than sense. Fervid. Foolhardy risk-taking. Burns self (and others) out.	Cautious, possibly even boring. Very 'physical'. Too predictable and habit-ridden.	Lives too much in the head, 'airy-theory', finds it hard to 'get real'. Up in the clouds.	Over-emotional. Too sensitive. Little sense of boundaries. Prone to water retention.
BALANCED (5-11 points)	Has drive without being too driven.	Practical without being dull.	Clear without being 'light'.	Responsive yet centred.

To COMPENSATE (in addition to making the most of what points there are, if any, in any Under-emphasized Elements OR being with people who have what you lack, or lack what you have, OR having a compensatory Element emphasized in their Chart):

EMPHASIS	FIRE	EARTH	AIR	WATER
UNDER	Look to the Sun, Mars and Jupiter, and any placements in 1st, 5th or 9th Houses,* and make more of them.	Look to Saturn and any placements in 2nd, 6th or 10th Houses,* and make more of them.	Look to Mercury and Uranus, and any placements in 3rd, 7th or 11th Houses,* and make more of them.	Look to the Moon and Neptune, and any placements in 4th, 8th or 12th Houses,* and make more of them. Detox regularly.
OVER	Make an effort to learn from experience and recognize the value of limitations. Consider others and their opinions.	Be less controlling, leave things to chance more, make room for the unexpected. Learn to trust the Unknown.	Recognize that life does not always go according to some plan or theory. Do the 'practical' and see what *really* happens.	Realize that you are more than just your feelings. Come to terms with childhood experiences that can make you overreact in the present.
COMPENSA-TORS	WATER & EARTH	FIRE & AIR	EARTH & WATER	FIRE & AIR

* These Houses correspond to these Elements because they themselves correspond to Signs of the same number in the Zodiac – i.e. 1st House corresponds to Aries because it is the 1st Sign and is a Fire House.

With our example we can see therefore that there is:
Over-Emphasis in Fire = Over-enthusiastic; possible Risk-Taking or Burn-out. Needs to listen to others. It is known that his wife Laura has strong influence over him. Laura Bush was born 4 November 1946 in Midland, Texas. Even with her birth time not known we can see that she has an Over-Emphasis of Fire-compensating WATER in her Chart (Sun, Mars and Jupiter in Scorpio, Moon in Pisces)

Under-Emphasis in Earth = Lack of practicality; poor sense of time (and timing?).

We will, therefore, according to the Compensation, look at his Saturn (in Cancer in the Twelfth House) and his 2ⁿᵈ, 6ᵗʰ and 10ᵗʰ Houses. The only one of these Houses with a Planet in is the 2ⁿᵈ – and it is Mars. We will bear all this in mind for the Synthesis, which follows in the next chapter.

Element Singletons

Occasionally you will find that there is one Planet (or even two) in one of the Elements. This is called a Singleton and would take on extra significance in that individual's Chart/personality/life.

In our Example there is a Singleton, Mars again – so we will keep this in mind as a very significant part of his Birth Chart.

2. Modes

There are three Modes in astrology: Cardinal, Fixed and Mutable. Each Sign belongs to one of these:

CARDINAL	FIXED	MUTABLE
Aries	Taurus	Gemini
Cancer	Leo	Virgo
Libra	Scorpio	Sagittarius
Capricorn	Aquarius	Pisces

They have these basic qualities:

CARDINAL	FIXED	MUTABLE
Initiating	Persisting	Varying
Promoting	Sustaining	Adapting

Assessing Modal Emphasis

As with the Elemental analysis above, equipped with Planetary Placements we can now calculate for the Chart the Planetary Weight of each Mode with the same point system: SUN and MOON = 4 points each

MERCURY, VENUS and MARS = 3 points each
JUPITER and SATURN = 2 points each
URANUS, NEPTUNE and PLUTO = 1 point each
ASCENDANT (Rising Sign) = 4 points
MIDHEAVEN = 2 points

So again, using our Example:

CARDINAL placements	pts	FIXED placements	pts	MUTABLE placements	pts
Sun in Cancer	*4*	*Mercury in Leo*	*3*	*Mar in Virgo*	*3*
Moon in Libra	*4*	*Venus in Leo*	*3*	*Uranus in Gemini*	*1*
Jupiter in Libra	*2*	*Pluto in Leo*	*1*		
Saturn in Cancer	*2*	*Ascendant in Leo*	*4*		
Neptune in Libra	*1*				
MidHeaven in Aries	*2*				
Total Cardinal	16	Total Fixed	11	Total Mutable	4

Again, as with the Elements, with the ten placements there is an overall total of twenty-four points, with the twelve there would be an overall total of thirty points. So we can, through the averages this time being roughly eight or ten points per Mode, assess the Modal Weighting as follows:

6 points or less makes that Mode UNDER-EMPHASIZED
16 or more makes that Mode OVER-EMPHASIZED
7-15 points makes that Mode BALANCED, with strength according to how near 7 or 15.

So this is what they would mean to the general disposition of the personality in question:

EMPHASIS	CARDINAL	FIXED	MUTABLE
UNDER (6 points or less)	Lacking initiative. Waits for or depends upon others to get things going.	Lacking persistence. Cannot, or finds it hard to, stand one's ground	Lacking flexibility. A bit one dimensional. Expects others to adapt.
OVER (16 points or more)	Good starter, bad finisher. Projects and relationships lack sustain or follow-through.	Stubborn. Slow to learn or change. Hangs on to things and people too long and too much. Retentive. Constipated.	Leaf in the wind. Indecisive and always adjusting to the requirements of others and circumstances.
BALANCED (7-15 points)	Healthy sense of initiative.	Firm yet open to changing if need be.	Moderately adaptable and alive to change.

To **COMPENSATE** (in addition to making the most of what points there are, if any, in an Under-emphasized Mode OR being with people who have what you lack, or lack what you have):

EMPHASIS	CARDINAL	FIXED	MUTABLE
UNDER	Either accept that you are a follower rather than a leader, or discover what you want enough to go it alone.	Determine your convictions and stick by them. Resist being a yes-person; there's seldom any future in it.	Ascertain what it was in your past that made you so resistant to change and bending a bit.
OVER	Try being more passive. Learn to delegate. Listen to others you trust. Over-managing life is counter-productive.	Ask yourself what you are afraid of happening if you let go. Find someone you can trust and let them take hold.	Build your own sense of values and foundation and trust them; do not let yourself or anyone else compromise them.

With our example, we can see therefore that there is:
Over-Emphasis in Cardinal = Good starter, bad finisher – but is this compensated for by healthy Fixed? Again, the Compensation points to the importance of having/listening to someone you trust. Again, Laura apparently acts as this 'braking influence' as do hopefully a few others.
Under-Emphasis in Mutable = Lack of flexibility; Expects others to adapt. Probably necessary in his job!
*But we further note that with both Earth and Mutable weak, it makes the Mutable Earth Sign Virgo his **weakest suit**, that Singleton that we have already strongly noted. This heavily stresses the significance of Mars in his Chart. Again, we will pick all this up later in the Synthesis.*

Mode Singletons
Occasionally you will find that there is one Planet (or even two) in one of the Modes. This would take on extra significance in that individual's Chart/personality/life.

Example: Mars again! (with Uranus).

3. Hemispheres

There are four Hemispheres in a Birth Chart, determined by the Houses contained therein (those in CAPITALS being their respective points of focus):

EASTERN	WESTERN	SOUTHERN	NORTHERN
Tenth	Fourth	Seventh	First
Eleventh	Fifth	Eighth	Second
Twelfth	Sixth	Ninth	Third
FIRST	**SEVENTH**	**TENTH**	**FOURTH**
Second	Eighth	Eleventh	Fifth
Third	Ninth	Twelfth	Sixth

They have these basic qualities:

EASTERN	WESTERN	SOUTHERN	NORTHERN
Identification with Self. Feels that it is oneself that is happening to life or making life happen.	Identification with Other. Feels that life is happening *to* oneself.	Identification with Outer World or public arena. Feels that life is happening 'out there'.	Identification with Inner World or private arena. Feels that life is happening 'in here'.

Assessing Hemispheric Emphasis

As with the Elemental and Modal analysis above, equipped with Planetary Placements we can now calculate for the Chart the Planetary Weight of each Hemisphere with the same point system:

SUN and MOON = 4 points each
MERCURY, VENUS and MARS = 3 points each
JUPITER and SATURN = 2 points each
URANUS, NEPTUNE and PLUTO = 1 point each
ASCENDANT and MIDHEAVEN do not count because they are the Eastern and Southern Points themselves, whilst their opposites, the DESCENDANT and LOWER MIDHEAVEN are the Western and Northern Points themselves.

---

* Be flexible with these approximate figures. Use your own judgement of the person concerned, and be aware how other factors in their Chart can compensate for under- or over-emphasis

With our Example we find the following (TIP: Go through House by House for each Hemisphere): using the Birth Chart itself, as with our example's on page 523).

EASTERN placements	pts	WESTERN placements	pts	SOUTHERN placements	pts	NORTHERN placements	pts
Uranus	*1*	*No Planets*	*0*	*Uranus*	*1*	*Mercury*	*3*
Sun	*4*			*Sun*	*4*	*Pluto*	*1*
Saturn	*2*			*Saturn*	*2*	*Venus*	*3*
Mercury	*3*					*Mars*	*3*
Pluto	*1*					*Neptune*	*1*
Venus	*3*					*Moon*	*4*
Mars	*3*					*Jupiter*	*2*
Neptune	*1*						
Moon	*4*						
Jupiter	*2*						
Total Eastern	24	Total Western	0	Total Southern	7	Total Northern	17

Check to see that you have included all the Placements; there should be **twenty,** two for each Planet, and a total of **forty-eight points**.

Now, unlike with the Elements and Modes, we are looking to see what Hemisphere/Hemispheres is/are most strongly emphasized in order to see what that person's natural 'bias' is. Balanced Hemispheres are not so desirable because such would not dispose the individual to any particular identification with how life operates. A kind of impasse or self-cancelling could be evident. And yet, such a person could be considered well-balanced providing they were happy to be so evenly spread, or that they were prepared to take their time owing to them not pushing that hard nor settling for one Hemisphere in particular.

With each Hemisphere having an average of **twelve** points (48 divided by 4), a Hemisphere Over-emphasis – around **sixteen** points or more* – is therefore quite advantageous, but when taken to extreme – around **twenty** points or more* – then some compensation definitely will be called for sooner or later. Compensation would mean the need to focus more on the opposite Hemisphere, like this:

EXTREME OVER-EMPHASIS OF	STRONG BIAS TOWARDS	COMPENSATE THROUGH
EASTERN HEMISPHERE	Self and promotion of its interests. Strong sense of identity. Egocentric or solipsistic. Feels only oneself is looking after oneself.	Learning to put self in others' shoes. Relationship challenges. Trusting in a Higher Power to sustain one.
WESTERN HEMISPHERE	Living through others. People person. Weak identity leading to loss of sense of self.	Taking responsibility for self. Determining one's own priorities. Following one's own star.
SOUTHERN HEMISPHERE	Objectivity and how things appear to be. People and things. Career person or globetrotter. Poor sense of inner being or 'soul-ground'.	Studying or returning to one's roots. Bringing the world to one's doorstep. Entertaining at home. Becoming more introspective.
NORTHERN HEMISPHERE	Home and family life. Identification with one's roots. Home-bug. Feels buried, gets stale and frustrated.	Travelling. Getting out more. Blowing away the cobwebs. Cutting the ties that bind. Dealing with fears of outside world.

Our Example, George Bush has:
Extreme Over-Emphasis in Eastern = Egocentric; Me, me, me > Need to consider opinions and needs of others; or to rely upon Higher Power/God. Yet again, it stresses the balancing influence of his wife, Laura. Does she compensate for these extremes? Astrologically and historically, it would appear so, as too does God with Bush's strong Christian beliefs.

Hemisphere Singletons

Occasionally you will find that there is one Planet (or even two) in one of the Hemispheres. This is called a Singleton and would be a point of focus in that individual's Chart/personality/life. For example, all the Planets in the Eastern Hemisphere except for, say, the Moon in the Western Hemisphere, would indicate that their Emotional Needs (Moon) were strongly dependent on Others (Western), despite the probable show of self-sufficiency that an Eastern emphasis displays. *In our Example: None.*

4. Lunar Nodes

The Lunar Nodes are the two points where the orbit of the Moon intersects the orbit of Earth around the Sun. The point where the Moon is moving northwards through the plane of the Earth's path is called the North Node or Dragon's Head, whereas the other, opposite point, where it is travelling southwards, is known as the South Node or Dragon's Tail.

Where they are in your Chart/Planetary Placements – depicted by ☊ for North Node and ☋ for South Node – shows, in the case of the North Node, your forward and favoured direction in life. The South Node, on the other hand, is your past, what is behind you – and in some cases, best *left* behind you. A graphic image of the Nodes that I find useful is to think of your personality as a boat travelling through the waters of life with the North Node being the prow and bow-wave, while the South Node is seen as the stern with the wash behind it. Essentially you cannot have the one without the other. The prow meets with resistance but it is that very resistance that is consistent with moving in the right direction. The stern, however, acts as a drag, but is also what gives stability and is where the rudder – one's ability to steer – is situated.

So, according to the House and Sign that the North Node is placed in you can gain information on your GO ZONE, that is, the greatest potential growth area of your life (House) and the way (Sign) in which that area can be realized. Conversely, the House position of the South Node will show the SLOW ZONE or area you have come from, know best, but that is in danger of dragging you backwards; and the Sign the South Node is placed in shows ways of going about things that are second nature, but again, could get you struck in a rut or leave you behind (like falling into the wash). If you believe in reincarnation, then the Nodes take on an added, and quite potent, meaning as the North Node comes to represent the theme and focus of your present life – what the Hindus call your *dharma*, your personal destiny and duty, in the sense of simply being *the right thing to do*. And the South Node is indicative of your karma, both positive and negative, of previous existence/s.

So, first determine the House and Sign positions of the North Node as given in the Planetary Placements of your Personality Profile.

Looking at our Example Chart on page 522 we see …
North Node ☊   Gemini ♊   20°34′ 11ᵗʰ
… telling us that it is in the Sign of Gemini in the Eleventh House.

Remembering that the South Node is always exactly opposite the North, and using this Table, we can deduce what House and Sign the South Node is in:

OPPOSING SIGNS		OPPOSING HOUSES	
Aries	Libra	First	Seventh
Taurus	Scorpio	Second	Eighth
Gemini	Sagittarius	Third	Ninth
Cancer	Capricorn	Fourth	Tenth
Leo	Aquarius	Fifth	Eleventh
Virgo	Pisces	Sixth	Twelfth

In our Example Chart the South Node is therefore in Sagittarius in the Fifth House. Note that the exact degree/minute position will be the same – 20°34' in this case – but in the opposite Sign.

Now using the lists of 'Sign Qualities' and 'House Fields of Experience' given on pages 34 and 35 you can assess what the Nodes mean in your own or anyone else's life.

So with our Example, G W Bush, we can say that with:

North Node in Gemini in the 11th House = GO ZONE = Politics through Communication
South Node in Sagittarius in the 5th House = SLOW ZONE = Furthering of Self; Gambling; Romance.

Obviously he has found his way, his 'dharma', with respect to politics, with his ability to communicate surprising quite a few people. One could say he has found his connection with himself. Conversely, his past was rather taken up with having a 'good time', but he turned that around. Whether 'furthering of self' is still more important than the interests of Ideals and the Group (11th House) could still be a question.

REMEMBER however, that the two Nodes are a mutually stabilizing pair of opposites which means to say that the South Node should not be left behind entirely; this would destabilize.

So, if our Example individual found he got lost amidst the needs and expectations of Politics and the Group, then pulling back to the Fun and Furtherance of his own Creative Self-expression (Sagittarius/Fifth House) would be necessary, along with the Gamble that this would involve.

Now, bearing all the above notations in mind, let us proceed with the Synthesis …

SYNTHESIS

All Profiles
The Personality Profile
The Timeline Profile
The Relationship Profile

One of the secrets of Synthesis – that is, interpreting a Birth Chart as a whole entity rather than just a collection of parts – is to get it to 'talk' to you. A Birth Chart is a magical thing, not just a diagram with symbols and figures on it. By getting to know the Chart through absorbing the various meanings given in a Profile, at some point that Chart starts to talk to you, telling you things that are not necessarily down in black and white in those interpretations. You could liken this process to the making of a cake. Every cake of a certain kind has the same ingredients, but how those ingredients are proportioned, prepared, mixed and baked can make all the difference to the quality of the cake. In other words, how you interpret the interpretations – mixing them with your own impressions and deductions, and your particular sense of what 'tastes' right – can give rise to a highly elaborate and unique description of a whole person. Another way of looking at this is to regard a person's Chart as a code you are trying to break. Once you have broken the code you have access; what is more, you have *earned* that access. Doing one's own Chart can be more difficult in this respect, however, because our own subjective idea of ourselves can get in the way of our 'inner truth' talking to us. Nevertheless, reading one's own Profile with an open mind will still help to reveal great, and often quite obvious, insights. In any event, do not be daunted by the welter of information, just endeavour to find one point that seems to be 'talking to you' and the rest will develop from there. This is because the magical Chart is also a hologram, and within each cell of a true hologram can be seen every other cell.

And whether it is your own or someone else's Profile you are looking at, there are some guidelines you can follow that facilitate the process.

1. ALL PROFILES

Personality Profile First
It is preferable to create and look at a Personality Profile first, that is, before doing a Timeline or Relationship Profile. This is because the Timeline and Relationship Profiles are *in relationship to* the individual personalities concerned. The relevant paragraphs below elaborate on this 'rule'.

Making Notes
As you read any Profile – Personality, Timeline or Relationship – make notes (as we already have in the Scene-Setting in the last chapter) on how you receive and understand certain interpretations, both in respect of your own impression of that person and how you see one component of the Profile compared to, or in the light of, one you have read previously. As you write – or even if you don't – you will begin to notice a **theme** emerging. Usually there will be more than one theme, complementing or in conflict with the other ones(s). Negatively, this could mean that the theme was that of two of more 'sub-personalities' vying for supremacy, or that the person was split, living two separate lives – neither an acceptable state. Such is often the case when there is a strong emphasis on one or more of the binary Signs. These are Signs that are composed of two factors, namely: Gemini (twins, obviously); Libra (weighing or making the choice between two opposites or extremes, hence the indecisiveness of this Sign); Sagittarius (horse and human, that is,

animal versus cerebral/spiritual impulses); Capricorn (from the original nature of this Sign, the Sea-Goat, with goat upper half and fish's tail, representing the earthly realm of commerce and practicality versus the dreamy, mystical and emotional world); Pisces (two fishes, one striving upstream, the other giving up/giving in, downstream fish). Another reason for 'splitting off' is a Chart where there are a lot of Opposition Aspects, or where there are possibly hidden or closed off areas such as Fourth, Eighth or Twelfth House placements can give rise to.

Intuition

For *The Instant Astrologer* it was tempting to use the by-line 'Just add intuition'. Whether or not this would have been good or bad taste, it is still true. Astrology without intuition is like mathematics without any sense of the value of numbers, or like following a recipe without any sense of what tastes right. However, the question arises as to what intuition actually is. Intuition is a sense of what is true – and therefore of what shall be – and not to be confused with instinct, which has more to do with a sense of survival. Someone might die for what they believe, or intuit, to be true, whereas instinct is used specifically to avoid dying. In other words, seeing what is written in a Chart for what it is – rather than what you'd like or fear it to be – is the key to intuition. Some people are more intuitive than others because they see the truth of the matter whether they want to or not. Such people usually make the best astrologers. At the same time, studying and using astrology will actually improve your intuition. It will also confront you with choices you made while interpreting a Chart that were wrong because a prejudice jumped in before your intuition – the word does, after all, mean 'pre-judgement'. In fact, prejudice could be said to be *false* intuition. For example, prejudging all attractive people as vain or confident would blind one to the truth of such a person's being.

This is all the more provocative and interesting when considering the theory that the very first idea or impression that one gets is usually the intuitive one, with an instinctive one close behind it (motivated by what we feel is 'safe'), and an intellectual deduction just behind that (motivated by what we think 'makes sense'). This is why, prejudice notwithstanding, people often curse themselves for not listening to their first choice. Likewise, when reading a Profile, your very first impression is probably the right one – again, prejudices notwithstanding! The catch is to not miss yourself actually having that first impression through identifying with the later one which you have been conditioned to believe is preferable, or through succumbing to one's prejudices – which we all have to a degree.

One more point concerning intuition has to do with the note-taking already described. Do not feel confined to keep to the astrological indication you are currently looking at. Allowing one's mind to spread across the page by free association – in words *and* pictures – is what reveals the various connections and themes within the personality you are studying. You might find that your paper is covered in a mass of arrows and jottings, doodles and sketches. To a conventional schoolteacher this might be unacceptable, but to the astrologer's mind this is the very way in which a personality is laid out and works. Also, feel free to pose questions as you go. These will either prove productive to ask the actual person, or the answer will appear later in one's study of the Profile(s). While making notes, it is strongly recommended that you use the ...

Keywords

These, and more about how to use them, are given on pages 553-557. You could call Keywords the Tools of Intuition because they act as a bridge between the pure symbolism that astrology effectively is, and the verbal interpretations.

Personal Advice

The subject of intuition becomes even more critical when or if you use astrology to counsel someone. Studying one or more Profiles by way of preparation for the counselling is obviously necessary, but one should be careful not to 'over-prepare' and get stuck with a 'script' of how we think that person 'works' and therefore how the consultation should go. This blocks intuition. Ultimately, human personality and fate, like life itself, is a mystery. The secret is to hold all the information gleaned from the Profiles in 'intuitive abeyance'. This means to say that you intuit the meaning of the Profile(s) but resist making any hard and fast conclusions. This does not mean to say that you do not have some very firm ideas of what that person is about or where they are at or headed. It is just that you do not deliver them as a *fait accompli*. Instead, it is better to begin with astrologically obvious generalities or a few potent suggestions until you receive a cue to introduce your more profound ideas to the person concerned. Then the way in which they respond to these will give one a further cue as to what is 'hot' and what is 'cold' with respect to your preparations. In other words, an astrological consultation should not be a monologue but a dialogue.

Soul Level

One of the hardest things to determine from a Chart alone is an individual's 'soul level', that is, the stage that they have got to in their individual spiritual awareness and evolution. This is so important because it is the 'inner dwelling being' within, behind, beneath and above the personality that in the end chooses what to do with that personality. On the face of it, the Chart merely describes that, the personality's potentials. For example, an unevolved individual with, say, the Aspect, Mars Square (challenging) Pluto (see pages 142 and 218) in their Chart could express such power psychopathically, whereas another, more evolved being, could express it as a healer, or even as someone who gets murdered in order to draw attention to some important human issue.

Apart from getting to know the individual personally over some period of time ('by their works shall you know them') – or through some more occult means such as the Mayan Sacred Calendar that will describe the type of soul and then enable you to see how well it has chosen its personality by comparing it to their Chart – we can yet again depend upon intuition. This is what the Synthesis does, for it is that inner dwelling being that talks to you through the Chart – or not, as the case may be.

2. THE PERSONALITY PROFILE

The Ruling Planet

This is the Planet that rules the Rising Sign or Ascendant, and is said to rule the Chart as a whole (as distinct from that which rules one's Sun Sign). The only trouble with this is that you do have to be sure that the birth time and therefore the Rising Sign is accurate and correct. If not, commence with resuming Setting The Scene, as given below. *In Bush's case this is quite reliable, and from his appearance quite obvious, that he is Leo Rising. His Ruling Planet is therefore the Sun. As the Ruling Planet stresses the significance and importance of how one's persona and identify find, express and prove themselves, in Bush's case it is through Cancer and the Twelfth House – Securing and Protection of and against the Unseen, and that Security and Protection have something to do with the Collective Unconscious, that he has to accomplish this on a spiritual level, that is, his freedom from Confinement is dependent upon everyone's. Quite a karmic task, Challenged by the Squares his Sun receives from his Moon and Jupiter in Libra, which can be seen as a Great Need for Comfort and the Familiar, the Securities of Home, Mother, Country, and above all To Be Liked. In other words, in order to accomplish his Hero's quest he has to forego these Lunar reassurances, yet at the same time they are the very things he is wanting to bring to the collective. His Sun is also Square his Neptune, which further stresses the spiritual and collective quality of his Purpose and Destiny. His Sun is Afflicted, as it has only Hard Aspects, and so has a fallen or failed hero karma about it.*

Setting The Scene
From **Setting The Scene** in the last chapter, for our example George W Bush (see Chart, Planetary Placements and Aspects on pages 522,524 and 525) we already have some pointers and possible **Themes**. Themes are so important because a Profile can offer such a mass of information that is otherwise hard to get a handle upon. So we recap what we established, and emphasize items to look at closely in the Profile, as well as adding further notes:

1. Elements
Over-Emphasis in Fire = Over-enthusiastic; possible Risk-Taking or Burn-out. Needs to listen to others. It is known that his wife Laura has strong influence over him. Laura Bush was born 4 November 1946 in Midland, Texas. Even with her birth time not known we can see that she has an Over-Emphasis of Fire-compensating WATER in her Chart (Sun, Mars and Jupiter in Scorpio, Moon in Pisces)
Under-Emphasis in Earth = Lack of practicality; poor sense of time (and timing?) According to the Compensation, look at his **Saturn (in Cancer in the Twelfth House)** *and his 2ⁿᵈ, 6ᵗʰ and 10ᵗʰ Houses.* **The only one of these Houses with a Planet in is the 2ⁿᵈ – and it is Mars.**

Element Singleton, Mars – a significant part of his Birth Chart.

2. Modes
Over-Emphasis in Cardinal = Good starter, bad finisher – but is this compensated for by healthy Fixed? Again, the Compensation points to the importance of having/listening to someone you trust. Again, Laura apparently acts as this 'braking influence' as do hopefully a few others.
Under-Emphasis in Mutable = Lack of flexibility; Expects others to adapt. Probably necessary in his job!

But with both Earth and Mutable weak, it makes the Mutable Earth Sign Virgo his **weakest suit,** *that Singleton already strongly noted. This heavily stresses the significance of* **Mars in his Chart.**

Mode Singleton: Mars *again! (with Uranus).*

3. Hemispheres

*Extreme (complete) Over-Emphasis in Eastern = Egocentric; Me, me, me > Need to consider opinions and needs of others; or to rely upon Higher Power/God. Yet again, it stresses the balancing influence of his wife, Laura. Does she compensate for these extremes? Astrologically and historically, it would appear so, as too does God, with Bush's strong Christian beliefs. So the role of Other (***Seventh House***), as the focus of the Western Hemisphere, is a significant compensation for his strong Eastern Hemisphere.*

4. Lunar Nodes

North Node in Gemini in the 11ᵗʰ House = GO ZONE = Politics through Communication
South Node in Sagittarius in the 5ᵗʰ House = SLOW ZONE = Furthering of Self; Gambling; Romance.

*Obviously he has found his way, his 'dharma', with respect to politics, with his ability to communicate surprising quite a few people. One could say he has found his connection with himself. Conversely, his past was rather taken up with having a 'good time', but he turned that around. Whether 'furthering of self' is still more important than the interests of Ideals and the Group (***11ᵗʰ House***) could still be a question.*

So, if GW found he got lost amidst the needs and expectations of Politics and the Group, then pulling back to the Fun and Furtherance of his own Creative Self-expression (Sagittarius/Fifth House) would be necessary, along with the Gamble that this would involve. This is further emphasized by having all that Leo in him, for the Fifth House is the Leo House (as it is the Fifth Sign)

Themes

Going over these notes, as well as emphasizing those astrological features that we want to look at more closely, we can identify issues that predominate – those all-important Themes. These are keys to the 'code-breaking' and so are more likely to get the Chart 'talking' to us.

Theme One

A Theme is already forming of a man who is very self-focussed, taking the initiative, possibly with burning zeal. When the Fire energy has something to burn on it no longer burns out the person. This is why Fire represents Vision and Adventure for it can express itself through them. But there is always that danger of going too far if there is not an equally compensating force or personality. One could also say that he needs or attracts a compensating force, either in the form of support or attack (Seventh House also represents Adversaries – page 35) – Mars?

Mars

Looking at his Personality Profile we see that his Mars is Unaspected – unsure of his masculinity and so possibly overcompensating with macho/warrior-like behaviour. He also is probably quite hard on himself as it is placed in Virgo – and exacting in his expectations regarding his Self-Worth as Mars is placed in the Second House. Whilst reading the Profile we also find out that Mars rules his MidHeaven because it is in Aries. This is all about status and being aggressive in order to prove oneself in the world. A question arises as to motivation here; is he fighting for an ideal or just trying to prove something to himself – or someone else?

Saturn

In his Personality Profile we find this Planet in Cancer in the Twelfth House and, like Mars, Unaspected. This all seems to support the idea of lacking confidence on the inside. This is emphasized by having his all-important Ruling Planet, the Sun (ruler of Leo his Rising Sign) also in this House. Both these Planets have to do with Father and Authority, so one is made to think that he is trying to prove himself to his father, but this might not ever work because it is the 'inner demon' of Saturn in the Twelfth House that he is trying to assuage. And talking of demons brings to mind Adversaries and...

The Seventh House

This is the focus of that compensatory Western Hemisphere. This is his wife Laura with her healthy support and counterbalancing – but it is also the House of Adversaries. Reading the Ascendant Profile we learn that the Seventh House cusp or Descendant is in Aquarius and that this refers us to that Sign's Rulers, Saturn and Uranus. Saturn we have already 'underlined' – and what it said in the Twelfth House concerning the need to depend upon a Higher Power rings a bell. GW is quite religious – Heavenly Father? And the Seventh House, being the House of the Projected Self, suggests that his inner demon (Saturn in the Twelfth) is projected onto someone or something else. But it (the Twelfth House) also refers to being open to unseen forces – who or what could that be? Hmmm. Is he his own man? Reading the Leo Ascendant and First House Planets in Leo (Mercury, Venus and Pluto) also stresses that confident exterior hiding a diffident interior (Twelfth House). But let's look at Uranus, which as it happens is in that other astro-factor we noted

The Eleventh House

This is the House of the North Node and Uranus. If you are technically or mathematically inclined you will note that they are very close (Conjunct) to one another. Uranus is the Rebel (see Keywords on page 555) and the Adversary (ruler of the Seventh House). From this it is again apparent that, psychologically speaking, GW is taking on his own Projected Self (Seventh House) which is felt by him as something trying to overthrow his own established order, which he feels is threatened – but truly this is **from within** (Twelfth House stuff). Destroy one outer demon and there will just be another and another outer *demon, ad nauseam, confronting him to be killed. This is like the Hydra, the many-headed serpent of Greek myth that Hercules had to slay. Symbolically, this is saying that the hero has to destroy his inner monster/demon in order to destroy the outer one, rather than pointlessly enduring the endless and exhausting task of trying to destroy the outer demon. This is like trying a new mirror because you don't like what you see in the old one. Interestingly, a sea-crab was sent to nip at his feet to hamper him in his attempts, but he despatched this also. Consequently, in honour of this, the crab was made into a constellation, Cancer, Bush's own Sun Sign. This means that he will succeed as long as he does not allow his Cancerian ego to dog his footsteps. It should not be overlooked that with his Uranus and North Node Conjunct to within one degree in the Eleventh House (Uranus's own) that his destiny is very much one of liberation. But it raises this whole philosophical question of genuinely freeing one's inner self or simply making a show of being a 'liberator' – welcome as that may or may not be.*

Theme Two
This is the unsure, very introspective person that he does not appear to be. His Pluto in the First House also lends weight to this astrological perception of his personality.

Theme Three
This is around his Moon, Jupiter, Uranus, Venus configuration (they all harmoniously Aspect one another and form a flat triangle (see the Aspect lines in the centre of the Chart – called a Mitre). This is all part of that very secure and self-assured, Texan, strong mother, moneyed, ex-president father, background. The House of Background, the Fourth, is ruled by Venus (see Lower MidHeaven, i.e. the Fourth House cusp, in his MidHeaven Profile), which in his Chart has only Soft (harmonious) Aspects – that is **Blessed.**

Themes One, Two and Three
Bush is triple-layered it would seem.

Outer layer: very confident, even vain (Theme One)
Middle layer: also very confident due to background (Theme Three)
Inner layer: very unsure and insecure (Theme Two). This is the part that, if he were 'in the chair', I would be focussing upon.
We will now employ another method of Synthesis …

The Holy Trinity
The 'Holy Trinity' is the three most important parts of a Birth Chart, namely:

> The Sun (Individuality – Father – Present) Chapter Two in Profile
> The Moon (Personality – Mother – Past) Chapter Three in Profile
> The Ascendant (Identity – Child – Future) Chapter One in Profile

Try to blend these Profiles together, imagine how they would interact. First consider the Sign positions, and in the case of the Sun and Moon, the House positions too, and any

Planets in the First House (as the Ascendant is the cusp of the First House).

In our example, GW has Sun in Cancer in the Twelfth House; Moon in Libra in the Third House; Ascendant in Leo. Here is someone whose main drive is towards Security and Protection (Cancer) particularly with regard to that which is Unseen (Twelfth House). Security (Moon) is sought through Being Liked (Libra) by those in his Everyday Life (Third House). The 'product' of this is a Sunny Exterior that Impresses (Leo) is Attractive (Venus in First House), Chatty/Talkative (Mercury in First House) but also Concealing (Pluto in the First House) of what is going on inside – the Unseen Realm (Twelfth House) where his Sun is placed.

This recalls or conforms the earlier intuitive sense that he was, karmically, a Hero who fell from grace 'previously' and that he is now trying to redeem himself. This he is doing by playing to the gallery, going with popular opinion and conforming to a gung-ho Hollywood hero image. The question arises as to whether this is the right way to redemption – or is it just making the same old mistake (See Ruling Planet above)? Nevertheless, he is embodying the archetype of American Hero, just when his country needs one following September 11th (see page 558). But is such a hero effective, any more than playing such a role is going to bring him what he is really after at a deep level – that redemption? Then again, maybe he is, for George W Bush is far more introspective than he appears to be, than his 'look at me and like me' persona would have one recognize. If he was 'in the chair' then I daresay I could get 'in there' and find out. But as he is not it is a case of time alone doing the telling.

Already we can see how this is supporting or confirming our findings with respect to those three Themes. This is so very important – these are the voices talking most loudly to us! Now let's look at the Aspects involved:

Solar Aspects

His Sun is Square to the Moon, Jupiter and Neptune – with no other Aspects. These are all Hard Aspects (see page 36) which makes his Sun what is called **Afflicted**. *An Afflicted Planet – that is, one receiving only Hard Aspects – is stressed and unstable (at least at first) and so more liable to behave negatively or attract negative experiences. As it is Sun in the Twelfth House, we could say that Protection (Cancer) from Unseen forces (Twelfth) is a critical, possibly neurotic, issue. We could also say that Unseen Protection figured somewhere too. The Square from his Moon in Libra would mean his need for things to be 'nice' would strongly contribute to this dilemma. This all further confirms Theme Two above, the inwardly unsure GW and his 'fallen hero' karma.*

Lunar Aspects

This is already covered by, and confirms, Theme Two above. This is a far easier place for him 'to be' than with that Sun in the Twelfth House. When his Hero received the 'call' on 11 September it was then that this Lunar, comfy/folksy, part of him wanted to run for cover. But it is evident that his Solar self rallied and responded to that call.

First House Planet Aspects

In addition to what we have already covered that parallels Themes One and Three, there is the Conjunct of Mercury and Pluto (see pages 109 & 217) which distinctly refers to the possessing of secret information. In his job as President of the United States of America, seemingly the most powerful man in the world, this is not surprising. Yet it also suggests that there is powerful and secret information that he will always be after, that is unknown to him. This is possibly why he gives the (mistaken) impression of being 'intellectually challenged'. His Chart says quite emphatically that he is not 'challenged' in this sense, but that he is challenged to transcend a mindset that is limited by his own inner self-doubt, which is in fact what is seen as being 'dumb'. It is not dumbness, just his own inner struggle (Sun in the Twelfth House) on display (Leo Rising).

What further conclusions can be drawn from this and from reading the rest of his Personality Profile are left to you, dear astrological seeker, dear planetary detective.

A Heading at the Top of the Page

Now as we get to the end of our Synthesis, we should endeavour to find a phrase that should begin to act as a heading that sums up the character and life so far of the person concerned.

I think, in GW's case, this could be (and note the question mark):

TWENTY-FIRST CENTURY AMERICAN HERO?

3. THE TIMELINE PROFILE

Looking at the Timeline for the period during which you are looking at a Chart is absolutely essential. Not only is it necessary in order to relate to where that person is at right there and then, but it also enables one to get a closer fix on the meanings of the Planets on their Personality Profile itself.

In our Example (see his Graphic Transits for 2003 opposite), GW has, at the time of writing – beginning of the Second Gulf War, March/April 2003 – two 'very strong influences', Jupiter Conjunct (intensifying) Pluto and Jupiter Conjunct (intensifying) Mercury – and one 'strong influence', Pluto Opposition (confronting) Uranus.

It can be seen from the Themes of the Jupiter influences or Transits that 'a powerful emphasis' is upon his Mercury and Pluto. This alludes to what we have looked at above, namely the 'secret information' – which it would seem has a lot to do with what he himself does not know (Where is Saddam Hussein? Where is Osama bin Laden? Where are Iraq's weapons of mass destruction, etc). These 'mysteries' are also written in his ongoing Neptune Opposition (confronting) Mercury and Pluto during late 2002/early 2003 and for the second half of 2003. From a psychological point of view, however, the real 'secret' is who George W Bush actually is! His heavily Transited Pluto is in his First House, which is all about an ongoing identity crisis.

George W Bush
Born Saturday 6 July 1946 07.26
New Haven, Connecticut 41N18 72W55

Year Transits from January 2003

2003			Jan	Feb	Mar	Apr	May	Jun	Jul	Aug	Sep	Oct	Nov	Dec
Jup	Tri	MC												
Sat	Sxt	MC												
Jup	Cnj	ASC												
Jup	Sxt	Sun												
Jup	Sxt	Moo												
Jup	Cnj	Mer												
Jup	Cnj	Ven												
Jup	Cnj	Mar												
Jup	Sxt	Jup												
Jup	Sqr	Ura												
Jup	Sxt	Ura												
Jup	Cnj	Plu												
Sat	Cnj	Sun												
Sat	Sxt	Ven												
Sat	Sxt	Mar												
Sat	Sqr	Nep												
Nep	Opp	Mer												
Nep	Opp	Plu												
Plu	Sxt	Moo												
Plu	Tri	Ven												
Plu	Sxt	Jup												
Plu	Opp	Ura												

The Pluto Transit to that other key Planet in his Chart, Uranus, is saying that the Adversary/Rebel is being confronted with Power (Pluto), with the whole issue of that 'inner demon' being intensified, as is Pluto's wont (see page 363). It remains to be seen what will ultimately be exposed.

Taking all of these powerful Transits (and the Personality Profile) into consideration, is it possible that something very dramatic and earth-shattering is to be revealed – to himself and/or the world at large – during 2003, particularly come August when he has Transiting Mars Opposition (confronting) Mars? Because Mars goes 'stationary' at this time, it'll last longer than the usual 3-5 days. So will this, for our 'American Hero', be his 'Gunfight at the OK Corral'? As it happens – and quite appropriately for someone whose fate is so bound up with the collective – August 2003 promises to be monumental in some way that also has to do with that 'secret information' which his Chart keeps pointing to.

4. THE RELATIONSHIP PROFILE

Laura, the wife of our example, G W Bush, is of unknown birth time, so we will calculate her Chart for noon, as is the rule (remembering to disregard the positions of her Ascendant and MidHeaven, all her House positions, and that the Moon's position will only be approximate). As stated above, this is 4 November 1946 in Midland, Texas, and gives her the following...

Planetary Placements

Planet/Point	Glyph	Sign	Glyph	Position	House
Sun	☉	Scorpio	♏	11°43'	10th
Moon	☽	Pisces	♓	11°40'	2nd
Mercury	☿	Sagittarius	♐	04°44'	11th
Venus	♀	Sagittarius	♐	01°20'R	10th
Mars	♂	Scorpio	♏	28°33'	10th
Jupiter	♃	Scorpio	♏	08°38'	9th
Saturn	♄	Leo	♌	08°39'	7th
Uranus	♅	Gemini	♊	21°12'	5th
Neptune	♆	Libra	♎	09°33'	9th
Pluto	♇	Leo	♌	13°20'	7th
Ascendant	AS	Capricorn	♑	14°56'	⌢
MidHeaven	MC	Scorpio	♏	03°31'	⌢
North Node	☊	Gemini	♊	12°08'	5th

On creating their Relationship Profile we see from the Inter-Aspects that over half of these (the valid ones for her unknown birth time) are Close Ones. This marks a strong, close relationship right away. Here we will compile a brief Synthesis drawn mainly from certain Close Ones and any Double Whammies. Make a point to read all these Inter-Aspects onscreen or here in the book.

Key Connections

GW's all-important Leo Stellium (star-cluster) of Mercury, Ascendant and Pluto, which we focussed on strongly in his Personality Profile above, makes a Close One Conjunct to Laura's Saturn. So that fiery
and historically troublesome part for him is disciplined, stabilized and matured by Laura – something to which he is probably the first to admit and be thankful for. This could be regarded as the most key of all the Key Connections and of the whole Relationship Profile therefore. The 'child' is taken in hand. It is not what one would call a romantic contact, but probably just right for a president and first lady. Then again, with this Key Connection being placed in Leo, it could well have a romantic connotation, but in quite a serious 'royal' way.

Relationship Challenges

GW's Pluto Square (challenging) her Sun is a tough one that can easily lead to a break-up – and they must have come quite close at some time. But as we will see in the Relationship Strengths, this one was taken care of.

The real 'terror' amongst the Challenges though, is his 'weak Mars' Opposition (confronting) her Moon. Despite her unknown birth time it is fairly safe to say that her Moon is a strong Planet in her Chart as it is Trine her Sun and Jupiter both. She has enormous inner (emotional/Water) confidence whereas GW does not. GW as we have seen has a strong persona (Leo stuff) but she apparently does not. Anyhow, because of her strong Moon and his weak Mars she would probably have won out in the battles that this Inter-Aspect guarantees!

Relationship Strengths

What ameliorates the above two Challenges are, firstly, GW's Sun Trine (harmonizing with) her Sun very closely, and probably Trine her Moon as well. These Planets fall in all the three Water Signs, that is, Cancer (his Sun), Scorpio (her Sun and Jupiter) and Pisces (her Moon). Furthermore GW's Unaspected Saturn in Cancer is Trine her Mars in Scorpio. The Water set-up is very strong in their relationship, making for profound emotional depth and intimacy – quite enough to put out any dangerous Fire! And, secondly, GW's troublesome Mars is Trine her Jupiter, so she would encourage and guide his actions and masculinity considerably.

There is also a Double Whammy of his Mercury Sextile (assisting) her Neptune and of her Mercury Sextile (assisting) his Neptune. Furthermore, they are almost both Close Ones. The key phrase of this Inter-Aspect is **Telepathically Attuned**, and so provides them with an extremely fine mutual understanding.

From perusing all of the Inter-Aspects there is not, as initially inferred, a great romantic thing going on here, although it is possibly romantic in the truer, heroic sense of the word. When all is said and done his Venus Sextile (assisting) her Uranus, the **Friendly Lovers**, is probably what sums them up as a healthy and longstanding relationship.

APPENDIX

1. TABLE OF CORRESPONDENCES

SUN	MOON	MERCURY	VENUS	MARS	JUPITER	SATURN	URANUS	NEPTUNE	PLUTO
Hot/Radiant	Cool/Receptive	Mutable	Warm/Soft	Hot/Sharp	Gaseous	Solid	Electric	Fluid	Nuclear
Spirit	Nature	Neutral	Feminine	Masculine	Sky	Land	Space	Ocean	Underworld
Life	Form	Connection	Magnetism	Dynamism	Scope	Boundaries	Infinity	Boundlessness	Intensity
Will	Feeling	Thinking	Attraction	Courage	Faith	Practicality	Intuition	Sensitivity	Insight
Creativity	Nurture	Reason	Aesthetics	Drive	Enterprise	Status	Progress	Universality	Fate
Fathering	Mothering	Communicating	Relating	Desiring	Expanding	Ordering	Awakening	Dissolving	Transforming
Dominating	Smothering	Over-analyzing	Seducing	Forcing	Overreaching	Suppressing	Disrupting	Undermining	Destroying
Governmental	Domestic	Commercial	Artistic	Military	Religious	Political	Esoteric	Spiritual	Occult
King/Hero	Queen/Heroine	Merchant/Scribe	Artist	Soldier	Priest	President	Inventor/Rebel	Musician/Mystic	Shaman/Healer°
LEO	CANCER	GEMINI VIRGO	TAURUS LIBRA	ARIES (SCORPIO)	SAGITTARIUS (PISCES)	CAPRICORN (AQUARIUS)	AQUARIUS	PISCES	SCORPIO
5th House	4th House	3rd & 6th Houses	2nd & 7th Houses	1st (& 8th) House	9th (& 12th) House	10th(& 11th) House	11th House	12th House	8th House

This Table serves to show the **interrelated structure** of astrological symbolism, the 'As Above So Below' of it all. Note that the Signs and Houses* given at the bottom of the Table are the ones ruled (or that used to be) by the Planet above it at the top of the table, because their qualities correspond to the nature of the Planet. Just pondering this Table of Correspondences should quite naturally in-form your mind, programming astrological thinking into it. To the same end, try this …

Correspondence Test
Think of anything you like (animal, vegetable, mineral, abstract) and then attempt to establish what Planet corresponds to it or rules it. 'Reading' or 'telephone' would be … Mercury. 'Epilepsy' would be … Uranus. It may be a combination of two or more Planets – like

'Unconditional love'? Neptune and Venus. Or a 'novelist' would be Mercury and Venus – and the Sun too, and if they were inspired and inspiring, Neptune would have to be there. 'Black humour'? Mercury, Uranus and Pluto? A 'writer of cookery books' would be Mercury and the Moon.

°Healing can apply to all the all three Outer Planets because they are all Transformative. However, Pluto is probably the most profoundly healing for it gets to the very root of a problem with great power and intensity.

*These are the generic House Rulers as distinct from the personal Rulers of these Houses (see 'Ruling Planet' in Glossary).

2. KEYWORDS

'PLANETS shine through SIGNS and live in HOUSES'

Remembering the above motto for keyword use, and having created a **Personality Profile** (or just a Birth Chart), we can employ the selection of keywords given on the next three pages to construct key phrases that describe and confirm known facets of personality, or we can use them to gain new insights into certain areas of personality. When doing this, bear in mind that you may need to 'turn' the keywords to get them to open the 'door' to meaning. So, for example, to someone with, say, Venus in Taurus in the Fifth House, we could turn a keyword like 'dance' (Venus) into 'dancer' or 'dancing' (because we know that that is what they are or do). Then joining that to the Taurus keyword 'sensually' and the Fifth House keyword the 'Stage', we get 'dancing sensually on the stage'. If, however, we were looking at Venus in Taurus in the Second House, we could choose 'dancing steadily income' turning it to 'dancing earned a steady income' or 'steadily the dancer made more money'.

You can have fun playing with keywords, tapping into meanings and quickening insights and solutions from out of your imagination, as well as maximizing opportunities and realizing potential. You can also use it for a **Timeline Profile** (in addition to using Transcan on page 380). For instance, right now I have Neptune Trine (supporting) Uranus, and my Uranus is in my Eleventh House. So I can then say that 'inspiration' (Neptune keyword) is supporting 'astrology' (Uranus) 'aspirations and goals' (Eleventh House). This really is *using* the Planets through the Signs in the Houses.

And we can use them with a **Relationship Profile** too. Say, for example, there is someone I am considering going into a venture with, who has their Saturn in Aries Conjunct (uniting with) my Moon in Aries in the Tenth House. This could be seen as their 'maturity' (Saturn) uniting with my 'child' (Moon), that is, their experience or position could meet my 'needs' (Moon), and in a forceful (Aries) manner, and thereby 'push' (Aries) my career or 'profession' (Tenth House). Yet at the same time I should be wary that they could be 'controlling' (Saturn) if I was too 'receptive' (Moon) to their 'forcefulness' (Aries).

Using keywords is rather like gaining a sense of the energies in play – whether in your own or someone else's personality, as a planetary influence happening at a certain time, or between two people. One then goes with it, but with a weather eye as to how those energies begin to take form. Back to the personality-as-sailboat metaphor used earlier, you gain an idea of the nature of the boat and the type of wind and conditions (and shipmates), and you set your sails and steer accordingly.

PLANETS – THE 'WHAT' OF ASTROLOGY

These Keywords are in the form of nouns as Planets describe ENERGIES, as things or beings, abstract or concrete, which find expression through the Sign and House in which they placed.

SUN	MOON	MERCURY	VENUS	MARS	JUPITER	SATURN	URANUS	NEPTUNE	PLUTO
Actor	Boat	Agent	Affection	Aggression	Abundance	Affliction	Abortion	Addiction	Atom
Aristocracy	Body	Breathing	Art	Anger	Academia	Age/Maturity	Alien(ation)	Asylum	Darkness
Back/Spine	Care	Calculation	Artist	Assertion	Advertisement	Authority	Alternatives	Atonement	Death
Blood	Child	Clerk	Beauty	Athlete	Belief	Coldness	Astrology	Conscience	Decay
Braggart	Comfort	Cleverness	Charm	Boy	Benevolence	Control	Aviation	Deception	Depth
Chief	Family	Communi-cation	Dance	Brutality	Church	Denial	Awakening	Escape	Destiny/Fate
Ego	Feelings		Erotica	Champion	Dogma	Discipline	Computers	Fantasy	Entropy
Energy	Female	Critic/Editor	Fancy	Conflict	Enterprise	Duty	Electricity	Healer	Espionage

Fame	Habits	Curiosity	Fashion	Conqueror	Excess	Fear	Engineer	Illusions	Evil
Father	Heroine	Dilettante	Flowers	Danger	Faith	Firmness	Explosion	Imagination	Extremism
Gambler	Home	Duplication	Gifts	Energy (raw)	General	Guilt	Fool	Insanity	Fiend
Generosity	Memory	Education	Girl	Exercise	God	Inadequacy	Freedom	Inspiration	Hell/Horror
Glory	Moods	Guide	Harmony	Fever	Goddess	Judgement	Intuition	Music	Intimacy
Gold	Mother	Insomnia	Indulgence	Fighter	Greatness	Learning	Inventor	Mystery	Intrigue
Heart	Nature	Intellect	Leisure	Force	Large things	Limitation	Magician	Mystic	Monster
Hero	Needs	Merchant	Love	Go-getter	Law	Materialism	Original	Peace	Obsession
King	Nourishment	Messenger	Lover	Hardness	Luxury	Mistrust	Outcast	Poetry	Occult
Life	Past	Nerves	Money	Heat	Organizer	Misuse	Outsider	Redemption	Power
Light	Phases	Reason	Ornament	Leader	Over-optimism	Objectivity	Paradox	Sacrifice	Psychology
Male	Predisposition	Senses	Pleasure	Pioneer	Philanthropist	Politician	Rebel	Sailor	Purging
Peacock	Princess	Thinker	Poise	Red(ness)	Philosopher	Pressure	Reform	Saviour	Secrecy
Prana	Queen	Trader	Relationship	Sharps	Prayer	Reality	Revolution	Sea	Sexuality
Pride	Response	Traveller	Sensuality	Strife	Preacher	Restriction	Science	Softening	Shaman
Prince	Reaction	Vehicle	Singing	Suitor	Priest	Rigidity	Shock	Spirituality	Sin
Radiance	Receptivity	Villain	Society	Tools	Priestess	Stability	Spasm	Suffering	Sorcerer
Ruler	Safety	Wit	Superficiality	Violence	Promise	Structure	Sudden	Surrender	Taboo
Spirit	Security	Words	Value	War	Prophet	Tests	Symbols	Undermining	Underworld
Star	Soul	Work	Vanity	Warrior	Providence	Trust	Truth	Vagueness	Vice
Vitality	Womb/Matrix	Writer	Vocal tone	Weapons	Wastrel	Weakness	Unusual	Victim	Wealth

SIGNS – THE 'HOW' OF ASTROLOGY

These Keywords are in the form of verbs or adverbs as Signs describe WAYS that qualify the expression of whatever Planet is placed in a particular Sign. Character traits are secondary to these because they are what are created by the combination of Planet in Sign. Characteristics merely characterize, and can become static, redundant, if not seen for what they are: the manifestation of qualified energy.

ARIES	TAURUS	GEMINI	CANCER	LEO	VIRGO
Actively	Crafting	Amusing	Accommodating	Acting	Analyzing
Championing	Cultivating	Communicating	Brooding	Boasting	Discerning
Courageously	Indulging	Connecting	Carefully	Confidently	Distilling
Dangerously	Lazing	Curiously	Catering	Creating	Healthily
Directly	Persevering	Dabbling	Gestating	Dominating	Improving
Doing	Possessing	Diversifying	Indirectly	Dramatizing	Industriously
Forcefully	Producing	Easily	Maternally	Entertaining	Purifying
Impatiently	Relishing	Flirting	Nurturing	Illuminating	Resolving
Impulsively	Sensually	Informing	Protecting	Patronizing	Serving
Independently	Slowly	Interesting	Reacting	Playing	Studying
Pushing	Stabilizing	Networking	Receptively	Radiantly	Training
Questing	Steadily	Skimming	Securing	Romantically	Withdrawing
Straightforwardly	Stubbornly	Splitting	Sympathetically	Ruling	Worrying

LIBRA	SCORPIO	SAGITTARIUS	CAPRICORN	AQUARIUS	PISCES
Allying	Coercing	Advertizing	Building	Civilizing	Addictively
Arbitrating	Covertly	Confronting	Climbing	Co-operatively	Dissolving
Artistically	Delving	Envisioning	Conforming	Cryptically	Eluding
Balancing	Desiring	Excessively	Controlling	Democratically	Escaping
Beautifying	Eliminating	Experiencing	Enduring	Humanly	Fascinating
Fashionably	Extremely	Exploring	Establishing	Innovating	Inspiring
Gracefully	Intensely	Furthering	Limiting	Liberating	Relieving
Harmonizing	Intimately	Galloping	Load-bearing	Paradoxically	Sacrificing
Nicely	Obsessively	Intuiting	Ordering	Reforming	Sensitively
Refining	Penetrating	Judging	Organizing	Refreshing	Soothing
Relating	Powerfully	Philosophizing	Presiding	Theorizing	Spiritualizing
Superficially	Sexually	Preaching	Restricting	Uniquely	Subtly
Vacillating	Transforming	Travelling	Setting	Unusually	Surrendering

HOUSES – THE 'WHERE' OF ASTROLOGY

These Keywords are in the form of nouns as Houses describe STATES, STAGES, PLACES, SITUATIONS or CONCEPTS where or through which the energy of the Planets, qualified by the Signs, are experienced, expressed or take form.

FIRST	SECOND	THIRD	FOURTH	FIFTH	SIXTH
Appearance	Self-worth	Breathing	Ancestors	Children	Apprenticeship
Attitude	Finances	Commerce	Buildings	Creativity/Art	Assimilation
Beginning	Earning power	Communication	Buried	Display	Cleaning
Birth	Income	Education	Devas	Fun & Games	Co-workers
Character	Property	Everyday thinking/life	Foundation	Gambling	Efficiency
Early environment	Talents	Media	Ground	Hobbies & Pastimes	Employment/Job
Eyes	Storage	Neighbours	Home/Family	Passions	Health
First impression	Accountancy	Nervous system	Inner/private life	Recreation/Vacation	Method
Identity	Bank	Routine	Mines	Romance/affairs	Pets
Persona	Ownership	Siblings	Nature	Self-expression	Preparation/Sorting
Physical body	Voice	Tracks & Ways	Parent (weaker)	Speculation	Psyche><Soma
Self	Material value	Travel (short distance)	Roots/Gene pool	Stage, the	Service/Agents
Window-on-world	Shopping	Vehicles	Subjectivity	Teaching	Welfare

SEVENTH	EIGHTH	NINTH	TENTH	ELEVENTH	TWELFTH
Adversaries	Contracts	Adventure	Achievement	Aspirations/Goals	Asylum
Alter ego	Death	Animals (large)	Authority	Associates	Collective Unconscious
Balancing factor	Divorce	Education (higher)	Celebrity	Brother/Sisterhood	Confinement
Better half	Hidden/Secret life	Foreign matters	Employer	Civilization	Conscience
Marriage	Intimacy	Higher Ground	Fame/Reputation	Clubs & Societies	Divine, the
Opposition	Joint ownership	Law	Objectivity	Friends	Institution/Hospital
Others	Occult	Morality	Outer life/world	Groups	Karma/Past
Partner	Other Side, the	Philosophy	Parent (dominant)	Hopes	Previous existence
Projected self	Property of others	Publishing	Profession/Vocation	Humanity	Subconscious
Public	Soul	Religion	Public Image/life	Ideals	Suppression
Relationships	Taxes/Inheritance	Ritual	State, the	Movements	Unlived life
Society	Transformation	Seeking	Status/Position	Politics	Unseen Realm
Strangers	Union/Sex	Travel (long distance)	Superiors	Science	Womb

3. SEPTEMBER 11th

This profound history-making event (11 September 2001 at 8.46 a.m. in New York City) was the focus of a major astrological configuration that was occurring from mid-2001 to mid-2002. This was Pluto in Sagittarius Opposition Saturn in Gemini. As can be seen from this graphic of the glyphs, the attack on the twin-towers of the World Trade Center by flying objects was astrologically represented in a frighteningly literal way.

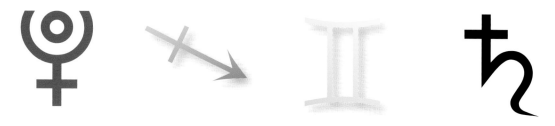

Pluto in Sagittarius Opposition (confronting) Saturn in Gemini

Using Keywords from the lists beginning on page 553 and from the Table of Correspondences on page 552, and then using Synthesis (page 537), we can see further into the meaning of this:

Pluto is *extremism, fiend, destroying* in (qualified by) Sagittarius, which is *religion, preaching, judging.*

Opposition is *confronting* and thereby *increasing awareness of two opposing factors*, of each other and themselves.

Saturn is *structure, materialism, authority* in (qualified by) Gemini, which is *commercial, reason, duality.*

From the impartial viewpoint that astrology engenders (and which the astrologer must endeavour to cultivate) it is borne in mind that Opposition only comes about because of two opposing viewpoints. And of course it goes both ways, with *deep religious convictions* (Pluto in Sagittarius) feeling opposed by the *control of materialism and commercialism* (Saturn in Gemini). Opposition is the demonstration that there are two sides to any whole. The trouble is that in human terms this too often leads to a dichotomy as opposed to an appreciation that it is differences that are integral to the making up of that whole. But you can see how this statement is a dichotomy in itself – the parts and the whole, which are in fact represented, respectively, by Gemini and Sagittarius. So this could be regarded as an Opposition within an Opposition, manifested by the presence of these two powerful Planets in these two Signs, which are in themselves both binary (see page 538).

Opposition also raises the issue of Projection (see Glossary), particularly where one party projects their desires and fears on to another, opposing, party. Essentially this Opposition between Gemini and Sagittarius is the age-old one of the *secular* versus the *religious*. Saturn is also secular in quality, so taking that end of the spectrum to its extreme. Pluto being the extreme anyway – which can be seen as Fate itself 'upping the ante' – drastically increases this polarization. Looking purely at the two Planets involved we can look at this polarity as *land* (Saturn) versus *underworld* (Pluto), or *suppressing* versus *destroying* – what feels downtrodden rises up from the *depths* to *destroy* the perceived *suppresser*, while the suppresser tries to bury or keep buried what it does not want to see.

In other words, September 11th was a fated event created by this enormous build-up of Opposition. The questions it poses are: Can we find a way of accepting and balancing out extremes of opinion, lifestyle and status? Can the 'haves' surrender their material control for the good of the whole? Can the 'have nots' take back their envy and resentment that they project upon the 'haves' under the guise of religious self-righteousness?

When all is said and done all these questions can only find an answer and resolution in one's own heart and mind. If you have an attachment to *material control*, or envy or resentment towards someone or something, then in effect you are contributing to the collective human problem for the simple reason that this is created by each and every individual human being. War-mongers must look to their own inner conflict; peace-marchers must find their own inner peace.

Astrology shows us how things are. Whenever there is Saturn Opposition Pluto (around every 34 years) there is a *power struggle* of some kind, according to the two Signs involved and any other concurrent planetary configurations. But the struggle – as every individual Birth Chart will tell you – is always and ultimately within. As far as Gemini and Sagittarius themselves are concerned there is no conflict, just polarity; and regarding Saturn and Pluto, they are just two lords of two intimately connected realms that, apart from the occasional earthquake and volcano, co-exist very well. But then again, using this telluric scenario as an analogy, that is in essence what September 11th was: a human earthquake or volcano releasing tensions and hidden, repressed material, with commensurate aftershocks and fall-out, contributing hopefully to a increased awareness that all of us are living on the same Planet, Earth.

4. GLOSSARY

AFFLICTED PLANET – A Planet that has only *HARD ASPECTS* from other Planets and as such renders the experience and expression of it negative, very difficult, neurotic or anti-social. Resolving the problem is best done by first being acutely aware of what it means in one's personality, and ultimately by expressing its qualities in a spiritual way. The opposite of a *BLESSED PLANET*.

AGE OF AQUARIUS – The *ASTROLOGICAL AGE* we are just entering, which is concerned with an awakening to the truth – especially regarding humanity and human nature, and which is necessarily disruptive. During this time we will increasingly free ourselves from the fears and illusions that have dogged humanity for so long (especially during the preceding Piscean Age), eventually giving rise to a peak in civilization.

ANGLES – Collective name for the *ASCENDANT, DESCENDANT, MIDHEAVEN* and *LOWER MIDHEAVEN*. Effectively the 'cross we bear'.

ASC or AS – Glyph/abbreviation of *ASCENDANT*.

ASCENDANT – The Eastern Horizon or point in a *BIRTH CHART* where the *PLANETS* and *SIGNS* are seen to rise. Also the First *HOUSE CUSP*. The Sign on the Ascendant at any given time is called the *RISING SIGN*.

ASPECT – A certain angular relationship between one *PLANET* and another. Aspects occur (1) between the *PLANETS* in an individual's *BIRTH CHART*, (2) between one Birth Chart and another *(INTER-ASPECTS)*, and (3) between the Planets passing through the sky at any given time, called *TRANSITS*, and the Planets in a Birth Chart. The ASPECTS used in this book are: *CONJUNCT* (0° between one Planet and another); *SQUARE* (90°); *OPPOSITION* (180°); *TRINE* (120°); *SEXTILE* (60°) – all within a particular *ORB*.

ASSISTING – Key phrase used for *SEXTILE*.

ASTROLOGICAL AGE – A 2160-year period of time which is governed by a certain *SIGN*, the quality of which determines the character of this evolutionary era. See also *AGE OF AQUARIUS*.

BIRTH CHART – A map of where the *PLANETS*, *SIGNS* and *HOUSES* are positioned at the time of birth. One's *CELESTIAL BLUEPRINT*.

BLESSED PLANET – A Planet that has only *SOFT ASPECTS* from other Planets and as such renders the experience and expression of it positive and relaxed, conferring talents and good fortune – but can incline one to laziness and apathy. The opposite of an *AFFLICTED PLANET*.

CELESTIAL BLUEPRINT – Poetic name for *BIRTH CHART*.

CHALLENGING – Keyword used for *SQUARE*.

CHARTWHEEL – The actual graphic of a *BIRTH CHART*.

CLOSE ONES* – *INTER-ASPECTS* that are within 3 degrees of exact and are deemed to form the central core of the chemistry between two people.

COMPENSATING ELEMENT* – That *ELEMENT* that compensates for *UNDER-EMPHASIS* in another.

COMPENSATION – What astrologer Liz Greene called the commonest human psychological trait, it describes how we respond to characteristics in others or ourselves by going to the opposite extreme. For example, one might feel shy or under pressure and compensate by being very bold and extrovert. Also, how one is liable to over-emphasize, or feel as over-emphasized, traits in one's *BIRTH CHART* that are in need of developing or overhauling.

CONFRONTING – Keyword used for *OPPOSITION*.

CONJOINING – Verb form of *CONJUNCT*.

CONJUNCT – One of the *ASPECTS* or *INTER-ASPECTS*. It intensifies the issues relevant to the *PLANETS* involved. Also called a *RETURN* when occurring as a *TRANSITING PLANET CONJOINING* the same *NATAL PLANET*, calling for some new form of expression or point of departure. For example, when Saturn *CONJOINS* itself after completing its 29.5-year orbit around the Sun, it is also said to be making its *RETURN*.

CONJUNCTION – Same as *CONJUNCT*.

CO-OPERATING WITH – Key phrase used for *SEXTILEE*.

CROSS-ASPECTS – Another name for *INTER-ASPECTS*.

CUSP – The boundary line between – and so therefore the end and beginning of – one *SIGN* or *HOUSE* and the next. See also *ASCENDANT, DESCENDANT, MIDHEAVEN* and *LOWER MIDHEAVEN*.

DAYLIGHT SAVING TIME (DST) – A *TIME STANDARD* that many countries adopt during the summer months to give more daylight at the end of the day by putting the clocks forward an hour. This always needs to be taken into consideration for the accurate calculation of a *BIRTH CHART*. Because this can vary from year to year, from place to place, this can be quite disconcerting and has been called the 'astrologer's bane' (at least, before modern computer software).

DES or DS – Glyph/abbreviation of *DESCENDANT*.

DESCENDANT – The Western Horizon or point in a *BIRTH CHART* where the *PLANETS* and *SIGNS* are seen to set. Also the Seventh *HOUSE CUSP*. The *SIGN* on the Descendant at any given time is called the *SETTING SIGN* and is always exactly opposite the *ASCENDANT* or *RISING SIGN*.

DIRECT – The usual, forward motion of a *PLANET* through the *ZODIAC* – as distinct from *RETROGRADE* or *STATIONARY*.

DOUBLE WHAMMIES – When you get the same *INTER-ASPECT* going both ways, for example, when you get *PERSON A*'s Venus *CONJUNCT PERSON B*'s Mars, and vice versa, that is, *PERSON B*'s Venus is *CONJUNCT PERSON A*'s Mars; this is a Double Whammy. This makes the meaning of this *INTER-ASPECT* especially significant and powerful in that relationship.

DRAGON'S HEAD – Another name for the North NODE of the Moon.

DRAGON'S TAIL – Another name for the South NODE of the Moon.

ELEMENTS – The four basic qualities of life: Fire, Earth, Air and Water.

GO-ZONE* – Fruitful area of experience represented by the North *NODE* of the Moon.

HARD ASPECTS – *ASPECTS or INTER-ASPECTS* which bring tension, conflict, challenge or confrontation to an individual or relationship, namely the *SQUARE, OPPOSITION* and some *CONJUNCTS*.

HARMONIZING – Keyword used for *TRINE*.

HEMISPHERE – The Eastern, Western, Southern or Northern half of a *BIRTH CHART*.

HOUSES – Twelve segments of space or time which represent the various fields of experience in life. Each House begins with a House *CUSP*. There are a number of methods used to calculate them; the one used in this book is Placidus, the most popular.

IC – Abbreviation of 'Imum Coeli' meaning *LOWER MIDHEAVEN*.

INTENSIFYING – Keyword used for *CONJUNCT*.

INTERACTION* – The chemistry between one person and another as determined by the effects of the *INTER-ASPECTS*.

INTER-ASPECTS – *ASPECTS* between the *PLANETS* in one person's *BIRTH CHART* and the Planets in another's, describing the chemistry between them.

INTERCHANGEABLITY* – An *INTER-ASPECT* where the effect of *PERSON A*'s *PLANET* is interchangeable with the effect of *PERSON B*'s Planet.

KEY CONNECTIONS* – The most immediately powerful *INTER-ASPECTS*.

KEYWORDS – Specially chosen words that focus the meaning of a particular *PLANET, SIGN, HOUSE* or *ASPECT* thereby triggering intuition and taking the symbolic meaning to the literal meaning.

LOWER MIDHEAVEN – An important, and the lowest, point in a *BIRTH CHART*, which is the CUSP of the Fourth *HOUSE*, the House of background, home life, etc. It is abbreviated to *IC*.

LUNAR NODES – See *NODES*.

MC – Abbreviation of 'Medium Coeli' meaning *MIDHEAVEN*.

MIDHEAVEN – An important, and the highest, point in a *BIRTH CHART*, which is the *CUSP* of the Tenth *HOUSE*, the House of profession, status, etc. It is situated exactly opposite the *LOWER MIDHEAVEN* and abbreviated to MC.

MIRROR* – The *MIRROR* is the means by which you can identify and take back your *PROJECTIONS*, thereby sorting out relationship difficulties at source, and empowering yourself at the same time. Its origins go way back to the Mayan and North American Indian cultures. The *MIRROR* that is a Sacred Symbol in the Mayan Sacred Calendar actually means 'Sword of Truth'.

MODES – The three basic *MODES* of life, astrologically speaking: Cardinal, Fixed and Mutable.

MOON'S NODES – See *NODES*.

MUTUALITY* – The point to remember that *ASPECTS* and *INTER-ASPECTS* go both ways. Planet A (or of *PERSON A*) is not only influencing Planet B (or of *PERSON B*) but vice versa as well.

NADIR – Another name for the *LOWER MIDHEAVEN*.

NATAL – Appertaining to the Birth Chart. Also called *RADIX*.

NODES – Two points of intersection between the Moon's path and that of the Earth around the Sun. The point of upward intersection is called the North *NODE* – see *GO-ZONE*. The point of downward intersection is called the South *NODE* – see *SLOW-ZONE*.

OPPOSING – Verb form of *OPPOSITION*.

OPPOSITION – One of the *ASPECTS* or *INTER-ASPECTS*. It increases awareness of the issues relevant to the *PLANETS* involved, often through CONFRONTING one with something or someone who appears to be opposing you.

ORB – Number of degrees allowed from the exact amount to make one of the given *ASPECTS* or *INTER-ASPECTS*. With a few exceptions, in *The Instant Astrologer* an Orb of 8 degrees is allowed for the *CONJUNCT, SQUARE, OPPOSITION* and *TRINE* for both *ASPECTS* and *INTER-ASPECTS*, whereas the *SEXTILE* has an Orb of 4 degrees as an *ASPECT* and 2 degrees as an *INTER-ASPECT*. With respect to the *ASPECTS* made by *TRANSITING PLANETS* an *ORB* of one degree is always used. However, as this relates to the duration of the *TRANSIT* in question it is somewhat arbitrary for such can vary quite considerably depending upon a number of factors for which a general rule cannot be made.

OVER-EMPHASIS – A surfeit of a particular *ELEMENT, MODE* or *HEMISPHERE*.

PERSON A and **PERSON B** – The general terms used to identify the two people involved in a relationship.

PERSONAL UNCONSCIOUS – See *the UNCONSCIOUS*.

PLANETS – The various energies or influences, along with the *SIGNS*, operating in and through a *BIRTH*

CHART. The term often includes the Sun, Moon and even the *ASCENDANT*. The *PLANETS* themselves are divided into the Inner Planets: the Sun, the Moon, Mercury, Venus and Mars, which govern those energies that are within one's personal control; the Social Planets: Jupiter and Saturn, which represent socio-cultural influences, along with the Outer Planets: Uranus, Neptune and Pluto, which also represent transformational, transcendental and evolutionary influences.

PROGRESSIONS – Symbolic positions of the *PLANETS* and their relationship to the *PLANETS* in one's *BIRTH CHART*. A *Progressed Planet*'s position for a certain number of years of age is calculated from the same number of days of age. For example, the Progressed positions for the thirtieth year of one's life would derive from the planetary positions of the thirtieth day of one's life.

PROJECTED SELF – The part of the self that is the *PROJECTION* that you make upon *another person or thing* – so much so that it actually becomes a part of the self.

PROJECTION – The psychological phenomenon of seeing in other people and the world at large what is actually or also a trait of one's own. This is done because that trait is regarded as either too bad or too good to belong to oneself. This is an *UNCONSCIOUS* function – until of course you become aware of it. This book is, to quite a degree, aimed at making you aware of it, simply because *your* planetary influences are happening *to you*, and therefore whatever happens is ultimately entirely of your *own* making or doing, consciously or unconsciously.

RADIX – See *NATAL*.

RETROGRADE – The apparent backward motion of the *PLANETS* as seen from the viewpoint of the Earth.

RETURN – See *CONJUNCT*.

RISING SIGN – The *SIGN* rising in the East, on the *ASCENDANT*, at any given time. This symbolizes your image, the manner in which you present yourself to the world around you, and how the world sees you. Your 'window on the world'.

RULING PLANET – The PLANET that rules your Chart/personality as a whole, usually the Ruler of one's *RISING SIGN*. Also, how certain *PLANETS* correspond to certain *SIGNS* in terms of quality and character, and are therefore said to rule them (see page 33). There are also the *PLANETS* that rule the *HOUSES* by virtue of ruling the *SIGN* on the *CUSP* of the *HOUSE* in question. This important factor is covered in *The Instant Astrologer* with respect to the Rulers of the *ANGLES*, but the other House Cusps (2nd, 3rd, 5th, 6th, 8th, 9th, 11th and 12th) are not dealt with directly because, firstly, they are a not within the scope of this book, and secondly, because these House Cusps (and therefore their Rulers) vary according to what *HOUSE* system is being used. If you have a

mind to, look on the *BIRTH CHART* to what *SIGN* is intersected by a particular *HOUSE CUSP* and then determine the Ruler. This can then be seen to have an important bearing upon that *HOUSE*, much in the same way that a landlord has on an apartment he or she rents out.

SETTING RULER – The *RULING PLANET* of your *SETTING SIGN*.

SETTING SIGN – The *SIGN* on the *DESCENDANT*, that is, setting in the West at any given time. This symbolizes the kind of people or relationships one attracts or is attracted to, and also, to a degree, one's *PROJECTED SELF* and *SHADOW*.

SEXTILE – One of the *ASPECTS* or *INTER-ASPECTS*. It brings efficiency and profit relevant to the *PLANETS* involved, but usually some kind of conscious effort is required.

SEXTILING – Verb form of *SEXTILE*.

SHADOW – The part of the self that you usually do not like to admit to having because it goes against the image you have acquired of yourself. The crucial point here is that your *SHADOW* also contains, in crude form, the part that you need to make yourself more complete and effective, both in terms of self-expression and of relating to others, and one other in particular. For instance, a common *SHADOW* is power, because having and using power means that you may have to be someone whom others do not like or approve of, and that power is something that only the government, state, church, boss, partner, etc has (over you, and it's bad) – in other words, you are disempowered. The *SHADOW*, in the unconscious state, always takes the form of a *PROJECTION*.

SIGNS – The twelve segments of space comprising a gigantic band encircling the Earth or following the ecliptic or path of the Sun. This is called the Zodiac of Signs (not to be confused with the Constellations of Signs which is the actual fixed stars with the same zodiacal names) and can be seen as the twelve seasons of the Sun. From our Earthly point of view, the influences of the *PLANETS* vary as they appear to orbit us, each one travelling through the *SIGNS* at their own individual rate.

SLOW-ZONE* – Potentially retrogressive expression or experience represented by the South *NODE* of the Moon.

SOCIO-CULTURAL INTERACTIONS* – Term used for *INTER-ASPECTS* between slow-moving *PLANETS* (Jupiter, Saturn, Uranus, Neptune and Pluto) that describe *INTERACTIONS* that are usually more to do with socio-cultural conditions than personal orientation.

SOFT ASPECTS – *ASPECTS* or *INTER-ASPECTS* which bring ease, inborn talent and natural harmony to an individual or relationship, namely the *TRINE*, *SEXTILE* and some *CONJUNCTS*.

SQUARE – One of the *ASPECTS* or *INTER-ASPECTS*. It challenges you with issues relevant to the *PLANETS* involved, usually prompted by an inner feeling of tension or blockage that needs to be overcome, although it can sometimes be felt as coming from without

SQUARING – Verb form of *SQUARE*.

STATIONARY – What a *PLANET* appears to do when it goes from *DIRECT* to *RETROGRADE*, or vice versa.

STELLIUM – Meaning 'star-cluster', three or more *PLANETS CONJOINING* one another, making for a powerful and complex dimension of personality.

SYNTHESIS – Putting together all the various factors in a *BIRTH CHART* into a whole.

THEMES* – An important part of *SYNTHESIS*.

TIME STANDARD – The time used in any place according to its Time *ZONE* which are 15-degree intervals of Longitude East or West of Greenwich (Mean Time).

TRANSITS – The ongoing positions of the *PLANETS* in the sky at any given time (following birth) and their relationship to the *PLANETS* in one's *BIRTH CHART*.

TRANSITING – Verb form of *TRANSIT*.

TRINE – One of the *ASPECTS* or *INTER-ASPECTS*. It provides ease, talent and good fortune with respect to the *PLANETS* involved.

TRINING – Verb form of *TRINE*.

UNCONSCIOUS, The – If human beings are seen as pieces in some gigantic cosmic game, then *THE UNCONSCIOUS* is what is actually playing that game. Your *PERSONAL UNCONSCIOUS* is your particular connection with *THE UNCONSCIOUS*, and therefore partly determines, along with your conscious will and senses, your Fate. Astrology is a map and mapper of *THE UNCONSCIOUS*, which is why it is able to predict or provide an insight into what is determining your Fate in terms of what your *BIRTH CHART* reveals as personality potentials, and through the events, possibilities and internal states indicated by *TRANSITS* and *PROGRESSIONS*. One can also view *THE UNCONSCIOUS* as a great sea upon which the little boat of your personality (a mixture of consciousness and unconsciousness) is floating or travelling, as it negotiates and navigates the planetary currents.

UNCONSCIOUS – Describing anything that lies in the *UNCONSCIOUS*.

UNDER-EMPHASIS – A deficit of a particular *ELEMENT*, *MODE* or *HEMISPHERE*.

UNITING WITH – Key phrase used for *CONJUNCT*.

UNKNOWN BIRTH TIME – If your birth time is not known it means that you will not be able to determine your *RISING SIGN*, *SETTING SIGN* or any other *HOUSE CUSPS* or positions. It may also give you a choice of two Moon Signs on days when the Moon changes *SIGNS*. However, by reading the interpretations for all Rising/Setting Signs and possibly two Moon Signs, you could come to some idea of birth time by working it backwards – or getting an experienced astrologer to do it for you.

ZENITH – Another name for the *MIDHEAVEN*.

ZODIAC – See *SIGNS*.

ZONE – The number of hours that a *TIME STANDARD* is ahead or behind Greenwich Mean Time.

* Terms exclusive to *The Instant Astrologer*.

5. RECOMMENDED READING

It is recommended that you look more deeply into whatever field or area of astrology takes your interest. Here are a few titles specific to some of these areas.

ASPECTS: *The Aspects in Astrology*
   by Sue Tompkins (Element Books, 1989)

DIVINATION: *The Astrological Oracle*
   by Lyn Birkbeck (Thorsons, 2002)

HOUSES: *The Twelve Houses*
   by Howard Sassportas (The Aquarian Press, 1985)

KEYWORDS: *Keywords For Astrology*
   by Hajo Banzhaf and Anna Haebler (Weiser, 1996)

MOON'S NODES: *Astrology For The Soul*
   by Jan Spiller (Bantam, 1997)

RELATIONSHIPS: *Dynamic Synastry*
   by Lyn Birkbeck (O Books, 2004)

RELATIONSHIPS: *Skymates*
   by Steven and Jodie Forrest
   (ACS Publications, 1989)

SCIENCE: *The Mayan Prophecies*
   by Adrian G Gilbert and Maurice Cotterell
   (Element Books, 1995)

SCIENCE: *The Scientific Basis Of Astrology*
   by Dr Percy Seymour (Quantum, 1997)

SUN, MOON & PLANET-SIGNS: *Do It Yourself Astrology*
   by Lyn Birkbeck (Element/Thorsons, 1996)

SUN-SIGNS: *Astro-Wisdom*
   by Lyn Birkbeck (O Books, 2003)

TRANSITS: *Planets in Transit*
   by Robert Hand (Whitford Press, 1976)

6. TAKING IT FURTHER

There are many other methods and fields of astrology that *The Instant Astrologer* has not, of necessity, used or looked into. Here are a few of the main ones, some of which may be covered in future add-ons to *The Instant Astrologer*.

Progressions

These are symbolic positions of the Planets that are usually arrived at by taking a 'day for each year'. If you were, say, thirty years old, then the positions of the Planets when you were thirty days old would be the Progressed positions. Where they were at that time in relationship to your Chart by Aspect – and to a lesser degree by House and Sign – would indicate significant events in your life. But as the Progressions are very slow moving, one would only really ever use the Progressed Sun, Moon, Mercury, Venus and Mars, because they move relatively quickly. Even so, the Progressed Sun takes around thirty years to go through a Sign.

Minor Aspects

As well as the five Major Aspects used in this book there are a number of lesser Aspects, with varying amounts of influence. The strongest of these is probably the Quincunx (150 degrees between one Planet and another). Minor Aspects can be quite significant when regarded as 'fine tuning'.

Lunations

These are the eight phases or relationships between the Sun and Moon as determined by the number of degrees the one is behind or ahead of the other. They indicate one's basic creative–emotional inclination. They are New Moon Phase (born with the Moon 0-45 degrees ahead of the Sun) – The Emerging or Budding Personality; The Crescent Moon Phase (Moon 45-90 degrees ahead of the Sun) – The Striving Personality; The First or Waxing Quarter Moon Phase (90-135 degrees) – The Deciding Personality; The Gibbous Moon Phase (135-180) – The Adjusting Personality; The Full Moon Phase (180-225) – The Realizing Personality; The Disseminating Moon Phase (225-270) – The Sharing Personality; The Second or Waning Quarter Moon Phase (270-315) – The Understanding Personality; and finally The Balsamic Moon Phase (315-360) – The Releasing Personality.

Composite Charts

This is the mathematical combining of two Birth Charts and creating of another one, the Composite. This is a Chart of the relationship itself as distinct from the Inter-Aspects used in this book. The Composite symbolizes the energy or purpose of the relationship itself, rather than how the two people get on.

Solar Returns

This is a Chart drawn up for when the Sun reaches the exact place it was when you were born, and symbolizes the nature of the coming year for you as an individual.

Horary Astrology

This is also called Traditional Astrology in that it was how astrology was mainly used in the past – that is, as a divinatory tool. The enquirer draws up a Chart for their question or for a significant event and, by following very closely proscribed rules, divines an answer.

Mundane Astrology

This is the astrology of nations and world events. Often thought of as what astrology is about for all astrologers whereas in fact it is a highly specialist branch of its own.

7. CALCULATION CHARTS FOR SETTING THE SCENE

1. ELEMENTS

Point System

SUN and MOON = 4 points each
MERCURY, VENUS and MARS = 3 points each
JUPITER and SATURN = 2 points each
URANUS, NEPTUNE and PLUTO = 1 point each
ASCENDANT (Rising Sign) = 4 points
MIDHEAVEN = 2 points

FIRE	EARTH	AIR	WATER
Aries	Taurus	Gemini	Cancer
Leo	Virgo	Libra	Scorpio
Sagittarius	Capricorn	Aquarius	Pisces

1. ELEMENTS of _____(name)

FIRE placements	pts	EARTH placements	pts	AIR placements	pts	WATER placements	pts
Total Fire		Total Earth		Total Air		Total Water	

4 points or less makes that Element UNDER-EMPHASIZED
12 points or more makes that Element OVER-EMPHASIZED
5-11 points makes that Element BALANCED, with strength of that Element according to how near 5 or 11 its weight is.

2. MODES

Point System

SUN and MOON = 4 points each
MERCURY, VENUS and MARS = 3 points each
JUPITER and SATURN = 2 points each
URANUS, NEPTUNE and PLUTO = 1 point each
ASCENDANT (Rising Sign) = 4 points
MIDHEAVEN = 2 points

CARDINAL	FIXED	MUTABLE
Aries	Taurus	Gemini
Cancer	Leo	Virgo
Libra	Scorpio	Sagittarius
Capricorn	Aquarius	Pisces

2. MODES of _____(name)

CARDINAL placements	pts	FIXED placements	pts	MUTABLE placements	pts
Total Cardinal		Total Fixed		Total Mutable	

6 points or less makes that Mode UNDER-EMPHASIZED
16 or more makes that Mode OVER-EMPHASIZED
7-15 points makes that Mode BALANCED, with strength according to how near 7 or 15.

3. HEMISPHERES

Point System

SUN and MOON = 4 points each
MERCURY, VENUS and MARS = 3 points each
JUPITER and SATURN = 2 points each
URANUS, NEPTUNE and PLUTO = 1 point each

NOTE – For Hemisphere assessment, ASCENDANT and MIDHEAVEN do not count because they are the East and Southern Points themselves, whilst their opposites, the DESCENDANT and LOWER MIDHEAVEN are the Western and Northern Points themselves.

EASTERN	WESTERN	SOUTHERN	NORTHERN
Tenth	Fourth	Seventh	First
Eleventh	Fifth	Eighth	Second
Twelfth	Sixth	Ninth	Third
FIRST	**SEVENTH**	**TENTH**	**FOURTH**
Second	Eighth	Eleventh	Fifth
Third	Ninth	Twelfth	Sixth

3. HEMISPHERES of _____(name)

EASTERN placements	pts	WESTERN placements	pts	SOUTHERN placements	pts	NORTHERN placements	pts
Total Eastern		Total Western		Total Southern		Total Northern	

A Hemisphere over-emphasis – around **sixteen** points or more – is quite advantageous, but when taken to extreme – around **twenty** points or more – then some compensation definitely will be called for sooner or later. But be flexible with these approximate figures. Use your own judgement of the person concerned, and be aware of how other factors in their Chart can compensate for under- or over-emphasis.

Other titles from

B O O K S

Also by Lyn Birkbeck

Astro Wisdom - Lyn Birkbeck

Revolutionary interactive astrology - all you need to know is your Star Sign and how old you are.

Obtain a wealth of information, unparalleled by any other Star-Sign book.
There are no calculations - just dip in and enjoy the following, mainly

interactive features:

Your Emotional Intent ~ Divine Do's and Don'ts ~ The Zodiacal Lifestream ~

Laws of Relating ~ As Time Goes By ~ Planets of Love.

ISBN 1 903816 56 4
Price: £9.99 $14.95

UK orders call: 01962 736880 ~ US orders call: 1-800-462-6420

OTHER TITLES FROM O BOOKS

The Reiki Sourcebook - Bronwen & Frans Stiene

The most comprehensive book on Reiki ever published, this is the ultimate resource for all Reiki beginners and practitioners. Bringing together every important piece of information that has been taught, discussed or written about Reiki since its development in the early 1900s, it includes information from sources such as living students of the masters Mikao Usui, Chujiro Hayashi and Hawayo Takata.

'What an incredible work... a must for all Reiki people - an informative, practical book...' Mari Hall, Bestselling Author and Founder of the International Association of Reiki.

Bronwen and Frans Stiene are the founders of the International House of Reiki, Australia. They have worked with Reiki and researched it in Europe, Asia, Australia and Japan for many years.

ISBN 1 903816 55 6
Price £12.99 $19.95

UK orders call: 01962 736880 ~ US orders call: 1-800-462-6420

Soul Power - Nikki de Carteret

How do you create inner stability in times of chaos? ~ How do you cultivate the power of presence? ~ Where does humility meet mastery? These are just some of the threads of spiritual inquiry that Nikki de Carteret weaves into a tapestry of Soul Power. Written in a poetic and meditative style this book is a discovery of spirit and of spiritual growth.

'A beautiful and touching expression of the spiritual journey.' Barbara Shipka, Author.

Nikki de Carteret's professional and mystical journeys intersect in business, media and spirituality. She is an international speaker, seminar leader, and teacher of mediation and leads workshops around the world on personal and organizational transformation.

ISBN 1 903816 36 X
Price £9.99 $14.95

The 7AHA!s of Highly Enlightened Souls - Mike George

7 moments of profound insight into our own lives, which we can all reach, which will open to us new ways of seeing our problems and our potential development. How do we begin to decide where to start our spiritual journey? What are the right methods? This book strips away the illusions that surround the modern malais we call stress.

Mike George is a spiritual teacher, motivational speaker, retreat leader and management development facilitator.

ISBN 1 903816 31 9
Price £5.99 $11.95

UK orders call: 01962 736880 ~ US orders call: 1-800-462-6420